Economic Liberalization, Distribution and Poverty

Economic Liberalization, Distribution and Poverty

Latin America in the 1990s

Edited by

Rob Vos

Deputy Rector and Professor of Finance and Development, Institute of Social Studies, The Hague, The Netherlands

Lance Taylor

Arnhold Professor of International Cooperation and Development, New School University, New York, USA

Ricardo Paes de Barros

Director of Social Studies, Institute of Applied Economic Studies (IPEA), Rio de Janeiro, Brazil

IN ASSOCIATION WITH THE UNITED NATIONS OFFICE FOR PROJECT SERVICES (UNOPS) IN REPRESENTATION OF THE UNITED NATIONS DEVELOPMENT PROGRAMME (UNDP)

Edward Elgar

Cheltenham, UK • Northampton, MA, USA

Published by
Edward Elgar Publishing Limited
Glensanda House
Montpellier Parade
Cheltenham
Glos GL50 1UA
UK

Edward Elgar Publishing, Inc.
136 West Street
Suite 202
Northampton
Massachusetts 01060
USA

A catalogue record for this book
is available from the British Library

Library of Congress Cataloguing in Publication Data

Economic liberalization, distribution and poverty: Latin America in the 1990s/edited by Rob Vos, Lance Taylor, Ricardo Paes de Barros.
p. cm.
(In association with the United Nations Office for Project Services (UNOPS) in representation of the United Nations Development Programme (UNDP).)
Includes index.
1. Latin America—Economic policy. 2. Latin America—Economic conditions—1982– . I. Vos, Rob, 1955– . II. Taylor, Lance. III. Barros, Ricardo Paes de, 1954– .
HC125.E37372 2003
330.98'0039—dc21

2002072176

ISBN 1 84064 871 6

Typeset by Manton Typesetters, Louth, Lincolnshire, UK.
Printed and bound in Great Britain by MPG Books Ltd, Bodmin, Cornwall.

Contents

Figures

Tables

Contributors

César Bouillon, Senior economist of the Poverty and Inequality Advisory Unit of the Inter-American Development Bank, Washington.

David Bravo, Researcher at the Universidad de Chile, Santiago.

Dante Contreras, Professor of Economics at the Universidad de Chile, Santiago.

Carlos Henrique Corseuil, Research associate at the Institute of Applied Economic Studies (IPEA), Brazil.

José de Gregorio, Governor of the Central Bank of Chile. Formerly Professor, Center for Economic Applied Research, University of Chile.

Juan José Díaz, Research associate of research center GRADE, Lima, Peru.

Roberto Frenkel, Director of CEDES, Buenos Aires, Argentina.

Enrique Ganuza, Regional Poverty Co-ordinator of UNDP for Latin America and the Caribbean, New York.

Martín González Rozada, Research associate, CEDES, Buenos Aires, Argentina.

Jeannette Larde, Researcher at the Department of Economics of the Univrsidad de Chile, Santiago.

José Antonio Ocampo, Executive Secretary, UN Economic Commission for Latin America and the Caribbean, Santiago and former Minister of Finance of Colombia.

Ricardo Paes de Barros, Director of social studies of the Institute of Applied Economic Studies (IPEA), Brazil.

Tomas Rau, Researcher at the Department of Economics of the Universidad de Chile, Santiago.

Jaime Ros, Senior research fellow, University of Notre Dame.

Jaime Saavedra, Director of research center GRADE, Lima, Peru.

Fabio Sánchez, UN Economic Commission for Latin America and the Caribbean and Professor of Economics, Universidad de los Andes, Bogotá, Colombia.

Alexander Segovia, Consultant UNDP, Guatemala.

Lance Taylor, Arnhold Professor of International Cooperation and Development, New School University, New York. Previously Professor of Economics at MIT, Cambridge (MA).

Máximo Torero, Research associate of research center GRADE, Lima, Peru.

Camilo Ernesto Tovar, Advisor to Executive Secretary, Economic Commission for Latin America and the Caribbean, Santiago.

Sergio Urzua, Researcher at the Department of Economics of the Universidad de Chile, Santiago.

Rob Vos, Deputy Rector and Professor of Finance and Development of the Institute of Social Studies, The Hague.

Preface

For some time now, the United Nations Development Programme (UNDP) and the UN Economic Commission for Latin America and the Caribbean (ECLAC) have engaged in carrying out comparative studies to obtain a better understanding of the interactions between economic reform policies and poverty and inequality.

Most multilateral organizations are heavily engaged in studies and debates about the globalization process. Globalization is of course also of great interest to the institutions that sponsored the present study. In Latin America the globalization process is reshaping the economies of the region in a major way. Since the late 1980s, the countries of the region have engaged in drastic economic reforms of striking similarity. Most particularly there have been fairly uniform patterns of trade and capital account liberalization. These reforms were implemented in conjunction with other market reforms, such as deregulation of financial and labour markets, privatization of state-owned enterprises and tax reforms. The process of economic opening though is commonly seen to have produced the most significant change in redefining the environment in which the economic actors in the region have to operate.

From the perspective of UNDP and ECLAC and their respective priority areas of activity, it was mandatory to raise the question how this process of balance of payments liberalization has affected income distribution and poverty.

Previous economic policy regimes implemented throughout the region have been criticized for failing to achieve efficient and sustainable patterns of growth and, as such, being incapable to reduce poverty and inequality. Excessive state control and protectionist import-substituting industrialization policies have been focal points of such critique. In this light, economic opening is seen as the key towards more efficient and competitive production, more adequate employment creation and, hence, poverty reduction and greater equity. Theoretical foundations for this hypothesis are found in traditional trade theory, which – under specific assumptions – predicts such benign outcomes following trade liberalization.

Many recent studies have questioned such pre-emptive conclusions. These empirical studies have cast some doubt on the prediction of unambiguously positive growth, distribution and poverty reduction effects following trade and financial opening. There is an increasing understanding that the interactions between the reform policies, structural adjustment, growth, poverty and inequality are much more complex, as much as context specific. We have only just started the undoubtedly long journey to a better understanding of these processes.

With this perspective in mind, and with the invaluable support of a network of experts of the Latin American economies, UNDP and ECLAC contracted an in-depth study of the poverty and inequality effects of the liberalization of the balance of payments during the 1990s. The network managed to cover 17 Latin American countries in great detail, providing an ample comparative perspective. The comparative perspective is enhanced by the fact that practically all countries took almost identical trade and capital account liberalization measures at the same point in time, that is the end of the 1980s and early 1990s.

Economic opening in Latin America went hand in hand with large capital inflows. This has brought new sources of economic growth, but also new factors of instability. Many countries in the region witnessed clear signs of economic recovery during the 1990s, but the road has been rocky as is evident from several crises with region-wide effects. The recent examples are Mexico's peso crisis and the subsequent Tequila-effect and Brazil's samba crisis. While the growth path has been somewhat unstable, the general perception is that income distribution has worsened as a consequence of the trade liberalization process, while poverty has fallen in some instances and increased in others. This book tries to trace in great detail the changes in economic conditions following the reforms, particularly the effects on growth, employment, labour earnings, distribution and poverty. Upon closer inspection, country experiences show quite a bit of diversity and the analysis benefits from the insights of 17 country papers written by outstanding scholars from the region. The country cases cover the effects of the reforms on the living conditions of nearly 90 per cent of the region's population.

Tracing the effects of reform policies on growth, distribution and poverty is complex because of the multiplicity of events taking place at the same time. The analysis will necessarily have to be done at several levels of aggregation.

In the first place, much of the impact of liberalization is macroeconomic in nature. There are effects on the overall level of economic activity, the inflation rate and other key macroeconomic price variables such as the real exchange rate, real wage, agricultural terms of trade and real interest rate. The evidence shows that liberalization has been associated with changes in the significance of national investment and saving, government spending and taxes, and exports and imports as (respectively) injections and leakages of effective demand. Although country experiences differ, clearly none of the Latin American countries has achieved a sustainable growth path, and income volatility persists and may even have increased as a consequence of the liberalization. Capital account liberalization has counteracted the objectives of trade liberalization in several instances. Contrary to the theory, liberalization has not produced a major export drive, with the exception of only a few country cases. Also, productivity growth in traded goods sectors has generally been disappointing in most cases. Insufficient employment growth in modern sectors has led workers to seek jobs in the informal employment sector. Expanding informal employment has been a common feature in almost the entire region in the 1990s. As the study shows, this has turned out to be an important source of growing inequality in earnings.

Second, changes in macro variables can have strong repercussions at the sectoral level. Economic indicators that can be affected include output levels, employment by skill or social type, functional income distribution and real wages, and (quite strikingly in the Latin American case) changes in levels and growth rates of labour and capital productivity. Labour migration across sectors can also have significant employment and distributional effects. Countries across the region show substantial differences in sectoral productivity growth and labour-intensity. Consequently, economic reforms (including labour market reforms) show different outcomes on employment and income distribution. Next to widening earnings differentials between formal and informal sector workers, another major source of inequality has been a rise in the skill-intensity of employment in Latin America. This went to the detriment of employment and wages for unskilled workers. While these are more or less generalizable labour market adjustment patterns, country experiences differ substantially in the details.

Finally, aggregate and sectoral labour market outcomes affect households in different ways, depending on asset and human capital endowments of families and household responses to changing market conditions (e.g. as expressed through shifts in labour participation rates). Application of an innovative method of counterfactual microsimulations allows for a decomposition of the various labour market outcomes on household welfare and poverty. Leaving aside some exceptions, the study generally finds that structural shifts resulting from the reform process (such as greater demand for skilled labour and labour-saving investments in modern economic sectors) are major underlying causes of greater inequality and poverty. These outcomes are most strongly associated with the process of trade liberalization. In some cases the positive impact of macroeconomic stabilization and expansion of aggregate demand on employment and real incomes has counteracted these negative outcomes. Capital account liberalization and the associated increase in capital inflows appear to be an important factor behind these more benign outcomes, but the same factors have also been a source of greater external vulnerability and macroeconomic volatility. These conclusions call for major amendments to the policy reforms – and hence to the so-called policy recommendations of the Washington consensus – as conducted in the 1980s and 1990s if growth, equity and poverty considerations are to be made more compatible.

Chapter 1 of the book provides an analytical framework for analysing the impact of the reforms and the major findings of the effects focusing on the macroeconomic variables and aggregate sector, labour market and income distribution variables. It provides summary narratives of the experience in 17 countries in Latin America and the Caribbean. It concludes with some important policy lessons. *Chapter 2* provides a comparative analysis of the results of the microsimulations. It shows how the different types of labour market outcomes of the liberalization process have affected welfare at the household level. The liberalization impact on poverty and inequality is measured this way. *Chapters 3 to 10* provide more in-depth and fuller country analyses for a selection of the countries, including in alphabetical order Argentina, Brazil, Chile, Colombia, Ecuador, El Salvador, Mexico and Peru.

Enrique Ganuza, Regional Poverty Co-ordinator of UNDP for Latin America and the Caribbean, took the initiative for the entire project, co-ordinated it and brought together a group of the region's best economic researchers. Without his stimulus this research would not have been what it has become. This book would also not have been possible without the work and talent of the authors of the country studies. The full list of authors and country papers appears at the end of Chapter 1. During almost two years these experts worked hard to reveal dark spots in our knowledge and understanding. They not only contributed their insights into the realities of their economies, but also helped to shape the analytical approach used in this book. As part of this road towards a better understanding, four workshops were held to discuss the work in progress. These workshops benefited from the support of the UNDP offices in El Salvador, Brazil, Guatemala and Argentina. We are also grateful to Barbara Stallings of ECLAC who actively participated in the workshops and provided valuable comments during the course of the project, as well as giving inputs from a large study on related issues which she co-ordinated for ECLAC. Samuel Morley of IFFPRI equally was an active participant at the workshops and generously put his vast experience and knowledge of the subject at the disposal of the group of researchers. Valuable inputs were also obtained from Miguel Székely of the Inter-American Development Bank, who contributed with helpful comments and wider perspectives over the course of the project. François Bourguignon, World Bank and Delta, participated in the workshop in Antigua, Guatemala and helped to shape the microsimulations method presented in Chapter 2. Werner Hernany helped to generate the microsimulation results for Honduras, which were used as input for Chapter 2. Ruth Rose was responsible for the translation from Spanish of all chapters, except for Chapters 1 and 7, and Rob Vos took care of the final editing.

While UNDP and ECLAC supported the project leading to this book throughout, both institutions ensured full independence of the work of the authors and editors.

Rob Vos
Lance Taylor
Ricardo Paes de Barros

The Hague, New York and Rio de Janeiro

1. Balance of payments liberalization in Latin America: effects on growth, distribution and poverty

Lance Taylor and Rob Vos

1.1 INTRODUCTION

Looking back from the end of the 20th century, the most striking aspect of economic policy in developing economies during the last 10–15 years has been the spread of packages aimed at liberalizing the balance of payments, on both current and capital account. Dramatic leaps toward external openness took place throughout Latin America, Eastern Europe, Asia and parts of Africa. Together with large but highly volatile foreign capital movements (often but not always in connection with privatization of state-owned enterprises), this wave of trade and financial deregulation redefined the external environment for a major part of the non-industrialized world. In Latin America, the stabilization and structural adjustment efforts immediately following the debt crisis of the early 1980s had focused mainly on fiscal and monetary adjustment and realignment of exchange rates. Then, in the late 1980s and early 1990s, came drastic reductions in trade restrictions and domestic and external financial liberalization, almost simultaneously in most countries. Steps were also taken toward restructuring tax systems and deregulating labour markets.

All these changes are very recent. It will take time before their full effects on growth, employment, income distribution and poverty can be fully assessed. Still, external liberalization marks a dramatic switch in development policies away from the traditional regime of widespread state controls and import-substituting industrialization. One would expect to see major consequences. The old regime had been criticized for failing to promote efficient and competitive industrial production, for creating insufficient employment and for failing to reduce income inequality. A fundamental question now is whether the liberalization of trade and capital flows will be better at meeting these goals. Will a world system in which national economies are highly integrated in commodity and capital markets (in terms of increased transaction flows and tendencies toward price equalization) promote equality and reduce poverty?

The reforms have been justified by expected increases in efficiency and output growth. Governments and international institutions promoting them have been less explicit about the distributional consequences. A predominant view is that liberalization is likely to lead to better economic performance, at least in the medium to long run. Even if there are adverse transitional impacts, they can be cushioned by social policies, and in any case after some time they will be outweighed by more rapid growth.

This policy view basically stems from supply-side arguments. The purpose of trade reform is to switch production away from non-tradables and inefficient import-substitutes toward exportables in which countries have a comparative advantage. Presumed full employment of all resources – labour included – enables such a switch to be made painlessly. Opening of the capital account is supposed to bring financial inflows that will stimulate investment and productivity growth. A recent defence based on cross-country regressions for Latin America (Londoño and Székely 1998) argues that equity is positively related to growth and investment. Higher growth and investment, in turn, are assumed to be associated with structural reforms, so that liberalization is seen to support low-income groups.

This story contrasts with findings of many other studies which, referring in particular to the effects of trade reforms, find that opening domestic markets to external competition is associated with greater wage inequality (Robbins 1996, Wood 1994 and 1997, Ocampo and Taylor 1998). Berry (1998) and Bulmer-Thomas (1996) corroborate this proposition with data for a range of Latin American countries, observing a shift in technology in favour of more capital- and skill-intensive production consistent with a rise in wage differentials. However, the evidence stems essentially from the 1980s and possibly captures more of the effects of short-run adjustment policies than of trade and capital account liberalization.

While there may be important supply-side effects to trade reforms, one should not overlook the effects of aggregate demand on growth and distribution and the impact of capital inflows on relative prices. The import-substitution model relied on the expansion of internal markets with rising real wages as part of the strategy. Under the new regime, controlling wage costs has come to centre stage. As long as there is enough productivity growth and no substantial displacement of workers, wage restraint need not be a problem because output expansion could create space for growth of real incomes. But if wage levels are seriously reduced and/or workers with high consumption propensities lose their jobs, contraction of domestic demand could cut labour income in sectors that produce for the domestic market. Income inequality could rise if displaced unskilled workers end up in informal services for which there is a declining demand.

Rising capital inflows following liberalization tend to lead to real exchange rate appreciation, which could offset liberalization's incentives for traded goods production and force greater reductions in real wage costs. On the demand side, capital inflows may stimulate aggregate spending through increased domestic investment (either directly or through credit expansion) and lower savings (credit expansion triggering a consumption boom). However, aggregate demand expansion may prove to be short-lived if the consequent widening of the external balance is unsustainable and volatility of short-term capital inflows and lack of regulatory control put the domestic financial system at risk.

The thrust of these observations is that the effects of balance of payments liberalization on growth, employment and income distribution come from a complex set of interactions involving both the supply and the demand sides of the economy. Income redistribution and major shifts in relative prices are endogenous to the process, and there are no facile conclusions about the effects of liberalization.

This chapter provides an overview of the recent experience with balance of payments deregulation in 17 countries in Latin America and the Caribbean. While their recent policies show a good deal of uniformity, outcomes are quite mixed. Overall one sees volatile growth and greater vulnerability to fluctuations in world trade and financial markets. Greater inequality, particularly at the level of primary incomes, is found in many instances, but the pattern is not uniform throughout the region.

A finding that can be somewhat more generalized is that – to the extent effects can be disentangled – it appears that the structural changes associated with trade liberalization have tended to cause a rise in income inequality, most pronounced in a widening of the income gap between skilled and unskilled workers. Capital account liberalization leading to greater capital inflows and, through that, aggregate demand expansion, employment growth and/or price stabilization has offset tendencies toward greater inequality and allowed poverty reductions in a number of instances. On the other hand, financial opening has also been associated with greater volatility, impeding sustained improvements in equity or poverty reduction.

The chapter is set up as follows. First we describe our basic methodological and analytical position, sketching a simple framework for assessing the impact of current and capital account liberalization on output, employment and real wages. We then give a quick comparative scan of the outcomes for the 17 country cases, followed by a summary interpretation of the experience of each country and results of counterfactual model simulations isolating the effects of liberalization for the country cases where such exercises are available. In the final section we try to draw some lessons from this recent experience of policy reforms and speculate about prospects for the new century.

1.2 ASSESSING THE IMPACT OF THE POLICY REFORMS

What is the Effect of Policy Changes?

How can we separate effects of specific policy changes from other factors such as external shocks and other policy initiatives? The country studies reviewed here faced this standard problem of economic analysis with a mix of the following elements:

- Well-informed country narratives discussing policy changes and observed outcomes in a before-and-after approach. The country stories started with a basic set of questions and hypotheses and a simple analytical framework suggesting possible channels of causation of the type outlined below.
- Still within the realm of before-and-after, a set of standardized decomposition analyses of aggregate demand, factorial income distribution, employment and productivity growth, respectively, were applied for all countries (see Appendix). These decompositions give in a disaggregated way essential comparative information about changes in output, employment and inequality that actually took place. Counterfactual policy simulations (with-and-without) were incorporated in a number of case studies based on country-specific models.
- Microsimulations analysing the impact on income distribution and poverty of changes in the labour market, which may be attributed to balance of payments reforms. This analysis uses household survey data as well as the results of the informed before-and-after or the model-based, with-and-without analysis. The simulations try to determine to what extent income distribution and poverty have changed as a consequence of changes in labour participation, unemployment rates and reform-related shifts in employment and remuneration levels by sector and skills.

It could be argued that, ideally, an approach based on formal modelling would be the better method to verify the effects of the various policy changes. A fair number of the case studies went through this costly exercise, providing some useful insights. While the models allow a more rigorous isolation of the effects of different reform measures, they have important limitations due to their assumptions about directions of economic causality and specification of parameters, as well as difficulties in describing changes in behaviour after liberalization and taking into account political economy. The hope is that a combination of methods can provide the ingredients needed to understand the underlying processes.

This chapter provides an overview of the main findings based on the application of the first three methodologies listed above, and thus focuses on the effects of balance of payments liberalization on labour market outcomes and primary income distribution. Chapter 2 provides the link to what happened to income distribution at the household level through the comparative analysis of the microsimulations.

A Simple Analytical Framework

A useful way to analyse the effects of balance of payments liberalization is in a model with traded and non-traded goods, as large shifts in price and quantity relationships between the two sectors have been observed in practice. Direct effects of removing barriers to trade and capital movements show up first in the traded (or tradable) goods sector, but spillovers in both directions with non-traded goods have been immediate and substantial. Amadeo and Pero (2000) and Ros (1999) point out the major connections in a similar fashion.

The framework is a fix-price/flex-price model à la Hicks (1965) and many others. Traded goods are assumed to be produced under imperfect competition. The simplest model involves a discriminating monopolist manufacturing goods that can both be exported and sold at home, as in Ocampo and Taylor (1998). Households at home buy both domestically made and imported consumer goods. Prior to liberalization, firms have established mark-up rates over variable costs in both their markets – levels will depend on the relevant elasticities. The market prices and productivity levels of unskilled labour and intermediate imports determine variable cost; skilled labour and physical capital are fixed factors in the short run. The traded goods price level P_t follows from the mark-up over variable cost.

With stable mark-up rates, traded goods comprise a Hicksian fix-price sector with a level of output X_t determined by effective demand. The level of production of non-traded goods is also determined by demand, but the sector may well have decreasing returns to unskilled labour in the short run. A higher production level X_n is made possible by greater unskilled employment L_n. However, cost-minimizing producers will hire extra workers only at a lower real product wage w/P_n, where w is the unskilled nominal wage and P_n is the price of non-traded goods. In other words, a higher price–wage ratio P_n/w is associated with greater non-traded goods production and employment and, if there are decreasing returns, reduced labour productivity. If P_n/w is free to vary, then non-traded goods aggregate into a flex-price sector (which we assume in the basic version of the model). With stable mark-up rates in the traded goods sector, the intersectoral price ratio P_t/P_n will fall as P_n/w rises, i.e. a rising price of non-traded goods is associated with real apprecia-

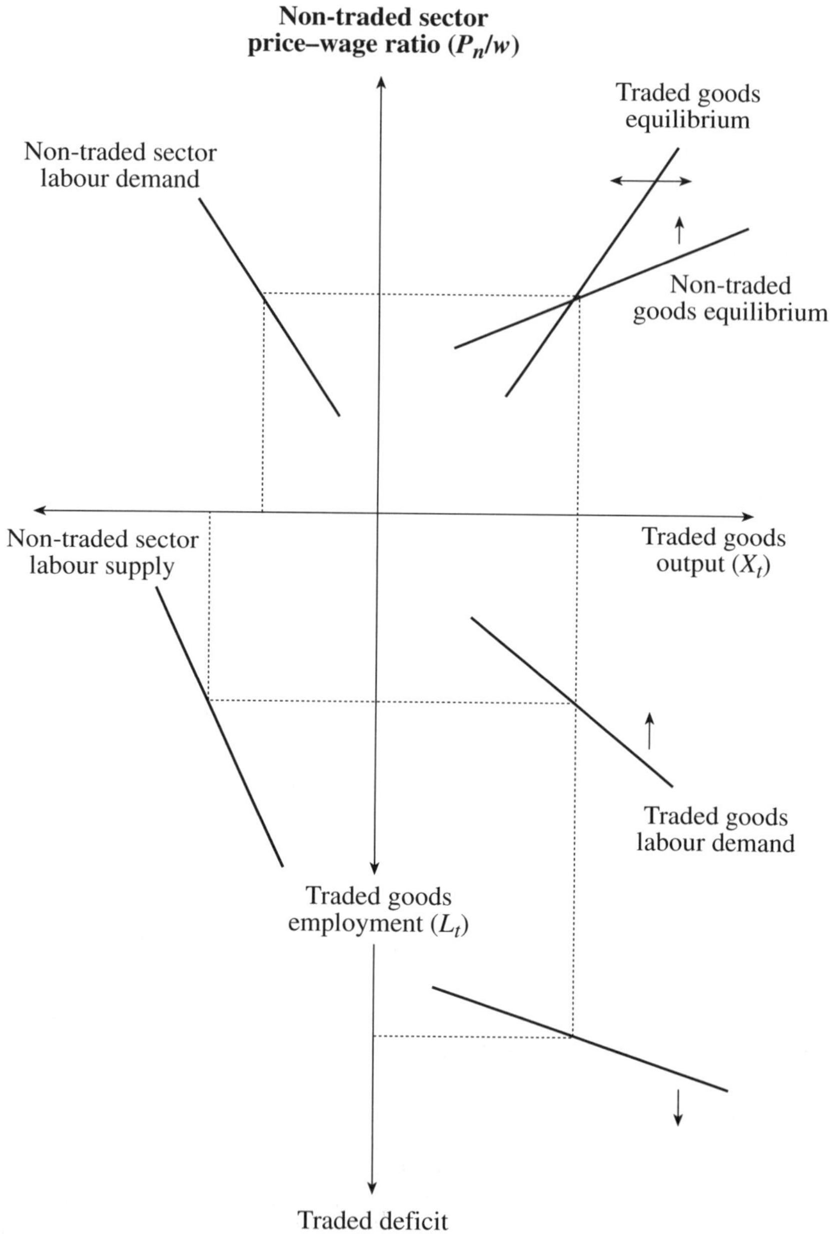

Figure 1.1 Initial equilibrium positions in traded and non-traded goods markets and probable shifts after current and capital account liberalization

tion as measured by the ratio of traded to non-traded goods price indexes (a commonly used proxy is the ratio of wholesale to retail price levels).

Figure 1.1 gives a graphical presentation of the model. The key quadrant lies in the extreme northeast. It shows how prices and output in the two sectors are determined. Along the schedule for 'Non-traded goods equilibrium', a higher traded goods output level X_t is assumed to generate additional demand for non-traded goods. As it is met by an increase in supply, the non-traded price–wage ratio P_n/w will rise. In the market for traded goods, a higher level of P_n/w can be associated with either higher or lower demand, depending on income effects. The 'Traded goods equilibrium' schedule illustrates the former case – demand for X_t is stimulated by an increase in P_n/w. As drawn in the figure, the short-run macroequilibrium defined by the intersection of the two curves is stable.

Effects of Liberalization

As indicated above, in most Latin American economies the current and capital accounts of the balance of payments were liberalized nearly simultaneously in the late 1980s to early 1990s. Given this history, one has to consider the two policy regime shifts together. However, for the sake of analytical clarity it is useful to dissect them one at a time. Effects of other reforms have to be considered as well, in particular domestic financial, tax and labour market deregulation. We begin with the capital account, followed by the current account, and end with some comments on the other sets of reforms.

Capital account liberalization

Upon removing restrictions on capital movements, most countries received a surge of inflows from abroad. They came in subject to the accounting restriction that an economy's net foreign asset position (total holdings of external assets minus total external liabilities) can only change gradually over time through a deficit or surplus on the current account. Hence, when external liabilities increased as foreigners acquired securities issued by national governments or firms, external assets had to jump up as well. The new assets typically showed up on the balance sheets of financial institutions, including larger international reserves of the central bank. Without a concerted effort at 'sterilizing' the inflows, they set off a domestic credit boom. Poorly regulated financial systems ran a high risk of a classic mania–panic–crash sequence along Kindleberger (1996) lines. The events in Latin America's Southern Cone around 1980 were only the first of many such disasters.

When the credit expansion was allowed to work itself through, interest rates could be low. However, other factors entered to push both levels off and the spread between borrowing and lending rates upward. One source of widening spreads is related to asset price booms in housing and stock markets, which forced rates to rise on interest-bearing securities such as government debt. Another source that sometimes played a role originated from central banks trying to sterilize capital inflows, thus pushing up rates as well. Finally, in non-competitive financial markets, local institutions often found it easy to raise spreads. High local returns pulled more capital inflows, worsening the overall disequilibrium.

Not surprisingly, exchange rate movements complicated the story. In many countries the exchange rate was used as a nominal anchor in anti-inflation programmes. Its nominal level was devalued at a rate lower than that of inflation, leading to real appreciation. In several cases the effect was rapid, with traded goods' variable costs in dollar terms jumping upwards immediately after the rate was frozen.

The same outcome also showed up via another channel. As countries removed capital controls and adopted floating rates, they lost a degree of freedom in policy formulation. From standard macroeconomic theory we know that, in a closed economy, the market for bonds will be in equilibrium if the money market also clears. When proper accounting restrictions are imposed on portfolio choice in an open economy, this theorem continues to apply (Taylor 1999) – that is, an open economy has just one independent asset market relationship, say an excess supply function for bonds of the form

$$B - B^d[i, i^*, (\varepsilon/e)] = 0$$

In this equation, B and B^d are bond supply and demand, respectively. The latter depends positively on the domestic interest rate i, negatively on the foreign rate i^* and on expected depreciation ε as normalized by the current spot rate e.[1]

For given expectations, the formula suggests that the interest rate and the spot exchange rate are inversely related. If, for the reasons mentioned above, the domestic interest rate i tended to rise, then the real exchange rate would appreciate or fall. Or, the other way around, if the exchange rate strengthened over time, then interest rates would be pushed upward (a tendency that would be amplified if real appreciation were expansionary in the short run). Abandoning capital controls made this trade-off far more difficult to manage. Some countries did succeed in keeping their exchange rates relatively weak, but they were in a minority.

To summarize, capital account liberalization combined with a boom in external inflows could easily provoke 'excessive' credit expansion. Paradoxically, the credit boom could be associated with relatively high interest rates and a strong local currency. These were not the most secure foundations for liberalization of the current account, the topic we take up next.

Current account liberalization

Current account deregulation basically took the form of transformation of quota restrictions (where they were important) to tariffs, and then consolidation of tariff rates into a fairly narrow band, e.g. between zero and 20 per cent. With a few exceptions, export subsidies were also removed. There were visible effects on the level and composition of effective demand, and on patterns of employment and labour productivity.

Demand composition typically shifted in the direction of imports, especially when there was real exchange appreciation. In several cases, national savings rates also declined. This shift can be partly attributed to an increased supply of imports at low prices (increasing household spending, aided by credit expansion following financial liberalization), and partly to a profit squeeze (cutting retained earnings) in industries producing traded goods. The subsequent decline in private savings was sometimes partially offset by rising government savings where fiscal policy became more restrictive. Many countries showed 'stop–go' cycles in government tax and spending behaviour.

Especially when it went together with real appreciation, current account liberalization pushed traded goods producers toward workplace reorganization (including greater reliance on outsourcing) and downsizing, such as in Mexican and Argentine manufacturing. If, as assumed above, unskilled labour is an important component of variable cost, then these workers would bear the brunt of such adjustments via job losses. In other words, traded goods enterprises that stayed in operation had to cut costs by generating labour productivity growth. Depending on demand conditions, their total employment levels could very easily fall.

The upshot of these effects often took the form of increased inequality between groups of workers, in particular between the skilled and unskilled. This outcome is apparently at odds with widely discussed predictions of the Stolper–Samuelson theorem, according to which trade liberalization should lead to an increase in the remuneration of the relatively abundant production factor in Latin America (unskilled labour) with respect to the scarce factor (capital or skilled labour). Of course, besides considering exchange rate and capital flow effects on remunerations, we depart from the standard Heckscher–Ohlin trade theory framework underlying Stolper–Samuelson by working with more than two production factors and allowing for factor immobility and product market imperfections. These considerations, along with changes in the sectoral composition of output such as emphasized in Figure 1.1, are important factors in determining the distributive effects of trade liberalization (see also Wood 1997). With liberalization stimulating productivity increases leading to a reduction of labour demand from modern, traded goods production, primary income differentials widened between workers in such sectors and those employed in non-traded, informal activities (e.g. informal services) and the unemployed.

Graphical illustration of the possible effects of BoP liberalization
It is easy to trace through the implications of these changes in Figure 1.1, beginning with the traded goods equilibrium schedule in the northeast quadrant. The sector was subject to several conflicting forces:

- By switching demand toward imports, current account liberalization tended to reduce output X_t. This demand loss was strengthened by real appreciation and weakened – or even reversed – by devaluation. Removal of export subsidies hurt manufacturing and raw materials sectors in some cases.
- Domestic credit expansion and a falling savings rate stimulated demand for both sectors, although high interest rates may have held back spending on luxury manufactured items such as consumer durables and cars (in countries where they were produced).

The outcome is that the shift in the traded goods equilibrium schedule was ambiguous, as shown by the double-headed arrow in the diagram. The contractionary forces we just mentioned did not impinge directly on non-traded goods; as shown, the corresponding market equilibrium schedule shifted upward. The likely results after both schedules were adjusted were a higher non-traded price–wage ratio P_n/w, a fall in the intersectoral terms-of-trade P_t/P_n and an ambiguous change in X_t.

Turning to employment and productivity changes, new jobs were typically created in the non-traded sector, i.e. L_n^d went up along the demand schedule in the northwest quadrant. With overall decreasing returns in the sector, its real wage w/P_n and labour productivity level X_n/L_n^d could be expected to fall.

Increased labour productivity meant that the traded goods labour demand schedule in the middle quadrant on the right moved toward the origin. Regardless of what happened to their overall level of activity, traded goods producers generated fewer jobs per unit of output. Reading through the lower quadrant on the left, L_n^s or unskilled labour supply in non-traded goods tended to rise. The effect on overall unemployment ($L_n^s - L_n^d$) was unclear. Only in a few cases did unemployment fall enough to generate strong wage pressure. Wage dynamics appeared to be driven by institutional circumstances in partly segmented labour markets, with details differing per country. In many cases, stable or rising unemployment and unresponsive wages caused the overall income distribution to become more concentrated. A typical case found in several instances has been that surplus labour was absorbed in the informal sector. This would put downward pressure on mean incomes of the self-employed in that sector and a widening differential between wage and non-wage labour incomes. The differential between skilled and unskilled wage rates tended to rise as well, the productivity switch being associated with greater skill-intensity of production.

The last curve to shift was the one setting the trade deficit in the extreme southeast quadrant: higher import demand and typically lagging exports meant that it moved away from the origin. The trade deficit thus went up for a given output level. The corresponding increase in 'required' capital inflows fed into the shifts in the capital account discussed above.

Other reforms

When assessing the effects hypothesized above in real country contexts, one has to take account of other measures that were implemented simultaneously in many of the countries and which compounded the effects discussed above. We briefly mention three other major areas of liberalization.

Domestic financial sector deregulation: The effects of capital account liberalization have to be understood in conjunction with the domestic financial sector reforms that also took place almost simultaneously in most countries around 1990 – with the exception of Colombia, Chile and Uruguay, which started in varying degrees as early as the 1970s. The lifting of interest-rate ceilings, lowering of reserve requirements, and easing of entry for new banks and other financial institutions were conducive to private credit expansion fuelled by foreign capital inflows. With inadequate bank regulation and supervision in most countries, these changes in regulatory policy exacerbated the risk of banking crises along the lines described above (Vos 1995).

Labour market liberalization: Thus far, the smallest changes have occurred in this area (IDB 1998). Only a few countries managed to make important moves toward increased labour market flexibility (Argentina in 1991, Colombia in 1990, Guatemala in 1990, Peru in 1991 and, at least on paper, Panama in 1995). Distributional outcomes will be strongly influenced by the degree of wage rigidity and labour market segmentation. In most cases, institutional wage setting in modern sector firms continues to prevail (as assumed above), as well as regulations stipulating high severance payments in employee dismissal cases. Strongly segmented labour markets are still a main characteristic in all countries. The bargaining power of organized labour is generally seen to have declined throughout the region, reducing the political space for real wage adjustments (IDB 1998, Morley 1999).

Tax reforms: Broadly speaking, countries have moved toward taxation of consumption through value-added taxes and away from direct taxation, roughly a shift away from taxing the wealthy and toward lower and middle income groups. Substantial lowering of marginal rates on income and corporate taxes has been common. In some cases – like Uruguay, Peru and, temporarily, Ecuador – personal income taxes were eliminated altogether.

1.3 CROSS-COUNTRY COMPARISONS

To trace through the sorts of changes described by the analytical framework presented in the previous section in detail, the first step is to examine how major economic aggregates shifted over time. To this end, the country papers deploy several simple time series and/or comparative static decomposition techniques. The essentials are outlined in the Appendix, beginning with effective demand and going on to employment, productivity growth and the functional income distribution.

Tables 1.1 through 1.4 and Figures 1.2 and 1.3 give a summary of some of the main findings per country. For now we look at three before-and-after comparisons: growth and equity; aggregate demand shifts; and productivity changes, sectoral production and employment reallocations. In Section 1.4 we summarize the specific country narratives in terms of the analytical framework outlined above. In Section 1.5 we discuss some counterfactual model analyses, trying to single out with greater sophistication how much of the observed changes can be attributed to the reform measures.

Growth and Equity

While most countries achieved moderate growth rates in the 1990s, except for a few exceptions it is hard to speak of a strong and sustained recovery from the dismal performance of the 1980s (Tables 1.1 and 1.2). What's more, toward the end of the decade growth had tapered off in many countries due to emerging domestic financial crises – as was the case in Paraguay, Colombia and Ecuador – or external events. Adverse foreign shocks included the impact of the Asian crisis on capital flows to Brazil with spillover effects on neighbouring countries, particularly Argentina, and of falling export earnings for most primary exporting economies due to plummeting commodity prices.

Capital inflows to most countries increased substantially and, as discussed in Section 1.2, brought both aggregate demand growth and real exchange rate appreciation (with a few exceptions, see below). The latter outcome has been consistent with reductions in inflation, which helped support higher average real wages in most countries. However, inequality of primary incomes increased almost across the board (Table 1.1). Virtually without exception, wage differentials between skilled and unskilled workers rose in the post-liberalization period. In a number of cases there were widening income

Table 1.1 Growth and inequality in Latin America in the 1990s

		INEQUALITY Overall primary incomes		
Change after liberalization		Rising inequality	Decreasing inequality	Unchanged
G	High (>5%)	ARG (91–94, 96–98)	CHI (92–97)	URY (90–97)
		CHI (76–81, 84–92)	ESV (91–97)	
R		COL (91–95)	PAN (90–94)	
		DR (91–98)		
O		PERU (91–97)		
	Moderate	BOL (89–97)	BRA (94–97)	URY (86–90)
W	(2–5%)	BRA (87–94)	CRI (87–92)	
		CRI (92–98)	CUB (94–98)	
T		ECU (90–97)		
		MEX (88–94)		
H		PAN (94–98)		
		PRY (88–91, 92–94)		
	Low (0–2%)	COL (95–98)	JAM (89–98)	
		ECU (95–99)		
		MEX (85–87)		
		PRY (95–98)		
	Negative (< 0%)	CUB (89–93)		
		MEX (94–95)		

		INEQUALITY Skill differentials		
Change after liberalization		Rising inequality	Decreasing inequality	Unchanged
G	High (>5%)	ARG (91–94, 96–98)	CHI (92–97)	
		CHI (76–81, 84–92)		
R		COL (92–95)		
		DR (91–98)		
O		ESV (90–97)		
		PAN (90–94)		
W		PERU (91–98)		
		URY (90–97)		
T	Moderate	BOL (89–97)	BRA (94–97)	
	(2–5%)	BRA (92–94)	URY (86–90)	
H		CRI (85–91, 92–98)		
		ECU (90–97)		
		MEX (88–94)		
		PRY (88–91, 92–94)		
	Low (0–2%)	COL (95–98)		
		JAM (90–92)		
		MEX (85–87)		
		PAN (94–98)		
		PRY (95–98)		
	Negative (< 0%)	JAM (93–98)		BRA (87–91)
		MEX (94–95)		

Notes: Inequality for primary incomes refers to per worker incomes of labour force. Skill differentials refer (mostly) to hourly incomes of all wage earners. Income distribution data based on household surveys. Due to data limitations, coverage is mostly for urban workers (see Table A1.1).

Source: Table 1.2 and country studies.

Table 1.2 Growth, employment and inequality

								Income inequality				Employment structure		
	Periods	Characterization	GDP growth	RER	Employ-ment rate	Wage share in GDP	Real wages	Overall p.c. house-hold income	Overall primary income (labour force)	Skilled/ unsk.	Formal/ inf.	Traded/ non-tr.	Skilled/ unsk.	Formal/ inf.
Argentina	90	Year before conversion plan	–1.3											
	91–94	Plan Conv, Expansion I	8.9	+	+/–		++	+	+	+		–		
	95	Tequila effect	–4.6	+	—		—	+	+	+		–		
	96–98	Expansion II	6.5	+	+		+	+	+	+		–		
Bolivia	80–85	Destabilization	–1.6	+	–		–							
	86–89	Stabilization	1.6	–	–	+	+	0/+	+	+		–	+	
	90–97	Post-liberalization	4.2	–	+	–	+/–	+	+	+		0/–	+	+
Brazil	82–86	Pre-reform period	4.4	+	+		+	0	0	–	–	–	+	+
	87–91	Liberalization	–0.3	–	0		–	+	0	0	+	–	+	+
	92–94	Post-liberalization I	5.4	–	–	–	+	–	0	+	+	+	+	–
	94–97	Post-liberalization II	3.2	+	–	–	+	0	0	–	–	–	+	0
Chile	70–74	Demand exp., hyperinfl.	1.0	+	+		—		–	–		+		
	76–81	Liberalization	9.4	+	+		++	++	++	+		–		
	85–89	Readjustment	8.4	–	++		+	–	+	+		–		
	90–97	Free trade agreements	9.4	+	+		++	–	–	–		–		
Colombia	92–95	Liberalization and boom	5.2	+	+	+	++	+	+	+	+	–	+	+
	95–98	Stagnation	1.4	+	–	–	+	+	+	+	+	–	+	–
Costa Rica	85–91	Trade lib. (CA)	3.7	+	+	+/0	–	–	–	+	+	–	+	+
	92–98	Further opening	4.3	0	+	0	+	+	+	+	+/0	—	+	+
Cuba	89–93	Opening forex market	–8.5	++	+/0	—	—	+	+		+	+	+	—
	94–98	Fiscal adj., informal activities	4.4	–/+	–/0	+	+	–	–		–	–	+	—
Dom. Rep.	91–99	Post-liberalization	6.5	++	+	+	+	–	+	+	+	–	+	+
Ecuador	88–91	Pre-reform	2.6	–	+/–	–	–	+	+	+	+	–	+	–
	92–98	Stabilization and liberalization	2.7	++	–/+	+/0	+	–/0	+	+	+	0	+	–
	98–99	Financial crisis	–7.0	—	—	–	—	+	+	+	+	0	+	–

El Salvador	80–82	BoP crisis	–9.5	+	—		–							
	83–89	War economy	1.3	++	–		–							
	90–95	BoP and financial liberalization	6.0	++	+		0/–	–	–	+		–	–	
	96–98	Demand contraction	3.0	+	0/–		0/–	–	–	+		–	–	
Guatemala	87–92	BoP liberalization	3.9	–		–	–				–	+		–
	92–97	BoP cum dom. fin. lib.	4.0	+		+	+				+	+		–
Jamaica	80–89	Pre-liberalization	1.6	+	+	—				+		–	+	+
	90–92	Financial liberalization	1.2	+	+	–	—	–		+		–	+	+
	93–98	Trade liberalization	–0.7	+	–	+	+	–		+		–	+	+
Mexico	88–94	Trade and financial lib.	3.9	++	+/–	+	+	+	+	+	+		+	
	94–95	Peso crisis and NAFTA	–6.2	—	—	–	—	+	+	+	+		+	
	96–98	Post-crisis	5.8	+	+	–	–							
Panama	86–90	Crisis	–1.7	0	—		–	+	+					
	90–94	Stabilization and recovery	6.5	0	+		+/0	–	–	+		–	+	–
	94–98	Trade reform	3.3	0	+/0		0	+	+	+		–	+	–
Paraguay	88–91	Trade and exch. rate reform	3.8	–	+/0	+	+	+	+	+	+	–	–	+
	92–94	MERCOSUR	3.6	+	0	+	+	+	+	+	+	–	+	–
	95–98	Financial reform	2.0	+	–	0	+/0	+	+	+	+	–	+	+
Peru	86–90	Hyperinflation	–1.1	++	–		—	+	0	+	–	–	+	–
	91–98	BoP liberalization	4.9	+/0	+		++	+	+	+	+	–	+	+
Uruguay	86–90	Pre-Mercosur	2.5	–	0	+	+	+/0	0/–	–	0	+/0	+/0	0
	91–97	MERCOSUR	4.3	+	0/–	–	+/–	+	+/0	+	+	–	+	0/–

Key to variables: ++ = strong increase; + = increase; +/0 = slight increase, almost stable; 0 = no change; 0/– = slight decrease, almost stable; – = decrease; — = strong decrease; +/–/+ = fluctuating trend (stop–go); growth = annual rate of GDP; RER = real exchange rate (+ = real appreciation).
Employment rate = change in employed as share of EAP (+ = rise in employment or decrease in unemployment).
Real wages = change in average wage rate.
Inequality = inequality of per capita household income (first column), per worker primary labour income (second column) (+ = rising inequality), change in ratio earnings of skilled and unskilled workers (third column) and change in ratio of formal and informal sector workers (fourth column).

Source: Country studies.

differentials between formal and informal sector workers, typically because of the type of employment reallocation along the lines of Figure 1.1. Either excess labour was typically absorbed in the non-traded, informal trade and services sectors (as in Bolivia, Colombia, Costa Rica, Ecuador, Panama and Peru), or in a few cases traditional agriculture served as a sponge for the labour market (Panama in the late 1980s, Guatemala and Mexico).

Primary income inequality increased for a variety of reasons. In Argentina, productivity increases in the traded goods sector affected workers of all skill levels. Wage rigidity being greater for unskilled workers, there was a reduction in earnings inequality in the sector, but greater inequality in Argentina was due to rising income concentration in the non-traded sector along with greater skill-intensity of new investment and the rise of unemployment in the traded goods sector. By contrast, in Mexico reorganization of manufacturing production was found to be a major source of greater skill demand, pushing up wage inequality in the traded goods sector with many of the displaced workers absorbed by agriculture, at least until 1994. In Brazil, productivity growth produced employment losses in the manufacturing sector. Labour demand fell for everyone in modern manufacturing, but skilled workers suffered the most. Real hourly wages fell for both skilled and unskilled workers in modern industry, but slightly less for unskilled workers, showing – as in Argentina – greater rigidity in wage adjustment at the lower end; hence skilled–unskilled income differentials showed a slight decline. As indicated, in most other cases such productivity growth in traded goods sectors pushed up skill differentials in that sector along with the gap between formal and informal sector workers.

The picture is not entirely gloomy as far as primary income distribution is concerned. In El Salvador, rapid employment growth of unskilled workers, particularly in export sectors, offset the widening gap between group skill differentials. In Chile, overall labour market tightening was probably the main factor behind reduction of wage differentials in the 1990s.[2] In Brazil, elimination of hyperinflation and labour demand shifts toward the unskilled have been factors underlying the dampening of primary income differentials. Trends have also been influenced by minimum wage policies, as in Ecuador, where upward adjustments in the minimum wage allowed for a temporary decline in earnings inequality (1992–95) despite an overall rising trend (1990–98). In Jamaica, real exchange rate appreciation implied a relative price shift in favour of non-traded activities, which in an overall stagnant economy attracted many unskilled workers from rural areas and the agricultural sector. As urban living standards are generally higher and real wages were allowed to grow, the sectoral employment shift explains the reduction in overall income inequality among workers despite the widening wage gap between the skilled and unskilled.

As shown by Figure 1.2, rising per worker differentials do not necessarily translate into rising inequality and poverty at a household level. The cases of rising inequality clearly predominate once more (east of the vertical axis), but so do episodes where poverty fell during the 1990s (south of the horizontal axis). Economic growth evidently helped reduce poverty, also where liberalization pushed toward greater inequality. Figure 1.3 sketches the broad picture of the inverse link between growth and poverty in Latin America during the 1990s. It is obvious that there are important deviations from the trend, and that the underlying mechanisms differ per country. Only in a few cases – particularly Chile and El Salvador – was poverty reduction associated with moderate to strong export-led growth and falling inequality. In most other cases, growth recovery following a surge in capital inflows allowed for an expansion of aggregate demand and sufficient overall employment growth or a rise in real wages to produce a reduction in poverty. As detailed further below, these particular domestic demand-led growth recovery patterns have been rather volatile and are unlikely to form sustainable paths of poverty reduction. In other cases, like Mexico and Argentina, the rise in inequality particularly associated with labour demand shifts favouring skilled workers and/or employment shifts into informal activities or unemployment caused a rise in poverty despite positive per capita growth. In other cases, changing labour market conditions have triggered strong labour supply responses, including rising female participation, as in e.g. Panama and urban Ecuador. Elsewhere, emigrant remittances (Central America, Dominican Republic, Cuba) or social security transfers (e.g. Costa Rica) have a strong positive influence on reduction of poverty and inequality at the household level. Chapter 2 discusses the relative importance of the various labour market adjustment mechanisms – aggregate labour demand, participation rates, demand shifts by sector and skill and remuneration structure – in full detail.

Macro Changes (Demand Decomposition)

Real exchange rate (RER) appreciation has been a pivotal characteristic of the post-liberalization period in most countries. Only where depreciation occurred or the currency was kept weak – as was the case in Bolivia, Chile, Colombia (1990–92), Mexico (post-1995) and Uruguay (1986–90) – did growth impulses come principally from export growth and diversification. Similar observations hold for countries that had credible incentive systems for non-traditional exports, like the Dominican Republic, Chile, Costa Rica and El Salvador.

Export-led growth was not central in all the other cases (Table 1.3). Rather, rising import leakages were commonplace, and stronger where RER appreciation and strong surges in capital inflows occurred. Higher import propensities offset the growth impacts of export expansions that nearly all

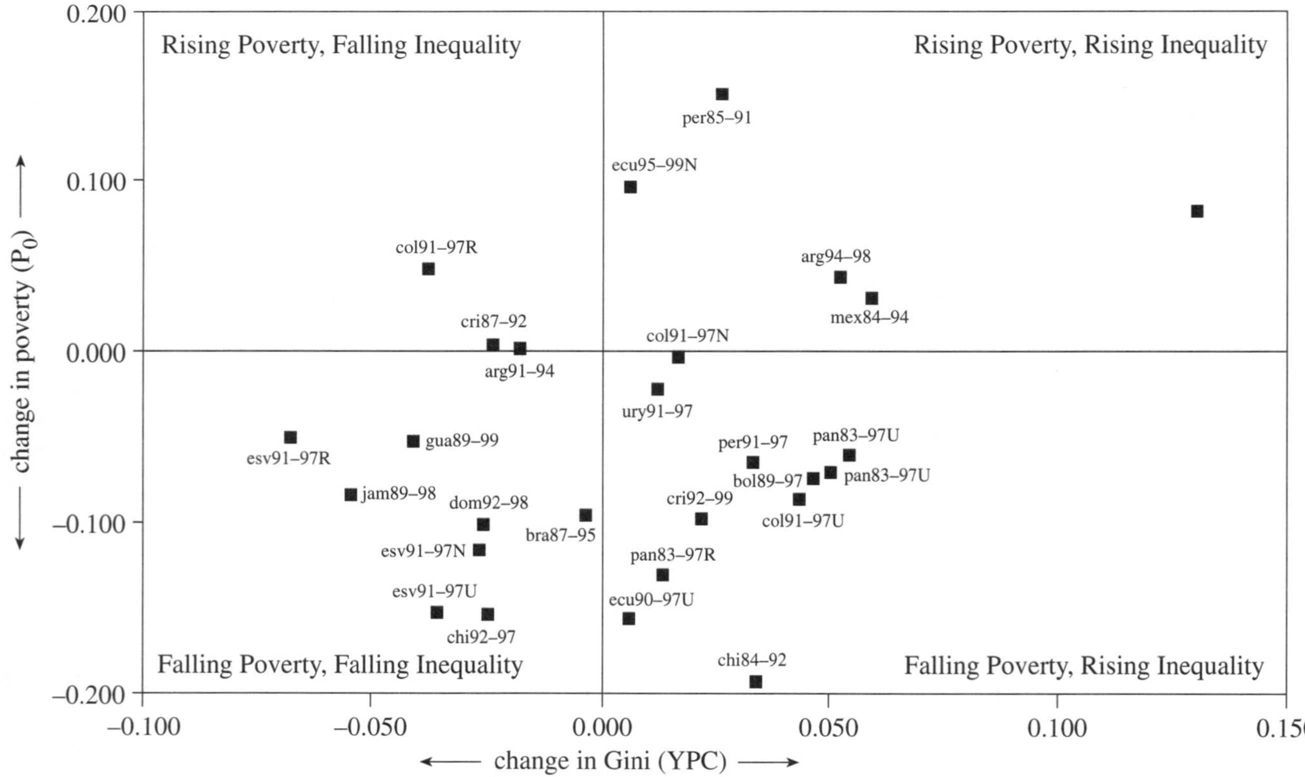

Figure 1.2 Poverty and inequality (of per capita household income) before and after liberalization

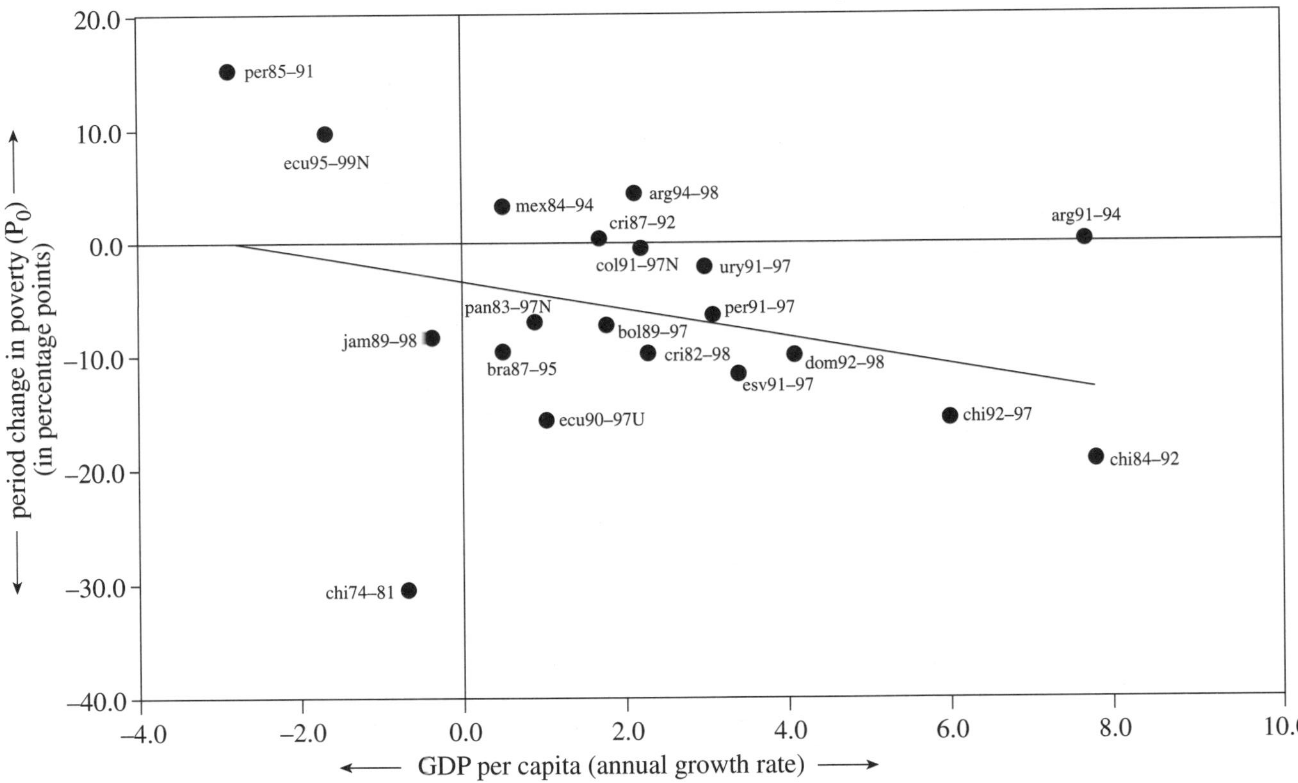

Figure 1.3 Growth and poverty in Latin America in the 1990s

Table 1.3 Factors of growth in the 1990s (by aggregate demand decomposition)

	Periods	Principal source of demand growth	Aggregate demand growth (*X*)	Direct multiplier effects			Leakages		
				I/s	*G/t*	*E/m*	*S*	*t*	*m*
Argentina	1990–94	Private consumption boom	8.9	++		0	—		+
	1995–96	Private demand contraction	–4.6	–		+	+		–
	1996–98	Private demand (C,I) recovery	6.5	+			–		+
Bolivia	1980–85	Private consumption and gov. spending	–1.5	+	—	+/–	—	0	–/+
	1986–89	Export led	2.1	–/+	0	+	+	0	0
	1990–97	Export led	4.8	+	+	+	+	0	+
Brazil	1982–86	Government spending and exports	–0.9	0	+	+	+	0	–
	1987–91	Government spending	3.0	–	+	–	+	+	+
	1992–94	Private spending and gov. spending	0.9	+	+	–	0	+	+
	1994–97	Private investment and consumption	5.2	+	–	–	–	0	+
Chile	1970–74	Private and government consumption	1.0	—	+	–	++	+/0	–/0
	1976–81	Consumption squeeze, export growth	9.4	0	+	–	+/0	+	–
	1985–89	Investment, exports	8.4	++	+/0	++	–/0	–/0	–
	1990–97	Investment, exports	9.4	++	+/0	++	+	–/0	–
Colombia	1990–92	Exports and government spending	2.2	–	++	+	+	0	+
	1992–95	Private consumption boom	9.6	–	+	+	—	+	+
	1995–98	Private demand contraction	1.5	—	+/–	+	0	0	+
Costa Rica	1985–91	Export led	5.7	+	+	++	+	—	+
	1992–98	Export led	6.5	+	+	++	–/0	–	+
Cuba	1989–93	Private demand squeeze	–13.7	—	—	++	++	–	++
	1994–98	Public spending and export recovery	7.0	++	++	+	—	+	+
Dom. Rep.	1993–99	Private demand and export led	7.5	+	–	+	+	0	+

Ecuador	1988–91	Private demand	4.4	+	0/–	–	–	+	0
	1992–98	Export led	2.9	–	0	++	+	0	0
El Salvador	1990–95	Investment and export	8.2	+	0	+	+/–	+	+
	1996–97	Export	0.1	—	+	++	–	–	–
Guatemala	1986–91	Consumption led	3.4	+	+/0	0	0/–	+/0	+
	1991–98	Consumption led	5.0	+/0	+/–/+	+	–	+	+
Jamaica	1980–89	Private consumption led	2.0	+	–	0	—	+	0
	1990–92	Export led	8.1	–	–	+	+	–	+
	1993–98	Private demand and export contraction	–3.1	+/–/+	+	–	–	–	–
Mexico	1988–94	Consumption boom	5.5	++	+/0	–	—	0	++
	1994–95	Crisis and cons. squeeze	–7.8	—	0	++	+	–	–
	1996–98	Investment recovery	8.3	+	+/0	0	+	0	++
Panama	1986–90	Crisis: private demand contraction	–5.4	++	0	+	–	0	+
	1990–94	Private demand and exports	5.7	+	0	+	+/0	0	+
	1994–98	Exports and private demand	4.9	+	0	+	–	0	0
Paraguay	1988–91	Private demand expansion	6.7	+	+	0/–	+/–	0	+
	1992–94	Private demand expansion	10.8	+	–	0/–	—	0	+
	1995–98	Private demand and export contraction	–0.6	+	+	–	–	+/0	–
Peru	1986–90	Collapse private demand	–1.9	++	+	–	–	–	–
	1991–97	Private demand recovery	5.6	++	+	–/0	+	+	+
Uruguay	1986–90	Export led, private demand squeeze	2.9	–	–/+/–	+	0	0	0
	1990–94	Private demand expansion	8.4	++	+/0	–	—	+/–	++
	1994–97	Private demand and exports	4.4	–/+	–	+	0/–	+/0	+

Key to variables: ++ = strong increase; – = increase; +/0 = slight increase, almost stable; 0 = no change; 0/– = slight decrease, almost stable; – = decrease; — = strong decrease; +/–/+ = fluctuating trend (stop–go).
Aggregate demand = GDP + imports (numbers refer to annual rates of growth).

Source: Country studies; see Appendix for demand decomposition methodology.

Table 1.4 Factors of productivity and employment growth

	Periods	Characterization	Productivity growth			Sector reallocation effects	Labour supply decomposition		
			Overall	T	NT	Employment	Particip. rate	Unempl. rate	Empl. rate
Argentina	1990–94	Plan Conv, Expansion I							
	1995–96	Tequila effect							
	1996–98	Expansion II							
Bolivia	1980–92	Destabilization/stabilization	–2.8	–2.9	–3.0	Large (toward agric., inf. trade)	+	+	–
	1992–97	Post-liberalization	1.0	1.0	0.8	Large (toward urban, inf. trade)	+	–	+
Brazil	1982–86	Pre-reform period	0.7	2.0	–0.4		+	–	+
	1987–91	Liberalization	–4.0	–2.4	–5.1		0	0	0
	1992–94	Post-liberalization I	4.4	2.4	4.6		+	+	–
	1994–97	Post-liberalization II	0.9	4.4	–1.2		0	+	–
Chile	1970–74	Demand expansion, hyperinfl.	0.8	0.1	1.3	Small	–	+	+
	1976–81	Liberalization	2.6	3.7	1.9	Small (–)	+	–	+
	1985–89	Readjustment	0.1	–1.2	0.9	Small (–)	+	–	++
	1990–97	Free trade agreements	3.9	4.8	3.5	Small (–)	+/0	–	+
Colombia	1992–95	Liberalization and boom	2.6	2.7	2.9	Small	+	+	+
	1995–98	Stagnation	2.0	2.8	1.9	Small	–	+	–
Costa Rica	1987–91	Trade lib.	1.5	2.3	0.9	Small	–	–/0	–/0
	1992–98	Further opening	0.6	3.0	–1.0	Small	+	–/0	+
Cuba	1989–93	Opening forex market	–8.3	–13.7	–5.0	0	–	+	+/0
	1994–98	Fiscal adj., flexibilization inf. activ.	4.1	11.1	0.1	0	–	–	–/0
Dom. Rep.	1991–96	Post-liberalization	3.5	5.7	2.3	Small	–	–	+

Ecuador	1992–97	Post-reform	0.1	1.3	–0.9	Large (away from NT)	0	–	+
El Salvador	1991–95	BoP and financial liberalization	14.3	–0.6	31.3	Large	–	–	
	1995–96	Demand contract	9.6	4.4	14.0	Small	–	–	
Guatemala	1987–92	BoP liberalization	0.4	–0.4	1.1	Large	0		
	1992–97	BoP cum dom. financial lib.	0.3	–1.3	0.8	Large	0/–		
Jamaica	1980–89	Pre-liberalization	3.2	1.7	0.9	Small	0	–	+
	1990–92	Financial liberalization	3.7	1.2	2.1	Small	0	–	+
	1993–98	Trade liberalization	–1.0	0.5	–1.6	Small	+	+	–
Mexico	1988–93	Financial liberalization	0.6	6.0	–0.5	Small	+	0	+
	1994–97	Peso crisis, NAFTA	–0.8	–0.2	–2.1	Small			
Panama	1991–94	Stabilization and recovery	0.2	4.3	–2.0	Large (out of agriculture)	+	–	+
	1994–98	Trade reform	0.2	1.2	–0.5	Fair (into informal services)	+/0	0	0
Paraguay	1982–92	Trade and exchange rate reform	–0.4	1.2	–2.5	Large (away from T)	+	+/–	–
	1992–97	Mercosur and financial lib.	–5.7	–2.1	–8.7	Large (away from T)	+	–/0	+
Peru	1986–90	High inflation period	0.7	1.1	0.6		–	+	–
	1991–98	BoP liberalization	0.6	1.1	0.5		+	–	+
Uruguay	1986–90	Pre-Mercosur	0.4	–0.7	0.6		+	–	–
	1990–94	Mercosur (I)	3.8	0.0	2.2		+	+	+/0
	1994–97	Mercosur (II)	2.7	6.5	2.4		0/–	+	–

Key to variables:
Productivity growth = annual rate of change of productivity (Q/L).
T = traded goods sectors.
NT = non-traded goods sectors.
Reallocation effects: see decomposition methodology in Appendix.

Source: Country studies. See Appendix for productivity and labour supply decompositions.

countries witnessed. Although exports gained importance as a source of growth, as expected, the gains, by far, do not seem to have been as strong as originally supposed by advocates of liberalization.

Public sector adjustment has been relatively less important in determining aggregate demand shifts in most countries, except for Cuba (1994–98). This outcome may be surprising, given the rhetoric about downsizing the state that accompanied the drive toward liberalization. Some countries even had a positive public sector demand effect, and others a stop–go pattern.

Without strong contributions from the foreign and public sectors, private sector demand growth emerged as the major driving force in many of the country histories. In particular, import-led consumption booms following trade and financial liberalization were the rule rather than the exception. They were triggered by both cheapening of imported traded goods (import liberalization and real exchange rate appreciation) and expansion of domestic credit supply (fomented by the surge in capital flows and domestic financial liberalization). As a result, private savings rates fell. Fewer cases were observed in which domestic demand was driven by expanding private investment, but where these occurred they have been more recent, as in Argentina (1996–97), Chile (1990–97) and Mexico (1996–98). Higher private capital formation could give hope for a brighter future were it not for a setback due to global instability in 1998–99.

Productivity and Employment Growth

So far, the liberalization attempts have yielded only modest aggregate productivity increases in most countries (Table 1.4). In most cases, as could be expected, there was greater productivity growth in traded than in non-traded sectors. The change in aggregate productivity is the result of the sum of productivity changes by sectors, weighted by sectoral output shares, plus the reallocation of labour from low- to high-productivity sectors (see Appendix). Findings from the country studies indicate that within-sector productivity shifts and output growth rates largely determined the aggregate outcomes. Typically, relatively small employment reallocation effects were found, but in a few cases – Guatemala, Mexico, Panama and Ecuador – there were important labour reallocation effects with low productivity agriculture or urban informal services serving as 'employers of last resort'.

1.4 SUMMARY OF COUNTRY EXPERIENCES

Despite some common features, country cases show important differences in experience. We briefly summarize the country narratives here. We cover 17

Latin American country stories here, eight of which are counted in detail in the country chapters.[3]

Argentina largely fits the line of argument of Section 1.2. After liberalization and imposition of an exchange rate freeze (the convertibility plan) in 1991, the economy continued an expansion that had started the previous year. In practice, convertibility turned the central bank into a currency board. Domestic credit creation was tied directly to foreign reserves, so that the volume of capital flows drove the level of economic activity.

In the first half of the decade, inflows were ample and the trade deficit widened. Growth continued until 1995, when the region was hit by what is known as the tequila crisis. Imports expanded rapidly until that crisis hit; exports jumped upward at mid-decade, stimulated by Mercosur and real appreciation in Brazil due to implementation of the anti-inflationary *Plan Real*. After the effects of the tequila shock dissipated, the economy started to grow again as capital inflows recovered, but entered into sharp contraction in 1998–99 with Brazil's slow growth and devaluation cutting into exports.

An early investment boom and perhaps a fall in the savings rate (not estimated independently in Argentine national accounts) led aggregate demand. The labour market apparently experienced a lagged adjustment to the wage and price realignments that took place rapidly after the exchange rate was pegged. During the 1990–96 expansion, industrial sector output grew at about 5 per cent per year due to higher local consumption and exports not fully offset by higher imports. The period saw a rapid labour productivity growth of about 6.6 per cent per year, which forced industrial employment to fall despite the output expansion.

The drop in industrial employment spilled over into other sectors, with an increase over time in open unemployment and 'involuntary underemployment' (the difference between the total employment rate and the rate for full-time jobs). Per capita incomes of the employed population rose until mid-decade but declined afterwards. Between 1991 and 1998, per capita income for the economically active population grew by 12.2 per cent. Without increased unemployment and labour market restructuring, the total would have been 29.4 per cent. Labour shedding in industry also took its distributional toll. Among the economically active population, the Gini coefficient rose from 0.471 in 1991 to 0.534 in 1998. As mentioned in Section 1.3, productivity increases in the traded goods sector affected employment at all skill levels. With wage rigidity greater for unskilled workers, this led to a decrease in wage inequality in this sector. Hence, unlike the model assumptions of Section 1.2, demand for skilled workers did not appear to move upward with new capital investment and skilled labour in the case of Argentine manufacturing. Rising inequality in Argentina is due rather to rising inequality in the non-traded sector along with greater skill-intensity of new investment in that sector, as well as the rise in unemployment in the traded goods sector.

By 1999 the economy was in deep recession with unemployment steadily rising. Eight years of convertibility ended up generating future prospects substantially worse than they were when the scheme was started.

Bolivia is often seen as one of the region's early reformers. Severe external shocks and poor domestic economic management drove the economy to hyperinflation by the mid-1980s. To redress the situation, the government implemented a drastic economic stabilization and reform programme in 1985 whose key features were the liberalization of the foreign exchange regime, major reduction of import restrictions and elimination of the export licensing system. The state-owned tin mines were closed as part of the stabilization programme, but privatization of public enterprises, the lifting of restrictions on direct foreign investment and further capital account liberalization did not get a major boost until the 1994 *Ley de Capitalización*. Major debt-reduction operations and massive inflows of development assistance helped turn the stabilization programme into a success, and inflation was brought back to single-digit levels by the early 1990s. Despite massive capital inflows (hovering around 6–10 per cent of GDP), economic recovery was initially slow but the pace of GDP growth settled at a moderate rate of about 4 per cent per year in the 1990s.

The opening of the economy brought a shift toward traded goods production and a change in export composition. Reliance on mineral exports became less important as there was a dynamic growth of non-traditional, agricultural exports. Growth of aggregate demand mainly relied on this growth of exports. Economic integration (Mercosur, Andean Pact) had a positive influence on both trade performance and real exchange rate depreciation. Despite the massive capital inflows, monetary authorities managed to keep the exchange rate competitive. Still, the structural adjustment did not alter the country's status as a primary commodity exporter, maintaining its vulnerability to external shocks. The external terms of trade fell by 32 per cent between 1990 and 1997, creating national income losses equal to US$ 560 million on an annual basis and hence offsetting inflows of foreign savings in aggregate terms.

Unemployment fell with overall economic growth during the 1990s. In urban areas, occupation rates increased for skilled workers, while demand for unskilled workers fell. Public sector reforms reduced government employment but did cause public sector wages to outpace those in the private sector. Within the private sector, skilled workers in small- and medium-sized enterprises saw the highest real wage increase, while average wages for mostly unskilled workers in both low-productivity family businesses and large-scale firms remained almost stagnant. On the whole, per capita income growth and falling unemployment helped reduce poverty, but at the same time income inequality increased mainly because of widening wage differentials in favour of skilled workers.

Brazil started trade liberalization in earnest in the early 1990s, in the context of regional integration in Mercosur. In the preceding decade, trade policies had been subject to macroeconomic considerations, particularly the use of quantitative import restrictions in response to foreign exchange constraints. Between 1988 and 1995/7 the average nominal tariff rate was brought back from 50 to 12.6 per cent. The major impulse toward capital account liberalization and stimulation of direct foreign investment came in 1991. Helped by global events, negative flows of private capital early in the decade were reverted to net annual inflows to the tune of US$ 25 billion in 1995–96. The heterodox macroeconomic policy experiments of the *Plan Cruzado* and *Plan Collor* of the late 1980s and early 1990s failed to bring stability. Monetary aggregates only came under control with the *Plan Real*, although fiscal problems were not fully controlled. The exchange rate appreciated with inflation under control and the nominal exchange rate being used as nominal anchor by the central bank. Growth of aggregate demand, driven mainly by private investment and consumption demand, recovered at an annual rate of 5.2 per cent during 1994–97. The private savings rate fell and the import propensity rose in a fashion similar to other experiences in which balance of payments liberalization produced real exchange rate appreciation and high capital inflows.

Lower inflation enabled a 6.5 per cent annual increase of real wages between 1992 and 1997, despite a drop in the employment rate and a slight rise in unemployment. Economic recovery and new capital flows allowed for productivity increases accelerating at an economy-wide rate of 4.4 per cent during 1992–94, slowing down to an annual 0.9 per cent during 1994–97 but with continued high productivity gains in the traded goods sector. Productivity growth created employment losses in the manufacturing sector, where 8.4 per cent of the workers lost their jobs between 1987 and 1997. Demand for labour fell for all types of workers in modern manufacturing, but skilled workers suffered the most. About 20 per cent of skilled and semi-skilled jobs in modern industries were lost in the course of the decade. Real hourly wages fell for both skilled and unskilled workers in modern industry, but slightly less for unskilled workers, showing as in Argentina greater rigidity in wage adjustment at the lower end; hence, skilled–unskilled income differentials showed a slight decline. On the other hand, employment and real wages in both non-traded and informal sectors increased along with aggregate demand in those activities.

The above-mentioned trends, especially the elimination of quantitative restrictions, appear to be most closely associated with the process of trade liberalization, as suggested by counterfactual model analysis. Productivity growth induced by greater trade competitiveness has caused employment losses of unskilled workers and real wage declines in the traded sector. In contrast, capital account liberalization and the associated rise in capital inflows appear to have had a positive impact on employment and real wages.

Chile: The liberalization process began in Chile in the mid-1970s, with rapid growth finally beginning after 1985. The history differed in several respects from the model sketched in Section 1.2. For example, drastic import liberalization in the 1970s was combined with maintenance of long-standing incentives, which helped provide the basis for rapid growth in non-traditional exports a decade later. Another important factor is that Chilean authorities managed to keep a weak exchange rate, despite capital inflows. There was significant appreciation only in the late 1970s, which fed into the massive financial boom-and-crash around 1980. In the mid-1980s, inflation stabilization relied heavily on de-indexation of wage contracts. Low-end wages served as a nominal anchor, allowing the weak exchange rate to be maintained.

Finally, after fully opening the economy to capital movements in the late 1970s, successive governments turned toward selective controls. Their effectiveness has been widely debated, but most scholars agree that they – perhaps weakly – helped hold down inflows at critical periods and lengthened the maturity of external debt.

Rapid output growth got underway in 1987, with non-traditional agro-exports playing a central role. Export and import shares of GDP increased, so that trade had a neutral effect on aggregate demand. With a low national savings rate, investment supported demand growth. Fiscal effects were expansionary in the late 1980s and contractionary thereafter.

Beginning from a low level, productivity growth was sustained in agriculture, including forestry and fishing, for three decades beginning in 1970. Despite its productivity improvement, agriculture generated substantial employment growth in the late 1980s, when overall employment grew at 2.1 per cent (the difference between 3.3 per cent annual growth in labour absorption and 1.2 per cent growth in labour market participation). In the 1990s productivity rose in both traded and non-traded goods sectors, and employment growth slowed to an annual 0.3 per cent.

Income inequality remains high despite Chile's impressive macro performance. Wage inequality initially shot up in the late 1980s after inflation stabilization, but gradually decreased thereafter, perhaps due to a tightening of the labour market.

Colombia: Economic performance followed along the lines of Section 1.2. Import restrictions and export promotion schemes were reduced sharply in the early 1990s. Capital movements were liberalized, although Chile-style restrictions on inflows were retained. Government spending, much of it directed toward social programmes, rose during the decade. The increase was largely financed by higher taxes, although the public sector did have a net expansionary effect on effective demand in the recessionary second half of the 1990s.

Macroeconomic performance was uneven – a 'go' phase in the early 1990s, then a prolonged stop. Effective demand was led by the external sector in the late 1980s. The subsequent liberalization phase (1992–95) was accompanied by a jump in private investment and a fall in savings, exchange rate appreciation and a demand boom for non-traded goods. Retrenchment began with monetary tightening in 1996. With some loosening in 1997, the monetary authorities held tight, throwing the economy into open recession in 1998–99.

One result of these changes was that the capacity of the economy to generate jobs deteriorated notably. There was labour productivity growth in both traded and non-traded sectors, in the range of 2.0–2.5 per cent per year. Demand growth for traded goods was negligible throughout the decade, while non-traded demand grew at an annual 4.5 per cent during 1991–95 and 2 per cent during 1995–97. As a consequence, overall employment growth was approximately zero during 1991–95, and –1.7 per cent during 1995–97.

Such poor employment performance hit workers with low educational levels the hardest. Demand for their services did not appear to be sensitive to wage changes either. The beneficial effects of liberalization appear to have been modest at best in terms of productivity growth, while tight money and capital inflows have been associated with an increasingly prolonged recession. For the decade as a whole, economic growth could make only a very small contribution to poverty reduction. The poverty incidence fell from 41.8 to 41.4 per cent between 1991 and 1997. Rising income inequality associated with the liberalization process explains the lack of trickling down of the benefits of growth. The Gini coefficient rose from 0.548 to 0.565, essentially as a result of rising earnings gaps between skilled and unskilled workers and employment growth favouring the better-educated workers.

Costa Rica: Like Chile, Costa Rica is remarkable because it retained export incentives and managed to avoid real appreciation despite substantial capital inflows since the mid-1980s. Its economic performance after liberalization got underway in the 1980s has been more successful than most countries in the region.

Foreign trade has generally been expansionary for demand, with export growth not being fully matched by higher import penetration. Despite a four-year political cycle around the presidential election, fiscal policy has generally been contractionary. Apart from an investment jump and savings fall associated with private capital flows (drawn by high interest rates) in the early 1990s, the private sector has not contributed positively to effective demand.

During the 1987–98 period, labour productivity grew at an annual 2.7 per cent for traded goods and –0.3 per cent for non-traded goods. Per capita output rose at an annual 1.4 and 2.1 per cent for the two sectors, respectively, so that most employment growth was generated by non-tradeds. In agriculture, productivity growth averaged an annual 3.5 per cent, as total employment in the sector fell. Job reduction in traded goods sectors was concentrated among the unskilled. Job creation in non-traded sectors tended to benefit the skilled. Overall, there has been moderate per capita income growth. Poverty fell as inequality did not worsen significantly, overall employment grew steadily and real wages and social security transfers expanded in the 1990s.

Cuba: The socialist model provided a basis for visible output growth through the mid-1980s, with average rates at 6.5 per cent (1971–80) and 8.5 per cent (1981–85). Thereafter, a tightening external constraint and rising fiscal deficits were associated with only 0.7 per cent annual growth between 1986 and 1989. The big external shock came between 1989 and 1993, when the import share of GDP fell from 29 to 12 per cent while per capita GDP declined by 30 per cent. The authorities chose to stabilize both employment and nominal wages. As a consequence, labour productivity and real wages declined in tandem with per capita GDP. With a basket of 'essential' goods provided through the pre-existing rationing system, prices of freely traded commodities had to jump to force the real wage reduction. The price index for informal markets rose from 100 in 1987 to 510 in 1992 and 1,553 in 1993.

After 1993 there was a strong push to develop export industries, along with relaxation of state controls over external transactions and opening up of national markets to foreign exchange. Greater access to foreign exchange through tourism and other exports along with newly liberalized flows of direct foreign investment and remittances from abroad permitted a gradual recovery of GDP after 1993. However, growth did not exceed 2.5 per cent per year between 1994 and 1998. The government was the main support for effective demand during the adjustment period, its spending substantially exceeding revenues. The private sector was the main beneficiary, hence its effect on demand was contractionary. Exports and imports have gone up together since the early 1990s, so their demand contribution has been neutral.

After 1993, annual economy-wide productivity growth averaged 4 per cent, and 11 per cent in traded goods sectors. These improvements took place in a rapidly evolving labour market. 'Other labour incomes' (of people selling products in free markets) rose from less than 20 to 40 per cent of GDP between 1989 and 1996, while the wage share fell from 60 to 45 per cent. The overall profit share went up after 1993, especially for traded goods and services such as mining and tourism.

The process of economic opening created a widening income gap between wage earners and more informal workers, although it has declined recently. Nevertheless, overall inequality was higher in the late 1990s than during the 1980s, with an increase in the Gini coefficient for primary incomes from about 0.24 to about 0.38. Provision of social services probably pushed the coefficient for secondary income down to about 0.3.

Dominican Republic: Tariff reduction and rationalization got underway in 1990, although some quotas were retained for agricultural products. Exchange controls and a dual exchange rate structure were retained, but restrictions on capital movements were lifted. The local financial sector became somewhat dollarized, with dollar deposits rising from 8 to 16 per cent of the totals outstanding between 1994 and 1998, while dollar loans went from 2 to 14 per cent. Short-term capital inflows were strongly positive during the 1990–93 period, only partly sterilized by the central bank. After an inflation stabilization package in 1990–91, the real interest rate went up to around 20 per cent per year. An index of the real exchange rate strengthened steadily from 100 in 1990 to 83 in 1997.

Throughout the 1990s, exports were flat at less than US$ 1 billion per year; imports rose from US$ 2 to 4 billion. The contractionary effect of the rise in the import share of output was offset by rapidly increasing private investment late in the decade. Between 1996 and 1998, annual output growth was in the 7–8 per cent range, led by construction, export processing zones and tourism. Demand growth in the US contributed to the Dominican Republic's strong performance.

The unemployment rate fell from 20 per cent in 1992 to 16 per cent in 1998. Substantial labour reallocation was involved. Agricultural output per capita grew at an annual 2.1 per cent between 1991–96, with productivity growth rate at a striking 6.3 per cent annual rate. Labour leaving agriculture moved predominantly to the booming service sectors, in which per capita output grew at an annual 4.4 per cent, with a productivity growth of 2.1 per cent. Agriculture was obviously serving as a source of surplus labour for the service economy, although the sources of its own rapid productivity growth remain unexplained. Whether the labour market adjustments characteristic of the 1990s can continue to provide high-skilled labour to the service sectors is unclear.

Ecuador: The liberalization process in Ecuador took place surrounded by an environment of strong external shocks, declining oil prices and the events of

El Niño. Trade liberalization got underway in 1990–92 under the flag of the Andean Pact, with capital market liberalization and a privatization scheme following soon after. Fiscal policy was tight until 1996, and then relaxed.

The effects of the package were along the lines sketched in Figure 1.1, with some demand expansion and employment growth after 1996 due to the fiscal stimulus. Both the real exchange rate and the P_t/P_n ratio declined steadily after 1990. Part of the fiscal imbalance was due to combined adverse effects of declining terms of trade and exchange appreciation on public receipts from the oil sector. In real terms, the fiscal balance was positive in the late 1990s, but negative in nominal terms because of the price shifts.

Effective demand was led by exports, with direct foreign investment (2.5 per cent of GDP after liberalization) helping build capacity in the oil sector. Despite liberalization and appreciation, the import share of GDP did not go up.

Productivity increased in sectors with relatively high output/labour ratios (oil, manufacturing) and fell elsewhere (especially other services). In the 1992–97 period, annual productivity growth rates were 2.4 per cent in traded goods, –0.9 per cent in non-tradeds and 0.1 per cent economy-wide. Informal employment rates rose in urban areas as the skill-intensity of production in traded goods went up. These changes were sharper in the early 1990s as intra-Andean group exports increased and Ecuador gained a competitive edge in particular manufactured intermediate goods and luxury consumption goods.

The share of wage earners in the labour force declined, while self-employment income as a proportion of value added went up. There was a trend toward greater wage inequality. However, urban poverty declined during 1992–97, perhaps because of changes in macro policy. Unfortunately, this trend was to be short-lived. By the end of 1998, external vulnerability and reduced fiscal discipline had pushed the external and public sector deficits to unprecedented heights. A currency crisis, a banking crisis and a surge in inflation followed in 1999 – partly because the financial sector was liberalized when it was virtually bankrupt and could only live off continued borrowing from the central bank. The liberalization episode did not budge the Ecuadorian economy from its historical position of being an unstable raw material exporter. In early 2000 a drastic move was taken by replacing the domestic currency for the US dollar. Over time this might generate greater price stability, but will expose the economy's structural weaknesses and external vulnerability even more strongly.

El Salvador has an economic performance that remains heavily dependent on foreign exchange availability and is strongly vulnerable to external shocks. During the 1980s massive inflows of foreign aid, mainly from the US, helped to keep the economy afloat during the civil war. The real exchange rate appreciation and the expansion of guerrilla warfare in rural areas led to a major export crisis by the end of the decade and, despite foreign assistance, to a foreign exchange shortage and a partial default on debt obligations. The end of the civil war allowed for a substantial economic recovery, helped by the need for post-war reconstruction, but particularly by a massive inflow of remittances from Salvadorian workers abroad. This source of foreign exchange fuelled a consumption and construction boom in 1990–95 along with the effects of trade and financial liberalization, which cheapened imports and eased access to consumer and other credits. Other economic reforms during this period included privatization of the banking system and elimination of the monopolies of the major traditional export products (coffee and sugar). GDP growth averaged around 7 per cent per year in this period.

After 1995, economic growth slowed down to a rate less than half of that achieved in the immediate post-war period. The use of the exchange rate as a nominal anchor is seen as a major factor limiting further demand expansion by imposing restrictions on fiscal and monetary expansion. The related rise in real interest rates negatively affected private investment and also coincided with a rise in the share of badly performing loans in total bank assets. Together with several cases of fraudulent banking practices, this undermined the credibility of the banking sector.

While private consumption and investment demand were major factors underlying aggregate demand growth in the immediate post-war years, export growth was the more consistent factor underlying growth dynamics throughout the 1990s. The dismantling of export monopolies and explicit export-promoting policies (export credits, export processing-free zones, tax breaks and foreign investment guarantees) stimulated the growth of non-traditional exports, particularly of maquila industries. Growth of worker remittance incomes as well as labour-intensive export growth benefiting especially female, unskilled workers helped reduce poverty and inequality during the period. The Gini coefficient for per capita household incomes fell from 0.534 in 1991/2 to 0.507 in 1997. The sustainability of this growth pattern very much depends on the prospects of further expansion of the maquila industry, which seem limited. The challenge would be to look for further export diversification, for which certain export incentives are in place, but with limitations being set on the macro side through high real interest rates and an appreciated exchange rate.

Guatemala: Liberalization of the current and capital accounts got underway in the late 1980s. The real exchange rate depreciated during 1985–90, but in 1991 macro prices shifted toward the familiar post-liberalization high interest rate/strong exchange rate combination. Because of extremely low tax receipts (8 per cent of GDP), the government has a chronic deficit which it financed during the 1990s by issuing short-term bonds. Coupled with high interest rates and large spreads between borrowing and lending rates (10 to 12 percentage points), the government bonds and a surge in private capital inflows provided the base for rapid expansion of credit to the private sector. Growth was led by private consumption throughout the 1990s, until it was cut off by a financial crisis in 1998. The overall growth rate fluctuated around 4 per cent per year, accompanied by a current account deficit of 4 per cent of GDP.

During the 1990s there was a shift in agricultural specialization away from food toward export crops. At the same time, foreign exchange revenues from maquila, tourism and remittances rose, but insufficiently to avoid a widening external deficit. In a non-standard pattern, productivity declined in agriculture, as the sector apparently absorbed workers displaced by slightly positive productivity growth in non-traded sectors. There was an increase in the spread in labour payments between more formal jobs in non-traded sectors and informal jobs elsewhere.

Jamaica was one of the worst economic performers in Latin America and the Caribbean during the 1990s. The economy stagnated during the 1980s and 1990s and real GDP growth effectively averaged zero per cent. The two decades were also characterized by a succession of structural adjustment programmes that were implemented rather unevenly, but included a sweeping balance of payments reform between 1991 and 1998. Remarkably, the poor economic performance did not have a negative impact on poverty and inequality. On the contrary, notwithstanding some volatility in the measures of poverty, household survey data suggest a clear reduction of poverty and, at the same time, inequality of per capita household resources also declined consistently, although less dramatically.

Since its first Stand-by Agreement with the IMF in 1977, Jamaica has implemented a whole series of stabilization and structural adjustment programmes. Implementation of structural reforms was lukewarm at best, particularly in the 1980s. Prior to 1990, reform largely consisted of fiscal contraction and some tariff reduction. Some privatizations were carried out in the late 1980s. From 1991 onwards, current account liberalization was implemented in earnest and exchange controls were removed. An orthodox stabilization programme was implemented alongside, with considerable yet gradual success.

The stabilization programme managed to bring down inflation and stabilize the currency, but at the cost of severe economic contraction. The ensuing disinflation, in the presence of lax bank regulation and weak capital adequacy, provoked a banking crisis later in the decade from which the economy has yet to recover. While one would expect the economic stagnation to negatively affect poverty, it has been the steady decline of the rate of inflation that seems to account for much, if not all, of the observed decline in poverty. However, the empirical evidence for Jamaica shows that inflation hurts skilled workers in the formal sector more than unskilled workers in the informal sector. Consequently, income inequality was sharply reduced when inflation soared between 1989 and 1991. But then, if the relationship also works the other way around, one would expect rising inequality thereafter when inflation was brought under control. In practice, however, inequality continued to decline, albeit only slightly, between 1992 and 1998. The explanation can be sought at least partly in the net outcome of opposite effects stemming from balance of payments liberalization. The static efficiency gains from trade and capital account liberalization seem to have produced an increase in the skill premium as observed elsewhere in the region. However, the real exchange rate appreciation associated with the capital inflows and capital account liberalization provoked a shift in both GDP and employment structure toward non-tradable services and away from agriculture and manufacturing, which offset this tendency toward greater inequality. Specifically, the underlying rural–urban migration has led the non-tradable services sector to become the one sector where most poor can now be found (it used to be agriculture in the late 1980s). However, because of the relatively better urban income opportunities, this migratory trend helps to explain why overall poverty and inequality fell at the same time.

Mexico: The liberalization process got underway in the 1980s as the economy was massively restructured after the 1982 debt crisis. It was largely complete by January 1994, when NAFTA went into effect. Financial liberalization had been completed a couple of years earlier.

There were two separate stages in Mexico's adjustment to liberalization, punctuated by the financial crisis of 1994–95. Beginning in the late 1980s there was a consumption boom associated with falling savings rates, rising import coefficients and capital inflows which fed into domestic credit creation. The strong exchange rate/high interest macro price tandem was very much in evidence. This phase ended with a 45 per cent real devaluation between 1994 and 1995. Between 1994 and 1998, exports rose from 17 to 29 per cent of GDP, while imports went from 22 to 29 per cent. As a consequence, the economy is now very open. In the late 1990s, foreign trade and investment led effective demand growth, private savings rates having recovered.

The first phase featured rapid productivity growth in mining and manufactures. Agricultural employment grew at 5.8 per cent per year during 1988–93, while output grew at 1.9 per cent; the sector thereby served as a labour sponge for workers displaced from the other traded goods sectors. Productivity growth in non-traded goods was –0.5 per cent per year. In the second phase, the economy-wide rate of productivity growth fell from 0.6 per cent per year in 1988–93 to –0.8 per cent in 1993–97. Most sectors had negative rates, although employment growth stopped in agriculture as its productivity growth rate rose to 1.2 per cent.

While these reallocations of the labour force were taking place, the distribution of earnings became more unequal, with a rapid increase in the wage premium for skilled labour. The skill mix shifted rapidly in traded goods sectors (except agriculture), with unskilled labour serving as a component of variable cost which had to be reduced in the face of a profit squeeze due to trade liberalization and a strong exchange rate. In manufacturing, the wage spread grew more rapidly in sub-sectors in which displacement of unskilled labour was greater.

Looking toward the future, the economy has recently been growing at an annual 5–6 per cent, with low levels of unemployment – that is, there is slow productivity growth. The big devaluation after 1994 clearly removed a fundamental inconsistency between liberalized markets and macro policy. Another major factor supporting Mexico's growth has been the long American upswing of the 1990s. When the US finally stops growing, the adaptability of the new Mexican model will face a major test.

Panama: In the 1980s Panama's economic development was characterized by economic stagnation. There was a deep economic and political crisis and authorities decided to default on external debt payments at the end of the decade. The old, dualistic pattern of growth in Panama proved to be unsustainable. The old growth model was based on the coexistence of an enclave export sector largely free of government intervention and a highly protected sector oriented toward the domestic market. Unemployment, poverty and inequality increased in the 1980s. The informal sector and self-employment were the sink of the labour market. Mean incomes of those employed in these activities decreased substantially in the period.

The government implemented a stabilization programme in the early 1990s and initiated a reform process geared toward economic liberalization in the spirit it was being implemented throughout Latin America. Trade tariffs were gradually reduced, whereas price controls were eliminated and a start was made with tax and public enterprise reforms. Most importantly, relations with external creditors and the Paris Club could be restored, leading to a recovery of capital inflows thanks to the rescheduling of debt obligations, a resumption of multilateral lending and bilateral aid flows and, with restored investor confidence, a resumption of private capital flows. Being an offshore banking centre and having the dollar as means of exchange, Panama's capital account was already open, but some further measures to promote direct foreign investment and privatization of public enterprises were introduced. The economy recovered along with the greater macroeconomic stability achieved in the early 1990s. The surge in capital inflows was the key factor underlying the boom in private consumption and in construction investment which drove the high growth performance between 1991 and 1994. The expansion of overall economic activity allowed for a reduction of unemployment and an increase of wage employment in the formal sectors. Both these labour market outcomes were conducive to a reduction in urban poverty and inequality between 1991 and 1994.

Growth slowed down by the mid-1990s and the trend toward less inequality and poverty was reverted. Starting in 1994 the government made more drastic moves toward economic liberalization. Some efficiency gains may have been achieved, but the reforms did not lead to an acceleration of the growth rate between 1994 and 1998. As a result, progress in the reduction of the urban unemployment and poverty problems also stagnated. Moreover, inequality increased in this period. Trade reforms shifted demand toward skilled labour, particularly in the metropolitan area and the canal zone, creating a surplus among unskilled workers. While both modern and informal services expanded, the latter sector absorbed much of the excess labour supply, resulting in widening income gaps both between skilled and unskilled workers and between wage earners and the self-employed. The Gini for per capita household distribution was pushed beyond 0.60, hence staying at the far extreme of countries with the most skewed income distribution.

Paraguay: The liberalization process got underway in the late 1980s, an important step along the way being Paraguay's entry into Mercosur in 1991. An inflation-targeted stabilization programme using the exchange rate as nominal anchor was put into place that year. After a previous phase of mild real devaluation, the exchange rate appreciated by 15 per cent between 1990 and 1991, and gradually grew stronger thereafter. The real annual interest rate on loans jumped to the 20 per cent range, with deposit rates around 10 percentage points lower.

Paraguay has long been a haven for 're-export' of goods among its neighbours, and thus errors and omissions figure prominently in its external accounts. Subject to this data problem, it appears that capital inflows (with a big component of direct foreign investment) rose during the 1990s. A domestic credit boom ensued, largely directed toward consumption. The major expansionary factor underlying effective demand was a fall in private savings rates, and the major contractionary force was an increase in import coefficients. The boom came to an end with two financial crises between 1995 and 1997. The central bank injected funds to the tune of 7 per cent of GDP as part of a bailout operation.

Economy-wide, productivity growth was –0.4 per cent per year between 1982 and 1992, and a dismal –3.1 per cent between 1992 and 1997. In the latter period, productivity growth in agriculture was 3 per cent per year. This apparent anomaly had two causes: mechanization in capital-intensive soybean production and a collapse of the *campesino*-dominated cotton subsector due to adverse shifts in the terms of trade, real appreciation and the spread of the boll weevil. Displaced labour was absorbed in the commercial and industrial sectors at the cost of sharp productivity reductions and increased informalization of the labour market. Real wages rose during the 1990s, probably due to lower inflation and a higher minimum wage. With unemployment and labour informalization also rising, the overall effects on income distribution were unclear. Rural poverty was rapidly going up, partly due to failed cotton growing.

Peru: Drastic liberalization and stabilization packages were imposed together in the early 1990s, as the economy emerged from hyperinflation in the late 1980s. The stabilization relied more on fiscal and monetary contraction than the use of the exchange rate as a nominal anchor. Nevertheless, the *sol* appreciated in real terms by about 50 per cent between 1988 and 1990, and continued to strengthen slowly thereafter.

Liberalization and exchange rate appreciation combined to generate an import boom led by consumer goods. Export growth resumed in 1993, largely due to favourable supply conditions in the traditional copper, gold and fishmeal sectors. Through 1996–97 the expanding current account deficit was covered more by capital inflows, partly spurred by privatization. The foreign funds fed into domestic credit expansion, with total loans to the private sector quadrupling between 1991 and 1997.

Effective demand was led by the private sector in the 1990s, in a shift from the historical pattern of fiscally generated demand. Both higher investment and lower savings rates were part of the aggregate demand shifts. Export growth was not sufficient to offset the demand leakages due to greater imports.

Output growth averaged an annual 6.4 per cent between 1993 and 1997, but tailed off in 1998–99 because of declining capital inflows and the effects of the weather shock caused by El Niño. Employment in Lima grew at an annual 4.9 per cent in 1993–97, with some reallocation from manufacturing toward other sectors. Job creation was more effective for the young than for workers 35 and older, who tended to be squeezed from the market as job-protection laws were wound up. In line with the slow growth of productivity, real wages did not increase substantially, although the premium for skilled workers appeared to rise. Inequality among both labour incomes and per capita household incomes rose in urban areas during the 1990s, as a result of rising demand for younger and more skilled workers and associated widening of earnings differentials. The strong overall employment growth and the recovery of real wages allowed for poverty reduction despite the loss of equity.

Uruguay: Along with its neighbours in the Southern Cone, Uruguay began liberalizing its economy in the 1970s. The process continued through the early 1990s, when the country joined Mercosur. Inflation was stabilized in the 1990s on the basis of capital inflows and slow nominal depreciation of the exchange rate. Between 1990 and 1995 the real exchange rate appreciated by about 45 per cent against the dollar, remaining stable thereafter. Against Uruguay's major trading partners in Mercosur, however, real appreciation was virtually nil and its exports benefited from trade preferences within the group. Interest rates remained relatively low, and real output grew at an annual 4 per cent between 1990 and 1997.

The economy opened substantially with regional trade integration. Between 1990 and 1997, imports tripled and exports expanded by 60 per cent. Capital account surpluses covered the growing trade deficit. Effective demand was led by the private sector, with its savings rate falling from 14 to 9 per cent between the 1980s and 1990s and investment rising from 11 to 14 per cent of GDP. Internal credit expansion fuelled the boom in demand. Fortunately, Uruguay managed to avoid a financial crash in the wake of the credit expansion.

Overall annual productivity growth in the 1990s exceeded 2 per cent. There was job shedding in industrial sectors due to stagnant output and positive productivity growth as Uruguay returned toward its traditional role as a raw material exporter. There was negative productivity and positive output growth in services, which picked up displaced labour. Real labour payments rose during the first part of the 1990s, and then stabilized or declined, especially in industry. Income inequality increased as labour demand shifted toward skilled workers as well as toward low-productivity informal sector jobs and self-employment. Nevertheless, poverty could fall during 1991 and 1997 with the growth of overall employment and of labour force participation. With Argentina and Brazil in recession in 1999, Uruguay's prospects for continued steady growth have been clouded since.

1.5 RESULTS FROM MODEL SIMULATIONS

The preceding discussion of results provides a first attempt at assessing the effects of balance of payments liberalization based on before-and-after approaches including decomposition analyses and country narratives. From this preliminary assessment no account can be given as to what part of the observed developments can safely be attributed to the market-oriented reforms. In principle, counterfactual simulations ('with-and-without') based on a rather diverse set of country-specific models can shed some more light on this question, albeit for only a reduced number of cases. The general view is that, except for Brazil, the balance of payments liberalization had an important influence on labour reallocation and the rise in inequality.

Simulations with a short-run macroeconometric model and an aggregate labour market model for Argentina (Frenkel and González 2000) show that most of the variance of economic growth is explained by capital flows. Related productivity growth created a large negative effect on labour demand in industry (–25 per cent), while import competition related to trade liberalization added another 8 per cent to the loss of employment in the sector. Both factors by far offset the employment growth due to domestic demand and export growth, leaving a net employment loss of 17 per cent between 1990 and 1996.

Effects of trade and capital account liberalization in Brazil appear to be rather small, according to a CGE model (Paes de Barros et al. 1999). As indicated, lifting trade restrictions, particularly quantitative ones, created negative employment effects, with most of the burden falling on unskilled workers in manufacturing. Greater wage rigidity for unskilled workers explains a drop in wage differentials. Capital inflows after capital account liberalization are associated with small but positive employment and wage effects.

Ocampo et al. (1999) find that the opening of the Colombian economy led to a rise in the employment–wage elasticity, particularly for workers with higher skills in the non-traded goods sector, explaining the observed rise in wage inequality. These results are based on a reduced labour market model, applying a technique of seemingly unrelated equations (SUR).

Simulations with a macroeconometric model for Costa Rica associate a slight fall in income inequality at the household level with the opening of the economy (Sauma and Vargas 2000). However, the observed trend is one of slightly rising inequality of per worker incomes and roughly stable per capita household income inequality. Institutional wage setting, social security transfers and non-modelled labour demand shifts by skill could explain the discrepancy.

A static neo-classical CGE for Jamaica suggests trade liberalization would have produced only very small effects on employment and output (King and Handa 2000). In contrast, the simulated capital account liberalization produces a strong aggregate demand effect favouring the traded goods sector. Capital account liberalization is associated here with a freeing of the foreign exchange market, elimination of the black market premium and, by the model's assumption, a removal of rent seeking from the service sector. The non-traded sector consequently shrinks, and since in Jamaica this is the more skill-intensive sector, the wage premium for skill falls and labour demand shifts in favour of the unskilled, yielding a drop in primary income inequality.

A structuralist CGE model for Paraguay suggests that trade and capital account opening had positive effects on growth and real wages at least in the short run (Gibson and Molinas 2000). The underlying consumption drive poses problems for the medium run, as there is insufficient productivity growth to sustain a widening external gap and rising labour cost.

Finally, a reduced-form econometric employment model for Peru shows a negative short-run effect of trade liberalization, but estimated long-run employment elasticities are projected to support positive urban job growth in the medium run (Saavedra and Torero 1999). The surge in direct foreign investment associated with capital account opening is found to be positively correlated with urban employment.

Clearly, these findings are not fully comparable given the model builders' different model choices, theoretical assumptions and parameter imputations. We will not go into these limitations here. Still, by and large, the simulation exercises provide supportive evidence to the conclusions of the country studies. As a broader generalization, the counterfactual simulations suggest that trade liberalization effects have predominantly caused a rise in inequality through the widening of skilled–unskilled wage gaps and by pushing unskilled workers into unemployment or informal activities. In addition, model simulation suggests that capital account liberalization and the associated rise in capital inflows contributed to an expansion of aggregate demand and lower inflation. These effects through employment growth and real wage increases contributed to lower inequality and poverty, not necessarily offsetting the effects of trade liberalization.

1.6 CONCLUSIONS

The usual caveats apply. Given the diversity of country experiences just reported, it is risky to generalize about lessons and conclusions. Of course, diversity of outcomes is a result in itself, and should negate the relevance of general sweeping statements about whether the reforms have been exclusively beneficial or costly in terms of growth, employment and equity.

However, if one is to sing a sad song, the evidence certainly shows that in the post-liberalization era none of the countries considered seem to have found a sustainable growth path. Employment growth has generally been slow to dismal, and rising primary income disparity over and above already high levels of inequality has been the rule. The positive note is that there are also cases in which renewed output growth went along with employment expansion, rising real wages and decreasing income disparity. These more benign outcomes were mostly observed in smaller economies. Their better performances were associated with a combination of (a) avoiding a macro price mixture of real exchange rate appreciation and high domestic interest rates, (b) maintaining a system of well-directed export incentives whether put in place at the national level or as part of regional integration agreements, (c) avoidance of steep falls in real wages, and (d) having a system of capital controls and prudential financial regulation capable of containing the negative consequences of capital surges. These factors appear to be behind the relative success stories – at least for parts of the 1990s – in Bolivia, Chile, Colombia (until 1995), Costa Rica, the Dominican Republic, El Salvador, Uruguay and Mexico (after 1995).

These countries all have problems and cannot be considered model cases that could stand as examples of success as we enter the next century. Moreover, a high hurdle to pursuit by others of their (relatively) successful policy mix comes from the fact that current orthodoxy insists on unregulated capital movements with resulting pressures toward high interest rates and strong exchange rates, as well as fully liberalized internal commodity and financial markets.

Finally, fundamental questions arise regarding social coherence and social policy. In the Introduction it was observed that the mainstream view of liberalization emphasizes its likely positive effects on economic performance. Adverse transitional impacts can in principle be smoothed by social policies, and in any case, after some time 'a rising tide lifts all boats'. Along with evincing a degree of scepticism about the inevitable benefits of liberalization, Sen (1999) and other observers stress that many people in developing and transition economies are in such difficult positions that they deserve social help on moral and ethical grounds.

More disquieting is a third view, broadly consistent with the results reported here. Liberalization can potentially unleash dynamic forces leading not only to an unimpressive aggregate economic performance but also to long-term slow employment expansion and increasing income concentration. For the majority of the countries considered here, and over a relatively short period of time, this 'sad song' is to the point – distributional equity has deteriorated, and in the face of lagging growth and rising unemployment social goals have become harder to achieve. Governments could conceivably put countervailing social policies into place, but in practice they probably lack the capacity to do so because of their own fiscal and administrative limitations.

Such constraints on social policy and burden-sharing can be reduced by investment in the capability of the state, as experience in now-industrialized countries demonstrated in the 19th century and again after World War II in the construction of welfare states (Polanyi 1944). However, an explicit political decision would be needed before such investments could be undertaken. It would be comparable in scope to the one that led to the worldwide spread of liberalization in the first place. Nevertheless, for those countries whose large populations make them representative of the whole Latin American region, the initial outcomes of liberalization suggest that a 'double movement' à la Polanyi, first toward and then away from an extreme liberal policy stance, could be forthcoming in the not-so-distant future. Inadequate social performance of any economic policy line ultimately leads to its reversal as society organizes to protect its own.

NOTES

1. Scaling the expected change in the exchange rate by its current level puts the quantity ε/e – the expected rate of return from capital gains on foreign securities – on a comparable footing with the two interest rates.
2. It should be noted that liberalization began in Chile in the 1970s and inequality increased considerably up to the end of the 1980s.
3. For the full set of papers see the list at the end of this chapter and Ganuza et al. (2001).

REFERENCES

Amadeo, Edward J. and Valeria Pero (2000) 'Adjustment, Stabilization, and the Structure of Employment in Brazil', *Journal of Development Studies*, **36** (4): 120–48.

Berry, Albert (ed.) (1998) *Poverty, Economic Reform, and Income Distribution in Latin America*, London: Lynne Rienner.

Bulmer-Thomas, Victor (ed.) (1996) *The New Economic Model in Latin America and its Impact on Income Distribution and Poverty*, London: Macmillan.

Hicks, John R. (1965) *Capital and Growth*, Oxford: Clarendon Press.

Inter-American Development Bank (IDB) (1998) *Economic and Social Progress Report of Latin America and the Caribbean 1998–9*, Baltimore: Johns Hopkins University Press.

Kindleberger, Charles P. (1996) *Manias, Panics and Crashes (3rd edition)*, New York: John Wiley and Sons.

Londoño, Juan Luis and Miguel Székely (1998) 'Sorpresas distributivas después de una década de reformas', *Pensamiento Iberoamericano-Revista de Económica Política* (Special Issue).

Morley, Samuel (1999) 'The impact of reforms on equity in Latin America', Paper for World Bank, World Development Report 2000, IFPRI, Washington D.C. (July).

Ocampo, José Antonio and Lance Taylor (1998) 'Trade liberalisation in developing economies: Modest benefits but problems with productivity growth, macro prices and income distribution', *Economic Journal*, **108** (3): 1523–46.

Ocampo, José Antonio, Camilo Tovar and Fabio Sánchez (1999) 'Cambio estructural y deterioro laboral: Colombia en los años noventa', CEPAL and Universidad de los Andes, Santiago de Chile and Bogotá.

Polanyi, Karl (1944) *The Great Transformation*, New York: Rinehart.

Robbins, Donald (1996) 'HOS Hits Facts: Facts Win: Evidence on Trade and Wages

in the Developing World', Harvard Institute for International Development, Cambridge (MA) (processed).
Ros, Jaime (1999) 'La liberalización de la balanza de pagos en Mexico: Efectos en el crecimiento, el empleo y la desigualdad salarial', Paper presented at UNDP-CEPAL-IDB conference on the *Effects of Balance of Payments Liberalization on Employment, Distribution, Poverty and Growth*, Rio de Janeiro, February.
Saavedra, Jaime and Máximo Torero (1999) 'Liberalización de la balanza de pagos. Efectos sobre el crecimiento, el empleo y la productividad. El case de Perú', Universidad del Pacífico, Lima.
Sen, Amartya (1999) *Development as Freedom*, New York: Alfred A. Knopf.
Taylor, Lance (1999) 'The Exchange Rate is Indeterminate in the Portfolio Balance and Mundell–Fleming Models – Each Has One Fewer Independent Equation than People Usually Think', New School for Social Research, New York (processed).
Vos, Rob (1995) 'Financial liberalization, growth and adjustment: Some lessons from developing countries', in: Stephany Griffith-Jones and Zdenek Drábek (eds) *Financial Reform in Central and Eastern Europe*, London: Macmillan, pp. 179–220.
Wood, Adrian (1994) *North-South Trade, Employment and Inequality: Changing Fortunes in a Skill-Driven World*, Oxford: Clarendon Press.
Wood, Adrian (1997) 'Openness and Wage Inequality in Developing Countries: the Latin American Challenge to East Asian Conventional Wisdom', *World Bank Economic Review*, **11** (1): 33–57.

LIST OF COUNTRY STUDIES

Argentina

Frenkel, Roberto and Martín González (2000) 'Comportamiento macroeconómico, empleo y distribución de ingresos: Argentina en los años noventa', CEDES, Buenos Aires.

Bolivia

UDAPE (2000) 'Bolivia: Efectos de la liberalización sobre el crecimiento, empleo y productividad', UDAPE, La Paz.

Brazil

Paes de Barros, Ricardo et al. (1999) 'Os efeitos da liberalição da balança de pagamentos sobre emprego e salários no Brasil', IPEA, Rio de Janeiro.

Chile

De Gregorio, José, Dante Contreras, David Bravo, Tomas Rau and Sergio Urzua (2000) 'Liberalización comercial, empleo y desigualdad en Chile', Universidad de Chile, Santiago.

Colombia

Ocampo, José Antonio and Fabio Sánchez (2000) 'Cambio estructural y deterioro laboral: Colombia en los años noventa', CEPAL and Universidad de los Andes, Santiago de Chile and Bogotá.

Costa Rica
Sauma, Pablo and Juan Rafael Vargas (2000) 'Liberalización de la balanza de pagos en Costa Rica: Efectos en el empleo, el crecimiento económico, la distribución de ingresos y la pobreza', Universidad Autónoma de Costa Rica, San José.

Cuba
Ferriol, Angela (2000) 'Apertura externa, desigualdad de ingresos y política social en Cuba', INIE, La Habana.

Dominican Republic
Aristy, Jaime (2000) 'Liberalización de la balanza de pagos: Efectos sobre el crecimiento, el empleo y el Bienestar. El case de la República Dominicana', Santo Domingo.

Ecuador
Vos, Rob (2000) 'Economic liberalization, adjustment, distribution and poverty in Ecuador, 1988–99', Institute of Social Studies, The Hague.

El Salvador
Segovia, Alexander and Jeannette Larde (2000) 'La liberalización de la balanza de pagos en El Salvador y sus efectos sobre el crecimiento, empleo y la distribución del ingreso', Antigua, Guatemala.

Guatemala
Fuentes, Juan Alberto (1999) 'Apertura y empleo en Guatemala', Guatemala Ciudad.

Jamaica
King, Damien and Sudhanshu Handa (2000) 'Balance of payments liberalization, poverty and distribution in Jamaica', University of West Indies, Mona.

Mexico
Ros, Jaime and César Bouillon (2000) 'Liberalización de la balanza de pagos en México. Efectos en el crecimiento, la desigualdad y la pobreza', University of Notre Dame, Notre Dame and IDB, Washington D.C.

Panama
Vos, Rob and Niek de Jong (2000) 'Economic reforms and rising inequality in Panama in the 1990s', Institute of Social Studies, The Hague.

Paraguay
Gibson, Bill and José Molinas (2000) 'Liberalización del sector externo en Paraguay: efectos sobre el crecimiento, la distribución de ingresos y la pobreza', University of Vermont (Burlington) and Universidad Católica (Asunción, Paraguay).

Peru
Díaz, Juan José, Jaime Saavedra and Máximo Torero (2000) 'Liberalización de la balanza de pagos. Efectos sobre el crecimiento, la desigualdad y la pobreza. El case de Perú', GRADE, Lima.

Uruguay
Bucheli, Marisa, Rafael Diez de Medina and Carlos Mendive (2000) 'Uruguay: Equidad y pobreza ante la apertura comercial de los noventa', Montevideo.

APPENDIX: DECOMPOSITION OF EFFECTIVE DEMAND, EMPLOYMENT, PRODUCTIVITY GROWTH AND FUNCTIONAL INCOME DISTRIBUTION

Effective Demand Decomposition

Over the liberalization period, there have been substantial changes in demand-side parameters like import coefficients and savings rates along with jumps in flows such as annual exports, investment, etc. It is illuminating to look at how output has responded to these shifts, using a simple decomposition of demand 'injections' (investment, government spending, exports) versus 'leakages' (savings, taxes, imports). The key point is that in macroeconomic equilibrium, totals of injections and leakages must be equal.

At the one sector level, aggregate supply (X) can be defined as the sum of private incomes (Y_p), net taxes (T) and imports (M):

$$X = Y_p + T + M \tag{A1.1}$$

The aggregate supply and demand balance can be written as:

$$X = C_p + I_p + G + E \tag{A1.2}$$

i.e. the sum of private consumption, private investment, government spending and exports. Leakage parameters can be defined as a function of aggregate output, yielding the private savings rate as $s_p = (Y_p - C)/X$, the import propensity as $m = M/X$ and the tax rate as $t = T/X$. From this one gets the typical Keynesian income multiplier function:

$$X = \frac{1}{s_p + t + m}(I_p + G + E) \tag{A1.3}$$

which can also be written as:

$$X = \frac{s_p}{s_p + t + m)} \cdot \frac{I_p}{s_p} + \frac{t}{(s_p + t + m)} \cdot \frac{G}{t} + \frac{m}{(s_p + t + m)} \cdot \frac{E}{m} \tag{A1.4}$$

where I_p/s_p, G/t and E/m can be interpreted as the direct 'own' multiplier effects (or 'stances') on output of private investment, government spending and export injections with their overall impact scaled by the corresponding 'leakages' (savings, tax and import propensities, respectively).

The country papers use equation (A1.4) in several ways. The simplest is a diagram of stances and total supply over time. In Mexico before 1994, for example, I_p/s_p was substantially higher than X, as the private sector pumped demand into the system, while $(E/m) < X$ meant that high import levels were cutting into demand. The roles of the private and foreign sectors reversed sharply after the 1994–95 devaluation. Another representation involves the levels of $(I_p - s_pX)$, $(G - tX)$ and $(E - mX)$, which from equation (A1.4) must sum to zero. Both such diagrams are helpful in identifying expansionary and contractionary factors in effective demand. Several papers apply discrete time 'first differencing' techniques to equation (A1.4) along the lines presented below. These show the contributions of shifting weights versus shifting multiplier impacts in determining X.

From the above equation system one can also derive the economy's real financial balance as:

$$\Delta P + \Delta Z + \Delta A = (I_p - s_p X) + (G - tX) + (E - mX) = 0 \qquad \text{(A1.5)}$$

where ΔP, ΔZ and ΔA stand for the net change in financial claims against the private sector, government debt and foreign assets, respectively. In continuous time, we have:

$$dP/dt = I_p - s_p X, \quad dZ/dt = G - tX \quad and \quad dA/dt = E - mX$$

A couple of points can be made here. First, claims against an institutional entity (the private sector, government or rest of the world) are growing when its stance with respect to X exceeds X itself. So when $E < mX$, net foreign assets of the home economy are declining, while $G > tX$ means that its government is running up debt. A contractionary stance of the rest of the world requires some other sector to be increasing liabilities or lowering assets, e.g. the public sector when $G > tX$. Because it is true that $dP/dt + dZ/dt + dA/dt = 0$, such offsetting effects are unavoidable.

Second, stock/flow disequilibrium problems threaten when ratios such as P/X, Z/X or $-A/X$ (or P/Y, Z/tX or $-A/E$) become 'too large'. Then the component expressions in equation (A1.1) and the accumulation flows in equation (A1.2) have to shift to bring the system back toward financial 'stock–flow' or 'stock–stock' equilibrium. Such adjustments can be quite painful.

Costs associated with the accumulation of net lending over time may imply important income redistribution effects between private and public domestic agents and the rest of the world. When taking such asset-related income transfers into account, we get the more familiar macroeconomic balances linked to expenditures and savings out of the disposable income of each institution, rather than from total supply as implied by equation (A1.5) above, i.e.:

$$\Delta D_p + \Delta D_g - (\Delta F_p + \Delta F_g) = (I_p - s_p X - iD_g + ei^* F_p) + (G - tX + iD_g + ei^* F_g) + (E - mX - ei^* F) = 0 \quad \text{(A1.6)}$$

where D_p, D_g and F ($=F_g+F_p$) stand for the stock of net private sector debt, net government debt and net external liabilities, respectively, as accumulated through the financing of the three gaps (in parentheses on the right-hand side) 'after transfers' over time. We can also define $NFA = -F$ as the net foreign asset position to get the 'after transfer' counterpart for A. The parameters i, i^* and e in equation (A1.6) stand for the domestic interest rate, foreign interest rate and the nominal exchange rate.

Employment Decomposition

Next, we take up decompositions of employment shifts. To save algebra, the formulas are *not* set up in exact form for the discrete changes of the variables that they contain. With enough patience in writing down discrete time first difference expansions, the right- and left-hand sides of all the decomposition expressions that follow can be made equal by balancing beginning and end-of-period terms. Such refinement is omitted here in the interest of ease of presentation.

In terms of notation, we consider changes from time $t - 1$ to t, or from time zero to time one. The difference operator is Δ, i.e. $\Delta X = X_t - X_{t-1}$, and we set $\hat{X} = \Delta X/X_{t-1}$ to indicate a growth rate (an alternative notation used in the literature and some of the papers is $X^* = \Delta X/X_{t-1}$). Let P be the population, E the economically active population, L the total of people employed, and U the total unemployed or $U = E - L$. The participation rate is $\varepsilon = E/P$ and the unemployment rate is $\upsilon = U/E$. The employment rate is $L/E = 1 - \upsilon = \lambda/\varepsilon$ with $\lambda = L/P$ as the employed share of the population. Evidently, we have $E = L + U$. Dividing by P allows this expression to be rewritten as $\varepsilon = \lambda + \varepsilon\upsilon$. Taking first differences and a bit of algebra we see that:

$$0 = (1-\upsilon)(\hat{\lambda} - \hat{\varepsilon}) + \upsilon\hat{\upsilon} = -(1-\upsilon)\hat{\varepsilon} + \upsilon\hat{\upsilon} + (1-\upsilon)\hat{\lambda} \quad \text{(A1.7)}$$

The first expression basically states that changes in the rates of employment and unemployment must sum to zero. The second further decomposes this condition in terms of the participation rate ε, the unemployment rate υ and the employed share of the population λ.

In turn, the employment ratio, $\lambda = L/P$, provides a useful tool to analyse job growth across sectors. Let L_i be employment in sector i, with $L = \Sigma L_i$. Let X_i be real output in sector i, and $x_i = X_i/P$ or sectoral output per capita. The labour/output ratio in sector i can be written as $b_i = L_i/X_i$, and let $\lambda_i = L_i/P$. Then we have:

$$\lambda = \sum (L_i / X_i)(X_i / P) = \sum b_i x_i$$

Taking first differences gives:

$$\hat{\lambda} = \sum \lambda_i (\hat{x}_i + \hat{b}_i) = \sum \lambda_i (\hat{x}_i - \hat{\rho}_i) \tag{A1.8}$$

so that the growth rate of the overall employment ratio is determined as a weighted average across sectors of differences between growth rates of output levels per capita and labour productivity (with productivity defined as $\rho_i = X_i/L_i$ and $\hat{\rho}_i = -\hat{b}_i$). Combined with equation (A1.7), equation (A1.8) provides a framework in which sources of job creation can usefully be explored. In expanding sectors relative to population growth, productivity increases do not necessarily translate into reduced employment; in slow-growing or shrinking sectors, higher productivity means that employment declines. Under liberalization, the interaction of non-traded and traded sectors can be traced in this fashion, along with the behaviour of sectors acting as 'sources' or 'sinks' for labour (agriculture has recently played both roles in different countries).

Labour Productivity Growth

One can also decompose growth of overall labour productivity $\rho = X/L = \Sigma X_i/\Sigma L_i$. The first difference version is:

$$\begin{aligned}\hat{\rho} &= \sum [(X_i / X)\hat{X}_i - (L_i / L)\hat{L}_i] \\ &= \sum (L_i / L)\hat{\rho}_i + \sum [(X_i / X) - (L_i / L)]\hat{X}_i \qquad \text{(A1.9)} \\ &= \sum (X_i / X)\hat{\rho}_i + \sum [(X_i / X) - (L_i / L)]\hat{L}_i\end{aligned}$$

The first line decomposes overall productivity growth into movements in output and employment, weighted by sectoral shares of these two variables. As discussed above, a common pattern under liberalization involved slow output growth and positive productivity growth in traded goods sectors, and faster output growth but low or negative productivity growth in tradeds. Across sectors, the outcome was fairly slow productivity growth overall.

The second and third lines show how overall productivity change can be written as a weighted average of sectoral productivity shifts plus a 'correction' term involving weighted reallocations of output or employment across sectors. The reallocation weights $[(X_i/X) - (L_i/L)]$ reflect differing productivity levels in different sectors. An output or employment loss in a low-productivity sector (agriculture, for example, with a negative value of

$[(X_i/X) - (L_i/L)]$) will add to overall productivity growth, as will an employment or output gain in a sector with a relatively high output/labour ratio. In the country studies such reallocation effects were observed everywhere, but were economically important in only a few cases.

Capital and Labour Productivity and Real Earnings

Assuming two labour-skill or ascriptive classes, total value-added nationally or in a sector can be written as $PX = \pi + w_1L_1 + w_2L_2$, where P is an output price index, w_1 and w_2 are wage levels for the two sorts of labour, and π stands for other payment flows (profits in a broad sense, perhaps self-employment income, etc.). Let $\theta_i = w_iL_i/PX$. The first difference version of the decomposition of payments is then:

$$0 = (1 - \theta_i - \theta_2)(\hat{\pi} - \hat{P} - \hat{X}) + \sum \theta_i[(\hat{w}_i - \hat{P}) - (\hat{X} - \hat{L}_i)] \qquad \text{(A1.10)}$$

If a breakdown of value-added by components is available, equation (A1.10) provides a useful means to think about productivity and payment shifts. If $\pi = rPK$, where r is the profit rate and K the level of capital stock, then $\hat{\pi} - \hat{P} - \hat{X} = \hat{r} + \hat{K} - \hat{X}$. With a rising capital/output ratio, a falling profit rate would be needed to open room for real product wage growth $\hat{w}_i - \hat{P}$ for labour type i to equal or exceed its productivity growth rate $\hat{X}_i - \hat{L}_i$. In the labour market itself, moderate wage and high productivity growth for skilled workers may combine with low or negative productivity and wage growth for the unskilled to maintain the equality in (A1.10).

Table A1.1 Income distribution and poverty in Latin America in the 1990s

	Coverage	Period	Gini labour incomes		Gini p.c. household income		Poverty (P_0)	
			First	Last	First	Last	First	Last
Argentina	Gran Buenos Aires	1991–94	0.471	0.490	0.485	0.467	9.6%	9.8%
		1994–98	0.490	0.534	0.467	0.519	9.8%	14.2%
Bolivia	Urban	1989–97	0.467	0.521	0.488	0.534	59.7%	52.4%
Brazil	National	1987–95	0.680	0.710	0.605	0.601	43.5%	33.9%
Chile	Gran Santiago	1974–81			0.458	0.541	78.0%	47.5%
		1984–92			0.566	0.600	62.3%	43.1%
		1992–97			0.565	0.540	36.7%	21.2%
Colombia	National	1991–97			0.548	0.565	41.8%	41.4%
	urban		0.448	0.503	0.498	0.541	37.5%	28.9%
	rural		0.440	0.400	0.479	0.441	55.0%	59.9%
Costa Rica	National	1987–92	0.389	0.363	0.401	0.378	29.0%	29.4%
		1992–98	0.363	0.375	0.378	0.389	29.4%	19.7%
Cuba	Urban	1989–98			0.250	0.380	6.3%	14.7%
Dom. Rep.	National	1992–98	0.480	0.496	0.482	0.456	36.6%	26.5%

Ecuador	Urban	1990–97[1]	0.466	0.494	0.488	0.494	44.8%	29.2%
	National	1995–99	0.555	0.562	0.529	0.535	31.9%	41.6%
El Salvador	National	1991–97	0.503	0.490	0.534	0.507	65.7%	54.1%
Guatemala	National	1989–98	0.580	0.649	0.587	0.540	63.0%	57.8%
Jamaica	National (cons.)	1989–98			0.436	0.381	25.0%	16.7%
Mexico	National	1984–94	0.465	0.553	0.476	0.535	28.5%	31.8%
Panama	National	1983–97			0.550	0.600	49.0%	42.0%
	urban[2]		0.460	0.474	0.470	0.524	28.0%	22.0%
	rural				0.550	0.563	74.0%	61.0%
Paraguay	National	1982–97				0.544		29.9%
Peru	Lima Metropolitana	1985–91	0.477	0.471	0.524	0.550	28.8%	44.0%
		1991–97	0.471	0.497	0.550	0.583	44.0%	37.6%
Uruguay	Urban	1991–97			0.407	0.419	18.1%	16.0%

Notes:
1. Gini of income earners (labour income) refers to 1990–98.
2. Gini of income earners (labour income) refers to 1991–98.

Source: Country studies.

2. Labour market adjustment, poverty and inequality during liberalization

Enrique Ganuza, Ricardo Paes de Barros and Rob Vos

2.1 INTRODUCTION

Trade and financial liberalization aims at improving economic efficiency and is thus expected to promote growth. In developing countries, economic growth is seen as a pivotal mechanism to reduce poverty. Attempts at economic liberalization are rarely justified when it comes to obtaining a more equitable income distribution. However, the traditional theory of international trade predicts through the Stolper–Samuelson theorem that trade liberalization improves income distribution, since remuneration of the relatively abundant productive factor (assuming this is unskilled labour) should improve with respect to the scarce factor (say, capital and/or skilled labour).

Several recent empirical studies have found an opposite trend, that is, inequality between labour and other factors seems to have increased in favour of skilled workers and capital income in many parts of the world, and most particularly in Latin America and the Caribbean (see Chapter 1). This difference between theory and practice has been explained by several factors, one of which is that in the 1980s, and especially the 1990s, many developing countries embarked upon macroeconomic adjustment processes and started a wide range of drastic economic reforms, trade liberalization being only one of them. As discussed in Chapter 1, the effects of balance of payment capital account liberalization on poverty and income distribution are not very clear. These effects seem to be heavily influenced by the degree of access to capital inflows and macroeconomic policies, which would allow for an expansion of aggregate demand while keeping inflation under control. If these conditions are met in practice, favourable macroeconomic effects such as less unemployment and higher real salaries would be supportive of a reduction in inequality and poverty. Capital inflows as well as macroeconomic policies in Latin America and the Caribbean have shown high degrees of volatility in the

1990s, for which reason it is difficult to predict the final result of current and capital account liberalization.

In this context, the question of which part of the increase observed in income inequality and change in poverty can be attributed to trade liberalization and which part is caused by other changes becomes a focus of interest. One way of answering it could be to build a computable general equilibrium (CGE) model in order to generate proper counterfactual situations that can unravel the effects of the different elements of the policy reforms. This alternative has some obvious limitations, including the difficulties that present themselves when trying to adequately model the economic behaviour before and after liberalization. Another limitation is that CGE models only model income distribution in terms of the income differentials between groups of workers and aggregate production factors and according to broadly defined categories of household groups, thus losing important dimensions of the full income distribution.

An alternative is to study in more detail the changes in income distribution and poverty among workers and households and which factors of the labour market can explain most of those changes. Having a better understanding of the types of change that have taken place and their importance could facilitate the formulation of better-specified hypotheses on how poverty and inequality have been affected by the various aspects of the policy reforms.

The counterfactual created using microsimulations, as we call the methodology used in this chapter, allows us to analyse what would have been the poverty and income distribution if the changes observed in the labour market had not taken place. In a way, it is a sophisticated before-and-after methodology. However, one can also apply the method jointly with a CGE model that has a sufficiently detailed labour market section. In that case, the changes observed in the labour market could be replaced by counterfactuals simulated with the CGE.

This chapter presents a comparative analysis of results based on microsimulations, which disentangle the main causes of the changes in income distribution and poverty in 17 countries of Latin America and the Caribbean during the period of drastic economic reforms of the 1990s. For each of the 17 countries selected, an analysis was made of the liberalization process of the balance of payments and a time interval was defined in which the process took place. The main interest of the analysis is to study the impact of liberalization on poverty and inequality. This impact can be transmitted through various channels. The country studies summarized in this chapter assume that the labour market is the main transmission mechanism of these effects.

Section 2.2 gives a concise presentation of the methodology used for the analysis of the effects, and describe the main components of the labour market through which the effects of liberalization are transmitted. Section 2.3 shows the comparative results of the case studies of the impact on inequality and poverty. The chapter concludes with a summary of the main findings regarding the effects of balance of payments liberalization on poverty and inequality and the extent to which these can be explained by the nature of the adjustment in the labour market.

2.2 THE MICROSIMULATIONS METHODOLOGY

The basic idea behind the microsimulations is to isolate the effects of each of the main determinants of the changes in poverty and inequality, and to associate those changes with the process of macroeconomic adjustment and stabilization as well as with the liberalization of the current and capital accounts.

The methodology was originally developed by Almeida dos Reis and Paes de Barros in 1991 for an analysis of the inequality of labour incomes. It was later generalized in order to analyse income inequality and poverty based on the total per capita household income (see Paes de Barros and Leite 1998, Paes de Barros 1999, Frenkel and González 1999). The methodology consists in creating a counterfactual in the form of labour market parameters that represent the employment and remuneration structure that would have prevailed had the liberalization not taken place. This counterfactual can be obtained in two ways. First, through the creation of a 'with-and-without liberalization' case using CGE or macro-model simulations (as was done in the studies on Brazil, Costa Rica, Jamaica, Paraguay and, to some extent, Chile). Second, by comparing the labour market structure at the beginning of the liberalization process to that at an adequate point in time after the reforms, thus generating a sophisticated 'before-and-after' comparison (as was done in the other country studies).

The structure of the labour market is defined in terms of the labour participation rate, unemployment, the employment and remuneration structure, and general remuneration level. The working-age population can be classified by types of individuals j, according to differences in gender and educational level (skilled versus unskilled). For all these types of individuals, the participation rate of the labour force and the unemployment rate are determined to identify part of the labour market structure. The employed labour force can be classified further by market segment k, defined by differences in economic sector of activity and occupational category. The average remuneration can be calculated for all these jk groups in the labour market, and these averages can be expressed as a ratio of the average for all workers. The structure of the labour market can thus be expressed by the following function:

$$\lambda = f(W, E, U, P, M)$$

where $W=[w_{kj}]$ represents the remuneration structure and the matrix $E=[e_{kj}]$ represents the employment structure, whose elements represent the share of type j individuals employed in segment k of the labour market. The vectors $P=[p_j]$ and $U=[u_j]$ represent, respectively, the participation rate vectors of the labour force and of the unemployment rate of type j individuals. Finally, the matrix M represents different socio-demographic characteristics such as the attained educational level.

The counterfactual simulations are carried out to obtain a new distribution of income in which one or several parameters of the labour market structure are changed. The problem lies in determining, for instance, what would be the income inequality if the labour market structure was determined by $\lambda^* = f^*(W^*, E^*, U^*, P^*, M^*)$ instead of being the real structure $\lambda = f(W, E, U, P, M)$. The changes in the parameters of the labour market structure can be analysed separately or sequentially. The impact of the increase in average wage incomes on poverty and inequality is also estimated.

The parameters of the labour market have been defined such that they include categories that best reflect the reality of the respective countries. In general terms, the following are included: (i) the participation rate P; (ii) the unemployment rate U; (iii) the employment structure by sector of economic activity S (in most countries defined as tradables/non-tradables) and by occupational category O (mostly wage earners/non-wage earners); (iv) the wage structure W_1 (labour income of each type of employment with respect to the mean average labour income); (v) the wage level W_2 for each type of employment; and, finally, (vi) the employment structure in terms of education M (skilled/unskilled). The latter category was excluded in most analyses because the behaviour of that variable is probably more associated with structural demographic changes and with long-term investment in education rather than with the effects of liberalization policies per se. The details on the definition of the labour market structure for each country can be found in the respective case studies.

For most of the country case studies, the 'before-the-liberalization' (initial year) parameters were applied to the 'after-the-liberalization' (final year) household survey information. This way, simulations are indicative of what the poverty and income distribution would have been if the changes in each of the parameters had not taken place during the analysed period. In some studies, parameter changes were generated through policy simulations with a CGE model, rather than taking observed 'before–after' changes. In all case studies, the simulations were done both separately for the change in each of the parameters and sequentially (in the order indicated above) to obtain results for the cumulative change.[1]

In order to assign the counterfactual values of the labour market to households and individuals in the household survey, a series of assumptions have to be made. First, we assume that the labour market is segmented, in the sense that workers do not move between the rural and the urban markets.[2] Second, given the lack of a complete labour market model, a random process is applied to simulate the effects of changes in the labour market structure. Random numbers are used to determine: (a) which working-age individuals change their position in the labour force, (b) which workers switched from one market segment to another (by economic sector or occupational category), (c) which employed individuals attained a different level of education, and (d) how the new, mean labour incomes are assigned to the individuals in the sample. It is assumed that, on average, the effect of randomized changes reflects the impact of the actual changes in the labour market.

The microsimulations were repeated many times – up to 5,000 – given that a process of random assignation was introduced. This way, 95-per cent confidence intervals could be obtained for effects of each parameter change on the inequality and poverty indices, except for the simulation of effects of change in the structure and level of remuneration, which does not involve random numbers. There is no predefined number of times that the simulations have to be repeated to obtain adequate confidence intervals, but experimental tests suggest that 30 repetitions should suffice.

The microsimulations method has advantages over other methodologies such as descriptive decompositions of inequality and poverty indices, as presented by Mookherjee and Shorrocks (1982), Shorrocks (1982) and Ferreira and Litchfield (1998), among others. This type of dynamic decomposition of inequality measures also allows for the separation of different effects on inequality, such as changes in the remuneration structure and in the relative importance of groups of workers and qualified individuals according to socio-economic characteristics. However, the advantage of the microsimulations approach over this type of method is that it takes account of the entire income distribution and not only sub-group averages. A further advantage of the microsimulations method is that it considers the effects of household composition and labour participation decisions. Therefore, the microsimulations method constitutes more than a purely descriptive analysis of the changes in labour structure.

Similarly, as indicated, CGE models only specify income distribution for aggregate groups of workers and households, emphasizing between-group income differentials. The microsimulations methodology has the advantage of simulating the impact on the full income distribution, taking into account between- and within-group differentials for the whole spectrum of labour and household characteristics. Another advantage is that this method requires relatively little information beyond that included in the household surveys.

The microsimulations methodology can be used even if access is limited to the micro data of one single survey, as long as one has additional summarized information on the parameters of an alternative, counterfactual structure of the labour market.

Weaknesses of the methodology are that the results may be path-dependent and, in a sequential simulation, sensitive to the order in which the various effects are analysed. Still, several sensitivity tests for a number of countries indicate that, in practice, this does not affect the total accumulated simulated values and hence the results are not path-dependent.[3] It can be shown formally that the order of sequence shows greater sensitivity when the interaction terms of the changes in the labour market variables are large (see De Jong 2001).

However, there is also an economic logic to the order in which the various effects need to be analysed. The sequence taken reproduces the steps used in many microeconometric models of the labour market. First, it is assumed that the agents decide first whether to participate (*P*) or not; then the market defines whether they can find employment (*U*). If they found employment, the adjustment process of the labour market defines in which sector (*S*) they will be located and in which occupation (*O*) they obtain employment. Obviously, their decisions as to whether to work or not can be influenced by the relative remuneration but, once the sector and the occupation in which they obtain employment are defined, the probability of the relative remuneration they will have becomes known. In other words, the proposed sequence has a logic that is used frequently in this type of analysis.

2.3 EFFECTS OF LABOUR MARKET ADJUSTMENT ON INEQUALITY AND POVERTY

We will now compare the results of 17 case studies, attempting to discover behavioural patterns between them.[1] In some of these 17 countries, outcomes for different periods were compared, the same period was analysed with alternative methodologies (described below), or a distinction was made between the effects at national, urban and rural levels.[5] A total of 31 observations or episodes were generated using the proposed general methodology.

The studies defined a specific time period within which the most important liberalization measures took place. Once these time intervals were determined, the poverty and distribution measures were calculated based on the observed data, both for the initial year (supposedly without liberalization or with restricted liberalization) and the final year (with liberalization completely or largely consummated).

Following the methodology described above, we simulated what would have happened to distribution and poverty in the final year observed if the liberalization were not to have taken place. As indicated in the Introduction, two procedures were used to this end. Some (see Table A2.1) used the final year's structure of characteristics of the household survey, analysing what would have happened with inequality and poverty had the economy in question not liberalized. Others (Brazil, Costa Rica, Chile, Jamaica and Paraguay) used general equilibrium models or econometric, partial-equilibrium models to simulate what would have been the structure of characteristics of the household survey in the final year had liberalization not taken place.

The first option implies that one has to assume that all the variations in the defined period were caused by liberalization. Some studies carried out both experiments. An exception is Jamaica. King and Handa (2000) start with end-of-period data (1998) and use a general equilibrium model to simulate what income distribution and poverty would have looked like if liberalization measures had not been implemented.[6] The methodology allows simulations of the effects of changes in specific variables, individually as well as sequentially and cumulative.[7] Below we analyse both types of simulations.

The studies assume that the key transmission channel of the effects of liberalization on inequality and poverty is the labour market. For this reason, the analyses focus on simulating the behaviour of labour market variables, more specifically the participation rate (P),[8] unemployment rate (U), employment structure (S, O), wage structure (W_1) and wage level (W_2). For some countries it was possible to do a more detailed analysis of some of the mentioned variables (especially, using further disaggregations of the employment structure per gender, skill, sector of economic activity and occupational category).[9]

As mentioned, without a CGE model, it is difficult to separate the effects of the different reform types. Nonetheless, following the analytical scheme of Taylor and Vos in Chapter 1, we may use the following hypotheses at the back of the analysis. Trade liberalization has mainly generated an impact on the employment structure by sector, occupation and skills and on labour income differentials (the remuneration structure) according to the same labour market characteristics. Thus, we assume that changes in the parameters S, O and W_1 are primarily associated with trade liberalization.

According to the analysis in Chapter 1, the transmission mechanisms of capital account liberalization have been largely macroeconomic. Surges in capital inflows mainly consisted of increases in portfolio investment (rather than direct investment). This affected the exchange rate, interest rates and, generally, facilitated fiscal expansion. The impact on the economy as a whole and the labour market depends on the macroeconomic adjustment process. Increases in capital inflows have allowed for an expansion of domestic aggregated demand, particularly of consumption and/or investment in construction, as well as inflation control. This scenario has led to increases in the participation rate (P), a decrease in unemployment (U) and increases in real wages (W_2). These processes generally produce a reduction in poverty and inequality. World financial markets have obviously been volatile during the 1990s. Many countries in the region have felt the effects of the crisis of the Mexican peso, the Asian crisis and the contagion of the Russian financial crisis toward Brazil. In response to this, macroeconomic policies became contractionary and, in some cases, more erratic. The impact on poverty and inequality thus becomes harder to predict and more specific to particular country conditions.

Simplifying, our hypotheses on the impact of the balance of payments liberalization are summarized in Table 2.1.

Table 2.1 Hypotheses regarding the impact of trade and financial liberalization on inequality and poverty

	IMPACT ON INEQUALITY	**IMPACT ON POVERTY**
Trade liberalization	INCREASES	AMBIGUOUS
Capital account liberalization and macro policies (*)		
expansive cycle	DECREASES	DECREASES
recessive cycle	INCREASES	INCREASES

Notes: * In the case of the expansive cycle, macroeconomic policies are assumed to facilitate the transmission of an increase in capital flows related to the financial opening into an expansion of aggregate demand, while maintaining adequate monetary control in order to reduce inflation. A reduction in capital inflows (recessive cycle) under such a macroeconomic regime would have an inverse effect on inequality and poverty due to the contraction of aggregate demand and employment.

We will now focus on summarizing comparative aspects. The peculiarities of each country can be found in the corresponding narratives of the subsequent chapters and in Ganuza et al. (2001). We have also limited the cross-country comparison of the effects on inequality and poverty to the simulated changes in the Gini coefficient of per capita household income and changes in the poverty incidence (P_0). In several of the country studies, the effects on inequality of primary incomes have also been simulated, using alternative inequality measures (in addition to the Gini coefficient, the Theil coefficient and others). The studies also show results for the effects on the gap (P_1) and severity of poverty (P_2). In general terms, the directions of the simulated changes do not differ if incidence or other poverty measurements are taken. The specific characteristics of the data and methodology used for each country are summarized in Table A2.1.

Verification of the Explanatory Power of the Method

A comparison between the accumulated result of the microsimulations and the observed values gives us an idea of the degree to which the labour market adjustment can explain the observed changes in inequality and poverty. The application of the method to the group of Latin American countries shows that a fairly good approximation is obtained of what happened with inequality. There is much less precision when simulating what happened to poverty (see the last columns of Tables 2.2 and 2.3).

The simulated adjustments in the labour market approximate the value of the inequality index at an approximate range of 5 per cent, except in a few cases (Colombia, Chile and the Dominican Republic) where the difference is larger but does not surpass 10 per cent. The simulated poverty index often differs significantly from the observed index. This could be explained by the fact that changes in household income due to other factors – e.g. income from secondary work and transfers such as remittances, pensions and others – are not being taken into account. Such factors are usually not directly related to the process of balance-of-payments liberalization. On the other hand, a limitation in the application of the method itself could also explain part of the difference. This holds in particular for the treatment of cases with zero income and the unemployed population.[10]

The method obviously has a margin of error. An obvious reason is the assumption that the changes in distribution and poverty are explained only by the labour market mechanism. As mentioned, omitted factors are transfers (such as retirement pensions, remittances, family support and others), other incomes (e.g. returns on financial assets) and demographic changes. As far as transfers and other incomes are concerned, these are important when trying to explain a large part of the margin of error in cases like Costa Rica (retirement pensions), El Salvador and the Dominican Republic (remittances). This holds despite the fact that the household surveys in question tend to show substantial under-reporting of these types of income (see e.g. Mejía and Vos 1997, Székely and Hilgert 1999).

In any event, we are primarily concerned here with the direction of the effects of the reforms on inequality and poverty, and which effect seems to predominate. We will now focus on these aspects.

Effects of Liberalization on Inequality

Table 2.2 summarizes the main results of the case studies. The table's final column compares the total cumulative sequential values with those observed in the final year. The data should be interpreted as follows. If the simulated

Table 2.2 Effects of liberalization on inequality

		Gini coefficient			
	Period	**Initially observed**	**Final**	**Simulated cumulative sequential**	**Simulated vs final observation**
Argentina	91–98	0.485	0.519	0.504	< 2.9%
Argentina	94–98	0.467	0.519	0.508	< 2.1%
Bolivia	89–97	0.488	0.534	0.513	< 3.9%
Brazil	88–96(1)	0.615	0.607	0.607	0%
Brazil	88–96(2)	0.615	0.607	0.610	> 0.5%
Colombia	91–97	0.548	0.565	0.536	< 5.1%
Colombia	91–97 u	0.498	0.541	0.519	< 4.1%
Colombia	91–97 r	0.479	0.441	0.482	> 9.4%
Costa Rica	88–98	0.402	0.394	0.394	< 0.1%
Costa Rica	88–98 c	0.402	0.394	0.396	> 0.4%
Chile	74–81	0.458	0.541	0.524	< 3.1%
Chile	74–81 c	0.458	0.541	0.583	> 7.9%
Chile	78–81	0.532	0.541	0.545	> 0.9%
Chile	84–92	0.566	0.515	0.542	> 5.2%
Ecuador	90–95 u(a)	n.a.	0.499	0.487	< 2.4%
Ecuador	90–95 u(b)	0.456	0.495	0.479	< 3.2%
Ecuador	95–99	0.529	0.535	0.536	> 0.2%
Ecuador	95–99 u	0.499	0.522	0.517	< 0.9%
Ecuador	95–99 r	0.464	0.465	0.471	> 1.4%
El Salvador	91–97	0.533	0.507	0.523	> 3.1%
Guatemala	89–98/99	0.582	0.540	0.556	> 2.9%
Honduras	90–99	0.599	0.581	0.584	> 0.5%
Jamaica	93/94–98 c	0.382	0.381	0.379	< 0.4%*
Mexico	84–94	0.476	0.535	0.506	< 5.5%
Panama	83–97 u	0.470	0.525	0.542	> 3.2%
Panama	83–97 r	0.550	0.564	0.590	> 4.7%
Paraguay	97	n.a.	0.544	0.579	> 6.5%
Peru	86–97	0.524	0.583	0.577	< 1.0%
Peru	91–97	0.550	0.583	0.586	> 0.5%
Dom. Republic	92–98	0.482	0.456	0.443	< 2.8%
Uruguay	91–97	0.407	0.419	0.402	< 4.2%

Notes: * Means that the opening reduced inequality. The characteristics of the data and simulation type can be found in Table A2.1.

Table 2.3 *Effects on inequality of changes in different labour market parameters (simulated values with respect to final year observations)*

					Wages (labour incomes)			Other	
	Period	**Partici-pation**	**Unemploy-ment**	**Employment structure**	**Total**	**Wage structure**	**Wage level**	**Education effect**	**Demographic effect**
Argentina	91–98	< 1.5%	n.a.	n.a.	n.a.				
Argentina	94–98	< 1.3%	n.a.	n.a.	n.a.				
Bolivia	89–97	< 2.2%	n.a.	n.a.	n.a.				
Brazil	88–96(1)	0.0%	0.0%	0.0%	0%	0%	0%		
Brazil	88–96(2)	< 0.2%	> 0.3%	0.0%	> 0.5%	> 0.2%	> 0.3%		
Colombia	91–97	< 1.0%	< 0.7%	< 2.7%	< 2.6%				
Colombia	91–97 u	< 0.5%	< 0.9%	< 1.8%	< 2.6%				
Colombia	91–97 r	> 2.0%	> 0.8%	> 5.2%	< 2.6%				
Costa Rica	88–98	> 0.4%	0%	> 0.7%		< 0.4%	< 0.1%		
Costa Rica	88–98 c	n.a.	< 0.4%	> 0.2%	> 0.3%				
Chile	74–81	< 0.5%	< 0.2%	> 0.4%		<7.5%	< 3.2%		
Chile	74–81 c	< 0.4%	< 0.8%	> 1.7%		> 5.7%	> 5.7%		
Chile	78–81	> 0.3%	> 0.8%	> 0.1%		< 0.8%	< 0.4%		
Chile	84–92	> 1.2%	> 2.0%	< 0.2%		> 2.1%	> 2.2%		
Ecuador	90–95 u(a)	> 0.7%	< 0.1%	< 0.3%* < 0.4%**		< 2.5%	> 0.5%		
Ecuador	90–95 u(b)	> 0.1%	0.00%	0.0%* < 0.1%**		< 3.6%	> 1.4%		
Ecuador	95–99	> 0.7%	< 0.4%	< 0.5%* < 0.2%**		> 1.1%	> 0.5%		
Ecuador	95–99 u	> 0.8%	< 0.7%	< 0.3%* < 0.1%**		> 0.9%	> 0.1%		
Ecuador	95–99 r	> 0.3%	> 0.9%	< 0.1%* < 0.3%**		< 2.3%	> 0.2%		
El Salvador	91–97	> 1.6%	> 1.8%	> 3.0%		< 2.8%	< 2.6%		
Guatemala	89–98/99	> 1.0%	> 0.1%	> 0.9%		> 1.6%	> 1.4%		
Honduras	90–99	< 1.2%	< 4.3%	< 3.8%		0.0%	> 0.2%		

Jamaica	93/94–98 c	n.a.	n.a.	n.a.	< 0.8%***				
Mexico	84–94	> 1.1%	< 0.1%	> 0.5%	< 7.7%				
Panama	90–97 u	> 3.4%	> 1.9%	< 0.3%* < 0.4%**		< 0.5%	< 0.1%		
Panama	90–97 r	> 2.4%	> 0.3%	< 0.2%* > 1.1%**		> 1.6%	< 0.3%		
Paraguay	97	> 2.9%	> 8.3%	> 8.0%	> 2.9%				
Peru	86–97	> 2.1%	< 1.7%	< 2.7%		< 4.3%	0		
Peru	91–97	> 6.0%	< 1.7%	< 2.7%		< 6.0%	0		
Dom. Republic	92–98	> 0.7%	> 1.3%	< 0.6%		< 5.0%	> 0.3%		
Uruguay	91–97	< 0.01%	< 0.8%	< 0.9%		< 0.3%	> 0.1%	> 0.1%#	< 1.8% ##

Notes:
* Employment structure by economic sector.
** Employment structure by occupational category.
*** Means the opening reduced inequality.
\# Demographic effect.
\## Educational effect.
The characteristics of the data and simulation type can be found in Table A2.1.

Table 2.4 Cumulative effects on inequality (Gini) of changes in different labour market parameters (simulated accumulated values with respect to final year observations)

Phase 1: participation
Phase 2: participation + unemployment
Phase 3: participation + unemployment + employment structure
Phase 4: participation + unemployment + employment structure + remuneration (4a: remuneration structure; 4b: remuneration level)

						Phase 4		
	Period	**Phase 1**	**Phase 2**	**Phase 3**		***Phase 4***	***Phase 4a***	***Phase 4b***
Argentina	91–98	< 1.5%	< 11.8%	< 11.2%*	< 10.6%**	< 2.9%		
Argentina	94–98	< 1.3%	< 11.2%	< 11.6%*	< 11.0%**	< 2.1%		
Bolivia	89–97	< 2.2%	< 0.9%	< 3.2%		< 3.9%		
Brazil	88–96(1)	0.0%	0.0%	0.0%		0.0%	0.0%	0.0%
Brazil	88–96(2)	< 0.2%	> 0.2%	> 0.2%			> 0.3%	> 0.5%
Colombia	91–97	< 1.0%	n.a.	n.a.		< 5.1%		
Colombia	91–97 u	< 0.5%	n.a.	n.a.		< 4.1%		
Colombia	91–97 r	> 2.0%	n.a.	n.a.		> 9.4%		
Costa Rica	88–98	> 0.4%	< 0.3%	> 0.4%			> 0.1%	< 0.1%
Costa Rica	88–98 c	0.0%	< 0.4%	0.00%		> 0.4%		
Chile	74–81	< 0.5%	< 0.6%	< 0.3%			< 7.6%	< 3.1%
Chile	74–81 c	< 0.4%	< 1.2%	> 0.3%			> 8.0%	> 7.9%
Chile	78–81	> 0.3%	> 1.2%	> 1.4%			> 0.5%	> 0.9%
Chile	84–92	> 1.2%	> 3.2%	> 2.9%			> 5.2%	> 5.2%
Ecuador	90–95 u(a)	> 0.7%	> 0.8%	> 0.5%*	> 0.3%**		< 2.5%	< 2.0%
Ecuador	90–95 u(b)	> 0.1%	> 0.1%	> 0.1%*	> 0.1%**		< 3.7%	< 2.3%
Ecuador	95–99	> 0.7%	> 0.5%	> 0.1%*	< 0.5%**		> 0.5%	> 1.0%
Ecuador	95–99 u	> 0.8%	> 0.1%	< 0.8%*	< 1.3%**		< 0.4%	< 0.4%

Ecuador	95–99 r	> 0.3%	> 1.9%	> 2.7%*	> 3.1%**				> 0.9%	> 1.9%
El Salvador	91–97	> 1.6%	> 2.0%	> 3.2%					> 3.4%	> 3.2%
Guatemala	89–98/99	> 1.0%	> 0.8%	> 1.8%					> 3.3%	> 2.9%
Honduras	90–99	< 1.2%	< 0.9%	> 0.2%					> 0.3%	> 0.5%
Jamaica	93/94–98 c	n.a.	n.a.	n.a.		n.a.				
Mexico	84–94	> 1.1%	> 0.8%	> 2.1%		< 5.5%				
Panama	90–97 u	> 3.4%	> 5.4%	> 5.0%*	> 4.7%**				> 3.6%	> 4.4%
Panama	90–97 r	> 2.4%	> 3.3%	> 2.8%*	> 3.6%**				> 5.4%	> 5.8%
Paraguay	97	> 2.9%	> 6.8%	> 10.4%		> 6.5%				
Peru	86–97	> 2.1%	>0.9%	< 1.9%					< 1.0%	< 1.0%
Peru	91–97	> 6.0%	> 4.8%	> 2.2%					> 0.5%	> 0.5%
Dom. Republic	92–98	> 0.7%	> 1.4%	> 0.7%		< 2.8%				
Uruguay	91–97	< 0.0%	< 1.2%	< 2.8%			< 2.8%#	<4.5%##	< 4.3%	< 4.2%

Notes:
* Employment structure by branch of activity.
** Employment structure by occupation.
\# Phase 3 plus salary structure/demographic effect.
\## Phase 3 plus salary structure/educational effect.
The characteristics of the data and simulation type can be found in Table A2.1.

INEQUALITY \ POVERTY	DECREASED	INCREASED
DECREASED	BRAZIL 88–96(2) COSTA RICA 88–98 COSTA RICA 88–98c CHILE 84–92 EL SALVADOR 91–97 GUATEMALA 89–98/99 HONDURAS 90–99 JAMAICA 93/94–98c DOMINICAN REPUBLIC 92–98	COLOMBIA 91–97r
INCREASED	BOLIVIA 89–97 COLOMBIA 91–97 COLOMBIA 91–97u CHILE 74–81 CHILE 74–81c CHILE 78–81 ECUADOR 90–95u(b) PANAMA 93–97u PANAMA 83–97r PERU 91–97 URUGUAY 91–97	ARGENTINA 91–98 ARGENTINA 94–98 ECUADOR 95–99 ECUADOR 95–99u ECUADOR 95–99r MEXICO 98–94 PERU 86–97

Figure 2.1 Observed changes in poverty and inequality

INEQUALITY	POVERTY: DECREASED	POVERTY: INCREASED
DECREASED	BRAZIL 88–96(2) COSTA RICA 88–98c CHILE 74–81c CHILE 78–81 CHILE 84–92 EL SALVADOR 91–97 GUATEMALA 89–98/99 JAMAICA 93/94–98c PANAMA 83–97u PANAMA 83–97r PARAGUAY 97 PERU 91–97	COLOMBIA 91–97r ECUADOR 95–99 ECUADOR 95–99r HONDURAS 90–99
INCREASED	BOLIVIA 89–97 COSTA RICA 88–98 CHILE 74–81 ECUADOR 90–95u(a) ECUADOR 90–95u(b) MEXICO 84–94 DOMINICAN REPUBLIC 92–98	ARGENTINA 91–98 ARGENTINA 94–98 COLOMBIA 91–97 COLOMBIA 91–97u ECUADOR 95–99u PERU 86–97 URUGUAY 91–97

Notes: For poverty, simulated values higher than observed values mean that liberalization decreased P_0, lower values mean that liberalization increased P_0. For inequality, simulated values higher than observed values mean that liberalization improved distribution (Gini decreased) and, if lower, liberalization worsened distribution (Gini increased).

Figure 2.2 Effects of liberalization on poverty and inequality (comparison between observations and simulations) value is higher than the observed value, liberalization is seen to have led to a lower Gini coefficient compared to a situation in which the economy had remained closed. In other words, liberalization would have contributed to a reduction of inequality. If, on the other hand, the simulated value is lower than that observed in the final year, this means that liberalization generated a higher Gini coefficient compared to the case without liberalization. Liberalization would thus have caused an increase in inequality.[11]

The country studies calculated a confidence interval for the different values obtained from the simulations. The following analysis probed all the estimated changes without limiting itself exclusively to those that are statistically significant.[12]

Table 2.3 summarizes the information available on the individual simulations that were carried out, varying – one at a time and without cumulating the effects – the selected variables of the labour market.[13] The figures express whether the simulated values are larger or smaller than the values observed in the final year, in percentage of value observed in the respective final year of the observation period. Table 2.4 summarizes the information on the simulated cumulative effects of changes in the various components (variables) of the labour market. Just as in Table 2.2, the figures express the percentage in which the simulated values are higher or lower than the values observed in the final year. Figures 2.1 and 2.2 summarize, respectively, the observed changes in inequality and poverty, and the total simulated effects of liberalization on inequality and poverty.

We can draw the following conclusions with regard to changes in inequality:

a. The inequality observed (Gini coefficients) during the liberalization period increased in 18 of the analysed periods and decreased in 10.[14] Using the country as a unit of analysis, the evidence is less conclusive. In eight countries inequality increased (Argentina, Bolivia, Colombia, Ecuador, Mexico, Panama, Peru, Uruguay) and in six it decreased (Brazil, Costa Rica, El Salvador, Guatemala, Honduras, Dominican Republic), whereas in Jamaica it remained unchanged and in Chile it varied differently, depending on the period of analysis.[15] The analysis here refers to the distribution of per capita household income. However, in those cases in which information is available, nearly all countries and episodes show an increase in inequality when analysing primary incomes (see Chapter 1).
b. With respect to the simulated effects on the Gini coefficient in 15 of the 31 simulated periods, inequality increased as a consequence of liberalization. With regard to the sample countries, in eight of them (Brazil, Chile, El Salvador, Guatemala, Honduras, Jamaica, Panama, Paraguay) the simulated effect of liberalization was to reduce inequality, and in

seven countries it led to greater inequality (Argentina, Bolivia, Colombia, Costa Rica, Mexico, Dominican Republic, Uruguay).[16] It is important to note that the range of variation of the percentage differences between the simulated values and the observed values in the analysed period's final year is relatively small. The changes in absolute values (independent of the sign) move between 0.1 and 9.4 per cent. For 17 of the 31 analysed periods, the difference is less than 3 per cent, and for 11 of them the difference is below 1 per cent.

c. Changes in wage differentials by sector and socio-demographic characteristics and changes in the average real wage are the single most important factors that drive the changes in inequality. This can be derived from Table 2.3, which shows the relative importance of the individual changes of the different labour market variables on inequality. In 17 out of 27 periods for which we have data, changes in wages (relative structure as well as level) are the most important determinant of the changes in inequality. In 12 cases the change in the relative remuneration structure predominates the inequality effect.[17] Looking at the countries, in 8 out of 14 countries for which complete information is available on the effects of all the variables, wage shifts form the single most important force underlying changes in inequality (Brazil, Colombia, Chile, Ecuador, Guatemala, Mexico, Peru, Uruguay). In five of these countries the changes in the remuneration structure are predominant.[18]

d. The analysis of the cumulative simulation results of the changes of the different labour market variables on inequality confirms the previous results. In 9 of the 15 countries for which information is available, the labour income changes produce the largest effect on the cumulative values within the total sequence. Hence, the changes in structure and/or wage level explain the major part of the effects of labour market changes on income inequality at the household level, more so than quantity changes in employment or labour participation. The conclusion holds two ways: both when inequality rises and falls.

e. The above does not mean that quantity effects have been unimportant. As analysed in detail in Chapter 3, the rise in unemployment caused by the industrial restructuring associated with the trade liberalization was the main factor underlying the substantial rise in inequality in Argentina during 1991–98. Quantity effects in labour demand also predominate in Honduras, with the shift in employment structure (favouring unskilled workers) contributing to the decline in income inequality in the 1990s. Liberalization is also seen to have contributed to falling inequality in Paraguay due to a fall in unemployment and a shift in labour demand towards informal workers. Shifts in the employment structure have been the predominant single factors in Colombia and El Salvador. In (urban)

Colombia rising demand for skilled labour due to liberalization is a major factor explaining the rise in inequality, while the inverse is true for El Salvador where the reforms-cum-export promotion favoured labour-intensive export industries. Participation rate effects have been important in only a few cases, most notably Panama, where the effect (by itself) contributed to a reduction in inequality.

According to the hypothesis presented in Table 2.1, the effects of trade liberalization can be seen mainly in the employment structure (*S*, *O*) and in relative remuneration (W_1). The influence of the liberalization of capital movements, together with the adopted macroeconomic policies, can be felt on labour participation (*P*), unemployment level (*U*) and remuneration level (W_2). The above findings confirm that outcomes can be ambiguous. In a majority of cases, shifts in the remuneration structure (often a larger skilled–unskilled wage gap) have contributed to greater inequality. We associate this with the trade reform. Shifts in employment structure often exacerbated the remuneration structure effect, but the impact of such shifts on distribution was less pronounced and in some cases even moved in an opposite direction. Where macroeconomic stability was achieved and aggregate demand could expand, real wages increased and unemployment could fall. In most cases where income inequality fell the (positive) wage effect was predominant. As discussed in Chapter 1, expansive macroeconomic cycles are associated with the capital account liberalization. Volatility of capital flows also implied stop–go patterns of macroeconomic adjustment, creating a similar instability in the distribution of income.

Effects of Liberalization on Poverty

Table 2.5 summarizes the results for the impact on poverty. As before, the table's final column compares the accumulated sequential values with those observed in the final year. A simulated value higher than the observed value means that, without liberalization, poverty would have been higher. In other words, liberalization would have contributed to poverty reduction. Inversely, a simulated value lower than that observed in the final year of the study period means that liberalization generated an increase in poverty. In contrast to the effects on inequality, the results for the changes in poverty are relatively easy to interpret.

Tables 2.6 and 2.7 represent the information on the effects of individual changes in the selected labour market variables on the incidence of relative poverty and the simulated effects of cumulative sequential changes in those variables, respectively.[19] The figures express whether the simulated values are higher or lower than those observed in the final year, expressed as a percent-

Table 2.5 Effects of liberalization on poverty

		Poverty incidence (P_0)			
	Period	**Initially observed**	**Final**	**Simulated cumulative sequential**	**Simulated vs. final observation**
Argentina	91–98	23.1%	27.5%	10.0%	< 63.6%
Argentina	94–98	23.0%	27.5%	13.9%	< 49.5%
Bolivia	89–97	59.7%	52.4%	52.4%	> 0.001%
Brazil	88–96(1)	34.8%	29.2%	29.2%	0.0%
Brazil	88–96(2)	34.8%	29.2%	30.2%	> 3.4%
Colombia	91–97	41.8%	41.4%	40.2%	< 2.9%
Colombia	91–97 u	37.5%	28.9%	28.4%	< 1.8%
Colombia	91–97 r	55.0%	59.9%	57.0%	< 4.8%
Costa Rica	88–98	27.4%	18.2%	23.9%	> 30.8%
Costa Rica	88–98 c	27.4%	18.2%	19.7%	> 8.0%
Chile	74–81	78.0%	47.5%	70.8%	> 63.5%
Chile	74–81 c	78.0%	47.5%	57.0%	> 20.0%
Chile	78–81	63.3%	47.5%	57.7%	> 21.5%
Chile	84–92	62.3%	43.1%	51.7%	> 19.8%
Ecuador	90–95 u(a)	n.a.	17.7%	28.7%	> 62.6%
Ecuador	90–95 u(b)	49.1%	29.2%	45.9%	> 57.2%
Ecuador	95–99	31.9%	41.6%	31.0%	< 25.5%
Ecuador	95–99 u	17.7%	29.3%	17.7%	< 39.6%
Ecuador	95–99 r	52.6%	59.5%	53.7%	< 9.7%
El Salvador	91–97	33.9%	31.2%	32.2%	> 3.0%
Guatemala	89–98/99	63.0%	57.8%	63.0%	> 9.0%
Honduras	90–99	73.6%	62.4%	62.2%	< 0.3%
Jamaica	93/94–98 c	20.7%	16.7%	16.4%	< 0.1%*
Mexico	84–94	12.9%	18.6%	19.0%	> 2.2%
Panama	83–97 u	28.0%	21.6%	28.4%	> 31.6%
Panama	83–97 r	74.0%	67.4%	72.7%	> 7.9%
Paraguay	97	n.a.	29.9%	45.0%	> 50.4%
Peru	86–97	28.8%	37.6%	34.4%	< 8.5%
Peru	91–97	44.0%	37.6%	50.8%	> 35.1%
Dom. Republic	92–98	31.7%	21.5%	29.8%	> 38.5%
Uruguay	91–97	18.1%	16.0%	13.8%	< 13.8%

Notes: * Means that the opening reduced inequality. The characteristics of the data and simulation type can be found in Table A2.1.

age of the value observed in the respective final year of the observation period. In this case it is also important to see the summary of results as presented in Figures 2.1 and 2.2.

In brief, the following conclusions can be drawn:

Table 2.6 Effects on the poverty incidence of changes in different labour market parameters (simulated values with respect to final year observations)

	Period	Partici- pation	Unemploy- ment	Employment structure	Wages (labour incomes) Total	Wage structure	Wage level	Other: Education effect	Demographic effect
Argentina	91–98	< 29.8%	n.a.	n.a.	n.a.				
Argentina	94–98	< 26.5%	n.a.	n.a.	n.a.				
Bolivia	89–97	< 1.9%	n.a.	n.a.	n.a.				
Brazil	88–96(1)	0.0%	< 0.7%	< 0.3%	0.0%	< 1.4%	< 1.4%		
Brazil	88–96(2)	< 1.0%	> 1.0%	< 0.3%	> 3.1%	0.0%	0.0%		
Colombia	91–97	< 1.4%	< 1.7%	< 3.5%	> 0.4%				
Colombia	91–97 u	< 1.3%	< 2.3%	< 2.7%	> 0.5%				
Colombia	91–97 r	< 1.6%	< 0.6%	< 4.9%	> 0.2%				
Costa Rica	88–98	> 8.1%	> 4.8%	> 8.4%		< 3.0%	> 33.0%		
Costa Rica	88–98 c	n.a.	> 2.4%	> 4.7%	> 8.1%				
Chile	74–81	> 3.8%	> 0.4%	> 0.2%		< 15.2%	> 45.3%		
Chile	74–81 c	> 0.4%	< 2.2%	> 0.06%		> 20.4%	> 20.4%		
Chile	78–81	> 3.2%	> 1.2%	< 0.04%		< 3.3%	> 18.4%		
Chile	84–92	> 1.8%	> 7.0%	< 0.9%		< 6.3%	> 13.2%		
Ecuador	90–95 u(a)	> 9.1%	> 0.1%	> 0.4%* < 0.3%**		< 15.2%	> 71.7%		
Ecuador	90–95 u(b)	> 2.8%	> 0.3%	> 0.3%* < 0.4%**		< 10.7%	> 65.4%		
Ecuador	95–99	> 4.4%	< 0.6%	< 1.8%* < 0.5%**		> 0.4%	< 28.2%		
Ecuador	95–99 u	> 5.3%	< 3.3%	< 1.9%* < 1.0%**		< 2.5%	< 36.7%		
Ecuador	95–99 r	> 3.7%	> 2.9%	< 1.3%* < 0.1%**		> 0.9%	< 14.0%		
El Salvador	91–97	< 1.1%	> 1.1%	> 4.3%		< 12.6%	< 4.1%		
Guatemala	89–98/99	> 0.9%	> 0.03%	> 1.0%		< 6.1%	> 7.2%		
Honduras	90–99	0.0%	< 3.5%	< 4.6%		> 0.8%	< 2.2%		

Jamaica	93/94–98 c	n.a.	n.a.	n.a.	< 1.8%***				
Mexico	84–94	> 20.5%	> 0.3	> 6.5%	< 31.1%				
Panama	90–97 u	> 23.5%	> 13.6%	< 1.9%* < 2.8%**		< 9.3%	> 1.5%		
Panama	90–97 r	> 5.4%	> 2.4%	< 0.3%* > 0.1%**		< 5.9%	> 2.4%		
Paraguay	97	< 4.3%	> 14.3%	> 19.7%	> 29.0%				
Peru	86–97	> 7.2%	< 4.0%	< 7.2%		< 7.7%	< 16.0%		
Peru	91–97	> 18.4%	< 4.0%	< 6.4%		< 4.3%	> 20.5%		
Dom. Republic	92–98	> 6.7%	> 8.0%	< 1.9%		< 9.3%	> 59.7%		
Uruguay	91–97	< 0.1%	< 4.7%	< 3.1%		< 0.7%	> 7.3%	> 0.3%#	< 4.3%##

Notes:
* Employment structure by economic sector.
** Employment structure by occupational category.
*** Means the opening reduced inequality.
\# Demographic effect.
The characteristics of the data and simulation type can be found in Table A2.1.

Table 2.7 *Cumulative effects on poverty incidence of changes in different labour market parameters (simulated accumulated values with respect to final year observations)*

Phase 1: participation
Phase 2: participation + unemployment
Phase 3: participation + unemployment + employment structure
Phase 4: participation + unemployment + employment structure + remuneration (4a: remuneration structure; 4b: remuneration level)

						Phase 4		
	Period	**Phase 1**	**Phase 2**	**Phase 3**		***Phase 4***	***Phase 4a***	***Phase 4b***
Argentina	91–98	< 29.8%	< 31.6%	< 35.6%*	< 40.0%**	< 63.6%		
Argentina	94–98	< 26.5%	< 26.9%	< 31.3%*	< 31.6%**	< 49.5%		
Bolivia	89–97	< 1.9%	> 3.8%	> 3.8%		0.0%		
Brazil	88–96(1)	0.0%	< 0.3%	< 0.3%			< 1.4%	0.0%
Brazil	88–96(2)	< 1.0%	0.0%	> 0.3%			> 0.7%	> 3.4%
Colombia	91–97	< 1.4%	n.a.	n.a.		< 2.9%		
Colombia	91–97 u	< 1.3%	n.a.	n.a.		< 1.8%		
Colombia	91–97 r	< 1.6%	n.a.	n.a.		< 4.8%		
Costa Rica	88–98	> 8.1%	> 5.7%	> 9.5%			> 3.1%	> 30.8%
Costa Rica	88–98 c	0.0%	> 2.4%	> 2.2%		> 8.0%		
Chile	74–81	> 3.8%	> 4.4%	> 4.4%			< 11.3%	> 49.1%
Chile	74–81 c	> 0.4%	< 2.2%	< 2.2%			> 20.1%	> 20.0%
Chile	78–81	> 3.2%	> 4.2%	> 4.4%			> 0.7%	> 21.5%
Chile	84–92	> 1.8%	> 8.2%	> 7.1%			> 0.4%	> 19.8%
Ecuador	90–95 u(a)	> 9.1%	> 9.2%	> 8.8%*	> 8.7%**		< 7.0%	> 58.6%
Ecuador	90–95 u(b)	> 2.8%	> 4.6%	> 4.8%*	> 5.0%**		< 5.4%	> 55.2%
Ecuador	95–99	> 4.4%	> 3.8%	> 0.3%*	< 1.1%**		< 2.8%	< 26.1%
Ecuador	95–99 u	> 5.3%	> 2.2%	< 3.3%*	< 4.8%**		< 5.3%	< 40.3%

Ecuador	95–99 r	> 3.7%	> 6.1%	> 4.5%*	> 3.8%**				> 1.4%	< 9.7%
El Salvador	91–97	< 1.1%	< 0.7%	> 2.8%					> 3.0%	> 3.0%
Guatemala	89–98/99	> 0.9%	> 1.1%	> 2.1%					< 3.5%	> 9.0%
Honduras	90–99	0.0%	> 1.4%	> 2.4%					> 3.3%	< 0.3%
Jamaica	93/94–98 c	n.a.	n.a.	n.a.		n.a.				
Mexico	84–94	> 20.5%	> 20.7%	> 31.7%		< 0.8%				
Panama	90–97 u	> 23.5%	> 36.4%	> 34.6%*	> 33.5%**				> 25.2%	> 26.1%
Panama	90–97 r	> 5.4%	> 7.6%	> 7.3%*	> 7.6%**				> 4.9%	> 5.0%
Paraguay	97	< 4.3%	> 9.0%	> 27.4%		> 50.4%				
Peru	86–97	> 7.2%	> 2.7%	< 4.3%					< 0.8%	< 8.5%
Peru	91–97	> 18.4%	> 14.6%	> 8.2%					> 9.8%	> 35.1%
Dom. Republic	92–98	> 6.7%	> 17.4%	> 14.2%		> 38.5%				
Uruguay	91–97	< 0.1%	< 7.1%	< 14.0%			< 15.8%#	<20.1%##	< 20.5%	< 13.8%

Notes:
* Employment structure by branch of activity.
** Employment structure by occupation.
\# Phase 3 plus salary structure/demographic effect.
\#\# Phase 3 plus salary structure/educational effect.
The characteristics of the data and simulation type can be found in Table A2.1.

a. The poverty incidence (P_0) diminished in 21 episodes and increased in eight during the liberalization period.[20] Using countries as a unit of analysis, poverty diminished in one country and increased in two (Argentina and Mexico). No unequivocal tendency could be determined in Peru and Ecuador as the movement went in different directions in the different sub-periods. No information is available for Paraguay.
b. With respect to the microsimulation results, in 19 of the 31 analysed periods poverty fell as a consequence of the combined effect of the balance of payments liberalization.[21] In 12 of the 17 sample countries (Bolivia, Brazil, Costa Rica, Chile, Ecuador, El Salvador, Guatemala, Jamaica, Mexico, Panama, Paraguay, Dominican Republic), liberalization contributed to poverty reduction. Liberalization is seen to have led to an increase in poverty in Argentina, Colombia, Honduras and Uruguay, while producing ambiguous results in Peru. The results for poverty show a wide range of variation for the relative difference between the simulated values and those observed in the final year. The 'error' ranges from –63.6 to +63.5 per cent of the observed poverty incidence. In 21 of the analysed periods the (absolute) percentage differences are larger than 5 per cent.
c. Changes in the level of average real wages dominate the simulated impact on poverty (Table 2.5). In 21 out of 27 analysed periods with available information, changes in the remuneration level or structure are the single most important factors. In 15 cases, the change in the wage level predominates.[22] With respect to countries, in 11 of the 14 countries for which complete information is available (Brazil, Costa Rica, Chile, Ecuador, El Salvador, Guatemala, Mexico, Paraguay, Peru, Dominican Republic, Uruguay), changes in the remuneration level or structure are most important. In seven of these the changes in wage level alone stand out.[23]
d. The price effects associated with changes in labour incomes and their distribution also dominate the poverty impact as measured by the cumulative, sequential simulations. The results show that in 13 out of 16 countries the changes in labour incomes show the largest changes within the cumulative simulated values. Again, in seven of these the change in real labour incomes by groups of workers is the largest component contributing to the overall effect.
e. Quantity effects predominate in a minority of cases only. Rising participation rates have helped to reduce poverty in Panama, Mexico and Peru, but only in Panama was this the major single factor, where falling unemployment also contributed mainly as a consequence of favourable macroeconomic conditions in the early 1990s. Shifts in the employment structure contributed as an important factor to increasing poverty in

Colombia and Honduras, while it helped reduce poverty in Mexico and Paraguay. In the case of Mexico, however, wage effects offset this to an important degree.

These findings seem to confirm once more the hypotheses of Table 2.1. The effect of trade liberalization on poverty has been ambiguous. On the one hand, it tends to increase inequality in the remuneration structure (with a negative isolated effect on poverty). In some cases this has been compensated by employment creation in favour of low-income groups (in which case it would have a positive effect on poverty). The latter (favourable) quantity effects have occurred in only a few cases, such as El Salvador, helped by special export incentives to labour-intensive industries. In most cases, the employment restructuring associated with trade liberalization contributed to a rise in poverty. However, the larger impact seems to have come from the liberalization of capital account and the corresponding macro policies. These determine whether the economic cycle is favourable (less unemployment, more participation and a higher average remuneration level) or not. In more than half of the cases these macroeconomic effects dominate the poverty outcome.

2.4 CONCLUSIONS

The results of the effects of liberalization are quite clear with regard to poverty. In most countries (12 out of 16) it decreased significantly. The analysis by periods leads to a similar conclusion, but also shows the transmission of macroeconomic volatility on poverty.

With regard to the impact on income inequality, the results are more ambiguous. The simulated effects across countries are split almost evenly in cases with greater and less inequality. In most cases the simulated changes were relatively small. On the whole, trade liberalization seems to have contributed toward increasing inequality, and sometimes to more poverty as well. Rising capital flows associated with capital account liberalization and macroeconomic policies controlling inflation and generating aggregate demand growth compensated, and at times even offset, this negative effect in several of the analysed episodes. On the other hand, several recession periods (as defined in Table 2.1) occurred, exacerbating the negative effects of trade liberalization and causing poverty and inequality to deteriorate simultaneously.

When analysing the presumed effects of balance of payments liberalization on inequality and poverty (Figure 2.2), we find seven country cases with positive effects on both counts: Brazil, Chile, El Salvador, Guatemala, Jamaica, Panama and Paraguay. At the opposite end of the spectrum, showing simulation results of more inequality and increased poverty, we have Argentina, Colombia, Peru and Uruguay. A reduction in poverty and an increase in inequality can be observed in Bolivia, Costa Rica, Ecuador, Mexico and the Dominican Republic. Honduras is the only country where inequality decreases and poverty increases. In rural Ecuador during the severe crisis of 1995–99 we see similar results, but this is likely a consequence of external shocks rather than reforms (see Chapter 7).

Price effects as expressed through the remuneration structure and level are found to be the predominant labour market changes explaining the differences between the simulated and observed values in the final year of the selected period. These are the single most important factors underlying the simulated impact on inequality and poverty. Although important to both indicators, poverty is most sensitive to such price effects, particularly to changes in the real wage level.

Finally, the country studies have allowed us to corroborate the meaningfulness of the methodology. Albeit not perfect, the microsimulations approach has been shown to be an effective tool to disentangle the influence of labour market variables on poverty and inequality at the household level.

NOTES

1. For a formal and detailed presentation of the practical application of the microsimulations methodology as applied to household surveys for Ecuador, see the Appendix.
2. This assumption is dropped in the simulations of the country as a whole.
3. See Vos and De Jong (2001) and De Jong (2001) for such experimental tests using data for Ecuador and Panama.
4. More detailed analysis can be found for eight countries in the subsequent chapters. A fuller account of 16 countries can be found in Ganuza et al. (2001). In addition, the Instituto de Pesquisas Económicas Aplicadas (IPEA) in Brazil has processed available data for Honduras, thus obtaining 17 country cases.
5. In some cases it was not possible to add the national-level information because there were no representative household surveys available for the population as a whole. In some case studies presented in the following chapters one can obtain further disaggregation by occupation or sector, nationwide estimates, and more details by skill level.
6. In other words, the authors simulated the 'opening' of the economy. Although these data are not entirely comparable, they are also presented in the following tables and sections to the extent they serve the comparative analysis.
7. In order to make the results comparable in the latter case, it is necessary for the sequence of changes in the variables – i.e. the order in which they are carried out – to be the same for each country case. The studies respected the agreed sequence.
8. The participation rate is defined as: (employed population + open unemployment)/working-age population.
9. On the other hand, for some countries it was not possible to separate the effects of the changes in wage structure and wage level, and the simulations appear under the generic term of 'wages'.
10. Such effects appear important where there have been strong increases in unemployment, such as, for instance, in Argentina and Ecuador during 1995–99.

11. As indicated above, the interpretation for Jamaica is different due to the use of a different methodology to simulate the process of economic opening.
12. The vast majority of the estimated values are statistically significant though.
13. For some countries, more detailed simulations are available for some of the variables, specifically employment and remuneration structure.
14. In Jamaica it remained unchanged, and in two analysed periods there is no estimate available for the observed inequality and poverty levels in the initial year.
15. For Paraguay there is no estimate available for observed poverty and inequality in the initial year.
16. There are no clear results for the total sequential effect in Ecuador and Peru. Chile is included in the group of eight countries that experienced a reduction in inequality, but there was an increase in inequality during the 1974–81 period.
17. The employment structure is the most important variable in four of the episodes, the participation rate in three and unemployment also in three. There is no information for four periods.
18. An analysis was also made of whether the changes in the different variables produced increases or decreases in inequality (i.e. whether the sign of the difference between simulated and observed values in the final year was positive or negative). No systematic pattern was found.
19. When analysing the changes in poverty, results for additional, individual and cumulative sequential variables were also obtained for the employment and remuneration structure.
20. There are no estimates for the initial years in some sub-periods for Ecuador and Paraguay.
21. The effect was zero in one of the periods for Brazil.
22. Employment structure is the most important variable in five of the observed cases, whereas the participation rate is the most important variable in one case. Unemployment is never the most important variable.
23. Neither in this case could we see any behavioural pattern as to whether the changes in the different variables produced poverty increases or decreases, that is, whether the sign of the difference between simulated values and those observed in the final year was positive or negative.

REFERENCES

Almeida dos Reis, J.G. and R. Paes de Barros (1991) 'Wage inequality and the distribution of education: A study of the evolution of regional differences in inequality in metropolitan Brazil', *Journal of Development Economics*, **36**: 117–43.

De Jong, Niek (2001) 'Decomposing changes in poverty and inequality: The case of urban Panama in the 1990s', The Hague: Institute of Social Studies (mimeo).

Ferreira, Francisco H.G. and Julie Litchfield (1998) 'Educación o inflación? Papel de los factores estructurales y de la inestabilidad mácroeconómica en la explicación de la desigualdad en Brazil en la década de los ochenta', in: Mauricio Cárdenas and Nora Lustig (eds), *Pobreza y Desigualdad en América Latina*, Bogotá: TM Editores, Fedesarrollo, LACEA, Colciencias, pp. 101–32.

Frenkel, Roberto and Martín González (2000) 'Liberalización del balance de pagos. Efectos sobre el crecimiento, el empleo y los ingresos en Argentina – Segunda parte', Buenos Aires: CEDES (mimeo).

Ganuza, Enrique, Lance Taylor, Ricardo Paes de Barros and Rob Vos (eds) (2001) *Liberalización de la Balanza de Pagos en América Latina y el Caribe: Efectos sobre el Empleo, la Distribución y la Pobreza*, Buenos Aires: Ediciones Universidad de Buenos Aires.

King, Damien and Sudhanshu Handa (2000) 'Balance of payments liberalization, poverty and distribution in Jamaica', University of West Indies, Mona.

Mejía, José Antonio and Rob Vos (1997) 'Poverty and Inequality in Latin America and the Caribbean: An Inventory 1985–95', INDES Working Paper Series I–4, Washington D.C.: Inter-American Development Bank.

Mookherjee, Dilip and Anthony Shorrocks (1982) 'A decomposition analysis of the trend in UK income inequality', *Economic Journal*, **92**: 886–902.

Paes de Barros, Ricardo (1999) 'Evaluando el impacto de cambios en la estructura salarial y del empleo sobre la distribución de renta', Rio de Janeiro: IPEA (mimeo).

Paes de Barros, Ricardo and Philippe Leite (1998) 'O Impacto da Liberalizaçao sobre Distribuiçao de Renda no Brazil', Rio de Janeiro: IPEA (mimeo).

Shorrocks, Anthony F. (1982) 'Inequality decomposition by factor components', *Econometrica*, **50** (1): 193–211 (January).

Székely, Miguel and Marianne Hilgert (1999) 'What's behind the inequality we measure? An investigation using Latin American data', Research Department Working Paper Series 409, Washington D.C.: Inter-American Development Bank.

Vos, Rob and Niek De Jong (2001) 'Rising inequality during economic liberalisation and crisis: macro or micro causes in Ecuador's case?', The Hague: Institute of Social Studies (mimeo).

APPENDIX: THE MICROSIMULATIONS METHODOLOGY

By way of example we spell out the steps taken in setting up the microsimulations using a particular case. The example refers to the application of the method using data for Ecuador for 1995 and 1999. The example is representative though for application in the other country cases.

The microsimulations were carried out at a national level and separately for urban and rural areas on the basis of LSMS survey data. Additional simulations were run for urban areas using either a combination of LSMS and urban household survey data, or the latter only. The following describes how the simulations were carried out for 1999 with 1995 parameters. The methodology for the other simulations is identical.

For 1999, an alternative labour market structure was defined on the basis of data from the 1995 LSMS. For each iteration of the microsimulations, a random number was assigned to each individual of a sub-group of the population in 1999. This number was used to rank the individuals. An analysis was made of the effects on poverty and inequality of the following changes in the structure of the labour market (considered separately or sequentially):

1. **Change in the participation rate of each *j* population group.**
   - *Objective*: To determine the indices of poverty and inequality if the participation rates in 1999 were to be equal to those in 1995.
   - *Procedure*: Within each *j* group, people ages 10 and older were ranked first according to labour force status – starting with the economically active – and then on the basis of the random numbers. Because for each *j* type the participation rate was lower in 1995 than in 1999, the last economically active *j*-type persons were reclassified as economically inactive and their labour income was set to zero.
2. **Change in the unemployment rate of type *j* economically active persons.**
   - *Objective*: To determine the indices of poverty and inequality if the unemployment rates in 1999 were to be equal to those in 1995.
   - *Procedure*: Only the economically active population was considered. Within each *j* group, the individuals were first ranked according to employment condition – starting with the employed – and then on the basis of the random numbers. For the *j* types with higher rates of unemployment in 1995 than in 1999, the last persons of each *j* type were reclassified as unemployed and their labour income was set to zero. In case of *j* types with lower rates of unemployment in 1995, the newly employed were grouped into deciles on the basis of the

random numbers and assigned the mean labour income of the corresponding decile of employed persons in 1999.

3. **Change in the sector of activity of *j*-type wage employees and non-wage workers.**
   - *Objective*: To determine the indices of poverty and inequality had the proportion of persons employed in the tradable sector not changed between 1995 and 1999.
   - *Procedure*: Only the employed population was considered. Mean incomes per decile of employed *j*-type persons in each sector were calculated for both occupational categories. Within each *j* group, the individuals were first ranked according to sector of activity – starting with the tradable sector – and then on the basis of the random numbers. For groups whose proportion of non-tradable sector workers was lower in 1995 than in 1999, the first non-tradable sector workers moved to the tradable sector. In *j* groups whose proportion of non-tradable sector workers was higher in 1995 than in 1999, the last tradable sector workers moved to the non-tradable sector. Within each *j* group, those persons who changed sectors were classified into deciles on the basis of their random number and their labour income was replaced by the corresponding mean income of the decile of those who were actually working in the sector of destination in 1999.
4. **Change in the occupational category of *j*-type employed persons in each sector of activity.**
   - *Objective*: To determine the indices of poverty and inequality if the proportion of wage employees in 1999 were to be the same as in 1995.
   - *Procedure*: Only the employed population was considered. Mean incomes were calculated per decile of *j*-type wage employees and non-wage workers in each sector of activity. For both sectors of activity within each *j* group, the individuals were first ranked according to occupational category – starting with the wage employees – and then on the basis of the random numbers. For groups whose proportion of wage employees was lower in 1995 than in 1999, the last wage employees became non-wage workers. For groups whose proportion of wage employees was higher in 1995 than in 1999, the first non-wage workers became wage employees. Within each *j* group, those persons who changed occupational category were classified into deciles on the basis of their random number and their labour income was replaced by the corresponding mean income of the decile of those who were actually working in the occupational category of destination in 1999.

5. **Change in the remuneration structure.**
   - *Objective*: To determine the indices of poverty and inequality if the structure of labour incomes in 1999 were to be that of 1995.
   - *Procedure*: Only the employed population was considered. Mean labour incomes were calculated for each of the 16 *jk* groups of employed persons, as well as an overall mean for both 1995 and 1999. The following relative mean incomes were subsequently calculated for 1995:

$$s_{jk} = \frac{\overline{yl95}_{jk}}{\overline{yl95}}$$

   The mean labour income in 1999 of each group was multiplied by the corresponding s_{jk} in order to obtain a new mean labour income for each *jk* group in 1999 prices:

$$\overline{yl}^{*}_{jk} = \frac{\overline{yl95}_{jk}}{\overline{yl95}} \cdot \overline{yl99}$$

   In turn, the new mean incomes of the *jk* groups were expressed as a proportion of the corresponding mean in 1999, and subsequently the 1999 labour income of each *i* individual in a *jk* group was multiplied by the proportion for the group:

$$yl^{*}_{jki} = \frac{\overline{yl}^{*}_{jk}}{\overline{yl99}_{jk}} \cdot yl99_{jki}$$

6. **Change in the level of remuneration.**
   - *Objective*: To determine the indices of poverty and inequality if the real incomes level of 1999 were to be that of 1995.
   - *Procedure*: Only the employed population was considered. New labour incomes were calculated by multiplying the 1999 labour income of each income recipient by the mean income ratio in 1995 (in sucres of 1999) to that in 1999:

$$yl^{**}_{jki} = \frac{\overline{yl95}}{\overline{yl99}} \cdot yl99_{jki}$$

7. **Change in the skill level of employed men/women in *k* segment.**
   - *Objective*: To determine the indices of poverty and inequality if the proportion of skilled workers in 1999 were to be the same as in 1995.
   - *Procedure*: Only the employed population was considered. Mean

incomes were calculated per decile of employed men/women in each *k* segment. Individuals within each group defined by gender and segment were first classified by skill – starting with the unskilled workers – and then on the basis of the random numbers. In groups whose proportion of skilled workers was higher in 1995 than in 1999, the last unskilled workers were reclassified as skilled. In case of groups with lower proportions of skilled workers in 1995, the first skilled workers move to the category of unskilled workers. Within each *j* group, those who went from unskilled to skilled were classified into deciles on the basis of their random number, and their labour income was replaced by the mean income of the corresponding decile of all those who were actually skilled in 1999. In the reverse case, the actual 1999 incomes were replaced by those of the corresponding decile of unskilled workers.

Table A2.1 Characteristics of the country studies

	Period	Coverage	Concept Used	Simulation Type
Argentina	91–98	Greater Buenos Aires	Real per capita household income	91 in 98
Argentina	94–98	Greater Buenos Aires	Real per capita household income	91 in 98
Bolivia	89–97	Urban	Real per capita household income	89 in 97
Brazil	88–96(1)	National	Real per capita household income	88 in 96 and counterfactual (model)
Brazil	88–96(2)	National	Real per capita household income	88 in 96 and counterfactual (model)
Colombia	91–97	National	Real per capita household income	91 in 97
Colombia	91–97 u	National	Real per capita household income	91 in 97
Colombia	91–97 r	National	Real per capita household income	91 in 97
Costa Rica	88–98	National	Real per capita household income	88 in 98
Costa Rica	88–98 c	National	Real per capita household income	counterfactual (model)
Chile	74–81	Greater Santiago	Real per capita household income	74 in 81
Chile	74–81 c	Greater Santiago	Real per capita household income	counterfactual (econometrics)
Chile	78–81	Greater Santiago	Real per capita household income	78 in 81
Chile	84–92	Greater Santiago	Real per capita household income	84 in 92
Ecuador	90–95 u	Urban (a)	Real per capita household income	90 in 95
Ecuador	90–95 u	Urban (b)	Real per capita household income	90 in 95
Ecuador	95–99	National (a)	Real per capita household income	95 in 99
Ecuador	95–99 u	National (a)	Real per capita household income	95 in 99
Ecuador	95–99 r	National (a)	Real per capita household income	95 in 99
El Salvador	91–97	National	Real per capita household income	91 in 97

Table A2.1 continued

	Period	Coverage	Concept Used	Simulation Type
Guatemala	89–98/99	National	Real per capita household income	89 in 98/99
Honduras	90–99	National	Real per capita household income	90 in 99
Jamaica	93/94–98 c	National	Real per capita household consumption	counterfactual (model)
Mexico	84–94	Urban	Real per capita household income	84 in 94
Panama	83–97 u	Urban	Real per capita household income	census 90 in 97
Panama	83–97 r	Rural	Real per capita household income	census 90 in 97
Paraguay	97	National	Real per capita household income	counterfactual (model)
Peru	86–97	Metropolitan Lima	Real per capita household income	86 in 97
Peru	91–97	Metropolitan Lima	Real per capita household income	91 in 97
Dom. Republic	92–98	National	Real per capita household income	92 in 98
Uruguay	91–97	Urban	Real per capita household income	91 in 97

Notes:
(a) Using LSMS surveys.
(b) Using labour force surveys.
(1) Using only the 1988 tariffs in the simulations.
(2) Using the 1988 tariffs and restricting the flow of capital in the simulations.
c Counterfactual.
u Urban.
r Rural.

3. Argentina: macroeconomic behaviour, employment and income distribution in the 1990s*

Roberto Frenkel and Martín González Rozada

3.1 INTRODUCTION

In the early 1990s, Argentina witnessed an impressive process of market-oriented reforms that focused on privatizing a large portion of state-owned companies and on liberalizing trade and capital flows. At the same time, the country put an end to a period of extreme price instability, which produced two brief episodes of hyperinflation in 1989 and 1990. Price stabilization went hand in hand with a strong growth recovery. However, on the downside there was a severe increase of unemployment and inequality.

Trade opening was a central component of the structural reforms of the 1990s. In 1988 some progress had been made in this direction, but the gradual approach was abandoned at the start of the new decade and the opening process accelerated. The average import tariff rate was reduced from 26.5 per cent in October 1989 to 9.7 per cent in April 1991. In addition, specific duties and quantitative restrictions on imports were eliminated.[1]

In addition, the privatization process started in 1990 with the transfer of the telephone company and the national airlines. In late 1994, most state-owned companies that produced goods or services had been sold, including the most important ones, i.e. the oil company, YPF, and electricity producers and distributors. This process covered a vast range of production areas, from iron and steel to petrochemicals and gas. In some cases – such as oil, trains, ports, highways, drinking water and sewerage, and television and radio channels – the government used concession mechanisms.

Several new laws marked the process of structural reform. First, the State Reform Act of August 1989 established the legal bases for the privatization of state-owned companies with the capitalization of public debt. Second, in order to improve the budget balance, the Economic Emergency Act of September 1989 suspended several subsidy mechanisms, such as those implicit in the industrial and regional incentive schemes. This law established equal treatment for domestic and foreign investment in productive activities in the country, and eliminated the need for prior approval of direct foreign investment. In addition, the deregulation decree of November 1991 eliminated a vast group of regulations for various economic activities.

The most important legal instrument of the stabilization process was the Convertibility Law of March 1991, which established parity between the peso and the dollar, and guaranteed foreign-currency contracts. This law established that the Central Bank had to back up 100 per cent of the monetary base with reserves in foreign currency. The new organic charter of the Central Bank (September 1992) abolished the government guarantee on deposits and fixed narrow limits within which the Central Bank could purchase public bonds and lend to commercial banks. The law also established the autonomy of the Central Bank. In practice, the Convertibility Law transformed the Central Bank into a currency board and completed the deregulation of the capital account of the balance of payments. In short, trade and capital flows were entirely liberalized from early 1991 onwards.

The research summarized in this chapter[2] analyses the growth process, the performance of the labour market, and the evolution of incomes and wages in the context of the structural reforms and the stabilization policies implemented in the 1990s. Following the Introduction, this article is divided into six sections. Section 3.2 presents some aspects of macroeconomic dynamics, mainly through graphs that facilitate comparison between the 1980s and 1990s and stress the stylized features of the latter period. In this abridged version of the research we present only the most relevant results of the employment and income analysis. Section 3.3 describes the behaviour of the national urban and Gran Buenos Aires (GBA) labour markets. The presentation compares the 1980s with the 1990s, and emphasizes the main stylized facts of the latter period. Section 3.4 includes the formulation and estimation of an econometric model for the national urban labour market. Section 3.5 uses GBA data to study changes in urban employment by economic sector and socio-demographic characteristics. The industrial sector is the most important tradable urban activity, and the analysis shows that the contraction of employment in this sector explains two-thirds of the contraction of full-time jobs in the 1990s. Section 3.6 studies trends in output, employment and productivity in manufacturing, using industrial survey data. Using an econometric model of labour demand we estimate and disentangle the various determinants of the contraction of manufacturing employment. Finally, Section 3.7 discusses the income distribution effects.

3.2 STYLIZED FEATURES OF MACROECONOMIC DYNAMICS[3]

Growth and the Business Cycle

Figure 3.1 shows the evolution of quarterly GDP (in logarithms) in the 1980s and 1990s. The trend is obtained through the Hodrick–Prescott filter (with the conventional parameter). As can be seen, in the 1980s GDP fluctuated around a stagnated trend, while in the 1990s the trend was clearly upward. The HP filter displayed in the figure indicates the new growth trend of the 1990s, equal to an annual rate of 4.8 per cent.

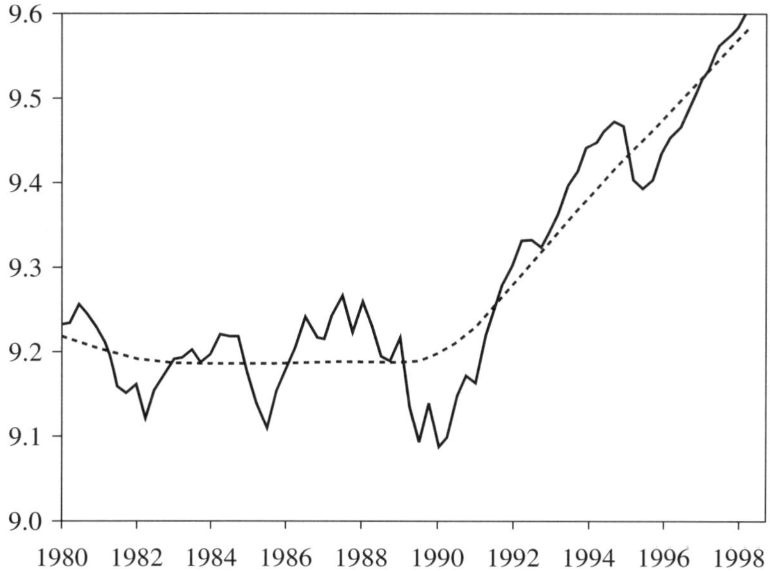

Figure 3.1 Log GDP and Hodrick–Prescott trend

The initial expansive phase lasted until 1994. Economic expansion started in the second semester of 1990, before the Convertibility Plan was launched, and peaked in the second semester of 1994.[4] Between the second semesters of 1990 and 1994, GDP (not seasonally adjusted) grew by 35.7 per cent, an average annual rate of 8 per cent. The second phase is the recession associated with the 1995 Tequila effect, which provoked a contraction of GDP of 6.8 per cent between the second semesters of 1994 and 1995. Recovery from the recession was completed by the second semester of 1996, at which point output had reached a level similar to that of the second semester of 1994.

Finally, we have the most recent expansive phase, with growth accelerating from the end of 1996 onwards, and stimulated by the strongest surge in capital inflows of the 1990s. Between the second semesters of 1996 and 1997, GDP grew by 9.2 per cent. The expansion decelerated from October 1997 onwards, coinciding with the Asian crisis. A new recession set in from the second semester of 1998 onwards.

Foreign Trade and the Balance of Payments

The export share of GDP at constant prices (see Figure 3.2) remained practically stagnant during the initial expansive phase. The coefficient jumped between 1994 and 1995, and stagnated again later on. The import share at constant prices increased strongly during the initial expansive phase, contracted during the recession, and showed a sustained recovery during the subsequent expansive phase.

The 1995 crisis constitutes a break in the pattern of balance-of-payments adjustment valued at current prices (see Figures 3.3 and 3.4). In the first phase, capital inflows showed a sustained growth until 1993 and declined in 1994, when the interest rates in the United States went up. The country-risk premium tended to drop until 1993, but increased in 1994 (see Figure 3.5). Further, the current account deficit widened during the initial expansive phase,

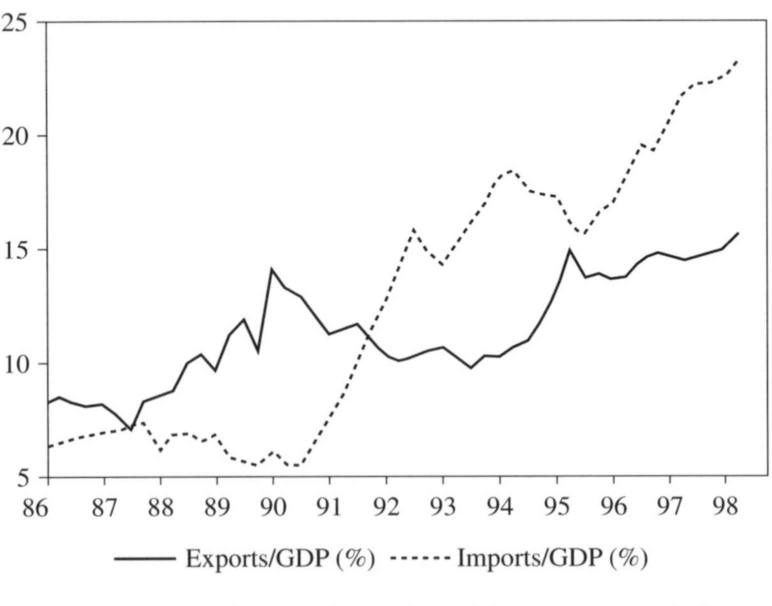

Figure 3.2 Export and import shares (% of GDP at constant 1986 prices)

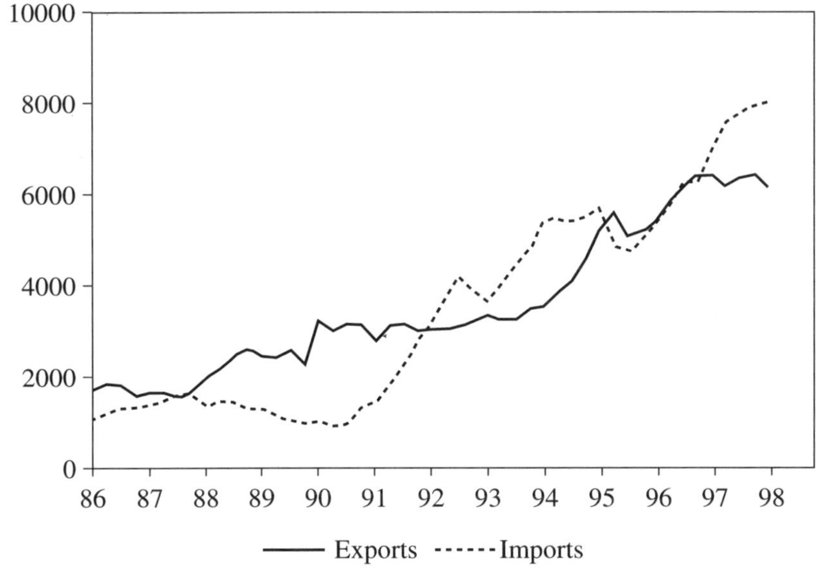

Figure 3.3 Exports and imports of goods (quarterly data at current price dollars, seasonally adjusted)

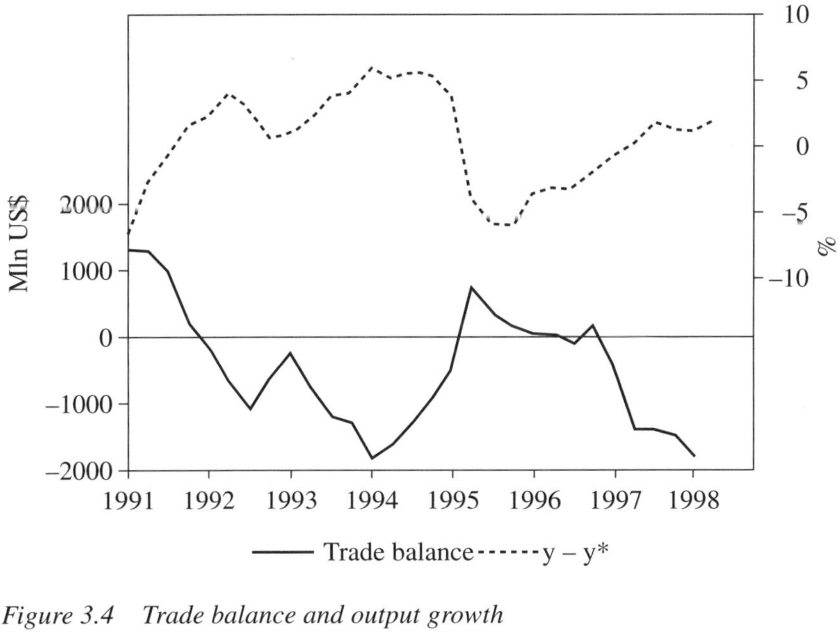

Figure 3.4 Trade balance and output growth

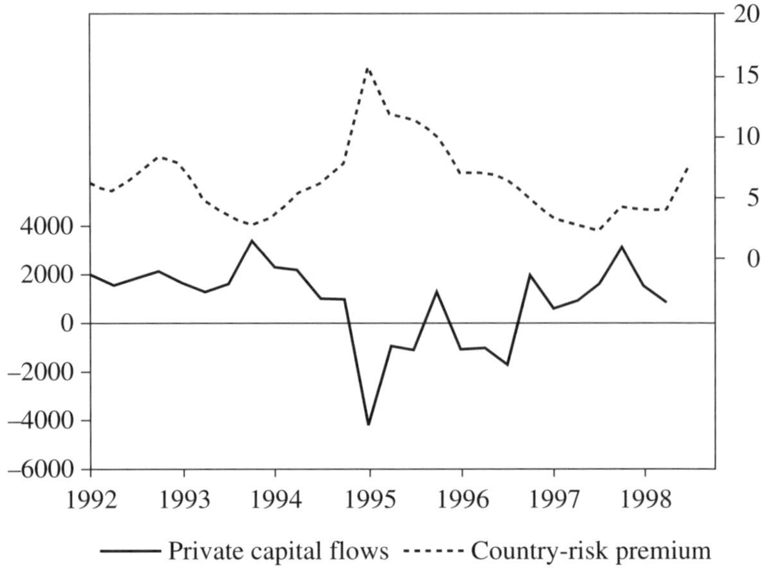

Figure 3.5 Net private capital flows and country-risk premium

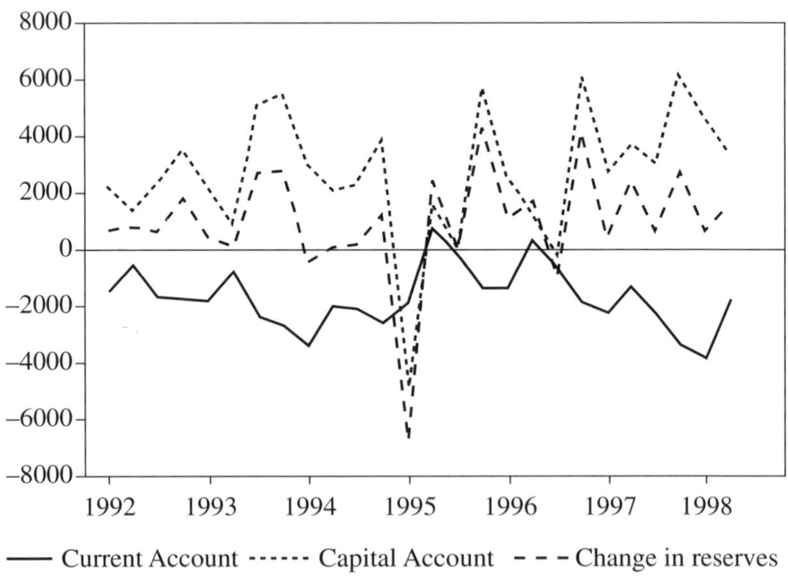

Figure 3.6 Current and capital account balance and change in reserves (millions of US$)

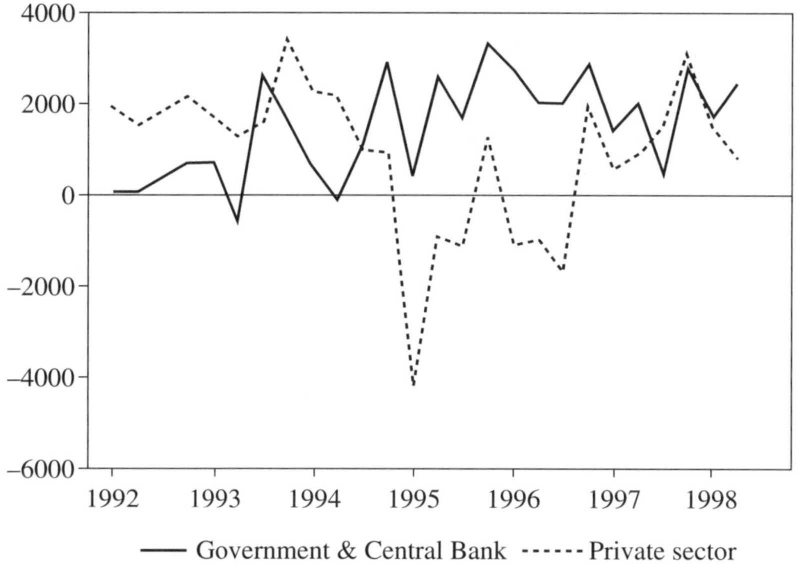

Figure 3.7 Net public and private capital inflows (millions of US$)

but until 1994 capital inflows – mainly private – systematically exceeded the current account deficit, and reserves increased (see Figures 3.6 and 3.7). With the drop of private capital inflows in 1994, reserve accumulation stagnated. This slow down in 1994 of the trends that characterized the early 1990s was followed in the first trimester of 1995 by sudden capital outflows and a contraction of reserves due to the so-called Tequila effect.

Following the Tequila crisis there was a transition phase in the evolution of the balance of payments, which continued until the third quarter of 1996. This phase is characterized mainly by a temporary reduction of the current account deficit, explained by the behaviour of the trade balance. The jump in the export volume, which was in part associated with the effects of the Brazilian *Plan Real* on Argentina, came on top of the rise in agricultural commodity prices, rising oil prices and the contraction of imports brought on by the recession. All these effects led to a temporary trade balance. In this phase, capital inflows are exclusively to the public sector, primarily as a result of the IMF-led rescue operation.

From late 1996 onwards, the evolution of the balance of payments returned to features similar to those of the first expansive phase of 1991–93. This recent expansive phase lasted from late 1996 until the Asian crisis. Net capital inflows, once again mainly from private sources, were similar to the peak levels prior to 1994. The current account deficit widened rapidly, mainly due to the increase of imports, but – just as was the case during the first expansive phase – capital inflows exceeded the deficit and reserves accumulated. The country-risk premium declined from 1995 onwards, reaching a low (similar to that of 1993) in the months preceding the Asian crisis. The deceleration of growth in late 1997 and the new recession phase in 1998 are linked to successive increases in the country-risk premium and a fall in private capital inflows.

Sources of Aggregate Demand Growth, Savings and Investments

During the first expansive phase, both consumption and investment growth[5] were the main factors contributing to the expansion of domestic absorption. At the end of the 1980s, the investment rate was at a historical low. It increased rapidly in this first phase, as it benefited from the appreciation of the exchange rate, which increased the purchasing power of (imported) capital goods in relation to the given savings rate. The 1995 crisis caused a simultaneous reduction of the consumption and investment shares. After the crisis, both components of domestic absorption increased their share in GDP, but the consumption share remained below the level achieved in the first expansive phase, while the investment rate kept rising.

During the first expansive phase, up to 1994, consumption dominated the increase of aggregate demand, particularly in the first two years, but the contribution of exports was negligible. With the 1995 crisis, the contraction of consumption and investment contributed in the same degree to the fall of the aggregate demand, whereas the expansion of exports played a significant countercyclical role for the first time. The recovery during the post-Tequila phase was led by consumption, but during the acceleration of growth in 1997 the contribution of investment growth was about the same as that of consumption.

The savings rate of the 1990s is systematically below that of the 1980s. The investment–savings gap widened during the first expansive phase, despite the rise in the savings rate in the second half of this phase. The gap closed during the 1995 crisis, due to the drastic contraction of investment, while the savings rate also fell. The adjustment mechanism was the contraction of output, together with a primarily exogenous export growth. The savings–investment gap widened again in the post-Tequila phase, reaching in 1997 a size similar to that of 1994.

Inflation

The dynamics of consumer prices (proxy of non-tradable goods) is typical of that observed as a result of shock-therapy stabilization plans which use the

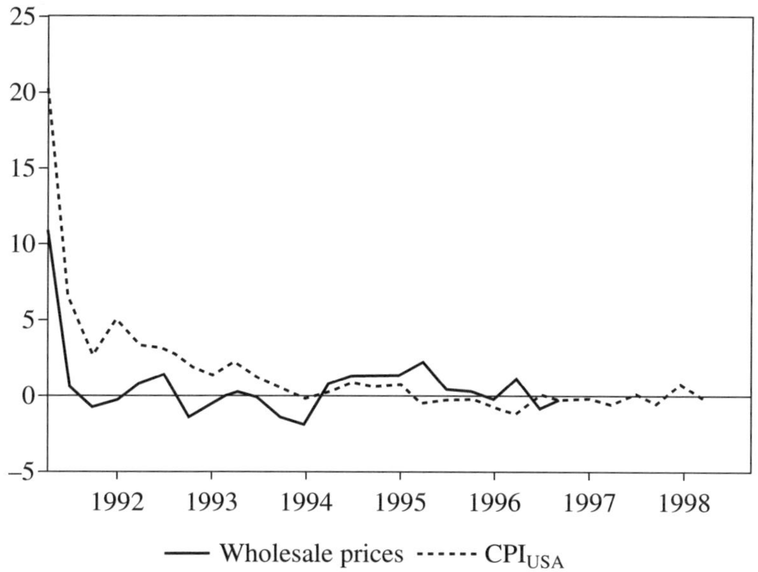

Figure 3.8 Difference between domestic and US inflation

exchange rate as nominal anchor (see Figure 3.8). The 'inflation inertia' remained for some time as a consequence of the survival of indexation mechanisms for wages and prices. Given that inflation decreased gradually in a context of substantial expansion of money, credit and demand, the process can only be attributed to the stabilizing role of the fixed exchange rate in a context of trade liberalization. Since the exchange rate was fixed, consumer price inflation converged gradually to international inflation. The convergence took about three years.

In contrast, the convergence of tradable goods prices was practically instantaneous. Wholesale prices serve as a proxy for tradable goods prices. The appreciation of the exchange rate (with a one-year lag) facilitated the convergence, as world market prices acted as an upper bound on domestic tradable goods prices from the beginning of the programme.

Relative Prices

The relative prices of the 1990s are very different from those typical of the preceding decade. The financial and trade opening affected macroeconomic behaviour and employment, mainly because of these changes in relative prices.

We take the launch of the Convertibility Plan as the start of the new regime. One can then see that most of the changes were produced in a

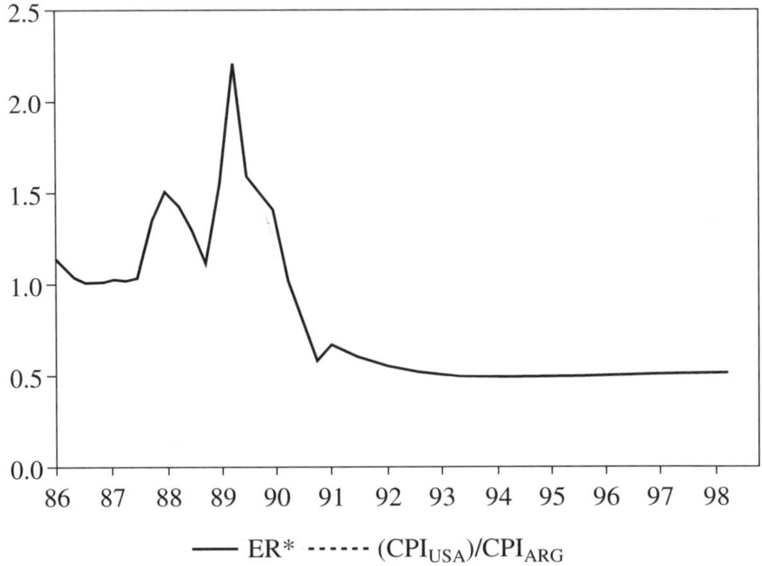

Figure 3.9 Real exchange rate (index, second semester of 1986 = 1)

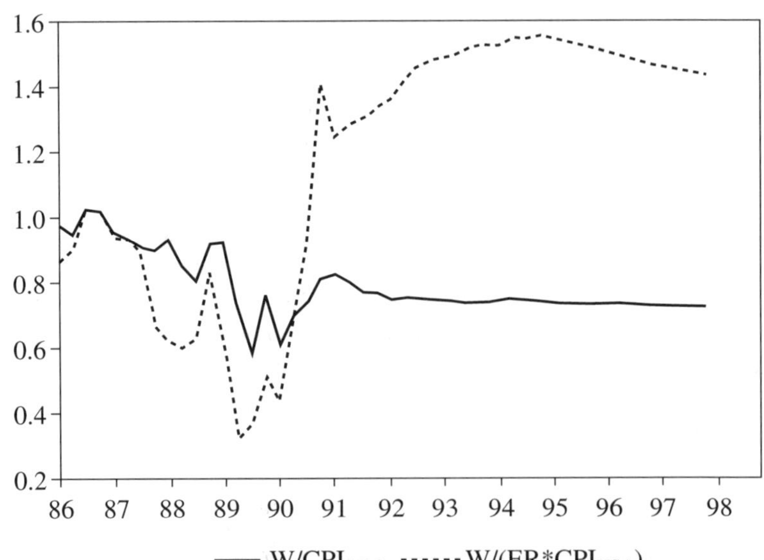

Figure 3.10 Real peso wage and real dollar wage

Table 3.1 Real exchange rate and dollar wage, 1986–98

	1986–90	1986–88	1990:4–91:1	1991:2–98	1994–98
Real exchange rate	1.22	1.16	0.62	0.50	0.49
Wage rate in constant US$	0.76	0.83	1.33	1.48	1.51

relatively short interval, including the months just before and after this launch. The change of relative prices was shock-wise, so that the new relative-price structure was established right from the beginning of the new regime. The price shifts produced in the course of the 1990s, starting in 1991, are small compared to those that took place at the very beginning of the period. These considerations hold most clearly for the exchange rate and the wage rate valued at constant dollars[6] (see Figures 3.9 and 3.10). Table 3.1 shows the mean values for the different sub-periods.

As the relative price change came as an initial shock, it is reasonable to assume that the observed shifts in the production structure, technology and industrial organization were adjustment processes to a shock, rather than marginal adjustments to gradual relative price changes.

3.3 URBAN EMPLOYMENT TRENDS

Figure 3.11 shows the evolution of the participation rate (NTPEAPOB), employment rate (NTASAN) and full-time employment rate[7] (NTASANPLE) starting in 1980, all as proportions of the urban population. The figure also shows the trends obtained through the Hodrick–Prescott filter.

The participation rate shows an upward trend from the mid-1980s onwards. The long-term growth trend (estimated with the HP filter) is 0.9 per cent per annum from the second half of the 1980s onwards. However, as the figure shows, the participation rate at the start of the 1990s was below the long-term trend. The growth trend estimated for the series after the second semester of 1990 is slightly above 1 per cent per year.

In the 1990s, the declining trend in full-time employment became more pronounced, and also total employment growth became negative, despite being cushioned by the increase of involuntary underemployment. The full-time employment curve for the 1990s shows a cyclical pattern with a peak in the second semester of 1992. Subsequently, it fell steadily until the second semester of 1996, with a steep decline in the first semester of 1995 associated with the recession of the Tequila effect. A recovery of the full-time employ-

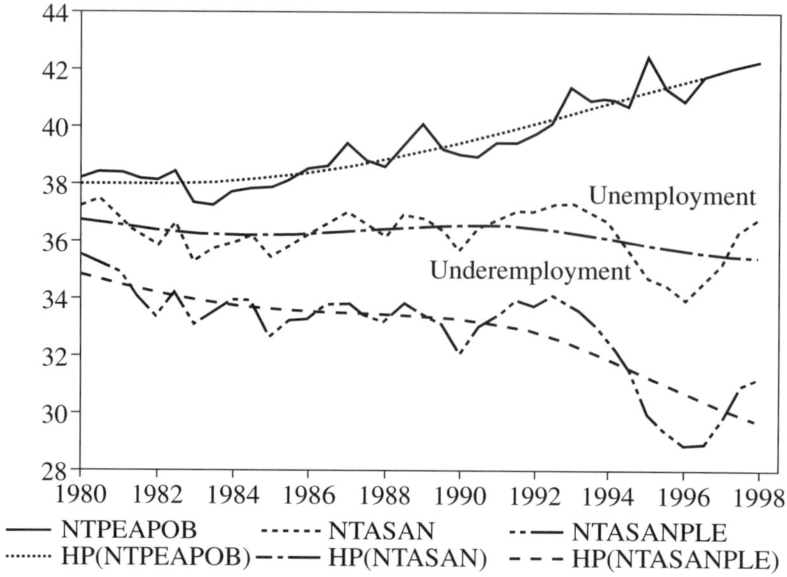

Figure 3.11 Participation, total employment and full-time employment rates (shares of urban population, %)

ment rate can be observed in 1997, and is linked to the strong output expansion mentioned above. This is a new phenomenon since the beginning of the fall in the employment rate, and has been subject to various interpretations and discussions, which we will comment on.

In Figure 3.11, the areas comprised between the curve for the participation rate and those for total employment and full-time employment refer to the unemployment rate (NTUNEMP) and the rate of involuntary underemployment (NTASANSUB), respectively, as shares of the urban population. The trends of the 1990s are clearly brought out, as well as the importance of the decline in full-time employment when explaining the increase in unemployment and involuntary underemployment.

The change in unemployment and involuntary underemployment measured as percentages of the economically active population in the 1990s can be summarized as shown in Table 3.2.

The contraction of full-time employment is the critical variable when explaining the increase of unemployment and involuntary sub-employment. Figure 3.12 shows the relation between the full-time employment rate and GDP (index, base = second semester of 1990). As can be seen, in the 1980s and up to the second semester of 1990, the full-time employment rate and output evolve with the same trend. In contrast, the trends diverge in the 1990s.

Table 3.2 Changes in unemployment and underemployment, 1990–98

	Average 1990–92:1	Average 1995–98:1	Difference
Unemployment (%)	6.9	16.1	9.2
Invisible underemployment (%)	8.6	12.8	4.2
Total (%)	15.5	28.9	13.4

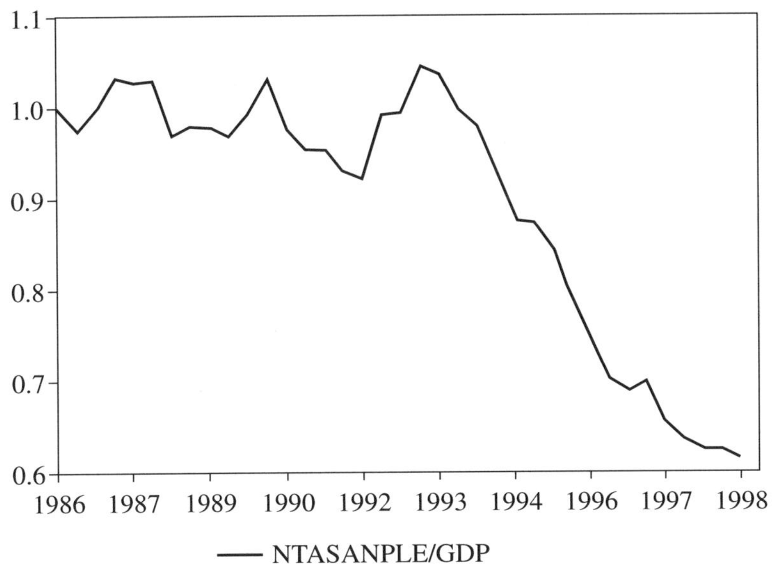

Figure 3.12 Full-time employment to GDP ratio

Data for Gran Buenos Aires

Figure 3.13 includes four charts for showing trends for the rates for total employment, full-time employment (35 hours or more), involuntary underemployment (TASANSUBI) and voluntary underemployment (TASANSUBV) as proportions of the population for Gran Buenos Aires in the 1990s.[8] The employment rate of the first chart is the sum of the other three components. First, full-time employment and voluntary underemployment tend to move together, peaking in the first semester of 1992 and reaching a trough in the second semester of 1996. In addition, involuntary underemployment varies anti-cyclically, with a trough around the second semester of 1992 and a peak

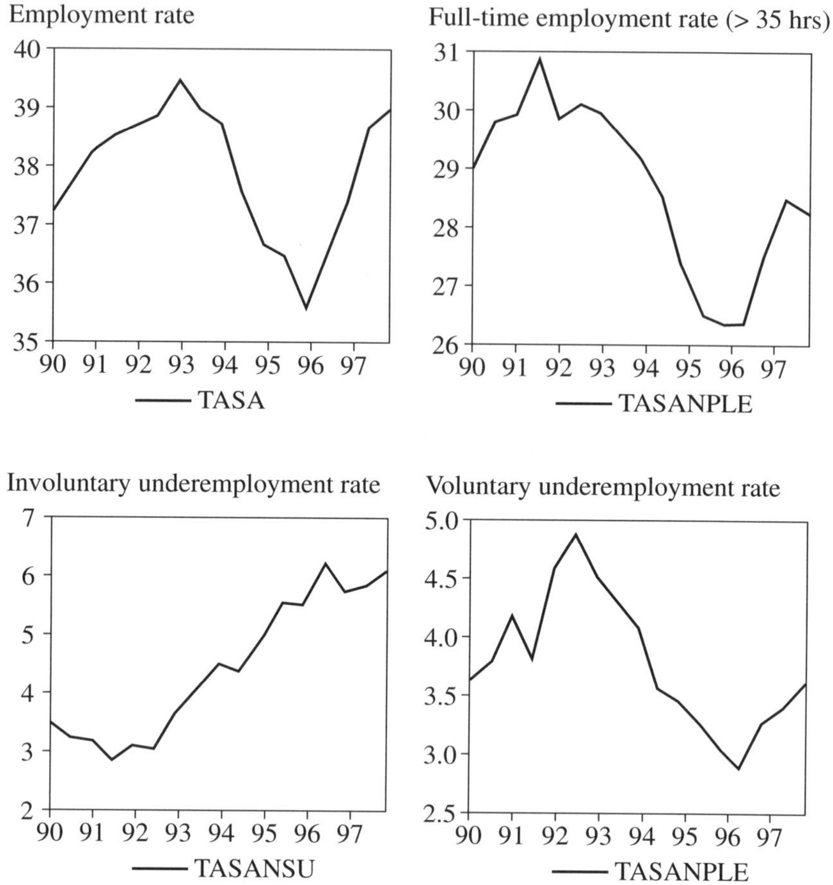

Figure 3.13 Employment trends in Gran Buenos Aires (shares of the GBA population, %)

in the second semester of 1996. Involuntary underemployment follows a trend similar to that of unemployment. These observations suggest that full-time employment and voluntary underemployment should be added as independent variables in the employment model, and that involuntary underemployment should be treated as a form of unemployment.

3.4 AN AGGREGATE MODEL OF THE LABOUR MARKET

The previous section clearly shows that there was a structural change in labour demand in the 1990s. External trade, domestic production, organization of production, technology and labour demand were restructured as a consequence of the type of incentives and constraints that emerged in the 1990s. We believe that the macroeconomic dynamics analysed in Section 3.2 was transmitted to firms mainly through the changes in aggregate demand and relative prices.[9] The incentives and constraints that prevailed in the 1990s did not emerge gradually. As said, new relative prices were set with a shock right from the start. Still, it is possible to conceive the restructuring of labour demand induced by the new incentives and macroeconomic constraints as a process that developed more or less gradually during the 1990s. We will analyse this question formally by first postulating the following equation for labour demand:

$$\log E = \alpha \log Y + \gamma \log(W/PK) + \delta$$

where E is employment, Y the product and W/PK the wage–capital price ratio. We define $t = 0$ as the period prior to the changes that occurred in the 1990s – say the 1980s – and $t = 1$ as the point in time at which the structural change processes of labour demand had advanced substantially – say 1996. Thus:

$$\log E_0 = \alpha \log Y_0 + \gamma \log(W_0/PK_0) + \delta_0$$

and

$$\log E_1 = \alpha \log Y_1 + \gamma \log(W_1/PK_1) + \delta_1$$

The difference between both observations is:

$$\Delta \log E = \alpha \Delta \log Y + (B_1 - B_0)$$

with

$$B_0 = \gamma \log(W_0/PK_0) + \delta_0 \text{ and } B_1 = \gamma \log(W_1/PK_1) + \delta_1$$

Given the fact that the relative price W_1/PK_1 remains practically defined for the entire currency-board period with a jump at the beginning of the period, we suppose that $B_1 - B_0$ follows a gradual adjustment in the course of the period, running a steady course:

$$d(B_1 - B_0) = \beta \quad \text{and, therefore} \quad \int \beta = B_1 - B_0$$

We then reformulate the employment equation as:

$$d\log(E) = \alpha d \log Y + \beta$$

with

$$\alpha > 0; \beta < 0$$

where β represents the gradual (contractive) adjustment of employment to the conditions of the 1990s. The estimates of this equation are based on bi-annual data for the periods 1980–98 and 1991–98. The equations for the first period are:

$$d\log(\text{NTASANPLE}) = \alpha d \log Y + \beta\text{DUM90S} + h\text{DUM97} + k$$
for the national aggregate

and

$$d\log(\text{TASANPLENO}) = \alpha d \log Y + \beta\text{DUM90S} + h\text{DUM97} + k$$
for Gran Buenos Aires

with

DUM90S = 0 between 1980 : 1 and 1990 : 2 and
DUM90S = 1 from 1991 : 1 onwards
DUM97 = 1 for both semesters of 1997 and
DUM97 = 0 for the rest of the period

DUM97 is a dummy variable that captures the additional growth of full-time employment in 1997. The statistical significance of the coefficient β in these regressions is a test for the structural change of the employment equation in the 1990s.

The regression equations for the bi-annual data for 1991–98 have the following specification:

$$d\log(\text{NTASANPLE}) = \alpha d \log Y + \beta + h\text{DUM97} \quad \text{for the national aggregate}$$

and

$$d\log(\text{TASANPLENO}) = \alpha d \log Y + \beta + h\text{DUM97} \quad \text{for Gran Buenos Aires}$$

Table 3.3 Regression coefficients for labour demand model

	1980–98 period		1991–98 period	
	National aggregate	Buenos Aires	National aggregate	Buenos Aires
α	0.275	0.277	0.336	0.287
β	–0.014	–0.016	–0.018	–0.018
h	0.039	0.047	0.038	0.047

Table 3.3 summarizes the estimates of the coefficients.[10]

The coefficients differ slightly. The coefficient for 1991–98 shows a significant short-term effect of 0.3. The fact that β is significant does not reject the hypothesis of structural change after 1991. The size of β indicates a declining trend of full-time employment rate at a rate of 1.8 per cent per semester, equivalent to an annual 3.6 per cent, and 24 per cent[11] for 1991–96. On the other hand, the estimator of h implies that, in the two semesters of 1997, the full-time employment rate increased on average 3.8 per cent (national aggregate) or 4.7 per cent (Buenos Aires) above the rate estimated by the employment equation. The constant term of the equation for both semesters of 1997 ($\beta + h$) is positive and equal to 2 per cent (national aggregate) or 2.9 per cent (Buenos Aires) per semester.

Additional information suggests that the significance of h reflects a transitory situation that can be explained by circumstantial factors of 1997. On the one hand, the equation for GBA 1991–98 shows an estimated β which projects the employment data of the first semester of 1998 with a residual lower than a standard error. This suggests that the effects of 1997 were transitory. On the other hand, analysis of the composition of full-time employment shows that the growth in 1997 can be explained by the rise of employment in manufacturing and in 'other services'. In the latter case, the growth benefited women in health and education services, and is probably a consequence of public subsidy programmes, which expanded in 1997, and of educational reform. Although these programmes continued at the same level thereafter, the effect on the full-time employment growth rate observed in 1997 was transitory.

The case of manufacturing is more important. For this sector we have additional employment data from the INDEC industrial survey. We have information on the number of unemployed persons and hours worked. The econometric analysis of the number of employed persons (an equation analogous to those estimated with the industrial production instead of GDP) yields a negative β coefficient, and for 1997 it shows a similar behaviour as the full-time employment rate of the household survey. The 1997 dummy is significant and positive, and its absolute value similar to that of the β coefficient. The same does not occur for hours worked, as the 1997 dummy is not significant. This indicates that the number of unemployed persons increased in 1997, whereas the number of hours worked per unit of output continued to fall at the same pace as the preceding years. In 1997, the number of hours worked per employed person dropped significantly. This can be explained by the more intensive use of temporary, low-cost labour contracts (effectively observed in 1997). This way of contracting workers seems to have come to replace increases in hours worked by permanent personnel, which the strong production growth of 1997 would otherwise have required. These forms of labour hiring were abolished by a labour legislation reform in 1998. In short, the declining trend in the employment/output ratio, measured by the number of hours worked, does not show a significant change in 1997. The shift in the trend of the number of employed persons resulted from a (transitory) substitution of additional hours for workers with permanent contracts for workers with temporary contracts.[12]

To examine the behaviour of involuntary underemployment, we estimate an equation for the national aggregate and for GBA, which relates the growth rate of the involuntary underemployment rate to that of the full-time employment rate. The results show that involuntary underemployment falls (grows) by about 1.6 per cent in response to a 1 per cent increase (fall) in the rate of full-time employment. Part of the contraction of full-time employment is thus not reflected in an increase in unemployment, but in a growth of involuntary underemployment. Conversely, when full-time employment increases, part of the increase comes from a reduction of the involuntary underemployment rate, so that it cushions the effects of the increase in full-time employment over the total employment rate.

3.5 ANATOMY OF THE DECLINE IN EMPLOYMENT

Figure 3.14 shows the employment rates disaggregated by gender and position in the household. Comparing the charts with those of Figure 3.13, we can observe that the employment rates of men and heads of household resemble the dynamics of the full-time employment rates. The information in Figures 3.13 and 3.14 suggests there are different phases in the employment cycle. We will now quantify the observed changes in the different periods, and analyse their composition by production sector, type of employment, gender and position in the household.

Frenkel and González Rozada (1999) analyse in further detail the labour market changes by sector, occupational category and gender. They show that in the expansion phase 1990:1–92:2, total employment grew by 1.66 percent-

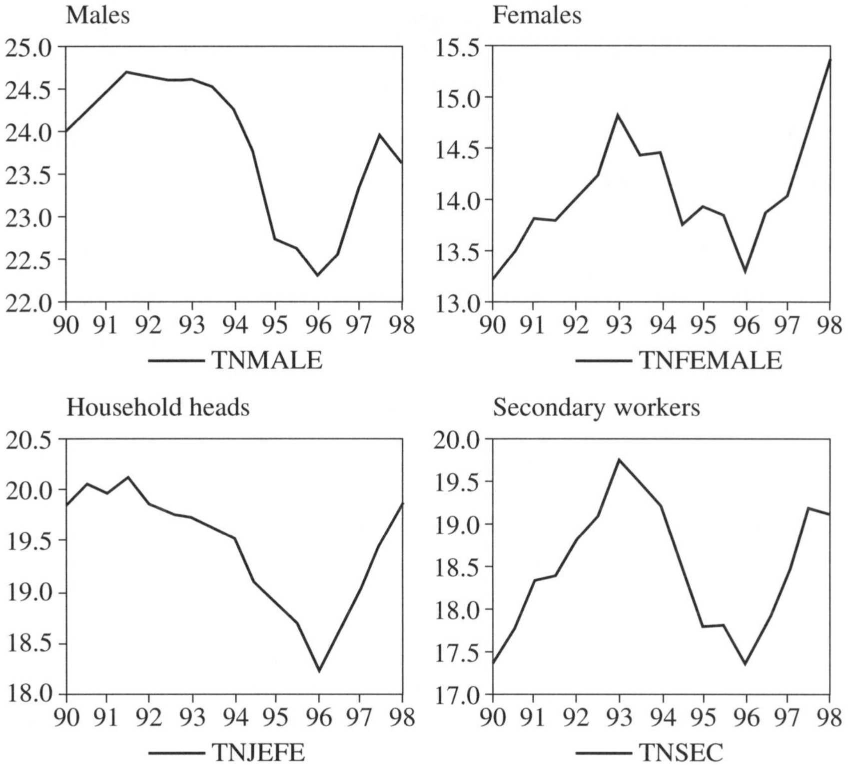

Figure 3.14 Employment rates for GBA by gender and position in household (shares of GBA population, %)

age points (pp) of the population. There was an expansion of full-time employment – slightly more than 1 pp – and voluntary underemployment, whereas involuntary underemployment shrank countercyclically. Most of the expansion came from the increase in employment in commerce, followed, in order of importance, by construction and manufacturing employment. It should be noted that the employment of household heads hardly increased.

In the contractive phase 1992:2–96:2, total employment dropped 2.43 pp. This fall seems to have been cushioned by the increase of involuntary underemployment. Full-time employment fell 3.75 pp and voluntary underemployment 2 pp, whereas involuntary underemployment increased 3.21 pp.

Two-thirds of the contraction of full-time employment concerns jobs in the manufacturing industry, and affected mainly men and household heads. Next in terms of importance are the losses of jobs in commerce and construction, with similar effects by gender and position in the household. There was also a contraction in jobs in other services, mainly affecting secondary workers in the household. On the other hand, full-time employment increased by slightly more than 1 pp in transportation and communications, and in financial services. In sum, the salient stylized facts of the drop in full-time positions are that two-thirds correspond to the manufacturing sector, two-thirds are men, and more than half are heads of household.

Mainly women and secondary workers are affected by the decline in voluntary underemployment. The reduction occurred in all sectors, but more than half is concentrated in other services, mainly women and secondary workers.

The fall in the sum of full-time jobs and voluntary underemployment amounts to 5.74 pp. Half the decline occurred in manufacturing, and after adding job losses in commerce and construction, two-thirds of the total decline is explained. The jobs lost in these sectors mainly correspond to men and heads of household.

We round up the analysis by examining the increase of involuntary underemployment. Half the observed increase occurs in other services, providing employment mainly to women and secondary workers. The other half is distributed across other economic sectors.

The characteristics of the drop in employment observed in the 1990:1–96:2 period are similar to those observed during the contraction phase. In short, the conclusions of this analysis emphasize the importance that the employment contraction in the industrial sector has had in the evolution of the overall employment rate of the economy. Employment in the commerce and construction sectors also shrank, albeit to a lesser degree. The decrease in the number of jobs involved mainly men and heads of family. In addition, more jobs became available in the transportation, financial services and utilities sectors. As a result, the drop in urban employment seems to have been mainly the consequence of the restructuring and concentration of production and trade activities that took place in the 1990s, particularly in manufacturing, i.e. the traded goods sector.

Full-time employment increased in the February 1996–97 period, as we already mentioned. Half the increase corresponds to other services and is constituted almost entirely of women. Slightly less than one-third corresponds to the manufacturing sector.

3.6 EMPLOYMENT, PRODUCTIVITY AND OPENING OF MANUFACTURING INDUSTRY

In this section we will analyse the mechanisms through which the conditions of the 1990s affected the behaviour of employment, production and productivity in the industrial sector.[13]

We assume that the change in industrial employment in the 1990s was the combined result of three factors. The first is output growth: the expansion of demand-induced production increases that, in turn, tended to increase labour demand. The second factor is the displacement effect of imports. The combination of the expansion of demand with the change of relative prices provoked a more than proportional increase in imports. These imports substituted domestic production in the total supply of industrial goods, causing at the same time a direct displacement effect of labour. The third factor is an autonomous process of reduction of employment per unit of output resulting from changes in the product mix, technology and industrial organization.

Putting aside the second effect, and given the observed increase in production, the other two factors can be expressed alternatively as a decomposition of the productivity increase. If the sensitivity of employment to output changes in the short run is different from zero, then the observed productivity increase can be decomposed into two elements: the increase attributable to output growth, and the productivity increase resulting from the changes in production mix, technology and industrial organization. The latter type of changes happened in order to gain competitiveness under the new regime. The first issue we will discuss in this section is the separation and estimation of the mentioned effects.

The Business Cycle and Employment and Productivity Trends

To separate the effects of the cycle and the trends in the employment dynamics, we estimate the following equation:[14]

$$d\log E = \alpha d\log Y - \beta$$

where E represents employed workers and Y gross production value, α is the partial, short-term employment output elasticity, and α is a constant in the period representing the tendency toward a productivity increase independent of the cycle.

We estimate the equation with semester-based data starting 1991:2. The regression result is:

$$d\log(E_t) = -0.009 + 0.210 d\log(Y_t)$$
$$(2.64) \quad (2.23)$$

$R^2 = 0.25$, *Sample*: 1991:2–96:2

The estimators of α and β are significant at the 5 per cent level. The partial employment output elasticity is 0.21 and the estimate of β is a trimester-based rate of –0.93 per cent, equivalent to an annual rate of –3.8 per cent.

We will now use the results to decompose the productivity increase (rate-wise) between a component attributable to the production increase and the autonomous component for the period 1990–96. Given that β is the estimator of the trimester-based rate of the autonomous productivity increase, we calculate $BETA = (1 + \beta)^{24} - 1$ as an estimator for the rate of change of autonomous productivity for the entire 1990–96 period (24 trimesters). With this estimator we calculate the component attributable to the output growth as a residual. The result is:

$$\begin{array}{ccccc} \Delta Q/Q & = & \Delta QC/Q & + & BETA \\ 47\% & = & 22\% & + & 25\% \end{array}$$

As can be seen, slightly less than half of the productivity increase of the period ($\Delta Q/Q = 47\%$) is attributable to output growth.[15]

We apply a similar process to decompose the employment contraction between 1990 and 1996 into a negative component determined by the tendency to reduce the labour force per production unit and a positive component attributable to the expansion of production:

$$\begin{array}{ccccc} \Delta E/E & = & \Delta EC/E & - & BETA \\ 17\% & = & 8\% & - & 25\% \end{array}$$

The reduction of employment at a constant output level would have been 25 per cent for the period as a whole. The production increase induced by the expansion of the demand implied a positive effect of 8 per cent, muffling the observed drop at 17 per cent.

Direct Employment Effects of Changes in Imports and Exports

We will now estimate the displacement effects of import growth and the expansive effect of export growth on output and employment in manufacturing industry for the 1990–96 period. To this end, we use the following identity:

$$\begin{array}{ccccccc} \Delta Y/Y & = & \Delta CA/Y & + & \Delta X/Y & - & \Delta M/Y \\ 35\% & = & 57.6\% & + & 10.2\% & - & 32.8\% \end{array}$$

where CA is the apparent domestic consumption of manufactured goods, X is exports and M imports. All variables valued at constant prices of 1986.[16]

Between 1990 and 1996, the increase in the domestic demand for manufactures was 57.6 per cent of the 1990 output level. The increase in manufactured exports added 10.2 per cent to total demand. In the same period, the increase in imports of manufactured goods amounted to 32.8 per cent of the 1990 production, so that the increase in the supply of imported goods satisfied nearly half of the increase in domestic demand. The changes in the components of aggregate demand and supply of manufactured goods determine the respective employment effects:

$$\Delta EC/E = EFCA + EFX - EFM$$
$$8\% = 13.3\% + 2.3\% - 7.6\%$$

The 8 per cent increase in industrial employment, induced by the production increase, results from two effects: a positive effect of 15.6 per cent derived from the increase of domestic demand and exports, and a negative effect of 7.6 per cent attributable to the increase of imports in the total supply of manufactured goods. The direct displacement of employment due to imports estimated this way is more than half the expansive effect attributable to the increase in domestic demand. In the following identity we summarize the decomposition of all effects on the employment change observed between 1990 and 1996:

$$\Delta E/E = -BETA + \alpha Y/Y = -BETA + EFCA + EFX - EFM$$
$$-17\% = -25\% + 8\% = -25\% + 13.3\% + 2.3\% - 7.6\%$$

3.7 INCOME DISTRIBUTION EFFECTS OF CHANGES IN THE EMPLOYMENT AND REMUNERATION STRUCTURE[17]

Per Capita Income of Employed and Active Population and the Effects of Unemployment

Figure 3.15 shows per capita income of the employed and economically active population. These are monthly-based data, expressed in constant pesos of May 1998.[18] Labour incomes followed a cyclical pattern correlated with GDP. In the first expansive phase, the increase peaked in the first semester of 1994. The subsequent contraction reached a low in the second semester of 1996. Obviously, due to the strong rise in unemployment, the contraction had a greater impact on the average incomes of the economically active population. The figure shows increases with respect to initial per capita income, at its peak level and at the end of the period. In 1998, the income of the occupied population was 22 per cent higher than that of 1991 and 5.8 per cent lower than the peak level of 1994. The mean income of the active population increased by 12.2 per cent over the whole period, and the drop with respect to the 1994 peak is 9.8 per cent.

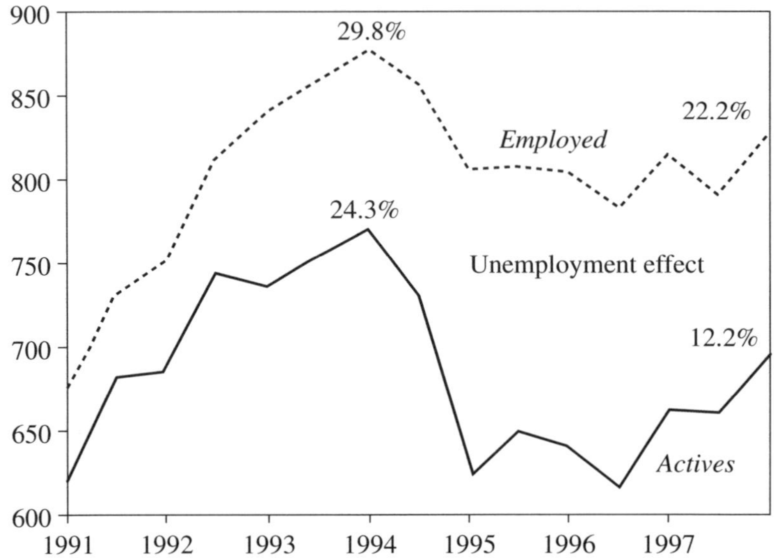

Figure 3.15 Per capita income of the employed and economically active population (monthly incomes at constant prices of May 1986)

The effect of the unemployment increase can be estimated by expressing the mean income rate of the economically active population as a function of the per capita income of the employed population and the rate of change of unemployment. Defining *A* as the economically active population, *D* as the unemployed, *YE* as the employed population's per capita income and *YA* as the per capita income of the economically active population, we arrive at the following equation:

$$\Delta YA/YA \cong \Delta YE/YE - \Delta(D/A)(YE/YA)$$
$$12.2\% \cong 22.2\% - 8.2\%$$

The percentages of the lower line correspond to the period changes. Had the unemployment rate not increased, the mean income of the active population would have increased 22 per cent. Instead, it increased 12.2 per cent. The difference of 10 percentage points – slightly less than half the increase of the employed population's income – reflects the income loss caused by the increase in unemployment. However, had the per capita income of the employed population remained constant, the effect of the unemployment increase would have implied an 8.2 per cent contraction in the mean income of the active population (the difference between –10 and –8.2 per cent is due to cross-effects).

Incomes of men and women show a trend similar to the aggregate income cycle, except that the peak income of women was reached in the second semester of 1994. In the contraction phase, the income of employed women dropped 6.7 per cent, compared to 5.9 per cent for employed men. Between 1991 and 1998 female unemployment increased 9.4 pp of the active female population, as against 6.4 pp for their male counterparts. For this reason, compared to 1991 the mean income of economically active women increased 14.7 per cent at the peak level of the 1994 maximum, and 8.2 per cent at the end of the period.

Nonetheless, it is important to note that the effect of unemployment on per capita income of the total active population is not explained by the increase in unemployment of the female active population. Indeed, taken over the entire period, the size of the unemployment effect on the mean income of active men is about the same as that of the entire active population.

Incomes by Occupational Category

Figure 3.16 shows the evolution of per capita income of the employed population by three occupational categories: full-time employees, full-time non-employees and involuntary underemployed. The per capita income of these three categories passed through a cyclical pattern peaking in the first semester of 1994. The figure shows the variations with respect to the first semester of 1991, the 1994 high, and the end of the period. In 1998, the income of the involuntary underemployed is practically the same as that of 1991, having shrunk 18.9 per cent with respect to the peak level. The increase over the whole period for full-time employees was 22.3 per cent, and the fall against the peak level 4.9 per cent. Full-time non-employees experienced a 49.2 per cent increase, and their income increased 8.5 per cent with respect to 1994.

Table 3.4 shows the decomposition of the period growth rate of per capita income of the employed population.

Every cell in the table can be read as the growth rate of mean income, which the employed population would have experienced if only the corresponding variable had changed. For example – all other things being equal – the drop of the full-time jobs of wage earners would have implied a 4.7 per cent income loss. If the 1991 employment structure had remained unchanged, per capita income would have increased by 29.4 per cent. The income effect of employment restructuring was negative: the decline in the share of full-time wage eaners and non-wage earners is associated with an income drop of 8.6 per cent. The total impact of the change in the employment structure is –4.4 per cent.

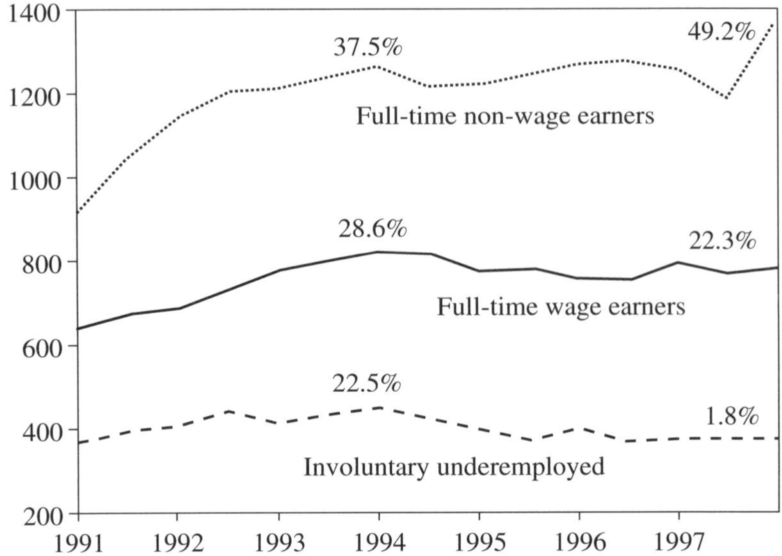

Figure 3.16 Average incomes by occupational category (monthly income at constant prices of May 1986)

Table 3.4 Sources of income growth by occupation

	Income contribution	**Employment contribution**	**Total contribution**
Full-time wage earners	14.9%	–4.7%	10.2%
Full-time non-wage earners	14.5%	–3.9%	10.9%
Involuntary underemployed	0.0%	4.2%	4.2%
Total	**29.4%**	**–4.4%**	**25.0% ≅ 22.2%**

We are now able to show the growth rate of the per capita income of the economically active population as a function of the increase in per capita income and the negative effects of the employment restructuring and the increase in unemployment:

$\Delta YA/YA$	≅	*Income effect*	+	*Employment restructuring effect*	+	*Unemployment increase effect*
12.2%	≅	29.4%		–4.4%		–10%

This summary result brings out the importance of the quantity effects. Had the shares of full-time jobs, involuntary underemployment and unemployment (in relation to the active population) remained the same as those of 1991, per capita income of the active population would have increased 29.5 per cent. The quantity effects of the loss of full-time jobs and the increase in unemployment and involuntary underemployment eliminated more than half of that increase.

Income Distribution

To conclude the analysis of per capita income growth, we now show the evolution of income distribution among the employed and active populations. For the latter, we assign zero income to the unemployed. Table 3.5 shows the income distribution of the employed population.

Table 3.5 Income distribution of the employed population

Income deciles for the employed population	**Cumulative percentage of total income**		
	1991:1	**1994:1**	**1998:1**
1	2.10	2.06	1.71
2	5.90	5.82	5.09
3	10.60	10.60	9.56
4	16.15	16.27	14.91
5	22.79	22.88	21.28
6	30.24	30.62	28.87
7	39.57	39.99	38.13
8	51.16	51.48	49.49
9	66.77	66.96	65.08
10	100.00	100.00	100.00
Gini coefficient	**0.423**	**0.420**	**0.456**

Between 1991 and 1994, the income distribution among the employed population remained stable. The bottom 40 per cent received 16.2 per cent of the total income in 1991 and 16.3 per cent in 1994. The top 10 per cent witnessed a minimal decline in income share, which went from 33.2 per cent in 1991 to 33.0 per cent in 1994. The Gini coefficient is practically the same at both points in time. The distribution deteriorated in the 1994–98 sub-period. In 1998, the share of the lower-income 40 per cent fell to 14.9 per cent, and the richest 10 per cent increased its share to 34.9 per cent. The Gini coefficient increased to 0.456.

The distributive changes are more acute if one calculates the income distribution between the active population in order to take into account the increase in unemployment. The distribution among the active population is shown in Table 3.6.

Table 3.6 Income distribution of the economically active population

Income deciles for the economically active population	**Cumulative percentage of total income**		
	1991:1	**1994:1**	**1998:1**
1	0.14	0.00	0.00
2	3.02	1.73	0.56
3	7.58	5.97	3.88
4	12.98	11.44	8.89
5	19.56	18.20	15.24
6	27.30	26.21	23.11
7	36.86	35.84	32.67
8	48.85	48.03	44.79
9	65.07	64.37	61.54
10	100.00	100.00	100.00
Gini coefficient	**0.471**	**0.490**	**0.534**

The income distribution among the active population deteriorated throughout the period. The poorest 40 per cent reduced its participation from 13.0 per cent in 1991 to 11.4 per cent in 1994 and to 8.9 per cent in 1998. The top 10 per cent increased its share from 34.9 per cent in 1991 to 35.6 per cent in 1994 and 38.5 per cent in 1998. The Gini coefficient went from 0.471 in 1991 to 0.534 in 1998.

When comparing the Gini coefficients in Tables 3.5 and 3.6, it is easy to note that the rise in inequality among the economically active population up to 1994 resulted exclusively from the initial phase's rise in unemployment. Later, between 1994 and 1998, the rise in inequality was mainly due to the joint effect of the increase in unemployment and widening income differentials among the employed population.

Microsimulations

We use the microsimulations methodology (see Chapter 2) to study the distributive impact of the economic processes that took place in the 1990s. We use data from the INDEC Permanent Household Surveys of October 1991, May 1994 and May 1998.

The inequality changes resulted from various economic factors such as employment structure per economic sector and per occupation, unemployment rate, wages and labour participation rate, as well as changes in other socio-demographic characteristics like age and household composition. The methodology takes these population characteristics as constant parameters, and estimates the individual and joint distributive impact of the economic factors, participation and education. In order to keep the socio-demographic characteristics constant, six demographic groups were defined based on three age and two gender classifications. The first demographic group corresponds to men in the age group 14–20, the second group to men aged 30–45, and the third to men older than 45. The remaining three groups were defined the same way for women. The employed population within each demographic group was classified into four sectors of economic activity – commerce, manufacturing industry, services and others. These branches were ordered within each demographic group according to average wage, showing first those belonging to the sector with the highest average salary, and last those belonging to the sector with the lowest. In practice, the sectors were ordered as follows: services, commerce, others and manufacturing industry. The unemployed and the economically inactive were added to these sectors. In other words, each demographic group is made up of people classified into six categories: four economic sectors, the unemployed and the economically inactive.

The microsimulations keep the 1998 population characteristics constant (a year of structural post-reforms and liberalization of the balance of payments). Subsequently, we determine what the income distribution would have looked like, if the wage structure, the sectoral composition of employment, the participation rate and the unemployment rate had not changed from those observed in 1991 (the first year of the structural reforms and the liberalization of the balance of payments) with respect to those observed in 1994 (the counterfactual year).

The comparison between 1998 and 1991 offers a balance of the distributive impacts of the processes that took place in the course of the entire period. The survey of May 1998 was conducted at the peak of the second expansive phase. Although GDP growth decelerated with the 1997 Asian crisis, economic decline only began in mid-1998. This way, the exercise compares the initial conditions with those of a boom period, experienced after the regime had gone through a complete cycle of expansion and recession.

The simulation with the 1994 parameters provides information at the intermediate point of the cycle, but at the same time can also be considered as a counterfactual exercise. The exchange-rate and monetary regime and the trade and financial opening were introduced as a shock early in 1991. By 1994, a large part of the process of privatization and deregulation had been completed and inflation had converged with that of the United States. Between 1991 and 1994, there was a surge in net capital inflows, and although the current account deficit was also widening, the reserve position strengthened nearly throughout the period. In 1994 the economy functioned with all the attributes of a Currency Board, and was at the peak of the expansive cycle that preceded the Tequila effect. In this sense, the simulation of the income distribution with the 1994 labour market characteristics – equivalent to a comparison between 1994 and 1998 – compares two cyclical peaks in a context of completed liberalization and external opening and in the presence of a volatile international capital market. Given this context, the 1994–98 comparison can be considered as representative of the regime's more structural trends, that is, beyond the initial or transitory effects of its first years of the reforms.

Confidence Intervals of the Estimates

In order to determine the effect of the changes in the labour market structure, we apply the microsimulations methodology by altering sequentially the participation rate, unemployment rate, employment structure (by sector), employment distribution (by occupation) and incomes recorded in 1998. These alterations were made within each of the previously defined demographic groups. In each case, the impact on the distribution of per capita family income was simulated. Since the methodology is based on the generation of random numbers, it is necessary to take into consideration the uncertainty this involves in the robustness of the effects. To this end, the microsimulations were replicated 5,000 times, obtaining 95 per cent confidence intervals for each calculated measure of inequality and poverty.

Results

Table 3.7 presents the changes in income distribution and poverty between 1998 and 1991, measured by the Gini coefficient in terms of per capita family income and the equivalent family income per adult[19] and by the poverty measures P_0, P_1 and P_2. P_0 is defined as the fraction of the population that is below the poverty line. P_1 is known as the poverty gap and attempts to capture the degree of poverty weighted for the poverty incidence. Contrary to the poverty incidence, P_0, the poverty gap attempts to capture what happens

Table 3.7 Effects on inequality and poverty of changes in the wage and employment structure between 1998 and 1991

	Per capita family income			Per adult equivalent family income			Poverty measures		
	Employed	Active	Total	Employed	Active	Total	P_0	P_1	P_2
Gini coefficient in 1998	**0.507**	**0.526**	**0.519**	**0.499**	**0.522**	**0.513**	**0.275**	**0.125**	**0.082**
P effect	**0.489**	**0.523**	**0.511**	**0.487**	**0.523**	**0.512**	**0.193**	**0.099**	**0.072**
	(0.481, 0.498)	(0.513, 0.530)	(0.502, 0.519)	(0.478, 0.495)	(0.514, 0.531)	(0.503, 0.520)	(0.184, 0.199)	(0.095, 0.103)	(0.069, 0.076)
P + D effect	**0.450**	**0.468**	**0.458**	**0.453**	**0.470**	**0.458**	**0.188**	**0.075**	**0.044**
	(0.444, 0.458)	(0.461, 0.474)	(0.451, 0.464)	(0.447, 0.460)	(0.464, 0.477)	(0.453, 0.466)	(0.179, 0.197)	(0.070, 0.079)	(0.040, 0.048)
P, D + R effect	0.453	0.470	0.461	0.454	0.471	0.461	0.177	0.072	0.043
	(0.446, 0.460)	(0.463, 0.476)	(0.455, 0.467)	(0.447, 0.461)	(0.464, 0.477)	(0.456, 0.468)	(0.168, 0.185)	(0.068, 0.075)	(0.040, 0.046)
P, D, R + E effect	0.457	0.474	0.464	0.458	0.475	0.464	0.165	0.067	0.041
	(0.449, 0.464)	(0.466, 0.481)	(0.459, 0.470)	(0.450, 0.464)	(0.467, 0.482)	(0.459, 0.472)	(0.158, 0.172)	(0.063, 0.071)	(0.038, 0.044)
P, D, R, E + W effect	**0.491**	**0.508**	**0.504**	**0.492**	**0.508**	**0.504**	**0.100**	**0.045**	**0.030**
	(0.474, 0.518)	(0.490, 0.535)	(0.489, 0.528)	(0.474, 0.518)	(0.490, 0.535)	(0.489, 0.528)	(0.092, 0.106)	(0.042, 0.049)	(0.027, 0.033)
P, D, R, E + WS effect	0.471	0.488	0.480	0.472	0.489	0.480	0.170	0.071	0.043
	(0.462, 0.483)	(0.479, 0.500)	(0.471, 0.489)	(0.463, 0.483)	(0.480, 0.500)	(0.472, 0.489)	(0.157, 0.178)	(0.067, 0.075)	(0.041, 0.047)
P, D, R, E +	0.490	0.506	0.502	0.490	0.507	0.502	0.105	0.046	0.030
WSO effect	(0.473, 0.515)	(0.489, 0.531)	(0.488, 0.525)	(0.473, 0.515)	(0.489, 0.531)	(0.488, 0.525)	(0.096, 0.112)	(0.043, 0.050)	(0.028, 0.033)
P, D, R, E +	0.494	0.511	0.507	0.495	0.511	0.507	0.105	0.048	0.031
WSOED effect	(0.477, 0.520)	(0.493, 0.537)	(0.492, 0.531)	(0.477, 0.520)	(0.493, 0.537)	(0.492, 0.530)	(0.096, 0.111)	(0.044, 0.051)	(0.029, 0.034)
P, D, R, E +	0.491	0.508	0.504	0.492	0.508	0.504	0.100	0.045	0.030
WSOEDR effect	(0.474, 0.518)	(0.490, 0.535)	(0.489, 0.528)	(0.474, 0.518)	(0.490, 0.535)	(0.489, 0.528)	(0.092, 0.106)	(0.042, 0.049)	(0.027, 0.033)
Gini coefficient in 1991	**0.480**	**0.491**	**0.485**	**0.473**	**0.486**	**0.479**	**0.231**	**0.084**	**0.045**

Notes: The effects are cumulative and their meaning is: P: participation, D: unemployment, R: employment structure by economic sector, E: employment structure by occupation, W: relative labour incomes, WS: relative labour incomes by gender, WSO: relative labour incomes by gender and by occupation, WSOED: relative labour incomes by gender occupation and education, WSOEDR: relative labour incomes by gender, occupation, education and economic sector.

if, for example, a certain policy affects only the poorest of the poor. P_2 is a generalization of the poverty gap. The P_1 measure takes into consideration the transfers between the poor and the non-poor, but a transfer between the poor will not have any effect in the poverty gap. The P_2 measure takes into account the inequality among the poor, i.e. it is a measure sensitive to the income distribution among the poor. If there no inequality among the poor, P_2 would be equal to P_1.

Table 3.7 emphasizes in **bold** the estimates that are statistically significant. The numbers in parentheses refer to the intervals of the estimates at the 95 per cent level of confidence, obtained after 5,000 simulations. Since we estimate the different effects sequentially, the confidence intervals measure the statistical significance of the effect analysed with respect to the preceding effect. As mentioned above, the experiment consisted of sequentially replacing within each demographic group the various characteristics of the 1998 population with the respective population characteristics at the beginning of the period of analysis, May 1991. First, the participation rate within each demographic group was altered, calculating the measures of inequality and poverty for the resulting population. By means of the comparison between the actual and counterfactual inequality measures, it is possible to quantify the impact of the change in the participation rate. The results are shown in Table 3.7 as 'P effect'. Then we take the population resulting after having changed the participation rate and the corresponding unemployment rate for each demographic group. The inequality and poverty measures were calculated for this new population, and are shown in Table 3.7 as 'P + D effect'. The confidence intervals that come with 'P + D effect' measure the statistical significance of this effect with respect to the 'P effect', this way giving a measure of the statistical significance of the change in unemployment rate. This is how the various characteristics of the actual population of 1998 were successively changed for those of the 1991 population, the resulting measures of inequality and poverty being shown in Table 3.7. The first line of the table shows the Gini coefficient in 1998, and the second part of the table shows the three measures of poverty using the actual population of 1998. The last line of the table contains the same calculations, this time for the 1991 population.

As can be observed in Table 3.7, the effect of the change in participation rate is not statistically significant for the active population or for the total population, but slightly increases the inequality for the employed population. This change in the participation rate also increases poverty, considering any of the three measures.

The unemployment effect is positive and significant in the sense that it increases inequality, although it has no significant effect on the poverty incidence. A positive and significant effect, in the sense of increasing poverty,

Table 3.8 *Effects on inequality and poverty of changes in the wage and employment structure between 1998 and 1994*

	Per capita family income			Per adult equivalent family income			Poverty measures		
	Employed	**Active**	**Total**	**Employed**	**Active**	**Total**	P_0	P_1	P_2
Gini coefficient in 1998	**0.507**	**0.526**	**0.519**	**0.499**	**0.522**	**0.513**	**0.275**	**0.125**	**0.082**
P effect	**0.490**	0.522	0.512	**0.487**	0.523	0.512	**0.202**	**0.101**	**0.072**
	(0.481, 0.498)	(0.513, 0.531)	(0.503, 0.520)	(0.479, 0.495)	(0.515, 0.531)	(0.504, 0.520)	(0.195, 0.209)	(0.097, 0.105)	(0.069, 0.075)
P + D effect	**0.454**	**0.471**	**0.461**	**0.457**	**0.472**	**0.461**	0.201	0.096	**0.067**
	(0.444, 0.459)	(0.461, 0.476)	(0.451, 0.467)	(0.447, 0.465)	(0.466, 0.477)	(0.453, 0.468)	(0.194, 0.210)	(0.092, 0.100)	(0.064, 0.069)
P, D + R effect	0.453	0.469	0.459	0.452	0.468	0.458	**0.189**	0.091	0.064
	(0.446, 0.459)	(0.463, 0.475)	(0.455, 0.465)	(0.447, 0.458)	(0.464, 0.474)	(0.452, 0.463)	(0.180, 0.196)	(0.088, 0.095)	(0.062, 0.067)
P, D, R + E effect	0.463	0.473	0.462	0.459	0.472	0.462	0.188	0.092	0.065
	(0.452, 0.467)	(0.466, 0.481)	(0.457, 0.470)	(0.451, 0.464)	(0.467, 0.480)	(0.459, 0.471)	(0.179, 0.194)	(0.089, 0.095)	(0.062, 0.068)
P, D, R, E + W effect	**0.477**	**0.522**	**0.508**	**0.479**	**0.523**	**0.508**	**0.139**	**0.075**	**0.056**
	(0.467, 0.490)	(0.512, 0.535)	(0.498, 0.519)	(0.467, 0.491)	(0.513, 0.536)	(0.499, 0.520)	(0.131, 0.147)	(0.071, 0.078)	(0.054, 0.059)
P, D, R, E + WS effect	0.472	0.516	0.499	0.473	0.518	0.499	0.190	0.094	0.067
	(0.460, 0.485)	(0.505, 0.530)	(0.490, 0.511)	(0.461, 0.487)	(0.506, 0.531)	(0.490, 0.512)	(0.182, 0.198)	(0.091, 0.098)	(0.064, 0.069)
P, D, R, E +	0.474	0.520	0.505	0.476	0.521	0.505	0.134	0.073	0.055
WSO effect	(0.463, 0.488)	(0.509, 0.534)	(0.495, 0.517)	(0.464, 0.489)	(0.509, 0.535)	(0.495, 0.518)	(0.126, 0.141)	(0.070, 0.076)	(0.052, 0.058)
P, D, R, E +	0.478	0.523	0.508	0.479	0.524	0.508	0.135	0.073	0.055
WSOED effect	(0.466, 0.491)	(0.512, 0.536)	(0.498, 0.520)	(0.467, 0.493)	(0.512, 0.537)	(0.499, 0.521)	(0.127, 0.142)	(0.070, 0.077)	(0.053, 0.058)
P, D, R, E +	0.477	0.522	0.508	0.479	0.523	0.508	0.139	0.075	0.056
WSOEDR effect	(0.467, 0.490)	(0.512, 0.535)	(0.498, 0.519)	(0.467, 0.491)	(0.513, 0.536)	(0.499, 0.520)	(0.131, 0.147)	(0.071, 0.078)	(0.054, 0.059)
Gini coefficient in 1994	**0.457**	**0.471**	**0.467**	**0.449**	**0.465**	**0.459**	**0.230**	**0.088**	**0.051**

Notes: The effects are cumulative and their meaning is: P: participation, D: unemployment, R: employment structure by economic sector, E: employment structure by occupation, W: relative labour incomes, WS: relative labour incomes by gender, WSO: relative labour incomes by gender and by occupation, WSOED: relative labour incomes by gender, occupation and education, WSOEDR: relative labour incomes by gender, occupation, education and economic sector.

is obtained for the poverty gap and for the P_2 indices, which would seem to imply that the unemployment effect on poverty occurs because the poor have become poorer. This effect also causes a rise in inequality among the poor. However, the changes in the sectoral structure and in the occupational structure of employment do not significantly affect income inequality. Both effects increase the poverty incidence, whereas – in general – there is no real significant effect on the other two poverty measures.

The income effect was calculated sequentially and is split into the effects corresponding to the various segments of the labour market – gender, occupation, education and economic sector. Table 3.7 shows that the total income effect reduces inequality for the three population groups, but has led to an increase in poverty as measured by any of the three indices.

Table 3.8 replicates the results of Table 3.7, this time for the changes registered between 1998 and the counterfactual population of 1994. The results obtained for this period are similar to those obtained using the initial population of 1991. Just as was the case between 1998 and 1991, the resulting change in the participation rate is not statistically significant, except for the employed population, where the effect tends to increase inequality. Poverty also increased, measured by any of the three indices, but this increase is smaller than for the entire period. The unemployment effect is positive and significant for the three analysed populations, in the sense that it increases inequality, but the levels are lower than those simulated for 1998 and 1991.

Just as was the case between 1998 and 1991, the change in the average wages reduced inequality for the three analysed populations, and the magnitude of this effect is greater for the entire period.

NOTES

* The authors appreciate the help of Carola Ramón and the comments of Lance Taylor and Rob Vos to a draft of this chapter. We are also grateful to the the participants for their comments provided at the seminars that took place in New York, Rio de Janeiro and San Salvador.

1. Between 1987 and 1988, the average tariff dropped from 43 to 30 per cent and quantitative restrictions were reduced. In October 1989, 807 tariff areas were subject to additional temporary duties, 122 to import licences, and 129 to specific duties. In April 1991, all areas subject to specific or temporary duties or to import licences were eliminated. Restrictions remained for only 25 product types (belonging to motor vehicles and parts) of a total of 10,000, and the special levies were maintained for cars and electronic equipment at a 35 per cent tariff. The tariff structure of April 1991 included three levies: zero for raw materials, 11 per cent for intermediate and capital goods, and 22 per cent for final goods. See Damill and Keifman (1993). Later, the tariff structure underwent some changes, and from 1995 onwards the Argentine tariff structure is that of Mercosur (with some exceptions).
2. The complete report can be found in Frenkel and Gonzáles Rozada (1999).

3. This and the following section draw on research results from a study that was done together with Mario Damill.
4. Since we only have bi-annual employment data at our disposal and to facilitate the analysis, it makes sense to characterize the evolution of GDP by semesters.
5. The Argentine National Accounts system does not have an independent estimate of consumption. The corresponding variable is calculated as a residual based on estimates of the other components of the accounts. The estimated consumption level includes the change in inventories. The investment variable refers to gross fixed investment.
6. The wage rate is defined here as the industrial wage published by FIEL, corresponding to a sample of large enterprises. For the 1990s, the observed wage dynamics differs from that observed in the wage data of the INDEC household survey, but this difference does not affect the point made about the structural change between the 1980s and the 1990s.
7. Full-time employment includes persons working 35 hours or more per week, as well as those working less than 35 hours but who do not want to work more hours. The data used correspond to the urban conglomerates covered by the INDEC household survey. These surveys are held twice a year, in April and October. Since these months are at the mid-point of each six-month period, we are presenting the analysis by semesters.
8. The participation and employment rates in GBA are higher than those at the national level, but the dynamics and the changes between the 1980s and 1990s are similar, so we will forgo commenting on them. When there are homologous series, the name of the series is maintained without the initial N (e.g.: TPEAPOB is the activity rate of Gran Buenos Aires, homologous to the national-level NTPEAPOB).
9. There are other changes that are probably also important (such as the availability of domestic and external credit, which facilitated the restructuring and imports of capital goods, or the changes in the regulatory framework of the labour market), but the restriction of degrees of freedom forces us to use a simple model that is compatible with the available semester-based employment data series.
10. All coefficients are statistically significant at the 5 per cent level of confidence. In the regressions for the entire period, the intercept term (not shown in the table) is not significant.
11. This is the trend of the employment rate. To obtain the trend for the number of jobs, one has to add the growth rate of the urban population:

$$-d\log(E/P) = -d\log(E) + d\log(P)$$

According to INDEC, the urban population growth rate is 2 per cent per year.
12. For a more detailed analysis, see the more complete report (Frenkel and González Rozada 1999).
13. The data come from the Monthly Industrial Surveys implemented by INDEC since 1990. The sample is national and includes about 1,300 establishments with more than 10 employees. The time series before 1990 are obtained by linking the old industrial survey with the one starting in 1990.
14. The basis is similar to that presented in Section 3.4. We assume a continuous, gradual adjustment to the conditions of relative prices current since 1991.
15. Using the estimate for β, $(1 - \alpha) = 0.79$ and $\Delta Y/Y = 22.5\%$, as a result of which the productivity increase attributable to output growth becomes 18 per cent.
16. The apparent domestic consumption is estimated as a residual on the basis of the production, export and import data. For this purpose, we use production data from the National Accounts at constant prices of 1986, which are different from the production data of the Industrial Survey. For several industrial branches, National Accounts figures reproduce the results of the Industrial Survey. In others, these data are complemented with additional information, which explains the differences. The employment and productivity estimates presented here are exclusively based on data from the survey. However, as mentioned, we use National Accounts production data for the decomposition of final demand.
17. For the sake of consistency, calculations in this section refer to cases with reported incomes only. The employment rate calculated this way is approximately 2 pp lower for

the entire period. The degree of change of the employment rate is not significantly affected.

18. We calculate labour and property incomes of the employed population. Incomes do not include social security transfers. The data are from INDEC's EPH for Gran Buenos Aires.
19. To obtain estimates by equivalent adult, household members are assigned different weights according to gender and age in order to reflect differences in needs. The coefficients used here correspond to those tabulated by the Ministry of Economy and Public Works in 1993 (CEPA, Documento de trabajo No. 2, 1993, p. 35).

REFERENCES

CEPA (1993) 'Evolución reciente de la pobreza en el Gran Buenos Aires. 1988–1992', *Documento de trabajo No. 2*, Buenos Aires: Ministerio de Economía y Obras y Servicios Públicos, Secretaría de Programación Económica.

Damill, M. and S. Keifman (1993) 'Trade Liberalization in a High-Inflation Economy: Argentina, 1989–91', in: M. Agosín and D. Tussie (eds) *Trade and Growth: New Dilemmas in Trade Policy*, New York: St. Martin Press.

Frenkel, Roberto and Martín González Rozada (1999) 'Liberalización del balance de pagos. Efectos sobre el crecimiento, el empleo y los ingresos en Argentina', *Serie de Documentos de Economía No 11*, Buenos Aires: Centro de Investigaciones en Economía, Universidad de Palermo – CEDES.

4. Brazil: economic opening and income distribution*

Ricardo Paes de Barros and Carlos Henrique Corseuil

4.1 INTRODUCTION

From the post-war period up to the late 1980s, the Brazilian economy was extremely protected with little exposure to international competition and a limited degree of regional integration. Starting in the early 1990s it went through an intensive liberalization process that encompassed trade opening and incentives for foreign investors.

Trade opening consisted of a reduction of tariff barriers and elimination of most non-tariff restrictions. The goal was to induce a substantial improvement in the efficiency of the Brazilian economy, which would generate a redistribution of factor incomes and, consequently, of individual incomes.

With capital account liberalization most restrictions on foreign capital inflows were eliminated. The aim of this component of the liberalization process was to support and create more favourable conditions to attain the objectives of trade opening. On the one hand, Brazil would attract additional financial resources, mainly portfolio investments. This would provide the funds to cover a potential trade deficit resulting from the expected increase in import growth. On the other hand, the economy would attract new technologies through a larger volume of direct investments, thus increasing its competitiveness in external markets. The increase in domestic competition would stimulate exports and thus sustain the process of trade opening.

The end result would be productivity gains – at least in the long run – and thus higher income growth, which together with the changes in the degree of inequality would have an impact on the country's poverty level. In the short run, however, a significant reallocation of resources, particularly of labour, between the sectors would be necessary. Labour cost would possibly rise for some segments of the labour force.

There is a major controversy about the outcomes of the trade opening policies, more in particular with regard to the impact on social welfare (see e.g. World Bank 1999). The objective of this study is to estimate the effects of the liberalization process on income distribution in Brazil. To some extent, the research is a pioneer study of its kind for Brazil, because the available studies to date have focused only on the labour market effects of trade liberalization (Barros et al. 1996, Moreira and Najberg 1997, Machado and Moreira 2000).

This chapter is organized in three sections in addition to the Introduction and Conclusions. Section 4.2 analyses the evolution of the economy's liberalization process starting in 1988 in the context of the macroeconomic adjustment that took place. Section 4.3 describes the methodology, and Section 4.4 presents the empirical results of the study.

4.2 ECONOMIC OPENING AND MACROECONOMIC AND LABOUR MARKET TRENDS

In this section we present the main objectives of the trade and financial opening policies and describe the observed macroeconomic and labour market trends for the period from 1987 to 1998.

Brazil's Opening Process

Brazil responded to the successive oil shocks of the 1970s with a large investment programme for the development of infrastructure and import-substituting production sectors. The programme was largely financed with foreign capital, which led to a rapid accumulation of external debt. In the early 1980s, the strong increase of international interest rates and the moratorium on debt-service payments declared by other highly-indebted countries affected the confidence of Brazilian creditors and caused an abrupt interruption of capital flows to Brazil, thereby creating a disequilibrium in the balance of payments.[1]

In 1983, an intensive emergency programme was implemented oriented at quickly raising exports and restricting imports. Under this new regime, various protectionist measures were taken. Specifically, tariffs on several products were raised and quantitative restrictions on imports were introduced. In addition, the government reintroduced a scheme of subsidies and tax exemptions favouring export firms and reducing investment costs in priority sectors.

The increased cost of the rescheduled external debt and the large volume of expected expenditures associated with the infrastructure investment programme of the decade before put high pressure on the fiscal balance. At the same time, the economic contraction caused by the measures taken to restore the external equilibrium led to a decline in tax revenues. As a result, the public deficit increased and inflation accelerated in a process that would continue until the mid-1990s. To avoid a negative impact of inflation on the trade balance, the government fixed the exchange rate through a system of pre-announced mini-devaluations in order to maintain the real exchange rate relatively stable. Wage increases were limited to stave off the inflationary effects of the devaluation. This produced an artificial fall in the relative price of labour.

Restoring the balance-of-payments equilibrium was the main focus of policy-makers in the first half of the 1980s. The subsequent debate on the performance of the economy concentrated, however, on the acceleration of inflation and the loss of external competitiveness of Brazilian firms. This went on until the introduction of the *Plan Real* in 1994. Table 4.1 shows the evolution of some of the main price indices between 1981 and 1998. At least three factors caused the inflationary spiral: (i) the protectionist policies raised the prices of imported inputs, thus increasing production cost; (ii) the fiscal imbalance persisted despite efforts to cut expenditures, resulting in increased money creation; and (iii) wage restrictions led to continuous workers' demand for wage increases when the economy started to recover. The latter induced the strengthening of indexation mechanisms for wages and prices, which continuously pushed up inflation and generated a process known as 'inertial inflation'. During the period successive economic plans of a largely heterodox nature were implemented. These were based mainly on price freezes, attempts to control public expenditures and monetary expansion. The objective was to control inflation, but none of the plans succeeded. Nevertheless, the effects of the interventions were felt in practically all relevant economic indicators.[2]

The measures to restore the external balance remained in place without major alterations until 1988. They ended up generating a significant loss of competitiveness of domestic firms and great difficulties for the domestic economy to reintegrate with the world economy. The degree of market concentration also increased as a result of the lack of competition from foreign companies, which in turn constituted an additional negative effect on price stabilization. In 1988 and 1989, the first steps were taken to create more transparency in the tariff structure and to lower the tariff rates. However, because most quantitative restrictions were maintained, trade liberalization only became effective starting in 1990, when Collor de Mello became president.

Several measures were taken to open the Brazilian economy to international competition: (i) gradual tariff reductions with an overall reduction in the average rate and in the differences in the tariffs applied to the various products;[3] (ii) elimination of remaining non-tariff barriers from previous periods; (iii) elimination of some special customs regimes; and (iv) introduc-

Table 4.1 Annual inflation rate, 1980–99 (percentages)

Period	INPC (IBGE)	IPCA (IBGE)	ICV (DIEESE)	IPC-SP (FIPE)
1982	97.9	103.3	103.0	94.6
1983	172.9	167.6	172.6	164.1
1984	203.3	208.6	204.0	178.6
1985	228.7	233.7	264.6	228.1
1986	57.9	72.5	96.5	68.1
1987	349.9	373.8	398.3	366.7
1988	993.3	981.2	921.2	891.7
1989	1863.6	1972.9	1946.3	1636.6
1990	1585.2	1621.0	1849.7	1639.1
1991	475.1	472.7	500.4	458.6
1992	1149.1	1119.1	1127.5	1129.6
1993	2489.1	2477.2	2702.7	2491.0
1994	929.3	916.4	1082.9	941.3
1995	22.0	22.4	46.2	23.2
1996	9.1	9.6	13.2	10.0
1997	4.3	5.2	6.1	4.8
1998	2.5	1.7	0.5	–1.8

Notes:
INPC (IBGE) = Measured change in prices of a consumer basket of goods and services for households with a monthly income of between one and eight minimum wages.
IPCA (IBGE) = Extended consumer price index. Index is calculated by the Brazilian statistical office (IBGE) and used for price corrections to the balance sheets and financial accounts of corporate enterprises.
ICV-SP (DIEESE) = Measured change in prices of a consumer basket of goods and services for households with a monthly income of between one and thirty minimum wages.
IPC-SP (FIPE) = Measured change in prices of a consumer basket of goods and services for households with a monthly income of between two and six minimum wages.

tion of a floating exchange-rate regime. These measures constituted a fundamental change in trade policies, taking the Brazilian economy to a phase of intense competition, both domestically and internationally. The price mechanism was rehabilitated as the central element in steering the policy of trade opening. In particular, the elimination of tariff and non-tariff barriers between member countries of Mercosur represented one of the most important achievements in the history of Brazilian trade policies.

Table 4.2 shows the evolution of import tariffs and the levels of effective protection between the pre-reform year 1988 and the reform year 1998. Substantial reductions can be observed in the nominal protection rate after the trade opening, although the trend seems to have changed in more recent

Table 4.2 Changes in protection rates of the domestic market

	Change 1987–90		**Change 1990–94**		**Change 1994–98**		**Change 1988–98**	
	Level	**%**	**Level**	**%**	**Level**	**%**	**Level**	**%**
Nominal tariffs								
Mean	–27.04	–47.0	–19.25	–63.2	4.36	38.9	–41.92	–72.9
S.D.	–6.36	–29.9	–9.06	–60.7	0.56	9.5	–14.86	–69.8
Maximum	–24.00	–23.4	–55.20	–70.1	14.60	62.1	–64.90	–62.9
Effective rate of protection								
Mean	–29.44	–38.2	–34.05	–71.4	6.77	49.7	–56.72	–73.5
S.D.	6.76	12.6	–52.22	–86.2	12.78	152.2	–32.68	–60.7
Maximum	43.00	14.0	–323.40	–92.1	101.50	366.4	–178.90	–58.1

Source: Based on Kume et al. (2000).

years.[4] The average tariffs on imported goods decreased by 72.9 per cent and the degree of sectoral dispersion of tariffs (measured by the standard deviation) dropped by 70 per cent. Reductions were not continuous, as duties and dispersion increased during 1994–98. The effective protection rate[5] fell most strongly in the 1990–94 period.

Liberalization of capital controls flows implied the elimination of another protectionist feature of the Brazilian policy regime of the 1980s. The share of foreign capital in domestic production has been of little significance throughout Brazil's history, especially when compared to other developing countries. This feature is the result of a combination of protectionist policies favouring domestic capital, discriminatory treatment against foreign capital, and restrictions on the access of foreign investors to domestic capital markets. The liberalization of the capital account of the 1990s tried to provide a direct stimulus to capital inflows (see Table 4.3). External finance was needed as domestic savings rates were at extremely low levels, mainly due to dissaving of the public sector. Broadly, the Brazilian government tried to stimulate the inflow of foreign capital through three principal measures: closure of the fiscal gap, as the gap implied high tax costs to potential investments in Brazil; constitutional reforms aiming to provide foreign investors with profitability conditions similar to those for domestic investors; and opening of the capital market to foreign investors.

Several administrative measures were also taken. These include easing of profit remittances and technical assistance between Brazilian branches of foreign-based companies. Further, foreign investments in non-tangible assets (transfer of technology, technical assistance, franchises, brands and patents)

Table 4.3 Incentives to capital inflows created in the 1990s

Group 1:
Tax exemption
1. Elimination of the additional income tax (between 40 and 60%) on dividends remitted to abroad larger than 12% of registered capital.
2. Elimination of the tax on liquid profits.
3. Income tax exemption at the source for earnings and dividends at the source.
4. Income tax exemption at the source for capital gains and profit remittances. The tax rates went from 25 to 15%.
5. Creation of the possibility of interest payments as a remuneration of own capital.

Group 2:
Constitutional reforms
1. Elimination of the exclusive right of state enterprises in the exploration and distribution of piped gas.
2. Elimination of the differentiation between companies with and without national capital.
3. Authorization to explore, produce and exploit mineral resource reserves by Brazilian enterprises with foreign capital.
4. Elimination of the exclusive right of national vessels in coastal and interior navigation.
5. Abolishment of the state monopoly of telecommunication services.

Group 3:
Opening of capital market
1. (1987) Regulation of the formation of Brazil-based Corporations and Investment Funds with foreign capital. Regulation of the Fund for Portfolio Diversification established abroad. All of these without a revaluation deadline for profits and taxation of capital gains and for tax on returns on fixed and variable interest-bearing assets.*
2. Flexibilization of the previous norm and authorization for foreign investment to operate in options/futures markets.**

Notes:
* Resolution no. 1289 of 20 March 1987 of the National Monetary Board.
** *Cédula del Inversionista Institucional* (better known as Annex IV).

in Brazil was made more easy. Guidelines were published for the registration of foreign participation in the capitalization of profits and reserves as well as for the process of corporate restructuring and capital reduction of companies receiving foreign capital. Finally, foreign investment would now also be allowed to enter the real-estate sector.

External loan contracts fall under a legislation of 1969. This law regulates debt reduction after a Central Bank authorization[6] or through emission of commercial papers, titles and private or public bond issues. As part of the opening process, major reforms took place in the regulation of credit allocation. Resolution 63 of the National Monetary Board (CMN) regulates the mobilization of resources to be transferred to domestic firms through investment or development banks for the financing of investment in fixed and financial assets.

In 1990, banks were allowed to mobilize resources in the form of commercial papers in foreign markets under the conditions and for the purposes as stipulated in Resolution 63. Later, the access to foreign finance for rural producers, agri-businesses and producers of fertilizers and insecticides (known as the *63 caipiras*) was regulated. Mobilization of external resources was also permitted for investment finance for construction or acquisition of new real-estate properties.

In 1995, foreign resource mobilization was authorized for lending to export sectors. Several decrees (CMN resolutions or memoranda of the Central Bank of Brazil) were issued in subsequent years to enhance the attractiveness of channelling funds through the credit system. Resources, as long as they are not transferred, can be transformed into federal titles and thus be used in the financial system. This typically helped financial intermediaries to make huge profits through arbitration.

Table 4.4 summarizes recent trends in the volume of foreign investment to Brazil. In the 1990s there is a steep increase in the net inflow of both portfolio investment and foreign currency credits, especially following the new facilities granted to the banks for mobilization of funds and allocation of credits.

Although the domestic interest rate is considered to be a major determinant of investment, the nominal rate was fixed passively until 1993. Traditional instruments of monetary policy were practically ineffective due to the high degree of indexation of the economy. The money supply was in effect 'endogenous'. With the stabilization of the economy, the interest rate turned into an important instrument to attract external resources to the Brazilian capital market. The volatility of the interest rate was put under stricter control as shown in Figure 4.1.[7]

The final aspect of the economic integration policies to be analysed refers to the changes in the exchange-rate regime. In December 1988, the

Table 4.4 Foreign investment (annual flows in millions of US$)

	Direct investment	Portfolio investment
1987	46	–
1988	46	16
1989	48	–5
1990	51	9
1991	51	48
1992	52	142
1993	55	554
1994	59	607
1995	63	191
1996	67	503
1997	98	442
1998	105	–154

Source: Central Bank of Brazil.

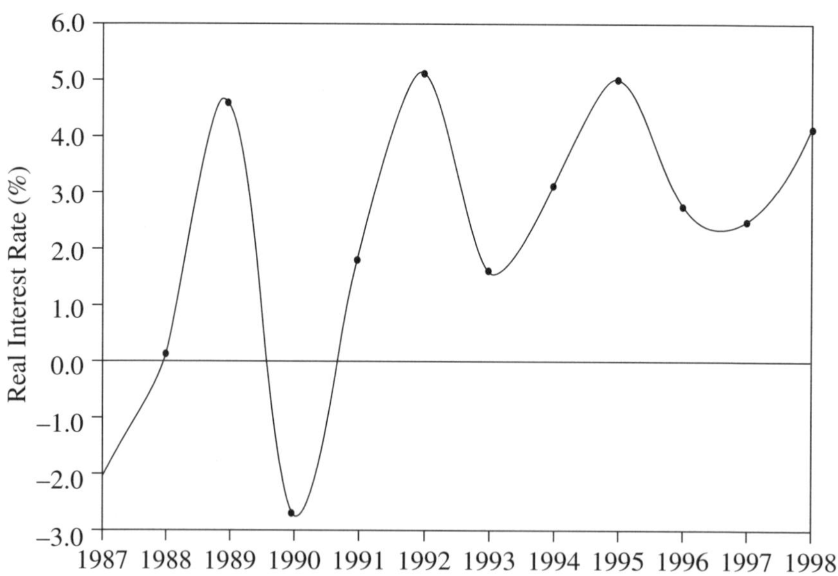

Source: Gazeta Mercantil newspaper.

Figure 4.1 Real interest rate (selic rate) (nominal rate deflation for CPI, IGP-DI)

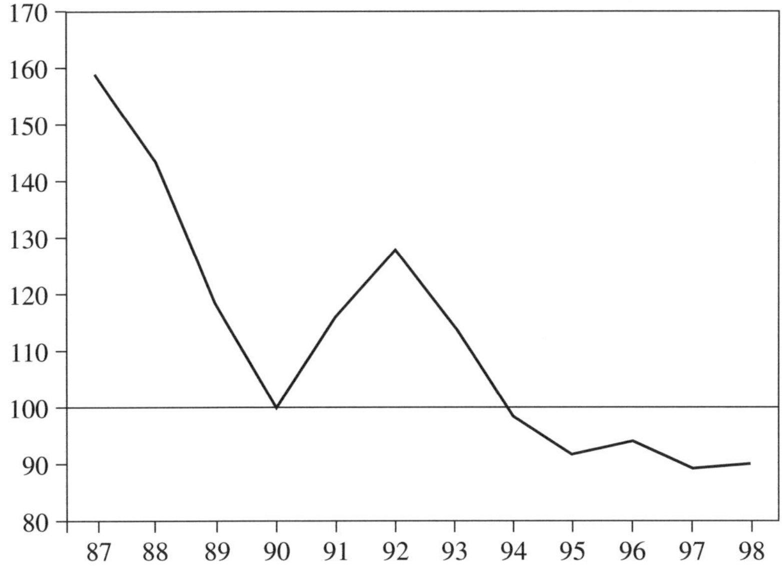

Source: Calculations based on data of the Central Bank of Brazil.

Figure 4.2 Real effective exchange rate (index, 1990 = 100)

CMN's decision to create a floating exchange rate (initially called *dólar turismo*) helped to stimulate capital movements between Brazil and other countries. At first the initiative should bring transparency to operations previously run through the parallel market, such as buying and selling of foreign currency by tourists. However, the floating-exchange rate allowed holders of foreign currency assets in Brazil to sell these to institutions accredited by the Central Bank without the need to show identification. This was the first step towards the repatriation of Brazilian capital deposited overseas. It also facilitated sending currency abroad, both for residents and non-residents. Figure 4.2 shows the evolution rate of real exchange over the past 15 years.

Macroeconomic Trends

As indicated above, the successive economic stabilization plans severely distorted economic indicators, making it difficult to attribute the observed variations solely to the opening process. Even so, the direction of change of most indicators is in line with what would be expected in theory from a process of economic opening.

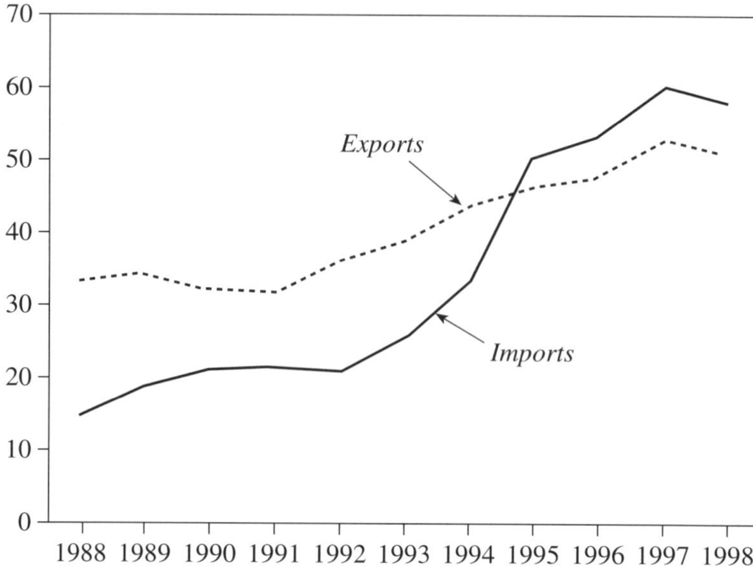

Source: Funcex.

Figure 4.3 Trends in exports and imports (millions of US$)

Figure 4.3 shows the evolution of the value of Brazilian exports and imports between 1987 and 1998. In general, exports followed an increasing trend, which can be explained by the combination of the increased competitiveness of the Brazilian economy and the effort to restore equilibrium in the balance of payments. The average annual growth rate of exports increased substantially from the 1980s (4.5 per cent) to the 1990s (7.8 per cent). Import growth accelerated after 1993, triggering trade deficits from 1995 onwards, after a decade of surpluses.

Figure 4.4 shows the evolution of the price and quantum indices of exports and imports between 1987 and 1998. We can see that export trends are influenced more strongly by volume growth than by price changes. The trend in the volume index of exports is more pronounced than its value index. The import volume oscillated throughout the period. In recent years the trend is related to substantial shifts in the composition of the imported goods. The increase in the import volume – over 250 per cent from mid-1993 to 1998 – strongly contributed to the trade deficits that were generated at the end of the period.

Figure 4.5 shows two indicators of trade penetration in the Brazilian economy during the 1985–98 period. The export coefficient exhibits a fluctu-

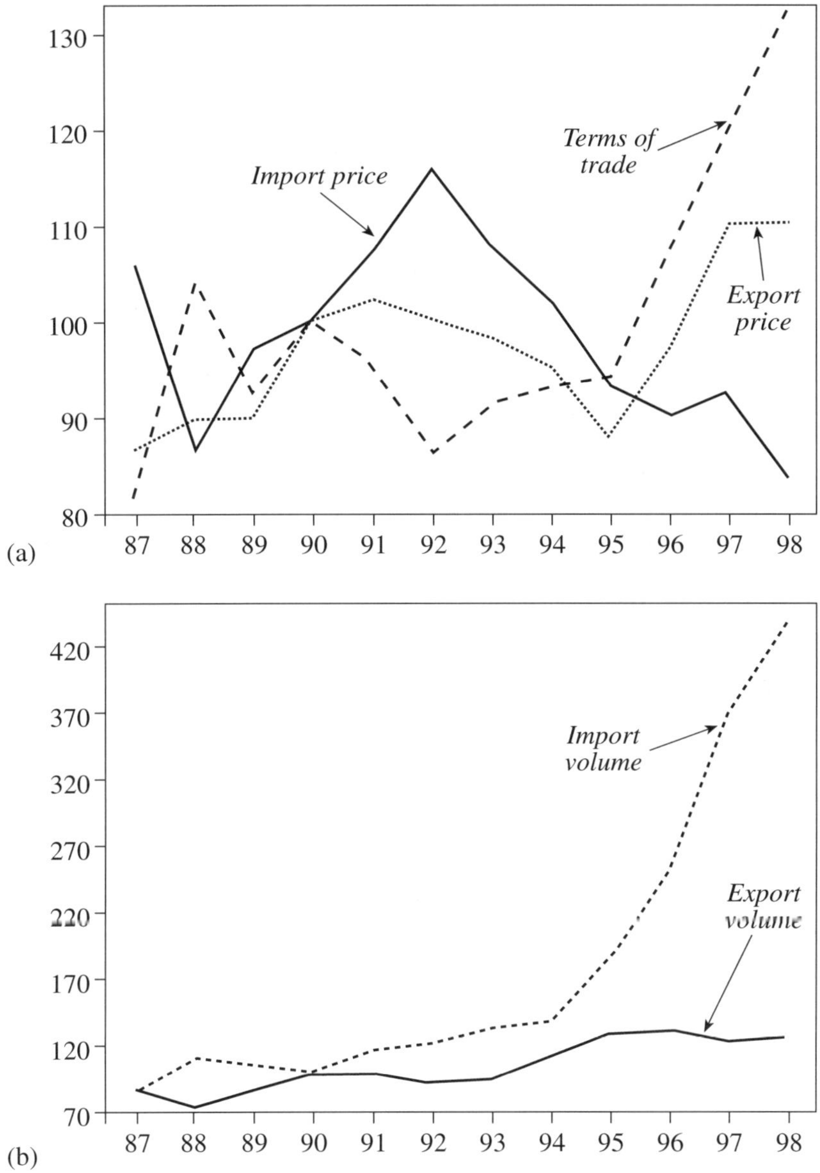

Source: Funcex/IPEA.

Figure 4.4 *(a) Export and import prices and terms of trade; (b) trends in volume of imports and exports (index, 1990 = 100)*

Source: Funcex/IPEA.

Figure 4.5 Import penetration and export coefficient

ating trend, showing a fall at the end of the period. The overall trend suggests not much progress was made in increasing the economy's export propensity, despite the observed export growth and the decrease of the anti-export biases during the 1990s. Much more so, trade liberalization produced an upward trend in the import penetration coefficient.

Table 4.5 shows Brazilian trade with Mercosur countries. Total exports of member countries increased significantly in aggregate terms starting in the 1990s. In 1996 the level of exports had increased by 85.7 per cent compared to the 1991–93 average. As happened in Argentina, the trade agreements between Mercosur countries provoked a shift in the direction of Brazilian exports from the United States and Europe to Mercosur and Asia.

Commodity flows between Brazil and Argentina accounted for almost 90 per cent of trade between the Mercosur economies in 1996, showing the overwhelming importance of the performance of both economies for the trade bloc. The composition of exports changed substantially during the 1990s. The share of primary products in Brazilian exports to Argentina fell strongly in favour of manufactured goods, particularly from large-scale industries.

The evolution of Brazilian GDP can be divided into two phases (Figure 4.6). During the first phase, which runs from 1987 until 1992, GDP is highly

Table 4.5 Trade between Brazil and Mercosur (in millions of US$)

	Exports			Imports			Trade balance		
	Mercosur	**World**	**% Mercosur**	**Mercosur**	**World**	**% Mercosur**	**Mercosur**	**World**	**% Mercosur**
1987	1388	26224	5.29	888	15051	5.90	500	11173	4.47
1988	1643	33789	4.86	1138	14605	7.79	505	19184	2.63
1989	1380	34383	4.01	2194	18263	12.01	–814	16120	–5.05
1990	1320	31414	4.20	2320	20661	11.23	–999	10753	–9.29
1991	2309	31620	7.30	2268	21041	10.78	41	10579	0.39
1992	4097	35793	11.45	2250	20554	10.94	1848	15239	12.13
1993	5395	38597	19.98	3378	25480	13.26	2017	13117	15.38
1994	5921	43545	13.60	4581	33079	13.85	1340	10466	12.80
1995	6154	46506	13.23	6821	49408	13.81	–667	–2902	22.99
1996	7305	47747	15.30	8267	53301	15.51	–962	–5554	17.32
1997	9044	52986	17.07	9625	61354	15.69	–582	–8368	6.95
1998	8877	51118	17.37	9425	57558	16.37	–548	–6440	8.51

Source: Ministry of Industry, Commerce and Tourism.

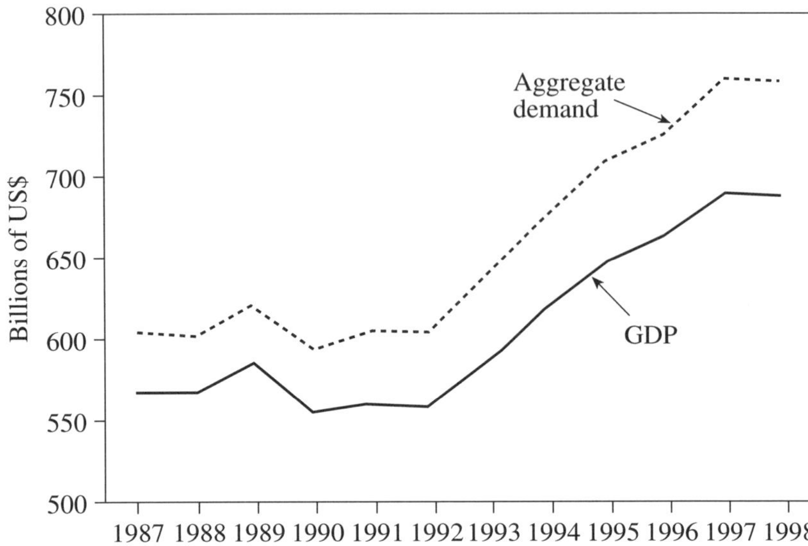

Source: National accounts.

Figure 4.6 Trends in GDP and aggregate demand

volatile and stagnant. Starting the next phase in 1993, GDP shows a steady, moderate growth rate. GDP increases by 21 per cent during this period. The volatility of output in the first phase is related to the inflationary process after the failure of the *Plan Cruzado* (1986) and to the adoption of the successive stabilization programmes. The economy recovered from 1993 onwards. Economic recovery was stimulated by more favourable international conditions – growing world demand and the return of capital flows to emerging-market economies – and the end to the political crisis experienced a year earlier. Recovery took place amidst high inflation. With the *Plan Real*, enacted in mid-1994, there was a strong increase in aggregate demand, essentially as a consequence of the sudden price stabilization that led to an increase in real incomes and more optimistic expectations of economic agents. Fiscal and monetary policies were restrictive in order to keep the level of reserves and balance of payments under control. The pressure on the external balance was caused by the real exchange-rate appreciation. The restrictive macroeconomic policies facilitated a moderate, but steady GDP growth in 1994–97.

To study the sources of aggregate demand growth, we apply the decomposition methodology explained in Chapter 1 (Appendix). Table 4.6 shows the trend of aggregate demand and its components. Despite the observed rise in the quantum and value index of exports, the figures suggest that the opening of the economy caused a decline in the export share in aggregate demand. It fell from 7.6 per cent in 1990 to 6.7 per cent in 1998. Similarly, the investment share went down. Government expenditures and household consumption increased their respective shares during the period.

It is interesting to note that the years when the export share in aggregate demand increased coincided with the recessions of 1988 and 1992–93. Consumption fell during the periods of high inflation (1988–89 and 1993–94), indicating that the composition of aggregate demand is clearly also linked to other types of macroeconomic shocks rather than just the trade opening.

Table 4.6(b) presents the trends in the leakage effects as the components of the aggregate demand multiplier – $1/(s+t+m)$ in the Appendix to Chapter 1 – and indicates that the import share (m) increased steadily since 1989. The tax rate (t) behaved erratically in the period, showing sudden jumps in the years of the major economic plans (1990 and 1994). The savings propensity shows a declining trend, probably as a consequence of the deceleration of inflation in more recent years and the surge in capital inflows, which diminished the dependence of investment finance on domestic savings.

The results of the dynamic decomposition of the components of aggregate demand growth are shown in Figure 4.7. The aggregate demand growth rate varies significantly at the end of the analysis period. It turned strongly negative during the 1990–92 recession and the period of capital market turbulence in emerging countries – the Mexican and Asian crises[8] – between 1996 and 1998. In a general sense, we can point out that the behaviour of demand was dictated mainly by investment, being counteracted by the anti-cyclical movement of government expenditures. Exports show less volatility, but with negative growth in the 1989 inflationary peak and a major increase in the beginning of the intensification of the opening process in 1990–93. With the *Plan Real*, the purchasing power of workers increased at first, redirecting part of the exported production toward the domestic market and interrupting the growth of exports.

The trend in the average productivity per worker – measured as the ratio between total output and the number of workers – can also be divided into two phases (see Figure 4.8). In the first stage, from 1987 to 1991, productivity falls, recovering later at a steady pace to reach a level of 6 per cent compared to that registered at the beginning of the period. This trend may be associated with the deepening of the trade opening process starting in the late 1980s. The access to higher-quality and lower-priced imported inputs and the drive toward greater competition forced domestic industries to improve their products and production methods and to reduce costs, including labour costs.

Table 4.6 *(a) Composition of aggregate demand, 1987–98; (b) macroeconomic leakages, 1987–98 (values in millions of reales at constant prices)*

(a)	**Consumption (*C*)**		**Investment (*I*)**		**Government spending (*G*)**		**Exports (*E*)**		**Aggregate demand (*X*)**
	Level	**% of *X***	**Level**	**% of *X***	**Level**	**% of *X***	**Level**	**% of *X***	
1987	345.95	57.12	131.85	21.77	71.91	11.87	55.93	9.23	605.65
1988	322.19	53.40	138.32	22.93	76.48	12.68	66.35	11.00	603.34
1989	317.89	51.37	157.63	25.47	90.93	14.69	52.40	8.47	618.85
1990	329.47	55.44	112.04	18.85	107.18	18.04	45.56	7.67	594.25
1991	345.58	57.05	110.96	18.32	100.47	16.59	48.70	8.04	605.71
1992	343.42	56.76	105.70	17.47	95.25	15.74	60.67	10.03	605.05
1993	351.92	55.07	122.10	19.11	103.46	16.19	61.52	9.63	639.01
1994	369.76	54.63	137.31	20.29	110.77	16.37	58.98	8.71	676.82
1995	386.91	54.69	144.03	20.36	126.65	17.90	49.92	7.06	707.51
1996	412.84	56.95	137.28	18.94	127.55	17.59	47.29	6.52	724.96
1997	435.43	57.40	146.36	19.29	122.24	16.45	52.01	6.86	758.56
1998	437.54	57.78	146.36	19.33	122.24	16.14	51.11	6.75	757.25

(b)	Imports (M)		Tax revenues (T)		Savings (S)		GDP (Y)
	Level	m	Level	t	Level	s	
1987	36.61	0.06	138.01	0.23	85.08	0.14	569.04
1988	34.69	0.06	132.82	0.22	113.65	0.19	568.66
1989	32.05	0.05	139.32	0.23	129.59	0.21	586.80
1990	38.68	0.07	164.45	0.23	61.65	0.10	555.57
1991	44.42	0.07	137.12	0.23	78.59	0.13	561.29
1992	46.81	0.08	139.34	0.23	75.48	0.12	558.24
1993	53.28	0.08	148.19	0.23	85.62	0.13	585.73
1994	56.80	0.08	172.98	0.26	77.27	0.11	620.01
1995	61.31	0.09	181.19	0.26	78.09	0.11	646.19
1996	60.95	0.08	187.19	0.26	63.98	0.09	664.01
1997	70.12	0.09	194.07	0.26	58.94	0.08	688.45
1998	69.43	0.09	204.97	0.27	45.31	0.06	687.82

Source: National Accounts.

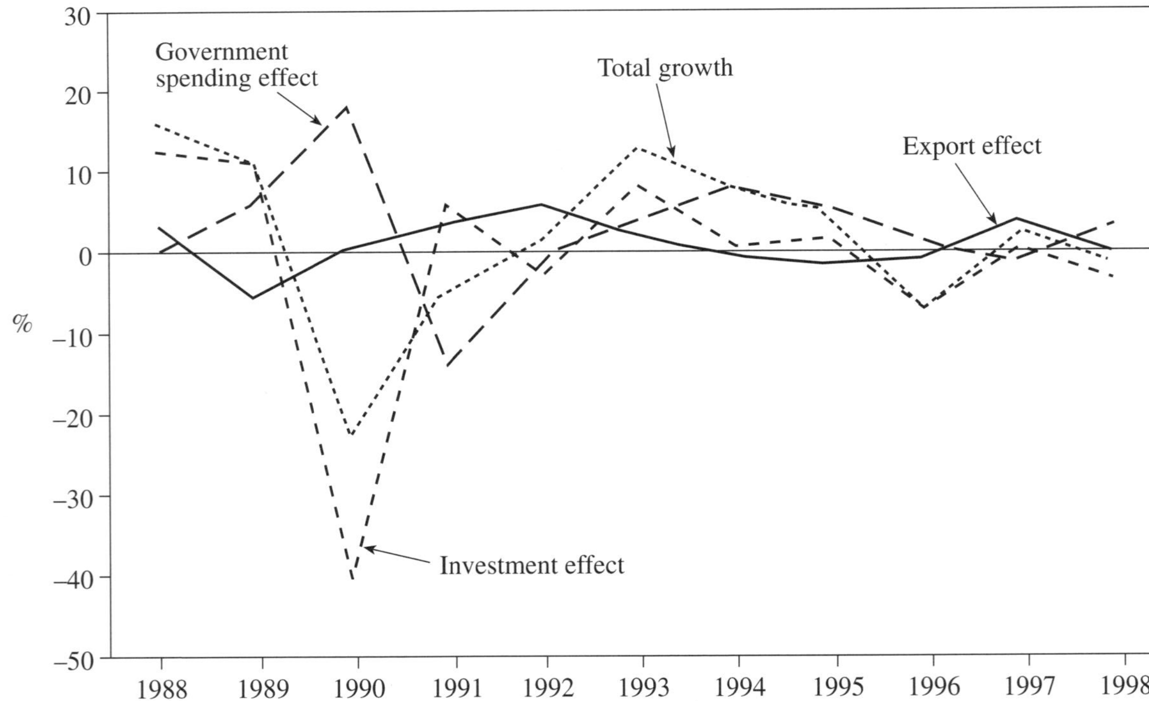

Source: National accounts.

Figure 4.7 Decomposition of aggregate demand growth

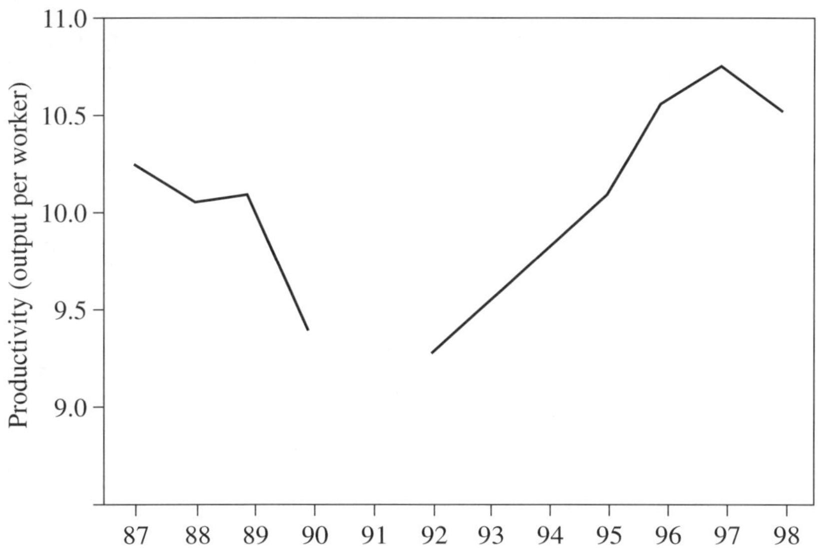

Source: PNAD.

Figure 4.8 Labour productivity trend

Labour Market Adjustment and Income Distribution

Employment increased between 1987 and 1998, as shown in Table 4.7. According to the PNAD household survey (*Pesquisa Nacional por Amostra de Domicílios*), 55.5 million people were employed in 1987, compared to 65.4 million in 1998. Real wages suffered drastic cuts during the recession of the early 1990s, recovering later to levels prior to 1987 at around R$ 450.00 in prices of September 1998.

Employment growth varies considerably for workers classified by educational level. Table 4.7(a) shows a reduction in the number of workers with lower educational levels and a substantial increase of skilled workers. This shift in employment structure is a reflection of the greater demand for skilled workers related to the adoption of new technologies after liberalization, as well as an increase in the educational levels of the Brazilian labour force throughout the period.

The number of formal sector wage earners with labour contracts[9] decreased in the recent period, whereas workers in the informal sector of the economy (those without *carteira* or self-employed) and public employees increased their respective shares. This feature suggests that private enterprises did not succeed in becoming more competitive while obeying labour

Table 4.7 *(a) Evolution of employment (millions of workers); (b) evolution of average labour incomes from main occupation (R$ of September 1998)*

(a)	1987	1988	1989	1990	1992	1993	1995	1996	1997	1998
Total	55.48	56.57	58.19	59.33	60.17	61.39	64.25	62.91	64.19	65.41
Sectors										
Agriculture	14.11	14.26	13.99	14.40	14.75	14.61	14.55	13.32	13.47	13.25
Manufacturing	9.70	9.70	10.30	10.03	9.32	9.48	9.52	9.33	9.38	9.13
Services	31.65	32.60	33.90	34.90	36.11	37.30	40.18	40.24	41.32	43.02
Other	0.01	0.00	0.00	0.00	0.00	0.00	0.01	0.00	0.00	0.01
Occupational category										
Self-employed	12.53	13.00	12.74	13.51	13.53	13.87	15.23	14.62	15.24	15.87
Formal wage earners	21.34	21.94	22.77	22.27	19.86	19.82	20.30	20.37	20.68	20.92
Employer	1.92	1.89	2.49	2.74	2.32	2.29	2.64	2.39	2.69	2.82
Informal wage earners	12.92	12.86	12.86	12.96	14.30	15.03	15.30	15.45	15.57	15.87
Unpaid workers	4.38	4.31	4.31	4.87	6.23	6.32	6.24	5.58	5.59	5.40
Public employee	2.37	2.58	2.58	2.99	3.92	4.04	4.54	4.48	4.41	4.50
Education										
No education	9.82	9.83	9.75	9.87	10.03	9.53	9.35	8.62	8.52	8.20
1–3 years	11.29	11.29	11.16	11.42	11.30	11.35	11.27	10.05	10.37	10.22
4–7 years	18.20	18.32	19.31	19.55	19.53	20.34	21.31	20.28	20.48	20.26
8–10 years	6.43	6.63	6.98	7.13	7.58	7.89	8.67	9.49	9.45	10.00
11 years or more	9.46	10.26	10.73	11.03	11.68	12.26	13.65	14.44	15.36	16.70

(b)	1987	1988	1989	1990	1992	1993	1995	1996	1997	1998
Total	458.23	425.89	480.17	423.34	355.83	370.44	452.70	473.37	470.60	461.71
Sectors										
Agriculture	223.15	191.52	226.06	184.22	158.86	168.86	177.11	187.22	181.48	173.63
Manufacturing	555.51	550.50	551.04	479.55	461.69	461.69	538.35	530.81	532.11	522.82
Services	533.04	491.08	563.10	505.62	426.14	426.14	531.91	554.56	550.70	537.07
Other	1012.04	2232.94	4613.38	2353.64	1744.01	2340.16	2340.16	2443.64	2111.84	3077.34
Occupational category										
Self-employed	429.16	367.10	453.03	388.90	326.64	360.19	441.59	493.19	456.74	419.92
Formal wage earners	588.72	572.63	575.79	502.86	481.14	479.56	537.95	539.03	543.32	542.28
Employer	1735.73	1590.42	1961.03	1551.08	1211.10	1406.16	1749.88	1863.79	1791.73	1663.27
Informal wage earners	193.38	168.99	190.38	179.53	163.34	168.44	221.89	241.64	242.47	248.70
Unpaid workers	–	–	–	–	–	–	–	–	–	–
Public employee	692.08	614.25	621.14	701.23	584.14	614.28	755.14	755.95	773.92	788.88
Education										
No education	171.30	144.22	162.23	147.45	135.67	132.62	158.28	169.71	160.28	157.16
1–3 years	249.83	214.44	248.66	216.35	182.32	180.33	214.73	229.43	224.82	210.87
4–7 years	349.65	312.77	356.96	320.73	270.74	269.83	321.36	330.69	316.73	303.87
8–10 years	510.46	458.83	511.40	447.12	392.21	382.35	451.83	457.52	447.58	417.10
11 years or more	1157.39	1089.41	193.56	1032.28	832.44	890.50	1056.60	1035.19	1028.01	983.30

Source: Own estimates based on household survey data (PNAD/IBGE).

laws, likely because of the high labour costs (wages and benefits) associated with formal labour contracts.

Employment and real wage trends differ across sectors, as can be seen in Figures 4.9 and 4.10. Manufacturing industry, which is the sector most exposed to the opening process, showed a reduction of 5.9 per cent in the number of employed between 1987 and 1998. Agriculture also suffered a 6 per cent drop in labour demand. The increase in overall employment is mainly on account of the services sector where labour demand increased by 36 per cent. Real wages are least volatile in the manufacturing industry. However, in all sectors real wages followed the mean trend and ended in 1998 at levels similar to those at the beginning of the period in 1987.

As the manufacturing industry was most affected by the opening process, and thanks to a greater availability of data, we provide some more detail of employment trends for the sector. Table 4.8 shows the trends in employment and real wages by industrial sub-sectors for 1987–98. First, the number of employees in the food industries grew most significantly from 1,461,073 to 1,732,468. Second, occupation levels remained virtually stable in a subgroup of industries, including paper and graphics, petrochemicals and oil extraction, pharmaceuticals, plastics, rubber and chemical products. Third, there is a large group of sub-sectors with declining employment levels, in-

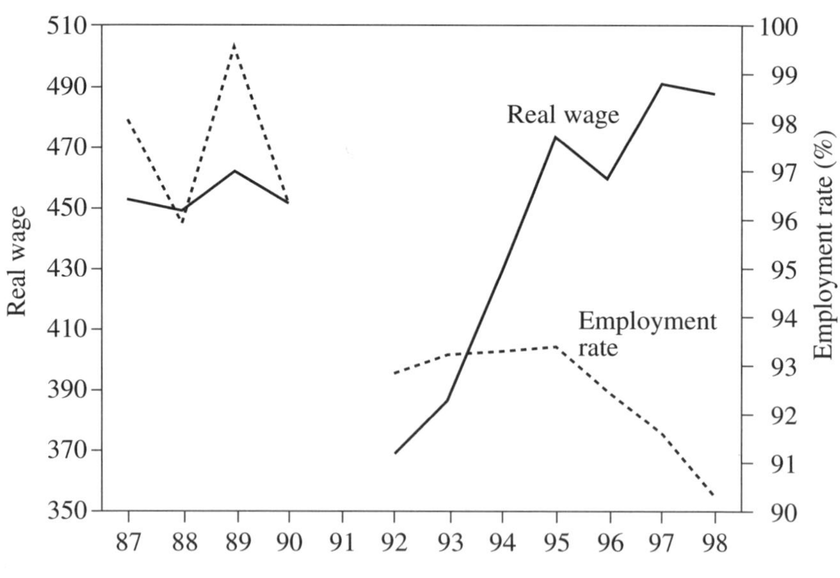

Source: PNAD.

Figure 4.9 Real wage (prices of September 1998) and employment rate (%)

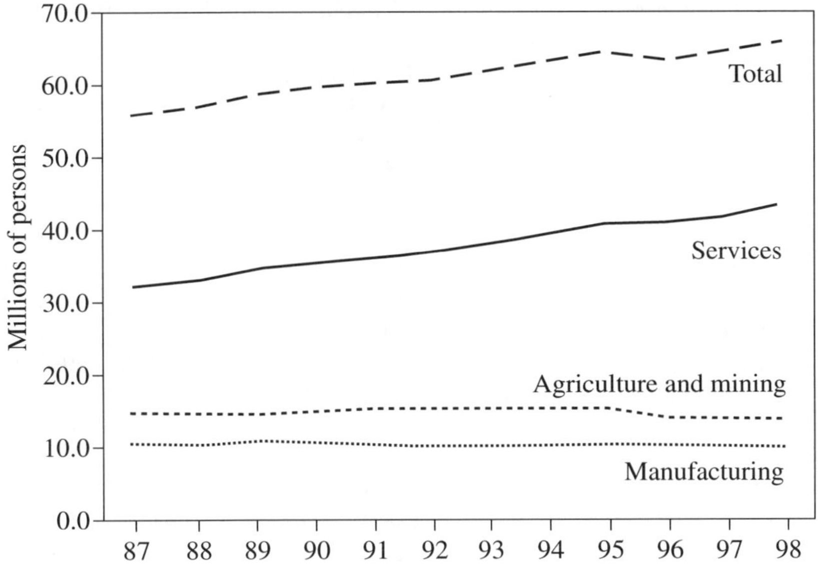

(a)

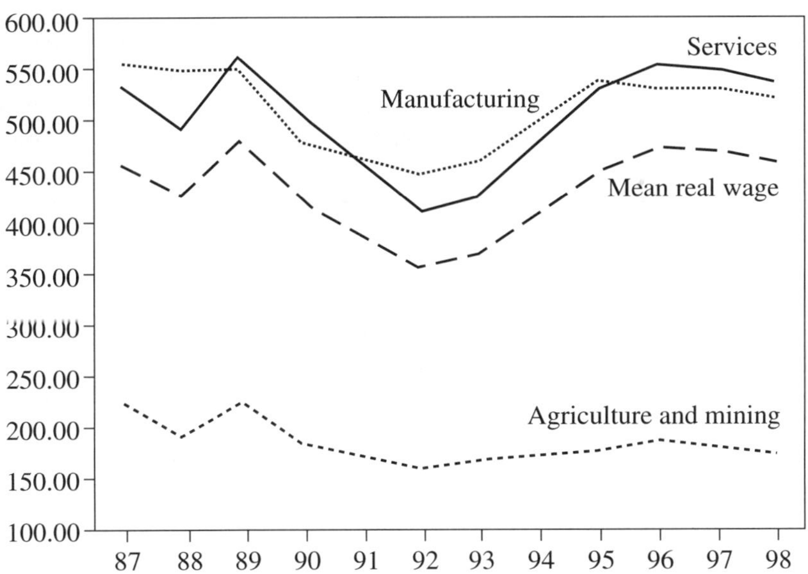

(b)

Source: PNAD.

Figure 4.10 *(a) Employment by sector; (b) real wage by sector (in R$ of 1998)*

Table 4.8 Employment and wages by manufacturing industries, 1987–98

	Employment (millions)		Real wages (R$ of 1998)	
	1987	**1998**	**1987**	**1998**
Total	**9704.2**	**9132.1**	**555.51**	**522.82**
Metal products	938.5	919.8	794.47	690.38
Mechanical products	465.0	374.8	898.88	722.23
Electronics	465.6	299.5	832.50	882.68
Transport equipment	552.1	411.2	884.80	992.98
Sawmills and wood products	1037.5	913.1	371.60	403.37
Paper and graphics	463.7	482.3	713.66	694.60
Rubber products	91.4	65.6	899.65	731.14
Chemical products	306.8	275.4	908.79	817.91
Plastics	188.0	182.2	661.94	625.46
Non-metallic minerals	625.7	557.7	415.88	435.59
Oil and petrochemicals	76.1	71.0	1682.38	1319.05
Pharmaceuticals	140.0	160.2	865.88	947.64
Textiles	627.7	347.4	416.38	446.50
Food products	1461.1	1732.5	460.20	430.64
Clothing	1567.1	1579.9	275.64	269.24
Footwear and leather products	425.7	414.8	341.15	326.01
Other industries	272.3	344.8	472.75	450.75

Source: Own estimates based on household survey data (PNAD/IBGE).

cluding transport equipment, mechanics, electronics, metallic and non-metallic minerals, wood products and furniture, steel, textiles and clothing.

Real wages[10] increased from R$ 458.23 to 461.71 during 1987–98. Manufacturing wages declined though, from R$ 555.51 to 522.82, that is a drop of 5.88 per cent. Four groups of industrial sub-sectors show a different behaviour. In the first group we have mechanics, petrochemicals and rubber, where real wages declined drastically, i.e. ranging from 18.7 to 21.6 per cent. In the second group, which includes chemicals and the steel and metal industries, the wage decline is somewhat smaller, ranging between 10 and 13.1 per cent. Real wage declines are relatively small in the third group, comprised of paper and graphics, plastics, food products, footwear and clothing. The decline in these branches is between 2.3 and 6.4 per cent. In the fourth group, which consists of textiles, pharmaceuticals, non-metallic minerals, wood products, transport equipment and electronics, real wages increased slightly in a range from 4.7 to 12.2 per cent.

Although the number of employed workers increased, the employment rate fell during 1987–98 (Figure 4.9) as a result of a more than proportional growth of the labour supply.[11] Both labour demand and supply effects may underlie this trend. Job creation may have fallen short of population growth, and/or labour participation rates may have increased. To see what happened, we will decompose the employment growth into these two factors. The employment rate (n) is given initially as the ratio between the number of employed (O) and the labour force (L) – also called the economically active population – which can be defined as:

$$n = \frac{O}{S} = \frac{O/L}{S/L} = \frac{o}{p}$$

where S is the total working-age population, o is the occupation rate (O/L) and p is the participation rate (S/L). From the previous equation we get:

$$\ln(n) = \ln(o) - \ln(p) \Rightarrow \Delta\ln(n) = \Delta\ln(o) + [-\Delta\ln(p)]$$

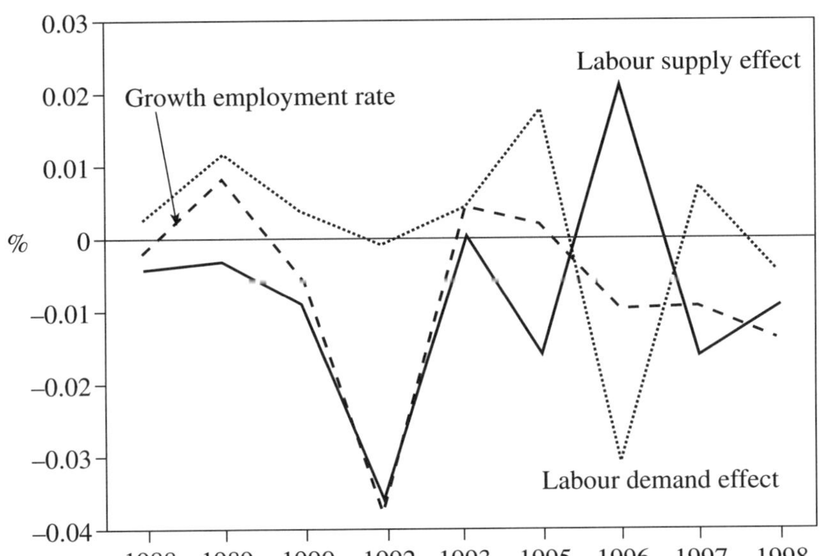

Source: PNAD.

Figure 4.11 Decomposition of the growth rate of employment

The logarithmic change gives a proxy of the rate of change in the employment rate. The first term on the right side of the final equation approximates the growth rate of the occupation rate and represents the previously described labour demand effect. The second term represents the role of labour supply in explaining the growth rate of the employment rate. Figure 4.11 shows the results of this decomposition and reveals that the labour offer was the main determinant of the employment rate growth during the 1990–92 crisis and of the recovery observed in 1993. Until that point, the demand effect followed the supply effect, but at a slower pace. Starting in 1994, employment rates plunged permanently and labour demand and supply started to move in opposite directions.

Finally, we look at the indicators of income distribution and poverty, presented in Figures 4.12 and 4.13. To measure inequality in per capita household incomes we use the Gini and Theil coefficients. Poverty is measured by the Foster–Greer–Thorbecke indicators P_0, P_1 and P_2, respectively, the poverty incidence, gap and severity. Figure 4.12 shows that inequality increased strongly during the period of high inflation in the late 1980s. In 1989, the Gini coefficient peaked at approximately 0.64 and the Theil coefficient surpassed 0.90. The *Plan Collor* brought distributional improve-

Source: PNAD.

Figure 4.12 Inequality trends of per capita household income

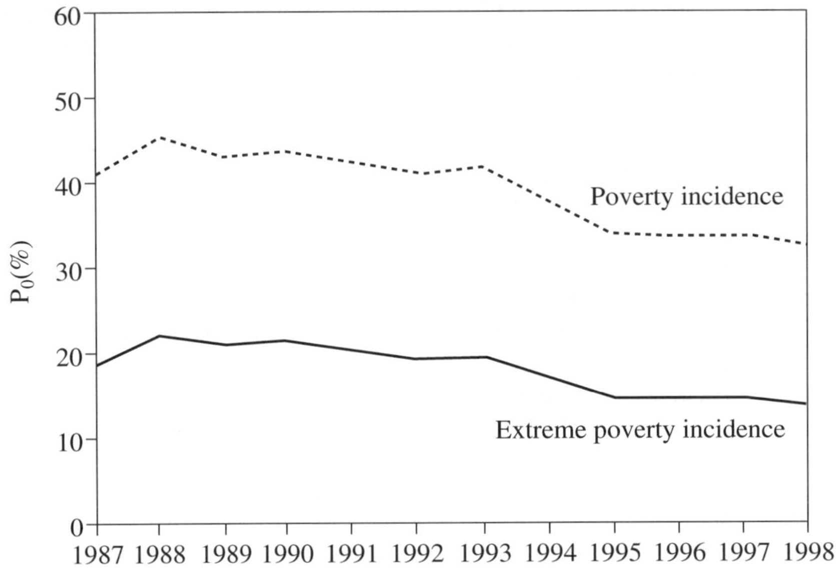

Source: PNAD Surveys from 1977 to 1998.

Figure 4.13 Poverty trend

ment, probably due to the strong income losses of the better off as a result of the monetary contraction. Inequality increased again in 1993. After the *Plan Real*, inequality stabilized around 0.60 (Gini) and 0.74 (Theil). Poverty indicators show a fairly steady poverty reduction since 1988, with a more pronounced fall between 1993 and 1994. The incidence of poverty and extreme poverty dropped to 32.7 and 13.9 per cent in 1998, down from, respectively, 45.3 and 22.1 per cent a decade earlier.

4.3 MODELLING THE IMPACT OF BALANCE-OF-PAYMENTS LIBERALIZATION

Research Strategy

The research strategy put forward to identify the impact of the liberalization process on income distribution follows the basic approach of the other country studies. Our approach consists of two steps. First, we estimate a 'with-and-without-counterfactual' scenario of how the Brazilian labour market would have reached its equilibrium had the liberalization process not taken place. Next, we identify how income distribution would have changed if the labour market situation went from a real to a counterfactual scenario.

Despite the apparent similarity with the approach of the other studies, this chapter differs from most of them with regard to the implementation of the first stage of the strategy. Rather than defining as the counterfactual scenario of the labour market structure the situation at the beginning of the liberalization process, we estimate the structure by means of a computable general equilibrium (CGE) model.

Among other results, the model provides new participation and unemployment rates, as well as a new employment and wage structure. The estimated values, which comprise a new structure for the labour market, will be used as input for the microsimulations (described in Chapter 2) that determine the changes in income distribution derived from the liberalization process. In other words, the CGE offers results on how the labour market reacts to the liberalization process, and then the microsimulation indicates how income distribution responds to these labour market adjustments.

CGE Approach to Simulating the Effects of the Liberalization Process

In this section, we describe the alternative policy simulations to isolate the effects of the liberalization process on the Brazilian economy. A brief description of the model can be found in the Appendix.[12] The simulations consist of allowing changes in the degree of trade protection (by changing tariff rates) and/or the capital flows coming from abroad (taking these as indicative of the capital account liberalization). The analysis contains more than one exercise, in order to identify the most relevant components of the liberalization process on income distribution.

The first simulation tries to interpret only trade liberalization. In this sense, the average values of the import tariffs of 1990 are applied to the products generated by each of the 42 sectors represented in the model.[13] It is important to point out that part of the Brazilian trade policy was to extinguish several non-tariff barriers. Further, the exchange rate was quite influential in determining the relative price of the imported product as against the national product. However, these shifts are not represented in our study because of the difficulty of properly simulating those effects in the model.

In the second simulation we add the financial component of the liberalization process to the trade component. Besides changing the import tariffs, the increase in direct foreign investment between 1990 and 1996 is deducted from the base-year value of foreign savings. This change in external savings we attribute to the capital account liberalization measures described in Section 4.2.

Thus, we simulate the hypothetical situation of the Brazilian economy in 1996 if tariffs and capital inflows had not changed since 1990. This way, instead of simulating an opening process, we simulate a process of closing the Brazilian economy. This has to be taken into account when interpreting the results. If the indicators to be analysed improved, we would infer that the opening worsens prosperity and vice versa.

4.4 SIMULATION RESULTS

Labour Market Adjustment

Before commenting on the results, it may be useful to explain how the simulations can affect the labour market parameters. In general, the simulations cause changes in the production structure, which in turn affects the demand for different labour categories. The transmission mechanisms can be presented as in Table 4.9.

Table 4.9 Transmission effects of a change in tariffs on labour demand

↑ tariff	↑ demand for domestic products	↑ labour demand	
	↑ government revenue	↑ government consumption	↑ labour demand
		↑ private consumption via government transfers	
		↑ investment via government savings	

The simulation that only involves tariffs induces consumers to substitute imported products for domestic. This, in turn, causes less government revenue despite the tariff increase, if the volume effect of the fall in import demand outweighs the price effect of the tariff increase. In this case, the government would either have to reduce expenditures or savings.

The demand for domestic products would decrease for two reasons. First, if there is a cut in government spending, social transfers to households would decrease and these would therefore consume less. Second, if the adjustment were through lower savings, there would be fewer resources available for

Table 4.10 *Simulated changes in labour market parameters*

	Base-year values (1996)		Increase in tariffs		Increase in tariffs and reduction in capital inflow	
	Skilled workers[a]	Unskilled workers[b]	Skilled workers[a]	Unskilled workers[b]	Skilled workers[a]	Unskilled workers[b]
Participation rate	75.3	54.8	75.1	54.7	75.8	55.2
Unemployment rate	6.9	7.0	6.6	6.7	7.8	7.8
Employment						
Informal wage earners	12.6	25.8	12.7	25.8	12.6	25.7
Formal wage earners	41.7	26.3	41.7	26.4	41.7	26.3
Public employees	19.3	3.2	19.3	3.2	19.4	3.3
Small-scale entrepreneurs	15.8	25.3	15.7	25.3	15.8	25.4
Large-scale entrepreneurs	4.2	0.7	4.2	0.7	4.2	0.7
Unpaid workers	6.4	18.6	6.3	18.6	6.4	18.7
Mean wages[c]						
Informal wage earners	506.0	184.0	506.0	183.0	506.0	172.0
Formal wage earners	784.0	337.0	785.0	335.0	737.0	319.0
Public employees	778.0	286.0	778.0	286.0	728.0	268.0
Small-scale entrepreneurs	959.0	341.0	956.0	340.0	903.0	322.0
Large-scale entrepreneurs	3307.0	2636.0	3282.0	2616.0	3297.0	2628.0
Unpaid workers						

Notes:

a. Skilled workers: 9 years or more of education.

b. Unskilled workers: 0 to 8 years of education.

c. Refers to labour incomes from the main occupation. Values in reales of September 1996. At that time the exchange rate to the dollar was close to one.

Source: Own estimates based on CGE model simulations.

investment, which in the model would mean less demand for products. Consequently, the effect on the aggregate labour demand is indefinite *a priori*. In turn, the demand for each labour category will also depend on the sectors that benefited most from the substitution of imports for domestic products, and the sectors that were most influenced by the change in government consumption or social transfers to households.

The only effect of the addition of the capital-inflow reduction in the simulation is that it diminishes the resources available to the government for spending or savings. As a result, the factors that cause a drop in labour demand increase in importance.

Table 4.10 shows that the variations of the model's labour market parameters are small. All parameters, for skilled and unskilled workers, show only minor variations from the base year.

The limited effect of the liberalization is even more evident in the simulation with only the tariff change. The results of undoing the trade liberalization suggest that government revenues fall due to higher tariffs, thus counterbalancing the positive effect that substitution of imports for domestic products would have had. Adding the 'closure' of the capital account leads to a further decrease in government resources. Now there is a general contraction in labour demand. Unemployment rises and labour incomes fall, both for skilled and unskilled workers.

Income Distribution Effects

Considering that the labour market parameters reacted only timidly to the simulations, income distribution is not expected to show significant variations either. In fact, Table 4.11 shows that both poverty and inequality indicators practically do not react to the new labour market conditions specified in the microsimulations. It is worth mentioning that the dispersion around this average result is extremely low, which makes it robust.

As expected, the reaction of the inequality measures to the alterations in the labour market parameters is most insignificant in the case of the tariff reform. In that case, inequality as well as poverty indicators only change by 0.1 percentage points.[14]

Looking at the combined effect of trade and capital account liberalization, the simulated closure of the economy produces a deterioration of the poverty and inequality indicators. This is not surprising, since we know that the simulation results were more unemployment and lower real wages. This should be interpreted as a reduction of poverty and inequality caused by the economic opening, albeit if anything only in a very minor way.

A subtle variation allows further exploration of the results in order to determine which labour market change affected income distribution most.

Table 4.11 Change in (a) inequality and (b) poverty due to a simulated 'closure' of the economy

	Tariff increase			**Tariff increase and capital flow reduction**		
(a) Inequality measures	***Mean***	***Maximum***	***Minimum***	***Mean***	***Maximum***	***Minimum***
Gini coefficient						
Original values	*60.7*	–	–	*60.7*	–	–
Change in P	60.7	60.8	60.7	60.6	60.6	60.6
Change in P + U	60.7	60.7	60.7	60.8	60.8	60.7
Change in P + U + O	60.7	60.7	60.7	60.8	60.8	60.8
Change in P + U + O + W_1	60.7	60.7	60.7	60.9	60.9	60.9
Change in P + U + O + W_1 + W_2	60.7	60.7	60.7	61.0	61.0	61.0
Change in U	60.7	60.7	60.7	60.9	60.9	60.8
Change in O	60.7	60.7	60.7	60.7	60.7	60.7
Change in W_1	60.7	–	–	60.8	–	–
Change in W_1 + W_2	60.7	–	–	61.0	–	–
Change in W_2	60.7	–	–	60.6	–	–
Theil coefficient						
Original values	74.2	–	–	74.2	–	–
Change in P	74.3	74.4	74.2	74.0	74.0	73.9
Change in P + U	74.2	74.2	74.2	74.3	74.4	74.3
Change in P + U + O	74.2	74.2	74.2	74.4	74.4	74.3
Change in P + U + O + W_1	74.1	74.1	74.1	74.9	74.9	74.9
Change in P + U + O + W_1 + W_2	74.2	74.2	74.2	75.3	75.3	75.2
Change in U	74.2	74.3	74.0	74.6	74.7	74.5
Change in O	74.2	74.2	74.2	74.2	74.3	74.2
Change in W_1	74.2	–	–	74.8	–	–
Change in W_1 + W_2	74.2	–	–	75.1	–	–
Change in W_2	74.2	–	–	73.9	–	–

(b) Poverty measures	Tariff increase			Tariff increase and capital flow reduction		
	Mean	*Maximum*	*Minimum*	*Mean*	*Maximum*	*Minimum*
Poverty incidence (P_0)						
Original values	*29.2*	–	–	*29.2*	–	–
Change in P	29.2	29.3	29.2	28.9	28.922	28.858
Change in P + U	29.1	29.1	29.1	29.2	29.281	29.205
Change in P + U + O	29.1	29.1	29.1	29.3	29.292	29.220
Change in P + U + O + W_1	28.8	28.8	28.8	29.4	29.390	29.317
Change in P + U + O + W_1 + W_2	29.2	29.2	29.1	30.2	30.256	30.183
Change in U	29.0	29.0	29.0	29.5	29.560	29.468
Change in O	29.1	29.1	29.1	29.1	29.160	29.131
Change in W_1	28.8	–	–	29.2	–	–
Change in W_1 + W_2	29.2	–	–	30.1	–	–
Change in W_2	28.8	–	–	27.8	–	–
Poverty gap (P_1)						
Original values	*13.6*	–	–	*13.6*	–	–
Change in P	13.7	13.7	13.7	13.5	13.478	13.435
Change in P + U	13.6	13.6	13.6	13.7	13.750	13.715
Change in P + U + O	13.6	13.6	13.6	13.7	13.764	13.729
Change in P + U + O + W_1	13.6	13.6	13.6	13.8	13.850	13.814
Change in P + U + O + W_1 + W_2	13.7	13.7	13.6	14.5	14.510	14.476
Change in U	13.6	13.6	13.5	14.0	13.982	13.923
Change in O	13.6	13.6	13.6	13.7	13.660	13.643
Change in W_1	13.6	–	–	13.7	–	–
Change in W_1 + W_2	13.7	–	–	14.4	–	–
Change in W_2	13.6	–	–	13.0	–	–

Table 4.11 continued

(b) Poverty measures	Tariff increase			Tariff increase and capital flow reduction		
	Mean	*Maximum*	*Minimum*	*Mean*	*Maximum*	*Minimum*
Poverty severity (P_2)						
Original values	*9.0*	–	–	*9.0*	–	–
Change in P	9.1	9.1	9.1	8.9	8.874	8.833
Change in P + U	9.0	9.0	9.0	9.1	9.108	9.068
Change in P + U + O	9.0	9.0	9.0	9.1	9.122	9.080
Change in P + U + O + W_1	9.0	9.0	9.0	9.2	9.178	9.136
Change in P + U + O + W_1 + W_2	9.0	9.0	9.0	9.6	9.598	9.557
Change in U	8.9	9.0	8.9	9.3	9.306	9.244
Change in O	9.0	9.0	9.0	9.0	9.023	9.007
Change in W_1	9.0	–	–	9.0	–	–
Change in W_1 + W_2	9.0	–	–	9.5	–	–
Change in W_2	9.0	–	–	9.6	–	–

Notes: P = participation rate; U = unemployment rate; O = employment structure by sector and type of occupation; W_1 = remuneration structure; W_2 = remuneration level.

Source: Own estimates based on microsimulations with household survey data (PNAD/IBGE).

With regard to inequality, the Theil index is more illustrative. It can be seen that the changes in the wage structure and wage level induce the greater impact on inequality. These variations are in the order of 0.5 and 0.4 points, respectively, and the cumulative change of this index in the sequential simulation is 1.1.

With regard to poverty, the analysis of any of the three indices shows that the change in wage level had the greatest impact of all labour market variables. The poverty gap (P_1) varies by 0.9 percentage points in the cumulative simulation. The change in the wage level explains 0.7 percentage points of this simulated variation.

The results show that trade liberalization had no effect on income distribution in Brazil. The capital account liberalization had a limited impact (reducing poverty and inequality). It may safely be concluded that the aggregate effect of the liberalization process was very small at best.

4.5 CONCLUSIONS

Theoretically, the main distribution effects of economic liberalization result from labour market adjustment. The employment and wage structure should change in response to trade liberalization. The results of this study are incompatible with this view. In the first place, we have observed that trade liberalization had significantly smaller effects than the surge in capital flows. It is important to mention that we did not consider the elimination of several non-tariff barriers, a relevant element of the trade opening. It is also worth mentioning that, in the long run, the simulated changes for capital account liberalization represent greater shocks than those changes simulated in the tariffs.

Second, we were also able to corroborate that the labour market was not affected in any major way by the liberalization process, and thus its effect on income distribution was also insignificant. The greatest variations on poverty and inequality indices do not reach one percentage point. This result makes it difficult to come up with any policy conclusions, since continuing the process in the moulds of the process recently experienced seems to bring neither costs nor benefits to society from a welfare point of view.

NOTES

* This study has benefited from contributions by Samir Cury, Carlos Frederico Souza, Carlos Hamilton de Araujo, Helder Mendonça, Maurício Cortez, Ricardo Henriques and Miguel Foguel. We would also like to thank Philippe Leite for his effort in carrying out the computer work that provided us with results, and Daniel Santos for his valuable contribution to this final version.

1. For a discussion on the Brazilian external debt crisis of the early 1980s, see e.g. Belluzzo and Coutinho (1983) and Castro and Souza (1985).
2. Lopes (1986) is an excellent study of the origins of the inflationary spiral of the 1980s.
3. An important aspect of the tariff reform was the reduction in the dispersion of the import tariffs between products. Between 1990 and 1994 the standard deviation of the tariff structure fell significantly from 20 to about 8 per cent.
4. It is worth mentioning that, in 1995, the government decided to increase tariffs as a response to the impact of the Mexican crisis. Although the increase did not change the tariff structure by sectors in any substantial way, some sectors experienced substantial variations in absolute terms, as was the case in the transport equipment and automobile industries.
5. The effective rate of protection takes into account both tariffs on final products and inputs. Tariffs on final goods provide protection, while those on inputs raise costs.
6. Applies only to non-financial enterprises.
7. During 1994–98, the Brazilian exchange-rate regime consisted of a crawling peg with a fixed, pre-announced average devaluation. The peg moved according to a band mechanism with a width established by the Central Bank. This way, the exchange-rate risk was kept within limits and incentives for emissions in the domestic capital market were determined almost exclusively by interest rates.
8. The Brazilian capital market crisis occurred after 1998 and is not included in this study.
9. Formal sector workers are defined here as those with a signed *carteira de trabalho*, that is, a work card or permit, which – according to Brazilian law – guarantees the formal status of the employee's job. The card needs to be signed by the employer for purposes of benefits and labour rights and obligations.
10. Measured in reales of September 1998.
11. Measured in reales of September 1998.
12. This description does not pretend to show the complete model due to limitations of space. The model description is limited to the components that differentiate the model from the typical CGE as described in the literature and the aspects that are important for the simulation exercises.
13. The year 1990 was taken as reference, because we believe that it was only then that the actual tariff reform became effective. Between 1988 and 1990, trade reform essentially consisted of eliminating tariff surcharges.
14. Except for P_0, which varies by 0.4 in response to the inclusion of the wage level change caused by the change in tariffs.

REFERENCES

Armington, Paul (1970) 'Adjustment of trade balances: some experiments with a model of trade among many countries', *IMF Staff Papers*, **17**: 488–523.

Barros, Ricardo Paes de and Rosane Mendonça (1997) 'Flexibilidade do mercado de trabalho brasileiro: uma avaliação empírica', Discussion Paper No. 452, Rio de Janeiro: IPEA.

Barros, Ricardo Paes de, Rosane Mendonça and Miguel Foguel (1996) 'O Impacto da Abertura Comercial sobre o Mercado de Trabalho Brasileiro', *Anales del XXIV Encuentro Brasileño de Economía – Anpec*, Águas de Lindóia.

Barros, Ricardo Paes de, Carlos Henrique Corseuil and Samir Cury (2001) 'Efeitos do salário mínimo sobre a pobreza no Brasil: estimativas a partir de um modelo de equilíbrio geral computável', Rio de Janeiro: IPEA (mimeo).

Beluzzo, Luiz Gonzaga and Luciano Coutinho (1983) *Desenvolvimento econômico no Brasil*, Campinas.

Blanchflower, David G. and Andrew J. Oswald (1994) *The Wage Curve*, Cambridge: MIT Press.

Castro, Antônio Barros de and Carlos Frederico Souza (1985) *A economia brasileira em marcha forçada*, Rio de Janeiro: Ed. Paz e Terra.

Cury, Samir (1998) *Modelo de equilíbrio geral para simulação de políticas de distribuição de renda e crescimento no Brasil*, São Paulo: Fundaçao Gutelio Vargas (Doctoral thesis).

Devarajan, Shantayanan, Jeffrey Lewis and Sherman Robinson (1991) 'From stylized to applied models: Building multisector CGE models for policy analysis', Department of Agriculture and Resources Economics, Working Paper 616, Berkeley: University of California at Berkeley.

Kume, Honório, Guida Piani and Carlos Frederico Souza (2000) 'A política brasileira de importação no período 1987–98: descrição e avaliação', Rio de Janeiro: IPEA (mimeo).

Lopes, Francisco (1986) *O choque heterodoxo: combate à inflação e reforma monetária*, Rio de Janeiro: Ed. Campus.

Machado, Ana Flávia and Maurício Moreira (2000) 'Os impactos da abertura comercial sobre a remuneração relativa do trabalho no Brasil', *Anales del XXVIII Encuentro Brasileño de Economía – Anpec*, Campinas.

Moreira, Maurício M. and S. Najberg (1997) 'Abertura Comercial: Criando ou Exportando Empregos?', Discussion Paper No. 59, Rio de Janeiro: Banco Nacional de Desenvolvimento Econômico e Social.

World Bank (1999) *World Development Report 1999*, Washington D.C.: World Bank.

APPENDIX: A GENERAL EQUILIBRIUM MODEL OF THE BRAZILIAN ECONOMY

General Characteristics of the Model

The model we used is based on the one developed by Devarajan et al. (1991), which solves endogenously the quantities and prices as well as institutional incomes.[1] It tries to grasp distribution effects, thus adopting a particular design that emphasizes disagreggation of production factors and institutions, especially workers and households. Labour is divided into seven categories, reflecting differences of insertion into the labour market (contractual relationship) and skill level.[2] This differentiation is essential when representing the Brazilian economy because several segments coexist in the market, absorbing structural shifts in the economy in a heterogeneous way.

Households are divided into eight classes, defined by income differentials, degree of urbanization, and type of household head.[3] This division allows a more precise perception of the dependence of households with respect to the various sources of income, including remuneration of production factors, social security benefits and returns on financial assets. This aspect is important because the liberalization process exerts a differentiated influence on the various income sources.

The model can be decomposed into two blocks: general equilibrium and income transfers between institutions. The first block is a specification of the neo-classical general equilibrium for most markets, where agents respond to relative prices as a result of the maximization of profit and utility, determining output and consumption levels. The only modifications incorporated are related to the supply of goods and the determination of the level of employment.[4] In the second block we incorporate information on the form of appropriation of factor income, as well as its redistribution among the agents/institutions represented in the model. These redistribution mechanisms are not present in Devarajan et al. (1991). Cury (1998) presents a large number of such mechanisms, which are extended in Barros et al. (2001). This way, the description of the first block is limited to a concise explanation of the production system and the labour market. We will now describe the second block in more detail.

General Equilibrium Block

Determination of output

The production function used in the model considers three types of factor inputs: labour, capital and intermediate inputs. The format of the function is structured in three steps. First, the various labour categories are added in a composite labour type for each sector, using a function of the Cobb–Douglas type.[5] In the second step, the composite labour factors and capital are aggregated, using a constant elasticity of substitution (CES) function to obtain value added.[6] The third and final step involves adding value added to intermediate inputs, using a Leontief-type function (with fixed proportion of the factors with respect to the total product).[7]

The model assumes that firms maximize profits and takes as given input and factor prices, as well as final product prices. While optimizing earnings, the firm has to take account of the technological restrictions defined by the indicated production function.

There are 42 sectors whose output can be exported or destined for domestic consumption.[8] The destination of output is determined by the producer, based on the comparison of the sales prices in international and domestic markets, in addition to a restriction related to the capacity of transferring sales from one market to another. Consumers choose between domestic and imported goods as imperfect substitutes, following the Armington specification (Armington 1970).

Behaviour of the labour market

One of the consequences of assuming profit maximization by firms is that the first derivative of the earnings function with respect to factor demand has to be equal to its remuneration. This is a necessary condition. In the model's specific case, the firm's behavioural rule, when applied to the seven labour factor categories, determines a relation between the wage rate and the value of the marginal product of each category and in each of the sectors.

CGE-type models traditionally model the labour market on the basis of labour demand functions of the indicated type and a given labour supply. In a market where equilibrium is determined by only these two aspects, there would be no involuntary unemployment. Since this result does not seem to reflect the labour market equilibrium of most countries – particularly that of Brazil – a third element is introduced, defined as the wage curve, which guarantees the existence of involuntary unemployment in equilibrium. The wage curve defines a negative relation between the unemployment rate (U_t) and the wage level (W_t), which can be described with the following equation:

$$\ln W_t = \alpha - \beta \ln(U_t)$$

The theoretical justification of this function can be based on the existence of wage rigidities due to either efficiency wage setting or trade union bargaining.[9] By the first argument, the firm motivates efficient behaviour by setting attractive wage levels. However, when the unemployment rate is high, the worker feels his job is threatened and tends to be naturally efficient, eliminating the need for the firm to offer attractive wages. Alternatively, firms may feel obligated to increase salaries when unemployment is low because workers' bargaining power increases in such situations. The wage curve can thus be interpreted as wage determination by firms, which takes into account the degree of competition among job seekers. When the need for jobs is large, i.e. in cases of high unemployment, firms can offer relatively low wages.

The relation of the wage curve to labour market equilibrium can be seen in Figure A4.1. Point *E* represents the equilibrium in full employment in a market hardly influenced by supply (L^s) and demand (L^d). With the introduction of the wage curve (*W*), equilibrium employment and wage levels are determined by *E′*, the point of intersection between the labour demand and wage curves. At wage *E′* there is excess labour supply, representing the unemployment level in the economy.

Contrary to the labour demand, labour supply and wages are not specified by sector, but only by occupational category. For this reason, as a first step, we derive aggregate employment, wage and unemployment levels. To determine employment and wage levels for each labour category, additional labour market assumptions are required.

We therefore complete the description of the labour market with the assumption that wages by labour category are sector-specific. In practical terms, this implies a sectoral segmentation of the labour market. For example, a semi-skilled, formal worker in the mechanics/automobile sector receives a

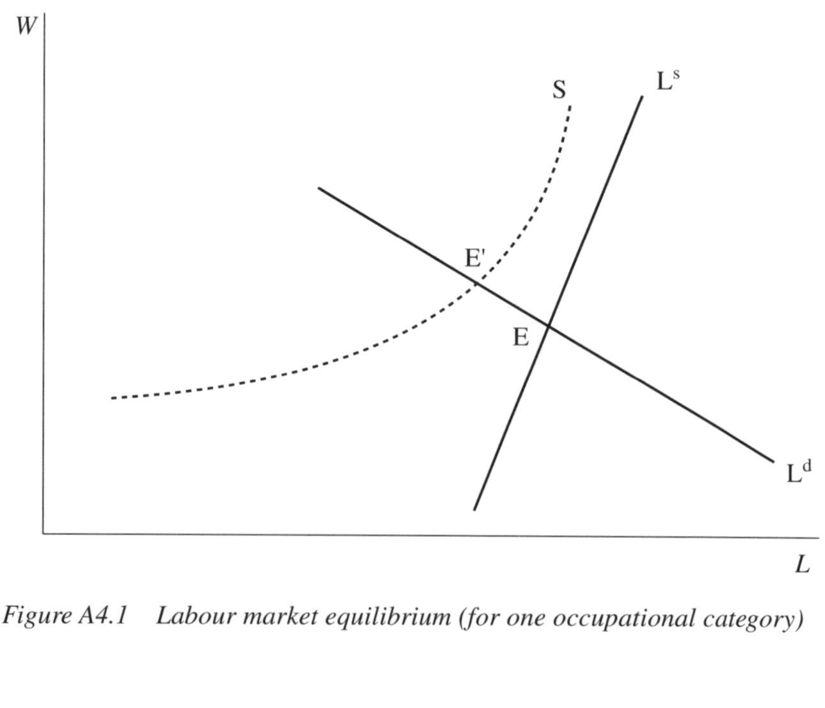

Figure A4.1 Labour market equilibrium (for one occupational category)

higher wage than the same type of worker in the clothing sector.[10] For this purpose, we introduce an exogenous variable in the function for the mean wage, namely a variable setting relative wage differentials between sectors (W_{il}).

The functioning of the labour market for public employees is similar to the process just described. Nominal wages for this labour category are fixed, above the market equilibrium, under the assumption of rigidity in the process of wage determination for public employees. This way, labour demand becomes endogenous and the difference between labour supply (exogenous) and demand determines unemployment.

Income Transfer Mechanisms

In this second block of the model we consider the income generation process of households, firms, government and the rest of the world. This process has two parts: the determination of income distribution generated in the production process and income transfers between the four institutional agents.

The first part consists of assigning capital remuneration to firms and labour earnings to households. The allocation of incomes of the seven labour categories to the eight household types is determined by the composition of households. It is worth mentioning that the model considers two types of firms: large enterprises (recipients of most of the capital remuneration) and small enterprises (recipients of the residual capital remuneration).

In the second part, income is redistributed among institutions. First, government collects direct taxes charged to firms and households,[11] duties charged on imported goods and contributions to the pension system.[12] Next, the government transfers resources to households either in the form of pension payments or as other government transfers (including all types of social benefits).[13] In addition, the government transfers resources to firms in the form of interest payments on domestic debt and for purchases of goods and services.[14]

To finance these expenditures, the government uses its tax revenue and external borrowing (capital flows). This external resource flow to the government is determined by the amount of resources needed to close the balance-of-payments accounts.

APPENDIX NOTES

1. The basic features of the model were developed by Cury (1998).
2. The labour types are unskilled informal, skilled informal, unskilled formal, semi-skilled formal, skilled formal, unskilled public employees and skilled public employees.
3. The household groups include: 1, poor urban whose head of household is active; 2, poor

urban whose head of household is inactive; 3, poor urban; 4, urban with medium income; 5, poor rural; 6, medium-income rural; 7, households with medium to high incomes; 8, households with high incomes.

4. This change is incorporated in Barros et al. (2001).
5. Here we assume that the function represents constant returns to scale, i.e. an equal increase of all labour types results in an equal increase of aggregate labour.
6. This function has a substitution elasticity different from one and reflects constant returns to scale.
7. Devarajan et al. (1991) use only the first and third step, combining capital with labour and value added with intermediate inputs, respectively.
8. Again, diversity becomes a virtue of the model, to the degree that the sectors are affected in a differentiated manner by the changes in trade policy as well as by foreign capital inflows.
9. Blanchflower and Oswald (1994) spell out the theoretical foundations of the wage curve, with estimates for some developed countries. Barros and Mendonça (1997) carry out an analysis applied to the Brazilian case.
10. The implicit hypothesis is that workers with the same educational level can receive different remuneration depending on the sector where they are employed, due to different productivity levels or simply due to geographical location.
11. Tax rates are defined as a fraction of the enterprise incomes, but differ for large and small companies as well as across the eight household groups.
12. The pension system is treated as a separate agent in the model. Not only does it manage a large volume of resources in Brazil, but the system also has a strong redistributive impact. Contributions to the pension system also affect firm incomes (again to a differentiated degree for large and small firms) and the determination of value added.
13. Allocation of these resources between household groups is fixed, using parameters based on 1996 data.
14. Allocation between sectors is analogous to that described for households.

5. Chile: trade liberalization, employment and inequality[1]

José de Gregorio, Dante Contreras, David Bravo, Tomas Rau and Sergio Urzua

5.1 INTRODUCTION

The Chilean economy went through important transformations in the last three decades. Following the import-substituting industrialization strategy, populist economic policies emerged in the early 1970s. Subsequently, Chile moved to an open and free market economy. As a consequence, economic performance has been quite irregular over the past three decades. Therefore, it is of some interest to examine the effects of trade opening on economic growth and inequality. It is also important to analyse the sectoral and macroeconomic transformations that took place during this period. To this end, after briefly discussing the main reforms and the macroeconomic policies, this study is divided into two main parts. The first deals with the macroeconomic effects of the opening process, while the second analyses the effects on welfare, using the methodologies developed in Chapters 1 and 2.

In the first part, we tackle the macroeconomic aspects along three lines of analysis. The first consists of decomposing aggregate demand to examine the determinants of economic growth. In order to accomplish this, it is necessary to build consistent time series for GDP from the 1970s onwards and to decompose growth by the main demand categories, i.e. exports, investment, private consumption and government spending. The second line involves an analysis of the changes in employment and labour productivity. The third line explores the effects of liberalization and stabilization on economic growth and inequality from a macroeconomic perspective.

The second part provides microeconomic evidence on the changes that took place in the labour market as a result of trade liberalization. Here we compare the structures of wages, employment, unemployment and labour participation before and after the opening of the economy. Based on these changes, we identify the fraction explained by the direct impact of liberalization, carrying out simulation exercises with counterfactual scenarios. In other words, we ask what would have happened to income inequality and poverty if the liberalization policy had not been implemented.

The structure of the chapter is as follows. Section 5.2 summarizes the structural reform and opening policies that took place in Chile in recent decades. Section 5.3 discusses the impact of trade liberalization on growth, employment, unemployment and total factor productivity from a macroeconomic perspective. In Section 5.4, we explore the impact of the opening on poverty and inequality through microeconomic analysis by modelling the changes in employment, unemployment, participation and wages. The conclusions are presented in Section 5.5.

5.2 ECONOMIC REFORMS AND TRADE LIBERALIZATION

Chile is usually mentioned as the first country to implement structural reforms among emerging-market economies. Chile's economic success during the 1990s tends to be attributed to these reforms, but one should keep in mind that they were started in the mid-1970s and it took years before they produced the expected effects. This period included two important recessions, stabilization policies, two periods of privatizations and a wide range of structural reforms.[2] This group of measures presented certain limitations when isolating the effects of specific policies on macroeconomic performance and prosperity. In fact, the benefits of the opening process are mixed with the costs associated with a wide range of policies. Hence, it is difficult to differentiate the various effects of the policies that were implemented. Even when an attempt is made to isolate certain elements, such as the reduction of inflation, many other effects cannot be properly identified.

Before 1974, Chile had maintained a long tradition of price controls. Starting that year, the first reform consisted of the liberalization of all prices in the economy. This was the first signal for a system based on the market as the channel for resources allocation. In addition, stabilization policies and policies to reduce the fiscal deficit were implemented. Indeed, the fiscal deficit dropped from 25 per cent of GDP in 1973 to 1 per cent in 1975, and inflation fell below 100 per cent in 1977 (see Figure 5.1).

In the period 1960–74, Chile was an example case of a country with an inward-looking development strategy based on import substitution. Exchange-rate adjustment served that purpose. In 1973, there were six official exchange rates, with a difference of 1:52 between the lowest and the highest rate. The average tariff rate was almost 100 per cent. After the military coup there was a large devaluation in order to re-establish competitiveness. The multiple exchange-rate system was limited to only three official rates and a crawling

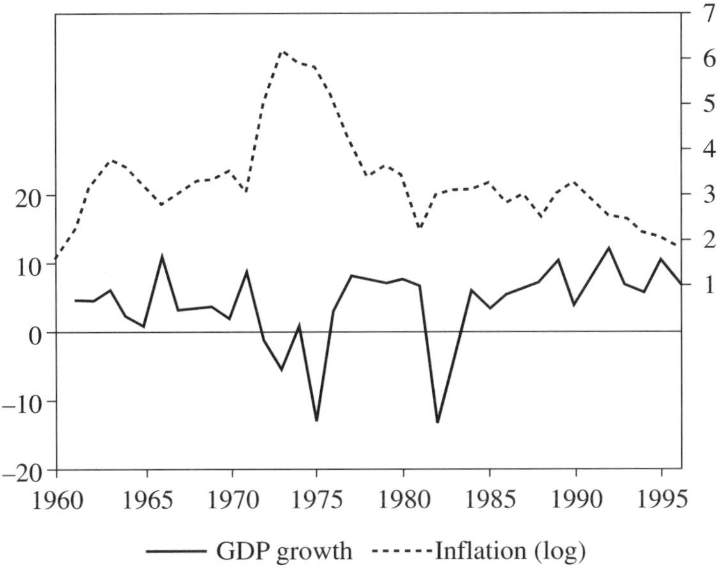

Figure 5.1 Inflation and growth

peg was introduced involving a devaluation every four months. The three rates were to converge to a uniform rate. In August 1974, the exchange rate for copper exports was unified and as a result only two exchange rates remained, one for trade and another for financial transactions. This helped achieve macroeconomic discipline, but inflation remained high despite considerable output contraction. In 1974, the real exchange rate witnessed the highest depreciation since 1960.

From the start, the military regime aimed at opening the economy. However, to compensate the reduction in tariff protection, authorities devaluated the exchange rate during the first phase of economic opening. To get the liberalization process started, tariff restrictions were eliminated, resulting in a reduction of the average tariff from 100 per cent in 1973 to a single and uniform rate of 10 per cent in 1979 for all goods and services, except for automobiles and certain agricultural products.

Figure 5.2 shows the trend in average tariffs and an index of trade liberalization. This index is a composite of indices for tariffs and quantitative restrictions. The index for quantitative barriers is based on Ffrench-Davis (1973) and De la Cuadra and Hachette (1990) and ranges between 0 and 20 points (20 indicating the absence of quantitative controls). De la Cuadra and Hachette (1990) also construct a trade liberalization index that summarizes the previous indicators and add a measure of the black-market premium, in

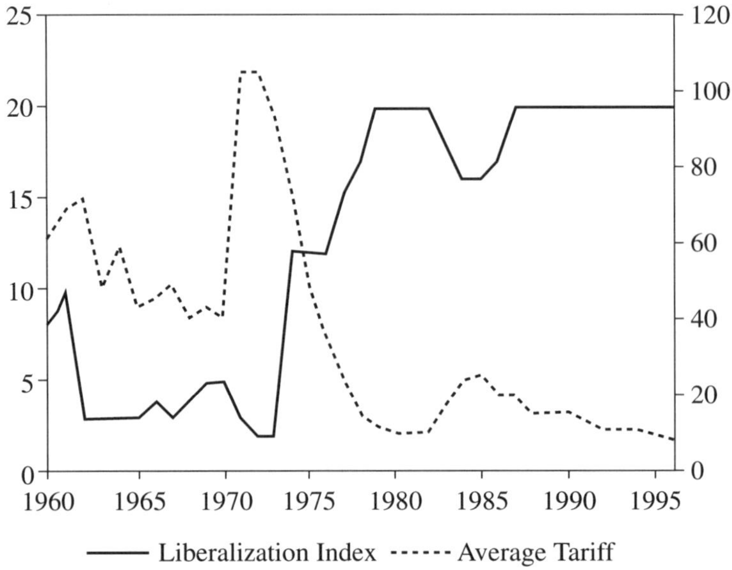

Figure 5.2 Trade liberalization

order to get a measure of the degree of opening and external market distortions. The resulting index also fluctuates in the previously indicated range, with a maximum of 20 indicating full opening (see Figure 5.2).

Trade liberalization was implemented in conjunction with other policies aimed at reducing transitional costs of reforms and obtaining support for them.[3] The most important policies were the major real exchange-rate depreciation and the privatization process (see Hachette and Luders 1992). Only after major cuts in government expenditures, monetary stabilization measures and negative external shocks, did the Chilean economy start to recover in 1975 and the initial reforms were consolidated. Trade opening was implemented during this period.

During 1978, economic authorities changed the exchange-rate policy. The target shifted from providing compensation for the opening process toward inflation control. This process culminated with a fixed exchange rate in June 1979 that lasted until June 1982. At that point in time, the economy had collapsed due to exchange-rate overvaluation, a growing trade deficit, massive indebtedness of the private sector, and a crisis in the financial sector and foreign-exchange market. Only in 1985, after a significant depreciation of the peso, did the economy manage to enter a new growth phase. After the debt crisis, tariffs were increased to 35 per cent and other duties were introduced in an attempt to compensate the most affected sectors and curb import growth. Later, tariffs were reduced to 11 per cent in 1992 and in 1998 a law was approved in order to reduce tariffs to a uniform rate of 6 per cent in 2003.

In the 1990s, the unilateral liberalization strategy was supplemented with free trade agreements. The original objective was to reach a free trade agreement with the United States and to enter NAFTA. This encountered many problems and the objective has not yet materialized. Nonetheless, Chile signed a series of trade agreements, among others with Canada and Mexico, and it became a special associate member of Mercosur during this period.[4]

PRINCIPAL ECONOMIC REFORMS IN 1974–85

- A large privatization programme that reduced substantially state participation in the production and distribution of goods and services.
- Labour market reforms that decentralized wage negotiations and increased labour flexibilization, modifying the power relationship between companies and unions. These policies were implemented in the early 1980s, as unions were suppressed before that.
- Financial sector reform. Prudential bank supervision was established after the financial crisis of the 1980s, which had been caused by the vast and unregulated liberalization process.
- Implementation of a private pension system based on individual contributions, to replace the traditional pay-as-you-go system.
- Trade reforms that substituted differential and high tariffs for low and uniform ones. These measures were accompanied by export-promotion policies aimed at making exports the engine of growth.
- Public sector reforms that tended to increase macroeconomic stability and the efficiency of the public sector. The Central Bank became independent in 1989 in order to ensure macroeconomic stability.

These measures had their greatest impact during the 1990s.[5] Indeed, during the 1987–96 period, the economy grew at an average annual rate of 7.1 per cent and income per capita increased by 5.4 per cent. As a result, the 1996 output level of 1996 was 70 per cent higher than that of 1986.[6]

After the 1982 debt crisis, the recovery of employment and the increase in the capacity utilization rate formed the main sources of economic growth in Chile. The unemployment rate was over 10 per cent each year between 1981 and 1987. Nevertheless, since 1987 productivity has been growing faster than 4 per cent per year and investment rates have increased considerably, reaching a record level of 28 per cent of GDP in 1997. The quality of investments has also increased. In 1996, about 58 per cent of investment was in machinery and equipment, up from 47 per cent in the second half of the 1980s. Growth was export led. Exports grew at an average rate of 9 per cent. Even though copper continues to play an important role in the Chilean economy, export growth is explained by both traditional and non-traditional exports. Since 1990, the volume of non-copper exports has grown by 11 per cent on average per year.

The establishment of an independent Central Bank in 1989 created an institutional structure that facilitated price stability. Since then, the Central Bank has conducted a countercyclical monetary policy of raising interest rates when growth of GDP or aggregate expenditures exceeds the target level consistent with a policy of inflation control. Since 1991, inflation has shown a downward trend, reaching one-digit levels by the end of the decade.

As already mentioned, around the late 1970s the economy allowed free capital movements and had a highly deregulated financial system. Controls were re-established after the debt crisis. The purpose of these controls was to prevent massive capital flight and to provide guarantees for foreign financing. With the surge in capital flows to emerging-market economies in the late 1980s and early 1990s, the capital account was liberalized and restrictions were lifted, for example those on foreign investments by pension funds, mutual funds and other investment institutions. However, the policy requiring foreign investors to hold on to their assets in Chile for a determined period of time was maintained. In addition, a non-interest-bearing reserve requirement, the *encaje*, was introduced in order to stem the massive entry of capital and avoid a real appreciation.[7]

5.3 TRADE OPENING AND MACROECONOMIC EFFECTS

This section examines the impact of trade opening on aggregate demand. First, we look at a decomposition of aggregate demand, under the assumption that the output is determined by aggregate demand. Next, we examine the changes in productivity and employment. Finally, we look at sources of growth from the supply side.

Demand Growth

To analyse the Chilean experience of the opening, it is necessary to go back to the early 1970s. There are no consistent national accounts from that time onwards, though, and the same goes for fiscal accounts. It is therefore necessary to adjust the long-term time series. The problems are largely found in the information on net government inflows (taxes minus transfers). We use the tax rate with respect to GDP of the 1970s, measured in dollars, to extrapolate the series in 1986 Chilean pesos consistent with national

Table 5.1 Contribution to aggregate demand (%)

	1970–74	1976–81	1985–89	1990–97	1970–97
Exports	24.9	39.5	46.8	47.1	41.4
Government expenditures	30.8	25.6	18.7	11.7	21.6
Investment	44.3	34.9	34.6	41.3	37.0

Source: Authors' calculations based on Ministerio de Hacienda and Banco Central. See text for more details.

Table 5.2 Decomposition of demand growth (%)

	1970–73	1976–81	1985–89	1990–97	1970–97
Exports					
Direct multiplier effects	–1.1	4.2	5.2	4.7	3.7
Leakage	–0.7	–3.8	–2.8	–2.1	–1.0
Exports subtotal	–1.9	0.4	2.4	2.7	2.7
Government expenditures					
Direct multiplier effects	2.0	0.5	0.5	0.4	0.5
Leakage	0.7	1.2	–0.3	–0.2	–0.1
Gov. spending subtotal	2.7	1.6	0.2	0.2	0.4
Investment					
Direct multiplier effects	–7.1	6.6	6.1	5.1	2.2
Leakage	7.3	0.8	–0.3	1.5	0.1
Investment subtotal	0.2	7.4	5.8	6.5	2.3
Total growth	1.0	9.4	8.4	9.4	5.4

Source: Authors' calculations based on Ministerio de Hacienda and Banco Central. See text for more details.

accounts. A similar adjustment was made for social and housing expenditures. For 1970–87, net government revenues were estimated by taking tax income minus social expenditure (excluding housing expenditures). For 1988–97 we used tax income minus social security contributions. Since most of the social expenditures correspond to transfers, this is a reasonable approximation. For 1998, the only year for which both series are available, the difference between them is equal to 0.3 per cent. A summary of the decomposition is presented in Tables 5.1 and 5.2. The 1970–97 period is divided into four sub-periods: 1970–74, 1976–81, 1985–89 and 1990–97. The two big recessions of the mid-1970s and 1982 are not included so as to avoid interpretation problems.

The results show that the importance of exports has grown since the stabilization and trade-opening period. Indeed, during the mid-1970s, exports contributed significantly to output. In contrast, we observe a reduction in the importance of public expenditures, which can be explained by the successive fiscal adjustments. The role of investment as a source of demand growth diminished during the liberalization period, but this was reverted during the 1990s.

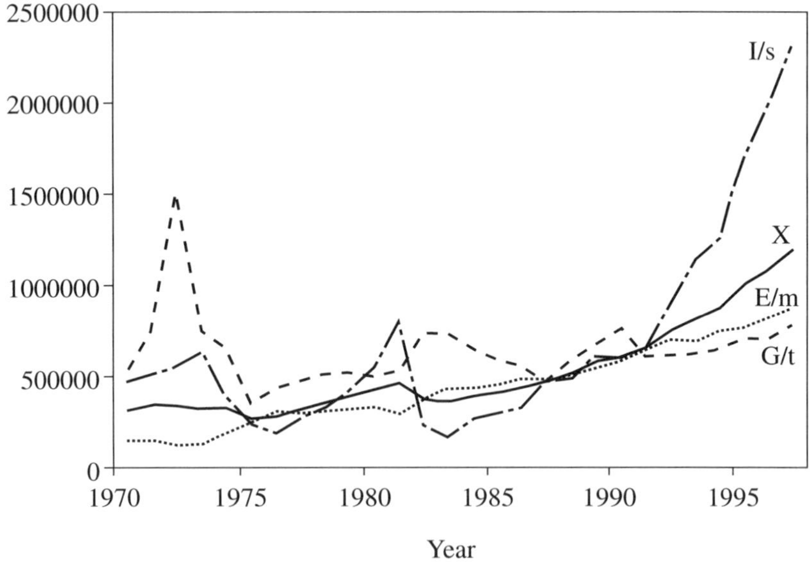

Source: Authors' calculations based on Central Bank data. See text for more details.

Figure 5.3 Output versus investment, trade and government spending multipliers (millions of Chilean pesos of 1986)

Figure 5.3 shows the annual trend of the own multiplier effects. This figure confirms the growth of the importance of exports and the reduction of the relative importance of public expenditures, as well as the growing importance of investment. This effect was not observed as clearly in Table 5.1, given that the importance of investments is diminished by the decrease in the coefficient $s/(s + m + t)$. This coefficient has decreased mainly due to the increase in the degree of opening of the Chilean economy, as reflected in m, as well as the decrease of s during the 1990s.

Figure 5.4 shows the evolution of the multipliers. This figure brings out the growth of the import multiplier since 1982, together with a significant increase in the export share. We can also see that the private savings multiplier starts to decrease after 1990. Still, the savings rate has remained relatively stable throughout the 1990s, whereas the import share in GDP increased considerably.

To analyse the changes in aggregate demand, it is worth examining whether the shares of the demand components have changed due to changes in their own multiplier or because of changes in the leakage factor caused by changing spending propensities. Expressing the demand decomposition equation (A1.4) in terms of percentage changes, we get:

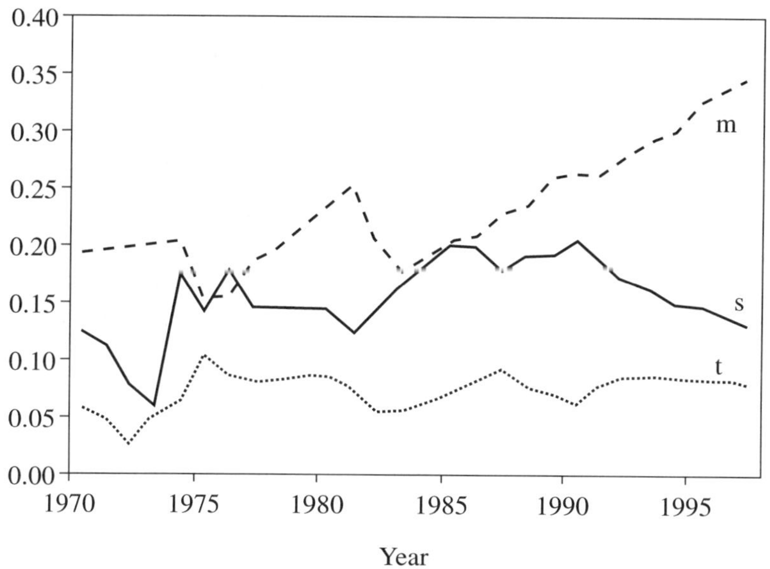

Source: Authors' calculations based on Central Bank data. See text for more details.

Figure 5.4 Import, savings and tax 'leakages'

$$\frac{\Delta X}{X} = \alpha_1 \Delta I - \beta_1 \Delta s + \alpha_2 \Delta G - \beta_2 \Delta t + \alpha_3 \Delta E - \beta_3 \Delta m$$

The supply of goods can grow because of a demand increase or a decrease in the leakage parameters. For example, output may rise because of a rise in investment or a fall in the savings propensity, which in turn increases the multiplier effect of investment growth.

Figure 5.3 shows this decomposition. The role of exports has clearly increased, despite the compensatory effect of a rising import coefficient. The import share increased particularly fast after trade liberalization between 1976 and 1982 (see Figure 5.4).

Investments constituted the main source of aggregate demand growth over the entire period. This can be explained by the low savings propensity, as compared with for instance the high import share. As a result, the investment rate has a strong impact on demand expansion. The public sector has played a minor role. In particular, the tax rate has remained relatively stable and fiscal expenditures have been relatively low as a percentage of aggregate demand. The only exception occurred during the Allende government (1970–73). In that period, aggregate demand expansion was mainly driven by the increase in public expenditures, while the decrease in exports became the main offsetting effect.

Employment and Labour Productivity Decompositions

Here we examine the changes in employment and productivity patterns for 1970–97 following the decomposition methodology of the Appendix to Chapter 1. Just as in the previous section, we exclude the two recessions. All years are included though when estimating averages for the entire period.

The results are presented in Tables 5.3 and 5.4. During 1970–97, the increase in the unemployment rate was small, whereas the labour absorption effect was fully offset by the labour supply effect. During 1970–73, unemployment fell due to supply factors, rather than absorption increases. During the recession of 1974–75, unemployment increased dramatically, mainly as a result of job losses while labour supply remained constant.

During the first phase of the liberalization process, the unemployment rate stayed high for Chilean standards, despite the drop in unemployment. This reduction in unemployment can be explained by a recovery of employment to normal levels, rather than by a direct employment-creating effect of trade liberalization. During the 1982 recession, unemployment increased due to the elimination of jobs. Figure 5.5 shows the drastic reduction in unemployment during the second half of the 1980s, which is mainly explained by the labour absorption effect. In 1989, the unemployment rate in

Table 5.3 Decomposition of the employment rate (%)

	1970–73	1974–75	1976–81	1982–84	1985–89	1990–97	1970–97
Growth of employment rate	0.4	–5.4	0.9	–2.1	2.1	0.3	0.1
Labour absorption effect	–0.7	–2.1	1.8	–4.8	3.3	0.9	0.5
Labour supply effect	–1.1	0.0	0.9	–0.6	1.2	0.5	0.4

Source: Authors' calculations based on Ministerio de Hacienda and Banco Central. See text for more details.

Table 5.4 Decomposition of labour productivity growth (%)

	Growth rate			Decomposition of participation	
	Production	**Employment**	**Labour particip.**	**Own effect**	**Reallocation**
1970–73	1.7	1.0	0.8	0.7	0.0
1976–81	6.5	3.9	2.6	2.6	–0.1
1985–89	5.6	5.5	0.1	0.4	–0.3
1990–97	6.4	2.5	3.9	4.0	–0.2
1970–97	3.8	2.2	1.6	1.7	–0.1

Source: Authors' calculations. See text for more details.

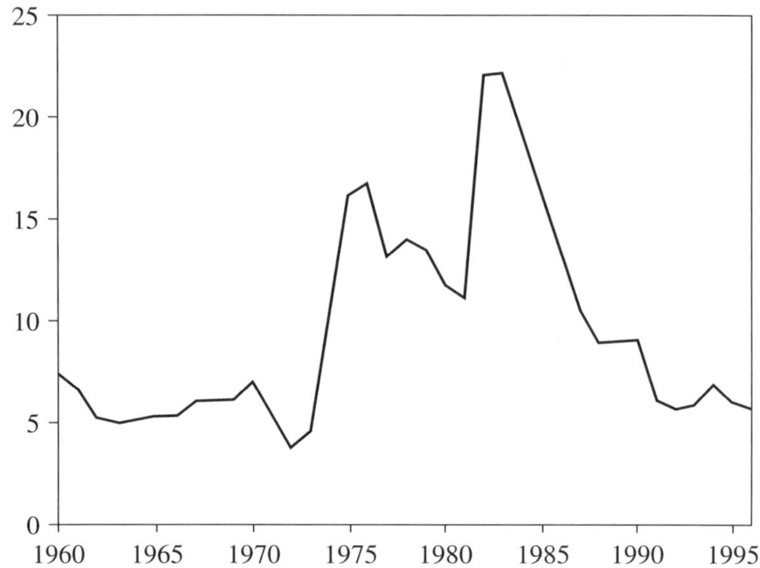

Source: Employment Survey for Gran Santiago, Universidad de Chile.

Figure 5.5 Unemployment in Gran Santiago (%)

Gran Santiago was below 10 per cent, a figure similar to that observed in 1974.

When extrapolating from the 1974–75 recession, the pessimistic predictions regarding employment after the debt crisis are understandable. After the first recession, the recovery of employment was slow compared to the recovery observed after the 1982 crisis, even though this last crisis was more widespread. There are three potential explanations for these findings. First, during the 1970s the economy underwent a series of changes in relative prices and sectoral incentives. The trade and financial opening could have curbed employment creation. In contrast, during the recovery after the 1982 crisis there was greater stability and this facilitated employment creation. Second, from the late 1970s up to 1981 the exchange rate appreciated, providing a disincentive to growth in the traded goods sector. In contrast, recovery in the 1980s took place in a context of exchange-rate depreciation and strong export growth. Third, and finally, in the late 1970s there were no labour institutions and labour negotiations were centralized, whereas in the 1980s the labour market functioned in a decentralized fashion.

Total Factor Productivity (TFP) Growth

To evaluate the performance of long-term economic growth, it is necessary to decompose the accumulation and growth of production factors in relation to the increase in the efficiency in the use of factors, that is the growth of total factor productivity. Here we present decompositions of output growth, which we will use to examine the impact of economic policies such as trade liberalization on total factor productivity growth and wage inequality. Let us take the following production function:

$$Y_t = A_t F(K_t, L_t)$$

where Y is GDP, A is a technological parameter or total factor productivity, K is the capital stock and L is employment. Further on, we will discuss whether employment is measured in units of labour or human capital. Under the assumptions of constant returns to scale and competitive asset and labour markets, it is possible to decompose the growth rate of output as:

$$\hat{Y}_t = \hat{A}_t + \alpha_t \hat{K}_t + (1 - \alpha_t)\hat{L}_t$$

where '^' indicates percentage change. The growth of the output can be decomposed into total factor productivity growth and factor accumulation, where each factor is weighted by its respective share in output: α for capital and $1–\alpha$ for labour. The α coefficient is measured in two ways. One method consists of obtaining the parameter directly from national accounts as the difference between GDP and labour remuneration.[8] An alternative method is to estimate the production function. Factor shares and the technology parameter, A, are obtained as a result. This method assumes that factor shares are constant through time, except for the productivity parameter, which is not realistic.

This study uses a third method. Following Sarel (1997), it can be held that factor shares change over time and per country due to changes in the composition of production by sectors. Factor shares are sector-specific. The method assumes that each factor share has the same production function across countries, except for A, for which reason it can be estimated with information per country. This way we estimate an average capital share of 41.2 per cent with a standard 1.1 per cent deviation.[9]

The capital measure is obtained as a mid-period estimate (Nehru and Dhareshwar 1993) In a steady state, there is a direct relation between growth, capital, investment and the depreciation rate (δ):

$$K_t = \frac{I_t}{\hat{Y} + \delta}$$

This relation is used to estimate K at a particular point in time.[10] For that we need the variable I_t, which can be obtained by estimating a regression of investment with respect to a time trend. The prediction of I for the average of the sample (1978 in our case) is used to obtain a capital stock series using a 5 per cent depreciation rate.

We do not have information on capacity utilization, which varies as a function of the economic cycle and could induce additional fluctuations in TFP. For example, in a recession unemployment will rise (L decreases), output will drop and, assuming constant capacity utilization, the change in K would be smaller than the actual change. This would exacerbate the decrease in TFP and underestimate the contribution of K. This effect is equivalent to using labour force instead of employment. The correction for this problem will be discussed later on.

With regard to employment, there are two measurement options. The first is to take total employment at the national level. This definition implies that, when estimating A, the variable will not only measure technological progress, but also improvement in the quality of labour (in terms of human capital) and capital. To measure the quality of labour we use the average years of education of the labour force. The production function can thus be written as:

$$Y_t = B_t F(K_t, S_t L_t)$$

where S refers to years of schooling and B is TFP, excluding human capital. Decomposing output we get the following relation between A and B:

$$\hat{A}_t = \hat{B}_t + (1 - \alpha_t)\hat{S}_t$$

The difference corresponds to the contribution of education to growth of per capita output.[11] The alternative expression for TFP measures not only technological improvements but also the reallocation of existing resources toward more productive activities. Certain economic reforms cause human capital to shift in the direction of new and more productive activities, but this should be reflected in an increase of TFP and not in a human capital contribution. However, as we will see below, reallocation across economic sectors does not explain productivity changes. A further disaggregation is needed to capture the effects of reallocation considering gross instead of net flows. The technology parameter thus captures not only the state of technology, but also the allocation of resources. Consequently, the shifts of production factors toward more productive activities resulting from the trade liberalization should be reflected in the growth of TFP.

Changes in the quality of capital should also be considered in TFP. There are several types of capital. Our study uses the one estimated by Roldos

(1997), completed with information supplied by Rojas et al. (1997), which in turn is based on the capital composition between machinery and equipment, on the one hand, and construction, on the other. In that case, the technological parameter C is estimated from the following production function:

$$Y_t = C_t F(Q_t K_t, S_t L_t)$$

where Q is the index of physical capital. We thus have three alternative measures of TFP: A, B and C. It is also necessary to control for capacity utilization. Since this information is unavailable for as far back as the 1970s, we assume that capacity utilization is proportional to the unemployment rate, which allows us to estimate the following regression for each TFP measure:

$$\log(TFP_t) = \phi_0 + \phi_1 U_t + \mu_t$$

The residual of this regression is an orthogonal component of the unemployment TFP (U), which is used as a measure of capacity utilization or, more appropriately, TFP controlled by the business cycle. Given our estimates of A, B and C, we define A_u, B_u and C_u, respectively, as TFP corrected by capacity use.

Table 5.5 and Figures 5.6 and 5.7 show the results of all the total factor productivity estimates. Given the long-term perspective, the information is presented in decades. According to all the definitions, TFP growth was practically nil from the 1960s until 1980. During the 1960s, TFP was relatively constant, and in 1970 the economy started to show a marked decrease in TFP in order to recover in the early 1980s. It has grown steadily since then. TFP started to increase systematically from 1983 onwards, reaching an average of

Table 5.5 Total factor productivity growth (%)

		A	B	C	A_u	B_u	C_u
1960s	Average	0.84	–0.08	0.12	0.67	–0.31	–0.07
	Std. Dev.	3.19	3.62	3.61	3.08	3.56	3.63
1970s	Average	0.13	–0.83	–0.42	0.65	–0.03	0.13
	Std. Dev.	5.76	5.86	5.86	5.12	6.02	5.82
1980s	Average	0.28	–0.61	–0.87	–0.27	–1.33	–1.46
	Std. Dev.	5.26	4.93	5.26	3.54	3.74	3.37
1990s	Average	3.18	2.55	1.28	2.67	1.86	0.77
	Std. Dev.	2.97	3.47	3.29	2.53	2.98	2.95

Source: Authors' calculations. See text for more details.

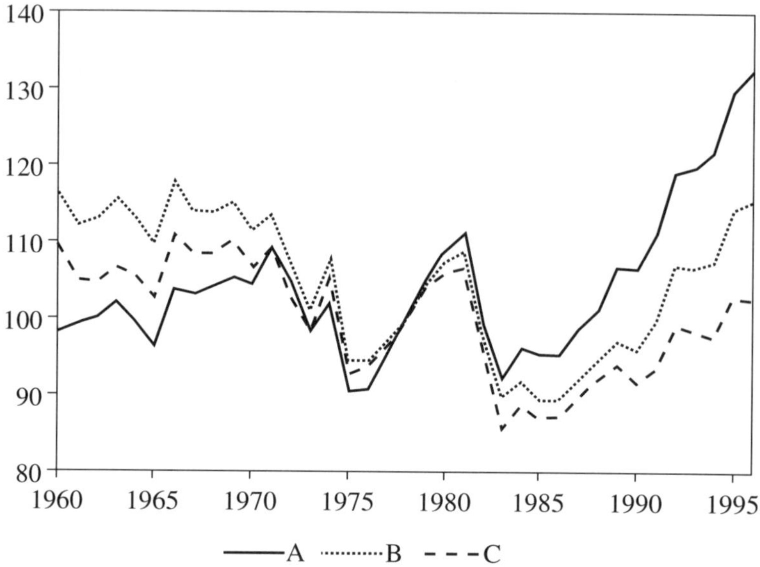

Notes:
A: TFP without adjustments.
B: TFP adjusted for labour quality.
C: TFP adjusted for labour and capital quality.

Figure 5.6 Total factor productivity (1978 = 100)

3.2 per cent for *A*, the most traditional measure, during the 1990s. These results are relatively consistent with the trend in labour productivity discussed above.

It is interesting to note that Chile shows three major reductions in TFP, which revert all the gains obtained in previous years. These events occurred in 1965, 1973–75 and 1983–86. Since then, the sustained TFP growth has been unprecedented. In general, when adjusting per factor quality, the average growth of TFP decreases. A similar effect is observed when controlling for capacity utilization, especially in the 1980s and 1990s.

Long-term Determinants of Growth and Inequality

Here we examine how economic conditions have affected the growth of TFP and inequality. Regression models are estimated for the first difference (log) of the total factor productivity and the contribution of capital to growth. This way we avoid unitary roots problems. To study wage inequality, we examine its level with the following model:

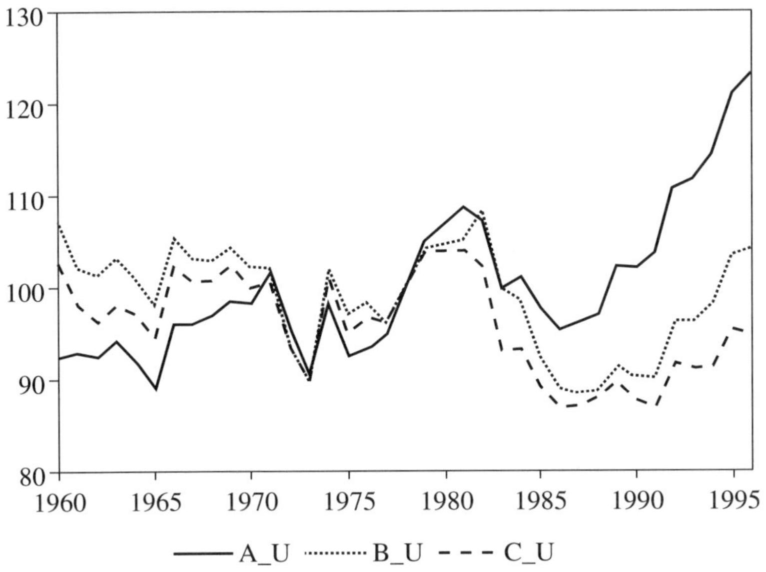

Notes: A, B and C are the same as in Figure 5.6, but adjusted by unemployment to control for capacity utilization.

Figure 5.7 Total factor productivity adjusted for unemployment

$$Y_t = \beta_0 + \beta_1 X_t + \mu_t$$

where *X* is a group of regressors. *Y* corresponds to two variables: the log of the difference in total factor productivity and inequality. Among the explanatory variables we include the trade liberalization index, the black-market premium as an indicator of the degree of control of the exchange rate and capitals flows,[12] the terms of trade as an indicator of world economic conditions,[13] the fiscal surplus and the share of government expenditures with respect to GDP. We also included variables that turned out to be insignificant, such as inflation, unemployment rate of Gran Santiago and the credit-to-GDP ratio corresponding to the credit of the banking system (excluding the Central Bank) and the non-banking private sector. The latter variable measures financial depth.

Figures 5.8, 5.9 and 5.10 show the changes in TFP and the contribution of capital and labour to growth. Figure 5.11 shows the evolution of two inequality measures. The first corresponds to the difference in log hourly wages of the 90th percentile with respect to the 10th percentile.[14] The second variable measures the variance of the logarithm of the hourly wage. Both indicators show a similar behaviour.

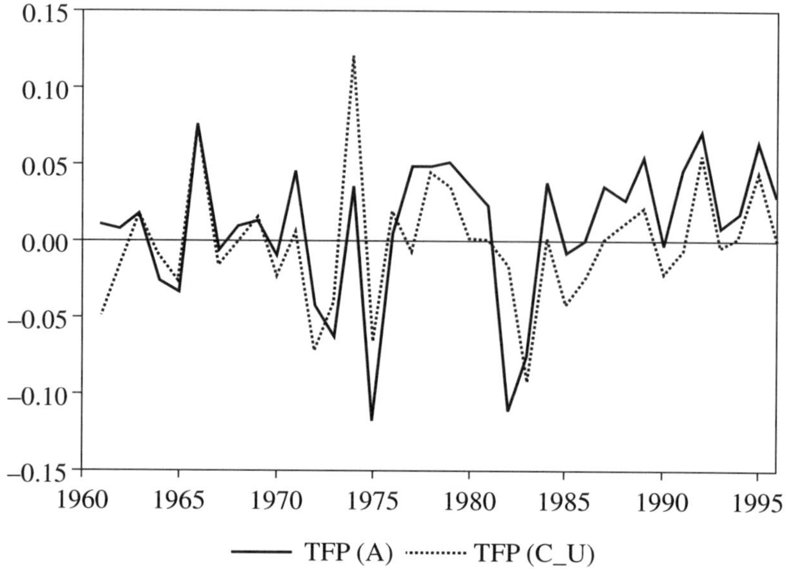

Figure 5.8 *Changes in the TFP (log differences)*

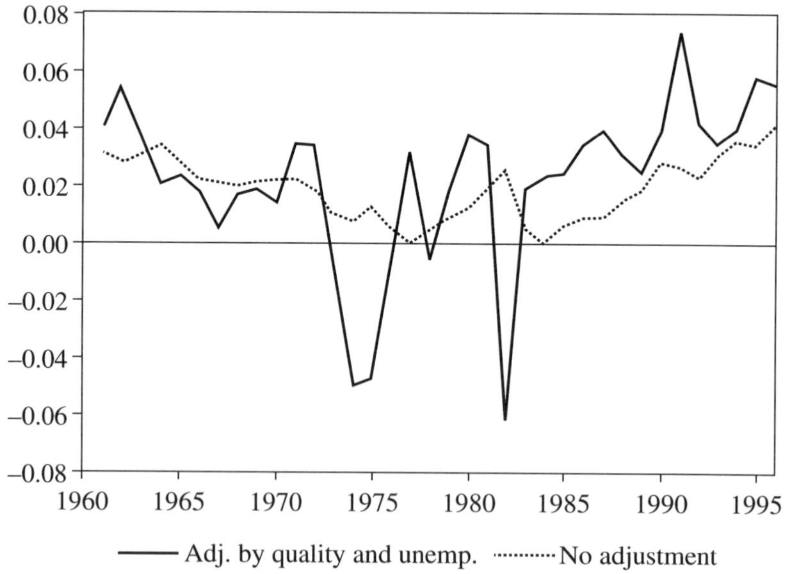

Figure 5.9 *Contribution of capital to growth ($\alpha \times$ percentage change in capital)*

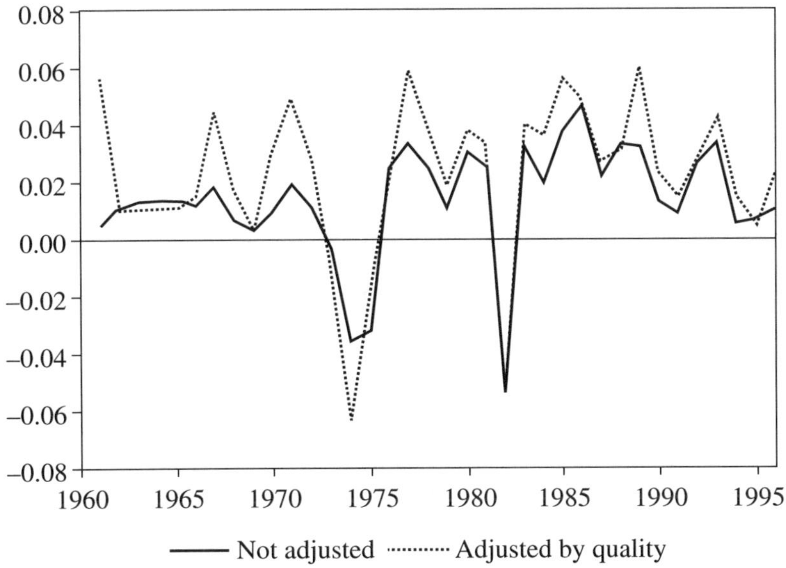

Figure 5.10 *Contribution of labour to growth ((1 – α) × percentage change in labour)*

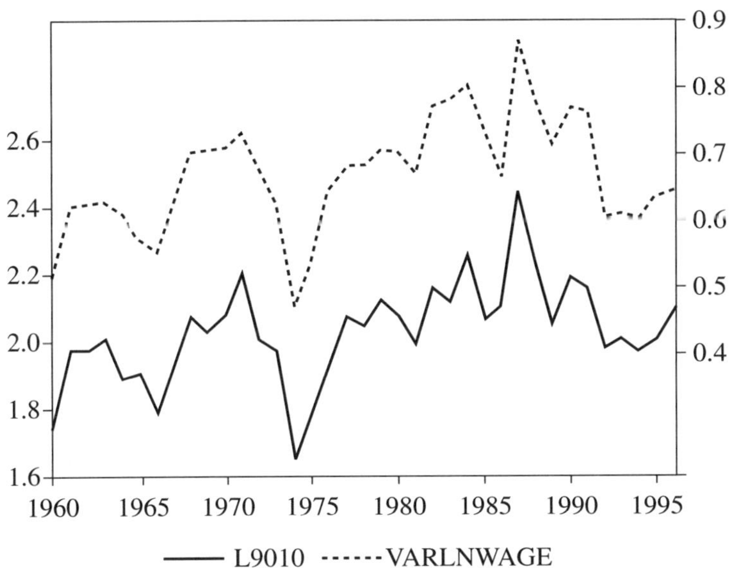

Figure 5.11 *Wage inequality*

We use two measures of the TFP variable: *A*, which does not consider adjustments for factor quality or capacity utilization, and C_u, which does consider these adjustments (see Figure 5.8). The annual contribution of capital is presented in Figure 5.9. As can be expected, the TFP measure without adjustments is more stable, in its assumption that capital is permanently used at full capacity. The contribution of labour and human capital (labour adjustment for education) is presented in Figure 5.10. A large part of the fluctuations are more in employment than in education, and both variables show a similar behaviour.[15]

Results are sensitive to periodization. In particular, the 1972–75 period is characterized by high inflation, a significant reduction in output, and inequality. For this reason we examine three periods. The entire 1960–96 period, the 1972–75 period (which is excluded in some regressions), and the 1976–96 period. Even when results change, the conclusions are relatively solid.

The TFP results are presented in Table 5.6. The first three columns show the results without adjustments for quality and factor utilization, the other columns take account of those adjustments. The regressions, as a function of the period and variable used, produce an adjustment of between 28 and 41 per cent of the TFP variance.[16]

In most TFP estimates, the trade liberalization index shows a positive and significant sign, which means that economic opening had a positive effect on productivity growth. When TFP is adjusted for quality and capacity utilization, the effect of the opening is still positive but weak, except when examining the 1976–96 period. In that case, the parameter is not statistically different from zero. These results suggest that the determining factor in TFP growth is the shift from a closed economy to an open one, rather than the existing tariff level. Indeed, the liberalization index changed from levels 2–5 (closed economy, 1960–73) to 17–20 (open economy, 1970–96). It is also difficult to identify effects that are associated with small changes in the degree of opening. Nevertheless, we can conclude that, as a result of the opening, technological progress accelerated and the allocation of resources improved.

On the other hand, inflation[17] seems to be negatively correlated with TFP growth when it is not adjusted for quality and capacity utilization. This result varies across the various periods. When we exclude the 1972–75 period, inflation does not seem to have a significant relation with TFP growth, even though its estimated parameter is negative. During 1976–96, inflation shows a significant and weak effect on TFP growth. In this period we may have a causality problem, though, as the rapid economic growth allowed for non-inflationary wage increases. In addition, the exchange rate appreciated, allowing a significant drop in inflation. This is of particular relevance to the 1990s. After adjustment of TFP, no relation is observed between inflation and

*Table 5.6 Determinants of total factor productivity growth**

Change in dependent variable	**TFP (A) [1]**	**TFP (A)** [2]**	**TFP (A)*** [3]**	**TFP (C_u) [4]**	**TFP (C_u)** [5]**	**TFP (C_u)*** [6]**
Liberalization index	0.556	0.652	–0.421	0.318	0.422	0.315
	(2.77)	(3.30)	(–0.60)	(1.67)	(2.52)	(0.573)
Inflation	–0.023	–0.028	0.091	0.004	0.001	0.006
	(–2.81)	(–1.12)	(–1.85)	(0.56)	(0.07)	(0.15)
Black-market premium	0.003	0.020	–0.074	–0.625	0.017	–0.159
	(0.67)	(1.36)	(–0.40)	(–1.44)	(1.39)	(–1.12)
Credit/GDP	–0.184	–0.193	–0.239	–0.118	–0.111	–0.082
	(–2.73)	(–3.00)	(–2.39)	(–1.85)	(–2.05)	(–1.05)
Change in exchange terms	0.073	0.071	0.070	0.082	0.114	0.036
	(1.43)	(1.19)	(0.74)	(1.68)	(2.26)	(0.49)
R^2	0.36	0.32	0.41	0.28	0.28	0.36
No. Obs.	36	32	21	36	32	21
DW	2.35	2.13	2.20	2.70	2.59	2.99

Notes:
t-statistics in parentheses.
* Change in the TFP log. A: without corrections for factor quality. C_u: corrects for quality and capacity utilization.
** Sample: 1960–71, 1976–96
*** Sample: 1976–96

TFP. The evidence shows a certain inverse relation – though not a very robust one – between inflation and TFP growth.[18]

The black-market premium does not seem to have an effect on TFP growth, and the terms of trade have a marginal effect. In most regressions, improvements in the terms of trade have a positive impact on TFP growth, but the effect is not significant. Interestingly, the credit/GDP variable is negatively correlated with TFP growth. This evidence somehow contradicts the relation between financial development and growth. Still, these results are consistent with those of De Gregorio and Guidotti (1995), which indicate that a strong expansion of credit and a significant drop in economic activity was observed during the debt crisis in Latin America. This evidence is related to financial crises in the context of poorly regulated financial markets, rather than to the sector's positive effects on growth.[19] In fact, except for the period of credit expansion and collapse (1979–83), this variable is statistically insignificant.

The determinants of inequality from a macro perspective are presented in Table 5.7. When looking at the complete sample, we can observe that inflation is inversely correlated with inequality. This is a counterintuitive result that has been documented previously by Marcel and Solimano (1994). The results depend on the period examined. Indeed, if we exclude the period 1972–75, inflation does not show a statistically significant effect on inequality.[20] The black-market premium in most specifications affects inequality negatively. Unemployment affects wage inequality negatively. In periods of high unemployment, wage dispersion also increases. This is not because the unemployed do not receive an income, but because inequality increases among occupied workers. Since productivity and unemployment are negatively correlated, these results can be interpreted as an effect of productivity on inequality. Regression [5] in Table 5.7 includes both variables and in consequence unemployment stops being significant. In general, these results show that wage inequality decreases at high income levels.

There is a large literature on the effects of liberalization on inequality. The macroeconomic evidence indicates negative and significant effects. However, we should not forget that inequality is affected by productivity and unemployment, variables that in turn are also affected by the degree of opening. Thus, we also need to examine the combined effects of these variables. A simple way of doing this is to take one equation and exclude those variables affected by trade liberalization, particularly TFP growth, and then examine the variable's coefficient. Taking equation [1] of Table 5.7 and excluding unemployment, which can be a proxy of TFP and is positively correlated to the liberalization index, we obtain a coefficient of 0.56 ($t = 3.5$) for 1960–96. For the period that excludes the years 1972–75 we obtain a coefficient of 0.75 ($t = 3.5$), and for 1976–79 a coefficient of 1.1 ($t = 0.9$). Consequently, the net effect for the entire period is a growth in inequality as a consequence of

Table 5.7 Determinants of wage inequality

Dependent variable:	VARLNWAGE	VARLNWAGE	VARLNWAGE	VARLNWAGE	L9010	L9010	L9010	L9010
Sample years:	60–96	6(–71, 76–96	60–71, 76–96	76–96	60–96	60–71, 76–96	60–71, 16–96	76–96
	[1]	[2]	[3]	[4]	[5]	[6]	[7]	[8]
Liberalization index	0.349	0.507	0.533	1.341	1.314	1.247	1.617	2.660
	(1.90)	(2.33)	(2.64)	(1.82)	(3.02)	(4.06)	(4.87)	(3.22)
Inflation	–0.048	–0.016			–0.093	–0.093	–0.065	–0.084
	(–4.06)	(–0.36)			(–4.27)	(–4.33)	(–0.90)	(–0.79)
Black-market premium	0.025	0.052	0.052	0.341	0.044	0.044	0.121	–0.189
	(3.53)	(2.35)	(2.43)	(1.15)	(3.52)	(3.61)	(3.30)	(–0.39)
Unemployment	0.758	0.705	0.664	0.622	–0.157			
	(3.02)	(2.60)	(2.73)	(1.55)	(–0.22)			
Total factor Pty.*					–0.577	–0.516	–0.530	–0.828
					(–1.62)	(–2.35)	(–2.40)	(–2.74)
R^2	0.50	0.44	0.43	0.36	0.51	0.50	0.48	0.42
n	37	33	33	21	37	37	33	21
D.W.	1.31	1.22	1.21	1.57	1.82	1.81	1.68	1.97

Notes:
t-statistics in parentheses.
* Total factor productivity without corrections: *A*.

liberalization. What makes the difference, though, is the change experienced from the 1960s up to the mid-1970s in relation to the change that occurred from the mid-1970s up to the 1990s. There was indeed a great leap in the liberalization index and an average reduction in wage inequality, which could be the joint result of reforms implemented and transformations that took place in the 1970s. We will now give a more detailed analysis of these effects at the microeconomic level.

5.4 TRADE OPENING AND MICROECONOMIC EFFECTS

This section examines the effects of trade opening on the structure of the labour market. The analysis allows an identification of the main changes in participation, employment, unemployment and wage structure, and their impact on welfare as measured by indicators of inequality and poverty. The effects associated with liberalization are analysed through simulation exercises that allow us to examine the impact of the opening process. We do this for two periods. First, based on the estimates of a trade liberalization index (see Figure 5.2), we simulate the effect of liberalization for 1974–81. A second set of simulations compares 1978 (before the opening) and 1981 (after the opening). In this second stage, we estimate the impact of liberalization using data from the EOUCH (Employment and Unemployment Survey for Gran Santiago of the Universidad de Chile) survey for the period 1965–90. In all exercises, we simulate separately the effects associated with the changes in labour participation, employment, unemployment and wages. We also include simulations of the cumulative effects. The entire section uses information from EOUCH data.[21] The survey data are only for the metropolitan area, since this sample provides the information needed to examine the impact of liberalization.[22]

Poverty and Inequality from a Long-term Perspective

Figure 5.12 offers the long-term trend in the poverty incidence and poverty gap. These indicators are constructed based on per capita income and the official poverty line currently used in the country. As can be expected, poverty indicators have shown a countercyclical behaviour for the last 40 years. Poverty levels rose significantly during the periods of economic expansion (1973–76 and 1982–86) and dropped during the periods of economic crisis. The considerable drop observed during 1987–97 is particularly striking.

Figure 5.13 shows the behaviour of the Gini coefficient for the same periods. When looking at the early 1960s and 1990s, we see relatively similar inequality levels with a Gini coefficient above 0.50 and below 0.55, respec-

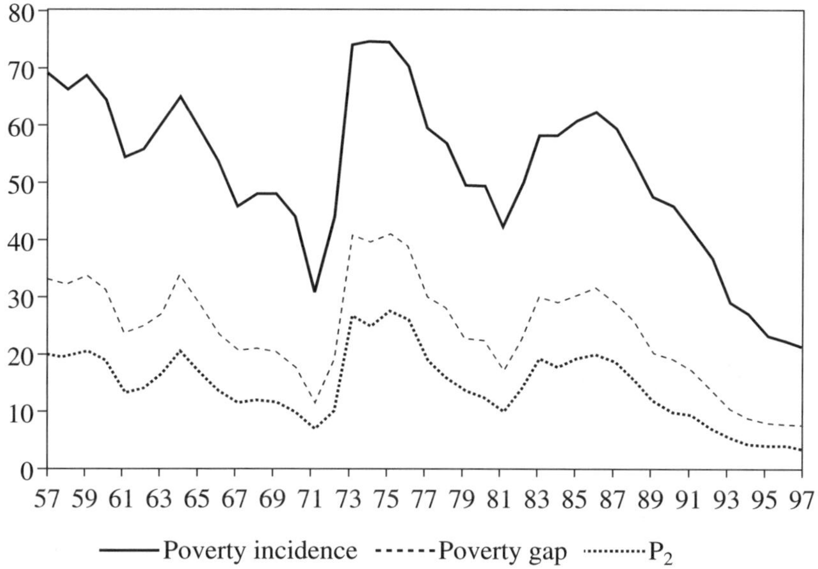

Source: Economics Department, Universidad de Chile.

Figure 5.12 Poverty in Gran Santiago, 1957–97 (poverty line, 1994 = 30100)

tively. Still, it is possible to observe significant variations in the inequality levels during the examined period. For 1975 we observe the lowest inequality of per capita household income, whereas in 1988 inequality reached an all-time high with a Gini coefficient of 0.65. From that year onwards we can observe a decreasing trend in inequality which 'stabilizes' in the 1990s. When comparing 1978 and 1981 – years that will be used to examine the impact of the trade opening – we see an increase in the inequality indicators and a drop in the poverty indicators.

Methodology

The simulation exercises that explain the changes in inequality and poverty are associated with changes in the wage and employment structure. This is why – based on the available information – different occupational categories were defined as a function of workers' educational levels, gender and economic sector of occupation. We first defined six types of workers, represented by the letter i, according to gender and education,[23] subdivided into primary (up to 8 school years), secondary (9 to 12 school years) and higher[24] (13 or

Source: Economics Department, Universidad de Chile.

Figure 5.13 Gini coefficient of per capita household income in Gran Santiago, 1957–97

more school years). This categorization allows a further definition of the following occupational categories: men with primary education; men with secondary education; men with higher education; women with primary education; women with secondary education; and women with higher education.

Once workers were classified, the following economic segments were defined: manufacturing industry, construction, personal and household services, community and social services, and others. The grouping of economic sectors in these categories can be justified for three reasons. First, we needed a minimum of observations for each category. Second, we defined groups so as to approximate tradable and non-tradable sectors. Due to the small number of observations for agriculture and mining we decided to include this as part of non-tradables. Further, because the sample is for the metropolitan area we chose to take manufacturing as a separate group (tradables), since it is the area's most important sector. The third group comprises the remaining sectors. Finally, this grouping yields 18 cells that define the structure of participation, unemployment, wages and employment of the metropolitan area, in other words with six types of workers per economic sector.

Measuring the Impact of Liberalization

To quantify the effect of liberalization from a parametric perspective, we estimated four different models according to the four previously mentioned economic variables – wages, employment, unemployment and participation.[25] These specifications do not come from any behavioural or structural model and should therefore be interpreted as correlation models.

(i) Wage equation

$$Ln(w_{ijt}) = \alpha_1 + \alpha_2 Age_{ijt} + \alpha_3 Age_{ijt}{}^2 + \alpha_4 Experience_{ijt} \\ + \alpha_5 Dum\_Lib + \alpha_6 Dum\_82:84 + \mu_1$$

(ii) Employment equation

$$Employment_{ijt} = \beta_1 + \beta_2 Employment_{ijt-1} + \beta_3 Age_{ijt} + \beta_4 Age^2_{ijt} \\ + \beta_5 Experience_{ijt} + \beta_6 Dum\_Lib + \beta_7 Dum\_82:84 + \mu_2$$

(iii) Unemployment equation

$$Unemployment_{it} = \phi_1 + \phi_2 Unemployment_{it-1} + \phi_3 Age_{it} + \phi_4 Age^2_{it} + \\ \phi_5 Experience_{it} + \phi_6 Dum\_Lib + \phi_7 Dum\_82:84 + \\ \phi_8 Ln(w_{s1,t}) + \phi_9 Ln(w_{s2,t}) + \phi_{10} Ln(w_{s3,t}) + \phi_{11} Ln(w_{it}) + \mu_3$$

(iv) Participation equation

$$Partici_{it} = \lambda_1 + \lambda_2 Partici_{it-1} + \lambda_3 Age_{it} + \lambda_4 Age^2_{it} + \lambda_5 Experience_{it} + \\ \lambda_6 Dum\_Lib + \lambda_7 Dum\_82:84 + \lambda_8 Ln(w_{s1,t}) + \lambda_9 Ln(w_{s2,t}) + \\ \lambda_{10} Ln(w_{s3,t}) + \lambda_{11} Ln(w_{it}) + \mu_4$$

The *Dum_Lib* variable represents a dummy for the effect of trade liberalization. Based on the liberalization index (see Figure 5.2), this variable takes the value of 1 for the period between 1974 and 1979. The variable *Dum_82:84* takes the value of 1 between 1982 and 1984, thus attempting to capture the crucial effect the world crisis of the early 1980s had on Chile.[26] In specifications (iii) and (iv) we see the variables $Ln(w_{s1,t})$, $Ln(w_{s2,t})$, $Ln(w_{s3,t})$ and $Ln(w_{it})$. The first three represent the natural logarithm of the average wage for each of the economic sectors (manufacturing, construction and services and the rest). The fourth represents the natural logarithm of the average wage per type of worker; this variable is constructed on the basis of the three educational categories (primary, secondary and higher education) by gender.

Table 5.8 Liberalization effect on labour market

Type I	Type II	Original 1981				Liberalization 1974–79			
		Wages	Empl.	Unempl.	Particip.	Wages	Empl.	Unempl.	Particip.
Ho-Pri-Ma	**Ho-Pri**	88.4	29%	10%	83%	104.0	29%	6%	83%
Ho-Sec-Ma	**Ho-Sec**	206.1	26%	9%	71%	223.8	27%	7%	70%
Ho-Su-Ma	**Ho-Su**	628.3	16%	4%	76%	605.4	17%	3%	74%
Mu-Pri-Ma	**Mu-Pri**	57.0	22%	9%	34%	66.9	23%	4%	36%
Mu-Sec-Ma	**Mu-Sec**	133.3	28%	14%	34%	172.7	28%	10%	35%
Mu-Su-Ma	**Mu-Su**	293.7	7%	4%	55%	423.3	8%	1%	54%
Ho-Pri-CS		98.4	37%			117.3	37%		
Ho-Sec-CS		137.0	22%			165.5	21%		
Ho-Su-CS		413.1	39%			583.7	35%		
Mu-Pri-CS		50.8	61%			61.2	62%		
Mu-Sec-CS		80.0	33%			101.2	32%		
Mu-Su-CS		216.1	71%			282.0	70%		
Ho-Pri-Re		22.9	34%			30.3	32%		
Ho-Sec-Re		90.6	53%			102.0	52%		
Ho-Su-Re		343.7	44%			386.6	43%		
Mu-Pri-Re		2.6	17%			3.1	15%		
Mu-Sec-Re		18.0	39%			19.8	41%		
Mu-Su-Re		46.3	23%			63.5	20%		

Notes:

1. The columns corresponding to the first scenario show the value of the wage, employment, unemployment and participation variables if we deduct the effect of trade liberalization from the observed situation of 1981. The liberalization effect refers to the period 1974–79. Counterfactual values are obtained from the parameters linked to dummy variable *Dum_Lib* in each of the regressions presented in Section 5.4.
2. Column 'Type I' shows the labour market categories (cells) corresponding to the wage and employment variables, whereas Type II refers to the unemployment and participation variables. Ho = men, Mu = women, Pri = primary education, Sec = secondary education, Su = higher education, Ma = manufacturing, CS = construction and services, Re = other sectors.
3. Monthly wages are expressed in thousands of pesos of 1996.

The subscripts used in the equations should be interpreted as follows: the use of $j = 1, 2, 3$ is related to the various economic sectors; $i = 1, 2, 3, 4, 5, 6$ correspond to the six different worker types; and $t = 65, 66, \ldots, 96$ correspond to the different years used. This way we obtain the liberalization effect conditioned for the various sectors and/or worker types, for which reason we only make six estimates for specifications (iii) and (iv).

Once the effect of trade liberalization is found,[27] it becomes possible to correct the vectors that describe our economy by simulating what the value on monthly wages and on employment, unemployment and participation rates would have been had the trade liberalization process not taken place. Table 5.8 shows the original vectors together with the counterfactual scenario, such that one can observe the direction of change per sector and per worker type of the different variables as estimated by the simulation exercise.

Microsimulations

For the simulations we classified the sample into six demographic groups and three economic segments. To this end we constructed socio-demographic cells in order to capture differences in participation, unemployment, employment and wages between different types of workers. This allows for a more accurate characterization of the labour market. Following the methodology set out in Chapter 2, we also constructed matrices and vectors that summarize the variables to be simulated. We have matrices for wages and employment per worker type and economic segment[28] and vectors for the unemployment and participation rates.[29] Once this was done for the two years of the study, we constructed alternative matrices and vectors for the same variables. These provide a counterfactual scenario with estimates of the variables if trade liberalization had not taken place.

The simulation process consisted of four stages.[30] In each, we simulated the effects on the poverty and inequality indicators of a change in each of the observed variables (unemployment or participation vectors, or wage or employment matrices) of the final year versus an alternative specification. This alternative specification has two possible origins: it is either a structure observed at a previous point in time, possibly the structure observed before the opening process started, or a counterfactual estimate to which the present structure would belong had the opening not taken place. The exercises were carried out separately (individually) and cumulatively. In order to generate confidence intervals for the inequality and poverty coefficients, we repeated each simulation 100 times. This allowed us to evaluate whether the estimated changes resulting from liberalization were statistically significant.

Impact of the First Liberalization Phase (1974–81)

We now present the results of the counterfactual analysis, examining what would have happened with income inequality and poverty had there been no opening. In other words, the impact of trade liberalization on welfare is identified, measured by poverty and inequality. It is important to note that we compare the pre-liberalization situation (1974 and 1978) to the situation one year after the liberalization. We selected 1981, because that year corresponds to a post-liberalization situation and is prior to the 1982–83 recession.

The microsimulations are done in two steps. First, we execute the simulations using the labour market structure observed in 1974 and 1978 with respect to the situation observed in 1981. This scenario assumes that all the changes observed between those years are due to the effect of the opening. In each exercise, the various 'phases' (participation, employment, unemployment and wages) are modelled separately as well as cumulatively. The simulation results are presented in Tables 5.9–5.12. We then proceed to use the regression methodology described above so as to identify the impact of liberalization.[31] The estimated impact of liberalization on the relevant parameters is 'deducted' from the observed value in 1981. Subsequently, we repeat the simulations as described above. These results for six simulations are presented in Tables 5.13 and 5.14. Before reporting the results of these microsimulations, it is necessary to shed light on some methodological procedures. The measures of poverty and inequality are estimated using the per capita income of individuals belonging to a household. The total household income is divided by the number of members in the household to obtain a per capita income, which is assigned to each household member.[32]

Before-and-after simulations

Tables 5.9 and 5.10 show the results of the simulations between 1978 and 1981, allocating the whole effect observed in 1981 as if it was entirely a product of trade liberalization. The first column shows poverty and inequality indicators. Among the first we include the poverty incidence, the poverty gap and the number of poor (unexpanded sample). Two inequality measures are also included: Gini coefficient and quintile ratio (Q5/Q1). The second and third columns show the previously described indicators using the per capita income effective in 1978 (before the opening) and 1981 (after the opening), respectively. Each indicator is estimated with its corresponding confidence interval based on 100 repetitions.[33] Columns 4–8 show the results of the different simulation phases. Column 4 shows the simulation results of phase 1, i.e. how inequality and poverty are affected when the participation structure of 1978 is applied to 1981. Column 5 shows the simulation of phase 2, i.e. the effect on welfare of imposing the unemployment structure of 1978 on

Table 5.9 'Before-and-after' microsimulations, 1978–81: separate effects

	Inequality and poverty measures	YPC observed 1978	YPC observed 1981	Phase 1	Phase 2	Phase 3	Phase 4a	Phase 4b
1.	**Gini Coefficient**	**0.5324**	**0.5406**	**0.5420**	**0.5450**	**0.5413**	**0.5365**	**0.5386**
				0.5390 0.5459	0.5426 0.5468	0.5402 0.5423		
2.	**Ratio Q5/Q1**	**15.8896**	**15.8054**	**16.0007**	**16.3526**	**15.8961**	**16.0256**	**16.5600**
				15.6937 16.2586	15.9701 16.6323	15.7993 15.9906		
3.	**Poverty Incidence**	**0.6333**	**0.4745**	**0.4895**	**0.4802**	**0.4743**	**0.4587**	**0.5616**
				0.4854 0.4946	0.4749 0.4853	0.4724 0.4755		
4.	**Poverty Gap**	**0.3116**	**0.1949**	**0.2044**	**0.2002**	**0.1956**	**0.1925**	**0.2639**
				0.2026 0.2072	0.1970 0.2032	0.1951 0.1961		
5.	**Number of Poor**	**8376**	**5584**	**5677**	**5533**	**5578**	**5398**	**6609**
				5614 5746	5458 5601	5556 5594		
6.	**Mean Income Q1**	**779**	**1148**	**1102**	**1114**	**1143**	**1140**	**868**
				1084 1117	1095 1137	1139 1147		
7.	**Mean Income Q2**	**1477**	**2161**	**2095**	**2128**	**2158**	**2193**	**1703**
				2076 2111	2100 2155	2154 2165		
8.	**Mean Income Q3**	**2301**	**3406**	**3304**	**3365**	**3406**	**3513**	**2750**
				3272 3328	3327 3396	3396 3416		
9.	**Mean Income Q4**	**4080**	**5673**	**5509**	**5643**	**5682**	**5934**	**4666**
				5449 5549	5597 5691	5661 5709		
10.	**Mean Income Q5**	**12380**	**18140**	**17630**	**18209**	**18169**	**18265**	**14374**
				17358 17811	18083 18319	18087 18276		

Table 5.10 'Before-and-after' microsimulations, 1978–81: cumulative effects

	Inequality and poverty measures	YPC observed 1978	YPC observed 1981	Phase 1 + 2	Phase 1, 2 + 3	Phase 1–3 + 4a	Phase 1–3 + 4b
1.	**Gini Coefficient**	**0.5324**	**0.5406**	**0.5471** 0.5431 0.5500	**0.5479** 0.5448 0.5516	**0.5433** 0.5395 0.5468	**0.5454** 0.5424 0.5489
2.	**Ratio Q5/Q1**	**15.8896**	**15.8054**	**16.6561** 16.3064 17.1118	**16.7283** 16.4396 17.1027	**16.9476** 16.4742 17.4746	**17.3225** 16.8965 17.7339
3.	**Poverty Incidence**	**0.6333**	**0.4745**	**0.4944** 0.4877 0.5009	**0.4952** 0.4896 0.5015	**0.4776** 0.4719 0.4856	**0.5765** 0.5728 0.5812
4.	**Poverty Gap**	**0.3116**	**0.1949**	**0.2096** 0.2071 0.2134	**0.2107** 0.2076 0.2138	**0.2068** 0.2032 0.2107	**0.2775** 0.2743 0.2812
5.	**Number of Poor**	**8376**	**5584**	**5611** 5537 5704	**5628** 5555 5730	**5421** 5335 5521	**6544** 6481 6617
6.	**Mean Income Q1**	**779**	**1148**	**1067** 1036 1088	**1062** 1040 1080	**1057** 1033 1085	**818** 796 835
7.	**Mean Income Q2**	**1477**	**2161**	**2064** 2027 2091	**2056** 2036 2081	**2095** 2063 2124	**1631** 1608 1655
8.	**Mean Income Q3**	**2301**	**3406**	**3267** 3230 3302	**3258** 3216 3291	**3372** 3334 3418	**2641** 2612 2675
9.	**Mean Income Q4**	**4080**	**5673**	**5486** 5425 5555	**5480** 5426 5539	**5744** 5693 5809	**4526** 4477 4558
10.	**Mean Income Q5**	**12380**	**18140**	**17770** 17490 18007	**17769** 17515 18021	**17915** 17681 18136	**14169** 14020 14327

Table 5.11 'Before-and-after' microsimulations, 1974–81: separate effects

	Inequality and poverty measures	YPC observed 1974	YPC observed 1981	Phase 1	Phase 2	Phase 3	Phase 4a	Phase 4b
1.	**Gini Coefficient**	**0.4583**	**0.5406**	**0.5377** 0.5348 0.5415	**0.5394** 0.5372 0.5413	**0.5430** 0.5415 0.5445	**0.5003**	**0.5235**
2.	**Ratio Q5/Q1**	**10.6831**	**15.8054**	**15.5841** 15.2740 15.8945	**15.7279** 15.5619 15.9137	**15.9429** 15.8694 16.0482	**12.8844**	**15.0581**
3.	**Poverty Incidence**	**0.7799**	**0.4745**	**0.4927** 0.4873 0.4985	**0.4765** 0.4738 0.4794	**0.4755** 0.4743 0.4771	**0.4022**	**0.6895**
4.	**Poverty Gap**	**0.4261**	**0.1949**	**0.2054** 0.2027 0.2076	**0.1966** 0.1950 0.1980	**0.1957** 0.1954 0.1960	**0.1486**	**0.3637**
5.	**Number of Poor**	**9193**	**5584**	**5728** 5657 5803	**5578** 5532 5624	**5591** 5576 5611	**4733**	**8115**
6.	**Mean Income Q1**	**573**	**1148**	**1100** 1086 1121	**1139** 1130 1150	**1145** 1141 1149	**1389**	**649**
7.	**Mean Income Q2**	**1057**	**2161**	**2088** 2071 2111	**2149** 2135 2162	**2156** 2151 2161	**2577**	**1247**
8.	**Mean Income Q3**	**1578**	**3406**	**3283** 3253 3317	**3391** 3370 3415	**3396** 3389 3405	**3963**	**1994**
9.	**Mean Income Q4**	**2513**	**5673**	**5411** 5363 5462	**5637** 5605 5672	**5650** 5636 5663	**6395**	**3312**
10.	**Mean Income Q5**	**6119**	**18140**	**17148** 16905 17433	**17921** 17762 18067	**18262** 18139 18385	**17894**	**9767**

Table 5.12 'Before-and-after' microsimulations, 1974–81: cumulative effects

	Inequality and poverty measures	YPC observed 1974	YPC observed 1981	Phase 1 + 2	Phase 1, 2 + 3	Phase 1–3 + 4a	Phase 1–3 + 4b
1.	**Gini Coefficient**	**0.4583**	**0.5406**	**0.5374** 0.5354 0.5400	**0.5389** 0.5368 0.5420	**0.4995** 0.4966 0.5024	**0.5236** 0.5209 0.5256
2.	**Ratio Q5/Q1**	**10.6831**	**15.8054**	**15.5626** 15.2866 15.8658	**15.6499** 15.2985 15.9108	**12.9419** 12.7395 13.1393	**14.9856** 14.7327 15.2134
3.	**Poverty Incidence**	**0.7799**	**0.4745**	**0.4952** 0.4936 0.4975	**0.4956** 0.4919 0.5001	**0.4210** 0.4173 0.4248	**0.7076** 0.7051 0.7114
4.	**Poverty Gap**	**0.4261**	**0.1949**	**0.2077** 0.2058 0.2095	**0.2083** 0.2066 0.2105	**0.1599** 0.1587 0.1613	**0.3767** 0.3751 0.3779
5.	**Number of Poor**	**9193**	**5584**	**5730** 5709 5770	**5745** 5686 5806	**4870** 4834 4912	**8190** 8150 8232
6.	**Mean Income Q1**	**573**	**1148**	**1091** 1075 1101	**1088** 1073 1101	**1308** 1297 1321	**625** 618 631
7.	**Mean Income Q2**	**1057**	**2161**	**2072** 2058 2090	**2067** 2052 2085	**2482** 2469 2498	**1200** 1195 1206
8.	**Mean Income Q3**	**1578**	**3406**	**3263** 3253 3276	**3255** 3245 3268	**3788** 3757 3812	**1912** 1897 1930
9.	**Mean Income Q4**	**2513**	**5673**	**5360** 5328 5402	**5355** 5303 5393	**6059** 6028 6082	**3152** 3126 3169
10.	**Mean Income Q5**	**6119**	**18140**	**16972** 16815 17143	**17032** 16841 17266	**16933** 16713 17145	**9365** 9304 9478

Table 5.13 'With-and-without' counterfactual simulation, 1981: separate effects

	Inequality and poverty measures	YPC observed 1981	Phase 1	Phase 2	Phase 3	Phase 4a	Phase 4b
1.	**Gini Coefficient**	**0.5406**	**0.5386** 0.5368 0.5399	**0.5361** 0.5343 0.5373	**0.5496** 0.5481 0.5512	**0.5713**	**0.5713**
2.	**Ratio Q5/Q1**	**15.8054**	**15.6212** 15.4881 15.7057	**15.3989** 15.1478 15.6370	**16.4073** 16.2963 16.5535	**22.4453**	**22.4318**
3.	**Poverty Incidence**	**0.4745**	**0.4762** 0.4744 0.4779	**0.4640** 0.4608 0.4668	**0.4748** 0.4733 0.4762	**0.5714**	**0.5714**
4.	**Poverty Gap**	**0.1949**	**0.1957** 0.1949 0.1965	**0.1876** 0.1857 0.1894	**0.1958** 0.1954 0.1964	**0.2834**	**0.2827**
5.	**Number of Poor**	**5584**	**5602** 5582 5621	**5515** 5470 5562	**5573** 5555 5590	**6725**	**6725**
6.	**Mean Income Q1**	**1148**	**1146** 1143 1149	**1182** 1166 1197	**1143** 1139 1149	**695**	**697**
7.	**Mean Income Q2**	**2161**	**2154** 2147 2163	**2219** 2209 2233	**2155** 2147 2161	**1639**	**1643**
8.	**Mean Income Q3**	**3406**	**3393** 3381 3402	**3480** 3459 3499	**3401** 3393 3408	**2668**	**2675**
9.	**Mean Income Q4**	**5673**	**5635** 5616 5653	**5763** 5730 5790	**5658** 5642 5671	**4623**	**4632**
10.	**Mean Income Q5**	**18140**	**17899** 17747 17998	**18196** 18107 18289	**18757** 18653 18893	**15607**	**15638**

Table 5.14 'With-and-without' counterfactual simulation, 1981: cumulative effects

	Inequality and poverty measures	YPC observed 1981	Phase 1 + 2	Phase 1, 2 + 3	Phase 1–3 + 4a	Phase 1–3 + 4b
1.	**Gini Coefficient**	**0.5406**	**0.5343**	**0.5438**	**0.5838**	**0.5834**
			0.5322 0.5356	0.5414 0.5465	0.5791 0.5875	0.5789 0.5868
2.	**Ratio Q5/Q1**	**15.8054**	**15.2633**	**15.9013**	**23.3418**	**23.3678**
			15.0694 15.4028	15.6470 16.0782	22.76803 23.7960	22.8948 23.9788
3.	**Poverty Incidence**	**0.4745**	**0.4639**	**0.4640**	**0.5698**	**0.5695**
			0.4598 0.4672	0.4603 0.4663	0.5668 0.5739	0.5658 0.5721
4.	**Poverty Gap**	**0.1949**	**0.1875**	**0.1887**	**0.2808**	**0.2807**
			0.1853 0.1891	0.1875 0.1904	0.2794 0.2823	0.2791 0.2822
5.	**Number of Poor**	**5584**	**5506**	**5494**	**6747**	**6742**
			5455 5552	5444 5520	6696 6785	6692 6769
6.	**Mean Income Q1**	**1148**	**1181**	**1174**	**705**	**705**
			1171 1194	1162 1184	697 713	696 714
7.	**Mean Income Q2**	**2161**	**2219**	**2211**	**1651**	**1652**
			2204 2240	2196 2226	1638 1666	1639 1666
8.	**Mean Income Q3**	**3406**	**3476**	**3470**	**2688**	**2689**
			3455 3495	3454 3499	2674 2703	2670 2703
9.	**Mean Income Q4**	**5673**	**5729**	**5731**	**4643**	**4662**
			5688 5773	5709 5760	4617 4669	4631 4699
10.	**Mean Income Q5**	**18140**	**18029**	**18670**	**16461**	**16472**
			17920 18105	18465 18836	16234 16748	16163 16775

1981. Column 6, phase 3, models the impact of employment resulting from liberalization.[34] The last two columns show the simulation corresponding to phase 4, which models the situation that would have taken place when imposing the wage structure of 1978 on 1981. This phase is divided into two stages: modelling changes in distribution or wage structure (phase 4a) and level (phase 4b). In addition, each simulation phase models a closing of the economy. Table 5.10 shows the same simulation exercises when done cumulatively.

Table 5.9 shows that there were no statistically significant changes in income distribution between 1978 and 1981. In fact, the Gini coefficient and the quintile ratio remain relatively stable between those two years, but there is a significant reduction in the percentage of individuals classified as poor. At the same time, the degree of poverty as measured by the poverty gap fell between 1978 and 1981.

The simulation exercises present other interesting results. The evidence indicates that the impact on the structure of labour participation, unemployment and employment had no significant effect on inequality and poverty. However, the results of phase 4b show that, had the economy not been liberalized, the effects of the changes in wage structure would have resulted in similar levels of inequality but not in significant reductions of poverty. Indeed, the inequality indicators do not change statistically, but poverty without liberalization would not have dropped the way it actually did with the liberalization. This suggests an important effect of the opening on the real wages level and not on their distribution, given that phase 4a linked to the structure itself produced similar indicators to those observed after liberalization.

Table 5.10 shows the results of the simulation for 1978–81, assuming that the entire effect observed in 1981 is a product of the trade liberalization. In contrast to the exercises shown in Table 5.9, this table shows the cumulative effect of the different phases.

In general, we can see that the Gini coefficient remains relatively stable, and only from the joint phases of the cumulative simulation exercises can we identify a statistically significant change. In particular, we see that the trade liberalization reduced inequality indicators marginally. This effect of less inequality is clearer in the quintile ratio: the cumulative effects indicate that if the opening had not taken place, the 1981 quintile ratio would have been 17.3, compared to 15.8 corresponding to the effective post-liberalization figures. Liberalization helped to alleviate poverty. We see that each phase, separately and jointly, tends to show a significant impact on the poverty indicators. It follows that, had there been no liberalization, the levels and degree of poverty in Chile would have been higher than those observed. In other words, the cumulative effects show that between 1978 and 1981 (without liberalization) poverty would only have been reduced from 63.3 per cent in 1978 to 57.7 per cent in 1981. This percentage is in significant contrast with the 47.5 per cent of poverty effectively observed in 1981, after the liberalization process.

Tables 5.11 and 5.12 show the same information as the previous tables, simulating the effects of the opening between 1974 and 1981. As we mentioned before, Figure 5.2 suggests that the level of opening was similar between 1974 and 1978, so it is interesting to examine the impact of the opening assuming 1974 to be a pre-liberalization year. Just as in the previous exercises, for analytical purposes 1981 is considered as a year to which the entire impact of liberalization can be attributed. Table 5.12 shows an increase in inequality levels when examining the effective situation between 1974 and 1981. The Gini coefficient increases substantially, from 0.46 in 1974 to 0.54 in 1981. The poverty incidence also drops in this period by 30 percentage points.

The simulation exercises on changes in participation, employment and unemployment do not show statistically significant changes in the inequality and poverty indicators.[35] Wage structure and levels do show important changes. Between 1974 and 1981, liberalization drove up inequality levels significantly. Phase 4a shows that, in the absence of liberalization, the Gini coefficient and the quintile ratio would have been 0.50 and 12.9, respectively. These figures are statistically significantly lower than those effective in 1981. Meanwhile, poverty would have reached a rate equivalent to 40 per cent of the population, and the gap would have reached about 15 per cent. These poverty indicators are lower than the effective ones, which correspond to 47 and 19 per cent, respectively. Simulation 4b shows that liberalization has a greater effect in reducing poverty levels and raising inequality levels. The Gini coefficient and the quintile ratio drop in the situation without liberalization, such that the poverty rate and poverty gap would have reached levels significantly higher that those observed after the opening.

Table 5.12 shows the cumulative simulation between 1974 and 1981. Similarly to the previous results, between these years and as a result of liberalization it is not possible to argue the occurrence of any changes in inequality. In other words, the trade opening had no significant effect on inequality. However, significant changes can be seen in the poverty indicators resulting from trade liberalization. The cumulative effects – that is, imposing the participation, unemployment, employment and wage structure of 1974 on 1981 – show that without liberalization the poverty incidence would have been 70 per cent, a figure significantly higher than the 48 per cent observed in 1981. Likewise, the poverty gap would have reached 38 per cent. It should be mentioned that this is the result when applying pre-liberalization income levels (phase 4b). The results change drastically when we simulate the changes in the remuneration structure (phase 4a).

Counterfactual with-and-without simulations

We now present the simulation exercises estimating the impact of trade liberalization, not assuming that the entire observed change is explained by the opening. The counterfactual is now derived from econometric techniques measuring the impact of liberalization on the metropolitan area's economic structure. The impact thus estimated is deducted from the observed parameter values for 1981. This allows the measurement of inequality and poverty levels in a hypothetical situation, i.e. had liberalization not taken place. Just as before, we compare the situation in terms of inequality and poverty indicators with and without trade opening for each phase and cumulatively.

Table 5.13 shows the simulations when comparing the 1974–81 period with the counterfactual information of the econometric analysis.[36] Phases 1 and 2 do not show any impact of poverty and inequality resulting from the opening. Phase 3 shows that the opening had a lesser effect in reducing indicators of inequality (quintile ratio) and poverty (gap).

Phases 4a and 4b, that simulate respectively the changes in the wage structure and level, indicate that without trade liberalization inequality would have been higher than that observed. In particular, the quintile ratio between the richer 20 per cent and the poorer 20 per cent would have been 22 times. The poverty incidence would have reached 57 per cent, that is 10 points above that observed in 1981. The poverty gap would have reached 28 per cent, in strong contrast with the 19 per cent observed in 1981.

Table 5.14 shows the cumulative simulation results. The results confirm those of the previous table. Inequality and poverty would have been higher had there been no liberalization. As a result of cumulating the effects, the size of the impact is higher than that presented in Table 5.14.

We can draw three conclusions from this analysis. First, as a result of liberalization, we observe a reduction of inequality levels. The cumulative effects generate larger changes than the individual effects. In addition, phase 4 contributes the largest effect, depending on the examined phase (be it 4a or 4b). These results suggest that the major labour market effects of liberalization took the form of changes in the wage structure, both in terms of wage level and wage distribution. Second, as a result of the trade opening it becomes possible to predict a significant reduction in poverty indicators. Examining both the individual and the cumulative simulations, we can see that the poverty incidence and gap have fallen as a result of trade liberalization.

Finally, the major impact of economic opening has come from changes observed in the wage structure. Indeed, the statistically significant changes in inequality and poverty are observed only when the last phase is included. This holds both for the separate and cumulative simulations. This means that, in the absence of the wage changes produced by liberalization, we would not have observed greater inequality and less poverty.

Welfare Impact of the Second Liberalization Phase (1984–92)

Mid-September 1984, the Chilean economy went through a second opening process with a compensatory exchange-rate adjustment. There was a significant tariff reduction and a proportional devaluation of the exchange rate. The purpose of these measures was to stimulate the export sector and increase the efficiency and competitiveness of the economy, thus achieving greater economic dynamics. This process was reversed to some extent in 1991, when tariffs were lowered. This period is labelled as the second opening of the Chilean economy.

Tables 5.15 and 5.16 show the separate and cumulative counterfactual simulations for 1984–92.[37] We assume that all the changes in the economic structure observed between 1984 and 1992 are a product of these reforms.

During this period we see that the second phase of the opening favoured a reduction in poverty and inequality. Indeed, except for phase 3, the exercises associated with the simulation of the effects of participation, unemployment and wages show that the inequality indicators would have been greater than those observed in 1992. In this last year, the Gini coefficient reached 0.514 and would have gone up to 0.526 without the second opening phase. The quintile ratio reached 14.2 and 16.1, respectively, for the same period. Poverty levels would have increased from 43 per cent in 1992 to a simulated 46 per cent due to changes in the unemployment structure, and would have dropped to 40 per cent in phase 4a and gone up to 49 per cent in phase 4b due to wage changes. In sum, the main effects of the opening are higher wages and lower poverty indicators. The size of the impact in this second phase is smaller.

Table 5.16 shows the cumulative effects. The results confirm the previous conclusions. In the absence of the liberalization measures, the Gini coefficient would have changed from 0.52 to 0.54. The poverty rate and poverty gap would have gone up by 8 and 6 percentage points, respectively, as compared to the observed values of 1992. These effects show significant welfare improvements for the Chilean society resulting from the opening process. Still, these results should be read with caution. We should keep in mind that these exercises assume that all the changes observed between 1984 and 1992 are a result of the second opening process.

Table 5.15 'Before-and-after' microsimulations, 1984–92: separate effects

	Inequality and poverty measures	YPC observed 1984	YPC observed 1992	Phase 1	Phase 2	Phase 3	Phase 4a	Phase 4b
1.	**Gini Coefficient**	**0.5661**	**0.5149**	**0.5211** 0.5181 0.5233	**0.5251** 0.5229 0.5284	**0.5138** 0.5129 0.5143	**0.5258**	**0.5262**
2.	**Ratio Q5/Q1**	**20.2586**	**14.1673**	**14.6906** 14.3619 14.999	**15.4428** 15.1950 15.8144	**14.1320** 14.0634 14.2467	**15.9174**	**16.1227**
3.	**Poverty Incidence**	**0.6234**	**0.4312**	**0.4389** 0.4323 0.4445	**0.4612** 0.4551 0.4659	**0.4275** 0.4250 0.4299	**0.4041**	**0.4882**
4.	**Poverty Gap**	**0.3218**	**0.1716**	**0.1765** 0.1735 0.1792	**0.1935** 0.1912 0.1963	**0.1699** 0.1694 0.1704	**0.1672**	**0.2128**
5.	**Number of Poor**	**6803**	**4460**	**4519** 4448 4580	**4536** 4453 4586	**4419** 4392 4446	**4180**	**5050**
6.	**Mean Income Q1**	**5025**	**9442**	**9217** 9118 9369	**8444** 8311 8609	**9480** 9409 9528	**9097**	**7572**
7.	**Mean Income Q2**	**10367**	**17544**	**17241** 17077 17427	**16374** 16238 16545	**17677** 17627 17721	**18265**	**15316**
8.	**Mean Income Q3**	**17405**	**27330**	**26878** 26682 27169	**25717** 25515 26034	**27532** 27472 27581	**28819**	**24395**
9.	**Mean Income Q4**	**30658**	**46449**	**46118** 45652 46735	**44344** 43962 44781	**46771** 46596 46951	**49039**	**41901**
10.	**Mean Income Q5**	**101800**	**133763**	**135397** 134066 136941	**130376** 129347 131575	**133965** 133384 134452	**144794**	**122073**

Table 5.16 'Before-and-after' microsimulations, 1984–92: cumulative effects

	Inequality and poverty measures	YPC observed 1978	YPC observed 1981	Phase 1 + 2	Phase 1, 2 + 3	Phase 1–3 + 4a	Phase 1–3 + 4b
1.	**Gini Coefficient**	**0.5661**	**0.5149**	**0.5315** 0.5294 0.5339	**0.5300** 0.5276 0.5323	**0.5417** 0.5389 0.5450	**0.5415** 0.5393 0.5434
2.	**Ratio Q5/Q1**	**20.2586**	**14.1673**	**16.0441** 15.7601 16.3188	**16.0245** 15.7790 16.3871	**18.2701** 17.9692 18.6061	**18.3279** 18.0325 18.5665
3.	**Poverty Incidence**	**0.6234**	**0.4312**	**0.4666** 0.4619 0.4719	**0.4618** 0.4571 0.4656	**0.4329** 0.4281 0.4374	**0.5166** 0.5127 0.5209
4.	**Poverty Gap**	**0.3218**	**0.1716**	**0.1974** 0.1945 0.2007	**0.1956** 0.1929 0.1980	**0.1919** 0.1884 0.1946	**0.2371** 0.2346 0.2396
5.	**Number of Poor**	**6803**	**4460**	**4562** 4499 4616	**4513** 4459 4558	**4233** 4162 4290	**5053** 5003 5116
6.	**Mean Income Q1**	**5025**	**9442**	**8285** 8147 8406	**8307** 8161 8429	**7907** 7746 8076	**6652** 6526 6736
7.	**Mean Income Q2**	**10367**	**17544**	**16173** 15966 16354	**16277** 16153 16463	**16750** 16523 16972	**14103** 13941 14269
8.	**Mean Income Q3**	**17405**	**27330**	**25386** 25152 25596	**25717** 25489 25966	**27022** 26765 27318	**23033** 22776 23262
9.	**Mean Income Q4**	**30658**	**46449**	**44499** 44040 45000	**45054** 44664 45436	**47936** 47498 48171	**41053** 40639 41464
10.	**Mean Income Q5**	**101800**	**133763**	**132912** 131497 133767	**133098** 132126 134107	**144446** 142300 145887	**121902** 121157 122788

5.5 CONCLUSIONS

This chapter analysed the impact of trade liberalization on variables such as growth, employment, productivity and welfare from various analytical perspectives. Starting in 1972, the Chilean economy went through a series of structural reforms oriented at creating a social market economy and liberalizing trade. We have tried to isolate the economic effects of the opening process.

The decomposition of aggregate demand showed a decrease in the relative importance of public spending on economic growth. Export growth contributed to the recovery from the two recessions of 1975 and 1982. However, investment was the main engine of growth in the 1990s. In fact, the multiplier analysis indicates that investment has been the most important factor in explaining output fluctuations. This growth-related impact has had a clear effect on the reduction of poverty, whereas the effects on inequality are less clear.

After the 1974 shock, unemployment increased rapidly, stayed at high levels, and increased even more during the 1982 crisis. The fast decline in unemployment in the second half of the 1980s came as a surprise and has not yet been given a definite explanation in terms of adjustment speed. The high initial unemployment level, the flexibility of the labour market and the strong economic growth explain the reduction per se. During the 1990s, changes followed a normal pattern with moderate reductions in unemployment rates.

Productivity growth accelerated during two periods, in 1976–81 (the opening period) and in the 1990s. When examining the growth in productivity at a sectoral level, we can see that most of the growth is explained by the overall productivity growth, rather than by the reallocation of resources between sectors. Possible effects of labour reallocation should not be dismissed though. Productivity may have increased due to reallocation within each sector, rather than a balanced growth between sectors. We are unable to evaluate this hypothesis with the available information for sector detail.

We assessed the performance of the Chilean economy in terms of total factor productivity growth and wage inequality by analysing their macroeconomic determinants. The evidence indicates that inflation has a negative effect on total factor productivity growth. Trade liberalization is positively correlated with productivity growth. The terms of trade, the black-market premium and financial development exercise only a small effect on productivity growth.

Wage inequality increased starting from the mid-1970s onwards. This is not solely the result of trade opening, but also influenced by the other reforms and transformations of the Chilean economy. The results show that inflation reduces inequality. However, these results vary by periods. In the early 1970s, there was high inflation, while inequality decreased. Higher income levels, explained by the levels of total factor productivity or low unemployment, reduce inequality, whereas a high black-market premium is associated with a rise in wage inequality.

The second part of our study examined the microeconomic impact of trade opening on welfare. To this end, we analysed the effects of the opening process on the labour market. Based on these estimates we carried out counterfactual exercises with respect to the changes that would have occurred in inequality and poverty had trade liberalization not taken place.

The empirical evidence is based on simulations for two time periods. For the first opening process we examined the periods 1974–81 and 1978–81. Two simulations were presented. One simulation assumed that all the observed changes are explained by liberalization and the second estimated the liberalization effect counterfactually using an econometric model. The second opening process is 1984–92, with tariff reductions and exchange rate increases, and simulations assumed that the entire effect observed between years is explained by trade liberalization.

The evidence suggests that trade liberalization reduced income inequality during the first liberalization process (for which we consider the 1978–81 period). The evidence becomes more patent when examining the cumulative effects. Besides, these effects are largely explained by the changes that took place in wage structure and wage levels. What is more, this inverse relationship between liberalization and inequality is most visible in the rich-to-poor quintile ratio, which means that the most significant changes took place at the extremes of the distribution. The results for the 1974–81 period suggest that liberalization led to an increase in inequality. During the second opening process (1984–92), liberalization seems to have led to less inequality, as evidenced by the results showing that in the absence of such policies the levels of inequality would have increased with respect to those observed in 1992. In sum, the effects on inequality are ambiguous and sensitive to the chosen period.

On the other hand, the impact of liberalization on poverty is somewhat more robust. Indeed, most simulations indicate that the effects of the opening process reduced poverty significantly. We use two poverty measures – poverty incidence and poverty gap – and both indicators suggest substantial welfare improvements due to trade liberalization.

Finally, changes in wage levels and remuneration structure dominate the analysed labour-market effects.

NOTES

1. We are very grateful to Claudio Bravo and Cristobal Huneeus for their excellent assistance, as well as to Enrique Ganuza, Ricardo Paes de Barro, François Bourguignon, Juan Alberto Fuentes, Rob Vos, Lance Taylor and participants for comments provided at the project meetings organized by UNDP.
2. For an additional discussion on the reforms, see Edwards and Cox-Edwards (1987) and Bosworth et al. (1994). This section follows Anríquez et al. (1998) and De Gregorio (1999).
3. Edwards and Lederman (1998) discuss trade liberalization at length.
4. Chile has decided not to become a full member of Mercosur to avoid the problems that increasing the tariffs to common market levels would create.
5. The Asian crisis was felt in Chile through the collapse of the copper price, and this effect, together with a restrictive monetary policy, caused a recession in 1999. GDP rose 3.4 per cent in 1998 and –1.5 per cent in 1999. This period is not included in the analysis because economic performance is a result of the effects of the business cycle rather than of the long-term effects of economic reforms.
6. The growth rate has not been stable, however, and fluctuated between a peak level of 11 per cent in 1992 and a low of 3.3 per cent in 1990.
7. The *encaje* has varied through time. Between 1992 and 1998 it consisted basically in the requirement to keep 30 per cent of capital inflows as a deposit in the Banco Central. The deposit is non-interest-bearing and hence entails a cost to the investor. The *encaje* operates as a fixed cost to capital inflows. We do not analyse the macroeconomic impact of the *encaje* here. However, see De Gregorio et al. (1998), who show that the impact of the reserve requirement on interest rates, capital flows and exchange rates is small, but nevertheless has extended the maturity of the external debt.
8. This method is subject to national accounting problems. In addition, small variations in the accounts may cause large enough changes in factor shares leading to substantial variations in the measure of total factor productivity. There are also serious measurement problems with regard to informal employment. If informal employment is included in the residual and not in the labour income, and if the degree of informality changes systematically with the degree of development, the factor share will be biased.
9. The relative stability through time is a consequence of the sectoral composition of production as reported in Section 5.4. These results are similar to those obtained through the production function estimation method. For example, Jadresic and Sanhueza (1992) find values of a between 0.29 and 0.38. Rojas et al. (1997) report a value of 0.35, whereas Roldos (1997) gets 0.44 with the assumptions of constant returns to scale. According to the national accounts the capital share is close to 0.5
10. This idea was originally put forward by Harberger (1978).
11. Education changes slowly through time.
12. The indicator is a proxy of the general distortions of the economy. This variable was included in the liberalization index, but is included in additive form so as to capture its direct impact.
13. Level values as well as first differences are used in the regression model.
14. Only considers full-time workers (working 30 hours or more per week).
15. We also ran regressions of determinants of the changes in the contribution of labour and capital, that is explaining unemployment and investment. The results were not statistically significant and are therefore not reported.
16. In some cases, these results are relatively good for the specification in first differences, but the model does not explain an important part of the relationship.
17. The results are basically the same when inflation is measured in levels or in logarithms.
18. In previous estimates we included unemployment as explanatory variable, which is already incorporated into C_u. The idea is to capture long-term determinants associated with the business cycle. In addition, there is a problem of endogeneity. A low TFP growth leads

to smaller employment creation. This is not the case for inequality. Unemployment has an important impact on inequality.

19. In Chile there was a strong expansion of credit, which reaches its peak in 1982, then diminishes, to expand again from 1990 onwards.
20. These outcomes are explained by the effect of the 1972–75 period. We excluded this period from the regressions (there were stabilization plans and inequality increased). We cannot exclude this period for the estimation of TFP and the growth equations.
21. The sample design of the survey includes a rotating panel of 25% of the total sample, each representing Gran Santiago. This practice has not been changed during the period of analysis. Hence the survey does not pose any sampling problems for our study. Even though the survey is repeated every quarter, we use the June data for each year given the access to the database.
22. There are other national-level sources of information for the 1990s, i.e. the period after the trade liberalization.
23. The educational cycles in Chile are as in our definition.
24. Higher education is defined by the number of school years and not by their type. It includes universities, professional institutes and vocational/technical centres.
25. As an alternative methodology we also applied VAR estimates of the time series. However, in our search for the best VAR estimation for various specifications, we were unable to capture more than 25 per cent of stationary processes (in the weak sense).
26. We also ran regressions including the liberalization index, but results were not satisfactory due to the minimal variation over time of the index. For this reason, we decided to use dummy variables to identify the changes in the degree of opening.
27. The effect corresponds to the coefficient linked to *Dum_Lib* in each of the estimated equations.
28. Matrix $W = [w_{ij}]$, where w_{ij} stands for the average wage of type-i workers in segment j of the market. An $E = [e_{ij}]$ matrix, where e_{ij} stands for the proportion of all type-i trained workers that are employed in segment j.
29. Vector $U = [u_i]$, where u_i stands for the unemployment rate of type-i workers. Vector $P = [p_i]$, where p_i denotes the participation rate for type-i workers.
30. The fourth stage corresponds to changes in the wage structure, and in turn is subdivided into two stages, that is changes in the wage distribution structure and changes in wage levels.
31. Let us not forget that, in this case, the effect of trade liberalization is quantified for the 1974–79 period.
32. The wage structure is calculated for those members participating in the labour market. Minors, housewives, and so on, are not counted in the previous tables. Poverty and inequality cannot be measured properly for a sample of these characteristics. To solve this problem, we identified each household member and all their income. Family income is then obtained from the sum of the individual income of each of its members. This allows us to carry out the simulation exercises without falling into these measuring problems. For example, if as a result of the simulation exercises a person becomes randomly unemployed, only this individual's income becomes zero and not the household income. This effect implies that the household income is reduced, increasing poverty. Similarly, if as a result of a simulation a household member who was not participating is 'made' to participate, the effect is modelled through an increase of individual labour income and its impact on poverty and inequality is measured by using the new per capita household income.
33. The fourth phase does not present confidence intervals because there is no generation of random numbers when simulating separately, given that only a wage structure is being allocated.
34. The intersectoral movements of workers resulting from the simulations of phases 1, 2 and 3 are determined by the ranking of sectors by mean income, so that a worker moves to an immediately adjacent sector depending on the established ranking.

35. Only a few exercises show marginal changes.
36. The estimated models incorporate a dummy variable for 1975 that accounts for the impact of the recession in that year.
37. In this case it was difficult to estimate this effect.

REFERENCES

Anríquez, G., K. Cowan and J. De Gregorio (1998) 'Pobreza y Políticas Macroeconómicas: Chile 1987–1994', in: E. Ganuza, L. Taylor and S. Morley (eds) *Políticas Macroeconómicas y Pobreza en América Latina y el Caribe*, Madrid: Mundi-Prensa (Published for UNDP).

Bosworth, B., R. Dornbusch and R. Labán (eds) (1994) *The Chilean Economy: Policy Lessons and Challenges*, Washington D.C.: The Brookings Institution.

De Gregorio, J. (1999) 'Exchange Rate Policy in Chile Since 1960: Political Economy and The Choice of Regime', Centro de Economía Aplicada, Santiago: Universidad de Chile (mimeo).

De Gregorio, J. and P. Guidotti (1995) 'Financial development and economic growth', *World Development*, **23**: 433–48

De Gregorio, J., S. Edwards and R. Valdés (1998) 'Capital Controls in Chile: An Assessment', Universidad de Chile, UCLA and Banco Central de Chile (mimeo).

De la Cuadra, S. and D. Hachette (1990) *Apertura Comercial: Experiencia Chilena*, Santiago: Universidad de Chile.

Edwards, S. and A. Cox-Edwards (1987) *Monetarism and Liberalization: The Chilean Experience*, Cambridge (MA): Balinger.

Edwards, S. and D. Lederman (1998) 'The Political Economy of Unilateral Trade Liberalization: The Case of Chile', NBER Working Paper No. 6510, Cambridge (MA): National Bureau of Economic Research.

Ffrench-Davis, R. (1973) *Políticas Económicas en Chile: 1952–1970*, Santiago, Chile: Editorial Nueva Universidad.

Hachette, D. and R. Luders (1992) *La Privatización en Chile*, San Francisco: International Centre for Economic Development.

Harberger, A. (1978) 'Perspectives on capital and technology in less developed countries', in M.J. Artis and A.R. Nobay (eds) *Contemporary Economic Analysis*, London: Croom Helm.

Jadresic, E. and G. Sanhueza (1992) 'Producto y Crecimiento Potencial en la Economía Chilena', Santiago: Banco Central de Chile (mimeo).

Marcel, M. and A. Solimano (1994) 'Developmentalism, socialism, and free market reform: Three decades of income distribution in Chile', in B. Bosworth, R. Dornbusch and R. Labán (eds) *The Chilean Economy: Policy Lessons and Challenges*, Washington D.C.: The Brookings Institution.

Nehru, V. and A. Dhareshwar (1993) 'A new database on physical capital stock: Sources, methodology and results', *Revista de Análisis Económico*, **8**: 37–59.

Rojas, P., E. López and S. Jimenez (1997) 'Determinantes del crecimiento y estimación del producto potencial', in F. Morandé and R. Vergara (eds) *Análisis Empírico del Crecimiento en Chile*, Santiago and Washington D.C.: Centro de Estudios Públicos, ILADES/Georgetown.

Roldos, J. (1997) 'El crecimiento del producto potencial en mercados emergentes: el caso de Chile', in F. Morandé and R. Vergara (eds) *Análisis Empírico del Crecimiento en Chile*, Santiago and Washington D.C.: Centro de Estudios Públicos, ILADES/ Georgetown.

Sarel, M. (1997) 'Growth and Productivity in ASEAN Countries', IMF Working Paper, WP/97/97, Washington D.C.: International Monetary Fund.

6. Colombia: structural change, labour market adjustment and income distribution in the 1990s[1]

José Antonio Ocampo, Fabio Sánchez and Camilo Ernesto Tovar

6.1 INTRODUCTION

Like other Latin American countries, Colombia was immersed in an intense process of structural reforms in the 1990s. On the external front, this process has had elements common to other regional experiences, such as trade reform and opening to direct foreign investments. There have also been contrasting elements, especially the maintenance of an active external-debt management. The reform process also included a modest labour reform and an ambitious reform of the social security system. The latter reform is part of a wider process of giving the private sector access to traditionally state-oriented areas. Major components of monetary and financial reforms include giving autonomy to the Central Bank and measures to increase competition among financial agents and improve prudential regulation and supervision. The most important difference with what has happened elsewhere in the region has been the combination of these economic liberalization processes with a significant growth of the size of the public sector, through an expansion of the supply of social services. Despite substantial growth of government revenue, rising social spending caused widening fiscal deficits, reflecting the difficulty faced by the Colombian government in reconciling economic liberalization with a more active social policy.

The economy grew at moderate rates in the 1990s. Growth was more volatile than in the past (especially in terms of aggregate demand behaviour), but with a gradual decline in inflation. Throughout the process, the sectors most exposed to external competition have weakened significantly. The labour market also deteriorated, as it went through a restructuring process accompanied by less job creation, especially in the production sectors most open to international competition (particularly agriculture and manufacturing industry). Labour market restructuring has manifested itself in the expulsion of unskilled labour, which has not been fully offset by rising employment for skilled workers. This suggests that the technological change since the early 1990s involved a shift toward more skill-intensive production activities, while labour-saving for all types of skills. These labour market shifts have had adverse effects on urban income distribution. Rising urban inequality has been stronger than the decline in inequality in rural areas. Rural areas have been deeply affected by adverse shocks in the rural–urban terms of trade and the ensuing crisis of commercial agriculture.

This chapter analyses the labour market changes and underlying behaviour in Colombia in the 1990s. It is divided into six sections, including this Introduction. Section 6.2 describes the reforms introduced in the 1990s. Section 6.3 briefly reviews macroeconomic trends and structural adjustment patterns. Using household survey data, Section 6.4 provides a detailed analysis of Colombian labour dynamics by economic sector, educational level and occupational position. After summarizing the state of the art of the literature on income distribution in Colombia, Section 6.5 presents the results of the microsimulation analysis. This analysis tries to identify the impact of the observed changes in labour market conditions (sectoral employment structure, relative wages, unemployment and labour participation) on income distribution and poverty for the population as a whole, as well as for urban and rural sectors. Conclusions are drawn in Section 6.6.

6.2 THE REFORMS

The process of structural reforms, known in Colombia as 'economic opening', began toward the end of the Barco administration and had its strongest impetus during the Gaviria administration (1990–94). The Samper administration (1994–98) took the reforms a step further, and these are being followed up by the Pastrana administration (1998–2002). The main element of this process was the liberalization of foreign transactions, i.e. the regimes of trade, currency exchange and direct foreign investment. The reforms were accompanied by economic growth as well as by structural changes and a redefinition of the functions of the public sector. All of this came in the context of a drastic state reform as defined by the new political charter of 1991. The processes also included a moderate flexibilization of the labour regime in 1990 and a more ambitious reform of the social security system in 1993 (Ocampo 1998).

The Liberalization of External Transactions

Trade liberalization had two basic components: liberalization of imports and the signing of a broad range of integration and free trade agreements. Both the liberalization programme started by the Barco administration in February 1990 and the more ambitious one announced a few months later by the Gaviria administration proposed a gradual tariff reduction, following the rapid dismantling of quantitative import restrictions. Macroeconomic problems led authorities to accelerate the liberalization process, which culminated in August 1991. In this 18-month period direct controls on imports were virtually eliminated, the average tariff was reduced from 44 to 12 per cent, and incentives to exports were cut from 19 per cent in 1990 to 6 per cent 1992. In order to ease the effects of international price fluctuations, a variable tariff system was adopted for agriculture. Trust legislation and safeguards against false competition accompanied this process. These new regulations were enforced modestly in subsequent years.

The intensification of the trade integration process was initiated in 1989, when the presidents of the Grupo Andino – which later became the Comunidad Andina – agreed to revitalize, intensify and reorient the process of subregional integration. Successive meetings led to an agreement in 1991 in favour of the establishment of a free trade zone that should become effective in 1992. In 1992, a free trade zone was established with Venezuela and Bolivia. Ecuador joined a year later. In late 1994, a common but restricted external tariff was adopted, which in practice only applies to Colombia, Venezuela and, to a very limited degree, Ecuador. This was complemented by other processes such as the signing of a free trade agreement with Chile in 1993 and Mexico in 1994 (the *Grupo de los Tres*, which also includes Venezuela), and the start of negotiations between the Comunidad Andina and Mercosur in subsequent years.

The main components of the capital account liberalization were the exchange reform and the opening to foreign direct investment (FDI). Freeing FDI flows was initiated in the late 1980s, but was only completed between 1990 and 1991 when all the corresponding restrictions were eliminated, except in the areas of security, toxic waste and large-scale mining investments. The regime of Colombian investments abroad was liberalized simultaneously. In the following years, new agreements for the mutual protection of foreign investments were signed.

The 1991 exchange reform decentralized the management of foreign-currency transactions by authorizing agents to handle transactions without control by the *Banco de la República*. However, a large part of the transactions were still regulated, including the obligation to channel these through financial agents legally authorized to operate in the market. A strict control was maintained on the end use of external loans (investments, exports and imports). Only in February 1992 did it become possible for the first time to contract short-term external credits to finance working capital. The exchange reform of September 1993 authorized financial agents to provide foreign-currency loans to domestic firms, regardless of the use of such credits, and substituted the previous regulatory system for one based in a reserve requirement for borrowers in foreign currency through an obligation to keep a deposit (*encaje*) in the Central Bank (*Banco de la República*). The objective of these measures was to control the amount and composition of the capital flows.[2] The size and terms of loans subject to the *encaje* became more restrictive in 1994. Restrictions were loosened in 1996, and tightened again in 1997. In May 1997, the system of external-debt management was simplified along the lines of Chile's system of the 1990s, requiring reserve deposits on all loans. The level of the implicit tax imposed by this system of capital controls was consistently higher than that of the Chilean regime during the years of booming capital inflows (an average of 13.6 and 6.4 per cent in 1994–98 for 12- and 36-month credits, respectively).[3] During the crisis of the late 1990s, the reserve deposit requirement was gradually decreased until its elimination in early 2000.

Growth, Structural Change and Redefinition of the Functions of the State

The Constitution of 1991 and other political decisions adopted throughout the decade had a significant impact on the structure of the state apparatus, altering the dynamics of public finances. As pointed out in the Introduction, the combination of this dynamics with the process of structural reforms is a peculiarity of the Colombian case in the Latin American context. The singularity lies in the fact that deregulation and privatization of the economy has been accompanied by a swelling of the size of the public sector, which expanded from 30 per cent in 1990 to 38 per cent of GDP in the late 1990s.

The increases in transfers to departments and municipalities financing rising social investment and an expansion of social security coverage had the largest impact on public finances. The 1991 Constitution and the ensuing laws (especially Act 60 of 1993, which started the new transfer system, and Act 100 of 1993, which created a new social security system) have led to a structural increase in government expenditure of about 4 per cent of GDP (Ocampo 1997). This is the main source of the total increase of non-interest central government expenditures. Despite its partial privatization, the social security reform also led to a parallel increase in benefits granted by the corresponding public agencies.

The rapid growth in expenditures was by and large offset by increases in tax revenue, particularly rising central government taxes, increased social security contributions and, to a lesser extent, higher municipal taxes. Indeed, the change in tax structure caused by trade liberalization, which introduced less dependence of import duties, was compensated by successive tax reforms (in 1990, 1992, 1995, 1997, 1998 and 2000) that served to finance, albeit partially, the increase in expenditures. Since the mid-1990s, the fiscal deficit increased, particularly that of the central government, reaching 3.9 per cent of GDP in 1998 and 5.2 per cent in 1999, when the recession caused a decrease in tax income. The consolidated public sector deficit reached 3.1 and 4.5 per cent of GDP in those years. The rising deficit and the persistent need to modify the country's tax structure are therefore a reflection of the difficulties the Colombian State has encountered in trying to reconcile an open economy with a more active social policy.

The growth of the size of the Colombian State was accompanied by a notorious change in its structure. The main elements include a drastic fiscal decentralization and giving the private sector access to sectors that were traditionally reserved exclusively for the state. The transfer of national funds to departments and, especially, municipalities has been the major component explaining the rise in national government spending. In turn, municipal expenditures, together with those of the social security system, showed the highest growth rates of the entire public sector. The processes of privatization, infrastructure concessions and the general opening of the infrastructure sector and the social security system to private investment are the most salient elements of the second wave of reforms. This process went together with the establishment of stronger regulating and supervising agencies in infrastructure, social security and financial sectors. In practice, the implicit strategy followed in all these areas was to leave in operation an important group of public agencies and enterprises to complement and compete with the private sector. In addition, the financial reform of the early 1990s aimed at increasing competition between different types of intermediaries, privatization of some institutions that had been nationalized during the financial crisis of the early 1980s, and full liberalization of foreign direct investment. The 1991 Constitution granted full independence to the *Banco de la República* to manage monetary and exchange-rate policies.

Labour and Social Security Reforms

The 1990 labour reform combined a partial flexibilization of the labour market with more protection of trade-union rights. In general, this reform implemented many of the proposals presented several years earlier by the *Misión de Empleo* (1986). The most important reforms in the first front included the flexibilization of temporal labour contracting, relaxation of dismissal of workers with more than 10 years of seniority (in exchange for higher severance payment and always subject to demonstration of just cause for dismissal), the adoption of an integrated wage system for higher-paid workers (more than 10 minimum wages) and the elimination of the excess costs of the previous regime of hiring and firing. This system of social benefits fixed the level of pay to the worker at a monthly wage per service year when leaving the company. However, the liquidation of workers' pension funds implied a cost increasing exponentially with the number of actual retirements. The reform substituted this system for one of mandatory savings in pension funds for new employees, and allowed negotiations between companies and more senior employees so that these could transfer to the new regime in exchange for a severance payment. In addition to these changes, which aimed at a more flexible labour market, the reform strengthened the right to unionize and was supplemented with legal instruments to effectuate this.

In practice, the resulting labour flexibility has not been limited, particularly due to the effects of the social security reform of 1993. Temporary employment increased as a share of total urban employment from 15.8 to 20 per cent between 1990 and 1997 (ILO 1998). This was no doubt a consequence of the legislative changes with respect to the regulation of temporary contracts. Nevertheless, the greater flexibility and the reduction of severance payments in comparison to the previous regime of dismissal have been offset by the increase in costs linked to hiring and firing of new employees. Indeed, increased costs of hiring are associated with the social security reform. The reform led to an increase in enterprise contributions from 13.5 to 26.5 per cent (13.5 per cent for pensions and the remaining 12 per cent for health),[4] thereby raising the share of social security contributions from 47.0 to 59.4 per cent of basic wages.

6.3 MACROECONOMIC TRENDS

The 1990s were characterized by strong stop-and-go cycles in macroeconomic policies. These cycles responded in part to external shocks, both positive and negative, especially those produced by the volatility in the international capital market. Other shocks were domestic in nature.

The decade started amidst growing inflationary pressures leading to a drastic adjustment programme announced at the end of 1990. The programme included a severe monetary contraction, a revaluation, moderate fiscal adjustment (Table 6.1) and the acceleration of the implementation of the trade reform. The adjustment programme caused a deceleration in economic growth, a break in the inflationary trends and a strong improvement of the current account balance.

The heavy pressure on international reserves and increasing quasi-fiscal costs caused by the monetary contraction during 1991 led the *Banco de la República* to accelerate currency revaluation and drastically cut interest rates. Simultaneously, growth of tax revenue led to an accelerated rise in public

Table 6.1 Macroeconomic policy variables and performance indicators, 1975–99

	1975–79	1980–85	1986–90	1991–99	1990	1991	1992	1993	1994	1995	1996	1997	1998	1999
Real exchange rate (1994=100)	81.0	73.0	103.1	103.0	114.9	113.0	106.8	107.5	100.0	102.3	98.8	93.3	98.3	108.2
Real interest rate														
Deposit rate (90 days)		10.3	6.4	6.2	4.9	4.8	–0.4	2.5	5.5	9.3	8.2	4.8	11.8	8.8
Average lending rate			14.1	14.9	12.6	12.9	8.1	10.9	14.4	18.2	17.7	13.6	20.7	17.4
Government spending (% GDP)														
DANE	20.3	28.1	30.1	31.7	30.4	31.0	31.1	31.3	31.3	34.1				
Central Bank (net of transfers)				31.9	30.4	31.8	31.0	31.3	31.4	34.0				
Ministry of Finance									30.3	32.0	35.8	37.2	36.0	
Fiscal balance, net of privatizations (% of GDP)	–1.5	–5.3	–1.5	–1.5	–0.4	0.0	–0.1	0.0	–0.1	–2.0	–2.0	–3.8	–3.9	–5.2
Central government	–0.2	–3.3	–0.9	–2.2	–0.6	0.4	0.1	–0.3	–1.6	–4.3	–4.3	–4.3	–5.6	–5.9
Rest public sector	–1.3	–2.0	–0.6	0.7	0.2	–0.4	–0.3	0.3	1.7	2.3	2.3	0.5	1.7	0.6
GDP growth	5.0	2.6	4.6	2.6	4.3	2.0	4.0	5.4	5.8	5.2	2.1	3.4	0.4	–4.5
Traded goods sectors	4.9	1.8	5.7	0.9	5.1	2.2	0.8	2.1	1.3	5.8	–0.6	0.9	1.4	–5.5
Non-traded goods sectors	5.1	3.2	3.7	3.4	3.2	2.0	5.4	5.3	7.6	6.4	4.8	4.7	–1.2	–4.4
Domestic aggregate demand growth	4.8	2.4	3.4	8.5	2.3	0.1	10.0	12.1	12.0	5.8	1.1	4.0	–1.1	–8.3
Inflation (CPI)	23.9	26.7	26.3	20.2	32.4	26.8	25.1	22.6	22.6	19.5	21.6	17.7	16.7	9.2
Exports (% GDP at 1975 prices)	15.0	14.4	18.5	22.9	20.7	22.7	23.1	23.3	22.0	21.7	23.3	23.2	23.1	24.2
External balance (% GDP at 1994 PPP exchange rate)														
Trade balance	3.5	–3.1	3.9	–1.2	4.3	6.2	2.3	–2.8	–3.3	–3.3	–2.9	–3.2	–4.7	0.4
Current account	1.5	–6.8	0.3	–3.1	1.2	4.9	1.7	–3.7	–5.2	–5.6	–5.6	–6.5	–6.2	–1.2
Gross fixed capital formation (% GDP at 1975 prices)	15.6	17.1	15.5	16.7	14.0	12.9	13.9	18.0	20.7	19.8	19.1	18.1	16.0	11.8

Source: Banco de la República (Central Bank), DANE (statistical office) and DNP (national planning office).

spending. The joint result of these policies was a boom in domestic and foreign indebtedness, causing an accelerated expansion of aggregate domestic demand in 1992–94. The demand growth was unprecedented in Colombia's post-war economic history. Economic activity and productive investment thrived amidst a considerable deterioration of the current account balance. Agriculture did not participate in the boom. Since the early 1990s, the agricultural sector had difficulties dealing with the external opening process in a context of low world market prices, especially coffee prices. Inflation was kept under control, and even declined slightly during the first phase of the boom, due to the revaluation and the rapid growth of imports. However, at the same time there was a boom in asset prices of real estate and stock market shares.

Monetary policy became increasingly contractionary throughout 1994 and 1995. The tight control of external indebtedness adopted in 1994 also contributed toward a slowdown of private demand growth. The policy avoided at the same time that monetary contraction would lead to a further real appreciation of the exchange rate. Aggregate demand started to slow down in 1995, and even more strongly in 1996, creating a strong deceleration of output growth and an interruption of the deterioration of the current account balance. The continued public expenditure boom was the key factor driving demand growth in this period.

The drop in interest rates throughout 1996 facilitated recovery of private demand and output in 1997. Public spending did not contribute to this expansion – on the contrary, during these years the first measures to curb growth of national government expenditures were adopted, as it became clear that the fiscal deficit was rapidly increasing. Tight controls on external borrowing alleviated the pressure towards real exchange-rate appreciation apparent in 1996 (but visible in the indicators of 1997). The current account experienced a moderate additional deterioration anyway.

Economic recovery did not last long due to the international crisis and the measures adopted to counter its consequences. The new policy measures were taken in a context of fragile external and fiscal balances. The restrictive monetary policy in response to the crisis managed to gradually depreciate the real exchange rate through successive changes of the exchange-rate band. It further led to a contraction of aggregate demand, improvement in external accounts and a reduction of inflation. The price to be paid was the worst recession in Colombian history and an accelerated deterioration of the portfolio of the financial system. Paradoxically, these measures of fiscal austerity were ineffective in terms of reducing the fiscal deficit. To the contrary, the drop in tax income caused by the recession, the increase in debt-service payments and the cost of the financial bailout worsened the fiscal situation in 1999. Improved competitiveness of the exchange rate and the fall in interest rates during 1999 facilitated a moderate output recovery during 2000.

On the whole, economic growth was slow compared to past experience and much more volatile. Average growth rates are strongly influenced by the severity of the recent crisis. Until 1997 there was moderate growth, only slightly lower than that of the second half of the 1980s. In contrast, the volatility of growth and aggregate demand, in particular, were salient features of the entire decade. This is the more noteworthy given the country's gradual and anti-cyclical policy stance, through which it had earned the reputation of being Latin America's economy with the least volatile business cycles. Other features are large current account deficits during most of the decade, partly linked to the real appreciation of the exchange rate and the structural deterioration of public finances.

The growth pattern was characterized by the rapid decline of the share of agriculture and manufacturing in GDP (see Table 6.2). This became evident during the boom period, when rapid growth concentrated in the expansion of service and construction sectors, i.e. in non-tradable activities. Some agricultural activities, especially crop farming of short cycles (grains and oil seeds), went through a deep crisis in the early 1990s. The domestic demand-led

Table 6.2 Employment and GDP by sectors (percentage shares)

	GDP (1975 prices)					**Employment**		
	1985	**1991**	**1995**	**1997**	**1999**	**1991**	**1995**	**1997**
Agriculture	21.9	21.8	19.3	18.8	19.9	26.7	22.2	22.9
Mining	2.3	4.6	4.3	4.7	5.7	1.2	0.8	0.7
Manufacturing	21.2	21.4	19.0	18.6	16.9	15.0	15.7	13.2
Electricity, gas and water	1.0	1.1	1.1	1.1	1.2	0.6	0.5	0.9
Construction	4.4	3.0	3.7	3.7	2.6	4.5	6.1	5.3
Commerce	12.1	11.5	11.9	12.0	11.5	20.7	21.7	21.9
Transportation	9.4	8.6	8.7	9.4	9.9	5.0	5.5	5.5
Financial services	14.2	14.6	16.3	17.3	16.5	3.6	4.6	5.0
Other services	13.2	13.2	12.9	14.5	16.1	22.6	22.8	24.7
TOTAL	100.0	100.0	100.0	100.0	100.0	100.0	100.0	100.0
Tradables	45.4	47.8	42.6	42.1	42.5	43.0	38.7	36.8
Urban						14.2	14.1	12.5
Rural						28.8	24.7	24.3
Non-tradables	54.3	52.0	54.7	57.9	57.6	57.0	61.3	63.2
Urban						43.9	47.0	49.4
Rural						13.1	14.3	13.8

Source: DANE, National Household Survey and National Accounts.

growth during the boom period is also reflected in the reversal of the rising export share witnessed from the mid-1980s to 1991 (see Table 6.1).

The shifts in the production structure that took place in the second half of the 1990s stem predominantly from the crisis in some of the sectors that expanded strongly in the first half of the 1990s (construction and, more recently, financial services) and the deterioration of the manufacturing industry (most pronounced during the recent crisis). Mining and some service sectors (transport and government services up to the start of the fiscal adjustment programmes) provided the only – albeit weak – growth engines during this period.

6.4 THE LABOUR MARKET

Overall Trends

Figure 6.1 shows the trend of the main labour market indicators in the seven largest cities since 1976, comparing it to the national indicators available only since 1991.[5] Urban labour participation increased rapidly in the 1980s mainly as a consequence of the rapid incorporation of women into the labour force which, in turn, was related to a drop in fertility. The slow growth of the economy in the first half of the 1980s caused sluggish employment creation in the seven largest cities. This dynamics, together with the above-mentioned participation behaviour, caused a considerable increase in the unemployment rate, which peaked in 1986. Since then, the labour market went into a tail-spin. The economy recovered its dynamism, employment creation accelerated, and this contributed to a reduction of unemployment.

These trends in the urban labour market were maintained until 1992, after which trends reversed again with the adoption of the structural reforms. Employment creation in the seven largest cities and the urban sector as a whole started to diminish after having reached a peak in 1993. The pace of job creation slowed down despite the continued boom in aggregate demand and rapid economic growth. At the same time, the upward trend in the participation rate came to an end. Reduced employment creation thus did not lead to higher unemployment for several years. In fact, the unemployment rate was 8.7 per cent on average in the cities during 1993–95, its lowest level since the early 1980s. In contrast, rural labour market conditions deteriorated as a result of a severe crisis in agriculture during these years. More specifically, rural employment diminished substantially between 1991 and 1993 and the unemployment rate increased during the first half of the 1990s, although at levels far below those of urban areas. Taking these opposite trends of urban and rural areas together we obtain a slightly descending trend in the employ-

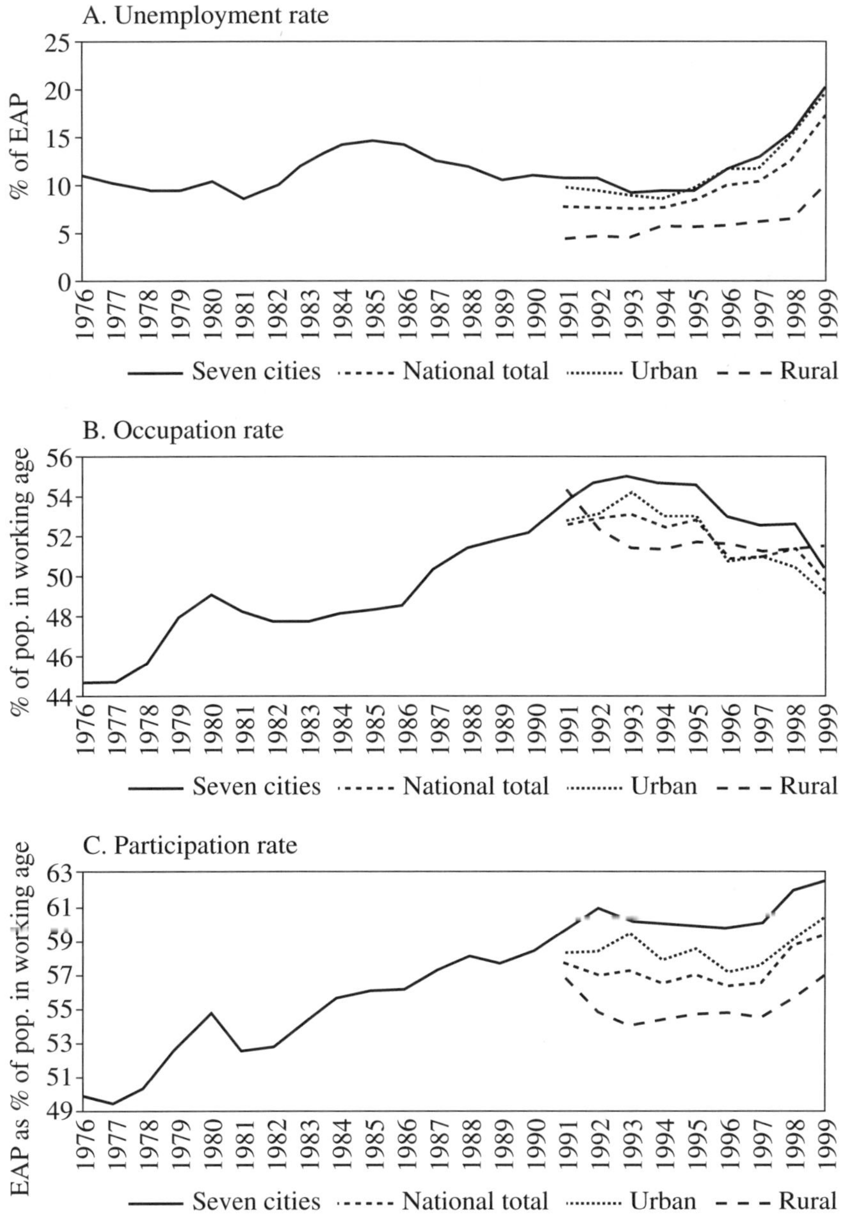

Source: DANE, National Household Survey.

Figure 6.1 Indicators of national, urban and rural labour market, 1978–99

Table 6.3 Main indicators of the labour market by gender, years of schooling and age, by area

	By area and gender, 1991 and 1997					By years of schooling and gender, 1991 and 1997			
	Area	**Gender**	**1991**	**1997**		**Years of schooling**	**Gender**	**1991**	**1997**
P	National	Men	78.4%	74.0%	**P**	≤ 9	Men	77.6%	71.7%
		Women	37.9%	38.3%			Women	32.7%	30.4%
	Urban	Men	73.1%	70.4%		10–15	Men	78.4%	77.7%
		Women	40.9%	41.5%			Women	53.6%	55.7%
	Rural	Men	84.4%	82.5%		> 15	Men	93.0%	90.0%
		Women	33.7%	28.3%			Women	81.8%	83.0%
U	National	Men	4.3%	6.8%	**U**	≤ 9	Men	3.5%	6.0%
		Women	10.7%	13.3%			Women	9.2%	12.3%
	Urban	Men	6.4%	8.7%		10–15	Men	72.1%	69.9%
		Women	12.7%	13.3%			Women	45.0%	46.2%
	Rural	Men	2.2%	2.9%		> 15	Men	90.1%	86.1%
		Women	7.6%	13.4%			Women	77.4%	77.6%
E	National	Men	75.1%	69.0%	**E**	≤ 9	Men	74.8%	67.4%
		Women	33.8%	33.2%			Women	29.7%	26.7%
	Urban	Men	68.4%	64.2%		10–15	Men	8.0%	10.1%
		Women	35.7%	36.0%			Women	16.0%	17.1%
	Rural	Men	82.6%	80.1%		> 15	Men	3.2%	4.3%
		Women	31.2%	24.5%			Women	5.4%	6.5%

By area and years of schooling, 1991 and 1997

	Area	Years of schooling	1991	1997
P	National	≤ 9	54.1%	50.2%
		10–15	64.9%	65.7%
		> 15	88.4%	86.9%
	Urban	≤ 9	49.2%	47.0%
		10–15	64.7%	65.7%
		> 15	87.9%	86.9%
	Rural	≤ 9	58.5%	56.2%
		10–15	65.5%	66.4%
		> 15	96.1%	88.4%
U	National	≤ 9	5.3%	8.0%
		10–15	11.7%	13.3%
		> 15	4.0%	5.2%
	Urban	≤ 9	8.4%	10.0%
		10–15	11.5%	13.3%
		> 15	4.0%	5.3%
	Rural	≤ 9	3.0%	4.8%
		10–15	12.2%	13.9%
		> 15	4.3%	2.0%

By area and age, 1991 and 1997

	Area	Age	1991	1997
P	National	12–24	45.7%	39.9%
		25–50	66.7%	66.8%
		50	47.4%	44.3%
	Urban	12–24	41.9%	37.5%
		25–50	67.1%	67.8%
		50	39.7%	40.2%
	Rural	12–24	50.2%	46.0%
		25–50	66.2%	63.9%
		50	55.5%	54.1%
U	National	12–24	14.1%	19.0%
		25–50	4.3%	7.0%
		50	2.0%	4.1%
	Urban	12–24	20.1%	22.9%
		25–50	5.8%	8.0%
		50	3.6%	5.1%
	Rural	12–24	8.3%	10.6%
		25–50	2.2%	4.1%
		50	0.7%	2.2%

Table 6.3 continued

	By area and years of schooling, 1991 and 1997					By area and age, 1991 and 1997			
	Area	**Years of schooling**	**1991**	**1997**		**Area**	**Age**	**1991**	**1997**
E	National	≤ 9	51.2%	46.2%	**E**	National	12–24	39.3%	32.3%
		10–15	57.3%	57.0%			25–50	63.8%	62.1%
		> 15	84.9%	82.3%			50	46.4%	42.5%
	Urban	≤ 9	45.1%	42.3%		Urban	12–24	33.5%	28.9%
		10–15	57.2%	57.0%			25–50	63.2%	62.4%
		> 15	84.4%	82.2%			50	38.2%	38.2%
	Rural	≤ 9	56.7%	53.5%		Rural	12–24	46.0%	41.1%
		10–15	57.6%	57.2%			25–50	64.8%	61.3%
		> 15	92.0%	86.6%			50	55.1%	52.9%

Notes:
P: Global participation rate.
U: Unemployment rate.
E: Employment rate.

Source: Calculations based on National Household Surveys.

ment rate at the national level. As said, employment fell despite booming economic activity. The slowdown of employment growth was accompanied by stagnation in the growth of the labour supply. As a result, the nationwide unemployment rate stabilized around 7 per cent.

In the second half of the decade, urban labour market conditions deteriorated starkly as a result of a dramatic fall in employment rates and a renewed increase in participation rates. This new dynamics entailed a steep rise in the unemployment rate starting in 1996, reaching an all-time high in 1999. Although the lack of dynamism in employment cannot be attributed exclusively to domestic demand, as we will see later on, this variable has undoubtedly played a decisive role in more recent years. The severest drops in the employment rate coincided with the deceleration and recession periods (1996 and 1999) and, in general, since 1996 there is a clear link between the behaviour of employment in the main cities and the trend in quarterly GDP (DANE 1999).

On the whole, employment rates fell during the entire decade. In the first half of the decade they fell in rural areas and in urban areas during the second half. For the country as a whole, the employment rate went down from 53 per cent in the early 1990s to a little under 50 per cent in 1999. The renewed trend toward rising labour participation manifested itself in an explosive growth of unemployment. As we shall see, these trends were accompanied by important changes in the sectoral composition of employment.

Table 6.3 gives more details of trends in labour market indicators for 1991 and 1997, the two benchmark years for the analysis of the effects of the reforms. In 1991, the trade reforms and the FDI liberalization were concluded and the new political charter was decreed. By 1997, the effects of the reforms have become visible and at that point in time it is also possible to isolate the effects of the severe crisis that affected the Colombian economy in recent years.

The indicators presented in Table 6.3 indicate that female participation rates are much lower than those of male workers. Nevertheless, labour participation of younger female generations has increased in urban areas thanks to the higher levels of education and lower fertility rates. During the period of analysis, we observe a drop in male participation in urban and rural areas and a drop in female participation in rural areas (Henao and Parra 1998, Farné et al. 1998, Ribero and García 1996).

Participation and employment rates increase with educational level, regardless of age, gender or area. Between 1991 and 1997, employment rates went down for all educational levels, except for higher-educated women. Unemployment was higher for women of all educational levels and for people with 10 to 15 years of education. In this period, unemployment increased for all educational levels, except for more skilled workers in rural areas.

However, this is due to their exit from the labour market, as the occupational rate of this type of workers decreased considerably. The rise in unemployment among men of 10 to 15 years of age is slightly higher than for the corresponding female group. The highest occupation and participation rates are observed among workers in the age group of 25 to 50 years, both in urban and rural areas. In contrast, the unemployment rates tend to fall with age.

Employment Trends

A more detailed view of national labour market dynamics can be obtained by decomposing changes in labour supply and demand by main structural factors.[6] The results are summarized in Table 6.4. The table shows that supply-side changes, due to demographic factors as well as changes in the global participation rate, should be equal to demand-side changes, due to changes in occupation and unemployment rates, both measured as proportions of the total population.

Three basic conclusions can be drawn from these results. First, labour supply increased at a moderate pace during the period. During 1991–95 the positive demographic effect was partly offset by the drop in labour participation. The demographic effect came to a complete halt in the middle of the decade, leading together with a continued decline in labour participation to a

Table 6.4 Decomposition of the global changes in the labour market (changes in percentage points, defined in relation to the total population)

	1991–95	1995–97	1991–97
Changes in labour supply			
Total[a]	1.2%	–0.6%	0.5%
Demographic	2.2%	–0.1%	2.2%
Participation	–1.0%	0.6%	–1.6%
Changes in labour demand			
Employment[a]	0.7%	–2.9%	–2.2%
Tradables	–3.9%	–3.0%	–7.0%
Non-tradables	4.7%	0.1%	4.8%
Unemployment	0.5%	2.1%	2.6%

Notes: [a] The decomposition excludes the joint effect of the changes in each of the two components.

Source: Own calculations based on National Household Surveys.

fall in labour supply in 1995–97. The fall in labour participation came to an end in 1998, which is beyond the reference period for purposes of analysis of the reform effects.

The second conclusion is related to labour demand. Employment creation was dismal during the entire period. Insufficient employment generation is reflected in the drop in the occupation rate by 2.2 percentage points of the total population between 1991 and 1997. Low employment growth is essentially due to a lack of labour demand in traded goods sectors. It should be emphasized that the loss of employment in the tradable sectors has been persistent throughout the decade, and because of its severity should therefore be linked to the effects of the structural reforms. Employment creation in non-traded goods sectors offset these job losses during the boom period, but ceased to absorb excess labour in subsequent years of slower economic growth. As a consequence, job losses in the tradable sector now became fully reflected in the overall occupation rate.

Finally, the favourable combination of falling participation and rising employment in non-tradable sectors had no effect on unemployment up to 1995, at which point it made a tailspin. As a result, unemployment levels rose by 2.1 percentage points of total population between 1995 and 1997. As indicated, the subsequent deep recession and the renewed rise in labour participation led to an explosive growth of unemployment in the years thereafter.

Trends in employment can be analysed further at the one-digit level of the economic activity classification. We apply a decomposition analysis of employment growth in terms of changes in the difference between per capita GDP growth and labour productivity growth weighted by sector. The results of this decomposition are presented in Table 6.5. It shows that the overall employment loss in agriculture and manufacturing was linked to a strong decrease in per capita output combined with substantial increases of labour productivity. As a result, the employment rate of the tradable sectors dropped as much as 7.0 percentage points of the total population between 1991 and 1997. In contrast, non-tradable sectors, especially services, showed a sustained increase in per capita GDP, especially during the boom period. During these years growth of per capita GDP was higher than labour productivity growth, allowing dynamic employment generation in these sectors. However, this process was interrupted and even changed direction in several sectors in subsequent years. The joint effects of the slow down in job creation in non-tradable sectors since 1996, linked to the deceleration of the economy and the long-term deterioration of employment in tradable activities thus explain the dramatic fall of total employment.

There are some relevant peculiarities about these overall sectoral trends. On the one hand, there is the stark decline in agricultural employment be-

Table 6.5 Decomposition of labour productivity, per capita GDP and employment growth

	1991–95	1995–97	1991–97
Growth of labour productivity			
Agriculture	18.7%	–4.1%	13.8%
Mining	65.6%	22.7%	103.2%
Manufacturing	–2.8%	18.4%	15.2%
Electricity, gas and water	34.1%	–38.6%	–17.6%
Construction	7.2%	14.1%	22.3%
Commerce	13.2%	1.1%	14.5%
Transportation	2.5%	10.6%	13.3%
Financial services	–3.0%	0.1%	–2.9%
Other services	11.7%	4.4%	16.6%
Total	**10.4%**	**4.2%**	**15.0%**
Tradables	12.0%	5.6%	18.3%
Non-tradables	10.8%	4.0%	15.2%
Growth of per capita output			
Agriculture	–0.7%	–3.9%	–4.6%
Mining	9.0%	8.5%	18.3%
Manufacturing	2.7%	–3.7%	–1.1%
Electricity, gas and water	11.7%	2.6%	14.6%
Construction	46.9%	–4.1%	40.8%
Commerce	19.8%	–0.9%	18.7%
Transportation	13.6%	6.1%	20.4%
Financial services	24.4%	4.4%	29.9%
Other services	13.4%	9.9%	24.6%
Total	**11.2%**	**1.2%**	**12.5%**
Tradables	1.7%	–2.6%	–0.9%
Non-tradables	19.8%	4.2%	24.8%
Change in employment			
Agriculture	–4.4%	0.0%	–4.3%
Mining	–0.4%	–0.1%	–0.5%
Manufacturing	0.8%	–2.9%	–2.1%
Electricity, gas and water	–0.1%	0.3%	0.2%
Construction	1.7%	–1.0%	0.7%
Commerce	1.2%	–0.4%	0.8%
Transportation	0.5%	–0.2%	0.3%
Financial services	1.0%	0.2%	1.2%
Other services	0.3%	1.2%	1.5%
Total	**0.7%**	**–2.9%**	**–2.2%**
Tradables	–3.9%	–3.0%	–7.0%
Non-tradables	4.7%	0.1%	4.8%

Notes: Employment growth does not coincide exactly with the difference between output and labour productivity growth due to interaction effects.

Source: Own calculations based on National Household Surveys.

tween 1991 and 1995. This is most visible in rural areas where the share of agricultural employment dropped by more than 4 percentage points in those years (see Table 6.2). On the other hand, between 1995 and 1997 employment losses in tradable sectors were concentrated in manufacturing. In this case, employment deteriorated in urban areas, reflecting the effects of the structural adjustment as well as the slow down of economic growth.

On the whole, the employment share in non-tradable sectors increased strongly from 57.0 per cent in 1991 to 63.2 per cent in 1997 (see Table 6.2). The pro-cyclical behaviour of employment was most noticeable in the construction sector. The sector boomed in 1991–95 and plunged into a recession thereafter. The employment share of the sector followed the same pattern as it went from 4.5 per cent in 1991 to 6.1 per cent in 1995, dropping to 5.3 per cent in 1997.

The preceding analysis can be extended to study the dynamics of job creation by sector, skill, occupational category and gender. Looking at employment growth by sector and educational level, we find two clear patterns (Table 6.6). First, the occupation rate of unskilled workers fell over the decade. The decline was most severe in tradable sectors. Second, employment creation for skilled workers concentrated in non-tradable sectors, especially in financial services and other services, whereas it stagnated in the tradable sectors.

The drop in the employment rate for unskilled workers – defined as those with primary education (0–5 years) or incomplete secondary education (6–10 years) – concentrated in agriculture between 1991 and 1995 and in manufacturing between 1995 and 1997. For non-tradable sectors we observe a clear cyclical behaviour in unskilled labour demand, closely linked to growth in the construction sector. Indeed, during the expansion phase this sector was the most dynamic in creating jobs for unskilled workers. In contrast, during the adjustment phase the decline in construction jobs for unskilled labour was second after that in manufacturing in explaining lower occupation rates. This dynamics of the employment rate for unskilled workers thus suggests that in non-tradable sectors the job creation for unskilled workers has been linked to the sector's own business cycle. In the tradable secto
mand showed a consistent decline.

Sectoral labour demand for skilled workers – de
incomplete (12–15 years) or complete (16 years or m
tion – has not increased very strongly, except in finan
In fact, job creation for skilled workers in financial
plains two-thirds of the increase in the employment
in the entire economy between 1991 and 1
secondary education (11 years), commerce
been the main source of employment creation,

Table 6.6 Changes in employment rates by educational level

	0–5 years			**6–10 years**			**11 years**		
	1991–95	**1995–97**	**1991–97**	**1991–95**	**1995–97**	**1991–97**	**1991–95**	**1995–97**	**1991–97**
Agriculture	–3.3%	–0.2%	–3.5%	–0.6%	–0.1%	–0.7%	–0.2%	0.2%	–0.0%
Mining	–0.2%	–0.2%	–0.4%	–0.0%	–0.1%	–0.1%	–0.0%	0.1%	0.0%
Manufacturing	–0.1%	–1.1%	–1.2%	0.1%	–1.3%	–1.2%	0.9%	–0.6%	0.3%
Electricity, gas and water	–0.0%	0.1%	0.0%	–0.0%	0.0%	0.0%	0.0%	0.1%	0.1%
Construction	0.8%	–0.5%	0.3%	0.6%	–0.6%	0.0%	0.2%	–0.0%	0.2%
Commerce	0.0%	–0.4%	–0.4%	0.0%	–0.4%	–0.4%	1.0%	0.1%	1.1%
Transportation	0.1%	–0.4%	–0.3%	0.2%	–0.2%	–0.0%	0.3%	0.2%	0.5%
Financial services	0.1%	0.0%	0.2%	0.2%	–0.1%	0.0%	0.3%	–0.0%	0.3%
Other services	–0.3%	0.1%	–0.3%	–0.2%	–0.2%	–0.4%	0.7%	0.3%	1.1%
Total	**–3.0%**	**–2.5%**	**–5.6%**	**0.3%**	**–3.0%**	**–2.7%**	**3.2%**	**0.3%**	**3.5%**
Tradables	–3.7%	–1.4%	–5.1%	–0.5%	–1.4%	–2.0%	0.6%	–0.3%	0.3%
Non-tradables	0.6%	–1.1%	–0.5%	0.8%	–1.6%	–0.7%	2.6%	0.6%	3.2%

	12–15 years			16+ years			TOTAL		
	1991–95	**1995–97**	**1991–97**	**1991–95**	**1995–97**	**1991–97**	**1991–95**	**1995–97**	**1991–97**
Agriculture	–0.1%	0.0%	–0.0%	–0.1%	0.1%	–0.0%	–4.4%	0.0%	–4.3%
Mining	–0.0%	–0.0%	–0.0%	–0.1%	0.1%	–0.0%	–0.4%	–0.1%	–0.5%
Manufacturing	–0.0%	–0.1%	–0.1%	–0.0%	0.1%	0.1%	0.8%	–2.9%	–2.1%
Electricity, gas and water	–0.0%	0.0%	0.0%	–0.0%	0.1%	0.1%	–0.1%	0.3%	0.2%
Construction	0.0%	0.0%	0.1%	0.1%	0.1%	0.1%	1.7%	–1.0%	0.7%
Commerce	0.1%	0.0%	0.2%	–0.0%	0.3%	0.3%	1.2%	–0.4%	0.8%
Transportation	–0.0%	0.1%	0.0%	–0.0%	0.1%	0.1%	0.5%	–0.2%	0.3%
Financial services	0.2%	0.0%	0.2%	0.2%	0.3%	0.5%	1.0%	0.2%	1.2%
Other services	–0.2%	0.5%	0.3%	0.3%	0.6%	0.8%	0.3%	1.2%	1.5%
Total	**0.0%**	**0.6%**	**0.7%**	**0.2%**	**1.7%**	**2.0%**	**0.7%**	**–2.9%**	**–2.2%**
Tradables	–0.1%	–0.1%	–0.2%	–0.3%	0.3%	0.0%	–3.9%	–3.0%	–7.0%
Non-tradables	0.1%	0.7%	0.8%	0.5%	1.5%	2.0%	4.7%	0.1%	4.8%

Source: Own calculations based on National Household Surveys.

Table 6.7 Employment growth by occupational status

	1991–95			**1995–97**			**1991–97**		
	Men	**Women**	**Total**	**Men**	**Women**	**Total**	**Men**	**Women**	**Total**
Unpaid family workers	–1.7%	–1.1%	–2.8%	0.0%	–0.3%	–0.2%	–1.7%	–1.3%	–3.0%
Private sector wage earners	1.5%	2.2%	3.7%	–2.4%	–1.0%	–3.4%	–0.9%	1.2%	0.3%
Public employees	–1.1%	–0.8%	–1.9%	–0.8%	0.5%	–0.3%	–1.9%	–0.3%	–2.2%
Domestic servants	–0.0%	–0.2%	–0.2%	0.1%	–0.3%	–0.2%	0.1%	–0.5%	–0.4%
Self-employed	1.1%	1.1%	2.2%	1.8%	0.0%	1.8%	2.9%	1.1%	4.0%
Employers	–0.5%	0.2%	–0.3%	–0.5%	–0.0%	–0.5%	–1.0%	0.1%	–0.9%
Total	**–0.8%**	**1.5%**	**0.7%**	**–1.8%**	**–1.1%**	**–2.9%**	**–2.6%**	**0.4%**	**–2.2%**

Source: Own calculations based on National Household Surveys.

Employment trends by occupational status and gender are characterized by three main features (Table 6.7). First, growth of wage employment shows a clear cyclical pattern. During the first expansion phase of the economy most employment creation benefited wage earners, whereas during 1995–97 this type of job suffered most from the contraction in labour demand. Second, self-employment increased strongly throughout the decade. The combination of these two factors during the years of declining growth hints at a process of informalization of employment. Finally, female employment rates increased relatively. In more recent years, though, the upward trend slowed down considerably.

Overall, the lack of dynamism in employment growth is closely linked to tradable activities. Non-tradable sectors were incapable of absorbing first-time job seekers and displaced workers from the tradable sectors during the boom period. The results also suggest that the change in employment trend by skill level is closely linked to the changes in the production structure. The decline of traded goods sectors (especially agriculture and manufacturing) has caused a permanent loss of jobs for unskilled labour, whereas output expansion in non-traded goods sectors (financial and other services) basically generated greater demand for skilled labour.

Changes in the Labour Productivity Growth

Labour productivity growth can be decomposed in three ways (see Chapter 1, Appendix). Table 6.8 shows the results of each. The first (A) decomposes the productivity growth as the sectoral sum of the difference between GDP growth and employment growth, each weighted by their share in total GDP and employment. The second and third (B and C) decompose the total labour productivity growth in a weighted average of productivity growth of each sector plus an inter-sectoral reallocation term for GDP or employment, respectively.

The results of the first decomposition suggest that overall productivity growth was due to a combination of factors. Productivity growth in traded goods sectors was important. However, in agriculture and manufacturing it was linked to a combination of low GDP growth and an accelerated drop in employment. This applies for agriculture particularly during 1991–95 and for manufacturing during 1995–97, that is the years during which these sectors faced strong adjustments. Mining's important contribution to the economy's overall productivity growth was associated with strong and steady growth of the sector's output. A similar phenomenon occurred in non-tradables during the boom period. The trend moved in the same direction until 1997, albeit at a slower rhythm.

The second and third decompositions are alternative, but equivalent exercises. The salient result is that sector-specific productivity growth is the main

Table 6.8 Decomposition of labour productivity growth (average annual growth rates)

	1991–95	1995–97	1991–97	1991–95	1995–97	1991–97	1991–95	1995–97	1991–97
(A)	**GDP {$(X_i/X)X_i^*$}**			**Employment {$(L_i/L)l_i^*$}**			**Total**		
Agriculture	0.4%	–0.0%	0.2%	–0.7%	0.4%	–0.3%	1.0%	–0.5%	0.5%
Mining	0.2%	0.2%	0.2%	–0.1%	–0.0%	–0.1%	0.3%	0.3%	0.3%
Manufacturing	0.5%	–0.0%	0.3%	0.5%	–1.2%	–0.1%	0.0%	1.2%	0.5%
Electricity, gas and water	0.1%	0.0%	0.1%	–0.0%	0.2%	0.1%	0.1%	–0.2%	–0.0%
Construction	0.4%	–0.0%	0.3%	0.5%	–0.4%	0.2%	–0.1%	0.4%	0.1%
Commerce	0.8%	0.2%	0.6%	0.7%	0.2%	0.5%	0.1%	–0.0%	0.1%
Transportation	0.5%	0.4%	0.5%	0.2%	–0.0%	0.2%	0.2%	0.5%	0.3%
Financial services	1.2%	0.7%	1.1%	0.3%	0.2%	0.3%	0.9%	0.5%	0.8%
Other services	0.7%	0.9%	0.8%	0.5%	1.0%	0.7%	0.2%	–0.1%	0.1%
Total	4.5%	2.4%	3.8%	1.9%	0.3%	1.4%	2.7%	2.1%	2.6%
Tradables	1.1%	0.2%	0.8%	–0.3%	–0.9%	–0.5%	1.3%	1.1%	1.3%
Non-tradables	3.5%	2.2%	3.1%	2.2%	1.1%	1.9%	1.4%	1.0%	1.4%
(B)	**Productivity weighted by GDP**			**Reallocation term**			**Total labour productivity**		
Agriculture	1.0%	–0.4%	0.5%	–0.1%	0.0%	–0.0%	0.9%	–0.4%	0.5%
Mining	0.7%	0.4%	0.8%	0.1%	0.2%	0.2%	0.9%	0.7%	0.9%
Manufacturing	–0.1%	1.8%	0.5%	0.2%	–0.0%	0.1%	0.0%	1.8%	0.6%
Electricity, gas and water	0.1%	–0.2%	–0.0%	0.0%	0.0%	0.0%	0.1%	–0.2%	–0.0%
Construction	0.1%	0.3%	0.1%	–0.2%	0.0%	–0.1%	–0.2%	0.3%	–0.0%

Commerce	0.4%	0.1%	0.3%	–0.7%	–0.1%	–0.5%	–0.3%	–0.1%	–0.2%
Transportation	0.1%	0.5%	0.2%	0.2%	0.2%	0.2%	0.3%	0.6%	0.4%
Financial services	–0.1%	0.0%	–0.1%	0.9%	0.5%	0.8%	0.8%	0.5%	0.8%
Other services	0.4%	0.3%	0.4%	–0.5%	–0.7%	–0.6%	–0.1%	–0.4%	–0.3%
Total	2.5%	2.1%	2.5%	0.0%	0.0%	0.0%	2.7%	2.1%	2.6%
Tradables	1.4%	1.2%	1.4%	0.1%	0.0%	0.1%	1.5%	1.3%	1.5%
Non-tradables	1.4%	1.1%	1.3%	–0.4%	–0.2%	–0.3%	1.0%	0.9%	1.0%

(C)	**Productivity weighted by employment**			**Reallocation term**			**Total labour productivity**		
Agriculture	1.2%	–0.5%	0.6%	0.1%	–0.0%	0.1%	1.3%	–0.5%	0.7%
Mining	0.2%	0.1%	0.2%	–0.2%	–0.2%	–0.2%	–0.0%	–0.0%	0.0%
Manufacturing	–0.1%	1.4%	0.4%	0.2%	–0.3%	–0.0%	0.1%	1.1%	0.3%
Electricity, gas and water	0.1%	–0.1%	–0.0%	–0.0%	0.2%	0.0%	0.0%	0.1%	0.0%
Construction	0.1%	0.4%	0.2%	–0.2%	0.1%	–0.1%	–0.1%	0.6%	0.1%
Commerce	0.7%	0.1%	0.5%	–0.3%	–0.1%	–0.2%	0.4%	0.0%	0.3%
Transportation	0.0%	0.3%	0.1%	0.2%	–0.0%	0.1%	0.2%	0.3%	0.2%
Financial services	–0.0%	0.0%	–0.0%	1.1%	0.5%	0.9%	1.0%	0.5%	0.9%
Other services	0.7%	0.5%	0.6%	–0.2%	–0.4%	–0.3%	0.4%	0.1%	0.3%
Total	2.7%	2.3%	2.4%	0.6%	–0.2%	0.3%	2.7%	2.1%	2.6%
Tradables	1.3%	1.1%	1.3%	–0.0%	–0.1%	–0.1%	1.3%	1.1%	1.3%
Non-tradables	1.5%	1.2%	1.4%	–0.2%	–0.1%	–0.2%	1.4%	1.0%	1.4%

Notes: Contribution of each sector to the growth of employment as a share of total population. The totals of the three decompositions do not coincide exactly because the discrete estimates do not include interaction effects.

Source: Own calculations based on National Household Surveys and national accounts.

determinant of overall productivity growth. Reallocation effects across sectors in terms of GDP or employment are small. Relatively rapid GDP growth and labour reallocation toward the financial sector was a source of productivity growth, but was offset by inverse trends in other non-tradable sectors, especially commerce and other services.

Wage Dynamics

Throughout the 1980s, labour incomes showed a moderate decline (Figures 6.2 and 6.3). Real labour incomes increased systematically starting in 1991, both by sector and skill level. Wages increased across-the-board in all sectors, but most strongly in government and financial services. Mean income in construction also increased considerably in the beginning of the decade, but this upward trend came to an abrupt halt by the end of the boom.

The picture for labour income growth by educational level is different (Figure 6.3). Labour income increased for all educational levels in the early 1990s, but this trend was short-lived. Starting in 1994, labour incomes stagnated for workers at all educational levels, except for those with university education. From 1996 onwards, there was a gradual drop in wages except for workers with a higher technical education (complete or incomplete). The post-1996 wage dynamics suggests that incomes of unskilled workers are more closely linked to the business cycle than those of skilled workers. Wages of skilled workers (completed university education) increased steadily with respect to labour incomes of workers at all other educational levels. This suggests that the relative demand for skilled labour has increased because of the sectoral reallocation toward tradable sectors and technological changes induced by the reform process. Another possible explanation could be that the supply of higher-educated workers has not responded at the same speed to these changes in the composition of labour demand.

This wage dynamics is at odds with minimum wage trends, which remained relatively stable after having fallen by 6 per cent at the beginning of the decade (between 1985–89 and 1991–92). Because of this difference in minimum and overall average wage trends, the share of workers with an income below the minimum wage has decreased. Indeed, estimates of the OIT (1998) indicate that the share of wage earners with incomes below two official minimum wages went from about 80 per cent in 1990 to only 63 per cent of total workers in 1997.

6.5 EFFECTS OF THE LABOUR MARKET IN INCOME DISTRIBUTION

A Brief Review of the Literature

Several recent studies conclude that urban income distribution in Colombia has improved during most of the 1980s; a trend that started in the 1970s. The studies also show that this trend reversed in the late 1980s toward a strong increase in inequality in the 1990s.[7] In rural areas we see opposite trends. Rural income distribution worsened between 1978 and 1988 followed by an improvement in the first half of the 1990s, to worsen again to some extent toward the end of the decade. Despite these offsetting trends, the worsening of urban income distribution prevailed over the nationwide trend in the 1990s (DNP 1998, Leibovich and Núñez 1999, Ocampo et al. 1998, Sánchez and Núñez 1999, Vélez et al. 1999). Table 6.9 shows that the primary distribution of income at the national level indeed deteriorated between 1991 and 1997 by slightly less than two percentage points of the Gini coefficient. This was a product of an adverse movement of more than four points in urban areas, which surpassed the effect of the nearly four-point improvement in rural areas. We should add though that the expansion of social spending and its better targeting toward the poor has redressed the trend in primary income distribution, that is the secondary income distribution improved (Sánchez and Núñez 1999). In other words, the overall distribution (primary and secondary) does not show any clear pattern during the decade.

These studies also indicate which are the determinants of the observed changes. These include shifts in the distribution and returns to education, employment opportunities, household characteristics (dependency rate and size), rural–urban terms of trade and the share of non-wage income (whose distribution is much less equitable than that of wages). Ocampo et al. (1998) and Sánchez and Núñez (1999) show that there was a massive redistribution of income between urban areas and the countryside. Urban high-income groups are the winners and rural high-income groups the main losers.[8] The former result largely reflects the rise in relative labour income of skilled workers and a downward levelling of rural incomes caused by the crisis of commercial agriculture, respectively. Vélez et al. (1999) show that income inequality among male workers decreased between 1978 and 1988, but increased notoriously between 1988 and 1995. In contrast, increasing concentration of incomes among female workers was a sustained trend of the entire 1978–95 period.

Ocampo et al. (1998) argue that falling urban inequality can be explained by a combination of increased levels and an improved distribution of education, favourable employment opportunities at the middle of the decade, and

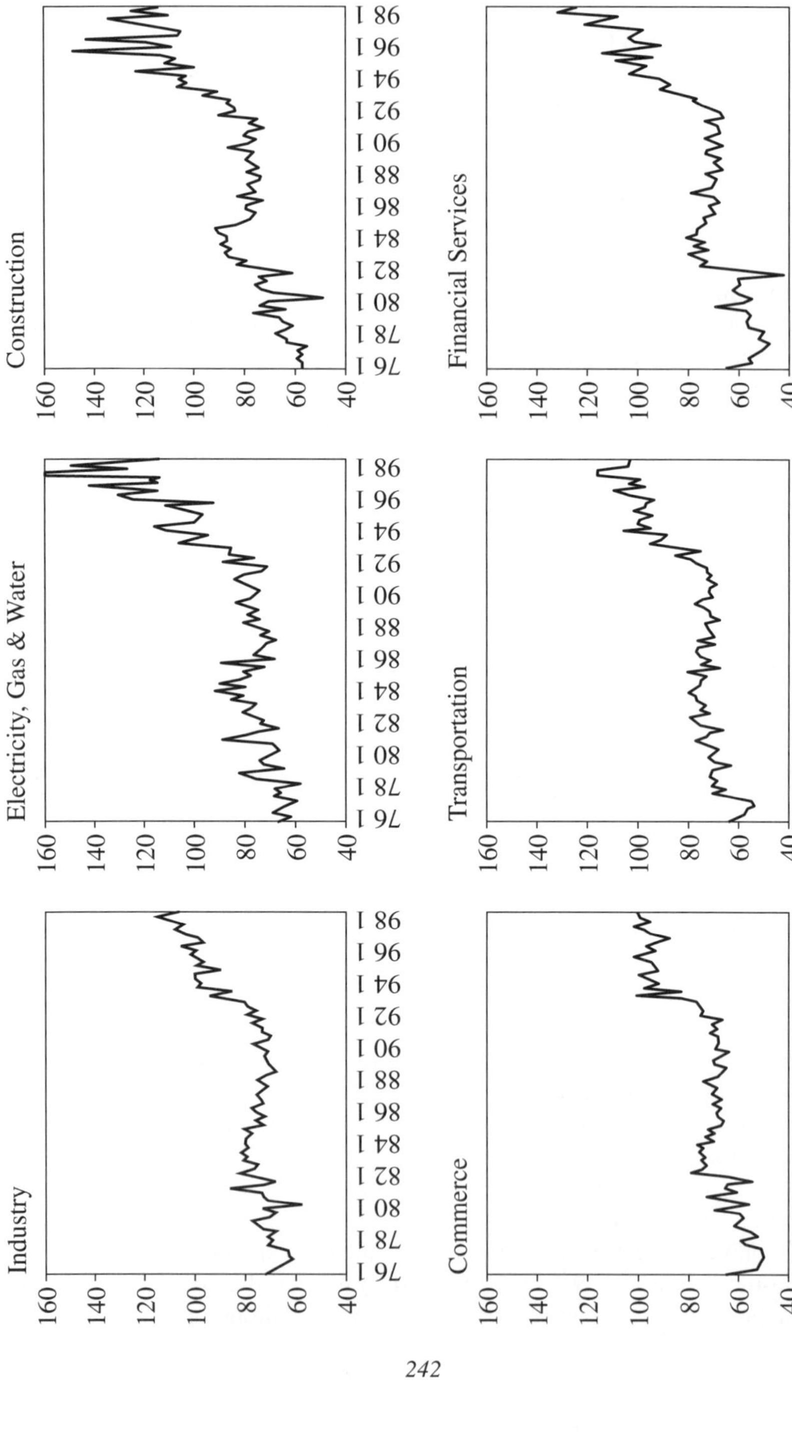

Industry
Electricity, Gas & Water
Construction
Commerce
Transportation
Financial Services
160
140
120
100
80
60
40
76 1
78 1
80 1
82 1
84 1
86 1
88 1
90 1
92 1
94 1
96 1
98 1

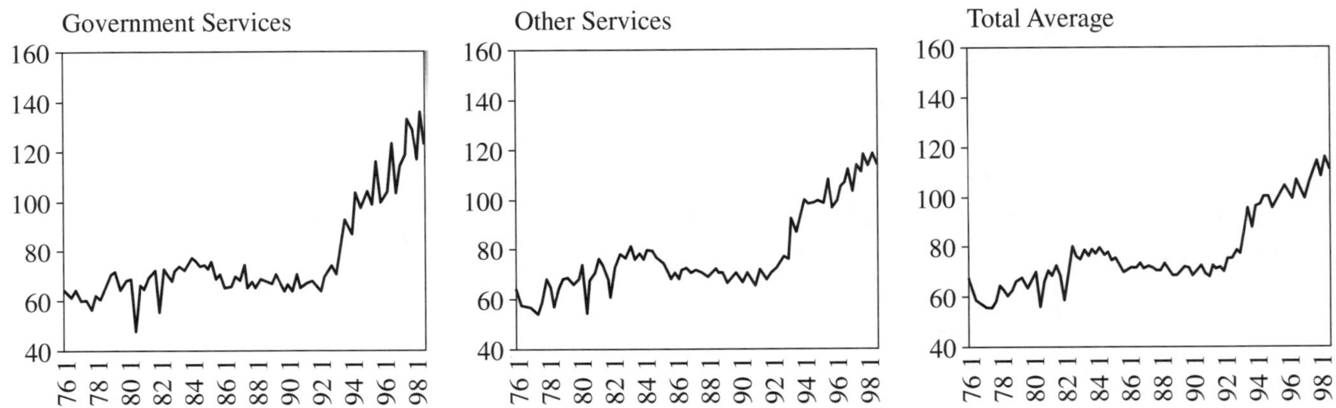

Source: DANE, National Household Survey.

Figure 6.2 Real wages by sector, 1976–98 (index, December 1994 = 100)

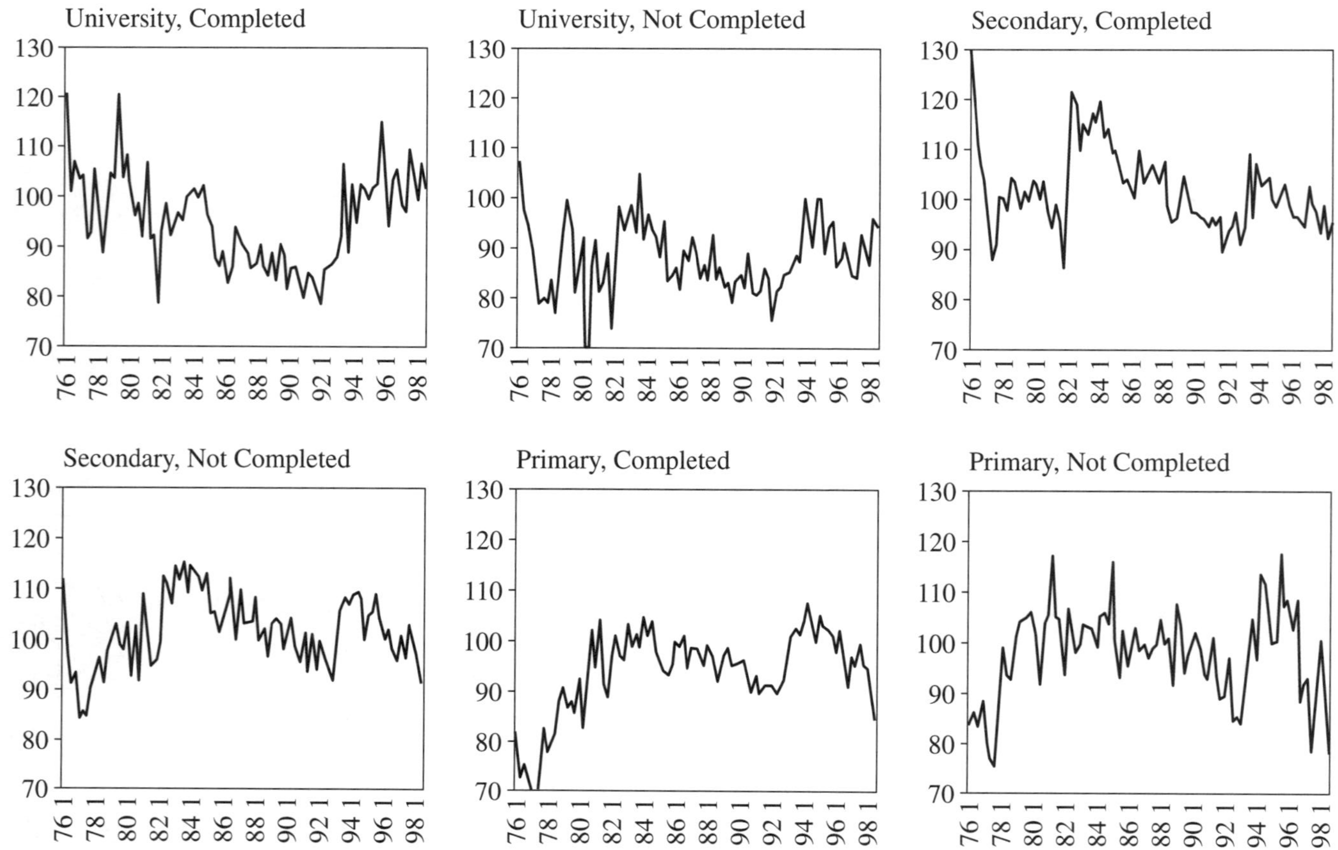
University, Completed
University, Not Completed
Secondary, Completed
Secondary, Not Completed
Primary, Completed
Primary, Not Completed
130
120
110
100
90
80
70
76 1
78 1
80 1
82 1
84 1
86 1
88 1
90 1
92 1
94 1
96 1
98 1

(a)

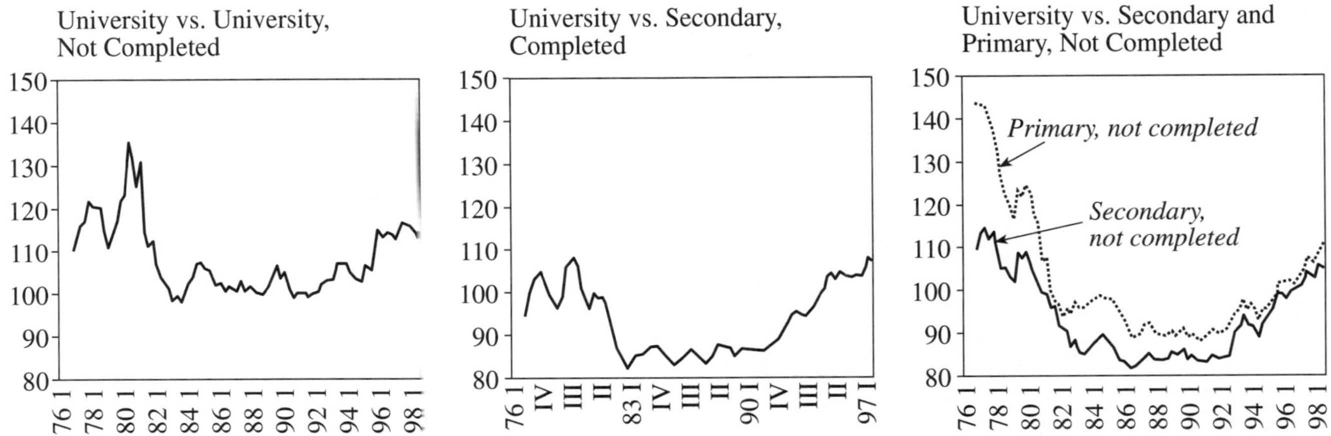

(b)

Source: DANE, National Household Survey.

Figures 6.3 (a) Trends in urban labour incomes by educational level, 1976–98 (index, December 1994 = 100); (b) relative urban labour incomes, 1976–98 reduced economic dependency rates of households. The demographic transition and the subsequent rise in female labour participation facilitated the fall in dependency rates. Reduced job opportunities, widening labour income gaps by educational level, and the relative growth of non-wage income were the adverse factors that determined the rise in income inequality in the 1990s. These effects predominated over the impact of favourable trends that continued – albeit more slowly – such as the improved levels and more equal distribution of education, the changes in demographic patterns, more female labour participation and decreases in average household size. According to this study, the trade opening produced major losses in profitability in rural areas, thus severely affecting large landowners and wage earners in commercial agriculture. Both groups belong to the highest deciles of rural income distribution. The net effect was a process of income equalization and inequality declined with falling mean rural income.

Distributional shifts in urban labour incomes are also reflected in substantial changes in rates of return to education. Educational returns declined in the 1980s and returns to higher education increased significantly in the 1990s (Sánchez and Núñez 1998). According to Sánchez and Núñez, these relative wage changes are unrelated to changes in the composition of labour supply. Rather, they are caused by labour demand shifts linked to changes in technology, production structure, relative factor productivity, economic opening and adjustment, and non-labour factor prices, especially the relative price of capital.

Leibovich and Núñez (1999) show that rural income inequality decreased for both wage earners and self-employed during 1988–95, male and female workers alike. Changes in endowments (particularly education and household size) and returns to education have positively influenced this trend. They further show that for both sexes inequality is lower among wage earners than among self-employed, both when measured by the Gini coefficient and entropy measures.

An essential part of the distributional changes is linked to the within-group income distribution of groups with the same basic characteristics (in terms of age, gender, education, experience, household head and residence).[9] According to Vélez et al. (1999), the greater within-group homogeneity explained an important part of the improvement in urban income distribution during 1978–88, and the greater heterogeneity explains the adverse trend of the subsequent period. For the recent period, Leibovich and Núñez (1999) find that less within-group inequality for workers with similar occupational characteristics was one of the determinants of the improvement in the distribution of rural income.

In turn, several studies have tried to explore the effects of the macroeconomic variables on income distribution. Bernal et al. (1998) find that a production shift towards tradable sectors tends to reduce the Gini coefficient, whereas higher inflation, higher unemployment rates and real devaluation tend to increase inequality. Results presented by Ocampo et al. (1998) do not support some of these findings, particularly not the supposed favourable distributional effects of lower inflation. Similar results are obtained with regard to the inequality-reducing impact of a resource shift toward tradables. The Ocampo study shows in particular that the trade opening led to rising income inequality, due to widening skill differentials. Increases in public expenditures in the 1990s had a similar effect. The former result also coincides with that obtained by Birchenall (1997), who used a methodology of probability functions and found that the trade opening induced a technological change that increased the demand for skilled labour in the seven main cities. Sánchez and Núñez (1999) found that, in the long term, the increases in unemployment rate, household size and real exchange-rate depreciation led to an increase in the number of poor households. They also found though that improvements in educational level, labour productivity and the rural–urban terms of trade help to reduce the poverty incidence in the main cities.

In sum, the existing studies associate the rise in urban inequality in Colombia during the 1990s with the strong shifts in labour earnings by skill level. The skilled–unskilled income gap increased. This is explained, alternatively, by increases in the relative demand for skilled labour resulting from trade liberalization, technological changes and greater public expenditures. Income distribution improved in rural areas, but this happened in a context of large income declines caused by the deterioration of the rural terms of trade and the ensuing crisis of commercial agriculture.

Labour Incomes and Income Distribution: Overall Effects

Table 6.9 shows the results of the microsimulations following the methodology spelled out in Chapter 2 and using data of the National Household Surveys (ENH) for September 1991 and 1997. The methodology consists basically in simulating what income distribution and poverty would have been in 1997 had the conditions of the 1991 labour market prevailed. These conditions are the participation rate, the unemployment rate, sectoral distribution of employment and labour income. The simulations are carried out for the national total and also for urban and rural areas. The effects of each labour market variable on income distribution are analysed first separately and then sequentially to obtain their joint effect.[10] The simulations were repeated 1,000 times in order to test the robustness of the estimates (MonteCarlo experiment).

The simulation results for individual parameter changes show that the national Gini coefficient would have been lower in all cases if the labour

Table 6.9 Microsimulations: labour market adjustment and inequality

	National	Urban	Rural
1991 Gini	0.5482	0.4977	0.4790
1997 Gini	0.5650	0.5411	0.4409
Difference	0.0168	0.0434	–0.0381
Participation			
Simulated	0.5595	0.5385	0.4498
Difference	0.0055	0.0026	–0.0089
% Explained	32.7%	6.0%	–23.4%
Unemployment			
Simulated	0.5613	0.5365	0.4446
Difference	0.0037	0.0046	–0.0037
% Explained	22.1%	10.7%	–9.8%
Employment			
Simulated	0.5495	0.5314	0.4638
Difference	0.0155	0.0097	–0.0229
% Explained	92.1%	22.3%	–60.2%
Wages			
Simulated	0.5504	0.5272	0.4295
Difference	0.0146	0.0139	0.0114
% Explained	86.5%	32.0%	30.0%
Sequential			
Simulated	0.5361	0.5187	0.4823
Difference	0.0289	0.0224	–0.0414
% Explained	171.9%	51.7%	–108.7%

Source: Own calculations based on National Household Surveys.

market conditions of 1991 still prevailed in 1997. Changes in the participation rate have led to an increase in the Gini coefficient by 0.0055 points (of 0.0168 observed). The rise in the Gini is 0.0037 for the effect of the unemployment rate, 0.0155 for the sectoral composition of employment and 0.0146 for wages. The results show that the latter two variables had the largest impact on income distribution during that period. The sequential simulation confirms these results. Had the overall 1991 labour market conditions prevailed in 1997, the Gini coefficient would have been even lower than that observed in 1991, i.e. 0.536 against 0.548.

The results of the simulations for the urban areas of the labour market conditions are similar to those found for the national total. The shifts in employment and wage structure explain, respectively, 22.3 and 32.0 per cent of the changes in the Gini coefficient. The sequential simulation explains 52 per cent of the increase in the Gini coefficient in urban areas, i.e. 0.0244 of a total increase of 0.0434 (from 0.497 to 0.541). This means that the greatest concentration of income was also due to other factors not considered in the labour market variables included in the simulations. These include the greater dispersion in earnings of workers with the same characteristics and the trend in non-labour incomes. In rural areas, the Gini coefficient dropped by 0.0381 (from 0.479 to 0.441). The changes in participation rates, unemployment and, most importantly, the composition of employment (which explains 60 per cent of the change in the Gini) largely explain the decrease in income inequality. Changes in wages show an opposite trend though.

The same methodology was applied to analyse changes in poverty. The results are much weaker than those for income distribution. According to Table 6.10, the percentage of poor households at the national level reached 41.4 per cent in 1997 as against 41.8 per cent in 1991, meaning that the incidence of poverty remained essentially the same. However, results differ for urban and rural areas. The share of poor urban households decreased from 37.5 to 28.9 per cent, but increased for rural households from 55.0 to 59.9 per cent. The simulation exercises indicate that, had the 1991 participation rate, unemployment rate and sectoral composition of employment prevailed in 1997, the poverty incidence would have been lower than that observed. The results of the simulation with the wage structure point in the opposite direction.

For the urban sector, the methodology has many limitations when it comes to explaining the strong reduction in poverty. Other factors must have been important to explain this trend. The work of Núñez and Sánchez (1999) shows that the decrease of the percentage of poor in the seven largest cities was basically due to changes in the relative prices of the consumption basket used to measure the poverty line. Of the 12 percentage points by which poverty decreased, about 8.4 are explained by the 'price effect', meaning that the inflation rate for the (food) poverty basket was lower than the average inflation rate.

The methodology explains changes in rural poverty better. The results of the simulation show that, had the 1991 rural labour market conditions prevailed in 1997, the percentage of rural poor would have been lower than that observed. In particular, the variable with the highest incidence on the increase of the percentage of rural poor was the composition of employment, which explains 60 per cent of the change in the poverty incidence (0.0293 of 0.0490 points). The sequential simulation, which takes into account the combination of the labour market conditions of 1991, shows that these variables explain jointly 59 per cent increase of rural poverty (0.0287 of 0.0490 points).

Table 6.10 Microsimulations: labour market adjustment and poverty

	National	Urban	Rural
1991 poverty incidence	0.4180	0.3750	0.5500
1997 poverty incidence	0.4140	0.2890	0.5990
Difference	–0.0040	–0.0860	0.0490
Participation			
Simulated	0.4081	0.2852	0.5893
Difference	–0.0059	–0.0038	–0.0097
% Explained	–146.7%	–4.4%	–19.7%
Unemployment			
Simulated	0.4071	0.2824	0.5953
Difference	–0.0069	–0.0066	–0.0037
% Explained	–171.6%	–7.6%	7.6%
Employment			
Simulated	0.3994	0.2811	0.5697
Difference	–0.0146	–0.0079	–0.0293
% Explained	–365.8%	–9.2%	–59.9%
Wages			
Simulated	0.4156	0.2905	0.6001
Difference	0.0016	0.0015	0.0011
% Explained	40.9%	1.8%	2.2%
Sequential			
Simulated	0.4020	0.2839	0.5703
Difference	–0.0120	–0.0051	–0.0287
% Explained	–300.1%	–6.0%	–58.6%

Source: Own calculations based on National Household Surveys.

Analysis of the Labour Market Effects by Income Decile

In order to obtain a better view of which groups have been most affected by the changes in the labour market, we have extended the simulation exercises to each of the income deciles for both urban and rural areas. We apply this for three cases: per capita total income, per capita labour income and income of the occupied population. The methodology is applied only to observe the isolated effect of each labour market variable. We did not perform the sequential simulation.

To better understand the simulation results, Table 6.11 shows some characteristics of the labour market per decile of total per capita household income. It can be observed that between 1991 and 1997, the participation rates de-

Table 6.11 Labour market indicators by income deciles, 1991 and 1997

	National		Urban		Rural	
	1991	**1997**	**1991**	**1997**	**1991**	**1997**
Participation rate (%)						
Decile 1	54.7	49.2	55.5	44.7	46.4	52.9
Decile 2	56.5	49.3	47.3	47.5	49.9	59.1
Decile 3	53.1	50.1	49.8	50.5	49.6	57.7
Decile 4	54.2	53.2	51.8	53.6	51.0	55.5
Decile 5	55.7	56.4	53.9	56.3	53.7	56.6
Decile 6	57.1	56.6	59.3	57.4	57.6	59.2
Decile 7	58.9	59.1	59.0	59.1	59.4	60.5
Decile 8	61.8	61.0	61.8	63.0	63.1	61.5
Decile 9	63.8	65.2	65.7	65.9	64.2	64.8
Decile 10	68.9	68.4	70.9	69.9	72.2	68.6
Unemployment rate (%)						
Decile 1	7.3	16.9	10.0	30.7	5.4	12.9
Decile 2	8.5	13.8	17.4	20.0	6.1	10.7
Decile 3	8.8	14.0	16.4	16.2	5.8	7.9
Decile 4	8.7	12.7	14.3	14.6	6.2	6.1
Decile 5	9.2	11.7	11.6	11.4	4.4	6.9
Decile 6	8.3	10.5	10.6	10.8	3.6	5.0
Decile 7	7.3	9.3	9.0	8.3	5.1	5.4
Decile 8	6.6	7.2	6.2	6.3	4.1	5.0
Decile 9	5.5	6.2	5.3	6.5	2.3	4.1
Decile 10	4.0	4.2	3.2	3.5	1.3	2.0
Labour incomes (thousands of pesos of 1997)						
Decile 1	54	44	107	137	33	54
Decile 2	62	92	125	156	42	66
Decile 3	106	124	159	172	73	84
Decile 4	130	142	186	196	98	102
Decile 5	150	167	205	208	113	110
Decile 6	167	190	217	243	122	120
Decile 7	186	223	252	264	140	122
Decile 8	211	261	287	311	147	133
Decile 9	262	348	371	418	162	151
Decile 10	601	851	782	940	186	197

Source: Own calculations based on National Household Surveys.

Table 6.12 Labour income adjustment, 1991 and 1997

	Change in share in total per capita household income			Change in share in labour per capita household income			Change in share in income of occupied		
	National	**Urban**	**Rural**	**National**	**Urban**	**Rural**	**National**	**Urban**	**Rural**
Participation rate									
Decile 1	0.05%	0.01%	–0.03%	0.01%	0.03%	–0.01%	0.06%	0.03%	0.04%
Decile 2	0.06%	0.02%	–0.07%	0.03%	0.04%	–0.02%	0.08%	0.06%	0.17%
Decile 3	0.05%	0.05%	–0.09%	0.02%	0.03%	–0.03%	0.11%	0.07%	0.13%
Decile 4	0.08%	0.04%	–0.11%	0.01%	0.06%	–0.03%	0.11%	0.01%	–0.01%
Decile 5	0.06%	0.04%	–0.11%	0.04%	0.06%	–0.05%	0.06%	0.01%	0.04%
Decile 6	0.04%	0.03%	–0.10%	0.05%	0.04%	–0.07%	0.10%	0.19%	0.08%
Decile 7	0.00%	0.00%	–0.11%	0.04%	0.04%	–0.02%	0.22%	0.05%	–0.10%
Decile 8	–0.02%	0.00%	–0.01%	0.02%	0.04%	–0.02%	0.09%	0.06%	–0.07%
Decile 9	–0.04%	–0.04%	0.19%	0.01%	0.04%	–0.03%	–0.02%	–0.02%	0.40%
Decile 10	–0.27%	–0.16%	0.45%	–0.24%	–0.39%	0.29%	–0.83%	–0.47%	–0.69%
Unemployment rate									
Decile 1	0.04%	0.01%	–0.03%	0.00%	0.01%	0.00%	0.07%	0.07%	0.06%
Decile 2	0.07%	0.02%	–0.07%	–0.01%	0.01%	–0.01%	0.12%	0.11%	0.12%
Decile 3	0.08%	0.04%	–0.09%	0.00%	0.02%	–0.02%	0.14%	0.16%	0.18%
Decile 4	0.08%	0.06%	–0.09%	0.00%	0.01%	–0.03%	0.18%	0.15%	0.20%
Decile 5	0.09%	0.05%	–0.13%	0.01%	0.00%	–0.01%	0.18%	0.20%	0.18%
Decile 6	0.05%	0.05%	–0.11%	0.01%	0.03%	–0.02%	0.22%	0.19%	0.22%
Decile 7	0.03%	0.03%	–0.10%	0.02%	0.00%	0.00%	0.18%	0.20%	0.21%
Decile 8	–0.04%	0.02%	–0.01%	0.00%	0.02%	0.05%	0.18%	0.15%	0.07%

Decile 9	–0.07%	–0.02%	0.17%	–0.02%	–0.03%	0.06%	0.10%	0.03%	0.09%
Decile 10	–0.33%	–0.27%	0.48%	–0.01%	–0.08%	–0.03%	–1.37%	–1.25%	–1.33%
Employment structure									
Decile 1	–0.02%	0.00%	–0.03%	0.13%	0.05%	–0.17%	0.07%	0.08%	0.05%
Decile 2	–0.05%	0.00%	–0.08%	0.16%	0.05%	–0.37%	0.14%	0.13%	0.16%
Decile 3	–0.02%	–0.03%	–0.09%	0.14%	0.09%	–0.37%	0.17%	0.17%	0.18%
Decile 4	–0.08%	0.02%	–0.13%	0.16%	0.08%	–0.33%	0.20%	0.21%	0.21%
Decile 5	0.05%	0.03%	–0.04%	0.16%	0.12%	–0.32%	0.24%	0.19%	0.23%
Decile 6	0.07%	–0.04%	–0.05%	0.18%	0.09%	–0.23%	0.22%	0.26%	0.25%
Decile 7	–0.08%	–0.04%	–0.03%	0.15%	0.10%	–0.24%	0.28%	0.25%	0.18%
Decile 8	–0.04%	–0.04%	0.17%	0.15%	0.09%	–0.30%	0.26%	0.21%	0.12%
Decile 9	–0.06%	–0.07%	0.14%	0.08%	0.05%	–0.14%	0.05%	0.02%	0.07%
Decile 10	0.22%	0.16%	0.14%	–1.30%	–0.72%	2.47%	–1.63%	–1.53%	–1.45%
Wages									
Decile 1	0.02%	0.03%	–0.02%	0.13%	0.05%	–0.17%	0.07%	0.02%	0.09%
Decile 2	0.03%	0.02%	–0.03%	0.19%	0.07%	–0.39%	0.11%	0.11%	0.20%
Decile 3	0.01%	0.04%	–0.05%	0.18%	0.08%	–0.42%	0.19%	0.13%	0.19%
Decile 4	0.03%	0.04%	–0.03%	0.16%	0.09%	–0.33%	0.17%	0.19%	0.20%
Decile 5	0.05%	0.05%	–0.05%	0.19%	0.10%	–0.36%	0.22%	0.26%	0.27%
Decile 6	0.05%	0.05%	–0.03%	0.17%	0.13%	–0.28%	0.32%	0.32%	0.29%
Decile 7	0.04%	0.06%	–0.03%	0.20%	0.12%	–0.22%	0.26%	0.23%	0.03%
Decile 8	0.02%	0.07%	–0.05%	0.18%	0.10%	–0.36%	0.17%	0.13%	0.22%
Decile 9	0.01%	0.03%	–0.06%	0.06%	–0.02%	–0.23%	–0.12%	–0.13%	0.15%
Decile 10	–0.28%	–0.38%	0.37%	–1.47%	–0.73%	2.77%	–1.40%	–1.27%	–1.65%

Source: Own calculations based on National Household Surveys.

creased considerably in the two lower-income deciles and to a lesser extent in the third to sixth deciles. In contrast, the participation rate in the higher-income deciles remained about the same. The corresponding changes have a distinct pattern for urban and rural areas. Whereas at an urban level labour participation fell in the poorest deciles and, to a lesser extent, in the higher deciles, the rural participation rate increased in all deciles, mainly in the poorest, and decreased in the higher-income decile.

Between 1991 and 1997, the national unemployment rate went up by about three points. This increase was concentrated among the poorest income deciles in both urban and rural areas, as can be seen in Table 6.11. Labour incomes increased for all urban income deciles (except for the poorest decile). The increase was highest for the highest deciles. In turn, labour incomes in rural areas increased for the first five deciles and decile 10, and decreased for deciles 6 to 9.

The effects of these labour market changes on total per capita income are shown in the left column of Table 6.12. Here we can see that, had the 1991 labour participation rates been maintained in 1997, the poorest deciles – particularly the poorest 60 per cent – would have increased their participation in the total income, thus improving income distribution. This is consistent with Table 6.11, which shows that labour participation decreased in these deciles. The same occurs with the simulated effects of the unemployment rate, although the greatest income effect appears to be concentrated in deciles 2 to 7. In turn, the simulated effect of changes in the sectoral composition of employment yields an increase in the share in total per capita income of deciles 5 and 6, and particularly of decile 10. Finally, had the 1991 wage structure prevailed in 1997, all income deciles would have increased their share in total income, except for the richest decile, which would have been the loser in this case.

The simulations of the labour market effects on the participation changes of the various deciles for urban areas confirm the results obtained in the previous section. Had the 1991 labour market structure been maintained in 1997 as far as urban participation rate, unemployment rate, sectoral composition of employment and wages are concerned, then the income share of the poorest 60 per cent would have increased and inequality would have decreased. This is consistent with the results of Table 6.11, which show that labour participation fell for the first six deciles 1–6, their unemployment rate increased and their relative labour income fell in relation to that of the higher-income deciles. However, deciles 3 to 6 – and not the poorest – would have benefited most.

Had the 1991 rural labour participation rate prevailed in 1997, the share of the bottom 80 per cent in rural income would have been lower (particularly that of deciles 3 to 7), while that of the top 20 per cent would have increased.

This would have entailed a higher Gini. A similar effect is found when simulating the effect of the unemployment rate. The changes in the employment and wage structure have led to a decline in the income share for the poorest quintiles and an increase in that of the richest, producing more income inequality. The simulated negative effect of sectoral employment shifts is greater in deciles 2 to 4, and the positive effects are concentrated in deciles 8 to 10. The wage effect yields a loss in income shares for all deciles, except for the richest 10 per cent. These results confirm the observed rural labour market trends between 1991 and 1997. They show relatively larger increases in labour participation and unemployment for the poorest income deciles, as well as labour income increases for deciles 1–5 and 10 and declines for deciles 6 to 9.

The middle columns of Table 6.12 show the simulation results for per capita labour income instead of total household income. The simulated effect of the participation rate and the unemployment rate on labour income shares is similar to that obtained for total income. The effects are smaller in size though, particularly for the unemployment effect. In contrast, the simulated effects of the employment structure and wage trend are larger. The table shows that the labour income share of all deciles would have been greater than that observed for both the national total and urban areas, except for the richest quintile (with only marginal changes for the ninth decile in urban areas). For rural areas, the effects of the employment and wage structure on rural income shares are also larger than those observed for total income. The labour income share would have fallen for all first nine deciles in favour of a substantial increase for the richest decile.

In turn, the simulations of the labour market effects on income shares of the national and urban occupied population yield results very similar to those obtained for per capita labour income. This does not apply for rural areas. These results are in the right-hand columns of Table 6.12. In particular, the labour market effects on the various income earners would have the same sign in urban and rural areas, and not the opposite sign, as is the case in the alternative simulations. A more accurate understanding of the reason for these opposite effects would require a detailed study of the changes experienced by the composition of rural households during the 1990s.

6.6 CONCLUSIONS

This study analysed the changes experienced by the labour market and income distribution between the beginning of the reforms in 1991 and 1997. During this period, economic growth was determined by strong fluctuations in domestic aggregated demand. The production structure also went through considerable changes. The share of non-traded goods sectors increased to the detriment of traded goods sectors, especially in agriculture and manufacturing.

The repercussions of these changes in the labour market were pervasive. The capacity of the economy to create employment deteriorated visibly. This is surely not a recent phenomenon. This became visible already during the spectacular boom of aggregate demand in 1992–95. At that time, it did not show up in the unemployment rate because of the favourable shift in labour participation. The deterioration of the job-creating capacity was severest in agriculture early in the decade and in manufacturing starting with the decline of the sector in the middle of the decade. This decline in tradable-sector employment was offset by the employment growth in non-tradables during the boom period of the early 1990s. The compensating effect disappeared with the exhaustion of the domestic demand boom in mid-decade.

The poor performance of employment has affected unskilled workers severely. The shifts in the production structure have dealt a real blow to these workers, as they were more sensitive to job losses in tradable sectors, whereas the increase in employment in non-tradable sectors mostly benefited skilled workers. Furthermore, technological changes have been capital-intensive and labour-saving at all skill levels, but affecting unskilled workers more. The bias generated by the economic opening process in favour of skilled labour demand is also reflected in the higher rates of return for higher education. The increase in the relative income of higher-educated workers thus negatively affected urban income distribution.

Between 1991 and 1997, the country witnessed an increase in income inequality as measured by the Gini coefficient, although with opposite trends in urban and rural areas. The microsimulations indicate the main impact of national and urban labour market adjustment on income distribution has been produced by sectoral employment shifts and changes in the remuneration structure. Changes in labour participation and unemployment rates have been less important. The simulations for rural areas show that the changes in the employment structure contributed to decrease the inequality. Poverty, especially in urban areas, fell drastically between 1991 and 1997. Poverty reduction was dominated by other than labour market effects, especially the strong reduction in the cost of the basic food basket. This favoured urban incomes at the cost of rural incomes.

NOTES

1. Section 6.5 was co-authored with Jairo Núñez. We are grateful for the comments of Jaime Aristy, Samuel Morley, Roberto Paes de Barros, Juan Carlos Ramírez, Lance Taylor, Rob Vos and other project participants to previous drafts. We also thank Piedad Urdinola for her assistance.

2. For a more detailed analysis of capital control regulations and their effectiveness in the 1990s, see Ocampo and Tovar (1999) and Villar and Rincón (2000).
3. We should add that in early 1997 there was also a short episode of explicit taxation of capital flows. This was subsequently declared non-executable by the Constitutional Court because of the procedure followed to decree it (the constitutional form of 'economic emergency').
4. See OIT (1998) and Reina and Yanovich (1998).
5. There are only two earlier national surveys, 1978 and 1988. The latter is not strictly comparable to the others, however, because for the urban area it only covers the seven largest cities.
6. This and the following section define the main labour indicators as related to the total population, and therefore differ from the traditional definitions of labour market studies which define such variables in relation to the working-age or economically active population. The methodology used is developed in the Appendix to Chapter 1 of this book.
7. A common feature of recent studies is to correct household surveys for non-response problems of higher income groups. The correction methods have become part of the typical processing problems of household surveys, which generate discrepancies between the estimates produced by different authors. The corrections are for non-response or under-reporting of incomes, consistency with national accounts, and so on.
8. These studies give different estimates for the size of the losses incurred by the rest of the rural income earners.
9. These effects appear in the residuals (unexplained effects) in the income generation functions.
10. The sequential simulation first calculates the effects of changes in participation. Once these results are obtained, unemployment simulations are made, and based on these results simulations of changes in sectoral employment structure are made. Finally, wage simulations are based on these last results.

REFERENCES

Bernal, Raquel, Mauricio Cárdenas, Fabio Sánchez and Jairo Núñez (1998) 'El desempeño de la macroeconomía y la igualdad: 1976–1996', in: Sánchez (1998).

Birchenall, Javier (1997) 'Income distribution, human capital and economic growth in Colombia', *Archivos de Macroeconomía No. 70*, Unidad de Análisis Macroeconómico, Bogotá: Departamento Nacional de Planeación.

DANE (1999) 'Evolución de la economía colombiana. Primer trimestre de 1999', Bogotá: Departamento Administrativo Nacional de Estadística.

DNP (Departamento Nacional de Planeación) (1998) *Informe de Desarrollo Humano para Colombia, 1998*, Bogotá: Misión Social-UNDP.

Farné, Stefano, Alejandro Vivas and Jairo Núñez (1998) 'La estabilidad laboral en el mercado de trabajo urbano en Colombia, 1984–1986', Bogotá (mimeo).

Henao, Marta Luz and Aura Parra (1998) 'Educación y mercados de trabajo', in: OIT (1998).

ILO (1998) 'Empleo: un desafio para Colombia', Project document ILO/Ministry of Labour/UNDP/95/003, Bogotá (mimeo).

Leibovich, José and Jairo Núñez (1999) 'The microeconomics of income distribution dynamics in rural Colombia (1978–1988–1995)', *Documento CEDE 99-12*, Bogotá: Universida de los Andes (August).

Misión de Empleo (1986) 'El problema laboral colombiano: diagnóstico, perspectivas y políticas', *Economía Colombiana, Separata No. 10*, Bogotá (August–September).

Núñez, Jairo and Fabio Sánchez (1999) 'Estimaciones trimestrales de la línea de pobreza y sus relaciones con el desempeño macroeconómico colombiano (1977–1997)', *Archivos de Macroeconomía No. 110*, Unidad de Análisis Macroeconómico, Bogotá: Departamento Nacional de Planeación.

Ocampo, José Antonio (1997) 'Una evaluación de la situación fiscal colombiana', *Coyuntura Económica*, **XXVII** (2) (June).

Ocampo, José Antonio (1998) 'Una década de grandes transformaciones económicas (1986–1996)', *Nueva Historia de Colombia. Tomo VIII*, Bogotá: Editorial Planeta.

Ocampo, José Antonio and Camilo Tovar (1999) 'Price-based capital account regulations: the Colombian experience', *Serie Financiamiento del Desarrollo 87*, Santiago: CEPAL (October).

Ocampo, José Antonio, María José Pérez, Camilo Tovar and Francisco Javier Lasso (1998) 'Macroeconomía, ajuste estructural y equidad en Colombia: 1978–1996', in: Enrique Ganuza, Lance Taylor and Samuel Morley (eds) *Política macroeconómica y pobreza en América Latina y el Caribe*, Madrid: Mundi-Prensa (for PNUD-CEPAL-BID).

OIT (Oficina Internacional del Trabajo) (1998) 'Empleo: un desafío para Colombia', Preliminary discussion paper, Project of the OIT/Ministerio de Trabajo/PNUD COL/95/003, Bogotá (mimeo).

Reina, Mauricio and Denisse Yanovich (1998) 'Salud, educación y desempleo: diagnóstico y recomendaciones', *Cuadernos de Fedesarrollo No. 4*, Bogotá: Fedesarrollo.

Ribero, Rocío and Juliana García (1996) 'Estadísticas descriptivas del mercado laboral masculino y femenino en Colombia: 1976–1995', *Archivos de Macroeconomía No. 48*, Unidad de Análisis Macroeconómico, Bogotá: Departamento Nacional de Planeación.

Sánchez, Fabio (ed.) (1998) *La distribución del ingreso en Colombia: tendencias recientes y retos de la política pública*, Bogotá: Tercer Mundo Editores-DNP.

Sánchez, Fabio and Jairo Núñez (1998) 'Educación y salarios relativos en Colombia, 1976–1995. Determinantes, evolución e implicaciones para la distribución del ingreso', in: Sánchez (1998).

Sánchez, Fabio and Jairo Núñez (1999) 'Descentralización, pobreza y acceso a los servicios sociales. ¿Quién se benefició del Gasto Público Social en los noventa?', *Coyuntura Social No. 20*, Bogotá: Fedesarrollo (May).

Vélez, Carlos Eduardo, Adriana Kugler and César Bouillón (1999) 'The reversal of inequality gains in urban Colombia, 1978–1995: a combination of persistent and fluctuating forces', Washington D.C.: The World Bank (mimeo).

Villar, Leonardo and Hernán Rincón (2000) 'The Colombian economy in the nineties: capital flows and foreign exchange regimes'. Paper presented at the Conference on Critical Issues in Financial Reform: Latin American/Caribbean and Canadian Perspectives, The Munk Centre for International Studies Program on Latin America and the Caribbean, Toronto: University of Toronto (June).

7. Ecuador: economic liberalization, adjustment and poverty, 1988–99[1]

Rob Vos

7.1 INTRODUCTION

Ecuador was a late reformer. Market-oriented reforms were implemented in earnest starting around 1992 with the liberalization of trade and capital flows. Adjustment policies in the 1980s in response to the debt crisis and falling oil prices had focused on short-term economic stabilization with only isolated and sometimes short-lived attempts at reforms of the protectionist trade regime. Historically, Ecuador's economy always seems to have survived difficult periods being 'bailed-out' by new primary export booms. High adjustment costs had to be paid in the 1980s, but cushions were found in the surge of shrimp farming, expansion of oil production and recovery of its position as the world's largest banana exporter. This has likely been a factor in slowing down the necessary policy reform process and kept the economy highly vulnerable to shocks in world demand and commodity prices.

Major reforms to the policy regime were implemented in the 1990s. Nonetheless, a main conclusion of this chapter is that, at the turn of the century, the Ecuadorian economy is still struggling to achieve macroeconomic stability, while volatile oil prices and the external debt overhang continue to be key determinants of the fiscal and external adjustment process. *Plus ça chan*ge? Some important changes have been observed, including a significant growth of non-traditional exports and substantial volume shifts in the macroeconomic balance. The real trade balance has moved to large surplus positions, while the real primary fiscal balance has also moved into surplus as a consequence of large cuts in the volume of government services. Adverse relative price shifts – falling terms of trade, real exchange rate appreciation – have made this adjustment look much less impressive in value terms, and have left the economy with persistent internal and external deficits. Vulnerability to external shocks, particularly commodity price volatility, remains one of the main weaknesses of the economy.

Underlying the large volume adjustments are production shifts toward greater export orientation. On balance, there has been a shift toward more capital-intensive production (oil, manufacturing, traditional agriculture), with the exception of a few agricultural sub-sectors (flowers, vegetables). The low productivity growth in the 1990s seems largely due to this sectoral shift, producing a relative decline in the overall demand for modern sector labour in the traded goods sector. The smaller demand for wage labour has become more skill-intensive, giving rise to larger wage inequalities and income differentials between wages and self-employed incomes. The weight of employment growth has been in informal jobs and for the self-employed. Together with dramatic decreases in the real wage, it has shifted factor income distribution away from wages and toward self-employed incomes. This distributional pattern was already predominant in the 1980s, when the recession and real wage declines pushed the wage share to very low levels. In the 1990s, the greater share of workers seems to have moved into the informal sector, but recovery of real wages in the first half of the decade allowed for a reversal in the downward trend of the wage share. In addition, urban household incomes move closely with adjustments in the institutionally set modern-sector minimum wage. This correlation appears to be associated with two factors: most wages and salaries in the modern sector are linked to the minimum wage, and urban self-employed incomes benefit from strong multiplier effects of real wage increases. The upshot has been declining urban poverty rates since 1992, the wage adjustment probably being more important than structural economic change.

All this changed at the end of the decade. In 1998–99 the economy was doubly hit by a steep decline in the oil price and the natural disaster provoked by the El Niño phenomenon. The ensuing fiscal and financial crisis revealed the economy's structural weaknesses as well as policy failures of the past. Rising inflation and falling employment undid the gains in urban poverty reduction in the preceding years. In early 2000, a bold move was made toward an official dollarization of the economy, but recovery from the crisis will probably take many years.

The analytics of the apparent unorthodox – and seemingly benign – outcome of adjustment in 1990–97 is complex. To simplify, we could use Figure 7.1 (simplified from Chapter 1) as a starting point. The figure provides a link between macroeconomic adjustment, sectoral productivity shifts and the labour market. The northwest quadrant assumes an increasing relationship between the output level and the trade deficit. Operating through reduced protection and appreciation of the real exchange rate, the balance of payments opening may well have shifted this schedule outward. Current account liberalization led to a bigger trade deficit; the deterioration was worsened by real appreciation induced by increased capital inflows and stabilization poli-

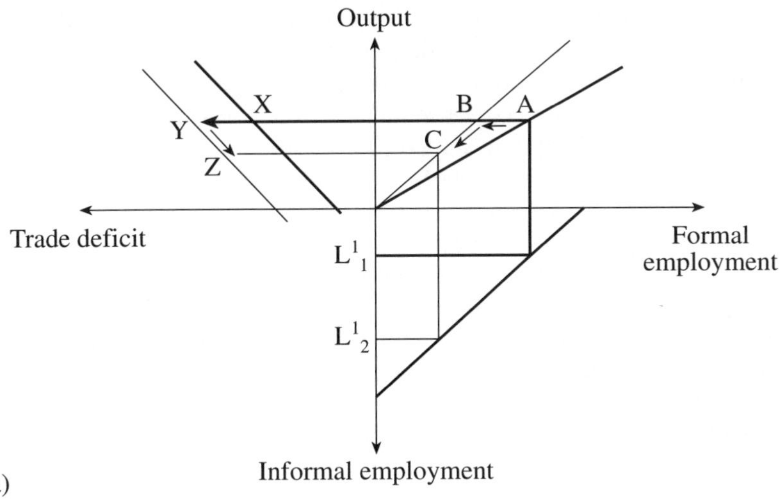

(a)

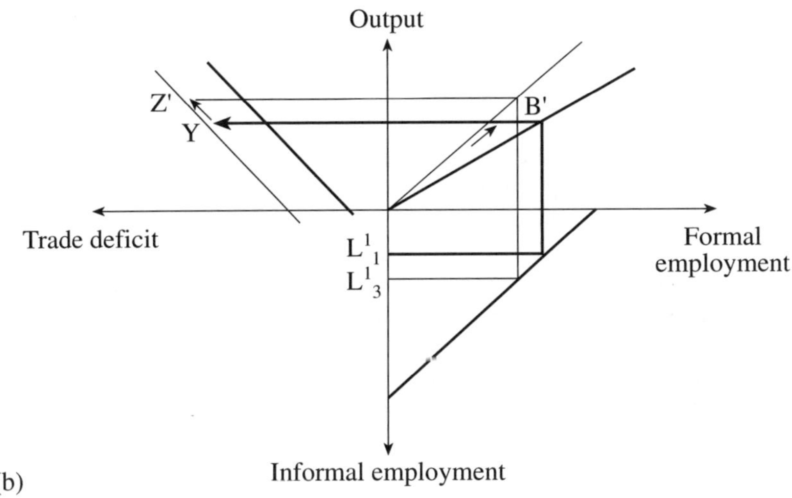

(b)

Figure 7.1 *Output and employment responses to macroeconomic adjustment policies and balance of payments liberalization: (a) opening and demand contraction; (b) opening and demand expansion* cies using the exchange rate as a nominal anchor, beginning around 1992. In the northeast quadrant, liberalization may well have led to less demand for formal employment at a given output level. Pressures toward cost reduction via enhanced labour productivity in tradable goods sectors along with growth of demand for relatively low-skilled jobs in non-traded sectors helped push this trend. As shown in the southeast quadrant, a reduction in formal employment is likely to be associated with an increase in informal jobs, greater self-employment and, given wage rigidity in formal sectors, higher unemployment. In stylized fashion, liberalization coupled with capital inflows initially led to a growth in productivity and a reduction in formal employment in a move from A to B. At the same time, the trade deficit worsened, jumping from X to Y. To avoid further expansion of the external disequilibrium, and to slash domestic inflation, authorities pushed toward fiscal austerity to cut back on aggregate demand and encourage further capital inflows. Output growth slowed, with formal employment decreasing during a policy-induced transition from B to C. At the same time, the trade deficit was contained in its move from Y to Z. We hypothesize that the story of Figure 7.1a is a stylized reflection of the events following the stabilization efforts and the trade and capital account opening of the Ecuadorian economy in the early 1990s.

After 1995 and up until mid-1998, fiscal discipline slipped and new rounds of wage increases were allowed, pushing domestic demand and the external deficit back in the direction of Z′ (in Figure 7.1b). Falling oil prices compounded the effect on the external balance. Demand expansion allowed for a recovery of formal employment (particularly in non-tradables) to B′, until new external shocks pushed the scheme back on a deep contractionary path.

The story could be formalized and elaborated further in a dependent economy model framework with labour and commodity market imperfections, including formal-sector wage rigidity, labour market segmentation and mark-up pricing in formal sectors, along lines such as those developed in Cox-Edwards and Edwards (1994) and Ros (1999). In these stories, if the non-tradables is the more labour-intensive sector – as is the case in Ecuador – then trade liberalization will reduce employment. Extending this to an intertemporal framework, Cox-Edwards and Edwards (1994) show that capital account liberalization in an economy with a minimum wage setting in the formal sector will lead to an increase in non-tradables employment through a positive expenditure effect (along the lines of Figure 7.1b).

These theoretical notions emphasize the importance of the starting conditions of a liberalizing economy, particularly factor endowments (including human capital and natural resources) and labour market imperfections, in predicting the probable outcomes of balance of payments liberalization on output and employment. We will not flesh out the theoretical notions in further detail, but rather keep the broader framework in mind when assessing trends in aggregate demand, employment and income distribution in Ecuador before and after the economic reforms.

This story is detailed in the following sections. The major policy changes and economic events since the early 1980s are summarized in Section 7.2. In Section 7.3, the main shifts in the macroeconomic balances and sectoral employment and productivity rates during the key period of economic reforms (1988–98) are analysed following the decomposition methodologies as suggested in Chapter 1. Section 7.4 analyses the consequences of the employment shifts for earnings and factor distribution, and develops some hypotheses as to how this has affected income distribution and poverty at the household level, further showing the impact of the recent economic crisis on poverty and inequality. The methodology of microsimulations (see Chapter 2) is applied in Section 7.5 to test these hypotheses and detect which macroeconomic adjustment and structural reform factors have contributed the most to poverty and inequality trends. Conclusions are presented in Section 7.6.

7.2 THE 'STOP–GO' PROCESS OF STABILIZATION AND OPENING OF THE ECONOMY

Ecuador has been a slow reformer. During the 1980s, adjustment focused predominantly on short-term economic stabilization, despite 'stop–go' rhetoric to liberalize the economy along the lines of the Washington consensus (see Table 7.1 for an overview of the major policy regime changes since 1982). As analysed in Jácome et al. (1998), economic stability remained a major concern of policymakers due to a succession of external shocks and erratic macroeconomic policies. In fact, by the end of the decade the inflation rate peaked at 75 per cent in 1989 and substantial fiscal and current account deficits were the main symptoms of overall economic instability. Both the fiscal balance and the external account have remained highly sensitive to oil price shocks and the external debt overhang. No major trade reform was undertaken to overhaul the 25-year-old import substitution regime. Instead, import restrictions were the major response to the pressure of the debt overhang to produce trade surpluses. The fixed exchange-rate regime was abandoned in 1983 and replaced by a crawling peg with periodical maxi-devaluations to align the real exchange rate, but multiple exchange rates continued to exist until the early 1990s. In effect, the traditional components of stabilization policies – fiscal, monetary and exchange rate policies – made up the toolbox of policy instruments applied in a stop–go pattern by successive governments. Responses to external shocks, IMF pressure and ever-returning populist tendencies determined switches between sub-periods of fiscal and monetary restraint and of macroeconomic expansion.

Table 7.1 Policy regimes, 1982–98

	1982–83 Stabilization Programme	**1988–90 Adjustment Programme**	**1992 Stabilization Plan**	**1998–2000 Economic Reactivation Programme (major amendments 1999–2000)**
Trade reforms	Increase in import restrictions	Tariff reductions and reduction of QR in context of Andean Pact. Average tariff at 13%	Further tariff reductions, 5–25% tariff range (with exceptions for luxury consumption goods)	Reorganization and stricter control of customs
Exchange rate regime	Crawling peg introduced	Crawling peg and periodical devaluations to align real exchange rate	Managed floating within fixed upper and lower boundaries	Managed floating. Maxi-devaluation (15% in September 1998). Flexible exchange rate introduced in February 1999 following effective 100% devaluation. During the rest of 1999, another effective nominal 100% devaluation. Official dollarization in January 2000
Capital account	Direct foreign investment and investment regulated through	In 1984, restrictions of DFI were abandoned and foreign investment	*Ley Liberalización de Flujos de Capital e Inversión* of 1992: full	Fully liberalized

	Acuerdo 24 of Andean Pact. No foreign investment allowed in oil and mining	in oil exploration permitted. Some controls on DFI re-established in 1988. Elimination of tax advantages for foreign investors. Strict tendering rules for DFI in oil sector	capital account liberalization	
External debt	Debt renegotiated with commercial banks and Paris Club. Private sector debt nationalized (*sucretización*)	Cap on interest payments (30% of exports) set unilaterally (default on all debt obligations in 1987). New Paris Club agreement in 1990	Agreement on Brady Plan terms and new Paris Club agreement	Partial default on US T-bill guaranteed Brady Bonds in September 1999. Creditors declare Ecuador in full default
Financial sector reform	No reform. Fixed interest rates	Interest rate liberalization, maximum spread set	Further financial liberalization and reduction of financial repression. Modernization of banking legislation. Some, but slight improvement banking supervision	Consolidation of financial reforms. Introduction of deposit insurance system. Recapitalization and bad debt takeover of range of ailing commercial banks. Creation of independent Central Bank. Financial crisis of 1999 leads to freezing of bank deposits,

Table 7.1 continued

	1982–83 Stabilization Programme	**1988–90 Adjustment Programme**	**1992 Stabilization Plan**	**1998–2000 Economic Reactivation Programme (major amendments 1999–2000)**
				bankruptcy and nationalization of major domestic banks by deposit insurance agency (AGD). Interest rates kept high in attempt to avoid capital flight.
Fiscal policies and reforms	Spending cuts and rise in state-controlled energy prices. No fiscal reform	Spending cuts and rise of state-controlled energy prices. Elimination of wheat subsidy. Modest first steps toward tax reform	Fiscal cuts. Elimination of gasoline price subsidy. Further, minor tax reforms (customs and tax collection)	Fiscal restraint. Freeze of public sector wages. Major tax reform: introduction of 1% tax on financial transactions, temporary suspension of income and profit tax. VAT increase (from 10 to 12%)
Domestic prices	Domestic price controls and subsidies on basic commodities	Gradual liberalization of some controlled prices	Liberalization of most domestic prices	Elimination of subsidy on natural gas and electricity. Compensation through targeted 'poverty bonus'

Wage policies	Minimum wages. Incidental nominal wage increases due to social pressure	Minimum wages. Incidental nominal wage increases due to social pressure	Minimum wages. Negotiated wage adjustments targeted toward maintaining or increasing purchasing power	Unchanged minimum wage legislation. Temporary wage freeze
Labour market reform	None. Protective labour legislation enforced mainly in small segment of large-scale modern sector. Weak enforcement of minimum wages	None. Protective labour legislation enforced mainly in small segment of large-scale modern sector. Weak enforcement of minimum wages. Attempts at reform fail. Dismissal of public employees but at high severance payments	None. Protective labour legislation enforced mainly in small segment of large-scale modern sector. Weak enforcement of minimum wages	None. Protective labour legislation enforced mainly in small segment of large-scale modern sector. Weak enforcement of minimum wages. Flexibilization of labour laws announced as part of dollarization plan (January 2000)
Privatization	None	None	Initiation of privatization programme (airlines, cement, fertilizers)	Speeding up of privatization programme announced (telecommunications, oil and energy)

On the whole, the overall structure of the economy underwent little structural change. Primary income distribution moved against urban wage earners, while there was a strong increase in the share of self-employment income in the informal sector. This distributional shift is explained by the continued squeeze of modern sector wages, employment losses in modern urban sectors (both traded and non-traded) and the consequent push of workers into the residual informal sector employment (Jácome et al. 1998). Modern sector enterprise profits were also affected by the economic crisis and it could barely maintain its share in added value, despite the steep fall in the wage share (see below).

Pressures toward more substantial reforms were resisted until the early 1990s. The regime of President León Febres Cordero (1984–88), who had entered into government with a strong neo-liberal rhetoric, did not achieve major economic reforms either. The regime started on a note of severe fiscal and monetary restraint but ended with a populist tune. Inflation accelerated to record heights toward the end of the decade.

The only major reform of the regime was the removal of restrictions on direct foreign investment as regulated through the Andean Pact (*Acuerdo 24*) and the opening of the oil and mining sectors to foreign investors. The latter helped boost oil production. Oil exports were the driving force behind the high growth in the 1970s, albeit with typical Dutch-disease effects (Vos

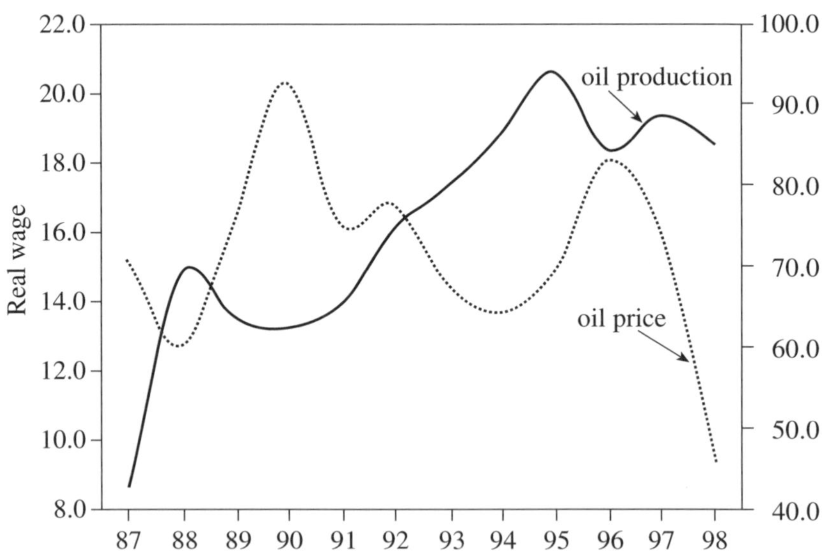

Source: Central Bank of Ecuador, monthly bulletins, various issues, 1987–98.

Figure 7.2 Crude oil export production and the oil price, 1987–98

1989), and remained a cushion during the 1980s. Opening the oil sector to foreign investors helped expand production capacity and eased the adjustment cost of oil price fluctuations. The management of oil revenues as a macroeconomic stabilization device is shown by the pattern in Figure 7.2, where oil prices and production show inverse trends. The need to accommodate oil production and exports to meet fiscal targets eventually forced Ecuador to give up its OPEC membership in 1992 (Sierra 1995). The policy secured a level of oil exports at US$ 1.2 billion per year and maintained fiscal dependence on oil revenues (Figure 7.3) but, as indicated, failed to ensure stability.

The external debt overhang was a major source of fiscal problems. Successive debt rescheduling brought little relief. Instead, the Central Bank took over most of the private external debt (labelled as the *sucretización*), along with a number of bad debts of ailing private banks. The upshot was growing operational losses of the Central Bank. Izurieta (2000) has estimated these losses, also labelled as the quasi-fiscal deficit, at 1 or 2 per cent of GDP during the 1980s, adding to already large non-financial public sector deficits (see Figure 7.4). However, when estimated by changes in the full net worth, the hypothetical quasi-deficit increased to over 20 per cent of GDP in 1987–88 due to the dramatic increase in the net external liability position of the

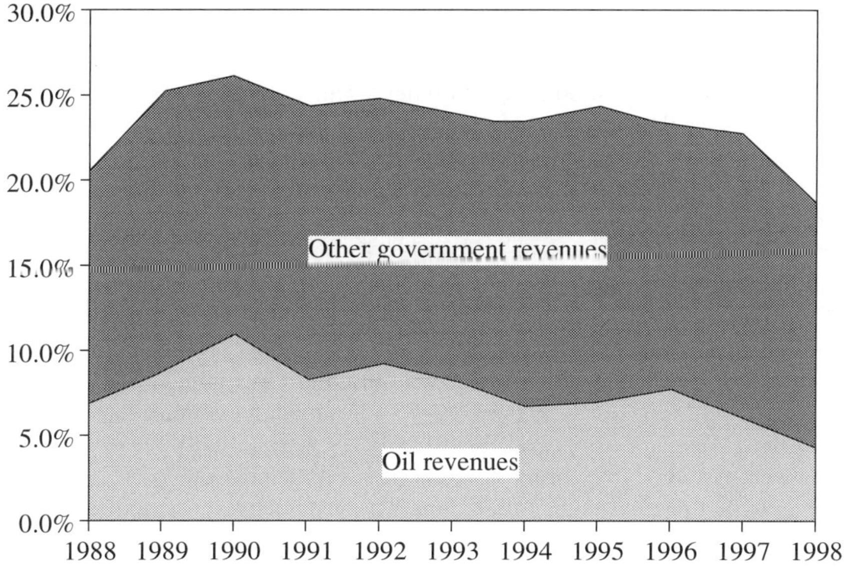

Source: Appendix Table A7.1.

Figure 7.3 Public sector revenue (% of GDP)

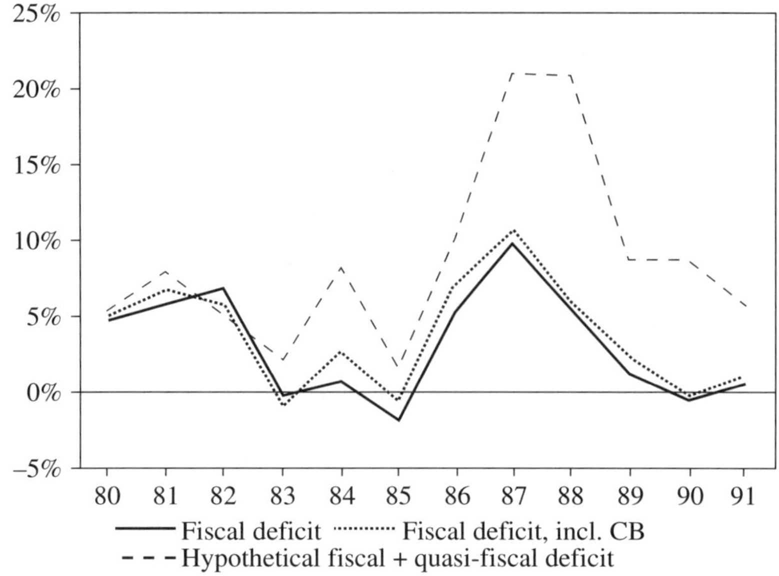

Source: Izurieta (2000).

Figure 7.4 Fiscal and quasi-fiscal deficit, 1980–91

Central Bank valued in domestic currency.[2] This is labelled the hypothetical deficit here, as the Central Bank did not show the appropriate asset revaluation in its balance sheets, in addition to the government opting to default on all its external debt obligations in 1987 and only part of the gap being monetized.

The centre-left government of Rodrigo Borja (1988–92) was left to deal with this enormous fiscal problem and record-high inflation, which reached a rate of over 80 per cent in late 1988. It promised to tackle the problems through an adjustment programme that would be neither orthodox nor heterodox, and in the end turned out to have a little bit of everything. Stabilization measures were very similar to the 1982–83 adjustment programme that counted with the IMF seal of approval. Fiscal policies were initially restrictive, but cuts were not enough to bring inflation below an annual rate of 50 per cent. The crawling peg exchange rate regime was sustained with periodical maxi-devaluations. Further orthodox measures included a gradual liberalization of some controlled domestic prices and a liberalization of interest rates, albeit subject to a maximum spread between deposit and lending rates. The regime of institutional wage setting in the modern sector (largely through minimum wage legislation) and a complex system of bonuses and cost-of-living compensation were maintained. Attempts at simplifying the system for public sector employees failed because of resistance from trade unions and the government bureaucracy itself. Real wages continued the decline that began in the early 1980s, as nominal wage adjustments to inflation were partial and lagged.

With regard to the balance of payments, the Borja regime reinstated some of the controls on direct foreign investment with strict tendering rules for the oil and mining sectors and elimination of tax advantages for foreign investors to put them on the same footing as domestic investors. Debt servicing payments were resumed after renegotiation of the Paris Club debt and restructuring of the commercial debt.

Trade liberalization was the major reform measure and was implemented between 1990 and 1992. The impetus came largely from the outside, as the Initiative for the Americas pushed for greater integration and economic liberalization of the Western Hemisphere. With the emergence of NAFTA and Mercosur, the countries of the Andean Pact tried to revive their free-trade zone, and average nominal import tariffs were reduced from 39 to 15 per cent.[3]

A more ambitious set of economic liberalization measures came with the government of Sixto Durán Ballén (1992–96). The trade reform was deepened, nominal tariffs were reduced further to a 0–35 per cent range, and the weighted average tariff fell to around 9 per cent (see Table A7.1). Fiscal policies were tightened more rigorously and the inflation rate could be halved to 25 per cent in 1996. The exchange rate regime shifted to a system of managed floating within a pre-established band. It was Ecuador's way of attempting to use the exchange rate as a nominal anchor to cut inflationary expectations. This succeeded only partially and thus the real exchange rate appreciated by some 15 per cent between 1992 and 1996 (see Figure 7.5). Besides the trade liberalization, a series of structural reforms in other areas were initiated.

The capital account was now fully liberalized under the *Ley de Liberalización de Flujos de Capital e Inversión* of September 1992. Simultaneously, the domestic financial sector was liberalized and steps – albeit modest – were taken to improve the bank supervision and regulation system. The politically controversial subsidy on domestic fuel prices was eliminated, but subsidies on other basic utilities such as electricity, cooking gas, water and housing remained intact. Although the benefits of these subsidies mainly accrue to the urban middle and higher income groups (World Bank 1996), attempts to liberalize these prices were successfully opposed by organized labour. A legal framework for the privatization of state enterprises was put in place, which led to the privatization of the national airline *Ecuatoriana*, one cement company, a fertilizer factory and a sugar refinery. In the aggregate,

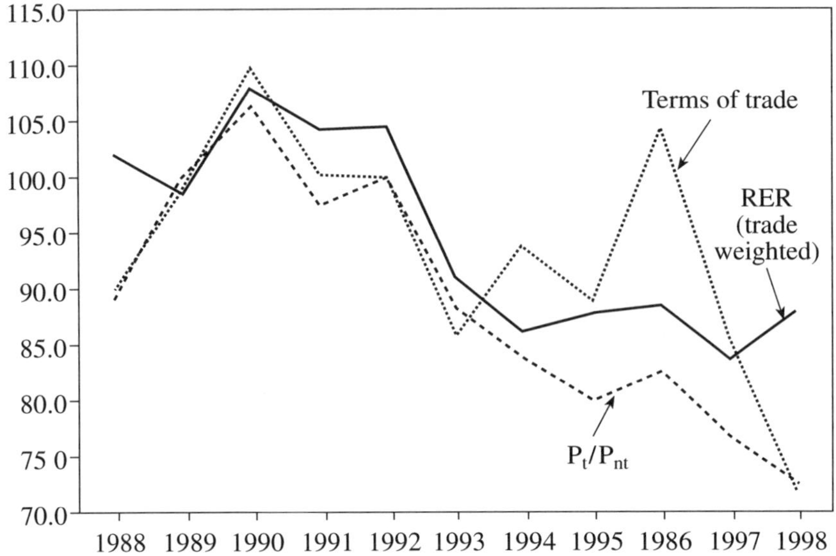

Source: Central Bank, National Accounts and monetary statistics.

Figure 7.5 External prices and real exchange rate (index, August 1992 = 100)

these only represent a small share of the public enterprise sector. Institutional reforms in other areas aimed at modernizing the state were formulated, but only very modest progress was made during the Durán government.

Most of the progress with the reforms was made during 1993 and 1994 with the new trade and exchange-rate regimes as central features. An important achievement in 1995 was a substantial debt reduction negotiated with commercial creditors within the framework of the Brady Plan. This helped reduce the external public debt burden from 88 per cent of GDP in 1994 to 78 per cent in 1995.

This positive event was counteracted by successive exogenous shocks that affected the policy reform process as much as they hurt the economy between 1995 and 1997. In early 1995 there was an armed border conflict with Peru that diverted attention from the economic adjustment process. Later that year, the main architect of the economic reforms and head of the economic team, Vice-president Alberto Dahik, fled abroad because of a corruption scandal. This brought political instability and, with upcoming elections in 1996, economic populism returned, leading to a more expansionary fiscal stance. The populist former mayor of Guayaquil, Abdalá Bucaram, won the elections.

The new regime was short-lived. Bucaram was ousted from office in February 1997, barely six months after coming to power. While elected on a populist platform, Bucaram's main economic advisor was Domingo Cavallo, who designed a stringent austerity programme and proposed the introduction of a currency board following the Argentine model. None of this actually turned into policies. Instead, widespread corruption and general chaos in the public administration provoked the mobilization of political forces in early 1997, and Bucaram went into exile.

After a short period of enormous political confusion, the allied political forces installed the speaker of Congress, Fabián Alarcón, as interim president. The new regime initiated a process of constitutional reforms, but at best proved to be a caretaker government in the economic sphere. It did re-establish better fiscal and monetary control that would be frustrated by two new exogenous shocks: a steep fall in oil prices and the natural disaster caused by El Niño in 1997–98. The direct cost of the drop in oil prices amounted to 1.0 per cent of GDP in 1997 and 2.7 per cent in 1998. The estimated foregone earnings[4] in agriculture, transportation and commerce due to El Niño have been estimated at somewhere between 1.1 and 10 per cent of GDP (Vos et al. 1998, CEPAL 1998). Obviously, even when taking the lower estimate, this produced a severe economic setback, with the non-financial public sector deficit climbing to 6.1 per cent of GDP and the external deficit to 11.9 per cent in 1998, up from a fiscal deficit of 3.0 per cent and an external surplus of 0.6 per cent of GDP in 1996.

The Economic Reactivation Programme of President Jamil Mahuad (1998–2000) promised a resumption of the reform process initiated in 1992. Trade and capital account liberalization would be consolidated and complemented with further institutional reforms in areas like customs administration and taxes. Further, the Central Bank was turned into an independent monetary authority and a new law to regulate the ailing domestic financial sector was announced. The process of privatization of public enterprises would be accelerated, particularly in the telecommunications and energy sectors. As has been the case with all previous programmes, the overwhelming initial concern of the Reactivation Programme was the short-term economic instability. The new government had to face bad weather, though – literally. Oil prices collapsed and most of the reconstruction costs of the damages caused by El Niño still had to be incurred.

The fiscal deficit in 1998 was back at its peak level of 10 years ago, when macroeconomic instability reached its most difficult point. Spending cuts and a nominal wage freeze returned as the conventional adjustment measures. The politically sensitive subsidies on natural gas and electricity were eliminated, and a modest targeted income transfer programme (*Bono Solidario*) was put in place to compensate low-income groups for the implied income loss. The exchange-rate system of managed floating was initially maintained, although a maxi-devaluation of 15 per cent in September 1998 was required to realign the real exchange rate to some degree (see Figure 7.5).

Low oil prices and incipient liquidity problems of the banking system led to a drain of monetary resources. In a desperate attempt to rescue the exchange rate and stem capital flight, monetary authorities increased short-term interest rates to 190 per cent in February 1999. The effort was doomed to fail because Ecuador lacks a market for domestic and international portfolio capital that could respond to the interest rate adjustment, and because the interest rate hike led to a domestic credit crush and put the long, latently insolvent banking sector into a state of panic.[5] The currency crisis thus became self-fulfilling and the exchange rate collapsed, ensuing high inflation and a full-blown economic and financial crisis. The bank crisis revealed the high indebtedness in dollar-denominated liabilities of the financial system, as well as its exposure to dollar-denominated assets outstanding with borrowers earning in domestic currency. The devaluation and the reduced capacity of the Central Bank to act as a lender of last resort tilted an already fragile system over the edge. Eight banks were declared bankrupt in February–March and, to avoid bank runs, deposits in all banks were frozen for 6 to 12 months. During the year, several major domestic banks failed and their deposits were taken over by the deposit insurance agency (AGD). Inflation accelerated to 65 per cent by late 1999 and GDP fell by 7.3 per cent that year. As the first country ever, Ecuador defaulted on payments on its Brady bonds in September 1999. However, neither this step nor the recovery of oil prices could stem the process away from deepening the crisis. The urban unemployment rate doubled to 14.5 per cent during 1999, real wages lost 25 per cent of their purchasing power, and the dollar value of the minimum wage dropped to US$ 40 per month. Negotiations with the IMF for a stand-by loan were delayed because of political obstructionism in the Ecuadorian congress, delaying the passing of a reform to the bank legislation and a reform of the VAT.

In January 2000, with no agreement with the IMF yet signed, nervousness in the exchange market led to the bold step of announcing the official dollarization of the economy in an attempt to provide more credibility to financial policies. President Mahuad needed to make such a step in an attempt to regain political credibility – to no avail it soon proved. An uprising of indigenous groups in mid-January 2000 received military support and led to the ousting of the president. United States pressure prevented the odd alliance of the Indian popular movement and the armed forces from forming an unconstitutional junta, and Vice-president Noboa was sworn in as president only a day after the uprising.

In sum, the 1990s witnessed important attempts at economic liberalization. Trade was almost fully liberalized by 1992, with high tariffs only applying to a limited number of luxury consumption goods. At the same time, the capital account and domestic financial sector were also liberalized and a dirty floating exchange-rate regime was established. Subsidies on domestic prices of basic commodities have now been eliminated, although successive governments only dared to take one or two at a time.

Reforms have been less far-reaching in other areas. In particular, the labour regime remained virtually unchanged throughout the 1980s and 1990s. Wage setting in the modern sector is governed by the minimum wage legislation. Base wages are set in reference to the minimum wage. In the modern sector there is a large wedge between the take-home wage and the base wage as a result of a complex system of mandated benefits, including thirteenth, fourteenth, fifteenth and sixteenth month salaries, a cost-of-living allowance, a complementary bonus and a transportation bonus. Some are a function of the minimum wage, some are lump-sum amounts, making administration and budget control a complex process. Some of the mandated benefits have been added over time as an alternative to an institutionalized wage indexation system. This minimum-wage level wedge has been increasing over time, reaching 700 per cent in 1998. Labour costs further include a 21.5 per cent social security tax, which is calculated over the base wage, excluding mandated benefits. Job security provisions present another potential source of labour costs: severance payments for 'unjustified' dismissal are 0.25 monthly salaries per year of service.

This cumbersome labour legislation has a potentially highly distortive effect on labour markets. However, enforcement of labour legislation is very weak and, as analysed by Cox-Edwards (1996), the actual additional costs of compliance with labour laws are actually in an order of magnitude of 8 per cent when comparing wage costs of complying and non-complying firms. Thus the costs created by labour market regulations are not as heavy as they may seem at first glance. This could explain why corporate enterprise managers do not see labour laws as a major concern for a firm's operations (Hachette and Franklin 1991). Compliance with labour legislation is mainly confined to the small segment of large companies. What's more, as analysed further below, the share of wages in total production costs during 1982–98 fell dramatically in nearly all economic sectors (except financial services). The employment effects of a liberalization of the labour market, both in terms of creation and relocation, are therefore likely to be small.

All in all, starting in 1992 Ecuador did make a serious move toward the type of economic reforms implemented elsewhere in the region. Yet, it may be symptomatic that the reform programmes ever since the debt crisis of the early 1980s were labelled as 'stabilization' or 'economic reactivation' plans, rather than structural reform programmes (cf. Table 7.1). In effect, macroeconomic stabilization problems have remained on the forefront, not in the least because vulnerability to external shocks, in particular oil prices, seems to have remained as strong as ever before. This could hint at the fact that little actual structural change occurred. As we shall see in the following sections, some real changes did take place, but they did not succeed in curing the fundamentals that underpin the stabilization problems and persistent income inequality of Ecuador's economy. Although the analysis stops in 1998, the events leading to the major economic crisis at the turn of the century merely reflect the prevailing fundamental weaknesses of Ecuador's economy, the attempts at liberalization notwithstanding.

7.3 ECONOMIC PERFORMANCE: LIBERALIZATION WITH LITTLE STRUCTURAL ADJUSTMENT?

Adjustment in Aggregate Demand

Economic growth during 1988–98 averaged a dismal 2.7 per cent per annum, with no notable difference between the pre- and post-liberalization periods (1988–91 and 1992–98). The economic reforms so far have therefore failed to enhance the overall growth rate. The drive toward liberalization has made the growth rate more dependent on exports. After accounting for multiplier effects, the contribution of exports to real aggregate demand increased from 48 per cent in 1988 to 60 per cent in the post-liberalization period (see Table 7.2). This export drive went largely at the cost of government spending, whose contribution fell from 30 to 20 per cent. The contribution of private investment remained stable and failed to recover from its decline during the 1980s adjustment.

This conclusion is derived from a simple decomposition methodology of effective demand (see Chapter 1). The methodology allows us to analyse the direct 'own' multiplier effects on aggregate demand of shifts in the exports volume, government spending and private investment, and shifts in import, tax and savings leakages, respectively. Table 7.2 and Figures 7.6 and 7.7 confirm that growth of the export volume (E) has been the most significant effective demand shift in the period of economic liberalization. Unlike experiences in other Latin American countries like Mexico and Nicaragua, there was no substantial increase in the import coefficient, as the external leakage parameter remained stable. Overall multipliers of government spending (G) and private investment demand (I_p) have been somewhat contractionary, with some fluctuations. The tax parameter (t), strongly influenced by fluctuating oil revenues, increased early in the period (1988–90) but fell thereafter. However, spending cuts, particularly in public investment – which fell by almost 30 per cent between 1988 and 1998 – outweighed this expansionary

Table 7.2 Decomposition of aggregate demand growth by effective demand components

	Contribution[1] (%)			Total aggregate demand	Growth of aggregate demand (Δ%)
	Private investment	Government spending	Exports		
1988	21%	30%	49%	100%	–
1989	23%	28%	48%	100%	0.9%
1990	20%	27%	53%	100%	1.9%
1991	24%	24%	52%	100%	6.9%
1992	22%	22%	55%	100%	3.0%
1993	21%	22%	57%	100%	2.1%
1994	21%	21%	58%	100%	4.5%
1995	22%	20%	58%	100%	3.5%
1996	20%	20%	60%	100%	0.8%
1997	22%	19%	60%	100%	4.1%
1998	23%	19%	58%	100%	2.2%

Notes: 1. Percentage shares correspond to the shares of the three right-hand side multiplier components of equation (A1.4) in aggregate demand (X).

Source: Central Bank of Ecuador, National Accounts.

effect of a reduced tax rate. The private investment volume (I_p) expanded at a rate of 4.5 per cent per annum, but its overall impact on effective demand stagnated as the private savings rate (s_p) increased. By implication, private consumption growth lagged behind income growth, which in turn is a consequence of further income distributional shifts against low-saving wage earners and in favour of higher-saving profit earners and informal sector workers (see below).

These volume shifts tell only part of the macroeconomic adjustment story. Export volume growth did not commensurately lead to greater foreign exchange earnings, as terms of trade moved unfavourably. While the volume export share in GDP (E/Q) rose steadily from 26 to 35 per cent, the value share showed greater volatility with an overall downward trend (Figure 7.8a). The import volume also showed an upward trend, but below export demand growth (Figure 7.8b). Consequently, the reform period yielded a doubling of the trade surplus in real terms (Figure 7.8c). This real domestic savings surplus did not translate into a comparable rise of dollar surpluses, though: net foreign exchange earnings were much more volatile, with the decline in

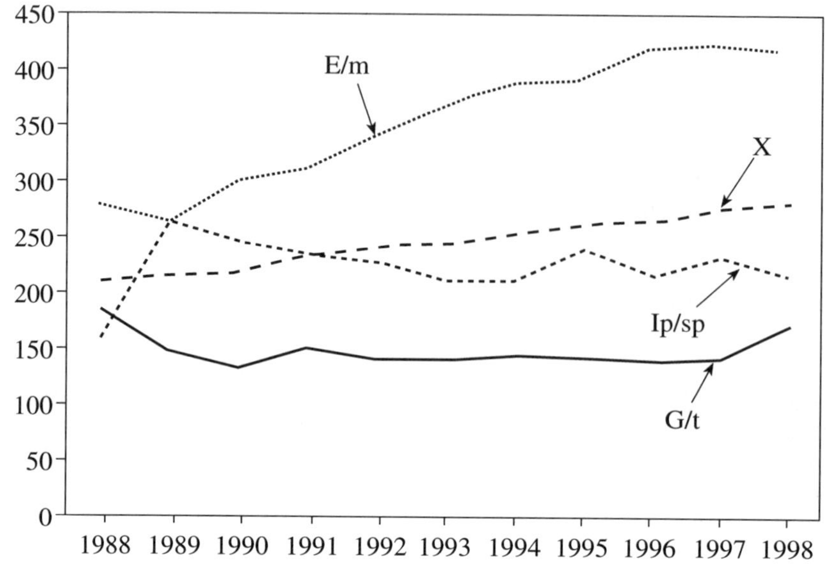

Figure 7.6 Direct 'own' macroeconomic multipliers

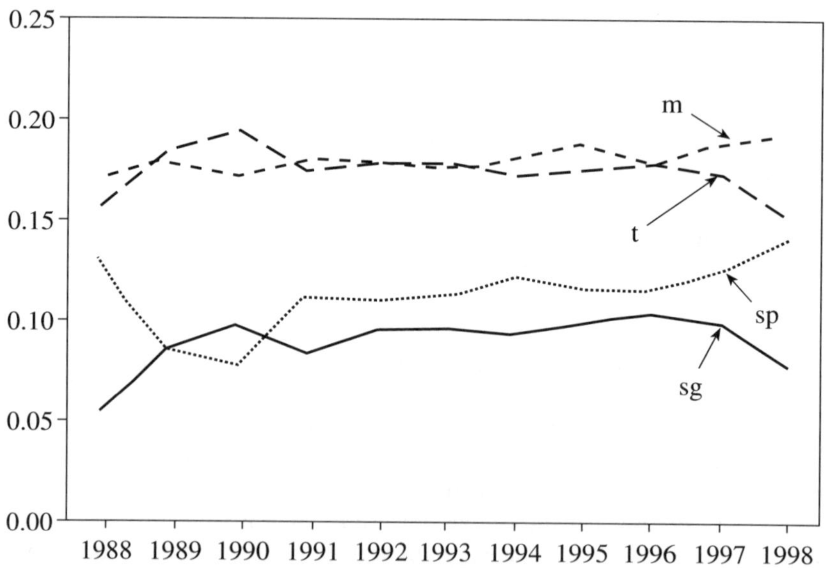

Figure 7.7 Leakages: average spending propensities

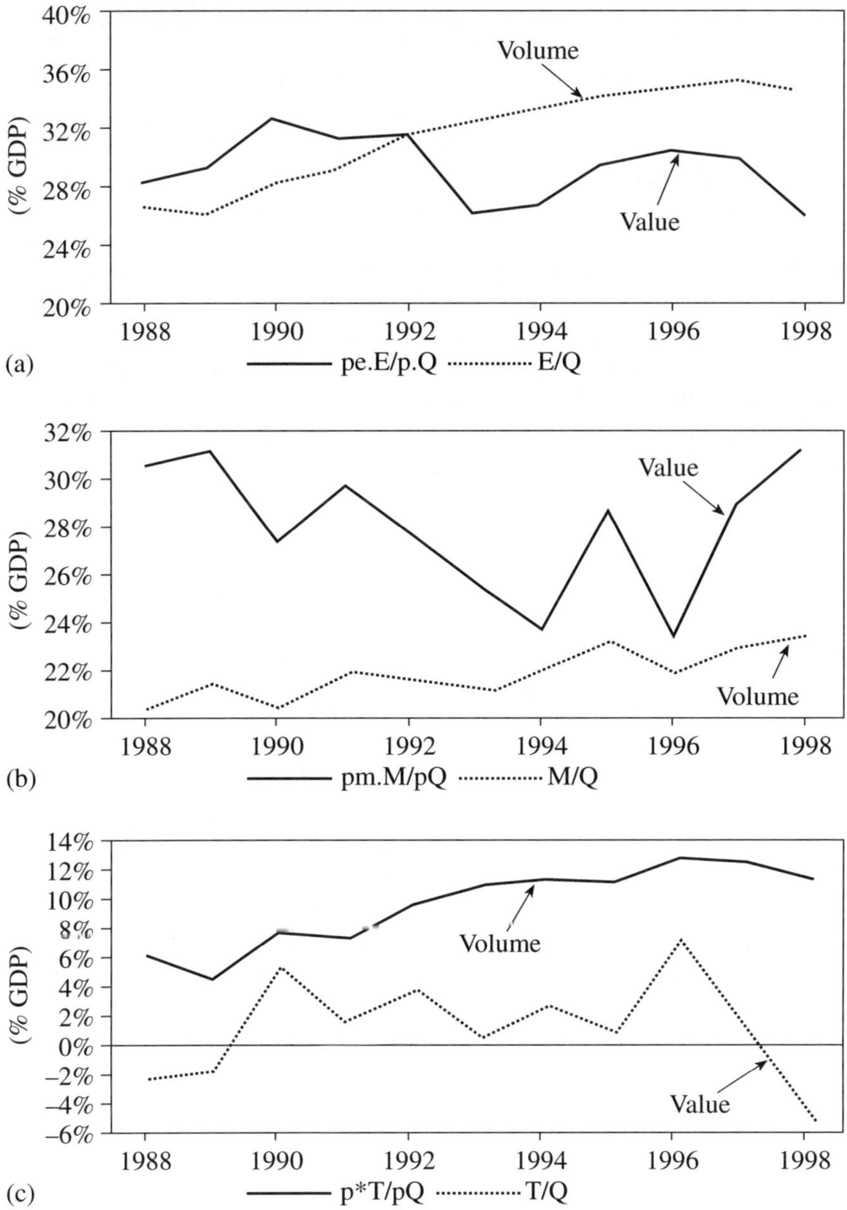

Figure 7.8 *(a) Export volume and value shares; (b) import volume and value shares; (c) trade balance (value and volume)*

oil and other commodity prices (partly due to the Asian crisis) moving the trade balance back into deficit in 1997–98.

It should be noted that the export volume expanded despite the substantial appreciation of the real exchange rate in the post-liberalization period (see Figure 7.5). Most of the volume growth comes from traditional exports, which typically have been fairly insensitive to the real exchange rate, particularly oil and shrimps. Another factor is related to the growth of intra-regional trade in the context of the Andean Pact, which was revived in 1990–91 with the harmonization of tariffs and culminated with the establishment of a common extra-regional tariff in 1995. In particular, manufacturing trade with Colombia developed favourably, partly due to a bilateral real exchange rate favourable for Ecuador. The role of the Andean Pact will be discussed in more detail below. Finally, there was a modest surge of new export sectors in agriculture (flowers, vegetables) with much of the seed money coming in the form of DFI.

Financing of Adjustment

As became clear in the previous section, there is an important real–nominal twist to the adjustment process in Ecuador. Relative price shifts (domestic/external, consumption/investment goods) may imply that large volume shifts are needed to achieve a small value adjustment in the finances required to accommodate the three macroeconomic spending gaps (private savings, fiscal and external; see Chapter 1, Appendix). Costs associated with the accumulation of net lending over time may also entail important income redistribution effects between private and public domestic agents and the rest of the world.[6]

Table 7.3 identifies the trends in the real and nominal financial gaps before and after the asset-related income transfers.[7] The results show once more the huge volume shift in the trade balance ($\Delta A'$) needed to achieve a much more modest dollar value trade surplus and to meet the external debt-servicing needs. This is also reflected in the country's external transfer problem. While the dollar-denominated debt-service burden ($\Delta NFA' - \Delta A'$) remained high at around 6 per cent of GDP, it fell considerably in commodity terms to mark the problems in converting production growth into foreign exchange earnings (Figure 7.9b). Private and public accumulation balances reflect the same pattern with the more noticeable adjustment in the fiscal balance. The private sector generated substantial savings surpluses in commodity terms ($-\Delta D'_p$), but remained a net borrower in money terms ($-\Delta D_p$) for most of 1988–98.

The government's primary surplus ($-\Delta Z = tX - G$) increased substantially around 1990 thanks to the rise in oil prices in the wake of the Persian Gulf War and the spending cuts of the 1988–90 and 1992 economic adjustment programmes. Various rounds of nominal wage increases and falling oil prices

Table 7.3 *Net financial claims*[1] *before and after transfers (percentage of GDP at current and constant prices)*

	Before transfers			After transfers		
	$I{-}s_pX$	$G{-}tX$	$E{-}mX$	$I{-}s_pX - iD_g + ei^*F_p$	$G{-}tX + iD_g + ei^*F_g$	$E{-}mX{-} ei^*F$
Current prices						
	ΔP	ΔZ	ΔA	ΔD_p	ΔD_g	ΔNFA
1988	5.6%	–3.5%	–2.1%	1.5%	5.3%	–6.8%
1989	11.9%	–10.1%	–1.8%	6.1%	1.2%	–7.3%
1990	6.7%	–12.0%	5.4%	3.8%	–0.5%	–3.4%
1991	9.3%	–11.0%	1.7%	5.5%	0.6%	–6.0%
1992	7.8%	–11.6%	3.8%	–0.2%	1.2%	–1.0%
1993	10.3%	–10.9%	0.6%	4.6%	0.1%	–4.7%
1994	5.4%	–8.4%	3.0%	4.7%	–0.6%	–4.1%
1995	5.5%	–6.6%	1.1%	3.0%	1.1%	–4.1%
1996	–0.2%	–6.9%	7.1%	–3.5%	3.0%	0.6%
1997	6.4%	–7.4%	1.0%	1.2%	2.6%	–3.8%
1998	9.1%	–4.0%	–5.1%	5.8%	6.1%	–11.9%
Constant prices						
	$\Delta P'$	$\Delta Z'$	$\Delta A'$	$\Delta D'_p$	$\Delta D'_g$	$\Delta NFA'$
1988	–3.8%	–2.4%	6.3%	–12.0%	5.7%	6.3%
1989	2.4%	–7.0%	4.5%	–4.5%	4.8%	–0.4%
1990	1.2%	–8.9%	7.7%	–2.9%	4.1%	–1.2%
1991	0.1%	–7.5%	7.3%	–5.4%	6.5%	–1.1%
1992	–0.7%	–9.0%	9.6%	–9.5%	6.5%	3.0%
1993	–1.8%	–9.1%	10.9%	–7.1%	3.1%	4.0%
1994	–2.5%	–9.0%	11.4%	–4.4%	–2.2%	6.7%
1995	–1.3%	–9.9%	11.2%	–7.1%	–6.0%	13.1%
1996	–2.6%	–10.2%	12.8%	–6.9%	–3.7%	10.5%
1997	–2.3%	–10.1%	12.4%	–7.6%	–4.2%	11.8%
1998	–4.0%	–7.3%	11.3%	–6.5%	–1.2%	7.7%

Notes: 1. If ΔP, ΔZ, ΔD_p, and $\Delta D_g > 0$, then they refer to an accumulation of domestic public and private debt, whereas if $\Delta NFA < 0$ it refers to an increase in foreign borrowing.

Source: Banco Central del Ecuador, *Cuentas Nacionales*, various issues and *Boletín Mensual*, various issues.

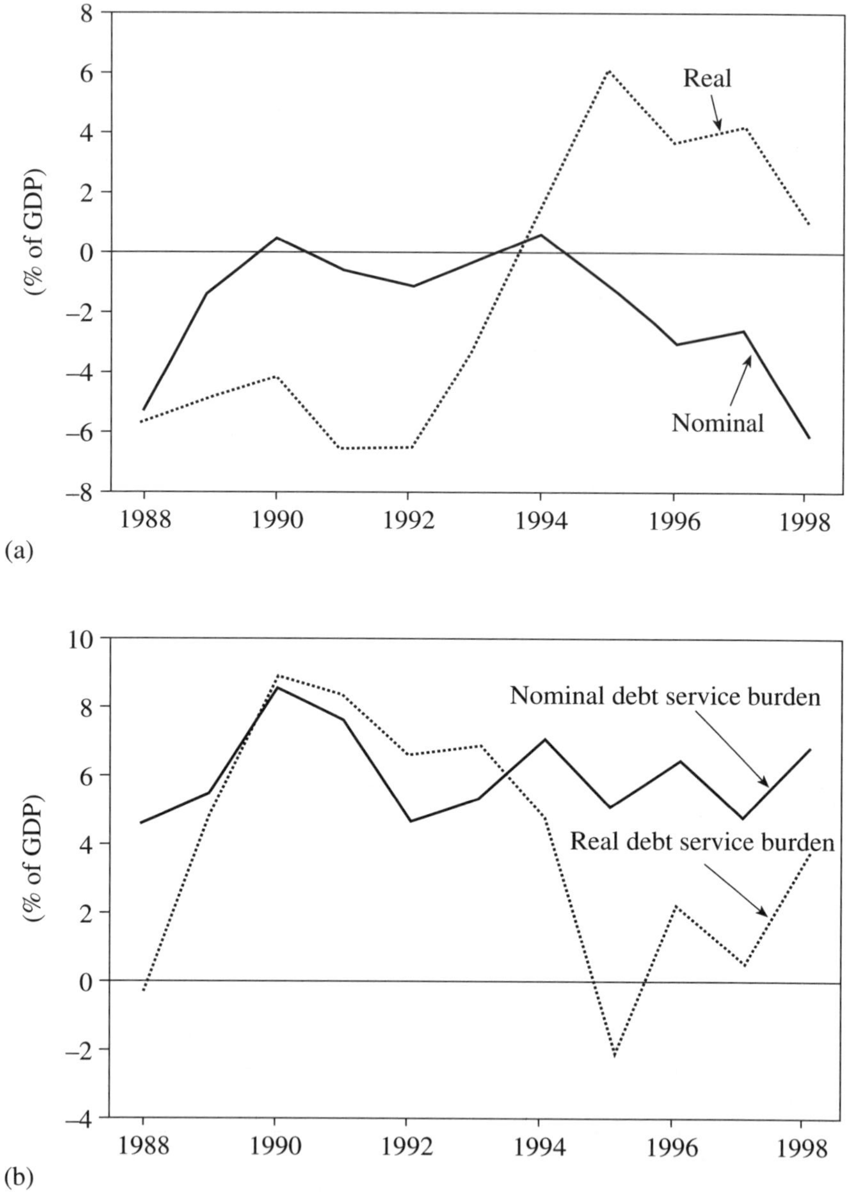

Figure 7.9 *(a) Nominal and real fiscal balance; (b) implicit and real foreign transfer burden*

after 1993 (with a temporary recovery in 1995–96) led to a decline in the primary surplus in nominal terms, as well as a rise in the overall nominal fiscal deficit (ΔD_g). In commodity terms, though, the fiscal balance shifted to a surplus reflecting both the impact of spending cuts in volume terms and the continued sensitivity of government finances to the oil price and exchange rate (debt burden; see Figure 7.9a).

The opening of the capital account has allowed for a different pattern of financing of the external deficits. During the 1980s, and in particular during 1987–91, Ecuador had little access to fresh sources of finance, despite large external deficits. In 1988–91, accumulation of arrears and refinancing of existing debt obligations were the main items on the capital account of the balance of payments (see Table 7.4). Most new disbursements came from multilateral institutions such as the IDB and the World Bank. The financial opening and lifting of restrictions on direct foreign investment allowed for a modest surge in private capital inflows. Direct foreign investment increased to around 2.5 per cent of GDP, up from historical levels close to 1.5 per cent. In addition, commercial bank credits toward the private sector resumed to around 3 per cent of GDP, but this was offset by about two-thirds by a resumption of capital flight as recorded in the balance of payments through the movements of short-term capital and errors and omissions. Most capital flight took place during 1995–97 (see Table A7.1), years of political turbulence due to the war with Peru, the voluntary exile of the vice-president and

Table 7.4 External financing, 1988–98

	1988–91	**1992–98**
Foreign savings	5.9%	4.1%
Portfolio investment	0.0%	0.0%
Direct investment	1.4%	2.7%
Net external borrowing	1.9%	3.1%
by public sector	1.8%	1.4%
new disbursements	1.2%	0.8%
refinancing	0.6%	0.6%
by private sector	0.1%	1.7%
new disbursements	0.3%	3.1%
refinancing	–0.2%	–1.5%
Arrears on external debt	4.0%	0.9%
Other short-term capital	0.7%	–1.9%
Change in reserves	–2.2%	–0.7%

Source: Table A7.1.

the 'Bucaramata'. Such political instability, weak institutions and the continued vulnerability of the economy to external shocks explain why the surge in capital flows has been much weaker than elsewhere in the region.

How much of the analysed shifts in effective demand composition can be ascribed to the process of economic liberalization? This is not easy to quantify. Nevertheless, up to this point we can infer the following from the analysis of the trends:

- The external (nominal) balance remains strongly sensitive to shocks in the external terms of trade (particularly oil prices).
- There has been a strong growth in the export volume since 1992, while import demand has remained fairly stable. The export volume growth is due, among other reasons, to increased oil production enabled partly by the opening to direct foreign investment in the sector, but oil export levels remain subject to macroeconomic policy considerations. As shown below, there has been some growth in non-traditional exports; this can be ascribed to the freeing of trade and capital. However, the growth of new export sectors has not been enough to reduce the economy's dependence on traditional primary exports.
- Unlike elsewhere in the region, trade liberalization has not produced an upward shift in the import demand curve.
- Fiscal adjustment is also still heavily influenced by external factors, i.e. oil prices on the revenue side and the external debt overhang on the expenditure side. Tariff reduction has not produced a substantial loss of government revenue.
- Capital account liberalization has allowed for a modest increase in capital inflows which helped support the relative stabilization of the nominal value of the sucre (at least during 1992–96), thus producing a real exchange rate appreciation.

The Supply Side: What Structural Adjustment?

The export drive following the economic liberalization is not reflected in major shifts in the sectoral composition of output. Non-oil traded goods sectors such as agriculture and manufacturing expanded at a pace similar to that of the non-traded goods sector (see Figure 7.10). Much of the export growth was concentrated on the traditional agricultural sector, e.g. bananas and shrimp. Non-traditional exports increased fivefold, albeit from small initial levels. Traditional exports such as oil, bananas, shrimp, coffee and cocoa are all primary commodities and still make up about 80 per cent of the total value of export earnings. The share of non-traditional exports did increase from 7 to 20 per cent between 1990 and 1997.[8] Some of this increase

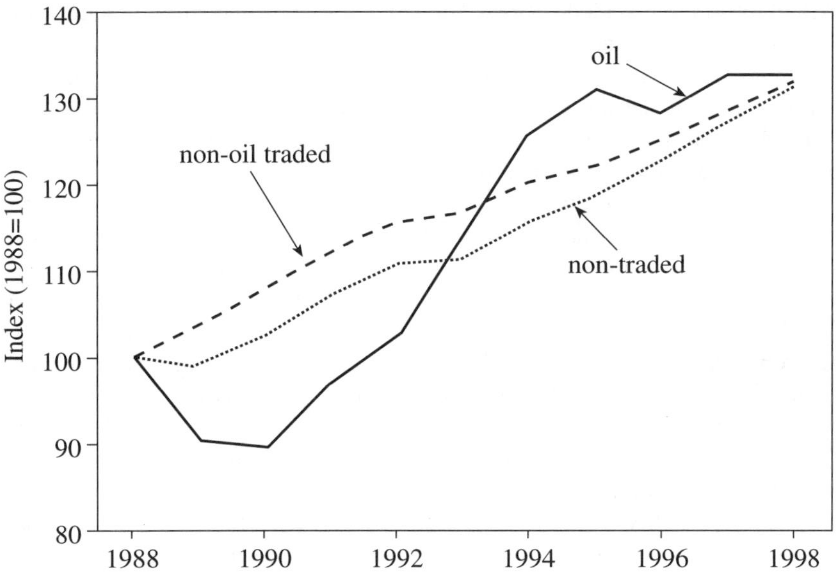

Source: Central Bank, National Accounts.

Figure 7.10 Traded and non-trade production growth (index, 1988 = 100)

is in new, labour-intensive agricultural products like flowers and vegetables, but an important share of the non-traditional export increase is in manufactured goods shipped to neighbouring countries of the Andean Pact. The main products include processed seafood, luxury consumption goods and vehicles, all characterized by capital-intensive production methods (see Vos 1987, Creamer et al. 1997).

The lowering of the tariffs and the reduction of the dispersion in tariff rates by commodity type did reduce dispersion of effective protection rates across manufactured sectors, but non-basic consumption and capital goods sectors still benefit from greater protection.[9] Export growth has been substantially larger in the more protected sectors. This bias in output expansion in the high-productivity, capital-intensive manufacturing sectors seems to have been part of a larger picture.

A decomposition analysis of productivity growth and sectoral employment reallocation confirms the pattern of adjustment following liberalization as sketched in the Introduction (Figure 7.1). In this story, liberalization may lead to relatively less demand for formal employment at a given output level through pressures toward cost reduction via enhanced labour productivity in tradable goods sectors, along with growth of demand for relatively low-skilled jobs in non-traded sectors. The reduction in formal employment would then likely be associated with an increase in informal jobs and greater self-employment in sectors such as commerce and services. As we shall see below, this explanation could apply to the early liberalization period (1990–95) – as depicted by Figure 7.1a – but more expansionary macroeconomic policies led to a partial reversal thereafter (Figure 7.1b).

Measurement of productivity growth is hampered by a lack of consistent employment data. To analyse what happened during the 1990s, only two sources provide nationwide employment data: the 1990 population census and the 1995 and 1999 living standards measurement surveys. Employment definitions are not strictly comparable, though, as the census data is likely to severely underestimate female labour participation and occupational rates. Using these sources would lead to implausibly high employment growth. The urban employment survey provides a more consistent source with data for 1988–97. Hence we recur to this source, keeping two drawbacks in mind: it only covers the urban workforce, and it requires using a proxy for 'urban' production which we equate with the non-agricultural sector. The latter assumption probably leads to an overestimation of productivity levels in some sectors, which are also important as sources of rural employment – particularly construction, commerce and services. The trend over time, however, is probably not affected by this assumption.

Bearing these limitations in mind, non-agricultural productivity growth since 1992 has been dismal, averaging 0.1 per cent per year.[10] As shown in Table 7.5, output growth in the traded goods sector outpaced employment growth, leading to an annual 2.4 per cent productivity increase. At the same time, there was a productivity decline in the non-traded goods sector, e.g. in construction, transport and other services. The transport sector – also closely linked to informal trade and services – and, especially, other services, absorbed a more than average employment growth, confirming the aforementioned hypothesis that the productivity growth in the traded goods sector may have pushed much of the labour force growth into informal employment.

Productivity growth in the traded goods sector is strongly influenced by the trend in the oil sector. As mentioned before, production in the oil sector was influenced by two factors in the 1990s. First, the policy target to maximize oil revenues led to hastened depletion of the natural resource. Second, the lifting of controls on foreign investment in the oil sector led to further productivity increases. The high volatility in the productivity levels suggests that the former factor still predominates. Productivity in the manufacturing industry increased at a 1.3 per cent rate between 1992 and 1997 after strongly declining trends in the 1980s caused by the recession and falling capacity utilization. This finding appears to be consistent with the increase in manufactured

Table 7.5 Decomposition of non-agricultural productivity growth, 1992–97

	1997 employment share L_i/L	1997 output/ labour ratio (sucres of 1975 × 10[3]) X_i/L_i	Output growth dX_i/X_i	Employment growth dL_i/L_i	Productivity growth ρ_i^*	Contribution to productivity growth $\Sigma\rho_i^*$	Weights of productivity change $(X_i/X).\rho_i^*$	Employment reallocation $(X_i/X–L_i/L)L_i^*$
Agriculture[1]	–	–	2.6%	3.4%	–	–	–	–
Oil and mining	0.4%	2795	5.3%	–3.0%	8.5%	1.0%	1.5%	–0.5%
Manufacturing	16.9%	68	3.2%	1.8%	1.3%	0.3%	0.3%	0.1%
Electricity, gas and water	0.3%	295	1.3%	–10.3%	13.0%	0.1%	0.2%	–0.1%
Construction	6.8%	27	0.9%	1.2%	–0.3%	–0.1%	0.0%	0.0%
Commerce	30.4%	37	3.0%	1.6%	1.4%	0.1%	0.3%	–0.2%
Transport and communications	6.1%	112	3.7%	3.8%	–0.1%	0.2%	0.0%	0.2%
Financial services	4.9%	114	1.8%	1.1%	0.8%	0.1%	0.1%	0.0%
Other services	34.1%	28	0.5%	5.1%	–4.4%	–1.6%	–0.7%	–0.9%
Total non-agricultural output	100.0%	58	2.9%	2.8%	0.1%	0.1%	1.6%	–1.5%
Traded goods	17.3%	28	4.2%	1.7%	2.4%	1.3%	1.8%	–0.5%
Non-oil, traded goods	16.9%	68	3.2%	1.8%	1.3%	0.5%	0.3%	0.3%
Non-traded goods	82.7%	44	2.1%	3.0%	–0.9%	–1.2%	–0.2%	–1.0%

Notes: See Appendix to Chapter 1 and text for estimation methodology.

Sources: Banco Central del Ecuador, *Cuentas Nacionales*; INEC, *Encuestas de Empleo Urbano*.

exports and the shift toward more capital-intensive sectors such as non-basic consumption goods and capital goods.

A decomposition analysis of the aggregate productivity growth[11] clearly shows that productivity increased in sectors with relatively high output/labour ratios such as oil and manufactures and fell in sectors with low labour intensity (especially other services; see Table 7.5). The shifts have been far from dramatic, though. Productivity gains have been small, and the largest productivity differentials have stayed the same since the 1970s – oil and manufacturing versus urban informal services (see Vos 1987, Jácome et al. 1998). During the 1970s and 1980s the incentive structure was also biased toward the more capital-intensive, non-basic industrial sector. In the 1990s, the institutional setting changed from a heavily protected inward-looking industry sector to a more export-oriented one, but the output dynamics remain concentrated where there is less employment creation, pushing excess labour into the urban informal services sector. From this perspective, the more recent sectoral reallocations seem like very little structural adjustment indeed.

Tables 7.6 and 7.7 further confirm the hypothesized labour market adjustment: a rising share in urban informal employment and increasing skill intensity in the production of tradables after the trade reform. Skill intensity fell in the non-traded sector, but the greater relative demand for unskilled workers was entirely concentrated in the services sector. The skill intensity increased in other non-traded sectors such as construction, commerce and financial services. This confirms the aforementioned hypothesis that informal services appear as the 'sink' of the labour market for the pool of unskilled workers. The implications for the distribution of factor incomes, inequality of household incomes and poverty are discussed in the following section.

Table 7.6 Urban informal employment (share of EAP)

	1990	1992	1995
Total	54.5%	58.1%	56.3%
Workers in micro-enterprises	27.4%	32.5%	31.6%
Domestic servants	4.5%	4.3%	4.8%
Unskilled independent workers and unpaid family workers	34.5%	34.3%	32.6%

Source: INEC, *Encuestas de Empleo Urbano*.

Table 7.7 Skilled–unskilled labour demand by sector,[1] 1990–99

	Ratio skilled/unskilled		
	1990	**1995**	**1999**
Agriculture	0.07	0.18	0.20
Oil and mining	0.55	0.89	1.18
Manufacturing	0.63	0.68	1.00
Construction	0.24	0.68	0.81
Commerce	0.76	1.53	1.14
Transport and communications	0.79	2.71	4.40
Financial services	5.62	7.70	8.74
Other services	1.56	0.44	0.46
Total	0.52	0.53	0.59
Traded goods	0.19	0.24	0.27
Non-oil, traded goods	0.19	0.20	0.22
Non-traded goods	1.01	0.85	0.99

Notes: 1. Unskilled workers are those with less than nine achieved grades of formal education (primary plus two years of secondary education); skilled workers have nine or more years (grades) of formal education.

Source: INEC, *Censo de Población* 1990; *Encuesta de Condiciones de Vida* 1995 and 1999. Data are national, i.e. covering the whole labour force, urban and rural.

7.4 WAGES, DISTRIBUTION AND POVERTY

Real Wage Trends and Labour Market Adjustment

The employment shift away from modern sector wage labour into informal sector and self-employed employment is a trend already present during the crisis of the 1980s. The share of wage earners in the urban labour force declined from 65.7 per cent in 1982 to 55.1 per cent in 1990 and further to 51.7 per cent in 1995, but increased again during the crisis to 57 per cent in 1999 (Table 7.8). In rural areas there seems to be a more secular decline in wage employment. The trend is related to falling employment opportunities, particularly in manufacturing, construction and government services, sectors with high shares of wage labour during much of the 1980s and 1990s. It is probably equally related to falling real wages that witnessed a declining trend from 1980 onwards. By 1992 the real minimum wage had fallen to a third of

Table 7.8 Share of wage earners in the labour force, 1982–99

	1982	1990	1995	1999
Urban wage earners (% of urban EAP)	65.7	55.1	51.7	57.1
Rural wage earners (% of rural EAP)	38.5	33.7	32.4	31.7

Source: INEC, Population Censuses, 1982, 1990 and INEC, *Encuesta de Condiciones de Vida*, 1995 and 1999. In the definition used here, wage earners do not include unpaid family workers and domestic servants.

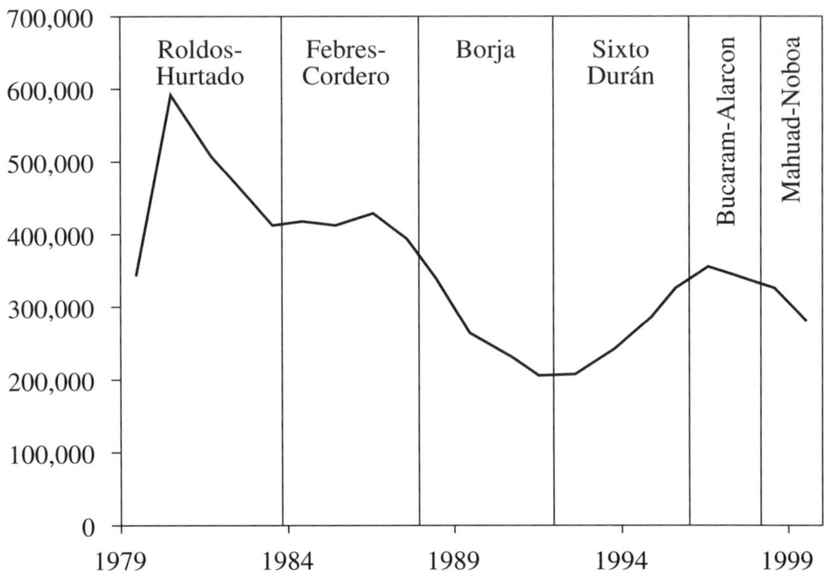

Notes: Nominal minimum wages include all bonuses and complementary remunerations as defined in minimum wage legislation. Base year for consumer price index is September 1994 through August 1995.

Source: Central Bank of Ecuador, *Información estadística mensual*.

Figure 7.11 Real minimum wage, 1970–99 (sucres per month at constant prices of 1994–95)

the 1980 level (Figure 7.11). As the minimum wage is indicative of the institutional setting of most wages and salaries, this severe drop in the return to wage labour is likely to have provided an incentive to find an income in other types of jobs. Various rounds of nominal wage increases decreed by the

Table 7.9 Trends in wage shares[1] by type of industry, 1980–95

	1980	1988	1992	1995
Traded[2]	20.4%	10.4%	7.3%	9.2%
Traded, non-oil	26.1%	9.9%	7.1%	8.9%
Non-traded	42.8%	27.0%	19.5%	21.4%
Non-traded, private[3]	31.8%	16.2%	12.1%	11.4%
Total	33.7%	19.9%	14.0%	16.5%

Notes:
1. Wage shares are taken as a percentage of value added at factor prices.
2. Includes agriculture, oil and mining, and manufacturing.
3. Non-traded goods sectors excluding government services.

Source: Banco Central del Ecuador, *Cuentas Nacionales*.

Sixto Durán government starting in 1992 supported a recovery of the real wage, without being able to restore it to the level reached in the early 1980s.

Declines in the share of wage employment and in real wages are reflected in a steep fall in the share of the overall wage bill in total value added (Table 7.9). The wage share fell from around 33 per cent of factor income to around 15 per cent between 1980 and 1995. In contrast, the share of self-employment income increased from 44 to around 70 per cent in the same period.[12] The corporate profit share also fell in favour of self-employed income. Since 1992, both the wage and corporate profit shares have regained some ground.

The decline of wage shares was substantial across all sectors during the 1983–92 adjustment period, except for financial services, where it increased (Table 7.9). The recovery of wage shares has been more differentiated. Much of the real wage increase accrued to public sector workers and is reflected in a rising wage share in the other service sectors after 1992. Traded goods sectors show only a slight recovery in the very low wage shares, from 7.3 to 9.2 per cent between 1992 and 1995. In agriculture, the wage share increased from 8.4 to 11.3 per cent of factor income in the same period, while in manufacturing it increased from 6.4 to 7.5 per cent. These are certainly no revolutionary changes. In effect, two partially offsetting tendencies were at work in the manufacturing industry: first, as analysed above, the sectoral effects of liberalization pushed toward less labour-intensive activities, creating a downward effect on the wage share. Second, the real wage hike pushed in the opposite direction and appears to have outweighed the former effect. By contrast, the agriculture industry saw a shift – albeit modest – toward more labour-intensive activities (flowers, vegetables, etc. for export production) which, combined with the wage, rose to a slightly higher wage share.

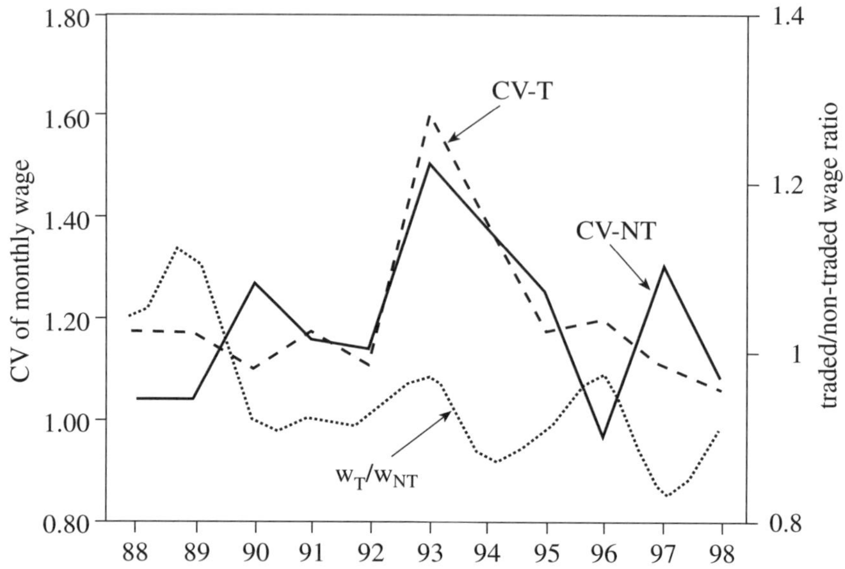

Note: CV = coefficient of variation of monthly wage per worker.

Source: INEC, *Encuestas de Empleo Urbano*.

Figure 7.12 Wage inequality in urban traded and non-traded sectors (private sector workers only)

On the whole, real wages in urban traded goods sectors declined by some 20 per cent as against those in the non-traded goods sector between 1988 and 1997 (see Figure 7.12). This is consistent with two earlier findings: the appreciation of the real exchange rate and the low wage share in the traded goods sector. The modest increase in the wage share in the non-traded sectors after 1992 is principally due to wage increases in public administration. As can be inferred from Table 7.10, the wage share in the non-traded market sector continued to fall after the 1992 reforms, which seems consistent with the hypothesis that liberalization brought a continued growth of informal sector employment.

Average wages disguise trends toward a greater wage inequality. The shift toward a greater skill intensity in traded goods sectors (see Table 7.7) is reflected in a rising dispersion of wage incomes in that sector. Recent data are only available for urban workers. Measuring wage inequality among private sector workers by the coefficient of variation (CV) shows a stronger widening in inequality in the traded goods sector until 1994, but the internal wage

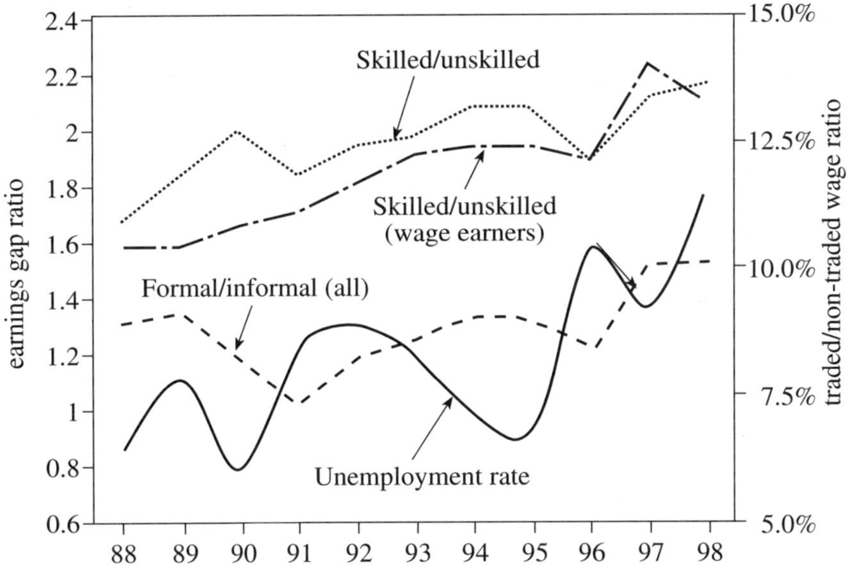

Notes: Earnings gap by skill level is defined as ratio of mean primary labour incomes of skilled and unskilled workers (all workers and private sector wage earners respectively). The earnings gap for formal/informal workers refers to the ratio of the mean income of private, modern sector wage earners to that of the informal sector's self-employed.

Source: INEC, *Encuestas de Empleo Urbano*.

Figure 7.13 Trends in earnings gaps between skilled and unskilled and formal and informal urban workers, 1988–98

inequality fell afterwards, most likely because of the equalizing effect of the minimum wage adjustment (Figure 7.12).

The wage differential between skilled and unskilled workers shows a more continuous rising disparity (see Figure 7.13). This wage gap increased from 58 per cent in 1988 to well over 100 per cent in 1997 and 1998. This tendency toward a widening earnings differential in favour of skilled workers is similar for private sector wage earners and all urban workers. A more detailed analysis of these income gaps shows that the inequality within groups fell for both skilled and unskilled workers (León and Vos 2000), so that the skilled–unskilled wage gap between groups is the persistent determinant of wage inequality despite the minimum wage increases between 1994 and 1997. This points toward a deepening of the existing segmentation of urban labour markets in Ecuador along human capital lines. Real wages fell significantly for both skilled and unskilled workers during the emerging economic crisis in 1998 and 1999. As Figure 7.12 also shows, this did not lead to a reduction of the wage gap, since both types of workers seem equally hit by the renewed acceleration of inflation and lagging nominal wage adjustments.

Similarly, the gap between formal and informal urban workers has maintained a rising tendency (Figure 7.13). This formal–informal income gap tends to move inversely to the open urban unemployment rate, which hints both at the residual character of the informal labour market segment and at the fact that the level of unemployment is an influential factor in formal sector wage-setting.

Returns to Education and Urban Labour Market Segmentation

Results of an application of Mincerian earnings functions[13] for urban workers confirm that returns to education for wage earners increased after 1992, but also show that male labourers were the only beneficiaries (Table 7.10). Returns for female wage earners and for the self-employed did not increase. The results also show that educational returns are higher for female workers than for male wage earners. This, together with substantially lower female participation rates, suggests that the urban labour market poses barriers to the entry of female workers. Returns to education are lower and declining for the self-employed, as expected, and the standard Mincerian function has much less explanatory power for this group of workers. This confirms the earlier conclusion of a continued and deepening labour market segmentation along the divides of human capital endowment and company type.

Table 7.10 Returns to education[1] for urban wage earners and self-employed workers, 1988–98

	1988	1990	1992	1995	1997	1998
Wage earners						
Males	7.8	7.9	8.7	8.4	8.4	8.5
Females	11.3	11.0	11.2	11.2	11.0	11.8
Self-employed						
Males	7.4	6.5	8.0	7.9	6.9	7.7
Females	8.6	7.3	7.3	6.2	7.4	7.5

Notes: 1. Returns to education refer to percentage increase in expected hourly income due to one additional year of schooling. Estimates obtained through Mincerian earnings functions. See León and Vos (2000) for details.

Source: León and Vos (2000) based on data from INEC, *Encuestas de Empleo Urbano*, 1988–98.

Labour Market Flexibilization, Employment and Distribution

Ecuador's cumbersome labour legislation could be expected to provide major distortions and cost-raising effects to the hiring of labour in the modern sector. At the same time, low and declining wage shares throughout the economy make it difficult to believe that labour market reform will have a major effect on overall economic performance. Moreover, as discussed in Section 7.2, compliance with labour laws is low, even in the modern sector. The labour cost-raising effect of the existing labour legislation is therefore believed to be small, and employers do not seem too worried about the existing labour regulations (see Cox-Edwards 1996). In a more stylized analysis, Rama (1996) does find some positive growth and employment effects following labour market reform, as it would shift workers from the informal sector to modern wage employment. Rama's model assumes full compliance with existing legislation so that it may overstate the likely impact of a labour market reform. Nevertheless, Rama (1996: 324) also states that one should not expect labour reform to be a panacea, and that a larger poverty-reducing impact should be expected from a long-term investment in education.

This is not to say that labour market reform would not be relevant and urgent. In particular, the existing payment system and institutional wage setting make the remuneration system complex and hardly transparent. Minimum-wage legislation with its mandatory benefits guides the payment pyramid in both public and private sectors. The historical pattern has shown that this makes modern sector nominal wage adjustments rigid and subject to political decision-making – the upshot being that, with inflation up, workers tend to lose purchasing power over time. This suggests that real wage trends are closely associated with urban poverty. Hence a more transparent system of remunerations could help maintain workers' purchasing power, as well as ease estimation of the production cost and budgetary implications of wage adjustments for private investors and the public administration.

Urban Income Distribution and Poverty

The aforementioned tendencies are further reflected in a growing inequality in urban incomes. Real incomes of the richest quintile (Q.V) recovered earlier and faster from the high-inflation episode of the late 1980s. Between 1994 and 1996, real income increases were stronger for the lowest quintiles (Q.I–III). The survey data also show a substantial recovery of real incomes of the urban poorest (Q.I). Per capita household incomes of the lower-middle income groups (Q.II–III) are the most closely related to the trends in the real minimum wage (Figure 7.14). This link is weaker for the poorest urban

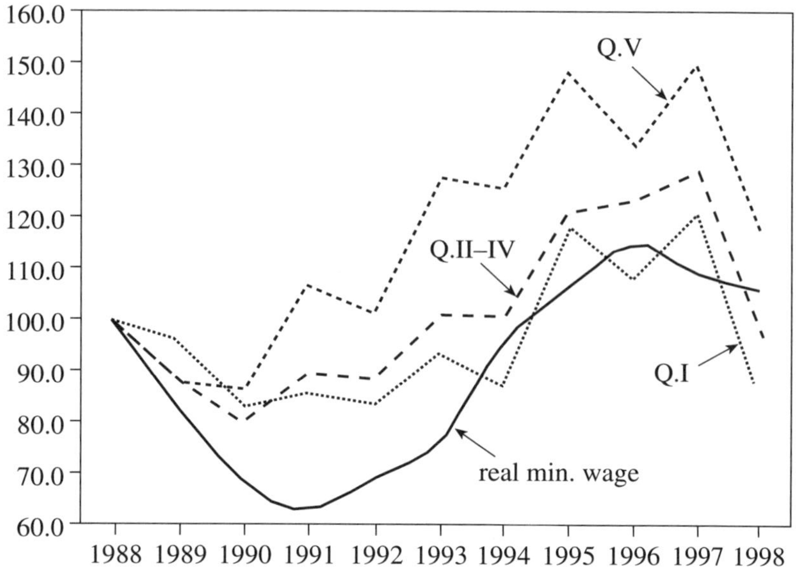

Notes: Min. wage refers to real effective minimum wage (including bonuses and additional monthly payments); Q.I = first quintile (poorest 20 per cent), Q.II–IV = second, third and fourth quintiles (20–60 per cent), Q.V = fifth quintile (richest 20 per cent).

Source: León and Vos (2000), based on INEC, *Encuestas de Empleo Urbano*.

Figure 7.14 Real urban per capita incomes by quintiles and the minimum wage, 1988–98 (index, 1998 = 100)

households, as a larger proportion of this income group is engaged as self-employed in informal urban activities.

The upshot of the aforementioned trends is that one can observe both a rise in urban inequality and a fall in the poverty incidence after 1992 and up to 1997. This is shown in Figure 7.15. The Gini for per capita urban household income increased from 0.44 to 0.48 between 1988 and 1992 and further to 0.50 in 1995. After 1995 there was a slight drop, possibly due to a loss of momentum in the liberalization process because of the political turmoil of 1995–96 and the subsequent decline in growth of traded goods production. Urban poverty declined substantially after 1992 and shows a close inverse correlation with the trend in real wages (Figure 7.15). Falling real wages and employment, along with rising inequality in per capita incomes in the emerging economic crisis of 1998, appear to have undone all the poverty reduction achieved during 1992–97.[14]

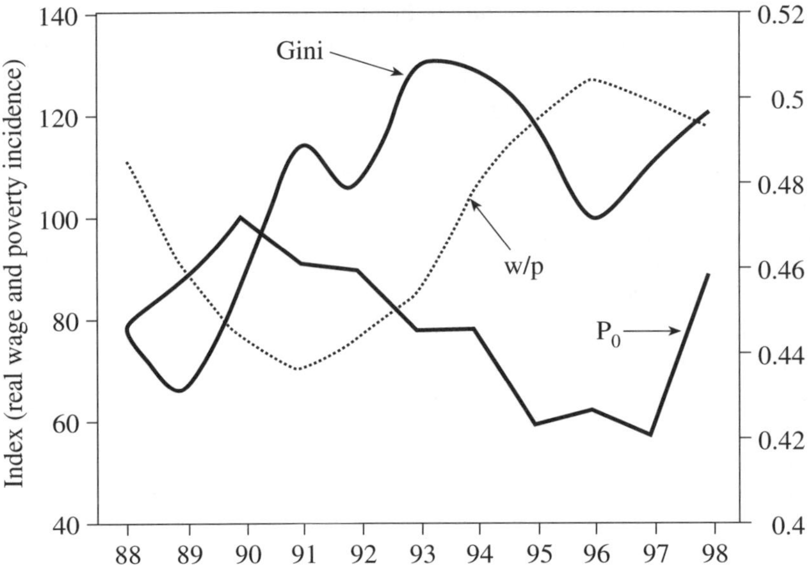

Notes: Real minimum wage (*w*/*p*) and poverty incidence (P_0) are expressed as indices (1990 = 100) on the left-hand scale. The Gini coefficient is on the right-hand scale. Reference period for all variables is November of each year.

Source: INEC, *Encuestas de Empleo Urbano*; León and Vos (2000).

Figure 7.15 Urban poverty, inequality and the minimum wage, 1988–98

Crisis, Inequality and Poverty

Urban households were hit the hardest by the economic crisis of 1998–99. Nationwide household surveys are only available for 1995–99. According to these sources, the poverty incidence increased by 10 percentage points, affecting about 1.2 million people nationwide (Table 7.11). While poverty remains more widespread in rural areas, the largest relative and absolute rise in poverty concentrated in urban areas. Income inequality also increased more steeply in urban areas. Poverty deepened in rural areas, but overall inequality remained roughly the same during the crisis. The data for 1999 in Table 7.11 represent the period October 1998 through September 1999 and hence do not yet show the full impact of the crisis that deepened during 1999 and early 2000, with the annual rate of inflation rising to well over 100 per cent.

The crisis was triggered by external shocks, but undoubtedly was also associated with the liberalization process. In particular, the lifting of financial

Table 7.11 *Poverty and inequality in Ecuador, 1995–99*

	National		**Urban**		**Rural**	
	1995	**1999**	**1995**	**1999**	**1995**	**1999**
Poverty						
Poverty incidence (P_0)	32%	42%	18%	29%	53%	59%
Poverty gap (P_1)	14%	17%	6%	11%	24%	27%
Poverty severity (P_2)	8%	10%	3%	6%	15%	16%
Inequality						
Gini of per capita household income	0.529	0.535	0.499	0.522	0.464	0.465
Gini of primary labour income	0.555	0.562	0.537	0.555	0.510	0.513

Notes: Poverty estimates are based on per capita household incomes and a poverty line of US$ 60 at PPP (as used for the urban survey data above).

Source: INEC, *Encuesta de Condiciones de Vida* (LSMS) 1995 and 1999.

controls in a context of weak bank supervision and a lenient lender-of-last-resort role of the Central Bank stimulated the fragile banking sector into more excessive risk-taking. The shocks exhausted monetary reserves and this pushed the financial system over the edge into bankruptcy. The transmission mechanisms of the crisis into poverty and inequality at a household level are most likely to go through macro variables, in particular the overall drop in real incomes (GDP per capita fell by 9 per cent in 1999) and the doubling of urban unemployment. Further, more excess labour was pushed into informal activities; this could explain at least part of the rise in urban inequality as well as poverty.

Macroeconomic changes were also important when attempting to explain the drop in urban poverty in the first half of the 1990s. Stabilization policies cutting inflation and domestic demand growth, facilitated by relatively favourable oil price and net capital inflows, led to real wage and employment growth. Trade liberalization also generated some export-led growth, but more importantly seems associated with some more structural labour market adjustment, creating greater demand for skilled workers in traded goods sectors and shifting the remuneration structure against unskilled workers and workers in informal service activities.

The microsimulations methodology (see Chapter 2) is applied in the next section to assess in greater detail the importance of shifts in aggregate labour demand, mean incomes, employment structure and earnings gaps on poverty and inequality.

7.5 SIMULATING THE EFFECTS OF MACRO ADJUSTMENT AND TRADE LIBERALIZATION ON POVERTY AND INEQUALITY[15]

The basic idea behind the microsimulations is to isolate the effect of each of the main determinants of the changes in poverty and inequality, and to associate these changes with the process of macroeconomic adjustment and stabilization as well as with trade and capital account liberalization. The methodology consists of creating a counterfactual in the form of labour market parameters representing the employment and remuneration structure, which would allegedly prevail had liberalization not taken place. This counterfactual may be obtained either by model simulations to generate a case of with-and-without, or by taking the structure prevailing at the beginning of the liberalization process to get a sophisticated before-and-after comparison. For lack of a sufficiently disaggregated and operational CGE model, the before-and-after option has been chosen here.

Chapter 2 spells out the methodology in general terms. Using the data sets for Ecuador, counterfactuals for the following labour market parameters are used: the rate of participation *P*, the unemployment rate *U*, the employment structure in terms of economic activity sector *S* (traded/non-traded) and occupational category *O* (wage and non-wage earners), respectively, the remuneration structure W_1 (labour income of each employment category vis-à-vis the mean), the remuneration level W_2 for each employment category and, finally, the employment structure in terms of education *M* (skilled/unskilled). The pre-liberalization (initial year) parameters are applied to the post-liberalization (final year) household survey data to simulate what poverty and income distribution would be had changes in each of the parameters not taken place during the period. Simulations are performed separately for each parameter change and in cumulative sequence in the indicated order.

The methodology was applied using the LSMS data for both urban and rural areas for the 1995–99 crisis period and, in combination with the urban labour force surveys, for urban areas for the 1988–90 and 1990–95 recession and liberalization periods. The year 1990 marks the beginning of the macroeconomic stabilization and liberalization process with most of the reforms being implemented in 1990–92. The 1988–90 period is one of economic recession and largely failed attempts at stabilization.

In order to assign the counterfactual labour market values to households and individuals in the survey data, a few important assumptions have to be made. First, the labour market is segmented, in the sense that workers are assumed not to move between urban and rural labour markets and unskilled workers not to move to skilled labour segments. Second, for lack of a full model of the labour market, a randomized process is applied to simulate the effects of changes in the labour market structure. That is, random numbers are used to determine which working-age persons change their labour force status, who will change from one segment of the labour market to another (sector or occupational category), which employed persons improved their level of education, and how new mean labour incomes are assigned to individuals in the sample.

Because of the introduction of a process of random assignation, the microsimulations were repeated several (32) times, so as to construct 95 per cent confidence intervals for the indices of inequality and poverty.[16] This was not required for the simulations of the effect of change on the structure and level of remuneration, which do not involve random numbers. In each simulation we calculated the incidence, depth and severity of poverty and the Gini and Theil coefficients of the distribution of both per capita income and primary incomes.[17]

Labour Market Changes

As mentioned, the effects of labour market adjustment on poverty and inequality during the period of stabilization and liberalization could only be simulated for urban areas, whereas for the 1995–99 crisis period outcomes for both the urban and rural population could be analysed.

Labour force participation (*P*) in the urban labour market increased for all groups of workers (skilled, unskilled, males, females) in all sub-periods. Unemployment (*U*) increased most strongly in 1988–90 and 1995–99, and barely changed in 1990–95. Sectoral labour demand (*S*) shifted toward the traded sector during 1988–90 and toward non-traded activities during 1990–95, only to move back into traded sectors during the 1995–99 crisis years. For most labour groups, a shift toward non-wage employment (*O*) was predominant in the 1988–95 recession and liberalization period, except for unskilled male workers who found more opportunities in wage employment. The share of skilled workers (*M*) in total employment increased for all groups of individuals throughout 1988–99.

The remuneration structure (W_1) among urban workers moved in opposite directions during 1988–95 and 1995–99. The greater shifts took place in the 1988–90 and 1990–95 recession and liberalization periods, most gains going to skilled non-wage earners in the traded goods sector. Unskilled male and female workers in the traded goods sector as well as unskilled female non-wage earners in the non-traded sector lost most ground in the primary income distribution in both the liberalization and the crisis periods. Mean earnings (W_2) increased for all types of workers in 1990–95, but fell strongly in 1995–99 for virtually all groups, especially female non-wage earners.

During the 1995–99 crisis years, nationwide labour force participation continued to increase, but notably most strongly among unskilled women in rural areas. At the same time, unemployment increased. Not all unskilled women in rural areas found employment as their unemployment rate increased, while for other types of rural workers unemployment actually fell. In urban areas, as expected, unemployment increased for all types of workers. The proportion of those working in the traded sector increased, except for skilled, female workers in urban non-wage activities. The highest increases were seen among other non-wage workers – in particular among less-educated women. When looking at shifts by occupational category, the prevalence of wage-employment diminished within several groups of employed persons. The pattern of the shifts is somewhat different for men and women. With respect to the skill composition, there was a large increase in skilled labour among female non-wage earners in the non-tradables sector. More generally, in terms of employment, skilled workers seem to have been less affected by the crisis than the unskilled, but this was not always the case in terms of remuneration. With some exceptions, the remuneration structure turned in favour of unskilled wage labour and against non-wage earners, especially women. In urban areas, women in non-wage activities were generally hit harder than men by the overall reduction in real labour income.

Simulation Results

What was the impact of these changes in the labour market structure on poverty and inequality? The results are presented in summary form in Table 7.12, while the main details for urban households during 1988–99 appear in Table 7.13 and those for all households during the 1995–99 crisis in Table 7.14. The outcomes have to be read as follows: we simulate what poverty and income distribution in, say, 1999 would look like should labour market conditions of e.g. 1995 still prevail. Thus, if we simulate the 1995 sectoral employment structure on the 1999 survey data and this yields a poverty rate lower than observed, this means that the shift in sectoral labour demand that took place between 1995 and 1999 has been poverty-enhancing.

Looking at the overall results (Table 7.12), it becomes clear that the urban labour market shifts that occurred during the 1990–95 liberalization period helped to reduce poverty (as shown by the '+' sign) and produced a rise in inequality in both per worker primary incomes and per capita household incomes. This result is consistent with the observed patterns described in the

Table 7.12 Microsimulations: impact on poverty and inequality of imposing an alternative labour market structure (sequential simulations: magnitude and direction of change relative to original value)

		Poverty			Inequality			
		P_0	P_1	P_2	**Gini YPC**	**Theil YPC**	**Gini YPI**	**Theil YPI**
LSMS surveys								
1999 (1995 parameters)	**National**	–	–	–	0	–	(–)	–
1999 (1995 parameters)	**Rural**	–	–	–	(+)	(–)	(–)	–
1999 (1995 parameters)	**Urban**	–	–	–	(–)	–	(–)	(–)
1995 (1990 parameters)	**Urban**	+	+	+	–	–	–	–
1995 (1988 parameters)	**Urban**	+	+	+	–	–	–	–
1999 (1988 parameters)	**Urban**	–	–	–	–	–	–	–
Labour force surveys								
1995 (1990 parameters)	**Urban**	+	+	+	–	–	–	–
1990 (1988 parameters)	**Urban**	–	–	–	–	–	(–)	–
1995 (1988 parameters)	**Urban**	+	+	+	–	–	–	–

Notes: P_0, P_1 and P_2 refer to FGT poverty indices (incidence, gap and severity). Inequality measures (Gini and Theil indices) refer to per capita household incomes (YPC) and primary incomes (YPI), respectively. A zero indicates a non-significant or near-zero effect; a sign in parentheses indicates a small effect (less than 2 per cent of original value); a minus sign has to be interpreted as a simulated increase in poverty during the period, a plus sign as a simulated decrease.

Source: Own calculations based on LSMS and urban labour force surveys.

previous sections. The more interesting aspects of the simulation exercise are in the details.

As shown by Table 7.13, the key factors underlying the observed reduction in poverty and rise in inequality during this period were:

- the rise in the level of remuneration, which by far explains most of the poverty reduction in this period while contributing to some reduction in inequality;
- the change in the remuneration structure (favouring skilled wage earners), which explains most of this period's rise in income inequality.

Other less important factors were:

- the contribution of the rise in the participation rate toward a fall in both poverty and inequality, while the greater supply of skilled workers helped reduce poverty but increase inequality;
- the shift toward non-traded employment which helped reduce poverty but probably led to an increase in inequality; the impact of both seems to have been rather small, though.

All in all, the macroeconomic factors underlying the real wage increases clearly dominated the urban poverty reduction achieved during the liberalization period, while the widening income gaps – by skill and between wage and non-wage income earners – associated with trade liberalization dominated the observed rise in urban inequality. The relative importance of these factors is similar for the other periods, plausibly because:

- the rise in unemployment and the fall in real wages contributed to the rise in urban poverty in the 1988–90 and 1995–99 recession periods;
- the shift in remuneration structure contributed to a rise in poverty and inequality during 1990–95, and the shift in the 1995–99 crisis period contributed to higher poverty despite producing lower inequality;
- rising participation rates in both periods helped reduce urban poverty and inequality, while rising skill levels of workers supported falling poverty but rising inequality.

The drop in mean income levels was also the predominant factor explaining the rise in poverty in both urban and rural areas during the 1995–99 crisis (Table 7.14). Consequently, inequality could potentially fall – as incomes tended to drop more pronouncedly among skilled workers and non-wage earners. The shift in remuneration structure was less favourable in rural areas, contributing to rising inequality, as unskilled female workers were among the

Table 7.13 Effects of changes in the labour market on urban poverty incidence and inequality

		Poverty (P_0)				Inequality (Gini of per capita income)			
		Labour force survey		LSMS		Labour force survey		LSMS	
		88–90	**90–95**	**90–95**	**95–99**	**88–90**	**90–95**	**90–95**	**95–99**
Value observed in final year		**0.4912**	**0.2921**	**0.1767**	**0.2931**	**0.4564**	**0.4946**	**0.4988**	**0.5221**
	–2%	0.4814	0.2863	0.1732	0.2872	0.4473	0.4848	0.4888	0.5117
	+2%	0.5010	0.2980	0.1803	0.2989	0.4655	0.5045	0.5088	0.5325
Values in case of changes in									
(1) rate of participation	Mean	**0.4926**	**0.3003**	**0.1927**	**0.3085**	0.4565	**0.4951**	**0.5023**	**0.5265**
	Lower limit	0.4922	0.2996	0.1915	0.3076	0.4563	0.4947	0.5039	0.5259
	Upper limit	0.4930	0.3010	0.1939	0.3093	0.4567	0.4955	0.5033	0.5271
(2) rate of unemployment	Mean	**0.4806**	**0.2929**	0.1768	**0.2835**	0.4519	0.4946	**0.4983**	**0.5182**
	Lower limit	0.4802	0.2927	0.1766	0.2829	0.4518	0.4945	0.4982	0.5181
	Upper limit	0.4811	0.2931	0.1770	0.2841	0.4520	0.4948	0.4985	0.5183
(3) employment structure (sectors)	Mean	**0.4891**	**0.2931**	0.1774	**0.2874**	**0.4557**	0.4946	**0.4972**	**0.5205**
	Lower limit	0.4885	0.2926	0.1767	0.2868	0.4555	0.4943	0.4963	0.5201
	Upper limit	0.4898	0.2935	0.1781	0.2880	0.4560	0.4950	0.4981	0.5209
(4) employment structure (occupational categories)	Mean	0.4917	**0.2908**	0.1762	**0.2902**	0.4561	**0.4942**	**0.4969**	**0.5215**
	Lower limit	0.4908	0.2905	0.1757	0.2895	0.4558	0.4941	0.4961	0.5211
	Upper limit	0.4925	0.2910	0.1767	0.2908	0.4565	0.4944	0.4976	0.5219
(5) remuneration structure		**0.4990**	**0.2607**	**0.1498**	**0.2857**	**0.4528**	**0.4770**	**0.4864**	**0.5270**
(6) level of remuneration		**0.4158**	**0.4830**	**0.3034**	**0.1854**	**0.4545**	**0.5016**	**0.5012**	**0.5226**
(7) employment structure (education)	Mean	**0.4863**	**0.3038**	**0.1856**	**0.2966**	**0.4555**	**0.4878**	**0.4937**	**0.5188**
	Lower limit	0.4856	0.3029	0.1848	0.2957	0.4551	0.4871	0.4923	0.5181
	Upper limit	0.4870	0.3047	0.1863	0.2975	0.4558	0.4886	0.4951	0.5196

Values in case of change of parameters									
(1–2)	Mean	**0.4823**	**0.3054**	**0.1930**	**0.2995**	**0.4519**	0.4952	**0.5028**	0.5226
	Lower limit	0.4816	0.3047	0.1917	0.2985	0.4517	0.4946	0.5019	0.5221
	Upper limit	0.4829	0.3060	0.1943	0.3006	0.4521	0.4958	0.5036	0.5232
(1–3)	Mean	**0.4683**	**0.3061**	**0.1922**	**0.2833**	**0.4496**	0.4950	**0.5012**	**0.5181**
	Lower limit	0.4673	0.3053	0.1909	0.2820	0.4492	0.4943	0.4999	0.5172
	Upper limit	0.4693	0.3069	0.1935	0.2846	0.4499	0.4957	0.5026	0.5190
(1–4)	Mean	**0.4743**	**0.3068**	**0.1921**	**0.2791**	**0.4478**	0.4949	**0.5003**	**0.5151**
	Lower limit	0.4731	0.3059	0.1905	0.2774	0.4472	0.4941	0.4987	0.5140
	Upper limit	0.4756	0.3077	0.1938	0.2807	0.4483	0.4957	0.5019	0.5162
(1–5)	Mean	**0.4878**	**0.2764**	**0.1644**	**0.2775**	**0.4460**	**0.4761**	**0.4865**	**0.5199**
	Lower limit	0.4866	0.2753	0.1629	0.2757	0.4455	0.4754	0.4848	0.5189
	Upper limit	0.4890	0.2775	0.1659	0.2793	0.4465	0.4767	0.4883	0.5209
(1–6)	Mean	**0.4032**	**0.4532**	**0.2802**	**0.1748**	**0.4438**	**0.4834**	**0.4888**	**0.5202**
	Lower limit	0.4020	0.4522	0.2788	0.1731	0.4433	0.4827	0.4871	0.5192
	Upper limit	0.4043	0.4543	0.2816	0.1766	0.4444	0.4840	0.4904	0.5212
(1–7)	Mean	**0.3978**	**0.4591**	**0.2874**	**0.1771**	**0.4436**	**0.4786**	**0.4866**	**0.5174**
	Lower limit	0.3966	0.4578	0.2857	0.1753	0.4429	0.4778	0.4847	0.5164
	Upper limit	0.3991	0.4604	0.2891	0.1789	0.4443	0.4795	0.4886	0.5185
Value observed in initial year		**0.3895**	**0.4912**	...	**0.1767**	**0.4446**	**0.4564**	...	**0.4988**

Notes: Normal values: difference not statistically significant. Bold values: difference statistically significant. Highlighted values: difference statistically significant and at least 2 per cent. Underlined values: poverty/inequality would have been higher if rate/structure were to be that of initial year. In case of changes in the employment structure, the mean incomes to be assigned were calculated for the employed persons in each sector of activity, occupational category or group of employed persons according to skill level, excluding labourers with zero incomes.

Source: Own calculations based on LSMS surveys of 1995 and 1999 and labour force surveys of 1988, 1990 and 1995.

Table 7.14 Microsimulations: labour market adjustment, poverty and inequality during the crisis

LSMS data		Poverty (P_0) National 95–99	Poverty (P_0) Urban 95–99	Poverty (P_0) Rural 95–99	Inequality (Gini of per capita income) National 95–99	Inequality (Gini of per capita income) Urban 95–99	Inequality (Gini of per capita income) Rural 95–99
Value observed in final year		0.4160	0.2931	0.5945	0.5349	0.5221	0.4645
	–2%	0.4077	0.2872	0.5826	0.5242	0.5117	0.4552
	+2%	0.4243	0.2989	0.6064	0.5456	0.5325	0.4738
Values in case of changes in							
(1) rate of participation	Mean	0.4342	0.3085	0.6166	0.5389	0.5265	0.4657
	Lower limit	0.4335	0.3076	0.6153	0.5384	0.5259	0.4642
	Upper limit	0.4350	0.3093	0.6180	0.5395	0.5271	0.4672
(2) rate of unemployment	Mean	0.4134	0.2835	0.6115	0.5330	0.5182	0.4689
	Lower limit	0.4128	0.2829	0.6105	0.5326	0.5181	0.4670
	Upper limit	0.4140	0.2841	0.6125	0.5333	0.5183	0.4708
(3) employment structure (sectors)	Mean	0.4085	0.2874	0.5870	0.5323	0.5205	0.4643
	Lower limit	0.4078	0.2868	0.5857	0.5318	0.5201	0.4628
	Upper limit	0.4091	0.2880	0.5883	0.5329	0.5209	0.4657
(4) employment structure (occupational categories)	Mean	0.4138	0.2902	0.5938	0.5337	0.5215	0.4631
	Lower limit	0.4133	0.2895	0.5927	0.5334	0.5211	0.4615
	Upper limit	0.4143	0.2908	0.5949	0.5340	0.5219	0.4647
(5) remuneration structure		0.4177	0.2857	0.6001	0.5410	0.5270	0.4540
(6) level of remuneration		0.2987	0.1854	0.5113	0.5377	0.5226	0.4655
(7) employment structure (education)	Mean	0.4216	0.2966	0.6004	0.5307	0.5188	0.4565
	Lower limit	0.4207	0.2957	0.5994	0.5300	0.5181	0.4557
	Upper limit	0.4224	0.2975	0.6015	0.5314	0.5196	0.4573

Values in case of change of parameters							
(1–2)	Mean	0.4317	0.2995	0.6306	0.5378	0.5226	0.4734
	Lower limit	0.4307	0.2985	0.6293	0.5370	0.5221	0.4719
	Upper limit	0.4326	0.3006	0.6319	0.5385	0.5232	0.4749
(1–3)	Mean	0.4174	0.2833	0.6211	0.5357	0.5181	0.4769
	Lower limit	0.4163	0.2820	0.6194	0.5347	0.5172	0.4748
	Upper limit	0.4185	0.2846	0.6228	0.5366	0.5190	0.4790
(1–4)	Mean	0.4115	0.2791	0.6169	0.5324	0.5151	0.4790
	Lower limit	0.4102	0.2774	0.6150	0.5312	0.5140	0.4766
	Upper limit	0.4128	0.2807	0.6187	0.5335	0.5162	0.4814
(1–5)	Mean	0.4045	0.2775	0.6026	0.5375	0.5199	0.4689
	Lower limit	0.4032	0.2757	0.6002	0.5365	0.5189	0.4669
	Upper limit	0.4059	0.2793	0.6050	0.5386	0.5209	0.4709
(1–6)	Mean	0.3074	0.1748	0.5369	0.5401	0.5202	0.4732
	Lower limit	0.3063	0.1731	0.5344	0.5391	0.5192	0.4714
	Upper limit	0.3085	0.1766	0.5395	0.5411	0.5212	0.4750
(1–7)	Mean	0.3101	0.1771	0.5371	0.5360	0.5174	0.4708
	Lower limit	0.3090	0.1753	0.5346	0.5349	0.5164	0.4688
	Upper limit	0.3112	0.1789	0.5397	0.5372	0.5185	0.4729
Value observed in initial year		0.3194	0.1767	0.5263	0.5290	0.4988	0.4639

Notes: Normal values: difference not statistically significant. Bold values: difference statistically significant. Highlighted values: difference statistically significant and at least 2 per cent. Underlined values: poverty/inequality would have been higher if rate/structure were to be that of initial year. In case of changes in the employment structure, the mean incomes to be assigned were calculated for the employed persons in each sector of activity, occupational category or group of employed persons according to skill level, excluding labourers with zero incomes.

Source: Own calculations based on LSMS surveys of 1995 and 1999.

major losers and skilled male workers in non-traded activities (commerce) among the winners. This trend toward greater rural inequality was offset by the effect of a falling unemployment rate. By contrast, urban inequality fell because of the shift in remuneration structure, but this effect was offset by the rise in unemployment and the reduction in the share of unskilled wage earners. The latter two factors were also important elements in explaining the rise in urban poverty.

In sum, the macroeconomic stabilization that supported real wage and employment growth during 1990–95 was strong enough to push for poverty reduction, despite the effects against equity of trade liberalization. This means that more poverty reduction could have been achieved had inequality not increased. During the crisis, the macro factors worked adversely without reversing the employment structure in a more equitable direction, hence both poverty and inequality worsened.

7.6 CONCLUDING REMARKS

An attempt has been made to trace the employment and income distribution effects of the current and capital account liberalization of Ecuador's balance of payments during the 1990s. The insistence of multilateral organizations, particularly the IMF and the World Bank, that developing countries should enforce trade and capital account liberalization is based on the notion that economic opening will bring important welfare gains. Countries often resist, as they fear important adjustment costs such as a short-term rise in unemployment. Textbook approaches to structural adjustment and liberalization of the external sector typically sidestep the question of unemployment and income distribution effects. In the orthodox approach, which takes the simple Heckscher–Ohlin model as a benchmark, these issues are non-existent. According to the simplest textbook approach, in a small developing economy with capital-intensive imports, mobile factors and flexible prices, a reduction of import tariffs will have no effect on total employment, not even in the short run. Trade liberalization would lead to a sectoral reallocation of resources, though, and – according to the Stolper–Samuelson theorem – redistribute income in favour of the input-intensive factor of exports production, i.e. allegedly unskilled labour in the case of developing countries. In the Latin American reality, adjustment and liberalization have naturally been accompanied by rising unemployment in many cases, while rising inequality between skilled and unskilled workers and between wage and non-wage earners has been found in countries with either labour- or capital-intensive exportables (Berry 1997, Ganuza et al. 1998). The nature of the labour market, with its typical wage rigidity in modern sectors and a good deal of labour market segmentation, is crucial in understanding the outcomes of the liberalization process on incomes and employment. Macroeconomic policies and vulnerability to external shocks will only compound such outcomes.

Ecuador's liberalization process did not start in earnest until the early 1990s. It has made the economy even more dependent on export growth. Some growth of non-traditional exports has taken place, but oil and other traditional primary exports remain the key source of foreign exchange earnings, as well as of the vulnerability to external shocks. We have an overall case of capital-intensive or natural resource-intensive exportables (oil, bananas), labour-intensive non-tradables and importables (domestic food and liberalized manufactures) as the second most labour-intensive sector. Trade models with wage rigidity predict that liberalization under such initial structural conditions will reduce employment (Cox-Edwards and Edwards 1994). In Ecuador we saw no steep increase in unemployment rates, but – with high poverty and no unemployment benefit schemes – a strong rise in urban informal employment in the initial years of the liberalization, following the broadly sketched pattern of Figure 7.1a. Capital account liberalization, real exchange rate appreciation, a return to expansionary fiscal policies and minimum wage increases reversed some of this trend in the mid-1990s, following the pattern of Figure 7.1b. Political conditions and external vulnerability make the situation quite volatile. Macro policies have been characterized by a 'stop–go' pattern ever since the early 1980s, and this has not changed in the post-liberalization era. Continued reliance on oil exports characterized the main source of external volatility. In the 1990s, negative terms of trade shocks more than offset large volume increases in traditional and non-traditional exports, while large volume adjustments also proved insufficient to protect the fiscal balance against declining oil revenues.

Urban wage earners suffered heavy income losses during the ill-conceived stabilization efforts of the 1980s but were able to regain some ground during the post-liberalization period, when inflation dropped and real wages increased. Contrary to popular perceptions in Ecuador, urban poverty appears to have declined between 1992 and 1997. From the aforementioned it follows that the major underlying cause should be found in macroeconomic policies rather than in the effects of liberalization per se. As indicated, the structural conditions predict a loss of employment and real wage declines following liberalization, at least in the short run. Macroeconomic policies helped to reverse the trend in mean real wages and thereby also helped reduce urban poverty. This happy outcome has proven to be unsustainable: the macroeconomic policies did not help decrease labour market segmentation or the trends toward rising wage inequality between skilled and unskilled workers and a rising wedge between formal and informal workers. In addition, sustained external vulnerability and slippage in fiscal discipline pushed the twin deficits to unprecedented heights by late 1998. This triggered a currency crisis, a full-blown banking crisis and high inflation in 1999. The subsequent drop in employment and real incomes undid most, if not all, of the urban poor's real income gains of the preceding years. Finally, vulnerability to external shocks remained. The 1998–99 crisis was not just caused by falling oil prices and El Niño. Sequencing of reform policies has been equally problematic. Specifically, the banking sector was liberalized at a point in which it was virtually bankrupt and could only live on continued borrowing from the Central Bank (Figure 7.4 and Izurieta 2000) for as long as the foreign reserve position could keep up. Real exchange rate appreciation and high real interest rates did not particularly help stimulate industrial restructuring toward more labour-intensive export activities.

While the functioning of the Ecuadorian economy underwent some fundamental changes as a consequence of the liberalization process, the old story of primary export-driven growth cycles has not lost its relevance. Given the other structural features, this is bad news for the long-term prospects of the poor's welfare. The very introduction of the dollar as the official means of exchange in 2000 will not resolve the structural problems. More investment in human capital is only one element that can clearly turn the story into a happier one. However, the fruits will only become visible in the medium term. Labour market reform and promotion of labour-intensive export production will help lay additional foundations for a growth pattern that may achieve more effective employment growth and poverty reduction. However, in the short run there is still the formidable task of achieving a sustainable macroeconomic stability and coping with the enormous costs of restructuring the bankrupt financial sector. A surge in oil prices would be a welcome cushion-providing event. However, if this positive external shock just meant a fallback to the type of complacency with reform policies of the past decades, such a short-term rescue would signify yet another delay of the structural type of change needed to achieve the indicated long-term development goals.

NOTES

1. I am most grateful to Niek de Jong for valuable research assistance in Section 7.5 and to Mauricio León for providing survey data and comments. I am further indebted to Lance Taylor, Jaime Ros, Roberto Frenkel and Geske Dijkstra for their helpful comments on a previous draft.
2. The Central Bank losses are estimated here as the change in net worth. The quasi-deficit does not include changes in net worth due to revaluation of assets and liabilities. The hypothetical quasi-deficit does include the revaluation. See Izurieta (2000) for the data and estimation methodology.
3. Tariff reduction also involved reduction of the dispersion in tariff rates across commodities. The tariff reform included a reduction of the upper and lower limits of nominal tariffs

from 0 per cent and 290 per cent to 0 per cent and 35 per cent, respectively. This substantially reduced the difference between Ecuador's tariffs and those of the rest of the world, and eliminated the dissimilarity between Ecuador's tariff structure and that of the other Andean region countries (Creamer et al. 1997).

4. That is, only prospective value-added losses are included in these numbers. Capital losses, reconstruction costs of damaged infrastructure, costs of evacuations, health care or lost lives, etc. are not considered here, but see Vos et al. (1998) for an analysis of the economic and social costs of the weather shock.
5. See Izurieta (2000) for an in-depth analysis of the factors underlying the financial sector fragility that had already built up in the 1970s and 1980s, when virtually all commercial banks relied on subsidized Central Bank loans to maintain liquidity.
6. When taking such asset-related income transfers into account, we get the more familiar macroeconomic balances linked to expenditures and savings out of the disposable income of each institution, rather than from domestic product as implied by equation (A1.5), i.e.:

$$\Delta D_p + \Delta D_g - (\Delta F_p + \Delta F_g) = (I_p - s_p X - iD_g + ei^* F_p) + (G - tX + iD_g + ei^* F_g) + (E - mX - ei^* F) = 0$$

where D_p, D_g and F $(=F_g + F_p)$ stand for the stock of net private sector debt, net government debt and net external liabilities, respectively, as accumulated through the financing of the three 'after transfers' gaps over time. We can also define $NFA = -F$ as the net foreign asset position to get the 'after transfer' counterpart for A. The parameters i, i^* and e stand for the domestic interest rate, foreign interest rate and the nominal exchange rate.
7. In the specification of equation (A1.6), only asset- and liability-related income transfers are highlighted. Other transfers (grants, workers remittances, etc.) are relatively small in the case of Ecuador and are therefore omitted in order to simplify notation. However, they are included in the estimates of Table 7.2. The constant price values for the accumulation balances were obtained by applying the appropriate deflators to each aggregate demand category using national accounts implicit deflators.
8. In 1998, non-traditional exports reached as much as a quarter of total export earnings, but this outcome is heavily influenced by the decline in oil prices and the impact of El Niño on banana, coffee and cocoa production. Shrimp cultivation benefited from El Niño's warmer water and a rise in productivity of about 25 per cent (see Vos et al. 1998).
9. 'Non-basic' consumer goods are defined as commodities with income elasticities with a demand larger than one, whereas basic goods are those with elasticities smaller than one. See Creamer et al. (1997) for an analysis of effective protection rates by commodities classified this way. The methodology and sector classification follows that set out in Vos (1987).
10. There is no major reason to assume strong productivity increases in agriculture as a whole either. Some export sectors (bananas, shrimp, flowers) probably showed productivity growth, but in other sectors (cocoa, livestock, domestic food crops) there has been little or no innovation. In fact, a simulated estimate of productivity growth for the economy as a whole using adjusted employment data for the 1990 census indicates that overall productivity growth was 0.2 per cent per year between 1990 and 1995, with agricultural productivity growing at 1.3 per cent. For this exercise, the employment data of the 1990 census were adjusted for the alleged under-reporting of female participation rates, and unpaid family workers in the workforce were included to make the data more comparable to the 1995 LSMS survey.
11. See Appendix to Chapter 1 for this decomposition methodology.
12. The data are derived from the Central Bank's national accounts, where the estimate of the share of self-employed income is obtained from the gross operating surplus of households and unincorporated businesses as reported in the household accounts. The usual caveats hold with regard to the residual nature of income components and household outlays in the national accounts.
13. The estimated functions reported here are quite standard: ln(W/hr) = f(S, E, E2, xi), where

the dependent variable is the log of earnings per hour, S is years of completed schooling, E is work experience, E2 is squared work experience and xi is a vector of appropriate dummy variables, including location (Quito), sector (government in the case of wage earners), etc.

14. In the light of this discussion (falling wage shares, rising informal, self-employed employment), the strong correlation between real wage trends and poverty may be somewhat counterintuitive. There could be a number of possible explanations for this finding. First, the survey data used here (INEC's *Encuesta de Empleo Urbano*) are subject to important limitations. These will not be detailed here; see León and Vos (2000) for an extensive discussion. Two important limitations are mentioned here: (a) incomes are likely to be strongly under-reported, particularly those referring to non-wage incomes; and (b) while questionnaires and sample design have been by and large unaltered, survey enumerators were better instructed starting with the 1995 survey which led mainly to a more concise registration of labour incomes. One should therefore assume that poverty indices are overestimated, while inequality measures may be understated. Nevertheless, after performing a sensitivity analysis for various types of adjustments for alleged under-reporting and observed non-reporting, Leon and Vos (2000) still find the same trends as reported in Figure 7.15. After adjustment, the rise in real per capita incomes and the fall in the poverty incidence from 1995 onwards become much less pronounced, but the observed trend remains unaltered. On these grounds, the results of Figures 7.14 and 7.15 seem defendable proxies of the direction of change.
15. See Vos and de Jong (2001) and the Appendix to Chapter 2 for a more detailed discussion of the methodology and simulation as applied to Ecuador.
16. Some simulations were also repeated more than 100 times, however producing the same outcome as for 32 repetitions.
17. Mean incomes per decile were calculated in the simulations. These means were assigned to the newly employed or to already employed individuals who changed their sector of economic activity or occupational category, or moved from one educational level to another. Theoretically, to assess the impact of changes in the labour market structure, one would have to calibrate the database prior to simulating the effect of said changes – that is, replace the original labour incomes by mean incomes per decile. A test showed that both the direction of change and the magnitude of the effect do not change if the original values of the labour incomes are used instead of calibrated values. Since this facilitates interpretation of the results, we depart from the original values.

REFERENCES

Berry, Albert (ed.) (1997) *Economic Reforms, Poverty and Income Distribution in Latin America*, Department of Economics, University of Toronto.

CEPAL (1998) 'Ecuador: evaluación de los efectos socio-económicos del fenómeno El Niño en 1997–8', Mexico: Comisión Económica para América Latina y el Caribe (June 22) (mimeo).

Cox-Edwards, Alejandra (1996), 'Determinants of hourly earnings in Ecuador: the role of market regulations', in: World Bank *Ecuador Poverty Report*, Washington D.C.: World Bank, pp. 265–94.

Cox-Edwards, Alejandra and Sebastian Edwards (1994) 'Labor market distortions and structural adjustment in developing countries', in: Susan Horton, Ravi Kanbur and Dipak Mazumdar (eds) *Labor Markets in an Era of Adjustment. Vol. 1: Issues Papers*, Washington D.C.: EDI/The World Bank, pp. 105–46.

Creamer, Germán, Kwan S. Kim and Clark Reynolds (1997) *Ecuador en el Mercado Mundial: el regionalismo abierto y la participación del Ecuador en el Grupo*

Andino, el Tratado de Libre Comercio de Norteamérica y la Cuenca del Pacífico, Quito: Corporación Editora Nacional.

Ganuza, Enrique, Lance Taylor and Samuel Morley (eds) (1998) *Política macroeconómica y pobreza en América Latina y el Caribe*, Madrid: Mundi-Prensa (for UNDP, IDB and CEPAL).

Hachette, D. and D. Franklin (1991) 'Empleo e ingresos en Ecuador en un contexto macroeconómico', AID, Quito (mimeo).

Izurieta, Alejandro (2000) *Crowding-out or bailing out? Fiscal deficits and private wealth in Ecuador, 1971–99*, PhD Thesis, The Hague: Institute of Social Studies.

Jácome, Luis, Carlos Larrea and Rob Vos (1998) 'Políticas macroeconómicas, distribución y pobreza en el Ecuador', *CORDES Documento de Trabajo No. 7*, Quito (also published in Ganuza et al. 1998).

León, Mauricio and Rob Vos (2000) *Pobreza urbana en el Ecuador, 1988–98: Mitos y realidades*, Quito: Abya-Yala Publishers.

Rama, Martin (1996) 'Ecuadorian poverty revisited: the impact of education, growth and deregulation', in: World Bank *Ecuador Poverty Report*, Washington D.C.: World Bank, pp. 311–34.

Ros, Jaime (1999) 'La liberalización de la balanza de pagos en México: Efectos en el crecimiento, el empleo y la desigualdad salarial', Paper presented at UNDP/IDB/World Bank/CEPAL Seminar 'Balance of Payments Liberalization, Distribution and Poverty in Latin America', Rio de Janeiro, Brazil, February 24–27, 1999.

Sierra, Enrique (1995) *Ecuador, Ecuador: Tu petróleo, tu gente*!, Quito: EDIDAC.

Vos, Rob (1987) *Industrialización. Empleo y Necesidades Básicas en el Ecuador*, Quito: FLACSO – Corporación Editora Nacional.

Vos, Rob (1989) 'Ecuador: Windfall gains, unbalanced growth and stabilization', in: E.V.K. FitzGerald and Rob Vos (eds), *Financing Economic Development*, Aldershot: Gower, pp. 187–232.

Vos, Rob and Niek de Jong (2001) 'Rising inequality during economic liberalisation and crisis: macro or micro causes in Ecuador's case?', Institute of Social Studies Working Paper Series No. 325, The Hague: Institute of Social Studies.

Vos, Rob, Margarita Velasco and Edgar de Labastida (1998) 'Efectos económicos y sociales del Fenómeno de El Niño en Ecuador, 1997–8', Paper presented at LACEA Annual Conference, Buenos Aires (October).

World Bank (1996) *Ecuador Poverty Report*, Washington D.C.: World Bank.

8. El Salvador: balance-of-payments liberalization, remittances, employment and poverty[1]

Alexander Segovia and Jeannette Larde

8.1 INTRODUCTION

Throughout its history El Salvador has suffered wide disparities in income and wealth distribution and severe social problems. Poverty affects a major part of the population, especially in rural areas. Empirical evidence for the 1990s indicates that the country's economic and social situation improved and that poverty decreased, essentially because of the reduction of urban poverty. Rural poverty decreased only slightly (Segovia 1998). Economic recovery and poverty reduction took place in a context of profound structural changes of the economy. These changes relate to massive internal and external migration, the crisis of the agro-export sector, the massive inflow of foreign resources originating mainly from remittances of Salvadorians living in the United States, and the implementation of major economic reforms. The reforms consisted of liberalization of the economy, renewed privatization of the banking sector and external opening.

This chapter analyses the effects of the liberalization of the balance of payments on economic growth, employment, poverty and income distribution in El Salvador in the 1990s. To this end, we carried out a simulation exercise which determines counterfactually what income distribution and poverty levels following the 1997 economic liberalization process would have been, if the 1991–92 pre-reform wage or employment structure were to have remained unchanged.[2] The study is organized into six sections. First (Section 8.2), we analyse the macroeconomic functioning of the Salvadorian economy, trends in aggregate demand and the main sources of growth. Section 8.3 deals with balance-of-payments adjustment in the context of the process of external opening and massive inflow of workers remittances. Section 8.4 analyses the behaviour of the labour market and wage trends. Section 8.5 studies the patterns of poverty and income distribution during the 1990s. Section 8.6 applies the microsimulations methodology to assess the impact of the liberalization of the balance of payments on inequality and poverty. Conclusions are in Section 8.7.

8.2 THE MACROECONOMIC FUNCTIONING OF THE SALVADORIAN ECONOMY

Business Cycles and Domestic and External Shocks

Since 1980, macroeconomic trends and economic policies in El Salvador have been largely determined by domestic and external shocks. In the 1980–98 period, episodes of economic recession and exchange rate and price instability coincided with foreign exchange shortage, whereas episodes of macroeconomic expansion and stability correlated with foreign exchange abundance. Employment and poverty trends followed the cyclical behaviour of the economy (Segovia 1998). The duration and intensity of the expansive and contractive economic cycles have also been influenced by the domestic social and political context and by the implementation of stabilization and adjustment programmes. Restrictive macroeconomic policies triggered recessions in some episodes and contributed to their prolongation.

Since 1980, El Salvador registered four economic cycles clearly related to the presence of domestic and external shocks and the shortage/abundance of foreign exchange.[3] The first cycle comprises the 1980–82 period, characterized by a highly conflictive social and political climate and by the existence of a severe balance-of-payments crisis caused by massive capital flight and the impact of a series of adverse external shocks (oil price increases, traditional commodity price declines, increase of international interest rates, and a halt of external financing to the country as a consequence of the political crisis). During this period, El Salvador faced an unprecedented and severe foreign-exchange constraint. This together with domestic social conflict led to a severe drop in GDP and employment levels. It put an end to the financial and exchange-rate stability that the country had enjoyed for more than 50 years. As a result, poverty increased significantly (Segovia 1998).

The second cycle encompasses the 1983–89 period when the country partially overcame the foreign-exchange constraint on growth due to the inflow of financial resources from the United States (starting in 1983). Most of the inflows took the form of donations (Segovia 1995, 1998).[4] The politically motivated capital inflow helped to keep the economy afloat during the war, despite the lack of necessary adjustment measures, the effects of several droughts, an earthquake in 1986, and the aggravation of the domestic civil strife (Segovia 1998).

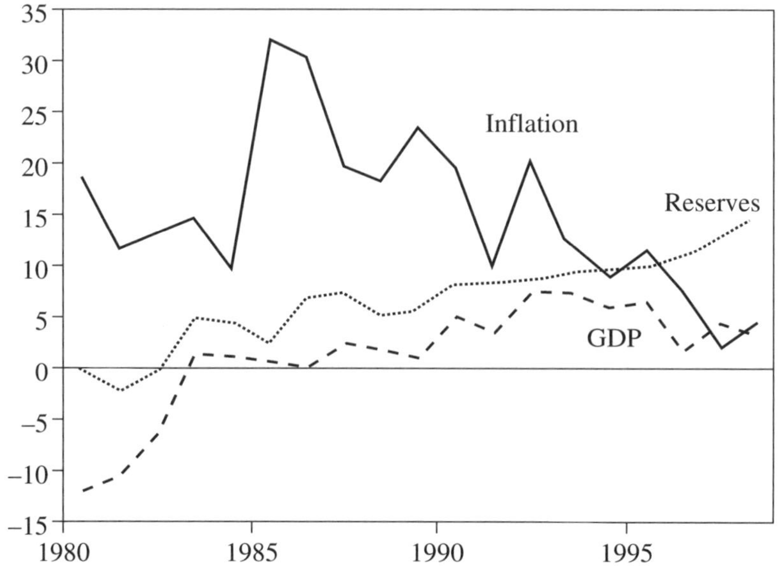

Source: Banco Central de Reserva of El Salvador.

Figure 8.1 Trends in inflation, real GDP and net international reserves, 1980–98 (growth rates in %)

As adjustment was postponed, macroeconomic imbalances worsened and inflation reached unprecedented levels (32 per cent in 1986, see Figure 8.1). The export sector suffered a profound crisis, largely a product of the overvaluation of the colon and the spread of the war to the country's rural areas. Foreign exchange shortages re-emerged in the final phase of this cycle. As a consequence, the government failed to meet external-debt obligations. This resulted in the suspension of disbursements by some international financial institutions.

During the third period, which ran from 1990 to 1995, the economy grew at an average of 6 per cent and reached growth rates over 7 per cent in some years. Growth trends reflected the strong post-war economic reactivation and the recovery of private investment (especially real estate), exports and consumption (especially of durable goods). The consumption boom was fed by the massive inflow of remittances and greater credit availability and accessibility. This was facilitated by the financial reforms, the process of trade opening, greater access to international capital markets, and cheapening of imports due to the fixed exchange rate and moderate inflation.

Price and exchange-rate stability accompanied the higher economic growth (see Table 8.1). Employment increased and poverty decreased (Segovia 1998).

Table 8.1 Selected macroeconomic indicators, 1989–98

Year	Exports (%GDP)	Imports (%GDP)	Real exchange rate (annual change)	Real lending rate	Real deposit rate	Public expenditure (%GDP)	Taxes (%GDP)	Fiscal balance (%GDP)	Real GDP	Inflation rate	Unemployment rate
1989	9.8	21.5	1.6	–7.2	–5.0	14.9	8.6	–3.7	1.0	23.5	8.4
1990	12.1	26.3	18.0	–1.3	1.8	15.7	9.1	–0.4	4.8	19.3	7.5
1991	13.6	28.5	–5.4	6.5	10.4	18.9	9.5	–2.8	3.6	9.8	8.7
1992	13.4	31.1	–6.7	–8.4	–3.5	20.6	9.6	–4.6	7.5	19.9	9.3
1993	14.9	30.9	–8.4	3.2	7.3	18.2	10.3	–1.6	7.4	12.1	9.9
1994	15.5	31.8	–1.7	4.7	10.1	18.2	10.9	–0.6	6.1	8.9	7.7
1995	17.4	35.0	–6.7	2.8	7.3	18.1	12.0	–0.1	6.4	11.4	7.7
1996	17.3	21.2	–4.8	6.6	11.2	20.2	11.3	–2.5	1.7	7.4	7.7
1997	21.6	33.4	–2.1	9.8	14.1	17.7	11.0	–1.8	4.2	1.9	8.0
1998	20.6	33.4	–1.7	6.1	10.8	18.6	11.2	–2.7	3.2	4.2	7.5

Notes: The data on exports and imports for 1989 and 1990 do not include maquila for lack of reliable data.

Source: Own calculations based on official data

During this period there was a substantial increase in foreign-exchange resources fuelled by higher levels of foreign aid for post-war reconstruction, private capital flows and workers' remittances. Restrictions on remittance receipts were eased. The massive inflow of foreign resources facilitated and, to some extent, accelerated the introduction of a programme of major economic reforms. The reforms concentrated on the liberalization of the economy, renewed privatization of the banking sector and elimination of monopolies in the foreign trade of coffee and sugar cane (see Section 8.3).

During the fourth and last period, 1996–98, economic growth decelerated, inflation dropped significantly and the de facto fixed exchange-rate regime was consolidated. The inflow of foreign resources remained high and restrictive economic policies targeted financial and exchange-rate stability. This contributed to the prolongation of the economic recession (Edwards 1999, PNUD 1999). As a result, domestic inflation fell to international levels, but real interest rates went up, real wages decreased and the fiscal situation deteriorated.

Financial problems emerged during this period as reflected in an increase of bad-performing loans in the portfolio of the banking system and the discovery of cases of financial fraud.[5] This affected the confidence in the banking system and exposed the weakness of the regulatory and supervisory institutional framework.

The economic slowdown has been subject to various interpretations. The more widely held view puts the blame on the loss of dynamism of the post-war reconstruction process (especially the end of the durable consumer goods and real-estate investment boom) and on the restrictive financial policy which was preceded by increases in public utility tariffs and the VAT (from 10 to 13 per cent).[6]

Several years of moderate growth have made clear that the Salvadorian economy is having serious difficulties returning to high and sustained growth under a fixed exchange-rate regime. The exchange-rate policy forced authorities to adopt restrictive financial policies in order to keep inflation at international levels. This limited private investment growth by pushing up real interest rates. Moreover, the scope for anti-cyclical fiscal policy has been limited due to the low tax burden.

Behaviour of Aggregate Demand during 1990–97

There is consensus in El Salvador that the high economic growth rates of the first half of the 1990s were partly the result of the post-war reactivation of domestic consumption. The process was facilitated by the opening of the economy and reinforced by rising workers' remittances. Additionally, the post-war reconstruction process is traditionally seen to have dynamized public and private investment. However, there is no consensus regarding the role of external demand in the growth process of the 1990s.

In order to determine the role of domestic and foreign demand in El Salvador's economic recovery in the 1990s, we analyse the behaviour of aggregate demand and its components for 1990–97 (see Chapter 1, Appendix). As can be seen in Table 8.2, during 1990–95 the annual growth rate of the demand (*X*) was high and sustained, coinciding with high GDP growth. In 1996, demand growth turned negative (–1.2 per cent) as a result of the negative growth of investment (–24.7 per cent) and exports (–1.4 per cent). That year, imports suffered a drastic contraction (–9 per cent) and GDP registered the period's lowest growth rate (1.8 per cent).

During the period, the composition of aggregate demand changed. The main component, consumption, lost ground as its share fell from 67.7 per cent in 1990 to 64.3 per cent in 1997. The investment share remained close to 11 per cent, but showed some volatility. The investment rate reached levels equal to or higher than 14 per cent in 1992, 1994 and 1995. Government expenditures showed a downward trend with a decrease of about one percentage point in their share in demand. Although exports decreased at the beginning of the period (1991–92), the export share increased starting in 1993, reaching 18 per cent in 1997.

The investment–savings gap (*I–sX*) widened throughout the 1990–97 period, although it narrowed somewhat in 1996–97 (see Table 8.2). The widening gap reflects the increase in the share of foreign savings to finance domestic investments. The gap between government expenditures and tax revenue (*G–T*) was reduced in 1990 and 1991, after which it became negative. This was the impact of the policy of austerity that kept public expenditures below tax income and stimulated government savings. The trade deficit (*M–E*) widened during the period.

The results of the demand decomposition are presented in Table 8.3. The table shows the sources of demand growth for the direct 'own multiplier' effects of each demand component and the observed changes in the expenditure categories. Results reveal that the external sector was the main driving force of aggregate demand in 1990–97. External demand expansion produced 24.5 per cent of aggregate demand growth, representing nearly 70 per cent of the total increase in demand (35.5 per cent). The good performance of the foreign sector is largely explained by dynamic exports, which contributed 28.4 per cent in aggregate demand growth. As we will see below, this dynamism is the result of the strong increase of maquila exports.

A more careful analysis of the annual results reveals that the external sector was not always the engine of aggregate demand growth. For example, in 1994 and 1995 the main source of growth was the private sector, private investment in particular. Public sector investment was also an important

Table 8.2 *(a) Behaviour of aggregate demand; (b) macroeconomic spending gaps, 1990–97*

(a) Percentage shares

	C	*I*	*G*	*E*	*M*	*GDP*	*T*	*X*
1990	67.7	10.6	7.6	14.1	23.8	76.2	7.0	100.0
1991	67.4	11.8	7.6	13.2	23.4	76.6	7.3	100.0
1992	66.8	14.0	7.1	12.1	24.5	75.5	7.3	100.0
1993	65.3	13.9	6.4	14.4	25.4	74.6	7.7	100.0
1994	64.5	14.6	6.2	14.8	26.0	74.0	8.1	100.0
1995	63.5	14.6	6.3	15.7	27.4	72.6	8.7	100.0
1996	66.3	11.1	7.0	15.7	25.2	74.8	8.4	100.0
1997	64.3	10.9	6.7	18.0	25.9	74.1	8.1	100.0

Annual growth rate

	C	*I*	*G*	*E*	*M*	**GDP**	*T*	*X*
1991	2.5	15.2	3.9	–3.9	1.2	3.6	8.2	3.0
1992	8.2	29.4	1.3	0.5	14.3	7.6	8.8	9.1
1993	6.3	7.7	–1.4	29.2	12.9	7.4	15.3	8.7
1994	5.5	12.4	3.4	9.4	9.4	6.0	11.6	6.9
1995	6.8	8.3	9.5	15.3	14.1	6.4	17.7	8.4
1996	3.2	–24.7	9.7	–1.4	–9.0	1.8	–4.9	–1.2
1997	2.4	4.2	1.6	21.5	8.2	4.7	1.8	5.6

(b)

	Values in million colones at constant prices of 1990			**Shares in %**		
	I–sX	*G–T*	*E–M*	*(I–sX)/X*	*(G–T)/X*	*(E–M)/X*
1990	4,336	288	–4,624	9.1	0.6	–9.7
1991	4,874	155	–5,029	9.9	0.3	–10.2
1992	6,755	–110	–6,645	12.5	–0.2	–12.3
1993	7,199	–760	–6,439	12.3	–1.3	–11.0
1994	8,205	–1,153	–7,053	13.1	–1.8	–11.3
1995	9,614	–1,675	–7,939	14.2	–2.5	–11.7
1996	7,391	–973	–6,418	11.1	–1.5	–9.6
1997	6,537	–998	–5,539	9.2	–1.4	–7.8

Source: Own calculations based on data from the Banco Central de Reserva of El Salvador.

Table 8.3 Decomposition of the sources of growth of aggregate demand, 1991–97 (percentages)

	Private sector			Public sector				Foreign sector			
	Private inv.[1]	Savings	Subtotal	Public inv.[1]	Cons.[1]	Taxes[2]	Subtotal	Exports[1]	Imports[2]	Subtotal	Aggregate demand
1991	3.2	4.5	–1.3	0.7	0.7	0.7	0.7	–1.4	–0.9	–0.5	–1.1
1992	5.4	3.4	2.0	2.6	0.2	0.0	2.9	0.2	2.1	–1.9	3.0
1993	1.8	0.7	1.2	0.5	–0.2	0.7	–0.4	7.9	1.6	6.3	7.0
1994	3.9	–1.2	5.1	–0.1	0.5	0.6	–0.2	3.0	1.0	2.0	6.8
1995	2.6	–1.5	4.1	0.0	1.3	1.2	0.2	4.9	2.3	2.6	6.8
1996	–9.0	–4.0	–5.0	0.4	1.4	–0.6	2.5	–0.5	–4.1	3.5	1.0
1997	1.6	3.4	–1.8	–0.5	0.3	–0.5	0.3	7.7	1.1	6.5	4.9
1990–97	9.0	4.8	4.2	3.7	5.3	2.2	6.8	28.4	4.0	24.5	35.5

Notes:
1. Corresponds to the direct 'own multiplier' effect of each demand variable.
2. Corresponds to the effect of the specific coefficient on the total multiplier of aggregate demand.

Source: Own calculations based on data from the Banco Central de Reserva of El Salvador.

source of aggregate demand expansion in 1992. The foreign sector only became the main engine of demand growth in 1993, 1996 and 1997.

8.3 ECONOMIC OPENING, MASSIVE INFLOW OF FOREIGN RESOURCES AND BALANCE-OF-PAYMENTS ADJUSTMENT

Institutional Reforms of External Sector

During the Cristiani administration (1989–94), El Salvador went through a programme of economic reform based on economic liberalization, trade opening and financial liberalization. Export diversification toward non-traditional exports and new markets was a specific goal of the reform process. To this end, state monopolies of foreign trade in coffee and sugar that had been in place since the 1980s were eliminated. Also price controls on nearly 200 products were lifted (leaving only six price-controlled products). New foreign trade legislation was also put in place, including laws for export promotion, guarantees for and promotion of foreign investment, and a decree regulating free-trade zones and tax havens.[7] A centre for export promotion (*Centro de Trámites de Exportación*, Centrex) was created, export taxes were eliminated and special export credit lines were opened.[8]

Mid-1990, the exchange rate was unified and a system of dirty floating was introduced aimed at maintaining a flexible and competitive exchange rate. Foreign-exchange transactions were also liberalized through the elimination of controls, quotas, licences, administrative procedures and other exchange restrictions. In May 1990, operation of the money-exchange houses was legalized. This measure was crucial in creating greater transparency in the foreign-currency market and in facilitating the channelling of workers' remittances through the formal foreign-exchange market. Family remittances started to feed the formal foreign-currency market from the early 1990s onwards, showing an impact on various accounts of the balance of payments. As a result, the foreign-exchange availability increased substantially. The black market, which had lived off the remittance flows, practically disappeared.

Exchange-rate policy changes took place in the context of wider financial reforms. Banks were privatized again after having been nationalized in the early 1980s. The financial reform also comprised the liberalization of interest rates, a change in the role of the Central Bank, and institutional changes to the system of bank supervision and regulation. External-debt management moved to a policy of aggressive renegotiations of the Paris Club debts with the United States, France, Japan and Spain totalling US$ 136 million. In addition, the United States cancelled 75 per cent of its concessional debt, equivalent to US$ 463 million, in 1992.

Trade reform included elimination of quantitative trade restrictions, elimination of tariff exemptions (except for CACM and free-trade-zone imports) and fiscal incentive laws, and the simplification and elimination of customs procedures. Import tariffs were drastically reduced, both in terms of tariff dispersion and nominal rates. In this sense, the trade reform process of the 1980s was deepened.[9] Tariffs were reduced from levels between 290 and 0 per cent to between 20 and 5 per cent.[10] Trade opening and tariff reductions were implemented in a very short period of time (just over two years) and measures applied uniformly for all sectors of the economy, except for some agricultural products.

In order to broaden trade relations, important steps have been taken in recent years toward strengthening Central American regional integration and El Salvador joined the GATT in 1992. Along these lines, trade agreements and partial agreements have been signed with several countries outside the CACM (Central American Common Market), including Panama, Mexico, Colombia and Venezuela.

Entry of foreign investment was eased with the law of incentives and guarantees for foreign investment, which also regulates rights and obligations of foreign investors. According to this law, foreign investors can participate in virtually any economic activity. Restrictions only remain for micro-enterprises and traditional fishing. In 1993 an intellectual property right law (*Ley de Propiedad Intelectual*) was passed, which also contributed to protect the interests of foreign investors.

Booming Remittances and the Balance-of-Payments Impact

The reform programme was carried out in a context of massive inflows of workers' remittances, foreign aid for post-war reconstruction, and private capital inflows attracted by the end of the war financial and exchange reforms. The huge inflows produced major macroeconomic effects, probably more far-reaching than those caused by economic liberalization itself. The amount of foreign resource inflows averaged 17.4 per cent of GDP in the 1990s, peaking at 19.2 per cent of GDP in 1992 (see Figure 8.2). Both the size and nature of the inflows have deeply affected the Salvadorian economy[11] and, more specifically, the trade sector.

Remittances formed the major component and produced a consumption boom. On average about 77 per cent of remittances are consumed. A significant part of these remittances have led to greater demand for imports, which in the context of slow export recovery produced an unprecedented widening of the trade deficit. El Salvador's enormous trade deficit represented the main

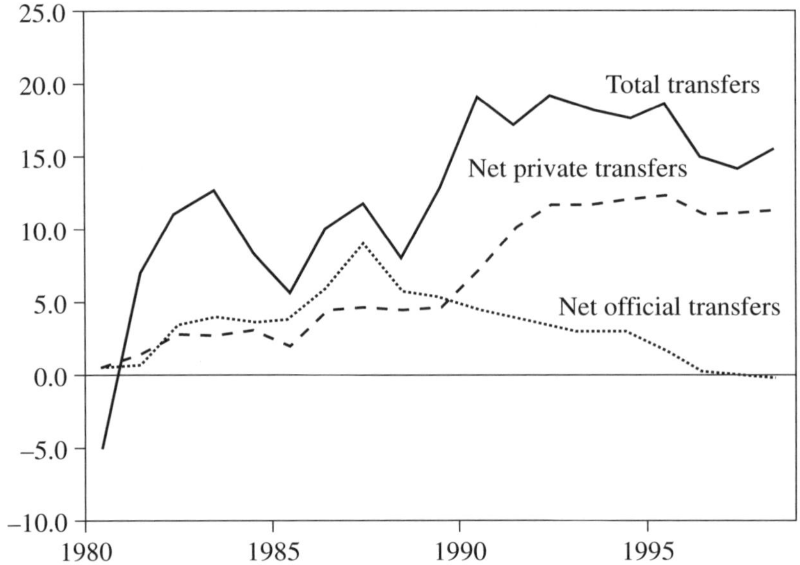

Source: Banco Central de Reserva of El Salvador.

Figure 8.2 Net official and private transfers, 1980–98 (% of GDP)

adjustment mechanism of the Salvadorian economy to the inflow of remittances (Harberger 1993a).

Rising domestic demand concentrated in non-tradables. Exports were affected negatively because of the effect on the real exchange rate.[12] The sectoral composition of GDP shifted in favour of non-traded goods, especially construction and services. El Salvador shifted from an agro-export economy to a service economy (Segovia 1995, 1998).

Table 8.4 shows the development of the balance of payments for 1990–98. As can be observed, the massive inflow of foreign resources has led to a deficit in the current account of the balance of payments as well as to an accumulation of reserves, although the first effect has been greater.[13] The increase in reserves reflected the policy of the open-market operations. This mitigated the negative effects of the massive inflow of foreign resources on the nominal exchange rate. However, it also created additional inflationary pressures, an increase in the quasi-fiscal deficit, rising interest rates,[14] and crowded out credits available for the private sector (Harberger 1993b, World Bank 1995, IMF 1998).

Table 8.4 Balance of payments, 1980–98

Year	Balance of goods, services and private transfers[1] Millions of US$ (1)	% of GDP (2)	Remittances Millions of US$ (3)	% of GDP (4)	Capital account balance Millions of US$ (5)	% of GDP (6)	Global balance[2] Millions of US$ (7)	% of GDP (8)
1980	12.4	–0.35	10.9	0.30	–226.7	–6.34	–196.2	–5.49
1981	–309.8	–6.01	42.2	1.23	171.8	5.00	–78.6	–2.29
1982	–301.6	–8.56	77.5	2.20	180.6	5.13	69.9	1.98
1983	–284.3	–7.19	92.4	2.34	228.3	5.77	200.5	5.07
1984	–347.1	–7.82	114.0	2.57	67.6	1.52	7.5	0.17
1985	–365.6	–6.81	101.7	1.90	–3.1	–0.06	–60.8	–1.13
1986	–241.1	–6.73	134.3	3.75	–6.8	–0.19	109.9	3.07
1987	–407.1	–9.85	168.2	4.07	–81.6	–1.97	57.8	1.40
1988	–429.3	–8.77	194.2	3.97	–116.3	–2.38	–63.8	–1.30
1989	–669.8	–12.92	203.5	3.92	150.9	2.91	–33.0	–0.64
1990	–669.7	–14.08	311.9	6.56	356.3	7.49	221.7	4.66
1991	–797.0	–15.12	504.8	9.58	159.8	3.03	91.1	1.73
1992	–1,065.3	–18.04	685.3	11.60	213.3	3.61	59.8	1.01
1993	–1,092.4	–15.85	790.3	11.46	237.1	3.44	155.3	2.25
1994	–1,265.9	–15.74	964.0	11.99	161.0	2.00	143.2	1.78
1995	–1,513.6	–15.99	1,062.6	11.23	403.1	4.26	146.5	1.55
1996	–1,317.3	–12.63	1,086.6	10.42	334.0	3.20	164.8	1.58
1997	–1,158.4	–10.14	1,199.0	10.49	266.5	2.33	362.5	3.17
1998	–1,331.1	–10.67	1,132.0	9.08	452.1	3.63	289.9	2.32

Notes:
1. Equal to the current account balance minus remittances and official transfers. We define official transfers as foreign financing, for which reasons they are included in the capital account.
2. A positive sign in column (7) indicates an accumulation of reserves.

Source: Own calculations based on data from the Banco Central de Reserva of El Salvador.

Trends in Foreign Trade

Exports recovered partially in the 1990s after the severe drop in the 1980s. This recovery is mainly due to the significant increase of maquila exports, which went from 2 per cent of GDP in the late 1990s to over 10 per cent of GDP toward the end of the decade (see Figure 8.3 and 8.4). The gross value of maquila exports increased from US$ 881 million in 1989 to US$ 1,189 million in 1998.[15] The value added of maquilas increased sizeably, from 131

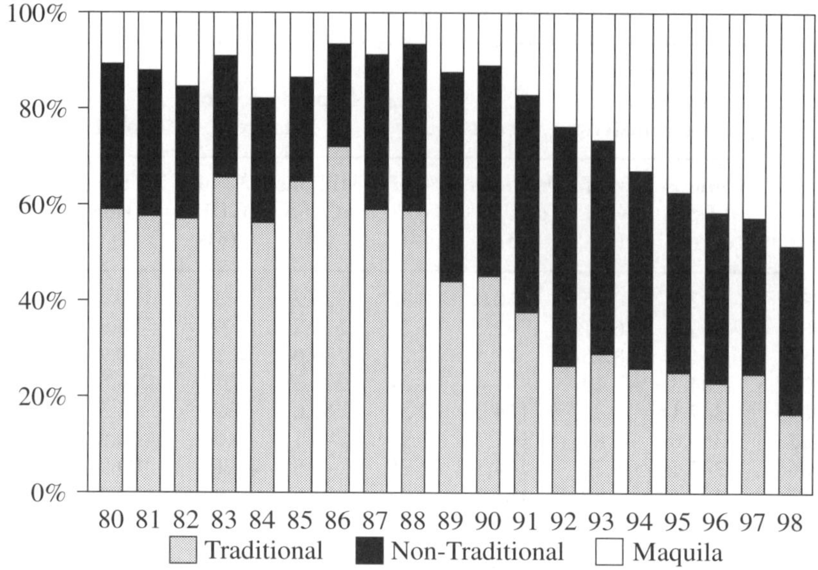

Source: Banco Central de Reserva of El Salvador.

Figure 8.3 Total exports including maquila, 1980–98 (percentage structure)

million colones at constant prices of 1990 (US$ 15 million) to 1,320 million (US$ 151 million).

Women newly entering the labour market were the main beneficiaries. Official data show that employment in maquila manufacturing increased considerably in the 1990s. Maquila employment increased from 6,117 to 69,700 workers between 1990 and 1998 (Ministerio de Economía and PNUD 1997).[16] The share of maquila products in total exports increased to nearly 50 per cent, to the detriment of traditional exports.

Despite the good performance of maquila exports, total exports as a share of GDP stayed well below their historical level. In 1998 total exports, including maquila, represented 20 per cent of GDP, whereas in 1980 this share was 34 per cent. Imports decreased in the 1980s, but to a lesser degree than exports, evidencing the strong dependence of the production apparatus on imports of intermediate and capital goods. Economic growth, depreciation of the colon, the private consumption boom and trade liberalization provoked a strong growth of imports. The import share in GDP reached 34 per cent in 1998, well over the 29.9 per cent registered for 1980 and the level reached in the late 1980s. Consequently, the country's trade

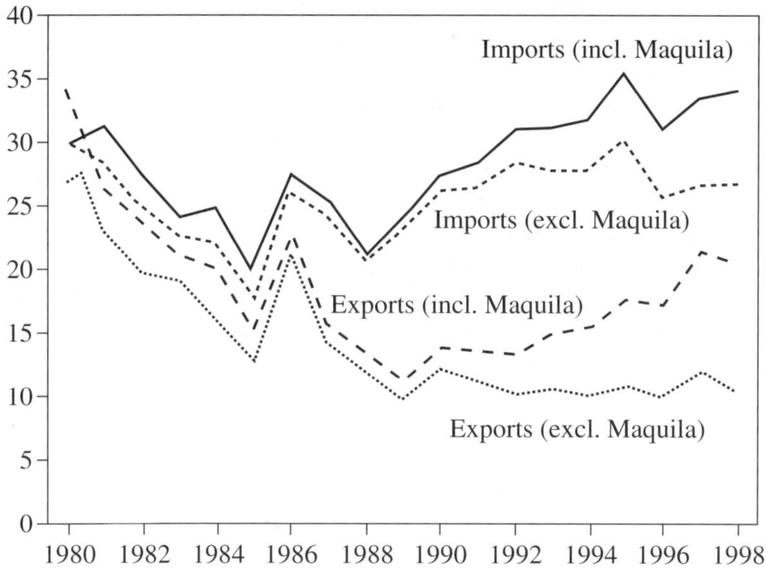

Source: Banco Central de Reserva of El Salvador.

Figure 8.4 Exports and imports, 1980–98 (% of GDP)

Table 8.5 Indicators of the maquila sector, 1990–98 (in millions of colones)

				Value added	
	Exports	**Imports**	**Net exports**	**At current prices**	**At 1990 constant prices**
1990	81.0	65.5	15.4	131.1	131.1
1991	132.0	107.0	25.0	179.2	164.6
1992	198.2	156.1	42.1	311.5	262.2
1993	290.1	220.0	70.1	485.7	420.8
1994	430.4	322.2	108.2	737.8	536.2
1995	646.6	473.0	173.6	1,032.5	724.4
1996	764.1	550.6	213.5	1,192.5	813.4
1997	1,056.8	765.7	291.1	1,631.2	1,100.2
1998	1,189.0	849.9	339.1	n.d.	1,320.2

Source: Banco Central de Reserva of El Salvador.

gap widened systematically over the past two decades, accelerating in the 1990s and reaching its highest level in 1992, when it represented close to 18 per cent of GDP.

Despite rising exports and imports in the 1990s, El Salvador has been unable to recover the degree of external openness of the 1970s and early 1980s (see Table 8.5). As can be seen in Figure 8.5, external openness measured by the sum of exports and imports was higher than 60 per cent in 1980. The percentage was almost halved in 1985, 1988 and 1989, to recover partially in 1990–98 to levels between 50 and 55 per cent.

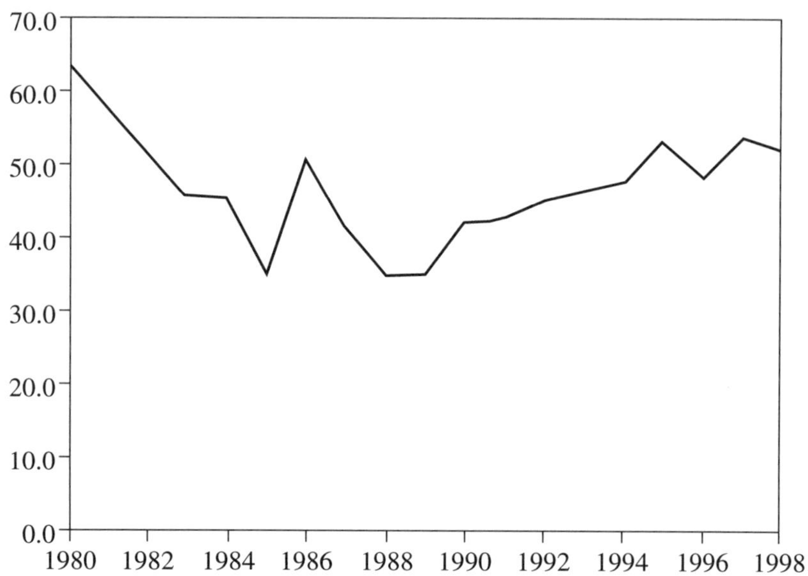

Source: Banco Central de Reserva de El Salvador.

Figure 8.5 Degree of economic openness, 1980–98

8.4 INEQUALITY, POVERTY AND LABOUR MARKET ADJUSTMENT IN THE 1990S

Inequality and Poverty

Employment and poverty are closely associated with the rate and pattern of economic growth in El Salvador (Segovia 1998). Poverty affects a majority of the Salvadorian population, especially those in rural areas. Segovia's study also showed that region (urban or rural), gender, educational level and economic sector are key determinants of poverty. Remittances form the main component of non-labour household income.

In this section, we analyse trends in inequality and poverty in the 1990s using information on the Multiple Purpose Household Surveys of 1991–92 and 1997. The analysis of income distribution does not pretend to establish causality, but rather to determine whether higher economic growth, employment expansion and poverty reduction have been associated with a decrease in inequality in the 1990s.

According to the 1999 Human Development Report (PNUD 1999), income distribution improved in El Salvador during 1990–97 as reflected by an inward shift of the Lorenz curve. The income share of the poorest 10 per cent was 1.9 per cent in 1997, up from 0.9 per cent in 1991–92. The richest decile saw its share fall from 41.5 to 32.8 per cent. Falling inequality is also reflected in a decline in the Gini coefficient from 0.53 to 0.51 between 1991–92 and 1997. The trend showed some fluctuation during the period.[17]

The poverty incidence, gap and severity decreased in both urban and rural areas. The reduction was greater in urban areas. The observed difference between the degree of urban and rural poverty reduction is consistent with previous studies (Segovia 1998). The difference is explained by the greater dynamism of non-traded goods sectors (especially commerce and services), which are mainly located in urban areas. The male rural poor have not benefited much from this growth because most are employed in agriculture, a sector which did not share in the economy's regained dynamism. According to Table 8.6, the share of the population below the poverty line fell from 65.7 to 54.1 per cent between 1991–92 and 1997. In urban areas the poverty incidence dropped from 59.7 to 44.3 per cent, and in rural areas from 71.2 to 66.2 per cent.

The Role of Remittances in Reducing Inequality

Rising remittances have led to an increasing share of non-labour incomes in total household incomes. Table 8.7 shows the proportion of households receiving remittances by deciles and the importance of non-labour incomes in the total income of households receiving remittances. Surprisingly, the share of households receiving remittances was higher in the upper deciles in 1991–92. However, between 1991 and 1997, this share increased for the first five deciles. This suggests that the rise in workers' remittances has contributed to the reduction in income inequality. This is further reflected in the rising share of non-labour incomes in total income of households receiving remittances, especially for the lower deciles. Table 8.7 also shows that the correlation between labour income and remittances is negative for 1991–92 and 1997,

Table 8.6 Inequality and poverty, 1991–92 and 1997

	1991–92			1997		
	Men	**Women**	**Total**	**Men**	**Women**	**Total**
Measured by per capita household income and official poverty line						
Gini coefficient						
Total	0.533	0.535	0.534	0.509	0.506	0.507
Urban	0.499	0.499	0.499	0.464	0.461	0.463
Rural	0.494	0.487	0.491	0.428	0.418	0.423
Poverty rate						
Total	0.651	0.663	0.657	0.536	0.545	0.541
Urban	0.596	0.598	0.597	0.437	0.447	0.443
Rural	0.699	0.725	0.712	0.650	0.674	0.662
Poverty gap						
Total	0.318	0.327	0.323	0.231	0.233	0.232
Urban	0.275	0.279	0.277	0.173	0.177	0.175
Rural	0.354	0.373	0.364	0.298	0.307	0.303
Degree of poverty						
Total	0.199	0.206	0.203	0.130	0.131	0.131
Urban	0.166	0.169	0.168	0.093	0.095	0.094
Rural	0.228	0.242	0.235	0.173	0.178	0.176
Measured by labour income of occupied workers and official poverty line						
Gini coefficient						
Total	0.507	0.483	0.503	0.488	0.484	0.490
Urban	0.480	0.465	0.484	0.461	0.475	0.475
Rural	0.467	0.459	0.469	0.411	0.386	0.410
Poverty rate						
Total	0.133	0.271	0.183	0.090	0.171	0.121
Urban	0.118	0.281	0.193	0.067	0.173	0.115
Rural	0.145	0.251	0.172	0.116	0.165	0.129
Poverty gap						
Total	0.060	0.111	0.079	0.043	0.064	0.051
Urban	0.049	0.114	0.079	0.031	0.064	0.046
Rural	0.070	0.105	0.079	0.056	0.064	0.058
Degree of poverty						
Total	0.038	0.061	0.046	0.026	0.033	0.029
Urban	0.030	0.061	0.044	0.019	0.033	0.025
Rural	0.045	0.061	0.049	0.035	0.032	0.034

Source: Own calculations based on data from Household Surveys of the Ministry of Economy.

Table 8.7 Remittances and household incomes (by deciles), 1991–92 and 1997

	Share of households receiving remittances		Share of non-labour income in total income for households with remittances	
Decile	**1991–92**	**1997**	**1991–92**	**1997**
1	0.03	0.05	0.43	0.59
2	0.07	0.10	0.36	0.57
3	0.09	0.13	0.32	0.44
4	0.10	0.15	0.34	0.52
5	0.11	0.15	0.32	0.37
6	0.14	0.14	0.30	0.36
7	0.15	0.18	0.28	0.37
8	0.18	0.18	0.27	0.36
9	0.19	0.19	0.24	0.28
10	0.22	0.15	0.24	0.26

	Correlation (labour income and remittances)	**Significance level**
1991–92	–0.0111	0.1249
1997	–0.0303	0.0056

Source: Own calculations based on Household Surveys data from the Ministry of Economy.

and statistically more significant for 1997. This means that, at least for 1997, the poorest households received the largest amounts of remittances, and confirms the hypothesis that remittances contributed to the decrease in inequality.

Labour Market Adjustment and Wage Trends

Educational attainment increased during 1991–97. Yet, the average skill level of the Salvadorian labour force is still rather low. The share of the economically active population (EAP) with little or no education (between 0 and 6 years of schooling) fell from 68.7 to 59.8 per cent between 1991–92 and 1997. Despite some improvement, poor educational levels in rural areas remain even more dramatic as 83.6 per cent of the EAP have less than 6 years of schooling, down from 88.7 per cent in 1991–92. The population share with

7 to 12 years of schooling increased from 24.4 to 30.4 per cent for the nationwide EAP, while that with 13 or more years of education went up from 6.9 to 9.8 per cent.

The national labour participation rate fell from 51.6 to 50.9 per cent between 1991–92 and 1997. Urban participation fell from 54.2 to 53.0 per cent and in rural areas it dropped from 49 to 48 per cent. This drop could be linked to the greater flow of remittances, since the high non-labour component of household income may have discouraged labour participation of household members. Table 8.8 shows that participation fell in both urban and rural areas, for both genders and for all educational levels, except for non-educated rural men and rural women with 1 to 6 years of schooling.

Open unemployment decreased slightly at the national level, dropping from 8.7 per cent in 1991–92 to 8.0 per cent in 1997. In urban areas the rate fell from 7.9 to 7.5 per cent and in rural areas from 9.7 to 8.7 per cent. Table 8.8 shows that lower unemployment mainly benefited female workers. Women, in urban and rural areas, are primarily employed in commerce and services, activities with expanding employment in the 1990s. In addition to this drop in unemployment, the employment structure shifted from tradable to non-tradable sectors. Employment went up in non-tradable sectors and decreased in tradables (Table 8.9).

Underemployment as defined by low-income levels seems to be a greater problem than open unemployment. In urban areas, underemployment represented 30 per cent in 1997, while income-related underemployment represented 87 per cent of total underemployment. The remaining 13 per cent correspond to visible underemployment defined as involuntary part-time work (Chacaltana 1998).[18]

Average real wages increased during the 1990s. However, there was an alarming increase in the wage gaps between urban and rural areas and between male and female workers. In 1991–92 urban wages were 2.03 times that of rural wages, and male wages were 1.24 times female wages. In 1997 these gaps increased to 2.20 and 1.36, respectively. While the average real wage increased, workers in non-tradable sectors and skilled workers with 7 or more years of schooling benefited most. In contrast, real wages for unskilled workers fell. Despite the wage decline for unskilled workers, employment for this type of worker increased strongly at the same time. Wages fell for rural and female workers (Table 8.10).

Table 8.8 *Unemployment and participation rates for urban and rural areas, 1991–92 and 1997*

	1991–92		**1997**	
	Unemployment	**Participation**	**Unemployment**	**Participation**
URBAN MEN				
Without schooling	0.10	0.71	0.09	0.67
1–6 years of education	0.09	0.58	0.09	0.56
7–12 years of education	0.08	0.70	0.10	0.70
More than 12 years of education	0.06	0.76	0.06	0.72
URBAN WOMEN				
Without schooling	0.04	0.40	0.01	0.40
1–6 years of education	0.06	0.39	0.03	0.37
7–12 years of education	0.11	0.50	0.09	0.46
More than 12 years of education	0.07	0.63	0.08	0.62
RURAL MEN				
Without schooling	0.10	0.83	0.11	0.85
1–6 years of education	0.09	0.70	0.09	0.68
7–12 years of education	0.12	0.71	0.10	0.71
More than 12 years of education	0.02	0.78	0.05	0.69
RURAL WOMEN				
Without schooling	0.09	0.26	0.04	0.23
1–6 years of education	0.11	0.23	0.04	0.24
7–12 years of education	0.15	0.28	0.10	0.28
More than 12 years of education	0.15	0.49	0.12	0.44

Source: Own calculations based on data from Household Surveys of the Ministry of Economy.

Table 8.9 Employment shares for urban and rural areas, 1991–92 and 1997

	1991–92		1997	
	Non-tradables	**Tradables**	**Non-tradables**	**Tradables**
URBAN MEN				
Without schooling	0.44	0.56	0.47	0.53
1–6 years of education	0.60	0.40	0.68	0.32
7–12 years of education	0.67	0.33	0.73	0.27
More than 12 years of education	0.82	0.18	0.86	0.14
URBAN WOMEN				
Without schooling	0.69	0.31	0.78	0.22
1–6 years of education	0.70	0.30	0.74	0.26
7–12 years of education	0.75	0.25	0.76	0.24
More than 12 years of education	0.90	0.10	0.92	0.08
RURAL MEN				
Without schooling	0.11	0.89	0.14	0.86
1–6 years of education	0.18	0.82	0.26	0.74
7–12 years of education	0.33	0.67	0.42	0.58
More than 12 years of education	0.74	0.26	0.74	0.26
RURAL WOMEN				
Without schooling	0.44	0.56	0.61	0.39
1–6 years of education	0.44	0.56	0.59	0.41
7–12 years of education	0.58	0.42	0.55	0.45
More than 12 years of education	0.88	0.12	0.92	0.08

Source: Own calculations based on data from Household Surveys of the Ministry of Economy.

Table 8.10 *Wages per occupied worker in urban and rural areas, 1991–92 and 1997 (constant colones of 1992)*

	1991–92		**1997**	
	Non-tradables	**Tradables**	**Non-tradables**	**Tradables**
URBAN MEN				
Without schooling	973	732	900	611
1–6 years of education	1,274	959	1,262	926
7–12 years of education	1,640	1,419	1,726	1,299
More than 12 years of education	2,860	3,673	3,727	3,500
URBAN WOMEN				
Without schooling	623	617	596	579
1–6 years of education	755	730	764	717
7–12 years of education	1,207	1,134	1,330	1,176
More than 12 years of education	1,773	1,809	2,352	2,928
RURAL MEN				
Without schooling	892	636	676	505
1–6 years of education	963	674	1,008	584
7–12 years of education	1,097	919	1,144	739
More than 12 years of education	1,476	1,168	1,785	1,508
RURAL WOMEN				
Without schooling	546	443	484	423
1–6 years of education	587	528	496	505
7–12 years of education	882	553	767	783
More than 12 years of education	1,276	671	1,745	1,553

Source: Own calculations based on data from Household Surveys of the Ministry of Economy.

8.5 EFFECTS OF LIBERALIZATION ON INEQUALITY AND POVERTY

In this section we will estimate the impact of liberalization on poverty and inequality levels as transmitted through changes in participation and unemployment rates and in the employment and wage structure.

Data and Methodology

We have used the databases of the Division of Social Information of El Salvador's Ministry of Economy for the years 1991–92[19] and 1997. These surveys have national coverage, which means they include both urban and rural areas. The methodology consists of determining what income distribution and poverty levels would have been if the 1991–92 wage or employment structure (pre-liberalization) still prevailed in 1997 (post-liberalization).

The microsimulations were based on the methodology as described in Chapter 2. Considering that the impact of liberalization may not be the same for the various categories of workers, the sample was divided into 16 demographic groups and two economic segments. The labour force was first classified by gender (men and women), completed years of schooling (none, 1 to 6, 7 to 12, 13 or more) and demographic area (urban, rural, national total). Then the labour market was divided into nine branches: agriculture, mining, manufacturing, electricity, gas and water, construction, transportation and communication, financial institutions, and services. These branches were subsequently grouped by tradable and non-tradable sectors.[20] As a result of these groupings we obtained the 32 cells (16 types of workers with two economic segments each) of Tables 8.8–8.10. Based on these socio-demographic cells of 1991–92 and 1997 we constructed matrices that represent the wage, total income and employment structure by type of worker and economic segment, as well as vectors for the unemployment and participation structures by type of worker. Next, based on the 1991–92 structures we proceed to do a series of microsimulations that compare the initial (1991–92) situation without liberalization to a final (1997) situation with liberalization.

The simulations are executed in four stages. We first apply the 1991–92 participation structure to the 1997 sample distribution and similarly for the employment and wage structures and wage levels. Each phase is done separately and cumulatively, simulating the effects on the Gini coefficient, quintile ratio (Q5/Q1), number of poor and poverty incidence, gap and severity. In order to generate confidence intervals for these indicators, we repeated each simulation 30 times. This methodology assumes that all the changes observed in the period are due to the liberalization effect.

We were unable to separate the effect of internal migration. However, in order to take into account the effect of workers' remittances sent by Salvadorians from abroad, the microsimulations are first carried out using per capita household income. To this end, total household income (including remittances) is divided by the number of household members, assigning the thus obtained per capita income to each household member. Subsequently, the microsimulations are carried out using per capita labour income for the occupied population only.

Simulation Results

Table 8.11 summarizes the results of the separate simulations. The sequential simulations are shown in Table 8.12. These tables also include the original values of the poverty and inequality indices.

The data show that between 1991–92 and 1997 there were important changes toward an improvement in the distribution of per capita household income. Phase 1 (Table 8.11) shows what would have happened to inequality and poverty measured by per capita household income if the participation structure of 1991–92 still prevailed in 1997. Without liberalization we would have seen increases in income concentration (measured by the Gini coefficient as well as the quintile ratio), a slight decrease in the incidence of poverty (P_0) and poverty gap (P_1), and no changes in the level of poverty (P_2), as against what actually happened in 1997. In other words, the impact of the opening on the participation structure improved income distribution, and the incidence of poverty and the poverty gap increased.

Phase 2 shows significant changes for all indicators. We can see that the impact of liberalization on the unemployment structure improved inequality levels and decreased poverty. Phase 3 simulates the employment structure, and results show that liberalization caused inequality and poverty to decrease significantly. Phase 4 applies the wage structure (phase 4a) and wage level (phase 4b) of 1991–92 to 1997. As can be seen, wages react contrary to the previous simulations. Had there been no liberalization, inequality, poverty indicators and the number of poor would have been lower. This fits with what actually took place in the labour market: a decrease in real wages of unskilled workers, an increase of wages for the skilled and semi-skilled labour force, and a rise in the urban–rural and male–female wage gaps. Liberalization drove up inequality and poverty indices through the wage structure and wage levels.

The results for labour income per employed individual (lower part of Table 8.11) show that the first three effects are statistically significant for the Gini coefficient and the quintile ratio as well as for the poverty rate, poverty gap, poverty severity and number of poor (except for the unemployment effect). In

Table 8.11 Effects of liberalization on inequality and poverty between 1991 and 1997 (each phase separately)

	Actual value						
	1991	**1997**	**Phase 1**	**Phase 2**	**Phase 3**	**Phase 4a**	**Phase 4b**
According to per capita household income							
Gini	0.533	0.507	0.515	0.516	0.522	0.493	0.494
			0.514 0.517	*0.516 0.517*	*0.520 0.523*		
Q5/Q1	18.486	15.034	15.880	15.945	16.610	13.908	13.739
			15.717 16.038	*15.823 16.139*	*16.418 16.781*		
P_0	0.657	0.536	0.530	0.541	0.558	0.468	0.514
			0.528 0.532	*0.540 0.543*	*0.556 0.560*		
P_1	0.322	0.230	0.229	0.236	0.249	0.190	0.213
			0.227 0.229	*0.235 0.237*	*0.247 0.250*		
P_2	0.201	0.130	0.130	0.135	0.145	0.104	0.117
			0.129 0.131	*0.134 0.136*	*0.143 0.146*		
No. poor	3,393,786	3,121,964	3,089,162	3,155,526	3,255,596	2,727,592	2,993,972
			3,076,981 3,101,321	*3,145,720 3,164,140*	*3,243,878 3,267,341*		

According to per worker labour income							
Gini	0.503	0.490	0.495	0.493	0.496	0.467	0.467
			0.494 0.497	*0.492 0.494*	*0.495 0.498*		
Q5/Q1	14.601	13.230	13.470	13.401	14.139	11.820	11.820
			13.381 13.571	*13.348 13.458*	*14.027 14.250*		
P_0	0.183	0.121	0.132	0.134	0.138	0.111	0.129
			0.131 0.133	*0.133 0.135*	*0.137 0.139*		
P_1	0.079	0.051	0.056	0.057	0.059	0.043	0.050
			0.055 0.056	*0.056 0.057*	*0.058 0.060*		
P_2	0.046	0.029	0.032	0.032	0.034	0.024	0.028
			0.031 0.032	*0.032 0.032*	*0.033 0.034*		
No. poor	326,220	249,278	254,779	247,629	257,142	206,803	239,619
			252,373 256,194	*245,116 249,740*	*255,029 259,996*		

Notes:
The confidence intervals are in italics.
Phases 4a and 4b show no confidence intervals because only the 1991 wage structure or level is applied, i.e. no random figures are generated.

Source: Own calculations based on data from Household Surveys of the Ministry of Economy of El Salvador.

Table 8.12 Effects of liberalization on inequality and poverty between 1991 and 1997 (cumulative phases)

	Actual value					
	1991	**1997**	**Phase 1, 2**	**Phase 1, 2, 3**	**Phase 1, 2, 3, 4a**	**Phase 1, 2, 3, 4b**
According to per capita household income						
Gini	0.533	0.507	0.517	0.523	0.524	0.523
			0.516 0.518	*0.522 0.525*	*0.522 0.525*	*0.522 0.524*
Q5/Q1	18.486	15.034	16.043	16.984	17.018	16.956
			15.871 16.183	*16.776 17.204*	*16.795 17.220*	*16.773 17.172*
P_0	0.657	0.536	0.532	0.551	0.552	0.552
			0.531 0.535	*0.548 0.554*	*0.548 0.554*	*0.550 0.555*
P_1	0.322	0.230	0.231	0.246	0.246	0.245
			0.230 0.232	*0.244 0.247*	*0.245 0.247*	*0.244 0.246*
P_2	0.201	0.130	0.132	0.143	0.144	0.143
			0.131 0.132	*0.142 0.145*	*0.143 0.145*	*0.142 0.145*
No. poor	3,393,786	3,121,964	3,103,489	3,213,707	3,216,683	3,216,807
			3,092,970 3,116,480	*3,196,121 3,227,610*	*3,196,486 3,231,179*	*3,203,671 3,232,820*

According to per worker labour income						
Gini	0.503	0.490	0.496	0.498	0.498	0.498
			0.495 0.498	*0.497 0.499*	*0.497 0.500*	*0.497 0.499*
Q5/Q1	14.601	13.230	13.558	14.245	14.216	14.083
			13.419 13.860	*13.498 14.535*	*13.472 14.480*	*13.400 14.470*
P_0	0.183	0.121	0.133	0.138	0.137	0.137
			0.131 0.134	*0.136 0.140*	*0.136 0.139*	*0.136 0.139*
P_1	0.079	0.051	0.056	0.059	0.059	0.059
			0.056 0.057	*0.058 0.060*	*0.059 0.060*	*0.058 0.060*
P_2	0.046	0.029	0.032	0.034	0.034	0.034
			0.031 0.032	*0.033 0.035*	*0.033 0.034*	*0.033 0.035*
No. poor	326,220	249,278	253,492	263,096	262,715	262,593
			250,383 255,778	*260,339 266,799*	*260,318 265,860*	*259,140 265,920*

Notes: The confidence intervals are in italics.

Source: Own calculations based on data from Household Surveys of the Ministry of Economy of El Salvador.

other words, liberalization decreased inequality and poverty indexes. Its impact through the wage structure was the opposite: as a result of liberalization there was an increase in inequality of labour incomes and an increase in poverty indexes. In general, the changes in the income distribution indicators are significant for the Gini coefficient as well as for the quintile ratio, which indicates that the trend toward equity affected all income quintiles. Similarly, all changes in the poverty indices are significant.

The sequential simulations (Table 8.12) show that the effects leading to greater inequality offset those reducing inequality. Without liberalization, the Gini coefficient and the quintile ratio would have increased significantly for per capita household incomes as well as for labour incomes per occupied worker. The poverty indicators would have increased as well. These results could be related to massive rural–urban migration and since urban living standards are higher. Urban workers have a higher participation rate, face less unemployment and have better wage levels.

Using per capita household income and applying the entire 1991–92 labour market structure to 1997, the Gini coefficient falls by one percentage point against the observed value of 1991. The poverty incidence, gap and severity show a reduction of 11, 8 and 6 percentage points, respectively. Again, this suggests that the increase in family remittances contributed toward decreasing inequality and poverty.

8.6 CONCLUSIONS

The analysis carried out in this study suggests that, during the 1990s, El Salvador was able to reverse by and large the deep economic and social crisis of the 1980s. The empirical evidence shows that, during the 1990–98 period, economic growth was accompanied by noticeable financial and exchange-rate stability, an overall reduction of poverty (mainly because of lower urban poverty) and probably a reduction in inequality. The microsimulation exercises suggest that economic liberalization had a positive cumulative effect on reducing inequality and poverty, although results are mixed when considering the participation, unemployment, employment and wage structures separately. On the other hand, analysis of the sources of growth of aggregate demand shows that the external sector was the main driving force during 1990–97, particularly non-traditional exports. This suggests that progress has been made in moving toward a new economic growth pattern based on the promotion of non-traditional exports.

Having arrived at this point, we should ask ourselves the question to what extent the described processes are sustainable in the medium and long term. Our analysis and that of other studies (Segovia 1995, 1998) show that the foundations for economic growth and macroeconomic stability are still fragile, and that the effects of growth and stability on poverty are still not large enough to see steady progress toward poverty eradication.

The Salvadorian economy slowed down in the second half of the 1990s. At this growth pace sustained poverty reduction will not be feasible. By the end of the decade, El Salvador was facing increasing difficulties to regain high and sustained growth. The fixed exchange-rate regime poses an important growth constraint, as it requires the adoption of restrictive demand policies to maintain inflation at international levels, thereby also harming private investment growth opportunities because of the resulting high real interest rates.

As also indicated by other studies (e.g. Segovia 1998), the rural poor have not really benefited from the overall dynamism of the economy. Most rural poor, especially the men, work in agriculture where growth has been markedly lower than in the rest of the economy. For this reason, El Salvador has to face the formidable challenge of regaining a high and sustained growth and implementing a development strategy aimed at a more balanced economic growth pattern. Such a strategy should explicitly target the achievement of greater welfare gains for the rural poor and, at the same time, ensure the conservation of natural resources.

Foreign resource inflows have had an important redistributive effect. Workers' remittances contributed to the reduction of poverty and inequality. However, the inflow of these resources has also had a negative effect on incentives to labour participation of recipients of remittances. Lower participation partly offset the positive effects of workers' remittances on poverty reduction.

Finally, the labour market analysis showed that, despite educational improvements, the overall skill level of the labour force remains very low. This limited human capital endowment is incompatible with a policy of sustained reduction of poverty and with the requirements of quality and competitiveness in production posed by globalization. To some degree, the low educational levels of the labour force are consistent with the growth pattern of the 1990s, which was based on growth of non-tradable sectors and maquila exports inducing increased demand for unskilled, low-paid labour. As the economic slowdown towards the end of the decade suggests, this is not believed to be a sustainable long-term growth pattern and investment in human capital is urgently needed to overcome structural poverty and improve El Salvador's competitiveness in global markets.

NOTES

1. We are grateful to Tomás Rau and David Bravo for their support in processing the microsimulations and for their helpful comments.
2. We used 1991–92 as the base year because we lack consistent comparative statistical information for previous years.
3. In a previous project (Segovia 1998), we identified only three cycles, as we looked then only at the trend in GDP.
4. In 1982 El Salvador signed an agreement with the IMF which allowed the government to reach its main goal of gaining access to foreign finance, particularly coming from the United States. These resources were mainly used to finance the fiscal deficit and the foreign-exchange gap. In this sense, it is no coincidence that US aid started to increase substantially in 1982. The economy improved thereafter.
5. In 1997 two cases of financial fraud were registered (FINCOMER and INSEPRO-FINSEPRO). Both cases were linked to illegal mobilization of funds from corporate firms with branches through which resources were mobilized outside the realm of financial regulation and supervision (PNUD 1999).
6. According to Corbo (1997: 19), the economic slowdown in 1996 was also related to the external shock caused by the major depreciation of the Mexican peso in late 1994. Producers of import substitutes and producers competing with Mexican exports lost competitiveness. The depreciation of the peso also led to a reorientation of maquila investments from El Salvador to Mexico.
7. These laws were, respectively, *Ley de Reactivación a las Exportaciones*, *Ley de Fomento y Garantía a la Inversión Extranjera* and *Ley del Régimen de Zonas Francas y Recintos Fiscales*. In 1998, the *Ley de Zonas Francas* was modified in order to accelerate the development of export industries and to protect some sectors, especially agriculture.
8. The exchange regime was unified and liberalized between mid-1989 and mid-1990. The banking system was initially authorized to operate in the currency market. The authorities re-imposed the system of multiple exchange rates after the guerrilla offensive of November 1989 and the introduction of a less restrictive credit policy in early 1990. This practice was short-lived. By June 1990 the exchange regime had been unified and a flexible exchange rate had been introduced.
9. Three moments can be distinguished in the trade liberalization process of Central America. The first corresponds to the elimination of some tariffs and restrictions to imports in the second half of the 1980s. The second moment occurs in the context of multilateral trade negotiations of the late 1980s and early 1990s, in which the opening is accompanied by increased access to world markets. The third phase takes place in the context of strengthening of regional integration and the intention of the member countries to participate in an integration plan for the Western Hemisphere.
10. In July 1998 the tariff on intermediate goods subject to a rate of 10 per cent was lowered to 7 per cent. The tariff on goods with a rate of 15 per cent was reduced to 12 per cent. Final goods subject to a tariff of 20 per cent saw the duty decline to 17 per cent.
11. A detailed analysis of the impact of foreign resource inflows on the Salvadorian economy can be found in World Bank (1995), Segovia (1998) and IMF (1998).
12. Harberger (1993b: 4–5) has noted the fact that only part of the foreign resources is spent in tradables means there is an increase in the supply of dollars that does not match the change in demand. This is why there is a downward trend in the real exchange rate.
13. During the 1990s, remittances facilitated the reduction in the current account deficit. In addition, following on recommendations by Harberger (1988), the authorities have used the reserves to make advance external-debt payments. This explains the overall balance-of-payments deficit registered in 1991–92.
14. The losses of the Banco Central de Reserva represented 0.8 per cent of GDP during 1991–92, dropping to 0.2 per cent of GDP in the two subsequent years (IMF 1998: 7).
15. The maquila industry was created in 1974 under the auspices of AID, thanks to the approval of a law that authorized operation of export-processing free-trade zones. The first

zone was established in the following year in San Bartolo, and its development was important up to 1979. Political instability caused many businesses to close, re-establishing activities in the 1990s. Maquila production in El Salvador took a tailspin in the late 1980s. The free-trade-zone project was picked up again and received an unprecedented amount of incentives. AID resources were channelled through the Ministry of Economy, FUSADES and the national banking system.

16. According to official statements, the alleged reduction in unemployment of 1998 was largely due to the employment growth in maquila industries. Maquila employment went up from 56,603 workers in 1997 to 69,700 in 1998, a 22 per cent increase in a single year.
17. In the 1990s the Gini showed a somewhat unstable trend, making it difficult to to draw solid conclusions about the overall tendency. Between 1991 and 1998, the values for the national Gini coefficient were as follows: 1991: 0.53; 1992: 0.52; 1993: 0.52; 1994: 0.53; 1995: 0.55; 1996: 0.50; 1997: 0.50; and 1998: 0.52.
18. Invisible underemployment is defined here as corresponding to those working at least 40 hours per week and receiving an income below the official minimum wage. Visible underemployment refers to workers who involuntarily work less than 40 hours per week.
19. Since we lack a comparable earlier survey, we assume that the 1991–92 survey represents the pre-liberalization situation.
20. The following production activities were defined as tradable: agriculture, forestry, fishing and hunting; mining; and manufacturing. The remaining sectors are taken to be non-tradables: electricity, gas and water; construction; commerce, restaurants and hotels; transportation, storage and communications; financial services and insurance; real estate and other services.

REFERENCES

Chacaltana, Juan (1998) *La Medición del Empleo y los Ingresos en El Salvador*, San Salvador: IDB, World Bank, CEPAL and DIGESTYC.

Corbo, Vittorio (1997) 'Una estrategia para consolidar la establidad, retomar el crecimiento y reducir la pobreza en El Salvador', FUSADES, San Salvador (November, mimeo).

Edwards, Sebastian (1999) 'Growth in El Salvador: Sources, Prospects and Challenges', San Salvador and Cambridge (MA): FUSADES and NBER (May).

Harberger, Arnold C. (1988) 'Informal Notes on Certain Issues of Diagnosis and Policy Recommendations', San Salvador: FUSADES (December).

Harberger, Arnold (1993a) 'Política Económica y Crecimiento Económico. Lineamientos a Seguir en El Salvador (hasta fines de la década de los 90)', Los Angeles and San Salvador: UCLA-FUSADES (mimeo, March).

Harberger, Arnold C. (1993b) 'Las Exportaciones y el Tipo de Cambio Real en El Salvador', Los Angeles and San Salvador: UCLA and FUSADES (mimeo, October).

IMF (1998) 'El Salvador: Recent Economic Developments', IMF Staff Country Report No. 98/32, Washington D.C.: International Monetary Fund.

Ministerio de Economía and PNUD (1997) *Informe sobre Desarrollo Humano en El Salvador*, San Salvador: UNDP.

PNUD (1999) *Estado de La Nación en Desarrollo Humano 1999*, San Salvador: UNDP (April).

Segovia, Alexander (1995) 'El Salvador: Macroeconomic Performance and Policies Since 1989', San Salvador (mimeo).

Segovia, Alexander (1998) 'Cambio Estructural, Políticas Macroeconómicas y Pobreza en El Salvador', in: Enrique Ganuza, Lance Taylor and Samuel Morley (eds)

Política Macroeconómica y Pobreza en América Latina y el Caribe, Madrid: Mundi Press (for UNDP), pp. 489–540.

World Bank (1995) 'El Salvador: Meeting the Challenge of Globalization', Country Economic Memorandum/Private Sector Assessment, Volumes I and II, Draft Report No 14109-ES, Washington D.C.: The World Bank (July).

9. Mexico: trade liberalization, growth, inequality and poverty[1]

Jaime Ros and César Bouillon

9.1 INTRODUCTION

Mexico provides a particularly interesting case for the analysis of the effects of the liberalization of the balance of payments. Not only were trade and financial liberalization measures in Mexico much more pervasive than in other countries, they occurred in a context of high mobility and volatility of foreign capital flows. These circumstances affected macroeconomic performance and thereby the effects of liberalization on the labour market, income distribution and poverty.[2]

This study analyses the effects of the liberalization of external trade and capital movements. Section 9.2 describes trade policy and financial liberalization reforms as well as the major shifts in the trends in foreign trade and capital flows. Section 9.3 analyses how capital flows and trade liberalization influenced macroeconomic behaviour through the real appreciation of the peso between 1988 and late 1994, the drop in profitability of tradable goods production and the collapse of private savings. It also examines how this macroeconomic performance affected sectoral employment and productivity. We will focus on the rapid growth of productivity and employment losses in manufacturing, which are associated with lower profitability and fast deepening of import penetration during 1988–94. Section 9.4 looks at the evolution of the wage structure since the late 1980s, linking it to the productivity and employment trends analysed in the previous section. The rise in wage inequality since the late 1980s has attracted the attention of many researchers, generating a wide range of hypotheses as to its causes. These hypotheses are discussed in this section, as an introduction to the analysis of Section 9.5 on the effects of labour market adjustment on inequality and poverty. Section 9.6 summarizes the main conclusions and discusses the prospects of the Mexican economy in the new context that emerged after the 1994–95 crisis.

9.2 LIBERALIZATION OF THE BALANCE OF PAYMENTS

In the mid-1980s, the Mexican economy was still suffering the effects of the 1982 debt crisis. On top of this, new difficulties emerged as a consequence of the collapse of international oil prices in early 1986. Three years later, the economy had found its way back to falling inflation and recovery of economic growth. This was due to a successful heterodox stabilization programme that was initiated in late 1987, the Brady agreement of debt relief and restructuring in July 1989, and the subsequent recovery of access to international capital markets. The main measures to liberalize the balance of payments were also adopted in the second half of the 1980s (see Box 9.1). These changes culminated in the North American Free Trade Agreement (NAFTA), which became effective in January 1994. Since then, NAFTA has constituted the institutional framework within which Mexico's foreign trade and capital movements operate. The framework includes a regime of virtually free trade and capital mobility between Mexico and the United States, its main trade partner and source of foreign investment.

BOX 9.1 MEXICO: MAIN POLICY MEASURES OF MACROECONOMIC STABILIZATION AND LIBERALIZATION OF THE BALANCE OF PAYMENTS

1985 July: first stage of the trade liberalization programme. Elimination of import licences for capital and intermediate goods, and reduction of the number of tariff categories.

1987 December: start of the stabilization programme (PSE) and second stage of the trade liberalization programme. The elimination of import licences is extended to imports of consumer goods. The degree of tariff dispersion and the average tariff are reduced.

1988 October/November: start of financial liberalization with the elimination of credit quotas (to high-priority sectors) and the obligatory reserve requirements. Eradication of some interest-rate ceilings.

1989 April: eradication of all interest-rate ceilings. May: reform of regulation of direct foreign investment. July: opening of stock market to foreign investors (through liberalization of the neutral-investment regime). Initial agreement on the external debt-reduction plan with creditor banks.

1990	February: signing of agreement on external debt reduction with creditor banks. Some restrictions on investment in bonds, stabilization bonds and treasury bills (except CETES) were already eliminated in July 1989. April: *Reglamentación S* and *Regla 144A* of the US SEC. December: opening of money market to foreign investors with the eradication of restrictions to portfolio investments in government bonds. Initiation of negotiations on free-trade agreement (NAFTA).
1991	February: recognition of the Mexican stock exchange as an offshore designated securities market by the US SEC. Privatization of TELMEX (initiated in December 1990) and privatization of main banks.
1992	April: 10 per cent ceiling on foreign currency deposits (and minimum requirement of investing 15 per cent of those liabilities in foreign currency). October: end of NAFTA negotiations. November: expansion of restrictions on foreign currency-denominated bank indebtedness (measures of April). December: signing of NAFTA by governments of the three member states.
1993	December: new Law on Foreign Investment, substituting the 1973 Act (which established as a general rule a maximum foreign ownership of 49 per cent of enterprise capital).
1994	January: NAFTA becomes effective.

Trade Opening and the Expansion of Foreign Trade[3]

The liberalization of external trade went through three stages. In mid-1985, the process of elimination of import permits and tariff reform (which had started slowly in 1984) accelerated as part of the stabilization programme of July that also comprised a devaluation of the exchange rate and fiscal adjustment. The coverage of permits, which had reached 100 per cent of the value of imports in 1982, was reduced to 37.5 per cent (see Ros 1994b and Villagómez 1998). The liberalization affected mainly intermediate and capital goods, as well as – more selectively – some consumer goods. The share of capital goods in the total controlled imports fell from 19 to 10 per cent, after having been as high as 31 per cent in 1982. At the same time, tariffs were increased in order to compensate for the elimination of direct controls. The weighted average tariff increased from 8.6 per cent in 1984 to 13.1 per cent in 1986. The new level was still below that of 1982 (16.4 per cent). Tariff dispersion was reduced. In 1986, 90 per cent of imports subject to customs duties were levied at three different rates (10, 22.5 and 37 per cent). In July 1986 the agreement to enter GATT was signed. This committed Mexico to continue substituting direct controls by tariffs and, later on, to reduce tariff rates.

The second stage was initiated in late 1987 as part of the *Pacto de Solidaridad Económica*, whose objective was to quickly reduce inflation through a temporary price, wage and exchange-rate freezes. The reform extended the elimination of import permits to a large part of manufactured consumption goods (which brought import licence coverage to only 20 per cent of the value of imports in 1988) and simplified the tariff system considerably. The dispersion of tariffs went down to a 0–20 per cent range with only five rates (0, 5, 10, 15 and 20 per cent), and the average tariff dropped to 10.4 per cent (non-weighted average) and 6.1 per cent (import value-weighted tariff). The measures also included suppression of practically all remaining official prices, which had traditionally constituted the basis for tariff payment. After these measures, the sectors that remained protected by import licensing represented nearly 25 per cent of the total tradable production, mainly agricultural products and a few manufacturing industries targeted by industrial promotion programmes (especially the automobile industry).

The third stage is linked to NAFTA. According to the OECD (1992), when negotiations on NAFTA started in 1990, Mexico was already one of the world's most open developing economies. The end of the negotiations and the signing of the agreement in late 1992, and the treaty becoming effective in January 1994, entailed additional steps toward trade liberalization. With more than two-thirds of its external trade with the United States, NAFTA largely means simply free trade for Mexico. Nonetheless, some trade restrictions were maintained in some sectors (equivalent to 6.8 per cent of the value of imports). These sectors include agriculture, particularly in corn production (where it was feared that fast liberalization would lead to massive labour migration), oil refinery (due to sovereignty considerations) and transportation equipment industry (where automobile enterprises had made investment decisions based on industrial programmes that guaranteed protection in exchange for achieving trade balance-related performance targets).[4]

There is no doubt that the trade liberalization process was successful in generating a rapid expansion of imports and exports. Total foreign trade (exports plus imports) went from 25.6 to 39.5 per cent between 1988 and 1994 and increased further to 55.2 per cent in 1997 (see Table 9.1). It is also clear that this expansion brought about strong imbalances between 1988 and 1994. Whereas the import share increased by 10.6 percentage points, exports only went up by 3.3 points. The rise in the export share only accelerated after the devaluation and crisis of late 1994, as it jumped from 17.2 to 29.5 per cent of GDP between 1994 and 1998 (see Table 9.1).

Liberalization of the Capital Account

Liberalization of foreign investment

The 1973 foreign investment law reserved certain economic activities to Mexican investment, and introduced as a general rule a maximum limit of 49 per cent on foreign ownership of companies.[5] Even though it was not until 1993 that the 1973 law stopped being the reference framework regulating foreign participation in the economy, the governments of Presidents De la Madrid and Salinas (starting in 1984 and 1989, respectively) gradually started interpreting the law less restrictively. The most far-reaching change within this process was the decree of May 1989 that abolished all administrative regulations and resolutions and presented a very liberal interpretation of the 1973 law.[6] New regulations established automatic approval of all foreign participation in investment projects of less than 100 million dollars, as long as these projects fulfilled a series of conditions (such as generation of foreign currency and regional development). The implicit goal of the new measures was to increase the share of direct foreign investment from 10 to 20 per cent of the total investment level prevailing in 1988.

The new law of 1993 incorporated the changes with respect to regulations of the recent past as well as NAFTA enactment in matters of national dealings with foreign capital. The 49 per cent limit disappeared as a general rule regulating the participation of foreign investment, and the number of sectors with some restrictions to foreign ownership was considerably reduced. The areas with limitations to a maximum of foreign participation included financial institutions, newspapers, fishing and harbours (all with 49 per cent), and national air transportation and co-operatives (25 and 10 per cent, respectively). The activities that remained restricted to foreign investment included radio and television (except for cable TV), ground passenger transportation, tourism and cargo, credit unions and development banking, and the distribution of gasoline and liquid gas. The sectors reserved exclusively to the state included oil and basic petrochemicals, electricity and nuclear energy, telegraph and mail, and radioactive minerals. It is worth mentioning that several post-1993 changes have allowed greater participation of foreign capital in some of these activities (see Villagómez 1998).

The opening of financial markets

The liberalization and opening of the local financial markets was initiated in 1988 with several measures that liberalized the obligatory reserve requirements and interest-rate ceilings, unified the free and controlled exchange

Table 9.1 Macroeconomic performance indicators since 1988

	1988	**1989**	**1990**	**1991**	**1992**	**1993**	**1994**	**1995**	**1996**	**1997**	**1998**
Growth rate (annual %)	1.2	4.2	5.1	4.2	3.6	2.0	4.4	–6.2	5.2	6.7	4.8
Inflation (annual %)	51.7	19.7	29.9	18.8	11.9	8.0	7.1	52.0	27.7	15.7	18.6
Real exchange rate (1988 index = 100)	100.0	94.6	89.9	82.0	75.0	70.8	73.6	106.6	96.7	85.5	86.4
Private savings rate (% of GDP)	17.5	14.8	13.2	10.6	10.5	11.6	11.4	15.8	16.7	17.2	17.4
Foreign trade (GDP percentages)											
Exports	13.9	14.0	14.1	14.2	14.4	15.2	17.2	23.9	26.8	27.9	29.2
Imports	11.7	13.2	15.0	16.6	19.2	19.2	22.3	20.2	23.5	27.1	29.5
Capital account (GDP percentages)											
Direct investment	1.6	1.5	1.1	1.8	1.6	1.5	3.5	3.1	2.9	3.7	2.9
Portfolio investment	0.5	0.2	1.4	4.9	6.6	10.1	2.6	-3.2	4.2	1.5	0.4
Loans	–1.8	0.4	4.7	3.1	–0.6	1.0	0.4	7.5	–3.8	–2.6	1.1
Debt (GDP percentages)											
Gross foreign	43.7	36.6	32.1	30.1	28.4	27.5	27.1	31.0	31.1	26.9	24.9
Gross domestic	22.4	23.4	20.9	16.8	11.8	10.2	10.8	9.5	6.9	7.3	8.7

Public finances (GDP percentages)											
Consolidated budget expenditure (total)	36.4	30.6	27.5	23.9	22.2	22.5	23.1	23.0	23.3	23.7	21.5
Current expenditure	12.5	11.2	10.5	9.9	8.8	9.1	8.9	8.2	8.1	8.3	7.2
Investment	2.9	2.4	2.7	2.9	2.7	2.5	3.0	2.5	2.9	2.5	1.8
Payment of domestic interests	12.5	9.0	6.8	3.1	2.2	1.5	1.1	2.6	2.3	2.5	1.5
Payment of foreign interests	3.6	3.3	2.3	1.9	1.5	1.2	1.2	2.0	2.1	1.6	1.4
Others	4.9	4.7	5.2	6.1	7.0	8.2	8.9	7.7	7.9	8.8	9.6
Consolidated budget revenues (total)	27.7	25.8	25.3	23.5	23.7	23.1	22.8	22.8	23.2	23.0	20.3
Federal government (total)	16.3	16.4	15.9	15.5	16.0	15.5	15.2	15.3	15.7	15.8	14.1
Taxes	11.4	11.1	10.7	10.7	11.3	11.4	11.3	9.3	9.0	9.8	10.4
Non-tax revenues	5.0	5.3	5.2	4.8	4.8	4.1	3.9	6.0	6.7	6.0	3.7
Labour market											
Urban open unemployment rate (%)	3.6	3.0	2.8	2.6	2.8	3.4	3.7	6.2	5.5	3.8	3.2
Average real wage	100.0	105.9	107.4	114.2	122.8	130.6	136.9	118.8	109.1		
Average real wage (manufacturing)	100.0	109.0	112.1	119.4	129.9	139.2	144.3	124.4	111.1	110.4	112.8
Real minimum wage	100.0	93.9	85.2	81.5	77.7	76.6	76.6	66.7	61.6	60.9	61.1

Source: INEGI National Accounts, Competitiveness Indicators; Banco de México, Economic Information; OECD Economic Surveys, several years; Revenue and Public Credit Secretariat, historical data; IMF, International Financial Statistics.

rates, and eliminated the exchange controls that had been adopted during the 1982 crisis. In 1989 and 1990 the main measures were taken which allowed entry of foreign portfolio investment to the stock market and money markets. The decree of May 1989 liberalized the so-called neutral investment regime (introduced in 1986) to stimulate the entry of foreign investors into the Mexican stock market (see SECOFI 1993). In addition, in late 1990 restrictions to the purchase of fixed-interest (government) bonds by foreigners were eliminated.

Together with changes in global markets (falling world interest rates and changes in the regulatory framework of portfolio investments in the United States),[7] these reforms contributed to a surge of capital flows to the country. Gross capital inflows increased from 3.5 billion US dollars in 1989 to 33.3 billion in 1993, before strongly contracting again in 1994 (Banco de México 1994). As Table 9.1 shows, the capital inflow increased from insignificant levels in 1988–89 to a peak of 12.6 per cent of GDP in 1993. Capital flows to Mexico presented a major share of the flows to Latin America, suggesting the presence of other Mexican-specific factors. For example, Mexico signed the first Brady agreement for restructuring and relief of public external debt, which was agreed in July 1989 and signed with the creditor banks in February 1990.[8] The agreement combined with the repayment of the external debt (financed with income generated by privatization and fiscal adjustment) and the reduction of international interest rates caused a substantial reduction in interest payment obligations both as a percentage of GDP and exports (see Table 9.1). This debt-service indicator, generally used by foreign and Mexican investors to evaluate country risk, dropped in the 1990s to below its level of the mid-1970s, prior to the balance-of-payments crisis of 1973–76. Another important fact was the start in the mid-1990s of the free-trade negotiations with the United States and Canada. The perspective of greater integration into the economic area of North America was frequently mentioned as an element that has contributed to rising capital flows to Mexico, particularly through the 'lock-in' effect on the economic reforms of the administrations of De la Madrid and Salinas de Gortari.[9]

Like foreign trade, the expansion of capital flows was unbalanced. Portfolio investment played a dominant and growing role early in the decade. From being almost non-existent in 1989, it increased to 3.4 billion US dollars in 1990 and 28.4 billion in 1993 (85 per cent of the total gross inflows).[10] Foreign investment only acquired greater importance than in the past starting in 1994, coinciding with the implementation of NAFTA and the approval of the new foreign investment law in 1993. Since then, direct investment averaged 3.3 per cent of GDP (about 20 per cent of total private investment), while other net capital flows reached about 1.7 per cent of GDP (see Table 9.1).

9.3 MACROECONOMIC PERFORMANCE DURING THE BOOM AND COLLAPSE OF CAPITAL FLOWS

For a while, capital inflows and the stabilization and reform programmes interacted brilliantly. The return to international capital markets was an indicator of the positive response of domestic and foreign investors to the economic reform and structural adjustment process that Mexico had undertaken since the mid-1980s. The reversal of the massive outward transfer of resources of the previous decade by itself put an end to the financial difficulties that followed the outbreak of the debt crisis in 1982. Capital inflows thus helped to ensure the success of the stabilization programme initiated in late 1987, which in turn reinforced the positive change in the perceptions about the prospects of the Mexican economy. At the same time, the liberalization process and the surge in capital flows were accompanied by trend changes in various macroeconomic performance indicators, which turned out to be decisive in the unfortunate end of the boom in capital inflows in late 1994.

Real Appreciation of the Peso, Declining Profitability and the 1994 Crisis

As the stabilization programme used the exchange rate as its nominal anchor, the surge in capital inflows contributed to a persistent real appreciation of the peso between 1988 and 1994 (see Table 9.1). The exchange-rate regime went through several changes, moving from a fixed exchange rate to a regime of daily mini-devaluations and, later, to a crawling exchange-rate band. Nonetheless, the real appreciation continued as inflation systematically surpassed the government's inflation targets. The peso appreciated by more than 40 per cent in real terms between 1988 and 1993. By 1993, the real value of the peso was only 10 per cent lower than that of 1981, the level just before the massive devaluations of early and mid-1982. Thus the exchange rate remained virtually unchanged despite the radical trade opening and lower oil export revenues the economy could count as compared to the early 1980s.

Trade liberalization and the real appreciation of the peso shifted relative prices against tradable goods, leading to a reduction of profitability. Table 9.2 illustrates this profit squeeze. The share of profits and interest income in total value added declined steadily between 1988 and 1994. The cumulative decline amounts to 7 percentage points. The shift in primary income distribution went to the benefit of skilled workers, whereas – as we will discuss in detail below – the income share of unskilled labour fell. The trend in the profit share differs between sectors. Overall, there has been a strong redistribution of profits from traded to non-traded goods sectors. The profit share of manu-

Table 9.2 Wage and profit shares, 1982–96

	1982–87	1988	1989	1990	1991	1992	1993	1994	1995	1996
Profits and interests[1]	53.4	56.5	56.0	54.5	52.9	51.8	50.4	49.8	54.6	55.9
tradables sector	*33.8*	*25.1*	*21.3*	*19.1*	*17.5*	*16.0*	*14.2*	*13.8*	*17.0*	*19.2*
non-tradables sector	*19.5*	*31.4*	*34.7*	*35.4*	*35.4*	*35.8*	*36.2*	*36.0*	*37.6*	*36.7*
Skilled labour[2]	8.2	9.8	11.7	12.3	14.0	15.6	17.2	18.2	16.6	15.5
Other labour incomes[3]	38.4	33.8	32.3	33.2	33.0	32.6	32.4	31.9	28.7	28.6

Notes:
1. Operating surplus (excluding oil, agriculture, trade and other services), minus property income paid to abroad plus public debt interest payments.
2. Estimate using the average wage of construction workers as the upper limit of remuneration for unskilled labour.
3. Remuneration of unskilled workers and independent workers. Estimated as a residual.

Source: Based on INEGI, National Accounts.

facturing and mining fell by more than 11 percentage points, while that in non-tradable goods production increased by more than 4 percentage points.

Foreign capital inflows generated a strong expansion of domestic bank credits, as the monetary effect was not completely sterilized. Part of this credit expansion was channelled toward financing new investments, but the most significant part ended up inducing a private consumption boom amidst an illusion of prosperity. The limited and deficient prudential supervision and regulation of the recently privatized banking system also contributed to excessive expansion of consumer credit, increasing the indebtedness of households and decreasing personal savings.

Growing household indebtedness was a source of declining personal savings, while the profit squeeze in the traded goods sector contributed to a drop in corporate savings. As a result, the private investment rate collapsed along with the domestic savings rate. The private savings rate dropped by 7 percentage points of GDP between 1988 and 1992 and recovered only slightly in 1993 and 1994 (Table 9.1). It is difficult to estimate the degree to which the consumption boom and the profit squeeze each contributed to the investment crisis (besides other potential factors).[11] Our own calculations suggest that distributive shifts and rising household indebtedness both played an important role.

The record level of current account deficits in a period of slow economic growth is thus explained by the steep fall in domestic savings, the real appreciation of the peso and trade liberalization. Current account deficits in the order of 7 to 8 per cent of GDP were exceptional in the past and typically a result of very rapid economic expansion (with GDP growth rates of more than 7 per cent). In the early 1990s, deficits of this size emerged in a quasi-stagnant economy and showed no signs of reversal when growth decelerated from 1991 onwards (see Figure 9.1 and, for a more extensive discussion, Ros 1994a, b and Lustig and Ros 1998).

The sources of the slow growth-cum-growing current account deficit pattern are shown in Figure 9.2. Using the aggregate demand decomposition (see Chapter 1), the figure shows the evolution of GDP and the impact of the fiscal stance (G/t), net exports (E/m) and private expenditure stance (I/s). GDP growth during the period was largely driven by private expenditure expansion. The expansionist stance of the private sector (increase in I/s) was in turn mainly due to the reduction of the private savings rate (s), rather than to the increase of private investment (I) or the investment rate (I/Y). The fiscal stance was only moderately expansionist between 1988 and 1994.[12] Foreign trade was contractionist for most of the period. The impact of export growth (E) was offset by the strong increase of the average import propensity (m). This explains the reduction of (E/m) in Figure 9.2. The combination of a strong rise in the import propensity and the collapse of the savings rate

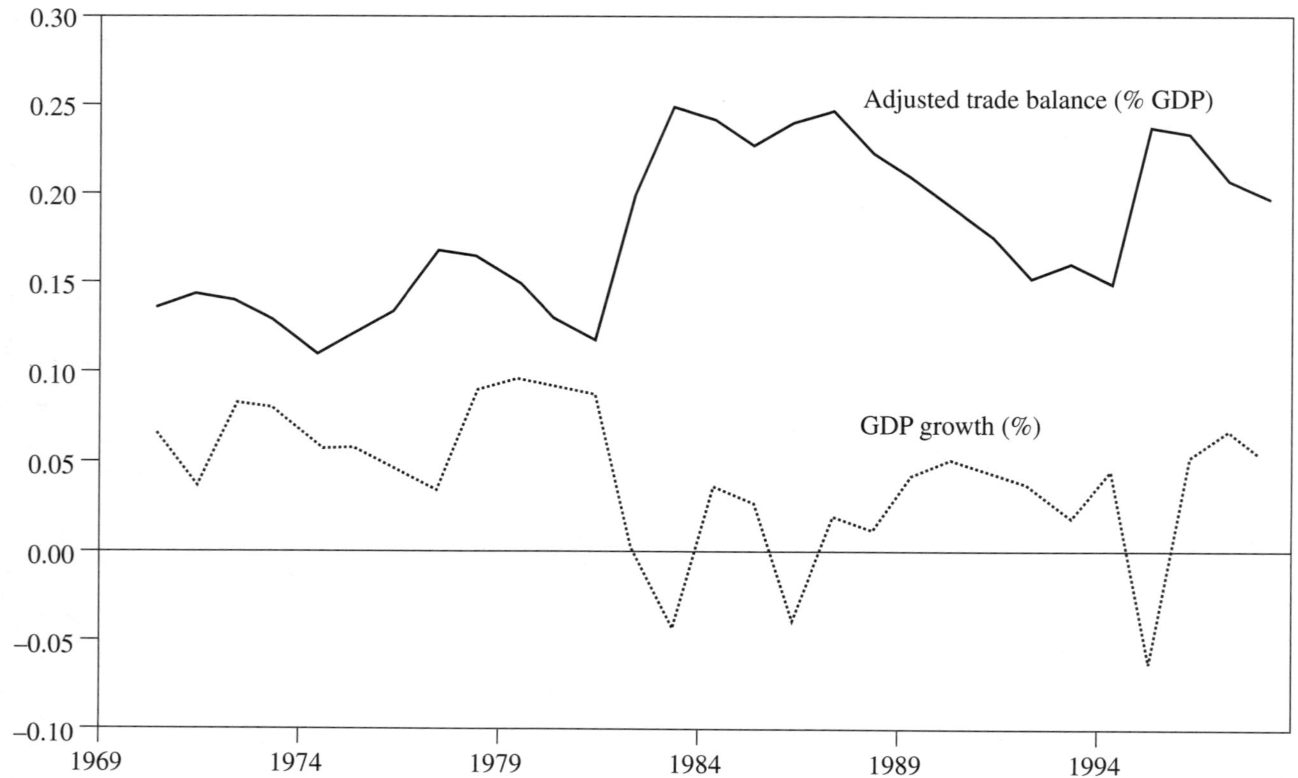

Figure 9.1 *GDP growth and trade balance, 1969–98*

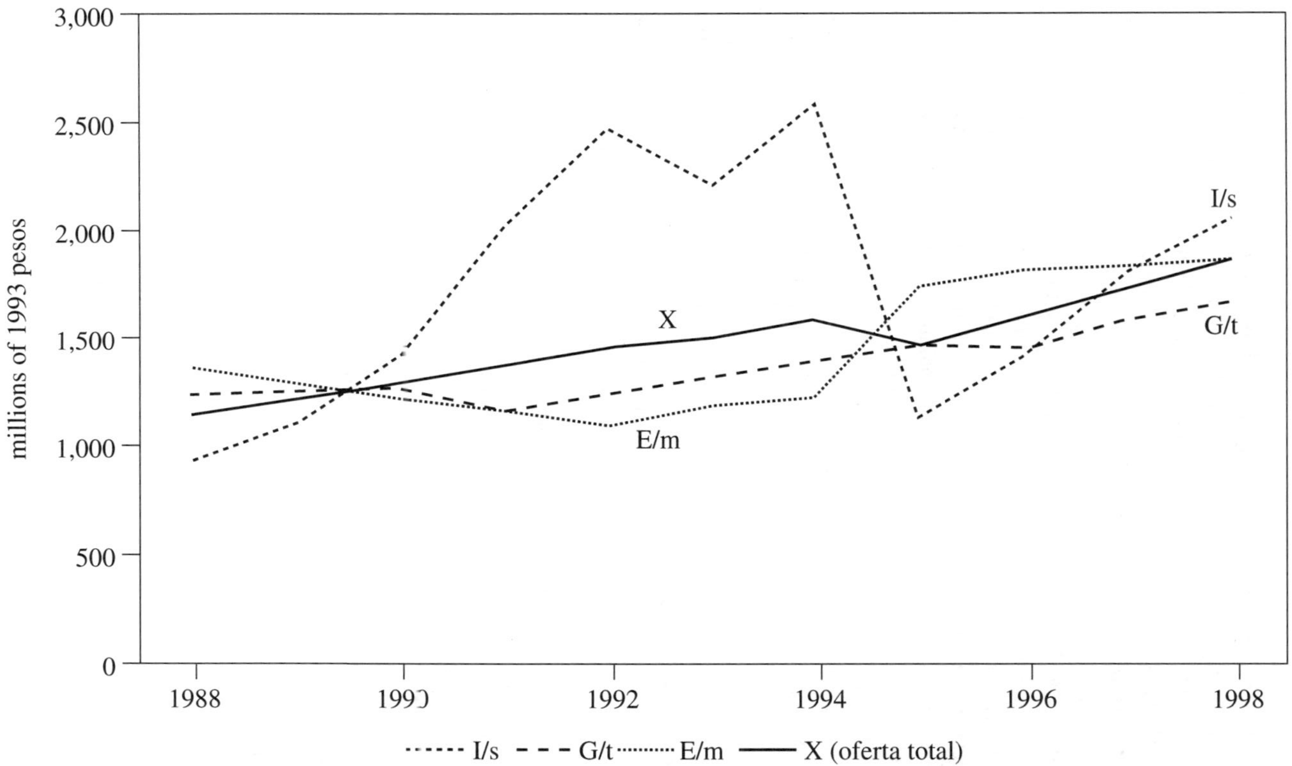

Figure 9.2 Sources of demand growth

explains the rapid deterioration of the current account amidst slow growth of GDP and production capacity.

This growth path of the economy was highly vulnerable, as it implied a continuous accumulation of external liabilities. Between 1989 and 1993, the current account deficit (excluding debt service) averaged 31.7 per cent of exports. Exports would need to grow at an average annual rate of 8.7 per cent (1989–93) for the ratio of foreign liabilities to exports to stabilize at a level of 3.6, as shown by the estimates of Dadush et al. (1994).[13] This ratio is much higher than the debt–export ratio of 2.2 or the debt–GDP ratio of 0.8, which the World Bank uses to classify a country as severely indebted. It is therefore rather unlikely that foreign creditors and investors would continue to supply the necessary financing to stabilize debt at the indicated ratio. This suggests that the economy would be facing severe balance-of-payment problems well before reaching the steady-state debt–export ratio.

Capital flows decelerated in 1994, but involved a series of speculative attacks associated with political events that took place in that year (in particular, the March assassination of the presidential candidate of the governing party). In an effort to stave off the deceleration of flows, the government took a series of economic policy decisions that created the conditions for financial crisis that emerged at the end of 1994.[14] First, the stock of domestic public debt was dollarized by converting payable peso-denominated *Certificados de Tesorería* (CETES) into dollar-indexed short-term bonds (*Tesobonos*). Second, the average maturity of government debt was shortened as the dollarization of the public debt was not only confined to CETES but also peso-denominated long-term bonds (*Bondes* and *Ajustabonos*) were converted to *Tesobonos*. As a consequence, a large amount of debt became due in 1995. Some 28.6 billion US dollars in *Tesobonos* were to expire in 1995, of which 35 per cent (US$ 9.9 billion) in the first trimester (see Cole and Kehoe 1996, Ibarra 1997).

In addition, the Banco de México decided to sterilize the effects on the money supply of both the international reserve losses resulting from speculative attacks (especially in March 1994 after the assassination of the presidential candidate of the governing party) and the more gradual losses resulting from the huge current account deficit and the slowdown of capital inflows. This prevented a contraction of the money supply and contributed to keeping interest rates down. Any other measures probably would have been ineffective to avoid a devaluation of the peso. However, reserves fell by US$ 20 billion during the year as a consequence. Together with an additional US$ 30 billion of dollar-indexed debt, this created the conditions for the financial panic following the devaluation of December 20. A rescue package of US$ 50 billion was needed to calm financial markets after the panic that followed the exchange-rate crisis. The need for adjustment was so large that the rescue operation could not avoid a deep recession in 1995. Real wages in manufacturing fell by more than 20 per cent. By the end of the decade, Mexican living standards had yet to recover from this negative impact.

Sectoral Employment and Productivity Trends

The real appreciation of the peso resulted in a low GDP growth, affecting tradable goods sectors in particular. Slow growth also affected employment creation, particularly in the manufacturing industry. Poor performance of manufacturing GDP was combined with a strong acceleration of productivity growth.

These trends are shown in Table 9.3, including the crisis and the post-crisis period (1993–97). The first column of the table shows employment growth for the economy as a whole and by sector as the difference between GDP growth (second column) and labour productivity growth (third column). The last column of the table gives a decomposition of the sources of the growth of labour supply (for 1988–93) as well as of the sources of employment creation. For example, the annual employment growth between 1988 and 1993, largely determined by socio-demographic factors, plus the growth of labour supply due to the expulsion of manpower in mining and manufacture, is equal to the employment creation in sectors with growing manpower (agriculture and non-traded goods sectors). The most salient feature of the 1988–93 period is the negative contribution of manufacturing to employment growth. As the second and third columns show, this is a result of the extremely high growth rate of labour productivity (an annual 6 per cent) in the context of slow GDP growth (an annual 4.2 per cent).

Productivity and employment in manufacturing industry

The relatively slow expansion of GDP and the rapid expansion of productivity in manufacturing seem to be closely linked to the reduction of profitability and the penetration of imports in the sector. The response to smaller profit margins varied per industry, depending on the size of the profit squeeze, the degree of import penetration and the sector's potential for intra-industry trade (see Table 9.4). In a group of industries (upper panel of Table 9.4), import penetration is inversely correlated with GDP and employment growth. Companies in these sectors reacted to the drop in profit margins with defensive productivity increases. Wherever the profit squeeze is very strong, variable costs are no longer recovered and firms go out of business. Employment losses are due in this case to the displacement effect of imports on local production. This holds for several segments of the textile, wood, and cement and glass industries.[15] Wherever the profit squeeze was moderate or even non-existent, as was the case in the food and paper and printing industries,

Table 9.3 *Growth of employment, productivity and GDP by sector (annual growth rates)*

Sector	Employment		GDP		Productivity		Contributions to employment	
	1988–93	1993–97	1988–93	1993–97	1988–93	1993–97	1988–93	1993–97
Total	3.1	3.2	3.7	2.4	0.6	–0.8	3.1	3.2
Mining[1]	–7.4	8.8	2.0	4.1	9.4	–4.7	–0.1	0.1
Manufacturing	–1.8	4.9	4.2	4.7	6.0	–0.2	–0.3	0.8
Agriculture	5.8	0.5	1.9	1.7	–3.9	1.2	1.5	0.1
Non-tradables	3.6[3]	3.9[3]	3.1	1.8	–0.5	–2.1	2.0	2.2
Construction	4.1	–1.7	4.9	0.1	0.8	1.8	0.2	–0.1
Transport and communications	5.0	2.7	4.1	5.0	–0.9	2.3	0.2	0.1
Commerce[2]	5.1	3.4	4.3	1.0	–0.8	–2.4	0.8	0.6
Services	3.0	5.5[4]	3.9	1.6[4]	0.9	–3.9[4]	0.8	1.7[4]
Government	0.8		0.9		0.1		0.03	

Notes:
1. Includes electricity.
2. Includes restaurants and hotels.
3. Includes non-specified activities.
4. Includes government.

General note: The contributions to employment are estimated using the following decomposition: $L^* = \Sigma(L_i/L)L_i^*$ where L^* is the growth rate of total employment, L_i the growth rate of employment in sector *i*, and (L_i/L) the participation of sector *i* in total employment. The contribution of each sector to employment growth is estimated as $(L_i/L)\ L_i^*$ and the sum of these contributions is therefore equal to the total in the first row. In turn, in each row the component (L_i^*) is decomposed per sector as $(Q_i^* - p_i^*)$ where Q_i^* is the growth rate of GDP and p_i^* the growth rate of labour productivity in the corresponding sector. The growth rate of GDP (Q_i^*) is shown in the second column and the growth rate of productivity is presented in the third column. The growth rate of variable *Y* between the years 0 and *t* is estimated as $(Log\ Y_t - Log\ Y_0)/t$ where log is the natural logarithm.

Source: 1997 National Employment Survey and INEGI, National Accounts.

also the slowdown of GDP and employment growth is less pronounced. In all these cases, the import coefficients are relatively low, indicating a high degree of protection of the domestic market. Export coefficients in these sectors are also low, suggesting a lack of business experience with export activities (see Table 9.4).

In a second group of industries (with the highest initial import and export coefficients, which suggest more potential for intra-industry trade than the

Table 9.4 Foreign trade, profit margins and productivity in manufacturing, 1988–94

Manufacturing industry branch	Year	Import coefficient	Export coefficient	Profit margin	Productivity growth[1]	GDP growth[1]
Non-metal mineral products, except oil and carbon derivates	1988	4.4	14.3	71.2		
	1994	12.0	12.5	60.5	7.2	8.9
Food, beverages and tobacco	1988	10.6	13.2	32.9		
	1994	19.8	9.7	35.2	3.5	5.0
Wood and wood products	1988	7.3	14.3	46.2		
	1994	27.8	11.0	33.8	4.2	2.3
Paper products, printing and publisher	1988	25.9	14.0	30.9		
	1994	41.2	6.3	26.7	1.7	3.4
Textiles and apparel	1988	11.5	16.6	36.3		
	1994	35.6	19.4	26.7	3.2	2.5
Chemicals	1988	31.5	23.0	36.0		
	1994	51.9	29.6	28.2	5.6	5.6
Metals	1988	44.4	41.3	35.9		
	1994	64.7	53.3	32.2	8.6	–1.6
Other manufacturing industries	1988	53.2	31.8	52.6		
	1994	76.4	43.6	34.6	0.4	8.8
Metal products, machinery and equipment	1988	67.5	56.1	21.5		
	1994	89.0	78.8	18.3	8.1	10.8
Total	1988	33.3	26.8	32.8		
	1994	54.7	34.1	28.5	5.4	4.2

Notes:
1. Annual growth rate (in %).
Import coefficient = *M*/(*VA* + *M* – *X*), export coefficient = *X*/*VA*, where *M*, *X* and *VA* are the 1993 constant-price values of imports by sector of origin, exports by sector of origin and gross value added, respectively. Profit margin = *EB*/(*R* + *CI*), where *EB*, *R* and *CI* are the values at current prices of the gross operating surplus, remuneration to employees and intermediate consumption, respectively.

Source: INEGI, National Accounts.

first group), import penetration is positively correlated with export growth. This group (lower panel of Table 9.4) includes chemicals, metal, machinery and equipment (related to the automobile industry) and other manufacturing industries. Productivity increases resulted from investment in labour-saving technologies, adoption of new hiring practices in order to reduce direct labour costs (personnel reduction and subcontracting), changes in the product mix (reducing diversity) and reduction of value added (using import supplements). This way, businesses in these sectors have been able to survive and prosper thanks to greater specialization in intra-industry trade. It also explains the rapid simultaneous growth of sectoral import and export coefficients, typical of performance during this period. In these cases, the import penetration led to higher export growth rates through a greater intra-industry specialization in international trade. In the first group of industries, productivity growth generally went hand in hand with slow GDP expansion due to import penetration. Here, productivity growth was defensive. In contrast, in the second group of industries technological changes linked to import penetration were almost always translated into the highest productivity and GDP growth rates within the manufacturing sector.[16]

Falling productivity growth in the economy as a whole

The acceleration of productivity growth in manufacturing did not lead to higher productivity growth for the economy as a whole. Paradoxically, compared to the second half of the 1970s, faster productivity growth in manufacturing between 1988 and 1993 was accompanied by a slower productivity growth rate for the economy as a whole. The reasons for this behaviour can be explained in the decomposition exercise presented in Table 9.5. Each sector's unadjusted contribution to total productivity growth is equal to the growth of its productivity multiplied by the share of the sector in total employment. The sum of these contributions is not equal to the growth of productivity in the economy as a whole (this explains the term 'unadjusted'), since part of the productivity growth results from labour reallocation effects from low-productivity sectors to high-productivity sectors. The effects of such reallocations equal the difference between the growth of productivity in the economy and the sum of unadjusted contributions. Its magnitude is shown in the last row of the table.

These reallocations were very important in the second half of the 1970s. The reallocation effect was even somewhat higher than total productivity growth. This can be explained by the drop in agricultural productivity, which offset productivity gains in other sectors, thus leaving reallocation effects as the sole source of net productivity gains. Although these reallocation effects were still positive during the 1988–93 period – which indicates that, on average, high-productivity sectors grew faster than low-productivity sectors –

their magnitude in this second period is much lower than that of the first period. The slowdown of total productivity growth can be explained entirely by the reduction of the reallocation effects. At the same time, the contribution of manufacturing to productivity growth increased substantially. The larger contribution of manufacturing was offset by productivity declines in non-traded goods sectors. It is important to note that the contribution of agriculture is not much less negative in the second period.

The smaller contribution to productivity growth of non-tradable sectors was certainly one of the causes for the reduction of the reallocation effects. This can be observed in the change of contributions adjusted to productivity growth (estimated such that the reallocation effect linked to the rapid growth of a high-productivity sector is added to this sector's direct or unadjusted contribution). The sum of the adjusted sectoral contributions is thus equal to the economy's productivity growth and the residual is zero. The results in Table 9.5 show that the greater contribution of manufacturing in the second period was indeed more than offset by the large drop in the adjusted contribution of non-traded goods sectors to productivity growth. The adjusted

Table 9.5 Sector contribution of GDP growth

	Growth of productivity		**Non-adjusted contributions**		**Adjusted contributions**	
Sector	**1974–79**	**1988–93**	**1974–79**	**1988–93**	**1974–79**	**1988–93**
Agriculture	–3.0	–3.9	–1.2	–1.0	–1.3	–1.4
Mining[1]	5.1	9.4	0.1	0.1	0.2	0.1
Manufacturing	1.9	6.0	0.3	1.1	0.8	1.1
Non-tradables[2]	1.3	–0.5	0.5	–0.3	2.0	0.8
Total	1.6	0.6	1.6	0.6	1.6	0.6
Reallocation effect			1.8	0.7	0.0	0.0

Notes:
1. Includes electricity.
2. Includes construction, transportation and communications, commerce, services and government.

General note: The unadjusted contribution of sector i to the growth of productivity in the economy as a whole is estimated as $(L_i/L)p_i^*$ where L_i/L is the share of sector i in total employment and p_i^* is the annual growth rate of productivity. The adjusted contribution of sector i to productivity growth is $(L_i/L)p_i^* + [(Y_i/Y) - (L_i/L)]Y_i^*$ where Y_i^* is the annual GDP growth rate of sector i and Y_i/Y is the share of sector i in total GDP. The growth rate of variable Y between the years 0 and t is estimated as $(Log\ Y_t - Log\ Y_0)/t$ where log is the natural logarithm.

Source: INEGI, National Accounts; 1997 National Employment Survey and ILO, Yearbook of Labour Statistics 1982.

contribution of agriculture to growth is negative at approximately the same size in both periods.

This reduction in the adjusted contribution of non-tradable sectors can be attributed to two factors. The first is the reduction in the relative productivity of these sectors between the two periods. The decline was due to the economic stagnation of the 1980s and contributed to reduce the effect of employment reallocation toward those sectors (productivity still being above average) and therefore limit its adjusted contribution to productivity growth.[17] The second factor is the slowdown of productivity growth in these sectors (from 1.3 to 0.5 per cent). This can be linked to the employment losses in manufacturing after 1988 as a result of the productivity increases in the sector. This led further to an increase in the rate of underemployment in services and commerce, which stood in the way of productivity growth in these sectors.

9.4 TRADE LIBERALIZATION, LABOUR MARKET AND WAGE INEQUALITY

The wage structure changed substantially in the period following trade liberalization. Income distribution shifted from unskilled to skilled labour between 1988 and 1994 (see Table 9.6). Figure 9.3 shows the reduction in relative labour remunerations in low-wage sectors (agriculture, construction, commerce and services with wages lower than the economy's average) since 1988. Figure 9.4 illustrates the rising trend of the white- and blue-collar wage ratio (or salary–wage ratio) in each branch of manufacturing industry. Several studies provide additional evidence on the increase in wage dispersion and see the widening gap between skilled and unskilled labour remuneration as the major source (see Hanson and Harrison 1995, Cragg and Epelbaum 1996 and Alarcón and McKinley 1997).

The employment and wage trends show that the rapid increase in the wage premium is caused by a change in the composition of labour demand. Table 9.6 indicates the importance of manufacturing labour demand. Indeed, the table shows that the change in the ratio of white- to blue-collar workers and the corresponding change in the income ratio of these two types of workers are positively correlated across industries. Industries that mostly displaced blue-collar workers (relative to white-collar workers) show the highest salary–wage ratios. If the substitution of unskilled labour with skilled labour (measured here by the white-collar to blue-collar worker ratio) were induced by supply factors, then we would expect a negative correlation between income and employment shifts across industries. That is, the increase in the salary–wage ratio is caused by the lower white-to-blue-collar worker ratio.

Table 9.6 *Trends in manufacturing wages and employment*

Branch of manufacturing industry	Salary/wage ratio[1]	White-collar to blue-collar worker ratio[1]	Growth of occupied personnel	Growth of occupied blue-collar workers[2]	Growth of occupied white-collar workers[2]
Metals	63.1	11.0	–5.7	–5.9	1.6
Textile and apparel	63.0	9.8	–4.4	–4.4	1.4
Non-metal mineral products (no oil/carbon derivates)	61.9	7.5	–2.6	–2.9	1.1
Paper products, printing and publishers	60.3	2.5	–2.5	–2.6	0.4
Chemicals	57.3	9.8	–1.8	–2.3	1.6
Food, drinks and tobacco	57.2	14.4	0.2	–0.4	2.1
Wood and by-products	35.4	–8.7	–3.6	–3.4	–1.2
Metal products, machinery and equipment	15.5	–18.5	–1.7	–0.9	–2.6
Other manufacturing industries	9.4	–18.6	1.3	2.3	–2.7

Notes:

1. Salary = remuneration of white-collar workers and Wage = remuneration of blue-collar workers. Refers to percentage change in the ratio during the period.
2. Annual rate.

Source: INEGI Monthly Industrial Survey.

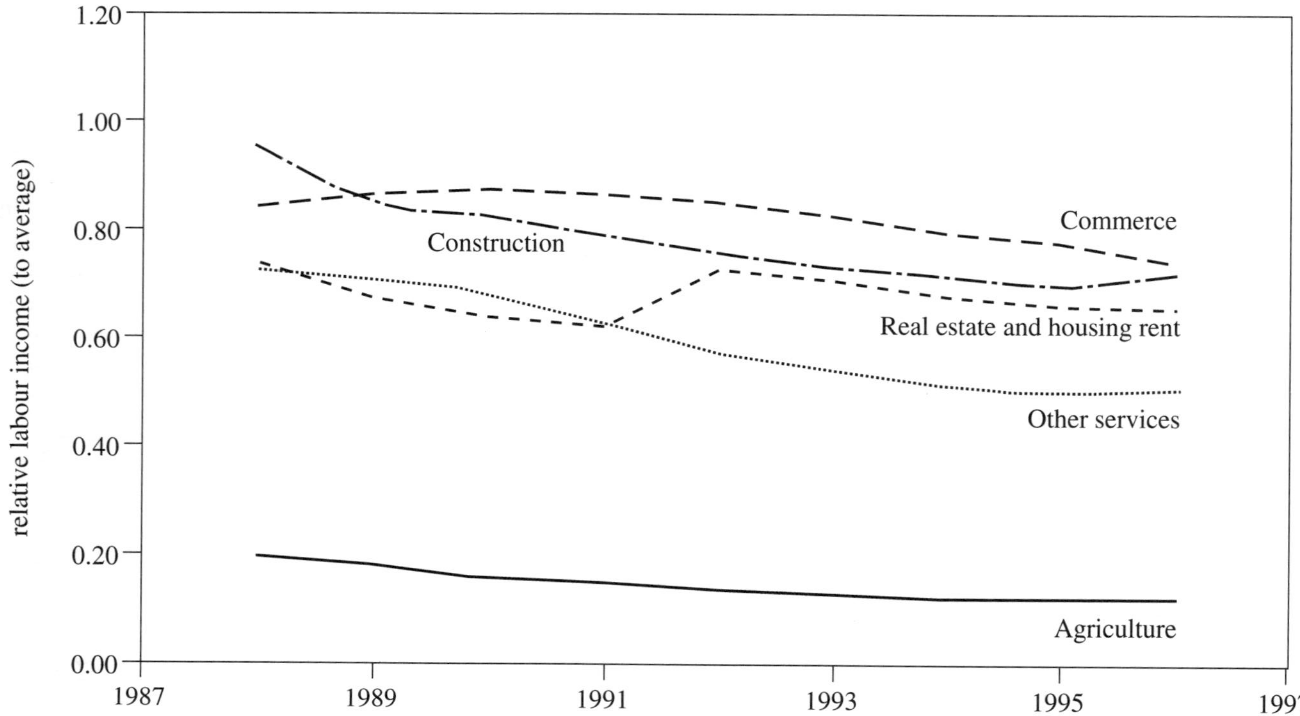

Figure 9.3 Relative labour income in low-wage sectors

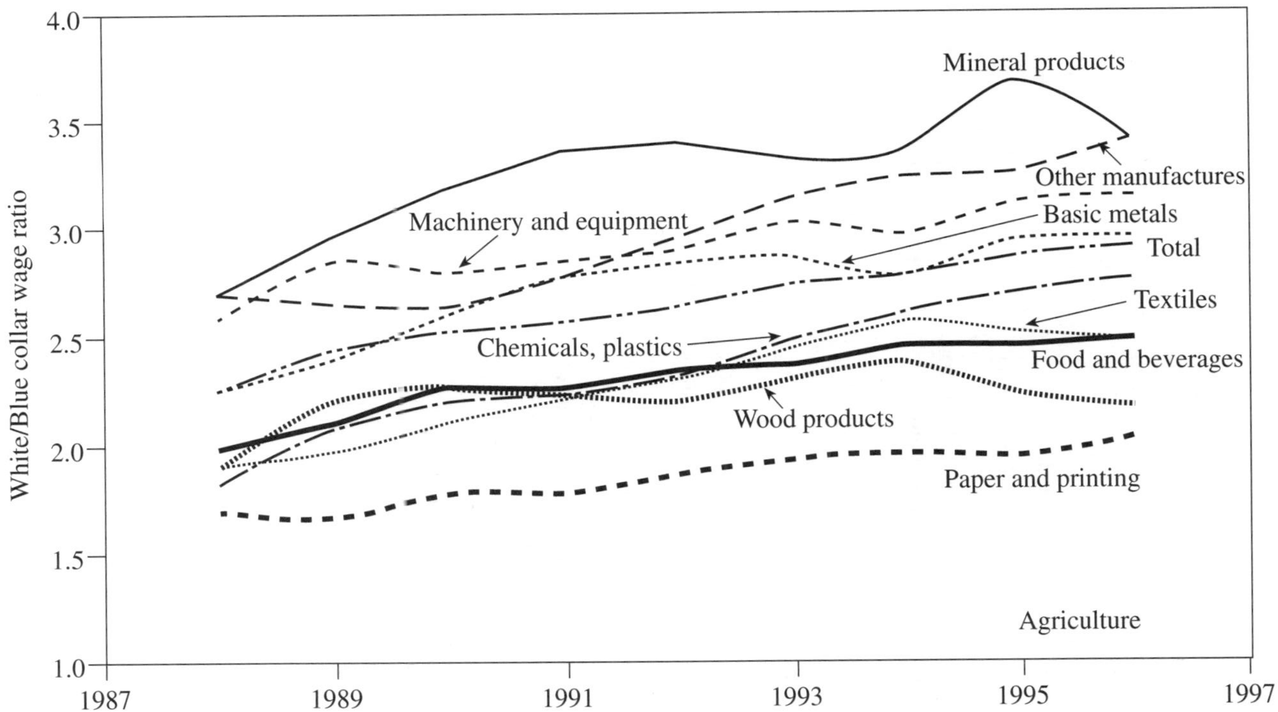

Figure 9.4 *White-to-blue-collar wage ratio in manufacturing, 1988–96*

Changes in the Composition of Labour Demand by Sector

Empirical evidence also suggests that the changes in the composition of labour demand are linked to intra-industry rather than inter-industry effects. Hanson and Harrison (1995) for 1984–90 and Cragg and Epelbaum (1996) for 1987–93 indicate that the net inter-industry effects do not really explain the labour demand shift in favour of skilled labour. Inter-sectoral employment shifts from unskilled to more skill-intensive industries explain little of the rise in the skilled–unskilled labour ratio and the wage premium. Hanson and Harrison state that these inter-industrial effects account for 7 to 20 per cent of the income share of white collar workers in total labour income. That is, 7 per cent when using information from the Industrial Census and 20 per cent when using a sample of medium-size and large enterprises of the Ministry of Trade and Industrial Development.

Not only the reduced magnitude, but also the sign of the inter-industry effects appear to be inconsistent with the predictions of orthodox trade theory. According to the Stolper–Samuelson theorem, trade liberalization should have raised the remuneration of the relatively abundant factor in Mexico (unskilled labour) in relation to that of the scarce factor (skilled labour). The mechanisms through which liberalization produces this result are well known. Assuming similar technologies in domestic and foreign production, trade opening leads to an increase in the relative price of goods intensive in the use of unskilled labour. Given the abundance of unskilled labour, these goods are produced by the domestic economy at relatively low costs. This relative price change leads to greater labour demand in unskilled-intensive industries, thereby provoking an increase in the wage of unskilled labour relative to that of skilled labour. Thus, the expected result of standard trade theory would be a reduction of the wage premium for skilled labour, rather than the increase observed in Mexico after trade liberalization.

Various hypotheses try to explain why inter-industry changes did not follow the Stolper–Samuelson theorem. First, the structure of effective protection in Mexico before trade liberalization may have favoured unskilled labour-intensive industries (see Hanson and Harrison 1995, 1999). Trade liberalization could thus have modified relative prices in the 'wrong direction' (i.e. in favour of skill-intensive goods). Second, the emergence in the last 20 years of new competitor countries with an abundance of unskilled labour and low wages could imply that, even though Mexico has a relative abundance of unskilled labour compared to its main trading partner (the United States), it does not with the rest of the world (Londoño and Székely 1997). Third, Mexico may not have a comparative advantage in several activities intensive in the use of unskilled labour despite its relative abundance. This may be the case because of differences in production functions (technological backwardness in unskilled labour-intensive industries) and/or reversibility in factor intensity. An example of reversibility of factor intensity may be agriculture, which sector has a relatively low skill-intensity in Mexico, but is relatively capital-intensive in the United States. The United States may thus have a comparative advantage over Mexico in the trade of agriculture products, despite Mexico's abundance of unskilled labour (see Larudee 1998).

Intra-industry Changes in the Composition of Labour Demand

The limited scope of the inter-industry effects must be consistent with substantial intra-industry and intra-firm effects explaining the increase in both the relative demand for skilled labour and the wage premium.

Cragg and Epelbaum (1996) suggest that the underlying mechanism should be sought in the effects of trade liberalization on the price of imported capital goods under the assumption that physical capital and skilled labour are complementary factors of production. The decrease in the relative price of imported capital goods as a result of trade liberalization stimulated the use of capital and skill-intensive technologies, given the complementarity of the two inputs. The resulting increase in the demand of skilled labour would have led to a rise in the wage premium.

A second hypothesis is that the greater competitiveness resulting from import liberalization accelerated the pace of technological change and reduced the demand for unskilled labour in manufacturing. This would have affected unskilled labour wages adversely.[18] This hypothesis can be developed further using a two-sector model of tradable and non-tradable goods in which the tradable goods sector operates under conditions of imperfect competition, where unskilled labour is its main variable input factor, and skilled labour is fixed in the short run and is a complement of physical capital in production.

Figure 9.5 shows the determination of wages and employment of unskilled labour in the tradable goods sector in such a model. The NN curve is a locus of combinations in which the non-tradables and unskilled labour markets are in equilibrium. The curve has a positive slope. An increase in employment in tradables leads to a drop in the supply of unskilled labour and a wage increase in the non-tradables sector (which in the final balance is transmitted to the tradables sector). The CC curve is a locus of combinations in which the market of importable goods is in equilibrium. The curve has a negative slope. An increase in wages for unskilled labour raises the cost and price of importable goods, thus reducing demand for such goods and employment in the sector.

The effects of trade liberalization on the labour market operate through three channels. The first channel is the reduction of the relative price of

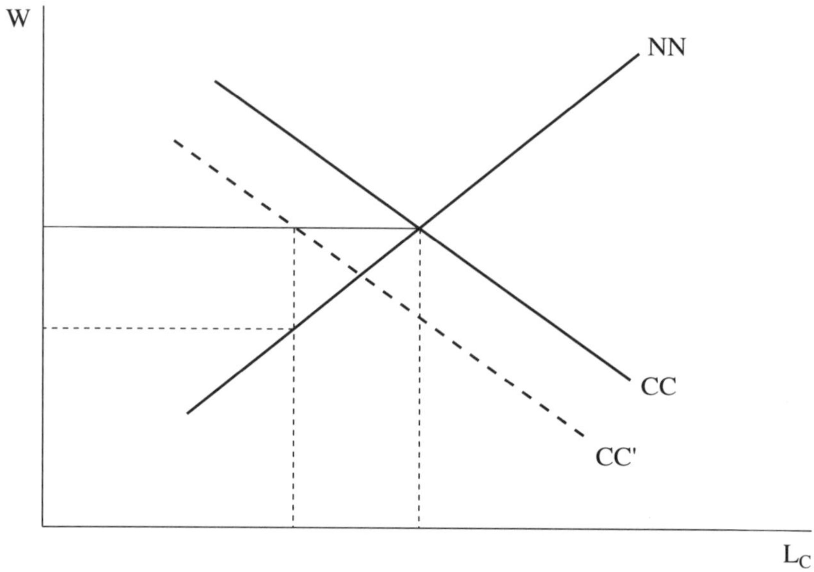

Figure 9.5 Trade liberalization and labour market adjustment

imported goods in relation to domestic product prices. The second is the increase in the import share in domestic markets (which goes beyond the change in relative prices) linked to greater preference for imported goods. The third is the increase of price elasticity of demand of firms producing importable goods as a result of intensified competition in domestic markets. These three mechanisms affect the position of the CC curve. The fall in the price of imported goods pushes the curve down (this holds when the substitution elasticity between imported and domestically produced, importable goods is larger than 1). Short-run employment and wage adjustment is as follows. If tradable sector wages do not drop immediately, sector employment contracts along the horizontal line, returning to the initial wage level. To the extent that the displaced workers become self-employed in informal activities of non-tradable sectors, informal incomes go down along the NN curve up to the point which full employment is re-established (at the intersection of the NN curve and the vertical line to the new employment level). This leads to a widening of the gap between the wage of unskilled workers in both sectors, which is consistent with the growing inter-sectoral wage inequality observed in the Mexican case (see Figure 9.3). It also widens the skilled–unskilled wage gap, as unskilled wages will tend to fall over time following excess unskilled labour supply in tradables sectors and the remuneration for skilled labour remains constant in this exercise due to the fixed-cost assumption of skilled labour. Figure 9.4 illustrates the increase in wage premium for skilled labour in non-tradable sectors. In the long-term, the income gap between formal and informal activities tends to close up through competition in the labour market, which in turn tends to re-establish the initial level of relative prices between imported and domestic goods and to shift the CC curve upwards.

Even if long-term adjustment restores the initial level of relative prices, the CC curve will not return to its initial position if the preference for imported goods increases as a result of liberalization (possibly as a result of the short-term adjustment and the disappearance of local substitutes for imported goods). In that case, the final equilibrium will be at a lower employment level in the production of importable goods and more employment in non-tradables.

The increase in the price elasticity of demand of firms in the importables sector has two effects. First, it tends to reduce the price of importable goods against non-tradables (which induces substitution in consumption between importables and non-tradables). Second, it reduces the price of importables against imported goods. Both effects tend to shift the CC curve upwards, reflecting that demand shifts toward domestic importable goods, which are produced at the initial wage level. The relative price shifts will also tend to offset the reduction of employment in the importable sectors (derived from the previous effects). However, in this case the long-term effects on investment of the decrease in profitability in the importables sector (with the greater price elasticity) tend to reinforce the sector's employment losses.

The marginal revenue curve of the representative firm in the importables sector will shift downward in response to a decrease in the price of imported goods and a greater preference for imported goods. The increase in price elasticity will be reflected in a change in the slope of the curve, which by itself will cause an increase in the volume of output. As suggested by the evidence, these effects did not offset the negative impact of the two previous mechanisms on employment and wages of unskilled labour in the importables sector. Moreover, the long-term dynamic effects of decreasing profit margins on sectoral investment levels exacerbated the adverse effects on employment and wages.

Both hypotheses regarding the impact of trade liberalization on the composition of labour demand (decreasing relative price of capital goods and intensification of foreign competition) emphasize, respectively, the positive effects of liberalization on skilled labour demand and the negative effects on unskilled labour demand. Both are consistent with the quantitative importance of the intra-industry effects indicated by Hanson and Harrison, as well as with the general increase of relative demand for skilled labour (within each manufacturing industry), as documented by Cragg and Epelbaum. Although these two mechanisms could have operated simultaneously, empirical evidence suggests – as we will see – that the effects of import penetration constituted the main form of labour market adjustment to liberalization.[19]

First, the hypothesis of increased competition of imported goods implies that the change in the composition of labour demand must be specific to the tradable goods sector and non-existent in the non-tradable goods sector (with no such increase in competition). Cragg and Epelbaum (1996) find as much. They show that the substitution of unskilled labour was much faster in the tradables sector, especially in manufacturing, and largely limited to this sector. If the main cause of the change in the composition of labour demand had been a drop in the relative price of imported capital goods, then the substitution of unskilled labour for skilled labour should have constituted a more general phenomenon encompassing both tradable and non-tradable goods. One could even argue that the phenomenon should have been more pronounced in the non-tradable sectors. As the allocation of investment probably changed in favour of non-tradables in view of the profit squeeze in tradables, the complementarity between physical capital and skilled labour should have induced a faster rate of substitution between both types of labour in the non-tradable sectors rather than in manufacturing industry.

Second, if the effects of trade liberalization were mainly channelled through import penetration, then we should observe that industries with more rapidly increasing white-to-blue-collar worker ratios should be those with faster reductions in employment. This would hold as under this hypothesis the change in the composition of demand reflects the changes in the variable factor, i.e. unskilled labour. This negative correlation between changes in the white-to-blue-collar worker ratio and employment changes can be observed in Table 9.6. The correlation does not support the alternative hypothesis. If the fall in capital goods prices and subsequent investment incentive was the main effect of trade liberalization on labour demand, then industries with faster growth of investment, production and employment levels should have larger increases in the white-to-blue-collar worker ratio, as these would benefit most from the decline in capital goods prices. In this case, the expected correlation is positive, not negative. Table 9.6 clearly shows that the increase in the white-to-blue-collar worker ratio is a result of a reduction of blue-collar employment, rather than due to an increase in the demand for white-collar workers. This fact seriously questions the explanation based on the decrease in the relative price of capital goods. This hypothesis suggests there should have been an absolute increase in the investment level and thus in the demand for skilled labour. It is worth observing that four of the five industries in the upper panel of Table 9.4 (where rapid import penetration is not linked to the expansion of intra-industry trade) are among the five industries that had the highest rate of employment reduction of blue-collar workers.

Within manufacturing industries, relative employment losses are positively correlated with the degree of the profit squeeze, with two exceptions.[20] This suggests that job losses were a response to the decline in profit margins related to the decrease in the relative price of importable goods. As the composition of labour demand is closely related to employment changes (Table 9.6), these two relations link the change in the composition of labour demand to the profit squeeze. The two exceptions are the two industries with the largest and smallest productivity growth during the period, i.e. metals and other manufacturing industries. This behaviour of profit margins is consistent with our hypothesis. Indeed, in our explanation the reduction of employment by firms is strictly an 'ex-ante' response to falling profit margins. That is, their fall before accounting for the more or less successful effect of employment reductions on 'ex-post' profit margins through their impact on labour productivity. If our hypothesis is correct, the industry with the highest growth rate of productivity (metals) can become an exception because it managed to compensate the effects of a strong 'ex-ante' fall with high productivity growth. This explains its relatively low ex-post reduction of profit margins in the context of a strong decrease in employment. The least successful industry as far as increased productivity is concerned (other manufacturing industries) could also constitute an exception, since the relatively low employment reduction determined a relatively strong ex-post fall of the profits margin.

While the change in the composition of labour demand in manufacturing played a decisive role in the increase of the wage premium of skilled labour, other supply-side factors also played a role. The changes in the composition of labour demand in manufacturing implied a change in the composition of labour supply growth for other sectors of the economy. Cragg and Epelbaum (1996) give evidence that the number of some low-skilled jobs (merchants and workers in transportation and services) expanded rapidly coupled with relatively low increases in remuneration between 1987 and 1993.

Trade liberalization did not benefit agriculture, an unskilled labour-intensive sector. As a consequence, the labour demand in this large sector of the economy was adversely affected and this led to a fall in the price of unskilled labour for other sectors. Combined with the other factors, including the change in the composition of demand in manufacturing, the result was the rapid widening of the wage gap between skilled and unskilled labour.

9.5 LABOUR MARKET, INEQUALITY AND POVERTY

The inequality in labour incomes and poverty went up considerably in Mexico after the trade reform and the liberalization of the balance of payments. As shown in Table 9.7, between 1984 and 1994 inequality in individual labour

Table 9.7 Inequality and poverty, 1984 and 1994

	1984	1994	Variation	
			Points	Average
Inequality: Gini coefficient				
Labour income	46.53	55.27	8.74	18.8
Per capita household income	47.62	53.31	5.89	12.4
Per capita household labour income	52.19	58.72	6.53	12.5
Per capita household non-labour income	65.15	62.94	–2.21	–3.4
Poverty				
Moderate poverty				
Poverty incidence	12.91	18.59	5.68	44.00
Poverty gap	3.69	5.76	2.07	56.10
Poverty severity	1.7	2.57	0.87	51.18
Extreme poverty				
Poverty incidence	2.39	5.24	2.85	119.25
Poverty gap	0.87	1.25	0.38	43.68
Poverty severity	0.46	0.47	0.01	2.17

Notes: The poverty rates were calculated using the INEGI poverty line for 1994. The moderate urban and rural poverty lines are 396.6 and 257.7 monthly pesos per capita of 1994, while the urban and rural extreme poverty lines are 198.3 and 147.3 monthly pesos per capita of 1994. Incomes were adjusted proportionately by the ratio of survey incomes to the total income of national accounts (GDP).

incomes increased by about 9 percentage points in terms of the Gini coefficient. The Gini measure of inequality of per capita labour income of the household worsened by 7 percentage points. This was offset somewhat by a decrease in the inequality of non-labour incomes. Overall, per capita household income inequality increased by almost 6 percentage points. As also shown in Table 9.7, the number of poor in the country went up by about 6 percentage points and those in conditions of extreme poverty by 3 percentage points between 1988 and 1994. The poverty gap and severity indicators also worsened both for all poor and for the extremely poor.

The previous section showed how trade liberalization has led to a widening wage gap between skilled and unskilled labour. The purpose of this section is to analyse the effects of the increase in the wage gap and other changes in the labour market structure on the increase in inequality of labour incomes and poverty. The data used are derived from the National Household Income and Expenditure Survey carried out by the statistical office (INEGI) of Mexico in 1984 and 1994. The exercise consists of simulating a counterfactual income distribution under the assumption that the post-reform labour market changes did not take place. To be more specific, the characteristics of the labour market in 1984 were imposed on the 1994 survey data, so as to simulate a new income distribution. The counterfactual scenario thus reflects the economy's conditions before the trade reform. The comparison between the original income distribution and that obtained with the counterfactual scenario allows us to estimate the changes in inequality linked to the changes in the labour market structure that took place between 1984 and 1994. The methodology allows us to isolate the effects in income distribution and poverty from changes in the participation and unemployment rates, in the wage structure and in the labour income structure.

Effects of the Labour Market Changes on Income Distribution

Table 9.8 summarizes the estimates of the effects of the various labour structure changes on inequality among employed individuals as well as the inequality of per capita household labour incomes and total per capita income. The table reports the simulated percentage changes between the Gini observed in 1994 and the one that would be obtained when allocating the 1984 labour market structure to that of 1994.[21] The most important result is the increase in inequality generated by the changes in the structure of average income per group of workers (grouped by gender, educational level and economic sector). The changes generate an increase in inequality of almost 10, 9 and 8 percentage points compared to the income level of employed workers, per capita household labour income and total per capita household income levels, respectively.

The change in participation rates appears to have the largest impact of all labour demand and supply variables. The participation rate went up for both men and women, as Table 9.9 shows. For women, the participation increases are positively correlated with educational levels. Participation of women with lower educational levels went up by about 5 percentage points, while that of educated women went up by 15 points. Participation levels of men with a secondary and higher education went up, the highest increase being found at about 16 percentage points for men with secondary education. These changes in the participation of the labour force after the reform did not lead to more income equality at the level of individual workers, but did lead to more equality at the household level, as Table 9.8 shows.[22] Although the changes respond mainly to changes in demographic variables such as educational level, number of children or household composition, the fact that the most

Table 9.8 Simulated inequality increases due to labour market changes after 1984 (in %)

	Individual effects			Cumulative effects		
	mean	**max.**	**min.**	**mean**	**max.**	**min.**
Labour income (individuals)						
Labour participation rate	1.75	2.22	1.40	1.75	2.22	1.40
Unemployment rate	0.35	0.46	0.23	1.94	2.33	1.47
Employment structure	–0.09	0.57	–0.92	–0.77	0.20	–1.75
Change in mean income	9.96			9.47	9.95	8.89
Per capita household labour income						
Labour participation rate	–3.95	–3.40	–4.37	–3.95	–3.40	–4.37
Unemployment rate	0.07	0.20	–0.06	–3.79	–3.31	–4.23
Employment structure	–0.57	–0.20	–1.25	–5.71	–4.69	–6.39
Change in mean income	9.10			3.40	4.07	3.02
Per capita total household income (individuals)						
Labour participation rate	–1.12	–0.65	–1.44	–1.12	–0.65	–1.44
Unemployment rate	0.14	0.25	0.02	–0.79	–0.33	–1.10
Employment structure	–0.49	–0.05	–0.98	–2.14	–1.39	–2.85
Change in mean income	7.66			5.27	5.77	4.92

Notes: The database has been normalized in order to avoid spurious changes in inequality resulting from the use of income percentiles in the simulations.

significant increases in labour participation are found among individuals with secondary or higher education may be associated with the economy's reform and modernization process. Rising inequality of per worker incomes resulted from the strong increase in male and female participation of individuals with secondary or higher education. The fact that these effects do not translate to greater inequality at the household level could be an indication that the changes in labour participation were in part a result of endogenous household decisions as a response to income changes.

In any event, the magnitude of these effects is much smaller than that of the changes in the remuneration structure, so that the equalizing effects did not offset the strong trend toward greater inequality generated by the changes in the average incomes per group of workers. On the whole, the labour market changes increased inequality in labour incomes of occupied individuals by 9 percentage points. The effect on inequality of per capita labour income of the household was 3 percentage points and that on total per capita household income inequality 5 points.

The analysis confirms the importance of the widening wage gap between skilled and unskilled labour as a major source of change in the structure of relative labour incomes, and therefore of the increase in inequality. Table 9.9 suggests that there could be three reasons underlying the inequality-increasing effects of the changes in remuneration structure across groups of workers. First, the large increase in incomes of higher-educated workers throughout most sectors of the economy (especially in the non-tradables sector, where the employment share of this group of workers increased significantly).[23] Second, the strong reduction of incomes of wage earners with secondary or lower education in manufacturing and mining. This reduction amounted to, respectively, 22 and 23 per cent for male and female wage earners with low education, and 2.5 and 10 per cent for male and female wage earners with secondary education. Third, the drop in average income of self-employed farmers. Although the income decrease in this sector was uniform for all educational levels, the sector uses mainly unskilled workers. Bouillon et al. (1999) and Legovini et al. (2000) have estimated the contribution of the deterioration of agricultural incomes to the increase of inequality in Mexico after the trade reform. They find that about 20 per cent of the increase in inequality between 1984 and 1994 can be explained by the deterioration of the conditions in the rural sector (especially in the south of the country). This deterioration is linked to the decline in world market commodity prices affecting farm incomes and to the dismantling of government support to the sector.

Effects of the Labour Market Changes on Poverty

Table 9.10 shows the simulation results for the poverty indicators. The joint effect of the labour market changes on poverty was very small for the moderate poverty incidence, but led to a 14 per cent reduction in extreme poverty. However, these rather general results hide two strongly diverging effects. By themselves, the inequality-increasing labour market effects, especially the changes in the remuneration structure, would have increased moderate poverty by 31 per cent and extreme poverty by 37 per cent. However, these effects were more than offset by the changes in labour participation, the unemployment rate and the employment structure, which induced a reduction of moderate and extreme poverty of 32 and 59 per cent, respectively.

The changes in the participation rate had an effect of reducing poverty mainly through the increase in participation of women with lower educational levels. This effect is equivalent to a decrease in moderate poverty of 21 per cent and extreme poverty of 42 per cent (see Table 9.8). The changes in

Table 9.9 Labour market characteristics, 1984 and 1994

(a) Mean income by educational level and economic sector

	Men			Women		
	1984	**1994**	**Change (%)**	**1984**	**1994**	**Change (%)**
Higher education						
Wage earners						
Agriculture	1,702.5	4,784.9	181.0	1,733.9	3,073.9	77.3
Mining and manufacturing	2,643.8	4,343.0	64.3	1,845.4	2,145.9	16.3
Services	2,366.1	3,925.4	65.9	1,509.4	2,260.0	49.7
Non-wage earners						
Agriculture	7,586.9	4,123.6	–45.6	n.a.	n.a.	n.a.
Mining and manufacturing	3,547.2	3,674.3	3.6	1,532.5	179.6	–88.3
Services	2,730.8	4,388.0	60.7	353.3	2,212.4	526.2
Secondary education						
Wage earners						
Agriculture	546.1	480.8	–11.9	269.6	205.5	–23.8
Mining and manufacturing	1,371.7	1,337.6	–2.5	269.6	205.5	–23.8
Services	1,306.9	1,255.4	–3.9	1,151.6	1,131.9	–1.7
Non-wage earners						
Agriculture, mining and manufacturing	2,195.2	1,146.5	–47.8	258.8	129.6	–49.9
Services	1,514.1	1,920.7	26.8	967.0	1,077.5	11.4

Lower education						
Wage earners						
Agriculture	484.7	463.1	–4.5	283.5	304.7	7.5
Mining and manufacturing	1,088.3	849.2	–22.0	816.5	545.0	–33.3
Services	958.3	935.3	–2.4	639.9	518.0	–19.1
Non-wage earners						
Agriculture	937.4	551.7	–41.1	314.8	113.6	–63.9
Mining and manufacturing	1,127.2	1,767.1	56.8	336.3	278.3	–17.3
Services	1,166.4	1,154.8	–1.0	507.4	491.2	–3.2

(b) Participation and unemployment rates by educational level

	Education							
	Total		**Lower**		**Secondary**		**Higher**	
	1984	**1994**	**1984**	**1994**	**1984**	**1994**	**1984**	**1994**
Men								
Unemployment rate	4.22	4.69	3.19	4.36	6.80	5.97	5.88	2.71
Participation rate	69.67	74.56	77.96	77.79	51.76	67.36	72.72	82.94
Women								
Unemployment rate	3.59	3.38	1.57	1.62	8.36	4.90	1.92	5.18
Participation rate	22.57	30.47	20.35	25.28	25.85	33.87	43.73	58.66

Table 9.10 Simulated poverty changes due to labour market changes after 1984 (in %)

	Individual effects			Cumulative effects		
	mean	max.	min.	mean	max.	min.
Labour participation rate						
Moderate poverty						
Poverty incidence	–20.53	–19.03	–22.28	–20.53	–19.03	–22.28
Poverty gap	–35.03	–33.22	–37.77	–35.03	–33.22	–37.77
Poverty severity	–52.32	–48.55	–56.72	–52.32	–48.55	–56.72
Extreme poverty						
Poverty incidence	–42.28	–38.70	–45.54	–42.28	–38.70	–45.54
Poverty gap	–87.21	–79.28	–94.59	–87.21	–79.28	–94.59
Poverty severity	–153.75	–137.22	–170.37	–153.75	–137.22	–170.37
Unemployment rate						
Moderate poverty						
Poverty incidence	–0.32	0.48	–0.96	–20.70	–19.50	–22.18
Poverty gap	–0.12	1.38	–1.44	–34.58	–32.68	–37.22
Poverty severity	–0.19	2.57	–2.75	–51.51	–47.19	–56.20
Extreme poverty						
Poverty incidence	0.94	4.18	–1.70	–40.52	–36.17	–45.40
Poverty gap	–0.01	5.48	–5.89	–85.16	–74.80	–92.11
Poverty severity	–3.56	4.52	–13.42	–153.67	–133.46	–170.43
Employment structure						
Moderate poverty						
Poverty incidence	–6.53	–2.90	–9.35	–31.68	–28.78	–34.51
Poverty gap	–9.32	–7.90	–12.39	–51.10	–47.94	–54.97
Poverty severity	–12.72	–9.91	–16.87	–73.94	–69.16	–79.87
Extreme poverty						
Poverty incidence	–8.55	–2.19	–14.53	–58.88	–52.19	–69.73
Poverty gap	–21.49	–16.47	–26.76	–119.57	–106.63	–131.81
Poverty severity	–32.65	–25.33	–39.10	–203.45	–181.80	–226.51
Remuneration structure						
Moderate poverty						
Poverty incidence	31.07			0.84	3.90	–3.14
Poverty gap	32.83			–13.62	–9.76	–17.97
Poverty severity	33.77			–31.08	–25.64	–36.76
Extreme poverty						
Poverty incidence	37.01			–13.94	–8.22	–19.30
Poverty gap	33.54			–67.63	–55.95	–77.53
Poverty severity	32.40			–139.90	–117.37	–160.97

Notes: The database has been normalized in order to avoid spurious changes in inequality resulting from the use of income percentiles in the simulations.

the participation rate greatly benefited the lower decile of the economy, which may explain its strong effect on the reduction of extreme poverty. It should be noted that the increase in participation of women with lower educational levels can be attributed to changes in demographic variables rather than to the economy's liberalization process.

The unemployment rate varied by less than half a percentage point for both men and women between 1984 and 1994 (see Table 9.9). For men with lower and secondary education, unemployment changed little (1 and –1 per cent, respectively), and for higher educational levels it went down by more than 3 per cent. For women we observe a slight drop in the overall unemployment rate, the net result of a reduction of nearly 3.5 points in the unemployment of women with secondary education and an increase of more than 3 points among women with higher education. The reduced size of all these changes, plus the fact that the major changes tended to appear among workers with higher educational levels (positive for men and negative for women) explains why the effects of unemployment changes on poverty were so limited (see Table 9.10).

The changes in the employment structure helped to reduce poverty, although not as much as the change in the participation rate. Moderate poverty decreased by 7 per cent and extreme poverty by 9 per cent as a result of these changes. The effects occurred mainly through the changes in the sectoral shares of unskilled workers by sector, more specifically the improvement in income of workers who migrated from the agricultural to the services sector.

9.6 CONCLUSIONS

No matter how one looks at it, the performance of the Mexican economy in the years following the balance of payments liberalization measures has been rather dismal. Once the difficulties linked to the debt crisis and the fall of oil prices were overcome, the economy grew at 3.5 per cent per year between 1987 and 1994. This is a slow growth rate, particularly if one considers the massive capital inflows during the period. The foreign savings helped to finance current account deficits of a magnitude that previously only occurred in a context of exceptionally high GDP growth rates.

The post-reform growth pattern had a particularly adverse effect on income distribution. Between 1984 and 1994, inequality measured by per capita household income went up by almost 6 points in terms of the Gini coefficient. Inequality at the household level was the result of greater inequality in the distribution of labour income. The evidence presented in this study indicates that trade liberalization contributed a worsening of the income distribution. The trade reform shifted labour demand against unskilled labour, resulting in an increase in the wage premium for skilled labour. This was the main source of rising labour income inequality. The effect of trade liberalization on increasing wage inequality was the main underlying factor.

The combination of slow economic growth and rising income inequality explains the increase in poverty. The number of poor increased by about 6 percentage points and those in conditions of extreme poverty went up by about 3 percentage points – this despite the fact that other labour market changes (particularly increases in the labour participation rates) were favourable to poverty reduction.

The dismal economic performance was partly due to the liberalization of the balance of payments in the context of persistent exchange-rate appreciation and highly volatile capital flows (see Section 9.2). The inconsistency between the exchange and foreign trade policies, and the vulnerability created by the massive inflows of short-term capital, came to an unhappy end in late 1994. After the deep recession in 1995, and contrary to what happened with the 1982 debt crisis, the economy has recovered at a rhythm of 4 to 6 per cent growth per year and the open unemployment rate has dropped to 3 per cent. How realistic is it to expect a scenario of sustained growth at a rate higher than that observed since the early 1980s?

Several factors indicate this could be a credible scenario. First, the international environment is presently more favourable than in the period following the 1982 debt crisis. The international rescue package was successful in keeping the post-crisis financial panic from degenerating into a shying away of international credit supplies (which, in the previous crisis, took almost a decade to revert). Compared to the early 1980s, international interest rates remain low and the Mexican government did not need to recur to excessively restrictive fiscal and monetary policies to mitigate the effects of the continuous capital volatility – despite the financial turbulence in the Far East and, more recently, in Russia and Brazil. As long as they can be kept within certain boundaries, such types of turbulence may contribute (as they have in the recent past) to prevent the reappearance of real exchange-rate overvaluation and the strong bias toward highly liquid, short-term liabilities that characterized the composition of the capital inflows in the early 1990s. Under such conditions, exchange and fiscal policies targeting a competitive real exchange rate and high levels of utilization of domestic resources have better chances of being implemented, thereby enhancing the probability of a sustainable recovery of economic growth.

Second, while taking into account the adverse short-term effects on living standards and income distribution, the crisis itself may have substantially improved the long-term macroeconomic perspectives. On the one hand, the large real devaluation of the peso eliminated at the roots the inconsistencies between the trade and exchange policies, which had played a major role in the process that led to the crisis. In addition, in a more open economy, a more competitive real exchange rate tends to have a positive effect on foreign trade.[24] On the other hand, given its magnitude, the real devaluation of the peso also contributed to turn around the factors that influenced the fall of private savings and the profitability in traded goods production (see Tables 9.1 and 9.2). The private savings rate went up considerably in 1995 after the strong real devaluation and kept increasing until 1997.[25] The depreciated real exchange rate led to an increase in profitability of the traded goods sector and this attracted more foreign investment. At the end of the 1990s, direct foreign investment represented nearly 20 per cent of private investment and about 60 per cent of total foreign investment (direct plus portfolio investments). The financing of the current account deficit has become less dependent on short-term capital and therefore is less vulnerable to new domestic or foreign shocks.

NOTES

1. The authors wish to thank José Montes, Maiju Perala and Esteban Rodarte for their assistance in the preparation and processing of the statistical database, and Bill Gibson, Jorge Katz, Nora Lustig, Lance Taylor and Rob Vos for their valuable comments. Many thanks are also due to the participants of the seminars in Rio de Janeiro, San Salvador, Antigua and Buenos Aires for their comments on previous drafts of this study.
2. Although the surge in capital inflows extended to the whole of Latin America in the early 1990s, Mexico clearly occupied a prominent position in this process. Nearly half the capital flowing to Latin America in the early 1990s went to Mexico. The contraction of capital movements in 1994 and 1995 started in Mexico and affected its economy quite severely. See Banco de México (1993), Calvo et al. (1992), United Nations (1993) and World Bank (1993).
3. For a more extensive and detailed discussion of the policy reforms, see Ros (1994a) and Lustig and Ros (1998).
4. In addition to the free-trade agreement with the United States and Canada, Mexico has signed bilateral free-trade agreements with Latin American countries. The agreement with Chile became effective in January 1992, and similar treaties with Bolivia, Costa Rica, Colombia and Venezuela became operational in 1995. In addition, in 1997 negotiations were started with the European Union in order to reach a bilateral and preferential trade agreement.
5. In practice, the law applied to new foreign investment projects, since the regulatory agency established by law – the National Committee for Foreign Investment (CNIE) – allowed companies fully owned by foreigners to maintain the capital structure in existence before the law became effective. The CNIE was also allowed to modify the 49 per cent general rule, taking into account a number of criteria that included complementariness of investments with national capital and its effects on transfer of technology, balance of payments and employment.
6. See Lustig (1992), Peres Nuñez (1990) and USITC (1990).
7. These changes (*Reglamentación S* and *Regla 144A*) encouraged portfolio investments in Mexico and other developing countries, particularly through the issuance of American Depository Receipts (ADRs) in the New York stock exchange and of country funds in US stock markets. See El-Erian (1992), Banco de México (1993), Ffrench-Davis and Reisen (1998) and CEPAL (1998).

8. For an analysis of the agreement, see Lustig (1992).
9. For an analysis of the subject, see Lustig et al. (1992) and Hufbauer and Schott (1993).
10. The magnitude of these inflows was such that, for a while, they 'overfinanced' the growing current account deficit and allowed the Central Bank to accelerate the accumulation of international reserves. The difficulties in sterilizing the effects of these strong reserve increases led the Central Bank to introduce temporary measures to limit foreign currency-denominated bank debt in 1992.
11. This is because there are no systematic estimates of business and personal savings (the National Accounts do not distinguish between these two sources of private savings) and, besides, the few available studies are contradictory due to the different information sources used. Székely (1998) gives estimates based on the Household Income and Expenditure Surveys of 1989 and 1992 and comes to the conclusion that the entire drop in private investment is due to the reduction of business savings. In contrast, Calderón (1997) – using flow-of-funds data – sees the decline in personal savings as the major cause of the reduction of private savings.
12. The reduction of the fiscal deficit shown in Table 9.1 does not contradict this expansionist stance. This reduction in the deficit was not caused by the contraction of expenditures in goods and services, but by the reduction in interest payments linked to disinflation and the agreement on external-debt reduction.
13. Ros (1994a,b) arrives at similar conclusions. See also McLeod and Welch (1992), Oks (1992) and Oks and van Wijnbergen (1992).
14. The sequence of events and economic policy dilemmas in 1994, which culminate with the December crisis, is examined in Lustig and Ros (1998) and Lustig (1998, chapter 7).
15. We emphasize the word *segments*. Other segments, as a more disaggregated analysis would reveal, followed a very different pattern that resembles more that of the second group of industries discussed further on. An example is the restructuring of the apparel industry, where several activities are successful cases of export-led growth. However, even in these cases the success became clear only after the devaluation of late 1994.
16. The exceptional productivity growth in other manufacturing industries and the metal industry will be discussed later (see Section 9.3).
17. The adjusted contribution of non-tradables is positive even though the non-adjusted contribution is negative, precisely because the productivity of the sector is above average.
18. Cragg and Epelbaum (1996) also suggest this as a possible mechanism, although they do not explore it.
19. Feenstra and Hanson (1997) suggest a third mechanism linked to the expansion of foreign investment in maquila industries. According to this hypothesis, the global process of growing subcontracting tends to shift production processes to developing countries, which in developed countries are relatively intensive in the use of unskilled labour, but – from the perspective of developing countries – are relatively intensive in terms of skilled labour.
20. The regression equation between the growth rate of occupied personnel (g_L) and the percentage change in the profit margin (g), excluding the two exceptions, is:

$$g_L = -0.006 + 0.116g \quad R^2\,(\text{adj.}) = 0.84$$
$$(-1.27) \quad (5.08)$$

t-statistics in parenthesis.
21. Since the simulation method (see Chapter 2) contains random components, we also present a confidence interval of maximum and minimum values of percentage changes in the indicators. The simulations were repeated 50 times in order to check the robustness of the results.
22. Legovini et al. (2000) also come up with these small equalizing effects for labour participation using the methodology proposed by Bourguignon et al. (1998).
23. The effects of the increase in returns to education on inequality in Mexico have been estimated by other studies. See Legovini et al. (2000) for nationwide estimates and

Bouillon et al. (1999) for estimates for male wage earners. Both studies use household survey data and the methodology proposed by Bourguignon et al. (1998).

24. A comparison of the performance of exports during the 1995 crisis and the 1983 recession illustrates the positive effect of combining a competitive exchange rate with trade opening. In 1995 the exchange rate went up by 86 per cent (at the end of the period). That year, non-oil exports (except for maquila) grew by 37 per cent, while maquila exports grew by 30 per cent. However, after a 466 per cent increase in the exchange rate in 1982, maquila exports went up by 29 per cent in 1992 and other non-oil exports fell by almost 6 per cent. In addition, the macroeconomic impact of export growth is enhanced in the context of a more open economy. As shown in Figure 9.2, net exports have had expansionist effects since 1995 (contrary to what happened between 1988 and 1994) and have constituted the main incentive for growth recovery since (the 1995 recession can be explained by the collapse of private investment).
25. Besides the real depreciation, an important factor in the increase of private investment has been the credit constraints caused by the crisis of the banking system. As credit restrictions eased, the rising trend in the savings rate could revert again. This could constitute a negative aspect of the economic recovery. In fact, the domestic savings rate fell sharply in 1998, largely due to a drop in private savings.

REFERENCES

Alarcón, D. and T. McKinley (1997) 'The paradox of narrowing wage differentials and widening wage inequality in Mexico' *Development and Change*, **28** (3): 505–30.

Banco de México (various years), *Informe Anual*, Mexico City: Banco de México.

Bouillon, C., A. Legovini and N. Lustig (1999) 'Rising inequality in Mexico: Returns to household characteristics and the "Chiapas effect"', Washington D.C.: Inter-American Development Bank (mimeo).

Bourguignon, F., M. Fournier and M. Gurgand (1998) 'Labor incomes and labor supply in the course of Taiwan's development, 1979–1994', Paris: DELTA (mimeo).

Calderón, A. (1997), 'Incomplete adjustment: Fiscal policy, private savings and current account deficits in Mexico since 1982', in: K. Jansen and R. Vos (eds) *External Finance and Adjustment. Failure and Success in the Third World*, London and New York: Macmillan and St. Martin's Press.

Calvo, G., L. Leiderman and C. Reinhart (1992) 'Capital inflows and real exchange rate appreciation in Latin America: the role of external factors', IMF Working Paper, Washington D.C.: International Monetary Fund (August).

CEPAL (1998) *Políticas para mejorar la inserción en la economía mundial*, Mexico and Santiago de Chile: Fondo de Cultura Económica.

Cole, H. and T. Kehoe (1996) 'A self-fulfilling model of Mexico's 1994–95 debt crisis', *Journal of International Economics*, **41** (November).

Cragg, M. and M. Epelbaum (1996) 'Why has wage dispersion grown in Mexico? Is it the incidence of reforms or the growing demand for skills?', *Journal of Development Economics*, **51** (1).

Dadush, U., A. Dhareshwar and R. Johannes (1994) 'Are private capital flows to developing countries sustainable?', World Bank Policy Research Working Paper 1397, Washington D.C.: The World Bank (December).

El-Erian, M.A. (1992) 'Restoration of access to voluntary capital market financing', *IMF Staff Papers*, **39**.

Feenstra, R. and G. Hanson (1997) 'Foreign direct investment and relative wages:

Evidence from Mexico's maquiladoras', *Journal of International Economics*, **42** (3/4): 371–94.
Ffrench-Davis, R. and H. Reisen (1998) *Capital Flows and Investment Performance*, Paris: OECD Development Centre.
Hanson, G. and A. Harrison (1995) 'Trade, technology and wage inequality in Mexico', NBER Working Paper No. 5110, Cambridge (MA): National Bureau of Economic Research (May).
Hanson, G. and A. Harrison (1999) 'Trade liberalization and wage inequality in Mexico', *Industrial and Labor Relations Review*, **52** (2).
Hufbauer, G.C. and J.J. Schott (1993) *NAFTA: An Assessment*, Washington D.C.: Institute for International Economics.
Ibarra, C. (1997) 'Three essays on the 1994–95 Mexican currency crisis', Notre Dame: University of Notre Dame (unpublished PhD thesis)
Larudee, M. (1998) 'Integration and income distribution under the North American Free Trade Agreement: the experience of Mexico', in: D. Baker, G. Epstein and R. Pollin (eds) *Globalization and Progressive Economic Policy*, Cambridge: Cambridge University Press.
Legovini, A., C. Bouillon and N. Lustig (2000) 'Can Education Explain Inequality Changes in Mexico', Washington D.C.: Inter-American Development Bank (mimeo).
Londoño, J. and M. Székely (1997) 'Persistent poverty and excess inequality: Latin America during 1970–1995', OCE Working Paper Series No. 358, Washington D.C.: Inter-American Development Bank (September).
Lustig, N. (1992) *Mexico: The Remaking of an Economy*, First Edition, Washington D.C.: The Brookings Institution.
Lustig, N. (1998) *Mexico: The Remaking of an Economy*, Second Edition, Washington D.C.: The Brookings Institution.
Lustig, N. and J. Ros (1998) *Economic Reforms, Stabilization Policies and the Mexican Disease* (forthcoming).
Lustig, N., B.P. Bosworth and R.Z. Lawrence (eds) (1992) *North American Free Trade*, Washington D.C.: The Brookings Institution.
McLeod, D. and J. Welch (1992) 'El libre comercio y el peso', *Economía Mexicana, Nueva Epoca,* **I** (1) (January).
OECD (1992) *Mexico*, Economic Studies of the OECD, Paris: OECD.
Oks, D. (1992) 'Stabilization and Growth Recovery in Mexico: Lessons and Dilemmas', Latin America and the Caribbean Regional Office, Washington D.C.: World Bank (January).
Oks, D. and S. van Wijnbergen (1992) 'Mexico after the debt crisis: Is growth sustainable?', *Journal of Development Economics*, **47** (1) (June).
Peres Nuñez, W. (1990) *Foreign Direct Investment and Industrial Development in Mexico*, Paris: OECD.
Ros, J. (1994a) 'Mercados financieros y flujos de capital en México', in: José A. Ocampo (ed.) *Los Capitales Externos en la Economías Latinoamericanas*, Bogota: Fedesarrollo and IDB.
Ros, J. (1994b) 'Mexico's trade and industrialization experience since 1960: A reconsideration of past policies and assessment of current reforms', in: G.K. Helleiner (ed.) *Trade Policy and Industrialization in Turbulent Times*, London and New York: Routledge.
SECOFI (1993) 'Evolución de la inversión extranjera en México durante 1992', *El Mercado de Valores*, **9** (1) (May).

Székely, M. (1998) *The Economics of Poverty, Inequality and Wealth Accumulation in Mexico*, London: Macmillan.
United Nations (1993) *World Economic Survey 1993*, New York: UN Department of Economic and Social Development.
United States International Trade Commission (USITC) (1990) 'Review of trade and investment liberalization measures by Mexico and prospects for future United States–Mexican relations, Phase 1: Recent trade and investment reforms undertaken by Mexico and implications for the United States', Investigation 332-282, Publication 2275, Washington D.C.: USITC (April).
Villagómez, A. (1998) 'El sector privado en México. Obstáculos a la inversión', Washington D.C.: Inter-American Development Bank (mimeo).
World Bank (1993) *Global Economic Prospects and the Developing Countries*, Washington D.C.: World Bank.

10. Peru: stabilization, liberalization and inequality[1]

Juan José Díaz, Jaime Saavedra and Máximo Torero

10.1 INTRODUCTION

The 1990s started with the implementation of structural reforms that fundamentally changed the functioning of the Peruvian economy. The economic reorientation consisted of increasing the role of the market so as to make relative prices the main resource allocation mechanism. The reforms aimed at establishing a relative price structure that reflected the relative scarcity and abundance of goods and services. The government started a series of reforms geared toward reducing government intervention and eliminating government-induced market distortions. The initial reforms comprised the liberalization of foreign trade, a tax reform, public sector restructuring and eliminating state monopolies in trade of fuels and some food products. Some reforms targeted market flexibilization and a beginning was made with the liberalization of the labour market. The financial system and the current account of the balance of payments were liberalized and deregulated. There was also an aggressive privatization of public enterprises.

At the beginning, the reform process encountered little political resistance because of the chaotic economic situation at the end of the 1980s. Hyperinflation caused a dramatic reduction of real incomes and informal employment expanded during the economic turmoil. Fiscal and external imbalances were generated under highly interventionist government policies. GDP fell by almost 20 per cent in real terms and inflation exceeded 7,000 per cent in 1988–90. In July 1990 a drastic stabilization programme was implemented to fix these imbalances. This initiated the reform process.

One of the main fears, and typically a source of resistance to such reforms, was that the structural adjustment would lead to massive employment losses and a rise in poverty. The macroeconomic mess that emerged in 1988, the hyperinflation of 1989–90 and the stabilization programme of August 1990 generated a severe output decline, prolonging the recession by another two years. A poverty-relief programme was implemented in 1991. The programme only provided little alleviation for the employment losses caused by the recession and steep fall in real incomes (with wages showing remarkable flexibility despite rigid labour regulations). During the recession, labour participation also declined as women decided to exit the labour market and young workers postponed their entrance. Employment increased by barely 1.2 per cent per year between 1988 and 1992, i.e. at a rate far below the growth of the population in working age. Employment did not decline in absolute terms due to the growth of self-employment. Rising self-employment and slower output growth provoked a severe drop in productivity in line with the decrease in real incomes.

At the same time, the structural reform programme, particularly trade liberalization and the reduction of the state apparatus, led to a realignment of relative prices and the production structure. The economic restructuring had a major impact on the labour market, particularly on the remuneration structure. Employment contracted in some branches of manufacturing and in the public sector. However, starting in 1993, the Peruvian economy recovered, leading to an increase in labour demand and employment. In the 1993–97 period, quantity rather than price adjustment ensured labour market equilibrium. Real income and productivity growth was dismal. The composition of labour demand changed in favour of skilled and younger workers as well as female workers. These groups of workers were the main beneficiaries in terms of income and employment.

The chapter begins with a summary of the changes in macroeconomic conditions and the structural reforms, emphasizing trade liberalization and other reforms that are essential to understand the changes in the production structure. This is followed by an analysis of the performance of key relative prices such as the real exchange rate, the real interest rate and the capital costs, which caused a reallocation of labour by sector. Further, we analyse labour market adjustment by sectors and various population groups. In subsequent sections we look at productivity trends through a decomposition analysis which identifies what proportion of productivity change is due to employment shifts and how much to output changes by sector.

Finally, following the methodology of Chapter 2, we apply a microsimulation procedure to estimate the effects of liberalization on inequality and poverty by individual workers and at the household level. We look in particular at the trends in the main labour market indicators (participation, unemployment, occupation and income) for the metropolitan area of Lima. We use the labour market structures of 1987 (a year of growth with still a closed economy) and 1991 (recession year with a closed economy) as our counterfactuals. These two structures allow us to compare what inequality and poverty would have been in 1997 (after opening and with a growing economy) if we still had the labour market structure of a closed economy (growing or in recession). This way we try to isolate – albeit partially – the effects of liberalization on inequality and poverty.

10.2 STRUCTURAL REFORMS AND MACROECONOMIC CONDITIONS

After the populist boom of 1987 the level of economic output fell dramatically, with negative growth rates for three consecutive years between 1988 and 1990. The fiscal and quasi-fiscal deficits surpassed 8 per cent of GDP since 1986. As a consequence, inflation reached cumulative levels of 1,722, 2,775 and 4,778 per cent in 1988–90. In June 1990, hyperinflation peaked at over 7,000 per cent. The stabilization programme of August 1990 demanded drastic fiscal and monetary adjustment. The government opted for a floating exchange rate and used a monetary target as a nominal anchor, because of the extremely low level of international reserves which impeded defending an exchange-rate target. Credit to the public sector fell to zero and Central Bank purchases of dollars were the only source of money creation. This adjustment helped to control inflation. By 1992, inflation had fallen to 57 per cent. The stabilization shock prolonged the recession and GDP stagnated between 1991 and 1992. In 1992, GDP per capita reached a low at a level similar to that of 1960 (see Figure 10.1).

Besides the stabilization programme, the government started a series of structural reforms that aimed at reducing government intervention in relative prices as well as in trade and production of goods. Trade reform and the opening of the capital account (which we will describe later) were followed by more reforms. These included a tax reform (which simplified legislation and created a new administration and tax fiscalization organism) and a state sector reform (which was later interrupted but which succeeded in dramatically reducing the oversized central government bureaucracy created by the Aprista government). All state monopolies in the distribution of goods and services were also eliminated. For many years, these monopolies fixed prices and dominated domestic trade in goods such as rice, sugar, wheat, tobacco and fuels. The government accelerated the privatization process. In addition to the closure of the development banks and the sale of government-owned banks, also energy enterprises, oil and mining production units and the telephone monopoly were privatized between 1991 and 1996. Liberalization of the labour market was another major reform affecting employment growth. The pension system was also reformed in 1993. The reform led to the creation of a private pension system (SPP) as the alternative to the pay-as-you-go public system of the Peruvian Social Security Institute.

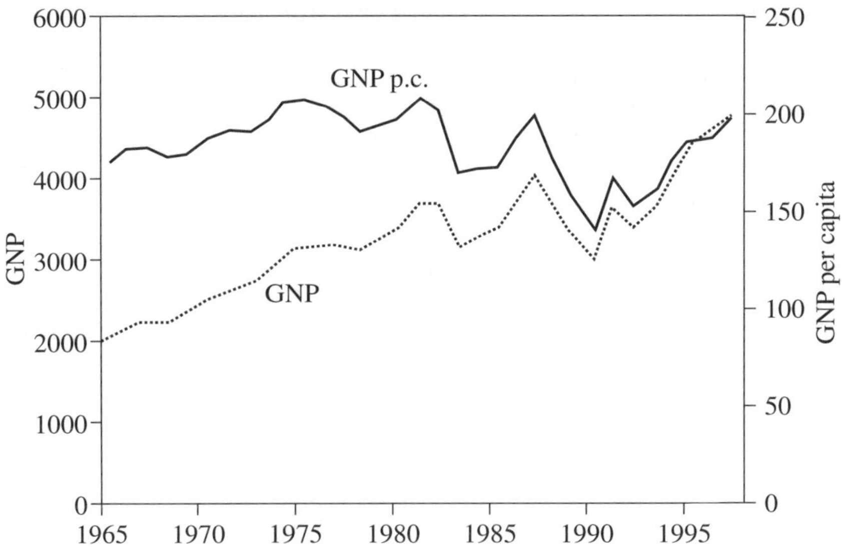

Figure 10.1 *Trends in GDP and GDP per capita, 1965–97 (new soles at constant prices of 1979)*

Output recovered from 1993 onwards. In 1994, the economy grew by 13.1 per cent, the highest growth rate in Latin America. Recovery was a result of the greater economic stability resulting from the reduction of inflation to 15 per cent, greater political stability linked to the defeat of terrorism (which reduced country risk), the reduction of interest rates resulting from capital inflows and increased access to credits due, among other factors, to the liberalization of financial markets. In 1995, the economy grew by an additional 7.2 per cent, partly due to the increase in the fiscal expenditure that preceded that year's presidential elections. In 1996, there was a deceleration precisely due to the need to correct the fiscal imbalance generated in 1995. Between 1993 and 1997, the average annual growth amounted to 6.4 per cent, one of the highest in the region. Those five years constituted the longest episode of consecutive growth of the Peruvian economy during the last 25 years. Only by 1995 was the economy recovered to the output level of 1987. Nonetheless, GDP per capita in 1997 was just about the level reached in 1973.

Trade Liberalization and the Foreign Sector

Trade liberalization, together with the other reforms that were implemented simultaneously, caused an important realignment of relative prices. This realignment had several objectives. The first objective was to increase competitiveness of the tradable sector in the medium run. The second objective was to limit the increase of domestic prices of tradable goods in the short run, in order to reinforce the disinflation process. The reform also intended to increase fiscal revenues through the elimination of quantitative restrictions and an increase in imports.

Prior to the structural reforms in August 1990, wide tariff dispersion and many quantitative restrictions characterized the trade regime. Apparel, food, drinks and tobacco, and dairy products were the most protected sectors with effective protection rates of over 180 per cent.[2] The trade reform started in 1990 and was consolidated the following year. During the first few months of the new government, the maximum and minimum tariff rates and tariff dispersion were reduced. The number of tariff rates was cut to three. A rate of 15 per cent applied to inputs (covering 41.3 per cent of products subject to tariffs), 25 per cent to capital goods (36.9 per cent) and 50 per cent to consumer goods (21.8 per cent). The average nominal tariff fell from 66 to 32 per cent (Table 10.1). The general tariff surcharge was replaced by a temporary 10 per cent surcharge, the number of prohibited import items was reduced to only 25, and import permit requirements and non-competition restrictions were suspended.[3] In November 1990 the 10 per cent surcharge was eliminated, reducing the average tariff further to 26 per cent. The standard deviation of the tariff structure dropped from the pre-reform level of 24 per cent to a post-reform level of 13 per cent.

The first measures were introduced gradually in line with the strategy to control inflation. Prices were expected to fall with increased competition in domestic markets. However, this did not happen initially for two reasons. The temporary surcharges provoked a speculative postponement of imports and the drop in incomes caused by the macroeconomic adjustment process significantly reduced the size of the domestic market. The reforms also faced resistance, especially in sectors producing for the domestic market, and specifically after publication of the tariff reduction timetable. Pressure from the private sector conditioned the changes in early 1991. An argument against intensifying the reform was the potentially adverse effect it could have on employment, particularly in manufacturing.

The change in the tariff structure reduced the overall level of effective protection, except in agriculture and in forestry and hunting. According to Escobal (1992), effective protection was negative for all sectors after accounting for lags in the exchange-rate adjustment.

During 1991–94, growth of consumer goods imports was spectacular, especially of consumer durables, as these increased by more than 100 per cent. Imports of raw materials and inputs went up by 30 per cent, whereas imports of capital goods (excluding transportation equipment) grew by less than 10

Table 10.1 Tariff level and structure, 1990–97

	1990				1991				1993	1997
	I	**II**	**III**	**IV**	**I**	**II**	**III**	**IV**	**Dec[2]**	**April**
1. Average tariff[1]	66	66	32	26	17	17	17	17	16	13
2. Standard deviation	25	25	17	13	4	4	4	4	3	3
3. Maximum tariff (w/o surcharge)	84	84	50	50	25	25	25	25	25	20
4. Maximum tariff (with surcharge)	110	110	60	50	25	25	25	25	25	25
5. Number of items with ad valorem rate										
a. From 0 per cent										
b. From (0, 10)	10	10	0	0	0	0	0	0	0	0
c. From (10, 20)	683	683	0	0	25	25	25	0	0	0
d. From (20, 30)	298	298	2,177	2,177	4,294	4,294	4,294	4,319	5,629	5,513
e. From (30, 40)	530	530	1,945	1,945	950	950	950	950	854	1,013
f. From (40, 50)	689	689	0	0	0	0	0	0	0	0
g. From (50, 60)	1,143	1,143	1,147	1,147	0	0	0	0	0	0
h. From (60, 70)	562	562	0	0	0	0	0	0	0	0
i. From (70, 80)	126	126	0	0	0	0	0	0	0	0
j. More than 80 per cent	285	285	0	0	0	0	0	0	0	0
TOTAL	940	940	0	0	0	0	0	0	0	0
	5,266	**5,266**	**5,269**	**5,269**	**5,269**	**5,269**	**5,269**	**5,269**	**6,483**	**6,526**

Notes:
1. Arithmetic average of nominal rate, including tariff surcharges.
2. Structure valid up to April 1997.

Source: Memoria Anual 1991, Banco Central de Reserva del Perú.

per cent (see Figure 10.2). According to Pascó Font (1998), the trend can be explained by a process of replacement of stocks of consumer goods among rich households and by the initiation of the process of industrial restructuring.

Mid-1995 there was a heated public debate among various economic interest groups whether a differential rate or a flat tariff should be established. The private sector strongly opposed a flat tariff because it objected to the lack of equity in the support to create competitive conditions between Peru and its trading partners in the Andean region and/or other countries. The government argued that past experiences of differential tariffs were inefficient as these favoured sectors without comparative advantages and generated corruption and tax-revenue losses. In the midst of this public debate the government agreed not to modify the tariff structure and a structure of 15 and 25 per cent was maintained until 1996.

In early 1997, the tariffs on items subject to 15 and 25 per cent were reduced to 12 and 20 per cent, respectively. The mean tariff fell from 16 to 13 per cent. The average effective protection rate dropped from 30.4 per cent in December 1990 to 14.4 per cent in April 1997. Even so, 65 items were transferred to the higher tariff rate (food products) and another 13 to the 12 per cent level (inputs for beer and food industries). As agricultural imports became subject to the higher rate (20 per cent), the effective protection rate for the agricultural sector increased to 15.5 per cent. These products were also subject to a 5 per cent surcharge and the proceeds were allocated to the support programme for the agricultural sector. The ban on used car imports was another change, which was interpreted by some sectors as a sign of policy reversal.

The main instrument of promotion of non-traditional exports, CERTEX,[4] was eliminated. In compensation, a tax rebate was authorized for exporters of non-traditional products.[5] Further export-promotion measures taken in 1991 included the elimination of all tariff-related restrictions on exports of goods and the removal of the legal obligation of exporters to submit foreign currency to the Central Bank. Starting in 1995, a drawback of 5 per cent of the FOB export value was introduced on all products with foreign sales of more than US$ 10 million.

The government did not take much serious action to promote non-traditional exports in the 1990s. Only in April 1996, the commission for export promotion (Prompex) was created as an autonomous state agency. With a limited budget, Prompex was to meet an ambitious agenda. Its tasks include to: enhance the supply of non-traditional export products as a function of the country's comparative advantages; search for new export markets with a growing demand, potential complementarity, options for international subcontracting and negotiation of bilateral or multilateral preferential tariffs;

facilitate and stimulate exports by formulating policies with an export bias; consolidate committees and consortia in priority sectors of small and medium-size businesses; and create an export mentality. In addition, the government created Centres for Transformation and Marketing (CETICOS). Under this system export firms would be exempted from all national and municipal taxes, duties or contributions during their first 15 years of operations.[6]

Export growth stagnated until 1993, but accelerated from 1994 onwards. The annual growth rate of exports was 19.3 per cent for traditional exports, especially copper, gold and fishmeal. The supply of the volume of exportable goods increased by 80 per cent between 1990 and 1997. In 1998, traditional exports decreased because of the El Niño phenomenon, which severely affected fishing and agricultural exports. Growth of non-traditional exports accelerated after 1993, reaching an average annual rate of 19.1 per cent. This growth came about in a context of greater diversification of exportable production and despite the exchange-rate appreciation. Despite the export growth, the trade deficit remained large and oscillated between 5.0 and 7.3 per cent of GDP (Figure 10.2). Despite the slight increase in the export share recently, the coefficient is still below that of the 1970s, when it increased strongly due to a positive price effect. The import share increased by almost 5 GDP points in the 1990s. It is important to note that the sum of the export and import

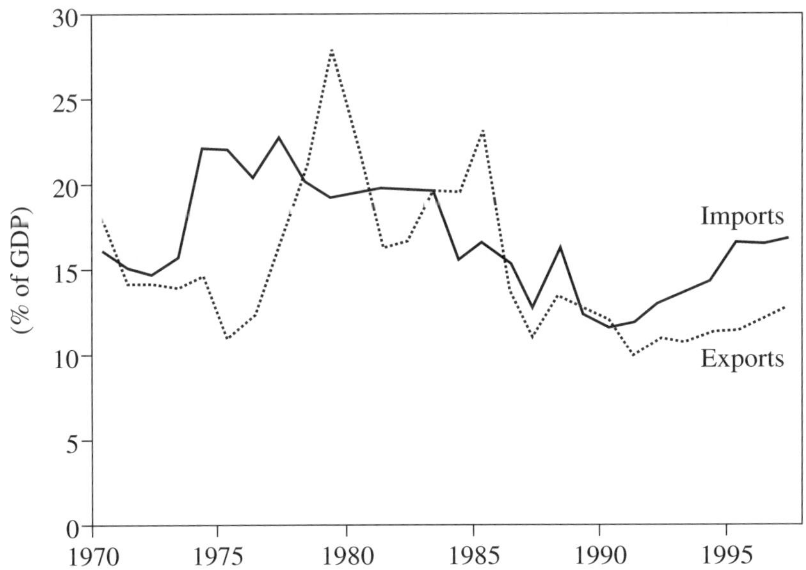

Figure 10.2 Export and import shares, 1970–97 (percentage of GDP)

shares is less than 30 per cent of GDP despite the reform measures toward trade opening and the observed export growth. In this sense, the Peruvian economy is much less open than other Latin American countries at the same level of development.

The Capital Account

As of 1991, residents and non-residents were free to open bank and portfolio accounts in Peru. This included permission to hold accounts in foreign currency. Giving equal rights to nationals and foreigners to operate financial institutions stimulated competition in the financial sector. The law on promotion of foreign investment allowed investors to enter any economic sector under any legal business form. Special facilities were created for foreign investors to pay taxes and the state was allowed to offer guarantees to acquisitions and investments. All of this was done in the context of an aggressive privatization process initiated in November 1991. As a result (shown in Figure 10.3), direct foreign investment grew from almost zero between 1988 and 1991 to an annual flow of more than US$ 1.5 billion since 1995. To this we should add US$ 4.8 billion in acquisitions by foreigners related to the privatization between 1993 and 1997. Long-term loans and the portfolio investment played a minor role in this surge in private external financing.

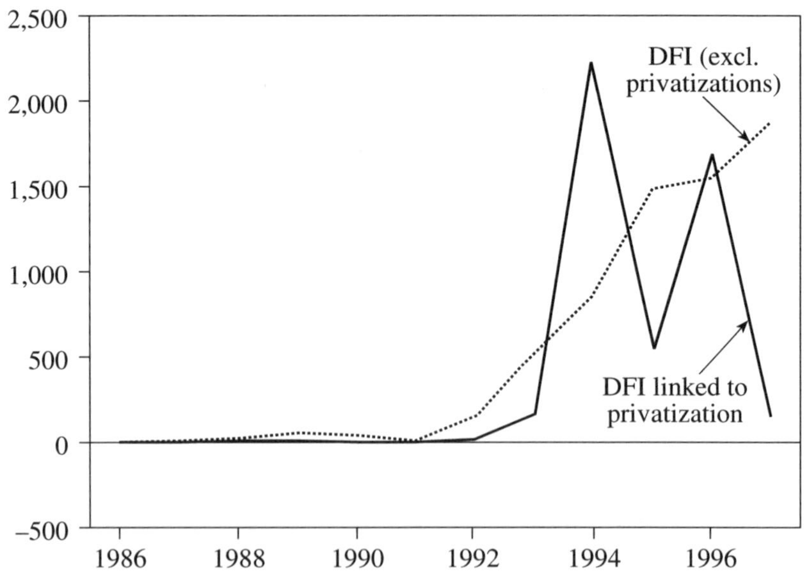

Figure 10.3 Direct foreign investment, 1986–97 (millions of US$)

Private capital inflows explain almost the entire surplus on capital account of the balance of payments, particularly between 1993 and 1996.[7]

Financial Liberalization

Financial liberalization aimed at the elimination of restrictions on access to financing, the development of the capital market and the reduction of transaction costs in financial operations. In 1990, new bank and stock exchange laws were passed. The role of state institutions in capital markets was redefined, including closure of the development banks, redefinition of the functions of the Banco de la Nación and COFIDE, and privatization or liquidation of branches of associated banking institutions. Interest rates were also liberalized,[8] the marginal reserve deposit requirement was gradually reduced and the public sector could no longer use domestic credits to finance its deficits.

Financial liberalization put an end to financial repression, under which regime interest rates were negative but the access to credit remained limited to only few borrowers and credit allocation was inefficient. From 1993 onwards, real lending rates turned positive. Nonetheless, credit to private enterprises increased and there was a modest growth of credit supplies to medium-sized enterprises.

Relative Price Adjustment

The trend in the real exchange rate is critical to the analysis of shifts in relative prices. This has to do with the difficulty of separating effects of the structural reforms from those derived from the macroeconomic stabilization process.[9] Edwards and Cox-Edwards (1995)[10] cite empirical evidence showing that one of the most important conditions in determining the success of a liberalization of external trade is to maintain a competitive real exchange rate. Real exchange-rate depreciation will induce a reallocation of resources toward the tradables sector, particularly toward export sectors. Rapid export growth will finance the import growth associated with the fall in the relative price of importables due to trade liberalization. In the case of Peru, even though the exchange rate did not depreciate sufficiently in the eyes of the exporters, at least it eliminated the strong anti-export bias caused by the policy of import-substituting industrialization.

Exchange-rate appreciation is seen to have been caused by the simultaneous liberalization of the current and capital account of the balance of payments, while Peru's country risk is seen to have been reduced as a result of political events. This generated substantial capital inflows leading to an increase in international reserves. This combination of factors inevitably led to a real exchange-rate appreciation. The Central Bank opted for a dirty float and

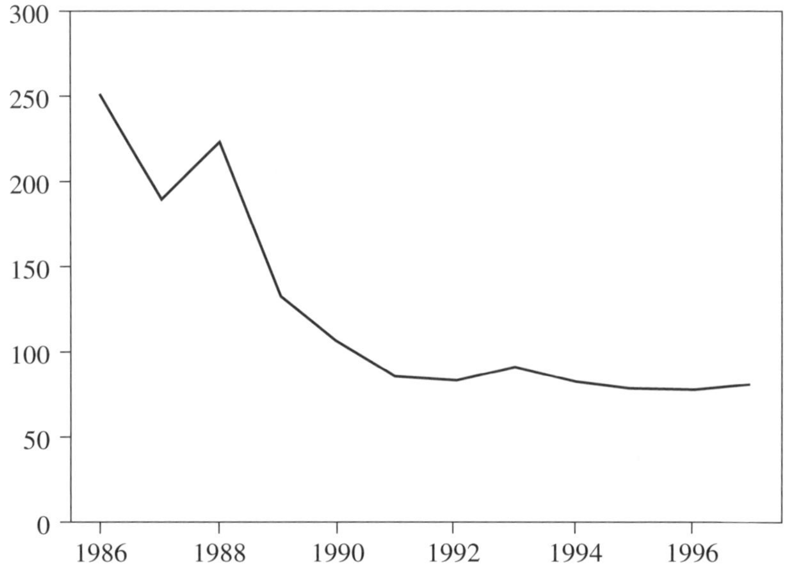

Figure 10.4 *Real bilateral exchange rate (average market price) (index, August 1990 = 100)*

intervened in the foreign exchange market in order to reduce the exchange-rate volatility, but such interventions did little to prevent the appreciation of the sol (Figure 10.4).

Generally speaking, relative prices moved closer to world market prices and the domestic economy dynamized its penetration in world markets. The realignment of the relative prices was also influenced by reforms in the non-traded goods market. Several state monopolies were liberalized and public transportation was deregulated. Together with the exchange-rate appreciation, which lagged behind domestic prices, this led to an increase of the relative price of non-tradable goods between 1992 and 1997.

10.3 CHANGES IN AGGREGATE DEMAND AND IN THE PRODUCTION STRUCTURE

The structural reforms had a strong impact on the structure of relative prices of the economy and thus on aggregate demand and the production structure. As indicated, from 1992 onwards, the economy started to expand as a result of the reduction of the inflation tax, the elimination of distortions in relative prices, and general greater economic and social stability. After dropping 1.8

per cent during 1992, in the two following years GDP expanded by 5.6 and 13.0 per cent. Growth of consumption and investment in an open economy with a smaller public sector and much less distortions to foreign trade will lead to a greater demand for tradable goods and thus to a trade deficit. In the non-tradable sector, increased demand will induce an increase in the relative price of non-traded goods and an output increase.

Sources of Aggregate Demand Growth

The decomposition exercise of aggregate demand is based on the methodology explained in Chapter 1 and assumes a short-run Keynesian model. Defining aggregate demand as X, we can decompose its growth rate disaggregating total investment into private and public components. We thus obtain:

$$X^* = \Delta I_{pub}\frac{\alpha_0}{\gamma X_0} + \Delta I_{priv}\frac{\alpha_0}{\gamma X_0} + \Delta G\frac{\alpha_0}{\gamma X_0} + \Delta E\frac{\alpha_0}{\gamma X_0} - \Delta s\frac{A_0}{\gamma X_0} - \Delta t\frac{A_0}{\gamma X_0} - \Delta m\frac{A_0}{\gamma X_0}$$

where I is investment, G government expenditure, E exports, s the propensity to save, t the average tax rate and m the propensity to import. Please note that α_0 is the sum of all leakages in the base year ($= s_0 + t_0 + m_0$), A_0 is the sum of exogenous demand components ($= I_0 + G_0 + E_0$) and $\gamma = \alpha_0(s_0 + t_0 + m_0)$. The first four terms include the demand growth originating from the change in each expenditure component, whereas the last three terms show the growth of aggregate demand originating from the multiplier effects of change of each component of the expenditure multiplier. For each component we construct a time series for the period 1971–98 and estimate the contribution to the change in aggregate demand as a percentage. Aggregate demand effects induced by private, public and external sectors can be identified as follows:

$$X^* = \underbrace{\Delta I_{priv}\frac{\alpha_0}{\gamma X_0} - \Delta s\frac{A_0}{\gamma X_0}}_{\textbf{Private sector}} \overbrace{+ \Delta I_{pub}\frac{\alpha_0}{\gamma X_0} + \Delta G\frac{\alpha_0}{\gamma X_0}}^{\textbf{Public sector}} \underbrace{- \Delta t\frac{A_0}{\gamma X_0} + \Delta E\frac{\alpha_0}{\gamma X_0} - \Delta m\frac{A_0}{\gamma X_0}}_{\textbf{External sector}}$$

The decomposition was done for 1971–98, in order to be able to clearly differentiate the 1990s from previous decades (Table 10.2).[11] During the pre-1990s economic boom, demand growth was driven by private demand, while public spending behaved pro-cyclically. This changed in 1990, when the public sector stopped being an important element in determining the changes in aggregate demand. Changes in demand growth during the 1990s related most strongly to trends in private consumption and investment and to a lesser degree to external demand. The 1990s also seem to mark a major break in the

Table 10.2 Decomposition of aggregate demand growth, 1971–97

	Private sector			Public sector				External sector			
	Savings	Investment	**Private sector**	Investment	Taxes	Current expenditures	**Public sector**	Exports	Imports	**External sector**	**Aggregate demand**
1971–76	0.9	2.5	**3.4**	1.6	0.8	1.2	**3.6**	–0.8	–1.1	**–1.9**	5.1
1977–80	–6.1	4.7	**–1.5**	–0.3	–1.1	0.0	**–1.5**	6.6	0.3	**6.9**	4.0
1981–85	2.1	–3.8	**–1.7**	0.0	0.4	–0.3	**0.1**	1.0	1.1	**2.1**	0.5
1986–90	3.0	–0.3	**2.7**	–1.7	2.1	–1.7	**–1.3**	–5.3	1.9	**–3.4**	–1.9
1991–97	0.1	5.0	**5.1**	0.9	–1.5	1.7	**1.1**	1.0	–1.6	**–0.6**	5.6
Boom periods	–1.4	5.9	**4.5**	1.0	0.5	1.6	**3.1**	–0.3	–0.3	**–0.0**	7.6
Recessions	2.7	–7.2	**–4.6**	–1.2	–0.5	–3.1	**–4.7**	1.2	0.9	**2.1**	–7.2
1971–80	–1.9	3.4	**1.5**	0.9	0.0	0.7	**1.6**	2.2	–0.6	**1.6**	4.7
1981–90	2.6	–2.1	**0.5**	–0.8	1.3	–1.0	**–0.6**	–2.2	1.5	**–0.7**	–0.7
1991–97	0.1	5.0	**5.1**	0.9	–1.5	1.7	**1.1**	1.0	–1.6	**–0.6**	5.6

Note: The boom periods are those in which aggregate demand growth was greater than 2 per cent, recession periods those with negative growth.

Source: BCRP Memorias, various years 1979–98.

state's role in the economy. Until 1991, the state was crucial in determining the macroeconomic fluctuations, wages and production of several sectors of the economy. Consequently, the demand generated by public investment and consumption (net of tax leakages) was crucial in the growth periods 1972–74, 1980–81, 1986–87 and in 1995. However, in all these cases government-induced demand growth proved to be unsustainable. Stabilization policies were typically postponed but were required in years following public spending booms. This is the case for 1978–79, 1984–85, 1990 and 1996. The state's retreat from production activities and the reduction of public expenditure fluctuations in the 1990s is reflected in a smaller impact of government spending on aggregate demand growth. The role of private sector spending becomes commensurately larger in this period. The propensity to import increased in the 1990s, returning to a level similar to the 1970s.

The external sector played an important but erratic role in determining aggregate demand fluctuations. The only regularity seems to be that external trade adjustment, caused by increases in world market prices of traditional exports, was instrumental in overcoming the crisis. For example, in the periods 1977–79 and 1984–85 such commodity price booms facilitated an increase (or a smaller reduction) in demand. In the period following the liberalization of foreign trade, the external sector does not seem to play an important role as an impulse or leakage of aggregate demand. The propensity to import increased in the 1990s, but export growth offset this negative effect on aggregate demand growth.

Analysis of the boom and recession periods reveals that public and private sector demand always moved in the same direction. Besides, no countercyclical role of fiscal policy can be observed. The external sector offset the negative effects of contraction of public and private spending during the recessions, but did not generate a major impulse to demand growth during expansive cycles.

Structural Change

The increase in the relative price of non-tradable goods and services and the drop in the price of importables, also reflected in the real exchange-rate appreciation, provoked a restructuring of the production apparatus. Manufacturing industry was the sector most sensitive to liberalization. Several manufacturing branches, such as the production of transport equipment (mainly assembly), domestic appliances and some metallurgic branches completely disappeared. Other manufacturing branches took advantage of their existing domestic distribution channels and turned into importers of the goods they used to produce as they lost competitive edge after liberalization. This happened to some branches in plastics, chemical and pharmaceutical products.

Other branches, such as shoemaking, changed product type and switched production toward lower-quality goods. Manufacturing output and employment declined during the first two years after liberalization (Saavedra 1996a, b). However, by 1994 it had already recovered to pre-reform production and employment levels. As Figure 10.4 shows, the share of manufacturing in GDP stabilized around 22 per cent during the 1990s. In effect, its share in total output fell by less than one percentage point (mainly because of the contraction in the capital goods sector).

In general, non-traded goods sectors, like construction, personal services, commerce and transportation, were able to recover quickly and their production was competitive enough to satisfy the increasing demand from 1993 onwards. Surprisingly, in the aggregate, the structural changes in production in the post-reform period have been far from dramatic (see Table 10.3). Rather, one observes a continuation of long-term trends in which manufacturing and agriculture are losing ground. Only the government services sector reduced its share as a direct consequence of the reforms.

Table 10.3 GDP by economic activity, 1986–97 (in percentages and millions of new soles of 1979)

	1986	**1990**	**1992**	**1995**	**1997**
Total GDP	3,904	3,244	3,287	4,243	4,662
Sectoral production	100.0%	100.0%	100.0%	100.0%	100.0%
Agriculture and fishing	12.1%	14.7%	13.8%	14.3%	14.2%
Mining	11.1%	9.6%	9.4%	8.3%	8.1%
Manufacturing industries	23.1%	22.1%	22.6%	22.7%	22.5%
Electricity, gas & water	1.2%	1.6%	1.7%	1.6%	1.7%
Construction	5.1%	5.9%	6.2%	8.5%	8.7%
Commerce, restaurants & hotels	18.1%	17.4%	17.1%	17.7%	17.9%
Transport & communications	6.6%	7.1%	7.3%	7.1%	7.4%
Finance & other business services	8.3%	9.4%	9.4%	7.9%	8.0%
Other services	6.8%	5.7%	6.3%	6.6%	6.4%
Public administration & defence	7.7%	6.7%	6.2%	5.3%	5.1%
Tradable sectors	46.2%	46.3%	45.9%	45.4%	44.8%
Non-tradable sectors	53.8%	53.7%	54.1%	54.6%	55.2%

Source: Banco Central de Reserva del Perú.

10.4 EVOLUTION OF THE LABOUR MARKET BEFORE AND AFTER LIBERALIZATION[12]

One of the main criticisms of the structural reform process was that these reforms would have a strong negative impact on employment and living conditions, particularly those of the poor. In practice, the major problems affecting Peruvians, inflation and terrorism, were put to an end toward the mid-1990s, several years after the start of the reforms. Opinion polls indicate that unemployment and 'lack of employment' had become the number one problems in the minds of the people (Saavedra 1998). Recent trends in urban employment show two different episodes. Between 1986 and 1992, total employment (occupied labour force) grew at an average annual rate of only 1.3 per cent (see Figure 10.5). Total employment did not vary much, despite the macroeconomic volatility caused by the populist boom of Alan García's government in 1987, followed by an inevitable recession during the period of hyperinflation (1988–90) and the subsequent recession caused by the stabilization programme (1990–92). Job creation accelerated from 1992 onwards. During 1992–98 employment expanded at an average annual growth rate of 5.3 per cent.

Employment trends by sector show that financial services, business services, transportation and commerce were the most dynamic activities during 1992–98 in the Metropolitan Area of Lima (see Table 10.4). Employment in

Figure 10.5 Lima Metropolitana: total employment and output growth

Table 10.4 Lima Metropolitana: sectoral distribution of employment, 1986–97

	1986–89	1991	1997
Total	**100.0**	**100.0**	**100.0**
Agriculture, hunting and fishing	1.1	0.8	1.2
Exploitation of mines and quarries	0.7	0.3	0.2
Manufacturing industry	21.7	17.2	16.1
Subtotal	*23.5*	*18.4*	*17.5*
Electricity, gas and water	0.5	0.5	0.3
Construction, restaurants/hotels	5.4	5.7	6.3
Wholesale and retail	29.9	33.7	35.8
Transportation and communications	6.6	6.9	9.0
Subtotal	*42.3*	*46.8*	*51.3*
Finance and business services	5.0	6.1	9.2
Personal and social services	23.2	23.9	18.3
Public administration	6.1	4.8	3.6
Subtotal	*34.3*	*34.8*	*31.2*

Source: 1986–95 MTPS Household Survey, 1996–98 INEI National Household Survey.

other services, such as non-personal services, consulting and so on, as well as construction, moved around the mean trend, whereas manufacturing and public administration showed much less dynamics.

This dynamics of job creation and losses – excluding agricultural and mining which are marginal in terms of employment in Lima – led to a decrease in the employment shares of manufacturing, personal and social services and public administration, in favour of employment in commerce, transportation and financial services. Manufacturing employment dropped to 16 per cent in 1997, down from 22 per cent of total employment in 1986–89. The share of personal services decreased from 23 to 18 per cent between 1992 and 1997.

Reducing the number of public employees through a scheme of economic incentives was an important element of the structural reform package of 1991. The incentives consisted of lump-sum cash transfers and improvements in employees' pension benefits. Even though many ministries and public institutions underwent strong reductions in personnel, the aggregate effect of the incentives was less than expected. Public employment at the national level fell by approximately 12 per cent between 1990 and 1993, despite the massive layoffs with the central government where employment dropped by 45 per cent. The offsetting effect came from strong employment growth in regional governments. Employment with local governments went up by 142 per cent, thus increasing the share in public employment from 16 to 44 per cent between 1990 and 1993. For Lima Metropolitana, public administration decreased steadily during the entire 1990s. Consequently, the sector's share in total employment dropped from 6.1 per cent during 1986–89 to 3.6 per cent in 1997. This trend reflects the reduction in central government employment and the disappearance of many public institutions established during the 1980s.

Commerce increased its share from 30 per cent in the late 1980s to 36 per cent in 1997. The employment share of financial services went up by almost five points and that of construction and transportation increased by one and three points, respectively.

Labour Participation, Unemployment and the Employment–Population Ratio

Participation rates in Lima Metropolitana behaved pro-cyclically with respect to GDP (see Figure 10.6). Two periods can be distinguished. In the first period (1986–92), output growth fell by 3.9 per cent per year, whereas the participation rate decreased by 1 per cent per year. As a consequence, the participation rate dropped from 0.60 in 1986–89 to 0.57 in 1992. As shown in

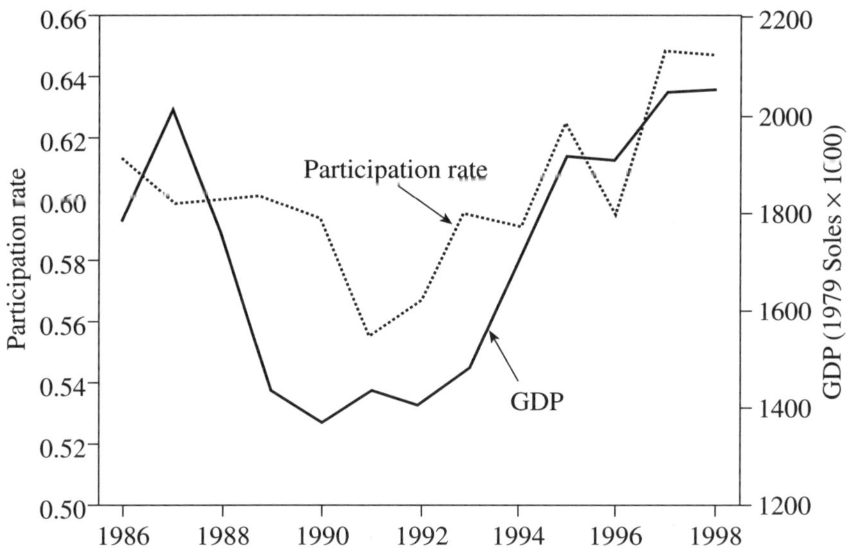

Figure 10.6 Lima Metropolitana: labour participation and output growth

Table 10.5 *Lima Metropolitana: participation rate by demographic groups, 1986–97*

	Participation rate			Annual percentage change		
	1986–89	**1992**	**1997**	**1992/86**	**1997/92**	**1997/86**
Total	**0.603**	**0.567**	**0.648**	**–1.04**	**2.72**	**0.65**
Gender						
Male	0.472	0.421	0.536	–1.92	4.96	1.15
Female	0.746	0.727	0.776	–0.42	1.31	0.37
Age						
14–30	0.535	0.498	0.614	–1.21	4.29	1.25
31–45	0.781	0.749	0.811	–0.70	1.61	0.34
46+	0.549	0.491	0.553	–1.84	2.41	0.07
Educational level						
Primary or lower	0.596	0.536	0.583	–1.76	1.71	–0.20
Secondary	0.571	0.546	0.627	–0.75	2.81	0.85
Higher	0.697	0.648	0.737	–1.20	2.59	0.50
Groups						
Young women, LE	0.559	0.541	0.554	–0.54	0.46	–0.09
Young women, SE	0.435	0.374	0.507	–2.46	6.25	1.41
Young women, HE	0.571	0.510	0.666	–1.86	5.48	1.41
Older women, LE	0.429	0.382	0.482	–1.94	4.79	1.06
Older women, SE	0.452	0.412	0.527	–1.53	5.05	1.41
Older women, HE	0.617	0.506	0.553	–3.26	1.79	–1.00
Young men, LE	0.842	0.738	0.755	–2.17	0.45	–0.99
Young men, SE	0.629	0.637	0.700	0.21	1.90	0.97
Young men, HE	0.718	0.680	0.814	–0.89	3.66	1.15
Older men, LE	0.802	0.749	0.738	–1.12	–0.31	–0.75
Older men, SE	0.884	0.839	0.841	–0.87	0.05	–0.46
Older men, HE	0.894	0.876	0.886	–0.32	0.21	–0.08

Note: LE = lower education, SE = secondary education, HE = higher education, university or other.

Source: 1986–1995 MTPS Household Survey, 1996–1998 INEI National Household Survey.

Table 10.5, it appears that this trend is explained basically by women exiting the labour force, especially younger (ages 14–30) and older (45+) women or women with either primary or university level education. This may be explained by the discouraged-worker hypothesis, which states that in periods of reduced income and employment possibilities, discouraged workers decide not to participate in the labour market. For men, the participation rate decreased slightly by 0.4 per cent per year, essentially due to a dropout of men with primary education. Labour participation among this demographic group continued to decline throughout the entire 1986–97 period.

In the second period (1992–97), output levels recovered and GDP grew at a 7.2 per cent annual rate and the participation rate increased at an average 2.3 per cent annual rate, partly as a reaction to the increase in labour demand. This increase was also explained by a rising trend in the female participation rate (at 4.1 per cent per year). Higher-educated women experienced the largest participation rate increase. Their participation rate surpassed that of 1986 by the end of the 1990s, thereby making up the ground lost in the late 1980s.

How did the Peruvian labour market absorb this increase in labour supply and what employment restructuring took place after the structural reforms of the early 1990s?[13] Figure 10.7 shows the decomposition of the changes in the participation rate into two components: changes in the unemployment rate and changes in the employment rate (the ratio of employed to population). In the 1980s, labour participation dropped slightly, due to a decline in both the employment and unemployment rate. In the 1990s, labour participation increased, resulting initially in rising unemployment. From 1993 onwards, the labour supply growth was largely absorbed by a rise in the employment rate.

On balance, unemployment increased in the 1990s. The unemployment rate started to increase in 1987, rising from 6.2 per cent in 1986–89 to 9.5 per cent in 1992, to drop slightly to 9.0 per cent in 1997. Rising unemployment has hurt mainly less educated and older male workers (see Table 10.6).

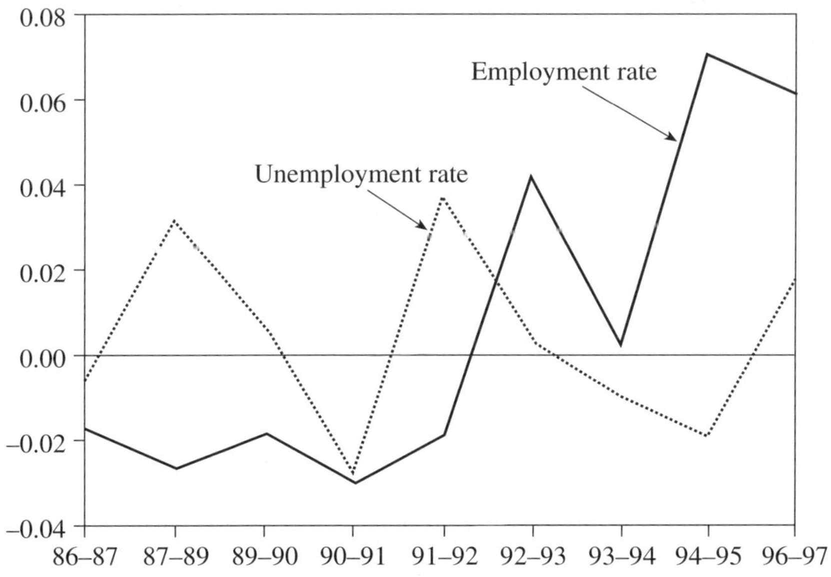

Figure 10.7 Lima Metropolitana: decomposition of labour supply growth, 1986–97

Table 10.6 Lima Metropolitana: unemployment rate by demographic groups, 1986–97

	Unemployment			Annual percentage change		
	1986–89	**1992**	**1997**	**1992/86**	**1997/92**	**1997/86**
Total	**6.2**	**9.5**	**9.0**	**7.5**	**–1.2**	**3.4**
Gender						
Male	8.6	12.7	11.3	6.6	–2.4	2.4
Female	4.5	7.6	7.2	8.9	–1.0	4.3
Age						
14–30	9.9	13.4	12.0	5.2	–2.3	1.7
31–45	3.3	6.3	6.2	11.3	–0.5	5.8
46+	2.7	7.4	7.1	18.2	–0.9	9.1
Educational level						
Primary or lower	3.8	8.0	8.1	13.4	–0.1	7.1
Secondary	7.7	10.2	10.8	4.9	1.2	3.2
Higher	5.4	9.4	6.4	9.8	–7.3	1.7
Groups						
Young women, LE	7.0	12.9	7.3	10.7	–10.7	0.4
Young women, SE	12.5	15.3	16.9	3.4	2.0	2.8
Young women, HE	11.2	18.5	8.5	8.7	–14.5	–2.5
Older women, LE	3.5	7.8	7.3	14.3	–1.3	6.9
Older women, SE	6.0	10.7	11.7	10.2	1.8	6.3
Older women, HE	3.1	6.0	6.4	11.6	1.1	6.7
Young men, LE	6.3	6.0	14.0	–0.8	18.5	7.6
Young men, SE	7.6	10.7	10.2	5.7	–0.9	2.7
Young men, HE	4.5	8.8	6.6	11.7	–5.6	3.5
Older men, LE	1.8	6.6	7.7	23.8	3.4	14.1
Older men, SE	2.7	4.6	3.4	9.8	–6.3	2.2
Older men, HE	1.7	4.7	4.7	18.3	–0.2	9.5

Note: LE = lower education, SE = secondary education, HE = higher education, university or other.

Source: 1986–1995 MTPS Household Survey, 1996–1998 INEI National Household Survey.

The employment rate, i.e. the ratio of total employment with respect to the working-age population, fell steeply between 1986 and 1992. Employment growth was very weak until 1992, while the working-age population increased at a rate of 2.7 per cent per year. This population growth did not lead to high unemployment rates as labour participation declined. The economically active population contracted even during 1990–92 because of the exit of women from the labour market and fewer young workers entering. This changed in 1993 when labour force growth accelerated, exceeding the growth of the population in working age. As a consequence, the employment rate increased in the 1990s.

Saavedra (1998) provides evidence that shows that 65 per cent of the reduction in the employment rate during 1986–92 can be explained by the decline in labour participation. The remainder is explained by the increase in unemployment rates. This pattern is found for all demographic groups, although among women the reduction in participation rates appears more important in explaining the drop in relative employment levels. The situation changed in 1992, when participation rates started to increase and unemployment rates decreased. Employment went up for all groups. This can be explained mainly by the rise in labour participation (65 per cent) and the reduction in unemployment (35 per cent).

The share of female employment went up for all groups, including for young and older women, mainly due to the increase in the participation rate. The male employment structure shows much less volatility than that of women. Male employment also recovered for all types of workers. However, for older men the recovery fell short of the initial drop in the employment rate. This is fully explained by a fall in labour participation for this group of workers.

Real Incomes

According to Saavedra (1999), wage flexibility has been one of the main adjustment mechanisms of the Peruvian labour market. As shown by Figure 10.8 and Table 10.7, the average real wage fell dramatically during 1987–90.

Figure 10.8 Lima Metropolitana: labour income and GDP growth, 1986–97

Table 10.7 Lima Metropolitana: real monthly labour income per demographic groups, 1986–97

	Real monthly income			Annual percentage change			Relative income		
	1986–89	1992	1997	1992/86	1997/92	1997/86	1986/89	1997	change 1997/86
Total	687	475	557	–6.0	3.3	–1.9	100	100	–
Gender									
Male	430	323	369	–4.6	2.7	–1.4	63	66	5.8
Female	850	562	690	–6.7	4.2	–1.9	124	124	0.1
Age									
14–30	487	346	436	–5.6	4.7	–1.0	71	78	10.3
31–45	806	555	669	–6.0	3.8	–1.7	117	120	2.4
46+	877	567	610	–7.0	1.5	–3.2	128	109	–14.3
Educational level									
Primary or lower	488	301	294	–7.7	–0.5	–4.5	71	53	–25.7
Secondary	609	392	423	–7.1	1.6	–3.3	89	76	–14.4
Higher	1,040	784	917	–4.6	3.2	–1.1	151	165	8.6

Groups									
Young women, LE	230	207	176	–1.7	–3.3	–2.4	33	32	–5.9
Young women, SE	364	248	300	–6.2	3.8	–1.8	53	54	1.3
Young women, HE	549	439	494	–3.7	2.4	–1.0	80	89	10.9
Older women, LE	357	230	209	–7.1	–1.9	–4.8	52	38	–27.8
Older women, SE	517	342	327	–6.7	–0.9	–4.1	75	59	–22.0
Older women, HE	784	672	739	–2.6	1.9	–0.5	114	133	16.1
Young men, LE	537	303	317	–9.1	0.9	–4.7	78	57	–27.4
Young men, SE	554	389	442	–5.7	2.6	–2.0	81	79	–1.6
Young men, HE	911	626	863	–6.1	6.6	–0.5	133	155	16.8
Older men, LE	674	402	419	–8.3	0.9	–4.2	98	75	–23.3
Older men, SE	963	520	570	–9.8	1.9	–4.7	140	102	–27.0
Older men, HE	1,693	1,185	1,364	–5.8	2.9	–1.9	246	245	–0.7

Note: LE = lower education, SE = secondary education, HE = higher education, university or other.

Source: 1986–1995 MTPS Household Survey, 1996–1998 INEI National Household Survey.

The decline is explained by the process of hyperinflation and the severe recession of the late 1980s caused by the cost of financing the artificial economic expansion of 1986–87.

The decline in real labour income of 6 per cent between 1986–89 and 1992 mainly affected male workers (–6.7 per cent), workers older than 46 years (–7 per cent), and those with primary education or less (–7.7 per cent) and secondary education (–7.1 per cent) (see Table 10.7). The strong income fall and the decline in the participation rate reduction explain the absence of a drastic rise in unemployment along with the drop in GDP and labour demand during the period.

This pattern changed in 1992. Monthly incomes increased at an annual rate of 3.3 per cent between 1992 and 1997. Female workers benefited most as their income growth averaged 6.1 per cent per year, along with highly skilled workers, whose incomes grew by 5.1 per cent. Further disaggregation shows that highly-educated women and young men were the winners during the 1990s. Older as well as unskilled workers witnessed some income recovery, but less than the income losses they had suffered in the previous period.

Real income trends mainly adjusted to labour demand and supply during the 1990s. Institutional wage setting stopped playing an important role. First, minimum wages were frozen in nominal terms between 1991 and 1995. Second, the bargaining power of trade unions practically vanished due to the elimination of collective wage bargaining at the sector level and the prohibition of wage-indexation mechanisms in private contracting. These measures radically changed wage determination in the formal sector and also influenced formal employment.

In the 1990s, productivity increases allowed for a rise in earnings despite the labour supply growth. Saavedra (1997) estimates that labour productivity per worker increased by 15 percent (11 percent if measured per worker/per hour) between 1990–93 and 1994–96. This productivity increase is in the order of magnitude of the observed rise in real hourly incomes in this period.

Income recovery in the 1990s was insufficient to compensate for the losses of the late 1980s. Mean labour income fell by 1.9 per cent per year between 1986 and 1997. The remuneration structure shifted in favour of women and young male workers with a higher education between 1986–89 (before the reform) and 1997 (post-reform). Unskilled workers were the main losers. More specifically, all male workers, except if highly educated and young, experienced a reduction of relative income, particularly those older than 36 years of age.

At the sector level, but excluding agriculture and mining, workers in construction, commerce and transportation suffered the strongest income losses. Their average incomes fell at an annual rate of –2.9 per cent between 1986–89 and 1997, while their employment share increased by almost 10 points

Table 10.8 Lima Metropolitana: real monthly earnings by economic sector, 1986–97

	Real monthly income			Annual percentage change		
	1986–89	**1992**	**1997**	**1992/86**	**1997/92**	**1997/86**
Total	687	475	557	–6.0	3.2	–1.9
Agriculture, hunting and fishing	792	719	405	–1.6	–10.9	–5.9
Exploitation of mines and quarries	1,628	2,038	2,964	3.8	7.8	5.6
Manufacturing industry	711	505	543	–5.5	1.5	–2.4
Subtotal	742	543	565	–5.1	0.8	–2.5
Electricity, gas and water	1,081	744	1,526	–6.0	15.4	3.2
Construction, restaurants/hotels	682	482	565	–5.6	3.2	–1.7
Wholesale and retail trade	622	408	425	–6.8	0.8	–3.4
Transportation and communications	956	640	673	–6.5	1.0	–3.1
Subtotal	692	457	498	–6.7	1.7	–2.9
Finance and business services	1,097	701	927	–7.2	5.8	–1.5
Personal and social services	518	399	457	–4.2	2.8	–1.1
Public administration	754	474	869	–7.4	12.9	1.3
Subtotal	645	462	642	–5.4	6.8	–0.0

Source: 1986–1995 MTPS Household Survey, 1996–1998 INEI National Household Survey.

(see Table 10.8). Labour incomes for workers in manufacturing fell by 2.4 per cent per year. Workers in financial, personal and government services witnessed the smallest income declines.

Returns to Education

As we have seen, relative earnings moved in favour of skilled workers. Figure 10.9 shows that there has been an increase in returns to education since 1991, except for 1996. Rising returns in part result from the recovery from drastic cuts in labour incomes in the period prior to 1991. Following Saavedra (1996a, b) and Díaz (1999), the trend can be further explained by the shift in labour demand toward more skilled workers. In most production sectors both employment and relative remuneration shifted in favour of skilled labour. This shift in labour demand can largely be explained by the decline in the relative price of capital caused by the trade liberalization and the real exchange-rate appreciation in the post-reform period and by the complementarity of capital and skilled labour in the adoption of new technologies.

Table 10.9 shows econometric estimates of the premium to education, as revealed by the trends in earnings by educational level.[14] The estimates of the coefficients indicate a falling educational premium between 1986 and 1993 and a rising premium between 1993 and 1997. In 1986, the premium for

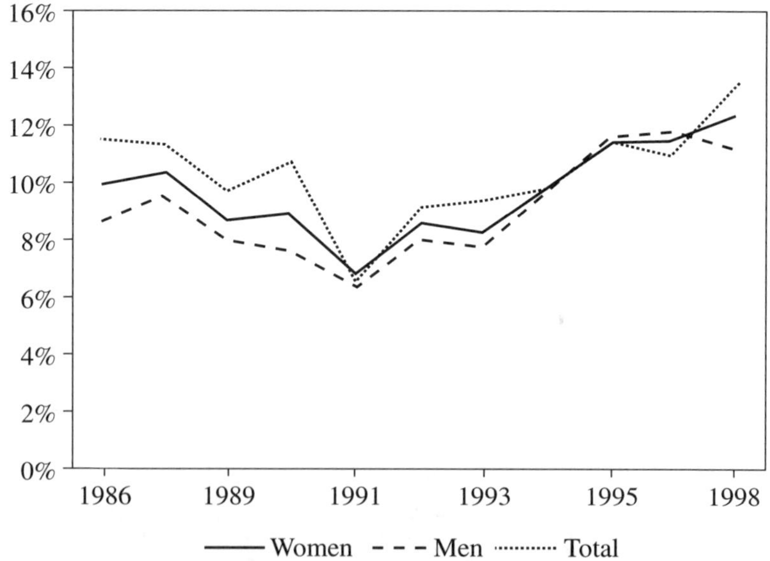

Figure 10.9 Lima Metropolitana: returns to education, 1986–98

Table 10.9 Lima Metropolitana: premium to education for female and male workers, 1986–97

	1986	1989	1991	1993	1995	1997
Women						
PE/SE	–0.136	0.322	0.218	-0.036	0.049	0.223
	[1.07]	[1.90]*	[1.26]	[0.26]	[0.32]	[0.99]
SE/PE	0.597	0.444	0.162	0.406	0.43	0.421
	[7.59]***	[5.41]***	[1.94]*	[5.00]***	[6.36]***	[5.54]***
HE/SE	0.696	0.601	0.437	0.58	0.713	0.662
	[10.60]***	[8.56]***	[6.08]***	[9.75]***	[13.52]***	[10.78]***
Men						
PE/SE	0.277	0.304	-0.041	0.098	1.061	0.12
	[2.24]**	[2.18]**	[0.13]	[0.50]	[4.50]***	[0.30]
SE/PE	0.304	0.207	0.178	0.231	0.298	0.219
	[5.98]***	[3.43]***	[2.52]**	[3.81]***	[5.37]***	[2.76]***
HE/SE	0.598	0.567	0.466	0.455	0.644	0.742
	[13.65]***	[12.09]***	[10.00]***	[10.85]	[16.55]***	[15.20]***

Notes: *t*-Statistics are in parentheses. Significance: * $p \leq 0.10$, ** $p \leq 0.05$, *** $p \leq 0.01$ Abbreviations: NE = no education, PE = primary education, SE = secondary education, HE = higher education.

Source: 1986–1995 MTPS Household Survey, 1996–1998 INEI National Household Survey.

female workers with a secondary education was 60 per cent relative to those with only primary education. Those with higher education earned 70 per cent more than those with a secondary education. For men, these premiums were 30 and 60 per cent, respectively. In the early 1990s, the income differentials by educational level dropped. The premium for female workers with secondary education dropped to 40 per cent and for those with higher education to 58 per cent. These premiums dropped to 23 and 46 per cent, respectively, for male workers. Between 1993 and 1997, returns to education increased. For example, the premium on higher education increased to 66 per cent for women and 74 per cent for men. The returns to secondary education show a growing but fluctuating trend during this period.

Saavedra and Díaz (1999) find that the premium on work experience declined almost continuously since 1986. This trend is consistent with a reduction of the relative incomes of older workers.[15] As shown in Figure 10.10, the monthly earnings gap between men and women increased in the 1990s, albeit showing some volatility. This trend is less pronounced when comparing hourly earnings differentials.

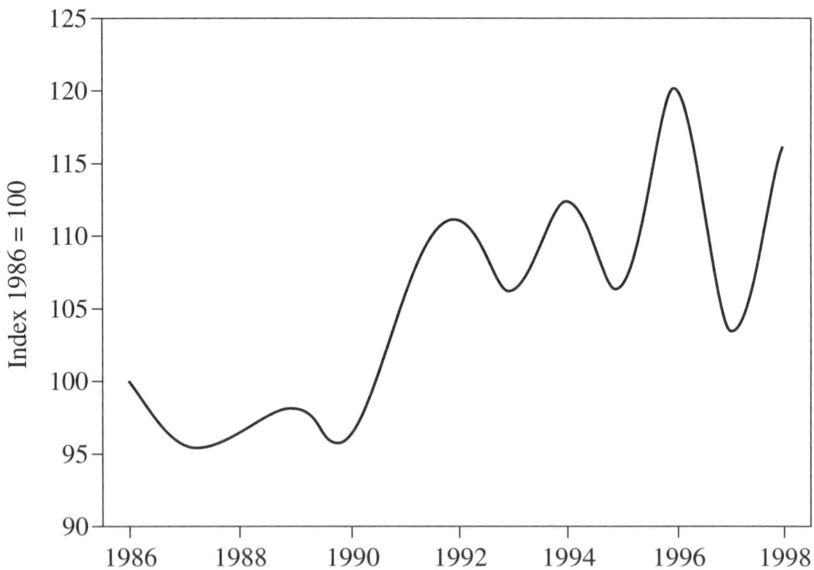

Figure 10.10 Lima Metropolitana: earnings gap between male and female workers

10.5 INEQUALITY AND ECONOMIC LIBERALIZATION

Labour income studies of urban areas in Peru show a slight reduction in income inequality in the post-reform period until 1996 (Saavedra and Díaz 1999). For Lima Metropolitana we find that the concentration of income decreased between 1985 and 1992 *or* 1994, depending on the data source (i.e. the National Household Survey or the National Living Standards Survey; see Figure 10.11). After that, labour income inequality increased. This trend seems consistent with the evolution of the returns to education. However, inequality measured in terms of per capita household labour income has shown a rising trend since 1987. The difference in the trend in per worker labour income and that of household labour income is a reflection of changes in employment composition of households by sex and age along the distribution of income. Inequality in labour earnings increased both at the level of households and individual workers in the second half of the 1990s, several years after the start of the reform process. It is not clear whether the degree of inequality is higher than that of the mid-1980s.

Poverty and underemployment move pro-cyclically (Figure 10.12). Both indicators fell in 1987 as a product of the populist boom induced by the García government, but doubled during the subsequent recession and

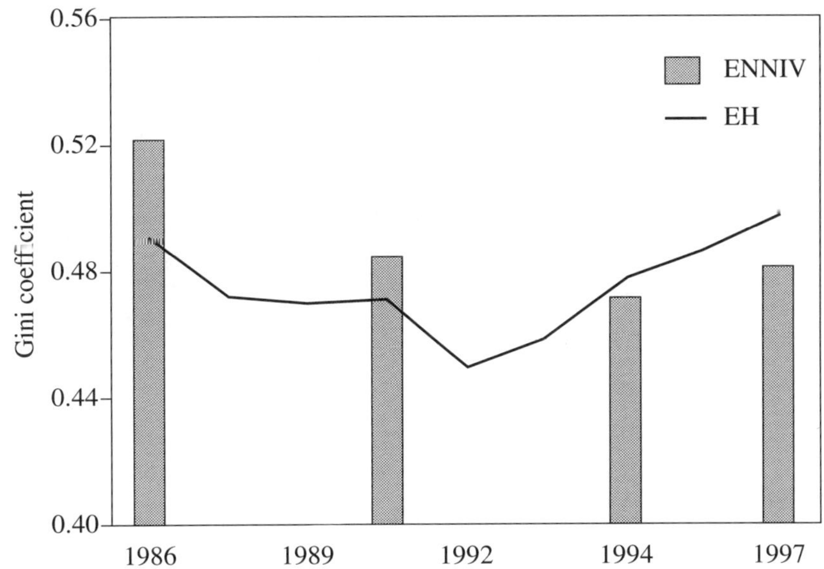

Figure 10.11 Lima Metropolitana: labour income inequality (Gini), 1986–97

Figure 10.12 Lima Metropolitana: labour income inequality (Gini) and invisible underemployment, 1986–97

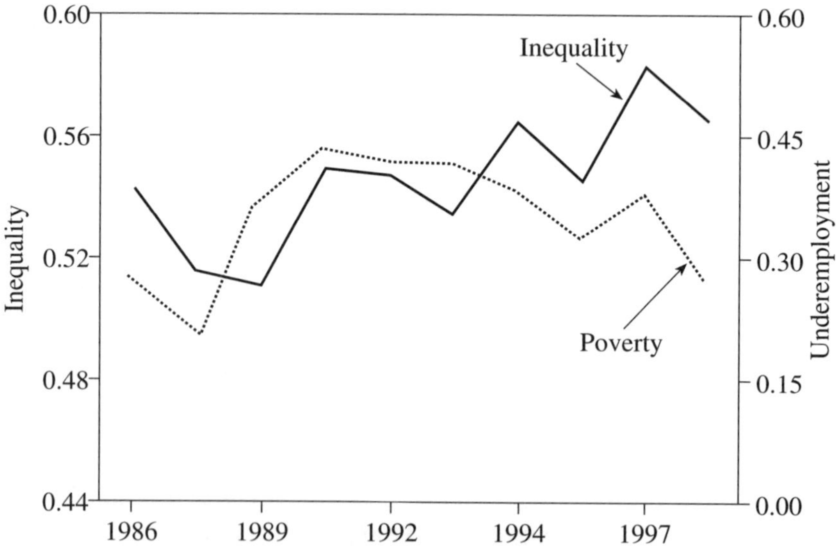

Figure 10.13 Lima Metropolitana: per capita household labour income inequality (Gini) and poverty incidence, 1986–97

hyperinflation period that lasted until 1991. Both poverty and underemployment declined after the introduction of the structural reforms and stabilization measures. Yet, the decline has been slight and poverty and underemployment are still well above the levels observed in 1986, a year of stability and moderate growth. In 1997, the underemployment rate reached almost 50 per cent and poverty affected 37 per cent of the population (Figures 10.12 and 10.13).

Following the simulation methodology of Chapter 2, we try to identify the effects of liberalization on inequality and income levels. The methodology assumes that the impact of liberalization on inequality and poverty can be isolated by taking the pre-reform employment and remuneration structure as a counterfactual. The methodology distinguishes four 'phases'. In sequential order, we change participation rates (phase 1), unemployment rates (phase 2), sectoral employment structure (phase 3) and sectoral remuneration structure (phase 4), replacing the observed data with that of the counterfactual years. For each phase we then estimate inequality and poverty indicators based on the simulated income distribution. The working-age population (14 years and older) is divided into 12 'demographic' groups defined by the combination of gender, age groups (14–34 and 35+) and three educational levels (primary or none, secondary and higher). Employment by economic sector is classified into three broad groups: (i) industry; (ii) electricity, gas and water, construction, transportation and commerce; and (iii) financial, government and other services. The methodology allows changing the labour income observed in 1997 if applying the counterfactual structure, but does not change non-labour incomes such as property income, interest or transfers. It is assumed that non-labour incomes are about 32 per cent of labour incomes for all years.

We show results for the Gini coefficient and poverty incidence for labour income per occupied worker and for per capita household income. The threshold income level used to determine invisible underemployment is taken as the poverty line for individual workers. Poverty in this case is thus the same as invisible underemployment. For households we actually estimate the poverty incidence. The simulation years are 1987 (a growth year with a closed economy) and 1991 (a recession year with a closed economy).[16] The 1987 simulations allow a comparison of what inequality and underemployment (or poverty) would have been in 1997 (when the economy was growing and had already gone through the liberalization process) if the labour market structure had been a closed but growing one. The 1991 simulations allow comparison of inequality and underemployment (or poverty) levels in 1997 had the labour market economy been closed and in recession.

In order to obtain a confidence interval for the results, the simulations of phases 1 and 3 were repeated 100 times each. We also carried out the same simulations with 500 and 1,000 repetitions, and the results were very similar

Table 10.10 Simulation of the effects of changes in the labour market structure on inequality and poverty

	Labour income per employed worker				**Per capita household income**			
	Gini	P_0	**Gini**	P_0	**Gini**	P_0	**Gini**	P_0
Observed								
1986	0.477	0.388			0.524	0.288		
1991	0.471	0.559			0.550	0.440		
1997	0.497	0.474			0.583	0.376		
Simulations								
Gini and P_0 of 1997 with the labour structure of:	**1991**		**1996**		**1991**		**1996**	
Phase 1: change in participation rate (100 times)								
Average	**0.496**	**0.454**	**0.496**	**0.465**	**0.618**	**0.445**	**0.595**	**0.403**
Range	0.012	0.020	0.012	0.016	0.021	0.030	0.016	0.024
Phase 2: change in unemployment rate (100 times)								
Average	**0.499**	**0.478**	**0.498**	**0.476**	**0.573**	**0.361**	**0.573**	**0.361**
Range	0.007	0.011	0.007	0.010	0.015	0.019	0.014	0.020

Phase 3: change in employment structure (100 times)								
Average	**0.477**	**0.444**	**0.476**	**0.448**	**0.567**	**0.352**	**0.567**	**0.349**
Range	0.010	0.012	0.010	0.015	0.014	0.016	0.011	0.017
Phase 4: change in wage structure (100 times)								
Average	**0.470**	**0.442**	**0.483**	**0.434**	**0.548**	**0.360**	**0.558**	**0.347**
Range								
Phase 5: change in mean income (100 times)								
Average	**0.497**	**0.558**	**0.497**	**0.378**	**0.583**	**0.453**	**0.583**	**0.316**
Range								
Phases 1+2								
Average	**0.497**	**0.456**	**0.497**	**0.466**	**0.611**	**0.431**	**0.588**	**0.386**
Range	0.015	0.021	0.010	0.014	0.026	0.026	0.014	0.024
Phases 1+2+3								
Average	**0.477**	**0.424**	**0.477**	**0.438**	**0.596**	**0.407**	**0.572**	**0.360**
Range	0.016	0.022	0.014	0.019	0.028	0.032	0.026	0.031
Phases 1+2+3+4								
Average	**0.441**	**0.362**	**0.457**	**0.367**	**0.586**	**0.413**	**0.577**	**0.373**
Range	0.021	0.041	0.012	0.034	0.023	0.030	0.016	0.032
Phases 1+2+3+4+5								
Average	**0.441**	**0.501**	**0.458**	**0.319**	**0.586**	**0.508**	**0.577**	**0.344**
Range	0.021	0.025	0.016	0.025	0.019	0.039	0.020	0.024

to those obtained with 100 repetitions. Cumulative simulations were executed so as to obtain inequality indicators for a counterfactual scenario in which the entire pre-reform labour market structure would still exist. These cumulative simulations were repeated 100 times.[17] The simulation results are presented in Table 10.10.

For labour incomes per employed worker we find that the changes in the participation or unemployment rates had no substantial effect on inequality or underemployment. The changes in wage and employment structure observed in the 1990s led to a somewhat higher income inequality but to less poverty than would have been observed in a closed economy in recession. The cumulative effect of the changes in the labour market (in participation and unemployment rate, in remuneration and employment structure and in mean income) can also be seen in Table 10.11. The effect of the economic liberalization is estimated on the basis of a comparison of the figures observed for 1997 and those obtained with the 1986 labour structure, when the economy was growing but remained closed to international competition. We found that, as a result of the economic liberalization, the Gini coefficient would have increased by 3.9 Gini points and there would be more poverty. The 'growth effect' compares two years with the same degree of opening and suggests that growth increases inequality slightly but strongly reduces poverty. The '1990s effect' allows us to show that, when simultaneously observing growth and liberalization, poverty is reduced, but at the cost of greater inequality.

We should mention that this study identifies the liberalization effect as the difference between the labour market structure of a growing and liberalized economy and that of a growing economy isolated from external competition (see Table 10.11). Specifically, this entails comparing the 1997 labour market with that of the 1980s. The weakness of this approach is that it cannot isolate the effect of the trade opening from other structural changes, particularly those in labour legislation. Important changes in the labour market include the increase in the participation rate and in returns to education. The first occurred mainly among women, who entered the labour market primarily in the services sector, not necessarily linked to the trade opening but rather to a general financial and economic deregulation. The increase of the returns to education was in part the result of trade liberalization, but – as we have seen – not exclusively.

Changes in the participation rate had an important effect on household incomes, and the changes observed in the 1990s would have reduced wage dispersion with respect to what would have been observed had the economy been closed, more so during the recession (see Table 10.12). Rising participation rates reduce poverty, as applying the labour market structure of the closed economy to the 1997 economy yields higher poverty rates than those observed. The changes in the employment and wage structure have yielded

Table 10.11 Simulated effects of liberalization and growth on inequality and poverty

	Open, growing economy (observed) (1)	Closed, growing economy (counterfactual) (2)	Closed economy in recession (counterfactual) (3)	Liberalization effect (1) – (2)	Growth effect (2) – (3)	1990s effect (1) – (3)
Labour income per employed worker						
Gini	0.497	0.458	0.439	0.039	0.018	0.057
Poverty incidence	0.474	0.319	0.502	0.155	–0.183	–0.028
Per capita household income						
Gini	0.583	0.577	0.586	0.006	–0.009	–0.003
Poverty incidence	0.376	0.344	0.507	0.032	–0.162	–0.131

slight increases in inequality and poverty, hence reversing the previous effect to some extent. As a consequence, the cumulative labour market changes do not indicate any substantial impact of liberalization or growth on income distribution. The changes in the remuneration structure (e.g. related to the increase in returns to education) tend to increase inequality. However, this rise in inequality appears to have been offset by the shifts in the participation rates of household members in working age.[18] Liberalization has produced a small rise in poverty, but in combination with the 'growth effect' poverty decreased substantially. In sum, the labour market changes observed in the 1990s have led to a reduction in poverty, while leaving inequality in per capita household incomes more or less unchanged.

10.6 CONCLUSIONS

Peru started the 1990s with the implementation of a major stabilization programme to repair the serious macroeconomic maladjustments that had been generated since 1988. Almost simultaneously, in the first half of 1991, a structural reform programme was introduced consisting of the freeing of foreign trade, public sector reforms, liberalization of the financial system, elimination of marketing boards and state monopolies, and far-reaching labour reforms. The simultaneous liberalization of the current and capital account of the balance of payments generated a surge in capital inflows leading to an increase in international reserves. The subsequent real exchange-rate appreciation caused effective protection rates to become negative once corrected for the exchange-rate effect. It further led to a boom in consumer good imports. Despite considerable export growth, the trade deficit widened.

Output recovered with a lag after the recession that was induced by the stabilization programme. This growth was a consequence of the greater economic stability that resulted from the reduction of inflation, greater political stability and reduced country risk, lower interest rates resulting from capital inflows, and increased credit supplies facilitated by financial liberalization. Despite the growth recovery, per capita income of 1997 was still no different from that of 1973.

Analysis of the aggregate demand components showed that growth in the 1990s was mainly driven by private sector domestic demand. Compared to previous decades, the role of the public sector was much less important. Greater import leakage in the post-liberalization period was partially offset by export growth. Growth decelerated markedly in late 1998 because of the El Niño phenomenon and the crisis in international financial markets.

Opposition to the reforms, especially to trade liberalization, stems from the expectation that these would have a strongly negative impact on employment and poverty. Two different periods mark recent urban employment trends in Peru. Between 1988 and 1992, total employment practically stagnated. Labour market adjustment took place through real incomes. Wages showed a surprising downward flexibility despite the fact that rigid labour regulations were still in place and despite a reduction in participation rates. In 1993, the situation changed and both employment and participation rates increased until 1997. Employment growth stagnated around 1998 as a result of the incipient economic recession.

Despite the overall employment growth, some workers, particularly older male workers, encountered more limited job opportunities. This can be explained by the process of privatization, the reduction of the state apparatus and the disappearance of manufacturing branches that had been protected for a long time. The introduction of new technologies and production processes induced by trade and financial liberalization led to an increase of demand for more skilled and younger workers. Direct foreign investment further helped to enhance employment opportunities for these types of workers in both tradable and non-tradable sectors, including brand new branches of services that were established. Older workers formed the only demographic group that did not benefit from higher employment and participation rates in the 1990s.

Employment expanded until 1997. However, the impact of economic liberalization on productivity growth and real income gains has been rather limited. In Lima Metropolitana, an area for which it is possible to calculate time series for labour market indicators, productivity grew at a modest annual rate of 1.2 per cent in the 1990s with the entire gain generated between 1993 and 1997. Productivity levels are still below those reached in the mid-1980s. Real earnings showed a similar trend with only modest improvement. Skilled workers benefited from the largest income gains, consistent with a rising trend in returns to education.

Despite this momentum in returns to education, evidence for urban Peru indicates that income inequality fell at least until 1994. Data for subsequent years reveal rising trends in income inequality of labour and household incomes. In addition, poverty and underemployment behaved pro-cyclically, increasing strongly in the early 1990s and falling slowly during the rest of the 1990s.

The microsimulations reveal that the inequality in labour incomes per employed worker increased as a result of changes in the labour market structure related to liberalization and, to a lesser degree, to growth. Invisible underemployment declined in the 1990s thanks to the increase in labour demand associated with liberalization and recovery of economic growth. The labour market changes did not yield a major cumulative impact on per capita household income inequality, but did help to reduce poverty. The analysis suggests that the structural change produced by liberalization appears to have had a small negative impact on poverty. Growth recovery was the major factor explaining the poverty reduction observed in the 1990s.

NOTES

1. The authors wish to thank Sam Morley, Rob Vos and Lance Taylor for their comments and Cybele Burga and Eduardo Maruyama for their valuable assistance.
2. The effective protection rate measures the percentage variation of a sector's value added, which results from applying various trade policy instruments (e.g. export tariffs, taxes and subsidies, and multiple exchange rates). See Armas et al. (1990).
3. This evaluation was carried out to determine whether a product was competing with any domestic product.
4. CERTEX (*Certificado de Reintegro Tributario*) is a transferable certificate that serves to pay taxes and which is calculated as a function of the FOB export value.
5. The refundable taxes would be VAT, FONAVI and the *ad valorem* import tax.
6. CETICOS are also considered primary custom zones, which means that merchandise entering such centres and having entered the country through the harbours of Ilo, Matarani or Paita is exempt from payment of tariff duties and other applicable levies, and may be redispatched abroad.
7. Short-term capital formed an important source of finance in 1992 and 1996, and showed a much more volatile behaviour.
8. Although the rates have reached high levels, this has happened because of the need of the banking system to cover its operational costs.
9. Real exchange-rate appreciation was observed under various stabilization programmes, especially in the Cono Sur (in which countries the exchange rate was used as a nominal anchor in order to combat inflation).
10. The cases that seem to go backwards are usually those in which the necessary macroeconomic balances to keep inflation under control are not maintained. This makes it difficult to maintain stability in any real exchange rate.
11. The calculations are based on official data of the Banco Central de Reserva del Perú (BCRP). Official figures are in constant 1979 prices. This generates certain distortions, particularly after the hyperinflation process of 1989–90. We also made the decomposition using the original series of the BCRP in soles of 1979, as well as alternative deflation methods of the series in nominal values, using price indices with 1994 as base year, but adjusted by a geometrical index calculated by Escobal and Castillo (1994). We made the estimations using the nominal series converted to constant-price dollars. In all cases the conclusions are by and large the same, except for the magnitude of specific demand impulses in specific years.
12. The analysis in this section refers to Lima Metropolitana, based on the time series of household surveys of the Ministry of Labour (MTPS), conducted between 1986 and 1995, as well as the national household surveys (ENAHO) of INEI/MTPS for 1996–98.
13. Pascó Font (1998) gives a summary of the structural reforms.
14. The premium (or income differential) of each educational level with respect to the level just below it has been estimated using cumulative dummy variables in the earnings functions. The modified earnings functions take the logarithm of the hourly income earned in the main activity as dependent variable and control for factors such as place of birth and experience. These dummies (one per differential to be estimated) acquire a value of one whenever the person has acquired a particular educational level, and zero if the level has not been attained. Each dummy represents one of the following pairs: 'primary education vs. no education' (PE/NE), 'secondary education vs. primary education' (SE/PE) and 'secondary education vs. higher education' (SE/HE). For example, if an individual in the sample has secondary education, the dummies corresponding to 'primary

education vs. no education' and 'secondary education vs. primary education' take a value of one, whereas the 'higher education vs. secondary education' dummy becomes zero.

15. In this case, experience is defined as the potential years of experience of workers, i.e. the difference between the age and the years dedicated to complete the attained educational level.
16. Although the legal changes related to the liberalization process took place that year, it is reasonable to assume that there were no important, immediate changes in the import structure.
17. Here we report the averages and range (maximum less minimum) of 100 repetitions of the simulations. The results of the simulations with 500 and 1,000 repetitions are available from the authors.
18. Changes in the participation rate will only affect income distribution, if participation rates differ by income level. Saavedra and Torero (1998) provide evidence on the importance of changes in labour participation. They find that changes in the employment rate have a significant impact on the transition from being poor to non-poor between 1994 and 1996.

REFERENCES

Armas, Adrian, Luis Palacios and Renzo Rossini (1990) 'El sesgo anti-exportador de la política comercial peruana: Un estudio de protección efectiva de minería', Lima: Instituto de Estudios Económicos Mineros.

Díaz, Juan José (1999) 'Estructura de ingresos en Lima Metropolitana 1986–1995', Serie Investigaciones Breves No. 11, Lima.

Edwards, Sebastian and Alejandra Cox-Edwards (1995) 'Monetarism and Liberalization: The Chilean Experiment', in: Sebastian Edwards (ed.) *Trade Policy, Exchange Rates and Growth*, Chicago: The University of Chicago Press.

Escobal, Javier (1992) 'Marzo de 1991, el mes de las reformas estructurales en el Perú', in: J. Vial (ed.) *¿Adónde va América Latina? Balance de las Reformas Económicas*, Santiago: CIEPLAN, pp. 233–60.

Escobal, Javier and Marco Castillo (1994) 'Sesgos en la medición de la inflación en contextos inflacionarios: el caso peruano', *Grupo de Análisis para el Desarrollo* Working Paper No 21, Lima: GRADE.

Pascó Font, Alberto (1998) 'Políticas de estabilización y reformas estructurales en Perú', Lima: GRADE (mimeo).

Saavedra, Jaime (1996a) 'Quienes ganan y quienes pierden con una reforma estructural: Un análisis de la estructura de ingresos en el Perú antes y después de las reformas', Lima: GRADE (mimeo).

Saavedra, Jaime (1996b) 'Apertura comercial, empleo y salarios', ILO Working Paper No. 40, Lima: Regional Office of the ILO.

Saavedra, Jaime (1997) 'Liberalización comercial e industria manufacturera en el Perú', *Investigaciones Breves* 2, Lima: Consorcio de Investigación Económica.

Saavedra, Jaime (1998) 'Crisis real o crisis de expectativas? El empleo en el Perú antes y después de la reformas estructurales', *Grupo de Análisis para el Desarrollo* Working Paper No. 26, Lima: GRADE.

Saavedra, Jaime and Juan José Díaz (1999) 'Distribución del ingreso y del gasto antes y después de las reformas estructurales', *Serie Reformas Económicas* No. 34, Santiago: CEPAL.

Saavedra, Jaime and Máximo Torero (1998) 'Labor Market Regulation and Employment in Peru', Lima: GRADE (mimeo).

Index